Praise for Juan
Harvest of

"A serious, significant contribution to understanding who the Hispanics of the United States are and where they come from."
—*The New York Times Book Review*

"A profound book with an equally profound message about the origins of Latino migration, domination, and colonization, and historical lessons not found in many American textbooks."
—*San Antonio Express-News*

"A compelling—and enlightening—chronicle . . . offers an insider's view of the rich and varied fabric of the people soon to be the largest minority in the United States."
—*The Miami Herald*

"Anyone who finishes *Harvest of Empire* will never again see Latinos as a monolithic group, but as a diverse society of citizens and future citizens, worthy of recognition and respect."
—*Fort Worth Morning Star*

"In what would seem an impossible task, journalist Juan Gonzalez tackles the entire history of Latinos in North and Central America in a single volume . . . illuminating."
—*Dallas Morning News*

"Required reading, not simply for Latinos but for everyone."
—*The Kansas City Star*

"Gonzalez's ever-enjoyable prose grabs the reader and fills in the gaps left by a traditional American history education."
—*In These Times*

"Here at last is the extraordinary saga of the Latinos in North America, brilliantly and compactly told. All the descendants of the old immigrants should read this book, to remind themselves of where they came from, and where all of us are going—together."
—Pete Hamill, author of *Snow in August* and *A Drinking Life*

"This excellent history of Latinos in North and Central America is fair-handed, extremely well-documented, and filled with the sort of details that explain rather than enflame."

—*Publishers Weekly*

"Juan Gonzalez brings us a sweeping account of the raw quest for empire that shaped the New World and is finally in our time transforming the United States. The history is often brutal, the experiences of the people caught up in the process wrenching. But Gonzalez paints a canvas that is in the end profoundly optimistic, for in the Latinization of the United States he sees the possibility of a renaissance of American democracy."

—Frances Fox Piven, coauthor of *Regulating the Poor*

PENGUIN BOOKS

HARVEST OF EMPIRE

Juan Gonzalez is the Richard D. Heffner Professor of Communications and Public Policy at Rutgers University and a longtime cohost of the radio/television news show *Democracy Now!*. He was a columnist with the *New York Daily News* for nearly thirty years, and is a two-time winner of the George Polk journalism award. Born in Ponce, Puerto Rico, he grew up in a New York City housing project, graduated from Columbia University, and was a cofounder of the 1960s Young Lords.

HARVEST
of EMPIRE

A HISTORY OF
LATINOS IN AMERICA

SECOND REVISED AND UPDATED EDITION

JUAN GONZALEZ

PENGUIN BOOKS

PENGUIN BOOKS

An imprint of Penguin Random House LLC
penguinrandomhouse.com

First published in the United States of America by Viking Penguin, a member of Penguin Putnam Inc., 2000
Published in Penguin Books 2001
First revised edition published 2011
This second revised edition published 2022

Copyright © 2000, 2011, 2022 by Juan Gonzalez
Penguin Random House supports copyright. Copyright fuels creativity, encourages diverse voices, promotes
free speech, and creates a vibrant culture. Thank you for buying an authorized edition of this book and for
complying with copyright laws by not reproducing, scanning, or distributing any part of it in any form without
permission. You are supporting writers and allowing Penguin Random House to continue to publish
books for every reader.

LIBRARY OF CONGRESS CATALOGING-IN-PUBLICATION DATA

Names: González, Juan, 1947- author.
Title: Harvest of empire : a history of Latinos in America / Juan Gonzalez.
Other titles: History of Latinos in America
Description: Second revised and updated edition. | [New York] : Penguin
Books, 2022 | "First published in the United States of America by
Viking Penguin, a member of Penguin Putnam Inc., 2000." |
Includes bibliographical references and index.
Identifiers: LCCN 2022008432 (print) | LCCN 2022008433 (ebook) |
ISBN 9780143137436 (paperback) | ISBN 9780593511473 (ebook)
Subjects: LCSH: Hispanic Americans—History. | Immigrants—United
States—History. | United States—Emigration and immigration—History. |
Latin America—Emigration and immigration—History. | United
States—Relations—Latin America. | Latin America—Relations—United
States. | United States—Territorial expansion—History. |
United States—Ethnic relations—History.
Classification: LCC E184.S75 G655 2022 (print) | LCC E184.S75 (ebook) |
DDC 973/.0468—dc23/eng/20220310
LC record available at https://lccn.loc.gov/2022008432
LC ebook record available at https://lccn.loc.gov/2022008433

Printed in the United States of America
6th Printing

Set in Vulpa Regular with Goudy Heavyface
Designed by Sabrina Bowers

The scorn of our formidable neighbor who does not know us is Our America's greatest danger. And since the day of the visit is near, it is imperative that our neighbor know us, and soon, so that it will not scorn us. Through ignorance it might even come to lay hands on us. Once it does know us, it will remove its hands out of respect. One must have faith in the best of men and distrust the worst.

—José Martí, January 10, 1891

Contents

PART I ✶ Roots (*Las Raíces*)

PART II ✶ Branches (*Las Ramas*)

PART III ⬙ Harvest (*La Cosecha*)

Introduction to the
Second Revised and Updated Edition

In June 2018, media reports revealed that U.S. Border Patrol agents had detained hundreds of Latino children inside chain-link cages at a warehouse in the southern Texas border city of McAllen. The disturbing images of terrified toddlers wailing for their parents provoked worldwide condemnation. The children had been initially seized with their parents, who were seeking to cross illegally into the country. Federal authorities then opted to jail and criminally prosecute the adults, while dispatching the children to makeshift detention sites for up to weeks at a time before transporting them to temporary care facilities around the country. Nearly two thousand minors were seized during April and May of that year, officials soon acknowledged, all part of a Trump administration "zero tolerance" policy aimed at stemming the sudden surge of migrants from Central America. The number detained eventually grew to more than four thousand, including some sixty cases of children whose families had been seeking asylum when apprehended.[1]

In the months that followed, six children died in U.S. custody, including seven-year-old Jakelin Caal Maquin in New Mexico. The public outcry prompted President Trump to quickly rescind his policy, yet more than two years later, hundreds of children had still not been reunited with their parents.[2] The family separation scandal was the most tragic example of decades of failure by political leaders in Washington to fashion a comprehensive and humane reform of the nation's immigration laws. No group was more directly affected by that failure than U.S. Latinos, given that nearly 80 percent of the nation's estimated eleven million undocumented migrants hail from Latin America.[3] Meanwhile, the Latinx population has continued to grow at a faster rate than the rest of the nation. It surpassed sixty-two million people in 2020—even more if you count some three million residents of Puerto Rico—thus increasing the pressure on the nation's leaders for immigration reform. Unfortunately, the Trump era produced far more heat than light on the issue of migration. Racially tinged anti-immigrant hysteria spread to large sectors of U.S. society, while restrictive policies on migrants became enshrined as official national policy, some of which persisted even after Democrat Joseph Biden succeeded Trump.

The main theme of this book when first published more than twenty years ago was that mushrooming migration from Latin America, Asia, and Africa to the rich nations of the world can only be understood—and, ultimately, will only be resolved—by a reckoning with the legacy of the colonial empires the United States and other Western nations created in those regions during the previous two centuries. Quite simply, the modern immigration crisis is a direct result of the political upheavals and wealth inequalities those empires produced and sustain to this day.

Throughout the Obama and Trump years, however, congressional leaders could not agree on how to overhaul the U.S. immigration system. They failed not just to resolve the fate of unauthorized migrants within the country, but also to modernize outdated guest worker programs, or to refashion processes for granting permanent visas and handling asylum seekers and refugees. They repeatedly deadlocked on such an overhaul precisely because the stakes are so high in an increasingly multiracial nation. Any comprehensive reform, after all, will determine who can legitimately become a U.S. citizen in the twenty-first century. It will reshape the nation's voting population for decades to come and will alter the distribution of political and economic power at both the national and local level. The Trump era produced instead a concerted effort by conservative whites to institute massive new crackdowns on both legal and unauthorized immigration, even on asylum seekers, along with the macabre expansion of a physical wall with Mexico. Trump earmarked some $15 billion for wall construction during his four-year term— none of it paid for by Mexico, as he had originally promised. When Joe Biden won the presidential election in 2020, only about 350 miles of the new barrier had been built, most of it replacing preexisting fencing or walls, and only 650 miles along the border had any kind of fencing at all.[4]

A few months after the family separation scandal erupted, voters shifted control of the House of Representatives from the Republicans to the Democrats in the November midterm elections. One under-reported result of that election was the extraordinary growth of turnout among Latinx voters, especially young people. An estimated 11.7 million Hispanics cast ballots in 2018, nearly double the number who did so in the midterm elections of 2014—*and almost as many as voted for president in 2016.* That unexpected increase was a major factor in Democrats achieving a net gain of forty-one seats in the House that year. Many young U.S. citizen Latinos were no doubt stirred to political activism in direct response to years of demonization of their community by Trump. Among the political activists to emerge that year was a twenty-nine-year-old New York–born Puerto Rican and democratic socialist, Alexandria Ocasio-Cortez, who toppled one of the most powerful Democrats in the House of Representatives in an upset primary victory. Ocasio-Cortez (she was soon dubbed AOC) went on to become the youngest woman ever elected to Congress, and she quickly captured national attention as the most charismatic figure among progressive Democrats nationwide. But her rise was not the only sign that Latinx voters were a growing political force. By the start of 2021, a record six Hispanics held seats in the U.S. Senate—four Democrats and two Republicans—and forty held seats in the House of Representatives.[5]

In the wake of Biden's presidential election victory, an avalanche of media reports all claimed that exit polls and voting returns showed a marked shift had occurred among Latinx voters toward more conservative views and in support of Trump, a narrative that captivated considerable attention. Those of us who have spent decades chronicling historical trends among Hispanic voters quickly recognized this as a false, or at best superficial, narrative. We saw instead a very different picture, one that stressed the main story as being the unprecedented increase in voting among Hispanics in 2020, an increase that had eclipsed even the historic overall jump in national turnout that year. We pointed out how Latinx voters had proved instrumental to Biden's victory in several key battleground states. And while it was true that there had been percentage increases in support for Donald Trump in some Hispanic areas, his share of the Latino vote remained squarely within historic parameters achieved by previous Republican presidential candidates (see chapter 10). In fact, the enormous attention suddenly devoted to how Latinos voted, or even the renewed skepticism expressed by some as to whether a cohesive Latinx community even exists, were themselves reflections of that community's rapidly growing importance in U.S. politics and society. We must not lose sight of the fact that even though nearly seven thousand Latinos held some kind of elected office in the country in 2020 (a record number), they still represented just about 1 percent of all officeholders, which is a tiny share when you consider that Hispanics composed 18 percent of the country's population. In other words, the greatest advances in Latino political representation have yet to come.

Even beyond politics, however, several other significant events and trends shaped the development of the U.S. Latinx community and of Latin America since the last edition of this book was published more than a decade ago. This revised and updated edition seeks to incorporate and assess those changes. The book's first two parts, "Roots" and "Branches," have remained largely the same, given that they trace the origins and evolution of the Latino community from colonial times through the early twentieth century. I have made only minor changes to correct factual errors somehow overlooked in prior editions, or to add vital new information from the explosion of research on the Latino experience that a raft of terrific new scholars produced in recent years. But the final five chapters of the book, composing Part III, "Harvest," have undergone more extensive revisions. There I have included the latest demographic and other data while also adding new narratives that aim to draw important lessons about the community's evolution. Given the complexity of the subject matter, any choice of such developments necessarily involves personal judgment. In my case, that judgment comes from a half century of being immersed in and studying the Latino experience through three distinct lenses—as a social activist, as a journalist, and as a scholar of its history. Thus, the main new trends I highlight in this edition are:

♦ The rise of anti-immigrant xenophobia as the cutting edge of neofascist populism in the United States, along with the mushrooming emergence of "border security" and the immigration detention system as a new arm of a racialized prison industrial complex.

♦ The phenomenal growth of climate refugees from Central America and the Caribbean, with masses of people fleeing not only gang violence and intractable poverty, but storms and drought disasters that have resulted from the planet's climate crisis.

- The emergence of Puerto Rico as a recurring national political issue, from the debt crisis of 2015, to the devastation of Hurricane María in 2017 and its aftermath, to the massive popular protest on the island in 2019 that ousted a sitting governor for the first time in U.S. history. Those successive upheavals sparked an unprecedented nearly 12 percent decline in Puerto Rico's population in just a decade, renewing a mass exodus from the island to the fifty states, especially to Florida and the South.

- The growing ethnic, racial, and class diversity of the Latino migrant population, with Central Americans now outnumbering even Mexicans in apprehensions by the Border Patrol for illegal entry, with Salvadorans surpassing those of Cuban descent as the third largest Latino group in the country, and with a new wave of more middle-class migrants and refugees from countries such as Venezuela, Colombia, and Nicaragua reviving existing conservative trends long espoused largely by Cuban refugees.

- The resurgence of right-wing neoliberal regimes in Latin America, with the new leaders moving rapidly to reverse the economic and social gains achieved by pink tide populist governments that came to power during the previous decade. This conservative movement gained force with the 2009 coup against Honduran president Mel Zelaya and the reign of terror in Honduras that followed, events that the Obama White House sanctioned. The movement then spread to coups or "lawfare" investigations that ousted progressive presidents in Brazil, Argentina, Bolivia, Ecuador, Peru, Uruguay, and Chile. Only Venezuela, Nicaragua, and Cuba managed to survive the new tide, with Mexico the sole nation to run counter to the trend when its people elected left-wing populist Andrés Manuel López Obrador as their president in 2018. Many of the new governments, however, were marked by persistent corruption, implicated in the rise of criminal gangs and drug trafficking in their countries, and the austerity programs they imposed only exacerbated economic inequality among their citizens to the point that in the wake of the COVID-19 pandemic, voters began returning leftist movements to power.

- The sudden emergence of the People's Republic of China as a new economic power on the Latin American stage. China's leaders repeatedly offered the region's economically burdened governments unprecedented sums of money in grants and low-interest loans to finance enormous infrastructure projects, often in exchange for long-term access to vital raw materials. The new Chinese presence allowed those governments to pursue policies more independent from Washington's dictates, thus marking the end of centuries in which Latin America was the uncontested backyard of the U.S. empire.

♦ Nowhere was the cultural diversity of the U.S. Latinx community more evident than in the field of culture, with the last decade witnessing a revolution in the arts spearheaded by a young Puerto Rican from the Dominican neighborhood of Washington Heights in New York City. In just a few short years, Lin-Manuel Miranda not only captured countless accolades for his artistic work, including the Pulitzer Prize and a MacArthur genius grant, he virtually transformed American theater and music through his hit Broadways shows *Hamilton* and *In the Heights*. He even prompted new approaches to how public schools teach U.S. history and the contributions of immigrants and people of color to the nation's development. Miranda and other new Latinx artists are not merely enriching U.S. culture, they are *reconstructing* it on a new foundation.

In the midst of such momentous change, even the *panethnic* term used to describe U.S. residents of Latin American descent has once again become a subject of debate. During the past decade, the term *Latinx* grew increasingly popular among young college-educated and professional Hispanics as a way to disrupt the gender binary and to be more inclusive of LGBTQ people. Still, only 3 percent of the nation's Latinos acknowledged in 2019 that they use the term to describe themselves, and only 23 percent have even heard of it.[6] Twenty years ago a similar controversy raged in some circles over whether *Hispanic* or *Latino* was more appropriate. Back then, I explained in the first edition of this book my belief that "needless time has been spent by Latino intellectuals debating which term . . . best describes us. Neither is totally accurate, but both are acceptable, and I use them interchangeably." That is still my view, which is why I have sought in this edition to incorporate *Latinx* as an alternative to *Hispanic* or *Latino*, especially when referring to more contemporary issues, but I have done so while still regarding both *Hispanic* and *Latino* as appropriate, if imperfect, terms. Moreover, most migrants from Latin America still prefer to identify themselves by their particular country of origin, or in the case of indigenous peoples, by their native heritage. Their U.S.-born-and-raised children, grandchildren, and great-grandchildren will increasingly adopt different views. Ethnic identity, after all, is a social construct, much like racial identity. It requires a dynamic and fluid approach, not a static and rigid one, with every generation free to reimagine and redefine its own place in society, though the actual economic and social conditions of any community should always take precedence over labels and intellectual descriptions.

As I was completing revisions to this edition, two historic upheavals shook the United States and the world, the reverberations of which will be felt for years to come. First was the COVID-19 pandemic and massive economic recession, followed by an unprecedented international protest movement for Black Lives Matter. This movement, energized by the brazen killing of George Floyd, an unarmed Black man, by a white Minneapolis policeman—all of it captured on video—sparked the largest street demonstrations on any issue in U.S. history, dwarfing even the giant women's rights protests at the start of the Trump administration, or the immigrant rights marches of 2006.

Both the pandemic and the racial justice marches underscored how historic inequities in U.S. society continue to afflict not just African Americans but Latinos as well. According to the federal Centers for Disease Control and Prevention, the Latinx community endured some of the worst outcomes during 2020 from COVID-19 of any ethnic or racial group in the country in both hospitalizations and deaths. Latinos were 3.1 times more likely to be hospitalized than non-Hispanic whites and 2.3 times more likely to die from the virus, rates that were slightly higher in both categories than for African Americans. Only Native Americans registered even more tragic results—3.7 times more likely than whites to be hospitalized and 2.4 times more likely to die. Moreover, nearly three months after health officials launched mass vaccinations, only 7.2 percent of those fully vaccinated were Hispanic and only 6.7 percent were Black.[7]

As for fatal shootings by police, an extensive *Washington Post* study of such incidents since 2015 showed that as of 2022 they occurred at a rate of thirty-eight per million among Black Americans and twenty-eight per million among Hispanics, compared with just fifteen per million among non-Hispanic whites and just five per million among other racial groups.[8] Blacks and Latinos, in short, were roughly twice as likely to be shot and killed every year by police as white Americans.

Over the past two decades, I have been repeatedly surprised by the number of complete strangers who recounted to me how *Harvest of Empire* awakened them to a new understanding of the Latino experience in the United States. The book's impact on Latinx college students and young university scholars has been especially gratifying, given the significant role those young people will play in shaping the nation's future. They are, after all, our greatest hope for a world without empires, without the exploitation and forced migration of millions.

—MARCH 2021

Introduction to the
Second Edition

Between March and May of 2006, an estimated three million to five million people, most of them Latinos, filled the downtown streets of some 160 U.S. towns and cities in the largest series of mass protests the nation had seen until that point.[1]

Not even during the heyday of the American labor movement in the 1930s, or during the high tide of civil rights protests and public opposition to the Vietnam War during the 1960s, had such astonishing numbers paraded peacefully in so many different localities over a common grievance. Never before had a group at the margins of U.S. society taken our political establishment by such complete surprise. Word of the mobilizations, it turned out, had spread largely via Spanish-language radio and TV and through social networks of young Latinos on the internet, so government leaders and the general public had little idea of what was happening until the huge crowds suddenly started to appear on our city streets.

The immediate aim of the marchers was to defeat a bill in Congress that would establish tough new criminal penalties for immigrants who were in the country illegally. The opponents sought not only to derail what came to be known as the Sensenbrenner bill, but to replace it with a comprehensive overhaul of U.S. immigration policy, one that would include a "path to citizenship" for an estimated twelve million undocumented workers already in the country. Protest leaders framed their effort as a moral call for compassion and respect, for *dignidad* for illegal immigrants. Many adopted the slogan *¡Si Se Puede!* (Yes We Can!), the nearly forgotten words that legendary Mexican American labor organizer Cesar Chavez had coined half a century earlier for his United Farm Workers organization.

Their message reverberated from the bustling streets of established

Latino neighborhoods in the major cities to scores of newly sprouted *barrios* in small towns and hamlets across the American heartland. The rallies they scheduled suddenly swelled with tens of thousands of maids, nannies, and maintenance workers, with lowly gardeners and day laborers, with restaurant busboys and dishwashers, with hotel waiters and bellhops, with hardened slaughterhouse workers and construction hardhats, many of whom had quietly led a furtive existence in the shadows of society, always afraid of being stopped by a local cop or sheriff, or of being caught in an immigration raid and hastily deported. Suddenly this brown-skinned and once-docile mass of humanity was parading through glistening city centers in broad daylight. With spouses and children at their side and their infants in strollers, they proudly marched with their entire Pentecostal or Catholic congregations, their ministers and church banners at the front, waving both the American flag and those of their native countries.

These were not simply gatherings of the undocumented, however. Hundreds of thousands of Latinos who had been born in the United States or become naturalized citizens, or who were longtime legal residents, also participated. And leading the way in virtually every protest were startling numbers of U.S.-born Hispanic high school and college students, many of them facing the prospect of being separated from their immigrant parents who could end up being deported.

All shared the same burning sense of outrage. All were fed up with the mainstream media's reigning stereotype that depicted hordes of Latinos and undocumented workers as a new menace engulfing the country.

And though Latinos made up the overwhelming number of marchers, they were hardly alone; joining them as well were thousands of Polish, Irish, Korean, Chinese, and Filipino immigrants, along with many white and Black religious and labor leaders and supporters.

The immigration protests of 2006 marked a rare example of an outcast group suddenly rising up and forcing the majority to rethink accepted notions of democratic and human rights. For most of the marchers, it was their first act of social protest, one that would permanently alter the way they viewed the world. For just as the 1963 March on Washington for Jobs and Freedom defined the outlook of many Black Americans, and just as the college rebellions of 1968 shaped the thinking of a generation of white Americans, so too did these protests represent a political coming of age for the nation's Hispanic minority.

The new movement burst on the scene with such unexpected force that it quickly gave rise to several contending narratives in the commercial media. On the one hand, scores of mainstream newspapers and television stations started for the first time to produce poignant and sympathetic stories about the lives of the undocumented, a perspective the press had largely ignored until then, preferring instead the stereotype of the "illegal alien." On the other hand, the fast-growing Spanish-language media offered a radically different narrative—one of solidarity, not of sympathy. From the scores of popular radio DJs around the country to the big television networks like Univision and Telemundo, from the hundreds of weekly Hispanic newspapers to the big-city dailies like *La Opinión* in Los Angeles and *El Diario–La Prensa* in New York City, the Spanish-language press openly extolled and promoted the movement. They depicted it as a heroic effort by Hispanic Americans to finally be recognized for their contributions to the nation.

But an equally powerful narrative emerged from right-wing talk radio and TV hosts like Rush Limbaugh, Bill O'Reilly, and Lou Dobbs. Seizing on the fact that some protesters proudly waved the flags of their home countries alongside the Stars and Stripes, these commentators openly sought to stoke public rage. They demanded tougher immigration policies and mass deportations and warned of an attempt by Latino radicals to reconquer the former Mexican territory of the Southwest as a Hispanic homeland.

Not surprisingly, anti-immigrant sentiment in the general population became more virulent, more sustained, and more overtly targeted at Hispanics. As it did so, local politicians around the country turned into overnight celebrities for instituting local crackdowns on immigrant communities. They included Joe Arpaio, the sheriff of Arizona's Maricopa County; Lou Barletta, the mayor of Hazleton, Pennsylvania; and Steve Levy, the Suffolk County commissioner on Long Island, New York. From across the political spectrum, many white and Black Americans angrily demanded stepped-up deportations and stiffer penalties on companies that employed undocumented workers. They urged a sealing of the U.S.-Mexico border through the rapid completion of a physical and virtual wall across its entire two-thousand-mile length.

The protesters and their allies, however, were equally defiant. Such was the force of their outcry that the Sensenbrenner bill died in the Senate. But so did a proposed bipartisan comprehensive immigration reform bill in 2007 that was backed by Massachusetts senator Edward Kennedy, Republican senator John McCain, and President Bush.

The new movement failed to achieve its main goal of immigration reform, yet it still left a deep and unexpected imprint on the entire country, for its stunning rise effectively marked the end of thirty years of conservative domination over national politics. Six months after the immigration protests, Democrats swept control of both houses of Congress, and one of the chief reasons for that historic power shift was the mushrooming Latino vote. The number of Hispanics casting ballots that November jumped by nearly 1 million over the previous midterm election—from 4.7 million in 2002 to 5.6 million in 2006. And in so far as the Republican Party was most closely associated with the Sensenbrenner bill, the percentage of Latinos who cast ballots for Republican candidates in the House of Representatives sank from 38 percent to 30 percent.[2]

Then, in 2008, Illinois Democratic senator Barack Obama, borrowing the same "Yes We Can!" slogan of Chavez's farmworkers and the immigrant rights movement, prevailed in the race for the White House. Obama owed his historic victory in no small measure to the overwhelming support he received from Latino voters. Some 9.7 million Hispanics cast ballots for president in 2008, 2.1 million more than in 2004. Obama garnered 67 percent of those votes, while Republican John McCain received just 31 percent, with McCain's share representing a significant drop from the 40 percent Latino support George W. Bush enjoyed in his 2004 reelection.

The 2.1 million additional Latino voters in 2008 mirrored a similar startling jump among African Americans; and along with a sharp increase of more than 300,000 Asian Americans, it produced the most diverse electorate in the nation's history and assured the victory of our first Black president. In the euphoric aftermath of Obama's inauguration, many claimed the United States had entered a new postracial era. A dispassionate review of voting statistics, however, did not provide such comforting visions of change, nor did the rise of the right-wing Tea Party movement soon after. Obama, after all, had received the support of only 43 percent of white voters, while John McCain amassed 55 percent. Such a yawning gap among whites would normally signal a Republican victory. Only the enormous turnout and overwhelming support Obama generated among the country's racial minorities—95 percent of African Americans voted for him, as did 62 percent of Asian Americans—made it possible for him to win the election handily.[3]

Obama's rise thus reflected how the country's electorate was changing, and not just in terms of greater opportunities for African Americans. The first decade of the new century saw the number of Hispanic elected officials nationwide surpass 6,600. Between 1994 and 2009, the number of Latinos in Congress climbed by nearly 50 percent—from 17 to 25—while the number of Hispanics holding elected positions in state governments increased by one-third—from 184 to 247. At one point during the past decade, a record three Latinos held seats in the U.S. Senate—Mel Martinez (R-FL), Ken Salazar (D-CO), and Robert Menendez (D-NJ).[4]

When I penned the first edition of *Harvest of Empire* at the end of the 1990s, the federal government was in the early stages of erecting a wall between Mexico and the United States, just south of San Diego. The makeshift barrier, I noted then, was not nearly as impressive as our planet's great testament to human insecurity, the 1,500-mile-long Great Wall that China's emperors spent centuries building against the Huns. Nonetheless, the American version was a clear indication that the U.S.-Mexico border had become the epicenter of momentous changes in our hemisphere: by day, a constant stream of trucks headed south, carrying goods to newly erected factories bustling with nearly a million low-wage workers; by night, a silent flood of people headed north in search of the U.S. wages that could spell survival for family members the migrant had left behind. Those movements were creating huge windfalls for tiny investor elites on both sides of the border, while leaving horrendous social conditions on the Mexican side.

The movement of labor northward, rivaling in size the great westward trek across the North American frontier by early European settlers, has produced a remarkable transformation—the Latinization of the United States. Unparalleled immigration has taken place from Mexico, the Caribbean, Central and South America since World War II, especially escalating since the 1960s. More than forty million foreigners settled here between 1960 and 2008, more than during any fifty-year span in the country's history, and half of those newcomers were from Latin America. Yet most experts were not fully grasping the magnitude of the change, despite a string of hyperbolic press accounts during the 1980s and 1990s that focused on Hispanic population growth.

The U.S. Census Bureau, for instance, has had to repeatedly revise upward its projection for the future growth of the Latino population. Its most recent estimate predicts the country's current Hispanic population, which was 46 million in 2009 (and that's without counting the 4 million residents of Puerto Rico who are U.S. citizens), will nearly triple to 132 million in 2050. At that point, Latinos could compose *nearly one-third of the entire U.S. population*; and together with African Americans and other nonminorities, they will make up more than half of all U.S. residents—235 million of 439 million people.

Whites of European descent, in other words, will cease to be a majority in the United States by midcentury, though they will no doubt remain the dominant racial group in terms of wealth and power. Looking out beyond 2050, it is now possible that by the end of this century a majority of the U.S. population will trace its ethnic heritage to Latin America, not to Europe.[5]

This is amazing when you consider that Latinos numbered a mere 9.1 million and represented just 4.5 percent of the population as recently as 1970. The Hispanic population explosion is no longer confined to the Southwest border region, or to a handful of big states like California, New York, and Florida. It has now extended to virtually every suburb, small town, and rural area of the country, with Mexican restaurants, Spanish bodegas, and Latin music now a ubiquitous part of life throughout the United States.

Such rapid change has understandably led to deep insecurity among non-Hispanic whites, even among some Black Americans. This is especially so for the large baby boomer generation, whose members grew up during the 1950s and 1960s when U.S. immigration rates were at the lowest levels of the twentieth century. The foreign-born population was not only tiny then, but the prevalence of racial segregation and the proliferation of all-white suburbs meant that both white and Black Americans had little social interaction with people who were culturally or linguistically different from themselves. The country, in other words, was racially divided but demographically homogeneous.[6]

Today, many of those older Americans are the ones voicing the greatest fear that Latino and Asian immigration will permanently alter the American way of life. A disturbing number started to believe in the 1990s that the country was under attack by modern-day Huns, hordes of Spanish-speaking "barbarians at the gate." Many came to regard the multicultural education movement in the public schools and universities as nurturing a divisive form of ethnic nationalism, one that is subverting the Euro-centered traditions of U.S. history and fostering such "un-American" reforms as bilingual education. Nothing seems to inflame advocates of our nation's Anglo-Saxon traditions so much as this issue of language. Given that a people's culture is inevitably expressed through its language, the growth of "foreign" language use somehow implies the growth of alien cultures. Hispanics, whether rightly or not, are now seen as the vanguard of a linguistic threat.

One manifestation of widespread insecurity is the rapid escalation in hate crimes against Latinos, with the FBI reporting a 35 percent jump between 2003 and 2006. Other studies suggest the bureau's tally drastically undercounts the extent of the problem, especially when it comes to Latinos. In 2008, for instance, the FBI reported 7,780 bias-crime incidents. That number, compiled from local police reports, has fluctuated between 6,000 and 10,000 throughout the decade. Only 11.5 percent of the 2008 incidents, according to the FBI, were because of ethnic or nationality bias.[7]

But a separate 2005 analysis by the Bureau of Justice Statistics claimed the real number of bias crimes has been far greater, averaging more than 190,000 annually for much of this decade. That study, based on the National Criminal Victimization Survey, revealed that nearly 30 percent of hate crime incidents between 2000 and 2003 involved ethnic bias. It also noted that more than half of bias crimes were never reported to police, with a major reason being that undocumented victims of such attacks are far less likely to file a police report than citizens or legal residents.[8]

At the same time, some local governments increasingly adopted laws targeting illegal immigrants. Perhaps most controversial was the law the Arizona state legislature passed in 2010 that authorized police to stop and question anyone who they had a "reasonable suspicion" was in the country illegally.

Our country is hardly unique, however, in its unease over Third World immigration. Since World War II, the shrinking of the modern world through air travel and mass communications and the ever-widening chasm between the rich developed countries on the one hand, and poverty-stricken Asia, Africa, and Latin America on the other, have fueled unprecedented immigration to the West. Invariably, the old colonial ties meant that immigrants from those regions gravitated to the metropolises of their former colonial masters. In Great Britain, burgeoning Pakistani, Indian, and Jamaican immigrant populations have unnerved native whites. In France, a new right-wing movement targets Algerians and Tunisians. In Germany, foreign nationals from Turkey, Africa, and Southeast Asia have drawn the ire of native citizens.

But how did the vast explosion in the Hispanic population of the United States occur? What were the forces that propelled so many Latin Americans to come here? Was it simply lax border enforcement and misguided federal immigration policies? Or was it something more fundamental to our own nation's very development?

The central argument of this book is that U.S. economic and political domination over Latin America has always been—and continues to be—the underlying reason for the massive Latino presence here. Quite simply, our vast Latino population is the unintended harvest of the U.S. empire.

Most of us are uncomfortable thinking of our nation as an empire, even if Wall Street speculators and investment banks have repeatedly shown their ability to wreck entire economies halfway around the globe in a matter of hours—a power far greater than the Roman or Ottoman Empires ever wielded. Our public schools have failed miserably in this regard, for they have taught us little about the machinations that accompanied our nation's territorial expansion or that helped bring about U.S. domination of the modern world.

Not too long ago, Latin America was generally pictured as our exotic backyard, a series of nondescript banana republics and semicivilized nations where Americans liked to travel for adventure or for vacations or to accumulate cheap land or to make their fortunes. The region's hapless governments became perpetual prey to the intrigues of competing circles of U.S. bankers and investors and to the gunboat diplomacy of U.S. presidents. But now Latino migrants, the product of those old relationships, have invaded the North American garden, kitchen, and living room. We are overflowing its schools, its army, even its jails.

Immigrants have existed, of course, from the beginning of civilization. And the basic reasons people move from one land to another have not changed—starvation or deteriorating social conditions, political or religious persecution, a chance to improve one's lot by starting anew somewhere else. But Latin American migration and the Latino presence in this country, as I attempt to show in this book, differed from that of the Europeans in several important ways.

First, the Latino migrant flows were directly connected to the growth of the U.S. empire and responded closely to its needs, whether it was the political need to stabilize a neighboring country or to accept its refugees as a means of accomplishing a broader foreign policy objective (Cubans, Dominicans, Salvadorans, Nicaraguans), or an economic need, such as satisfying the labor demands of particular U.S. industries (Mexicans, Puerto Ricans, Panamanians).

Second, once the Latin Americans got here, they moved not from an immigrant to a mainstream status, but to a linguistic/racial caste status, mostly as a result of how language and race conflicts have been dealt with throughout United States and Latin American history.

Third, most Latin Americans arrived here when the United States was already the planet's dominant superpower, as our society was entering a postindustrial period and as our gap between rich and poor was growing, which meant that the unskilled factory jobs European immigrants had utilized to rise into the middle class were no longer a major option.

But as our corporations and financial institutions penetrated ever more deeply into Latin America, they fueled an unprecedented movement of labor from the south to the north. Government policies aimed at promoting greater economic integration only ended up exacerbating income and wealth disparities between inhabitants of the two regions. This is especially true in those countries most under the sway of Washington and Wall Street. As a result, our economy became an irresistible magnet drawing low-wage labor from the poorest areas of our "common market."

In 1990, for instance, four years before the North American Free Trade Agreement (NAFTA) took effect, federal estimates of the number of immigrants living in the United States illegally ranged from 3.4 million to 5.5 million. Most reliable estimates today place that number around 11 million, with Mexico being, at least until recent years, the source for more than two-thirds of those migrants. Before NAFTA took effect, an average of 350,000 Mexicans were migrating to the United States annually. During the early years of this decade, that number climbed to nearly 500,000 per year. Mexico holds the dubious distinction of sending more of its nationals to work abroad than any other country in the world, including China and India.[9]

But grasping the underlying causes of Latino immigration is just the start. It is equally important to recognize the flesh and blood stories behind this enormously complex phenomenon. Why did each Latino group come when it did? Why did some come and others not migrate at all? What did the pioneers of each group find when they got here? How did they interact with other Americans? How did they build their communities? Why did some retreat into ethnic enclaves and others not? How are Latinos changing the nation, and how do Anglo-Americans, white and Black, feel about those changes?

This book seeks to answer many of those questions by presenting an integrated historical look at both Latin America and Latinos in the United States—how both contributed to and were affected by the development of American ideals and American reality. It is divided into three main sections, which I have called "Roots," "Branches," and "Harvest."

"Roots," composed of three chapters, traces the long and tortuous relationship between Latin America and the United States. The first chapter, covering the colonial period, summarizes how Latin America and the United States developed into such radically different societies from the 1500s to independence; the second, how the United States expanded into an empire during the nineteenth century through seizing and exploiting Latin American territories; and the third, how our leaders turned the Caribbean region into a U.S. protectorate in the twentieth century. Admittedly, reviewing five hundred years of New World history in three short chapters is a daunting task, so be forewarned: I attempt to focus on key lessons and patterns that I have culled from various histories by both Anglo-American and Latin American authors, with an eye toward what light can be shed on our contemporary situation.

The second section, "Branches," is composed of six chapters, each devoted to one of the major Latino groups in the country. Here I combine the research of others on the modern migration saga with my own oral history interviews and investigations as a journalist. The immigration story of each Latino nationality is unique in the times it occurred, the class and type of people who came, and the way they dealt with their new environment. Our immigrant tales are as varied as those of the Swedish, Irish, Germans, Poles, and Italians who preceded us. No doubt, several books could be devoted to each Latino group, but I chose to focus my individual chapters on a family or a few individuals who tend to reflect the general migration story of that group, especially in its early years. I have tried to zero in on immigrants who became leaders or pioneers of the migration, and who have thus spent some time consciously digesting their own experiences. Most of them are people whom I have met during more than thirty years working as a journalist here and in Mexico, Central America, and the Caribbean. They are not the usual ethnic politicians whom outsiders look for when they want a quick read on how a community feels or acts. Rather, I have focused on grassroots leaders, people who clearly have earned the respect of their fellow migrants, but who rarely get interviewed or known outside their own communities.

The final section, "Harvest," is about Latinos in America today. It is composed of five chapters on some of the most pressing issues the average American usually associates with Latinos—politics, immigration, language, and culture. In addition, I have added a chapter on a key cause of Latin American migration over the past sixty years—U.S. trade policy, or what should more properly be called globalization. Finally, there is a chapter on Puerto Rico. Why a whole chapter? Well, that tiny island in the Caribbean was a bigger source of profit for U.S. investors during the twentieth century than any other country in the world. It also happens to be the last major American colonial possession. Yet it receives very little attention commensurate with its importance. Ending colonialism there is an issue with far-reaching repercussions, and not just for the nine million Puerto Ricans here and on the island. Until Puerto Rico is decolonized, American democracy will not be complete.

Developments in Latin America and the United States over the past ten years have produced a wealth of new evidence to support my original "harvest of empire" thesis. In this revised edition, I have sought to trace those key developments. The book's first two sections have remained the same except for minor stylistic improvements. I have extensively revised and updated, however, the five chapters in the final "Harvest" section, supplementing them with more up-to-date data and with accounts of key incidents and trends that are shaping the Latino community's evolution. Among the most noteworthy of these over the past decade have been:

- The post-9/11 crackdown on illegal immigration by both federal and local governments and the unprecedented immigrant rights movement it sparked.

+ The growing influence of the Latino electorate in the nation's political life, perhaps best symbolized by President's Obama's historic appointment of the first Hispanic Supreme Court associate justice, Sonia Sotomayor.

+ Puerto Rico's extraordinary four-year battle to get the U.S. Navy out of Vieques, as well as the island's deepening economic crisis and still unresolved status issue.

+ The disastrous impact of U.S. free trade policies on Latin America and on immigration to our shores in the wake of NAFTA.

+ The emergence of left-leaning populist governments throughout Latin America and how that sea change has affected the Latino population of the United States.

No nation, of course, is as crucial to U.S. relations with Latin America, or to establishing control of our immigration flow, than Mexico. The exodus of that country's workers to El Norte has become so massive that a few years ago Mexico moved into first place as the nation supplying the largest number of *legal* immigrants to the United States since the federal government began keeping statistics in 1820. It has now surpassed even Germany, the United Kingdom, Italy, and Ireland in this regard.

NAFTA, which was supposed to spur more new jobs in Mexico and thus slow the pressure on Mexicans to emigrate, has instead led to a greater exodus to the United States. Meanwhile, American corporations have sharply expanded their control over Mexico's manufacturing, banking, and agricultural sectors, and they now dominate its trade. Foreign banks moved into the country in a big way after the 1994 peso crisis, to the point that Citigroup is today one of Mexico's largest banks, while a handful of U.S. and other foreign firms now control more than 80 percent of that country's banking assets.[10]

Tens of thousands of subsistence farmers in the Mexican countryside have been driven to near ruin. Instead of planting traditional beans and corn, they have been increasingly lured by violent drug cartels to switch to marijuana and opium crops. Some officials estimate that as much as 30 percent of Mexico's farmland is now devoted to illicit crops. Large numbers of unemployed men in border cities like Ciudad Juárez, Tijuana, and Matamoros have become easy recruits for the private armies of the drug cartels. Spiraling drug violence in those cities has become a harrowing replay of the tragedy that engulfed Colombia in the 1980s.[11]

The book is aimed at the general reader who wishes to deepen his or her understanding about Hispanics as well as at the growing number of Latino students, professionals, and intellectuals who may know a great deal about their particular ethnic group—Chicanos, Puerto Ricans, Cubans, for instance—but little else about any other Hispanics.

So who am I to undertake such an ambitious task? Well, I was born in 1947 to working-class parents in Ponce, Puerto Rico. My family brought me to New York City's El Barrio the following year, and I have lived in this country ever since. As a journalist, and before that as a Puerto Rican community activist who helped found and direct two national organizations, the Young Lords in the 1960s and the National Congress for Puerto Rican Rights in the late 1970s, I have spent decades living in and reporting on scores of Latino communities throughout the United States and Latin America, devouring in the process every study or account of the Latino experience I could find.

At some point, I grew tired of having our story told, often one-sidedly, without the passion or the pain, by experts who had not lived it. There have been several such well-intentioned efforts for the general reader over the years, but too many fell into what I call the safari approach, geared strictly to an Anglo audience, with the author as guide and interpreter to the natives encountered along the way.

In our universities, meanwhile, many fine historians have broken important ground in recent decades with their research into Latino life in this country, and this book would not have been possible had they not paved the way. But many of those efforts focused on one Latino group, or on a specific area such as culture or politics, or a specific period of history. Few have attempted to sketch a broader canvas, to connect the past to the present, to cut across academic disciplines, while still making the entire process coherent to both Latinos and Anglos. Few attempt to understand our hemisphere as one New World, north and south. Even fewer trace the seamless bond between Anglo dominance of Latin America—two hundred years of massive and ever-increasing transfers of wealth from south to north, what Uruguayan Eduardo Galeano has called the "open veins of Latin America"—and the modern flood of the region's people to the United States. It is the view of this book that one would not exist without the other.

If Latin America had not been pillaged by U.S. capital since its independence, millions of desperate workers would not now be coming here in such numbers to reclaim a share of that wealth; and if the United States is today the world's richest nation, it is in part because of the sweat and blood of the copper workers of Chile, the tin miners of Bolivia, the fruit pickers of Guatemala and Honduras, the cane cutters of Cuba, the oil workers of Venezuela and Mexico, the pharmaceutical workers of Puerto Rico, the ranch hands of Costa Rica and Argentina, the West Indians who died building the Panama Canal, and the Panamanians who maintained it.

In this country, just how white and Black America cope with the mushrooming Latin American population will determine whether our nation enjoys interethnic tranquility in the twenty-first century or is convulsed by conflicts such as those that tore apart the multiethnic states of Eastern Europe, the old Soviet Union, and elsewhere.

I hope the reader will find in these pages not facile solutions to complex problems but a frank attempt to make sense of both the Latin American and North American experience. It has not been easy to separate my head from my heart as I sought to chronicle this story. I have met too many Latinos throughout my life who struggled and sacrificed far beyond the endurance of most of us to create something better for their children, yet found no respite and little respect, only to be, as the late poet Pedro Pietri once wrote, "buried without underwears." The deeper I delved into the two-hundred-year record of shenanigans by our statesmen, businessmen, and generals in Latin America, the angrier I became, especially because those leaders never seemed to learn from the past. My anger, however, is not tainted by hate; it comes from the frustration of seeing how bountiful our nation's promise has turned out for some, how needlessly heartbreaking for others, and it is tempered by the conviction that the American people still cling to a basic sense of fairness, that once they understand the facts, they rarely permit injustice to stand, which is in part why I have included in the book a host of facts not commonly known about Latinos.

Hopefully, by the time you have finished this book, you will see the Latino in America from another viewpoint. We Hispanics are not going away. Demographics and the tide of history point only to a greater not a lesser Latino presence throughout this century. Ours, however, is not some armed *reconquista* seeking to throw out Anglo occupiers from sacred lands that were once Latino. It is a search for survival, for inclusion on an equal basis, nothing more. It is a search grounded in the belief that, five hundred years after the experiment began, we are all Americans of the New World, and our most dangerous enemies are not one another but the great wall of ignorance between us.

A word about language usage. I believe needless time has been spent by Latino intellectuals in this country debating whether the term *Hispanic* or *Latino* best describes us. Neither is totally accurate but both are acceptable. Much as Blacks in this country went from being comfortable with *colored*, then *Negro*, then *Black*, then *African American*, so will U.S. Latin Americans pass through our phases. I remember back in the mid-1980s attending a joint conference in Mexico of Mexican and U.S. Hispanic journalists. The small Indian town where the conference was being held organized a reception for us visitors one night. The town square was decorated with a huge banner that read: "*Bienvenidos, periodistas hispano-norteamericanos*" ("Welcome, Hispanic–North American journalists"). So to each his own labels.

Likewise, we all know the word *America* has been unfairly appropriated by the people of the United States to refer to this country when it actually denotes the entire hemisphere. Latin Americans, meanwhile, refer to the United States as *Norteamérica*, or North America, and to U.S. citizens as *norteamericanos* (apologies to Canadians). And in Mexican American communities here, whites are sometimes called Anglos. Here, too, I have eschewed purism, using Americans, North Americans, and Anglos interchangeably.

I have used Mexican Americans or Chicanos to refer to Mexicans born and raised in the United States, *mexicanos, tejanos, californios* to refer to those Mexicans who lived in the country before the Treaty of Guadalupe Hidalgo made them U.S. citizens, and have italicized Spanish words that are not commonly known to an English-reading audience.

That said, I ask you to travel back with me to tear down some walls and begin a new journey through the American story.

PART I

Roots

(Las Raíces)

1

CONQUERORS AND VICTIMS:
The Image of America Forms
(1500–1800)

We saw cues and shrines in these cities that looked like
gleaming white towers and castles: a marvelous site.
—BERNAL DÍAZ DEL CASTILLO, 1568

The arrival of European explorers to America began the most astounding and far-reaching encounter between cultures in the history of civilization. It brought together two portions of the human race that until then had known nothing of each other's existence, thus establishing the basic identity of our modern world. French writer and critic Tzvetan Todorov has called it "the discovery *self* makes of the *other*"; while Adam Smith labeled it one of "the two greatest and most important events recorded in the history of mankind."[1]

Of the Europeans who settled America, those who hailed from England and Spain had the greatest impact. Both transplanted their cultures over vast territories. Both created colonial empires from whose abundance Europe rose to dominate the world. And descendants of both eventually launched independence wars that remade the political systems of our planet.

That common history has made Latin Americans and Anglo-Americans, like the Arabs and Jews of the Middle East, cousins in constant conflict, often hearing but not understanding each other.

Most of us know little of the enormous differences between how the Spanish and English settled America, or how those disparities led after independence to nations with such radically divergent societies. For just as adults develop key personality traits in the first years of childhood, so it was with the new nations of America, their collective identities and outlooks, their languages and social customs, molded by centuries in the colonial womb.

This first chapter seeks to probe how both Latin American and Anglo-American cultures were shaped from their colonial beginnings in the 1500s to the independence wars of the early 1800s, particularly how each culture took root in separate regions of what now makes up the United States.

What kind of people were the original English and Spanish settlers and how did the ideas and customs they brought with them affect the America they fashioned? What was the legacy of the settlers' religious beliefs, racial policies, and economic relationships? How did the colonial systems of their mother countries influence their political traditions? How were the rights of individuals regarded in the two groups of colonies? How did divergent views toward land, its ownership and its uses, promote or retard the development of their societies? To what degree did the various Amerindian civilizations the Europeans conquered influence the settlers' own way of life?

WHEN WORLDS COLLIDE

The native population at the time of first contact has been much debated. Estimates vary wildly, though there seems little doubt that it equaled or surpassed that of Europe. Most likely, it was around 60 million; some scholars place it as high as 110 million.[2] The greatest number, perhaps 25 million, lived in and around the Valley of Mexico, another 6 million inhabited the Central Andes region, while the territory north of the Rio Grande was home to perhaps another 10 million.[3] A bewildering level of uneven development prevailed among these Native Americans. The Han and Capoque were still in the Stone Age, nomads foraging naked along the bayous of the North American Gulf Coast. The slave-based city-states of the Aztecs, Mayas, and Incas, on the other hand, rivaled the sophistication and splendor of Europe. The Aztec capital of Tenochtitlán was a bustling metropolis. Meticulously designed and ingeniously constructed in the middle of a lake, where it was accessible only by well-guarded causeways, it contained some 250,000 inhabitants when Hernán Cortés first entered it. (London's population at the time was a mere 50,000 and that of Seville, the greatest city in Castile, barely 40,000.) The Spaniards were awestruck. One of Cortés's captains, Bernal Díaz del Castillo, left a vivid description of what he and his fellow Spaniards beheld that first day from the top of the central Aztec temple:

> We saw a great number of canoes, some coming with provisions and others returning with cargo and merchandise; and we saw too that one could not pass from one house to another of that great city and the other cities that were built on water except over wooden drawbridges or by canoe. We saw ... shrines in these cities that looked like gleaming white towers and castles: a marvelous sight.
>
> Some of our soldiers who had been in many parts of the world, in Constantinople, in Rome, and all over Italy, said they had never seen a market so well laid out, so large, so orderly, and so full of people.[4]

But Aztec civilization could not compare in grandeur, archaeologists tell us, to its predecessor, the city-state of Teotihuacán, which flourished for several centuries before it collapsed mysteriously in AD 700, leaving behind soul-stirring pyramids and intricate murals and artifacts as clues to its resplendent past. Nor did the Aztecs approach the sophistication of the Maya, America's Greeks, whose mathematicians and astronomers surpassed any in antiquity and whose scholars invented during their Classic Period (AD 300 to 900) the hemisphere's only known phonetic script.

Farther north, beyond the Rio Grande, hundreds of native societies existed when the Europeans arrived, all with their own languages and traditions, though only the Pueblos of New Mexico and the Iroquois Confederation in the Northeast approached the level of civilization reached by the natives of Mesoamerica and South America. The Pueblos were descended from the even larger and more advanced Anasazi, who flourished in present-day Colorado, New Mexico, and Arizona during the twelfth and thirteenth centuries AD before they, too, mysteriously vanished. By the time the first Spaniards arrived in the region in 1540, the Pueblos numbered around sixteen thousand. They were living in small cities of multilevel adobe apartments built on high plateaus, among them Acoma, Zuni, and Hopi. A peaceful, sedentary civilization, the Pueblos survived off the expanse of barren scrubland and buttes by planting extensively in river bottoms. They practiced a complicated animist religion that revolved around their ceremonial center, the kiva, where they taught their young that "competitiveness, aggressiveness and the ambition to lead were . . . offensive to the supernatural powers."[5]

The Iroquois Confederation, formed around 1570 by the Mohawk shaman, or chief, Hiawatha, was the largest and most durable alliance of native societies in North American history. Its influence stretched from the hinterland of Lake Superior to the backwoods of Virginia. Feared by all other Indians, the Iroquois became gatekeepers to the huge fur trade and a decisive force in the competition between the English and French for its control. They lived in towns of up to several thousand residents in wooden longhouses protected by double or triple rings of stockades. Social authority in each of the five Iroquois nations was matrilineal. Women chose the men who served as each clan's delegates to the nation's council, and each nation, in turn, elected representatives to the confederation's fifty-member ruling body, the Council Fire. That council decided all issues affecting the confederation by consensus.

The Europeans who stumbled upon this kaleidoscope of Amerindian civilizations were themselves just emerging from a long period of backwardness. The Black Death had swept out of Russia in 1350, leaving twenty-five million dead. There followed a relentless onslaught of epidemics that so devastated the continent that its population declined by 60 to 75 percent in the span of a hundred years. So few peasants were left to work the land that feudal society disintegrated, the price of agricultural labor soared, and new classes of both rich peasants and poor nobles came into being. The sudden labor shortage spurred technical innovation as a way to increase production, and that innovation, in turn, led to the rise of factories in the cities. The social upheaval brought about a new mobility among the long-suffering peasantry, and with it a new aggressiveness. Rebellions by the starving poor against their feudal lords became more frequent. Some even assailed the all-powerful Catholic Church, whose bishops preached piety to the common man while surrounded by the privileges of the nobility.[6]

By the fifteenth century, the frequency of plagues had ebbed, population had rebounded, and the continent had emerged into a dazzling era of artistic and scientific achievement. The first printing presses disseminated the new knowledge widely, through books written in scores of vernacular languages, ending forever the monopoly of

Latin and the stranglehold of the clergy on learning. In 1492, as Columbus launched Europe's historic encounter with the Amerindians, Renaissance geniuses like Hieronymus Bosch and Leonardo da Vinci were at the apex of their fame; the German master Albrecht Dürer was twenty-one; Niccolò Machiavelli was twenty-three; Dutchman Desiderius Erasmus was twenty-six; the Englishman Thomas More was fourteen; Copernicus was only nineteen, and Martin Luther a boy of eight.

The revolutions in production and in knowledge were reflected in politics as well. For the first time, strong monarchs ruled England and Spain, kings who were determined to create unified nations out of fiefdoms that had quarreled and warred against one another since the fall of the Roman Empire.

Foremost among those monarchs were King Ferdinand of Aragon and Queen Isabella of Castile, who joined their twin kingdoms and finally ousted the Moors in 1492 from the Kingdom of Granada, the last Arab stronghold in Europe. For most of the previous eight centuries, Moors had occupied the Iberian Peninsula, where they withstood fierce but intermittent crusades by Christian Spaniards to reclaim their land. Those crusades—the Spanish call them *La Reconquista*—had succeeded over the centuries in slowly shunting the Moors farther south, until only Granada remained in Arab hands.

Ironically, the Moorish occupation and *La Reconquista* prepared Spain for its imperial role in America. The occupation turned the country and the city of Córdoba into the Western world's premier center for the study of science and philosophy, while the fighting engendered a hardened warrior ethos in the hidalgos, Spain's lower nobility. It was those hidalgos who later rushed to fill the ranks of the conquistador armies in the New World. The wars provided vital practice in colonization, with Spanish kings gradually adopting the practice of paying their warriors with grants of land they recovered in battle. Finally, *La Reconquista* reinforced a conviction among Spaniards that they were the true defenders of Catholicism.

Unlike Spain, which grew monolithic through *La Reconquista*, England emerged from the Middle Ages bedeviled by strife among its own people. The most bloody of those conflicts was the thirty-year War of the Roses, which finally drew to a close in 1485 when Henry Tudor of the House of Lancaster vanquished Richard III of the House of York. Henry VII quickly distinguished himself by creating a centralized government and reliable system of taxation, the first English monarch to do so. His success was due in no small measure to the prosperity of English farming, to the flowering of English nationalism, and to his enlightened concessions to local self-government. Henry's subjects proudly believed themselves to be better off than any people in Europe, and they were largely right, for neither the widespread class divisions nor the famine and squalor that afflicted much of the continent during the fifteenth century could be found in England. Slavery, for instance, did not exist in the kingdom, and English serfs already enjoyed greater liberties than their European counterparts.[7] The yeomanry, small farmers who composed a large middle class between the gentry and the serfs, fostered economic stability and provided a counterweight to curb the power of the nobility. At the same time, Parliament and the traditions of English common law accorded the average citizen greater protection from either the king or his nobles than any other political system in Europe.

Such were the conditions in 1497 when Henry, fired by news of Columbus's discoveries, dispatched explorer John Cabot to America. Cabot landed in Newfoundland and laid claim to North America for the British Crown, but he perished in a subsequent trip before establishing a colony. That failure, along with the discovery of gold and silver in Mexico and Peru a few decades later, permitted Spain to catapult to the pinnacle of sixteenth-century world power. Meanwhile, the English, bereft of colonies and increasingly consumed by religious and political strife at home, were reduced to sniping at Spanish grandeur through the exploits of their pirates.

When they finally did embark on a New World empire a century later, the English brought with them not just their tradition of local self-government but the vestiges of their domestic conflicts as well, most important of which were the religious schisms and sects that arose after Henry VIII broke with the pope in Rome and established the Church of England. Among those sects, one in particular, the Puritans, was destined to leave a vast imprint on American society.

Another "British" conflict that was to greatly influence the New World was the colonizing of Catholic Ireland and the bloody repression that accompanied it. By their callous treatment of the Irish, Anglo-Norman Protestants set the stage for the massive Irish flight that followed. English leaders justified that occupation by claiming that the Irish were a barbarian people, but in doing so, they gave birth to notions of Anglo-Saxon superiority that they would later use to justify their conquest of Native Americans.[8]

EARLY SPANISH INFLUENCE
IN THE UNITED STATES

The textbooks most of us read in grammar school have long acknowledged that Spanish conquistadores crisscrossed and laid claim to much of the southern and western United States nearly a century before the first English colonies were founded at Jamestown and Massachusetts Bay. But most Anglo-American historians have promoted the notion that the early Spanish presence rapidly disappeared and left a minor impact on U.S. culture when compared with our dominant Anglo-Saxon heritage.

Those early expeditions, however, led to permanent Spanish outposts throughout North America, to the founding of our earliest cities, Saint Augustine and Santa Fe, and to the naming of hundreds of U.S. rivers, mountains, towns, and even several states. Moreover, they led to a Spanish-speaking population—more accurately, a Latino/mestizo population—that has existed continuously in certain regions of the United States since that time. That heritage, and the colonial society it spawned, has been so often overlooked in contemporary debates over culture, language, and immigration that we would do well to review its salient parts.

Juan Ponce de León was the first European to touch what is now U.S. soil. His fruitless search for the Fountain of Youth led to his discovery in 1513 of Florida. He returned eight years later but was killed in battle with the Calusa Indians before he could found a settlement.

Nearly two decades after Ponce de León's death, Francisco Vásquez de Coronado and Hernando de Soto, their imaginations fired by the treasures Cortés had seized in Mexico, each led major expeditions in search of the fabled cities of gold. Starting from central Mexico in 1539, Coronado and his men marched north into present-day Arizona, New Mexico, Texas, Oklahoma, and Kansas, planting the Spanish flag wherever they went. By the time the expedition returned in 1542, the Spaniards had discovered the Grand Canyon, crossed and named many of the continent's great rivers, but discovered no gold. The same year Coronado set out, de Soto led an expedition out of Cuba that explored much of Georgia, South

Carolina, Alabama, Mississippi, Arkansas, and Louisiana, but he and half his men perished without finding any treasure.

The most extraordinary exploit of all, however, was that of Álvar Núñez Cabeza de Vaca, who arrived in Florida in 1527—fifteen years before de Soto—as second-in-command to Pánfilo de Narváez, the bungling onetime governor of Cuba whom King Charles of Spain authorized to complete the colonization of Florida. After landing on the peninsula's western coast, Narváez led a three-hundred-man expedition inland near present-day Tallahassee, then foolishly lost touch with his ships and was killed. His men, unable to withstand the constant Indian assaults, headed west along the Gulf Coast on makeshift barges.

Only four survived the ordeal, among them Cabeza de Vaca and a Spanish Moor named Estevanico. The four spent the next seven years wandering through the North American wilderness. Their six-thousand-mile trek, one of the great exploration odysseys of history, and the first crossing of North America by Europeans, is preserved in a report Cabeza de Vaca wrote for the king of Spain in 1542. At first, they were separated and enslaved by coastal tribes, where Cabeza de Vaca was beaten so often his life became unbearable. After a year in captivity, he managed to escape and took up the life of a trader between the tribes: "Wherever I went, the Indians treated me honorably and gave me food, because they liked my commodities. I became well known; those who did not know me personally knew me by reputation and sought my acquaintance."[9]

His rudimentary medical knowledge enabled him at one point to cure some sick Indians. From that point on, the tribes revered him as a medicine man. Once a year, when the various tribes gathered for the annual picking of prickly pears, he was reunited with his fellow Spaniards, who remained enslaved. At one such gathering in 1533, he engineered their escape and they all fled west through present-day Texas, New Mexico, and Arizona. As they traveled, word spread of the wondrous white medicine man and his companions, and soon thousands of Indians started to follow in a caravan of worshippers. The four did not finally reconnect with Spanish civilization in northern Mexico until 1534. By then, Cabeza de Vaca had been transformed. He no longer regarded the Native American as a savage, for he now had an intimate understanding of their culture and outlook. Instead, the barbarity of his fellow Spaniards toward the Indians now filled him with despair. His description of his trip through an

area where Spanish slave traders were hunting Indians remains a
powerful revelation into the nature of the Conquest:

> With heavy hearts we looked out over the lavishly watered, fertile, and
> beautiful land, now abandoned and burned and the people thin and
> weak, scattering or hiding in fright. Not having planted, they were re-
> duced to eating roots and bark; and we shared their famine the whole
> way. Those who did receive us could provide hardly anything. They
> themselves looked as if they would willingly die. They brought us
> blankets they had concealed from the other Christians and told us how
> the latter had come through razing the towns and carrying off half the
> men and all the women and boys.[10]

THE TOLL OF CONQUEST

The devastation Cabeza de Vaca warned of still defies comprehension. By the late 1500s, a mere century after the Conquest began,
scarcely two million natives remained in the entire hemisphere. An
average of more than one million people perished annually for most
of the sixteenth century, in what has been called "the greatest genocide in human history."[11] On the island of Hispaniola, which was
inhabited by one million Taínos in 1492, fewer than 46,000 remained twenty years later.[12] As historian Francis Jennings has
noted, "The American land was more like a widow than a virgin.
Europeans did not find a wilderness here; rather, however involun-
tarily, they made one."

Fewer natives perished in the English colonies only because the
Amerindian populations were sparser to begin with, yet the macabre percentages were no less grisly: 90 percent of the Indian population was gone within half a century of the Puritan landing on
Plymouth Rock; the Block Island Indians plunged from 1,500 to 51
between 1662 and 1774; the Wampanoag tribe of Martha's Vineyard
declined from 3,000 in 1642 to 313 in 1764; and the Susquehan-
nock tribe in central Pennsylvania nearly disappeared, falling from
6,500 in 1647 to 250 by 1698.[13]

Much of this cataclysm was unavoidable. The Indians succumbed
to smallpox, measles, tuberculosis, and bubonic plague, for which
they had no immunity, just as Europeans had succumbed to their
own epidemics in previous centuries. But an astounding number of

native deaths resulted from direct massacres or enslavement. If the Spaniards exterminated more than the British or French, it is because they encountered civilizations with greater population, complexity, and wealth, societies that desperately resisted any attempt to subjugate them or seize their land and minerals.

The battle for Tenochtitlán, for instance, was rivaled in overall fatalities by few in modern history. During the eighty-day siege of the Aztec capital by Cortés and his Texcoco Indian allies, 240,000 natives perished.[14] A few Indian accounts of the battle survive today thanks to Franciscan missionaries like Bernardino de Sahagún and Diego Durán, who as early as 1524 developed a written form of the Nahuatl language, the lingua franca of central Mexico. The missionaries urged the Indians to preserve their tragic songs and reminiscences of the Conquest, and several of those accounts, such as the following section from the *Codex Florentino*, vividly describe what happened at Tenochtitlán:

> Once again the Spaniards started killing and a great many Indians died. The flight from the city began and with this the war came to an end. The people cried: "We have suffered enough! Let us leave the city! Let us go live on weeds!"
>
> A few of the men were separated from the others. These men were the bravest and strongest warriors. The youths who served them were also told to stand apart. The Spaniards immediately branded them with hot irons, either on the cheek or the lips.[15]

Less than a quarter century after the arrival of Columbus, the Indian genocide sparked its first protest from a Spaniard, Fray Bartolomé de las Casas, who had arrived in Santo Domingo as a landowner but opted instead to become a Franciscan missionary. The first priest ordained in America, he quickly relinquished his lands and commenced a campaign against Indian enslavement that made him famous throughout Europe. As part of that campaign, he authored a series of polemics and defended the Indians in public debates against Spain's greatest philosophers. The most famous of those polemics, *A Short Account of the Destruction of the Indies*, recounts scores of massacres by Spanish soldiers, including one ordered by Cuba's governor Pánfilo de Narváez, which Las Casas personally observed. In that incident, according to Las Casas, a group of natives approached a Spanish settlement with food and gifts, when the

Christians, "without the slightest provocation, butchered before my eyes, some three thousand souls—men, women and children, as they sat there in front of us."[16]

Las Casas's untiring efforts on behalf of the Amerindians led to Spain's adoption of "New Laws" in 1542. The codes recognized Indians as free and equal subjects of the Spanish Crown, but landowners in many regions refused to observe the codes and kept Indians in virtual slavery for generations. Despite his heroic efforts, Las Casas, who was eventually promoted to bishop of Chiapas in Guatemala, also committed some major blunders. At one point he advocated enslaving Africans to replace Indian labor, though he ultimately recanted that position. While his polemics were among the most popular books in Europe and led to widespread debate over the toll of colonization, they greatly exaggerated the already grisly numbers of the Indian genocide, thus making Las Casas the unwitting source of the Spanish "Black Legend" that would later be propagated by Dutch and British Protestants—the view that the Spanish Conquest was somehow more ruthless and savage than that of other European colonizers.[17]

Spain, of course, had no monopoly on settler barbarism. In 1637, the Puritans of the Connecticut Colony mistakenly concluded that local Pequot had killed two white men, so they set out to punish them. Assisted by other Indian enemies of the tribe, the Englishmen stormed the Pequot village on the Mystic River while its braves were absent, and roasted or shot to death between three hundred and seven hundred women and children before burning the entire village.[18] Forty years later, during King Philip's War, colonists and their mercenaries conducted similar vicious slaughters of women and children. An estimated two thousand Indians perished in battle and another thousand were sold into slavery in the West Indies during the conflict.[19] And South Carolina's Cherokee War (1760–1761) turned so brutal that a colonist defending a fort against Indians wrote to the governor, "We have now the pleasure, Sir, to fatten our dogs with their carcasses and to display their scalps neatly ornamented on the top of our bastions."[20]

This type of savagery, often reciprocated by Indians desperate to defend their land, became a hallmark of Anglo-Indian relations far after the colonial period. A particularly gruesome example was carried out by Andrew Jackson in 1814. Settlers and land speculators from the Carolinas had started moving into the territory shortly

after the War of Independence. When the settlers tried to push out
the Indian inhabitants, the Creek resisted, and the U.S. Army, led
by Jackson, intervened. During the war's decisive battle at Horseshoe Bend, Alabama, on March 27, 1814, Jackson's men massacred
and cut off the noses of 557 Creek, then skinned the dead bodies to
tan the Indian hides and make souvenir bridle reins.[21]

THE ROLE OF THE CHURCH

While all European settlers justified the Indian conquest and genocide as God's will, the Spanish and English differed substantially in
their methods of subjugation, and this eventually led to radically different colonial societies. English kings, for instance, commanded
their agents to "conquer, occupy and possess" the lands of the "hea-
thens and infidels," but said nothing of the people inhabiting them,
while Spain, following the dictates of Pope Alexander VI, sought not
only to grab the land but also to make any pagans found on it "embrace the Catholic faith and be trained in good morals." In Spain,
both Crown and church saw colonizing and conversion as a unified
effort. Priests accompanied each military expedition for the purpose
of Christianizing the natives. Within a month of landing in Mexico,
Bernal Díaz reminds us, Cortés presided over the first Indian baptisms, of twenty women given to the Spanish soldiers by the Tabas-
cans of the coast: "One of the Indian ladies was christened Doña
Marina. She was a truly great princess, the daughter of Caciques and
the mistress of vassals . . . they were the first women in New Spain to
become Christians. Cortés gave one of them to each of his captains."[22]

As the Conquest proceeded, priests performed such baptisms by
the thousands. Before the holy water could dry on their foreheads, the
Indian women were routinely grabbed as concubines by Spanish soldiers and settlers. The priests even performed occasional marriages
between Spaniards and Indians, especially among the elite of both
groups, thus fostering and legitimizing a new mestizo race in America. For example, Peruvian historian Garcilaso de la Vega, called El
Inca, was born in 1539 to a Spanish officer and an Incan princess,
while the parish register of Saint Augustine, Florida, recorded
twenty-six Spanish-Indian marriages in the early 1700s, at a time
when only a few hundred natives resided near the town.[23] Far more
important than legal marriages, however, was the extraordinary

number of consensual unions. Francisco de Aguirre, among the conquistadores of Chile, boasted that by fathering more than fifty mestizo children, his service to God had been "greater than the sin incurred in doing so."[24]

The first English colonies, by contrast, began as family settlements. They maintained strict separation from Indian communities, sometimes even bolstered by segregation laws.[25] In North America, Indians rarely served as laborers for settlers or as household servants, and unmarried sexual unions between natives and whites were rare except for captives of war.

The English, furthermore, never saw proselytizing among the Indians as important. True, the Virginia Company listed missionary work as one of its purposes when the Crown granted Jamestown its charter in 1607. And nine years later, the Crown even ordered funds raised from all parishes in the Church of England be used to erect a college for the natives. But the company never sent a single missionary to Virginia, and the college was never built. Officials simply diverted the money for their own ends until an investigation of the fraud prompted the Crown to revoke the company's charter and take over direct administration of the colony in 1622.[26]

Likewise, the New England Puritans segregated themselves from the Indians, not even venturing out of their settlements to win converts until decades after their arrival. In 1643, sections of Harvard College were built with money raised by the New England Company among Anglicans back home. While donors were told the funds would be used for Indian education, some of the money ended up buying guns and ammunition for the colonists.[27] So minor was Puritan concern for the Indians' souls that by 1674, fifty-five years after the founding of Plymouth Colony, barely a hundred natives in all New England were practicing Christians.[28]

At one time or another, clerics Roger Williams of Rhode Island, Cotton Mather of Massachusetts Bay, and Samuel Purchas of Virginia all vilified the natives as demonic. The Reverend William Bradford, one of the original Pilgrim leaders, insisted they were "cruel, barbarous and most treacherous . . . not being content only to kill and take away a life, but delight to torment men in the most bloody manner."[29] Throughout colonial history, only Williams's Rhode Island colony and the Quakers of Pennsylvania showed themselves willing to coexist in harmony with their Indian neighbors. Despite their low regard for the Indians, the English settlers did not try to incorporate them as subjects of colonies. At first, they merely purchased or finagled choice parcels of land from some tribes and pressured others to move toward the interior.

In the Spanish colonies, however, the natives were far more numerous, and the policies of the Catholic Church far more aggressive. Church leaders did more than merely recognize Indian humanity or accommodate *mestizaje*. The church dispatched an army of Franciscan, Dominican, and Jesuit monks who served as the vanguard of sixteenth-century Spanish colonialism. The monks who flocked to America perceived the chaotic rise of capitalism in Europe as auguring an era of moral decay. In the Native Americans they imagined a simpler, less corrupted human being, one who could more easily be persuaded to follow the word of Christ. So they abandoned Spain to set up their missions in the most remote areas of America, far from the colonial cities and *encomiendas*.

Those missions—the first was founded by Las Casas in Venezuela in 1520—became the principal frontier outposts of Spanish civilization. Many had farms and schools to Europeanize the Indians and research centers where the monks set about learning and preserving the native languages. Quite a few of the monks were inspired by Thomas More, whose widely read *Utopia* (1516) portrayed a fictional communal society of Christians located somewhere on an island in America. One of More's most ardent admirers was Vasco de Quiroga, who established a mission of thirty thousand Tarascans in central Mexico and rose to bishop of Michoacán. Quiroga, like More, talked of trying to "restore the lost purity of the primitive Church." Given that Indians had no concept of land ownership or money, the missionaries easily organized cooperative tilling of the land and even communal housing, just as More espoused.

The natives proved less malleable and far less innocent than the Europeans imagined, so much so that early colonial history is filled with countless stories of monks who met hideous deaths at the hands of their flocks. Despite those tragedies, the monks kept coming, and as the years passed, some of their missions even prospered. That prosperity enraged colonial landowners, who increasingly regarded mission Indian labor as unwanted competition for the products of their plantations. In 1767, the colonial elite finally succeeded in getting the Jesuits, the most independent of the monastic orders, expelled from the New World. By then, 2,200 Jesuits were working in the colonies and more than 700,000 Indians resided in their missions.[30]

Long before those Jesuit expulsions, Spanish monks played a

crucial role in colonizing major parts of the United States. Most important were the Franciscans, who founded nearly forty thriving missions in Florida, Georgia, and Alabama during the 1600s and numerous others in the Southwest. Saint Augustine was the headquarters for the Florida missions, in which as many as twenty thousand Christianized Indians lived.[31] While most of the Florida missions eventually were abandoned, several in the Southwest later turned into thriving towns, with Spanish monks today recognized as the founders of San Antonio, El Paso, Santa Fe, Tucson, San Diego, Los Angeles, Monterey, and San Francisco.

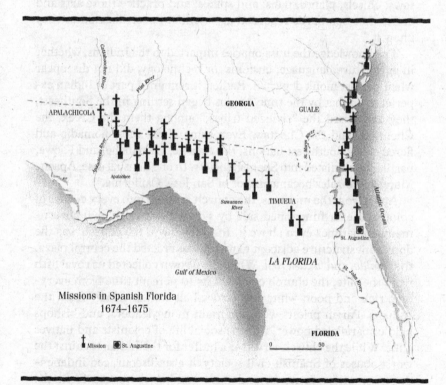

Missions in Spanish Florida
1674–1675

† Mission   ◼ St. Augustine

0 ———— 50

The Florida missions and settlements left a greater imprint on frontier American culture than we might believe. That influence was not always a direct one. Rather, it came by way of the Indians and Africans who remained after the missionaries were gone and who carried on some of the customs they learned from the Spanish settlers. Indians who traded with Europeans at Pensacola in 1822 were "better acquainted with the Spanish language than either the French or English," notes historian David Weber, and Englishmen who settled in Virginia, Carolina, and Georgia encountered Indians who were already cultivating peach trees the Spanish had introduced from Europe. Weber notes that the missionaries of Florida and New Mexico "taught native converts to husband European domestic animals—horses, cattle, sheep, goats, pigs, and chickens; cultivate European crops, from watermelon to wheat; raise fruit trees, from peaches to pomegranates; use such iron tools as wheels, saws, chisels, planes, nails, and spikes; and practice those arts and crafts that Spaniards regarded as essential for civilization as they knew it."

The knowledge the missionaries imparted to the Indians, whether in agriculture, language, customs, or technology, did not disappear when the last monk departed. Rather, it remained part of Indian experience so that by the time Anglos began settling in the Southeast, they discovered the "civilized tribes," among them the Creek, the Cherokee, and the Choctaw. Even some of the most nomadic and fierce of the Southwest nations, the Apache, Comanche, and Kiowa, partially assimilated into Spanish society. In one unusual case, Apache Manuel González became mayor of San Jose, California.[32]

Apart from the missions, the church reached into every corner of colonial life. It functioned side by side with Spanish civil government, sometimes even above it. In every town, the church was the dominant structure adjacent to which was erected the central plaza, the *cabildo*, and *la casa real*. While the Crown collected its royal fifth from the elite, the church collected its 10 percent tithe from everyone, rich and poor, white and colored, as well as tribute from the Indians. Parish priests were the main moneylenders, and bishops held unparalleled power over the social life of colonists and natives alike. While the church served as a buffer for the Indians against the worst abuses of Spanish civil society, it also discouraged independence or self-sufficiency, and it demanded obedience from the natives it protected.

Even Europeans who dared question church authority or doctrine were liable to be called before the all-powerful Inquisition, which could threaten anyone up to the governor with excommunication or prison, and which routinely prohibited the circulation of thousands of books and works of art it deemed sacrilegious. Its demand for blind faith toward church doctrine impeded for centuries the spread of tolerance, ingenuity, and creativity in Latin American thought.

No English colonial church enjoyed a monopoly power approaching that of the Catholic Church in the Spanish territories. The proliferation of sects among Protestants meant each denomination, even when its leaders wished to set up a theocratic colony, could do so only within a circumscribed area, as the Puritans did in Massachusetts and Connecticut. The Puritan witch trials of the early 1690s in Salem and surrounding Essex County rivaled the worst atrocities of the Inquisition. Twenty men and women were executed and more than 150 imprisoned, but the fanatics proved incapable of controlling everyone. Long before the witch trials, Roger Williams rebelled and founded the Rhode Island colony, where he permitted all manner of worship, and other colonies followed similar liberal policies. Catholic Maryland enacted a religious tolerance law and Quaker William Penn set up his Pennsylvania colony, which, likewise, welcomed all believers. New York City turned into such a hodgepodge of religious groups that its English governor reported in 1687: "Here, bee not many of the Church of England, [and] few Roman Catholicks, [but] abundance of Quakers—preachers, men and women, especially—singing Quakers, ranting Quakers, Sabbatarians, Anti-sabbatarians, some Anabaptists, some Independants, some Jews: in short, of all sorts of opinions there are some, and the most part of none at all."33

After Parliament declared religious freedom in the colonies with the Toleration Act of 1689, the emigration of sects from Europe soared. Thousands of Germans, among them Lutherans, Moravians, Mennonites, and Amish, settled in the Middle Colonies and the hinterlands of the South, as did Scotch-Irish Presbyterians in the South.

THE ROLE OF RACE

Beyond their religious practices, the English and Spanish colonial worlds diverged substantially in their attitudes toward slavery and race. The long period of Arab domination left an indelible legacy of racial and cultural mixing that the Spanish immigrants carried to the New World. Moorish occupiers of the Iberian Peninsula had invariably taken Spanish wives, setting off an era of miscegenation so extensive that "by the fifteenth century there were dark-skinned

Christians, light-haired Moors, hybrids of every shape and complexion in Castile," according to one historian. Some Muslims, called
Mudejares, continued to live under Christian rule, while some
Christians, called Mozarabs, learned to speak Arabic and adopted
Muslim habits. The dress, foods, and traditions of Moors and Spaniards permeated each other's societies. In architecture, for instance,
the horseshoe arches, tiled floors and walls, and open interior court-
yards so commonly associated with Spanish design in America, all
drew from Arabic inspiration.[34]

This tradition of racial mixing made it more acceptable for Spanish settlers to engage in sexual unions with both Amerindians and
Africans. This was especially true for settlers from Andalusia in
southern Spain, the province that endured the longest period of
Moorish occupation, and which supplied nearly 40 percent of the
early settlers to America.[35] At the beginning of the Conquest, Seville, Andalusia's main port, was Spain's most cosmopolitan city and
the nexus for commerce with Africa. It quickly turned into the bustling crossroads for transatlantic trade as well. By the middle of the
sixteenth century, the city counted nearly one hundred thousand inhabitants from all parts of Europe and the Mediterranean, including
six thousand enslaved Africans.[36]

But racial mixing did not mean racial equality. As the Indian
population of America gradually rebounded, and as Black slave labor
assumed a greater role in colonial plantation production, the Spanish and Creole upper classes became increasingly fearful of revolt—
so fearful that after the Haitian revolution, the Council of the Indies,
the Crown's administrative body for colonies, banned all marriages
between whites and free Blacks or *mulatos*. Despite the ban, the
practice of mixed racial marriages continued, with dispensations
often granted in cases where the honor of the woman was at stake.
Upon denying one such request in 1855, the civil governor of Ori-
ente province in Cuba remarked, "There is little doubt that the dis-
semination of ideas of equality of the white class with the coloured
race puts in jeopardy the tranquillity of the Island, the largest proportion of whose population consists of the said race."[37]

Apart from the ban on unions between whites and nonwhites, the
institution of marriage itself played a distinctive role in Spanish society. It was one of the many avenues the church utilized to mitigate
the worst aspects of slavery that were so evident in the English colonies. The church would not permit slave owners, for instance, to separate married couples, and it sanctioned marriage between slaves

and free persons. Historian Herbert Klein reports that in selected parishes of Havana between 1825 and 1829, more than a third of all marriages were between slaves, and nearly a fifth were between a slave and a free person. In many parts of Cuba, the marriage rate among slaves was equal to or higher than among whites.[38]

Perhaps even more important than formal marriage, however, was the social impact of consensual unions. No European society before the nineteenth century witnessed the level of free unions found in Latin America. Illegitimate births among free persons of all classes were close to 50 percent. Among the white upper classes, they were higher than among any other European elite.[39] Those unions, which were invariably between white men and nonwhite women, were preferable to official marriage because they did not subvert the class structure.

The prevalence of both consensual unions and miscegenation, along with the strong influence of the Catholic Church, led to major differences between how the English and Spanish regarded the rights of slaves, especially toward the end of the eighteenth century. Until then, all colonial powers had allowed masters to free their slaves. But after the Haitian revolution, the British, French, and Dutch started to restrict manumission, while the Portuguese and Spanish colonies promoted and codified the practice.

As a result, only in the Portuguese and Spanish colonies did giant classes of free Blacks develop, and with them the *mulato* group (in some countries they were called *pardos* or *morenos*) that so distinguished Latin America's rainbow racial spectrum from North America's stark Black-white system of racial classification. In the United States, for instance, the first federal census in 1790 reported that "free coloreds" were less than 2 percent of the population, while enslaved Blacks were 18 percent.[40] The same proportion of free Blacks to slaves was roughly true in the British, Dutch, and French Caribbean colonies. But the opposite trend prevailed in the Spanish and Portuguese colonies, where free Blacks or coloreds outnumbered slaves, with perhaps 40 to 60 percent of free Blacks able to purchase their emancipation outright.[41] The viceroyalty of New Granada, which included Colombia, Venezuela, and Ecuador, had 80,000 slaves and 420,000 free coloreds in 1789.[42] Cuba had 199,000 slaves and 114,000 free coloreds in 1817.[43] By 1872, free coloreds composed 43 percent of Brazil's population, outnumbering both pure whites and enslaved Blacks.

Color and status so deeply demarcated the English colonies,

however, that the free colored class was considered an abnormality only barely tolerated.[44] A drop of Black blood made you Black in Anglo-Saxon society, while in the Portuguese and Spanish world, mestizos and *mulatos*, no matter how dark, were invariably regarded as part of white society, although admittedly second-class members.

Racism persisted in both groups of colonies, but in the Iberian ones it assumed a muted form, its operation rendered more complex by the presence of a huge mixed-race population. The quest for white purity in Latin America became confined to a tiny upper class, while dispensations for lower-class whites to marry outside their race were routinely granted. The reasons were simple. For rich whites, marriage was first and foremost a manner of securing inheritance lines. Racial mixing was not allowed to subvert the class structure, though on occasion even some of the elite officially "recognized" their mixed-race children, ushering them partially into white society. The arcane types of mixed-race offspring that developed in Latin America were astounding. Beyond mestizos and *mulatos*, there were *zambos* (Indian and Black), *coyotes* (mestizo and Indian), *salta-atrás* (those with Black features born of white parents), *chinos* (offspring of Indian and *salta-atrás*), *cuarterones* (quadroons), and even more exotic distinctions.

For the Anglo-Saxon colonies, on the other hand, interracial marriage was taboo, by any class of whites. Even after independence and emancipation, it remained banned, and while rape or unsanctioned unions obviously occurred, Anglo-Saxons almost never recognized their mixed-race children, no matter how light-skinned the offspring or how poor the father.

LAND AND POLITICS IN THE TWO SOCIETIES

Beyond religion and race, the Spanish and English colonies diverged radically in the way they managed their economic and political systems. Spain's colonies were royal affairs from the start. Conquistadores functioned as direct agents of the Crown. And Spain's main object, at least for the first century, was gold and silver; by 1600, its colonies had already produced more than two billion pesos' worth, three times the total European supply before Columbus's first voyage.[45] (The total surpassed six billion pesos, mostly in silver, by 1800.) The flood of silver coin, however, only led to massive inflation at home. Domestic industry and agriculture stagnated as more than two hundred thousand Spaniards left for the New World during the first century of colonization. Countless others fled the Spanish countryside and flocked to Seville and Cádiz to engage in mercantile trade.[46] The Crown's expulsion of the Moors and Jews only exacerbated the economic crisis, because those two groups had provided much of the country's professional and commercial vitality. Jewish merchants fled with their wealth to the financial centers of London, Amsterdam, and Genoa.[47] With Spain forced to resort to huge loans from foreign banks to meet the spiraling costs of administering its vast empire, much of the production from the mines of Mexico and Peru passed into the coffers of Dutch and English bankers and went to pay for manufactured goods to supply the colonies.

When they finally started their own American colonies nearly a century after Spain, the English and the Dutch rejected Spain's state-sponsored approach. They relied instead on rich nobles financing individual colonies and on a new type of business venture— the joint stock company. The London Company, the Plymouth Company, the Virginia Company, and the Dutch West Indies Company all secured charters from their monarchs to populate the new territories.

While the Pilgrims and other colonists indeed fled religious persecution, the same cannot be said of the companies that transported them. Utopia for these new capitalist concerns was far less spiritual in nature. It meant the chase for enormous profit: from trading for furs with the Indians; from wood and iron and other raw materials that could be shipped to England; and from charging hefty rates for relocating England's malcontents and dissidents to the New World. In 1627, for instance, the London Company declared one of its objectives to be "the removing of the surcharge of necessitous people, the matter or fuel of dangerous insurrections, and thereby leaving the greater plenty to sustain those remaining with the Land."[48]

The mass exodus from England and Europe, however, was not simply a spontaneous emigration of the continent's persecuted and destitute, as immigrant myth would have us believe. More than half the population of the thirteen colonies before 1776 was composed of indentured servants. Among these were fifty thousand convicts who were released from English jails during the seventeenth century to populate the Maryland and Virginia colonies, and a considerable number of children who had been kidnapped and sold into servitude.[49]

Land speculators who worked in tandem with merchants orchestrated and engineered much of the exodus. Labor agents scoured the British Isles and the Rhineland for recruits to work the huge tracts of American land the speculators owned, enticing farm families to sell their property and seek instant wealth in the New World.[50] William Penn, for example, employed recruiting agents in London, Dublin, Edinburgh, and Rotterdam. Penn's merchant friend in Rotterdam, Benjamin Furly, was so successful advertising the colony in the Rhine Valley that he turned Pennsylvania into the center for German immigrants to the colonies.[51]

At first, England left colonial administration in the hands of the companies because the Crown was preoccupied with its own domestic strife and religious battles. But by the end of the seventeenth century, Parliament assumed direct administration through its Board of Trade, the counterpart to Spain's Council of the Indies. Even then, however, England kept its New World bureaucracy rather tiny.

The Spanish empire, on the other hand, spawned such a huge colonial bureaucracy that 1.1 million people held religious office of some kind in the Spanish colonies by the seventeenth century, and nearly half a million held government jobs.[52] Like most bureaucracies, the colonial church and civil government slowed the pace of decision making, buried innovation under mountains of reports and edicts, and stifled all manner of dissent. In fairness to Spain, its empire was the largest the world had ever seen. From Oregon all the way to Patagonia, it stretched over some of the world's most impassable mountains, longest rivers, and most forbidding deserts and impenetrable jungles. The population of its colonies, ten times that of the mother country, required far more effort to control than the more compact and less densely populated English colonies east of the Allegheny Mountains.

Latin America's great size and mineral wealth required an enormous supply of laborers. Indians and mestizos mined the empire's gold and silver, built its cities and churches, tended its herds, and grew its food. And once mining waned in importance, enslaved Africans harvested the new gold and sugar, as well as tobacco, cocoa, and indigo. For a Spaniard in America to engage in hard labor was almost unheard of.

In the English colonies, on the other hand, Amerindians never emerged as a central or principal labor force, though some recent scholars have documented significant use of Indians as servants and slaves by New England's colonial elite, as well as by European settlers in other regions that would later form parts of the United States.[53] The colonial economy largely depended on three groups of workers: free white farmers, propertyless whites (both indentured and free), and enslaved Africans. Nearly 70 percent of all white immigration to the colonies until the Revolution was made up of indentured servants. Those servants, having completed their required years of work, became free artisans in the cities or moved to the frontier to start their own farms. By the time of the Revolution, the majority of the white population comprised independent yeomen, small farmers, and fishermen.[54] That agrarian group—simple, unassuming, skeptical of far-off government control, and determined to create a new life out of an immense and fertile wilderness—would form the cultural core of the new North American society, or at least of its white majority.

Radically different land policies further demarcated English and Spanish colonial society. Frenzied speculation in land was ubiquitous in the English territories.[55] "Every farmer with an extra acre of land became a land speculator—every town proprietor, every scrambling tradesman who could scrape together a modest sum for investment," says one historian.[56] Both the English colonial administrators and, later, the state and federal governments fostered speculation. Time and again, those in charge of government created overnight fortunes for their friends and themselves through corrupt schemes aimed at amassing huge holdings. By 1697, for example, four Hudson Valley families, the Van Cortlandts, Philipses, Livingstons, and Van Rensselaers, had amassed for themselves 1.6 million acres spanning six present-day counties in mid–New York State, creating that state's new landed aristocracy.[57]

Where the English had their tradition of land speculation, the Spaniards had the opposite, the *mayorazgo*, in which a family's rural and urban holdings were made legally indivisible, handed down from generation to generation through the eldest son. Other family members could be assigned portions of the family estate to administer and profit from, but they could never own and, most important, could not sell that portion.

The biggest *mayorazgos* went to the original conquistadores. More modest allotments were assigned to their lower-ranking soldiers, and even smaller grants to civilian settlers. As the generations passed, intermarriage within the elite created labyrinthine mergers of old estates. Merchants, miners, and later immigrants often tried to purchase titles or marry into the established *mayorazgos*. The giant estates only got bigger, never smaller, and individual buying and selling of land for quick profit was rare.[58] The *mayorazgos*, together with the labor system of the *encomiendas*, thus became the basis for Latin America's latifundio system, in which a tiny portion of the white population owned most of the land and all others were reduced to laborers.

In contrast to both the English and Spanish, Native Americans invariably saw land as a resource to be used by all and owned by none. Even in the most stratified Indian societies, land was owned ultimately in common. Among the Aztecs, for instance, the *calpulli*, or extended clan, apportioned land to each member. The members, in turn, remitted a portion of their crops to clan leaders, who used that portion to pay the emperor's tribute.[59] No matter how many treaties the Indian nations may have signed to appease white settlers, they invariably saw themselves as ceding *use of the land*, not perpetual ownership.

Finally, and perhaps most important, the English and Spanish settlers brought with them vastly different political traditions. When each group attempted to transplant those traditions in the New World, they found themselves deeply influenced by the Amerindians who had preceded them. In Mexico, for instance, the Aztec ruler, chosen from within the royal family by a council of nobles, stood atop a highly differentiated class society. He exacted tribute from his own people and from conquered or dependent city-states like Tacuba, Texcoco, Tlaxcala, and Tarasca. The Spaniards did not dismember those centralized structures of power; instead, they appropriated them from above, erecting the scaffolding of their colonial organization, from viceroys to middle-level *corregidores*, over an already autocratic Indian foundation. And they astutely relinquished control of the *cabildos* (town councils) outside of the major cities to the Indian majority, turning the traditional chiefs into political mediators and into suppliers of Indian labor to the *encomiendas*.

The Aztecs, as we have seen, were far different from the Iroquois with whom English settlers alternately fought and allied for 150 years before independence. Lewis Henry Morgan, the founder of American anthropology and the first to systematically study the

Iroquois, wrote in 1851, "Their whole civil policy was averse to concentration of power in the hands of any single individual, but inclined to the opposite principle of division among a number of
equals."[60]

The Iroquois constitution, preserved over the years in oral tradition and recorded on wampum belts, led to a unique brand of democracy, which was based on consensus decision making by elected
representatives. Their confederation, according to Morgan, contained "the germ of modern parliament, congress, and legislature."
Since Morgan, numerous scholars have documented how the Iroquois influenced the democratic ideas of our own Founding Fathers.[61] This country's fierce devotion to individual rights, insists
historian Felix Cohen, has its roots in Iroquois thought, as does
"universal suffrage for women . . . the pattern of states within a state
we call federalism, the habit of treating chiefs as servants of the people instead of as masters."[62]

Some go even further. "Egalitarian democracy and liberty as we
know them today in the United States owe little to Europe," argues
anthropologist Jack Weatherford. Rather, "they entered modern
western thought as American Indian notions translated into European language and culture."[63] Several of the Founding Fathers were
influenced by the Iroquois system of checks and balances. Benjamin
Franklin published the first Indian treaty accounts in 1736, and he
studied native societies extensively while serving as Indian commissioner for Pennsylvania in the 1750s. During one Anglo-Indian conference in 1744, he was so moved by the oratory of Iroquois shaman
Canassatego, who urged the colonies to form their own federation,
that he began advocating such a system for the colonies.[64] Thomas
Jefferson frequently delved into the traditions of the Iroquois, and he
praised their morality and oratory in his *Notes on the State of Virginia*. And Charles Thompson, secretary to the Continental Convention, admiringly described the Iroquois government as "a kind of
patriarchal confederacy."[65]

Other Iroquois principles that have found their way into American democracy are the separation of military and civilian power (the
code of Hiawatha required Iroquois sachems and war chiefs to be
elected separately) and the impeachment of elected leaders. In some
ways, the five tribes were far ahead of the Founding Fathers, for
they prohibited slavery and they recognized the voting rights of
women. Settlers who came to know the simplicity of Iroquois society were invariably impressed with its ability to blend individual

liberty and the moral authority of the clan to restrain antisocial behavior. Crime, for instance, was almost unknown among them.

England founded colonies throughout the world, but only in North America did the traditions of English common law, local control, and parliamentary representation flourish, and a good part of that is due to the influence of Iroquois traditions on the settlers. By comparison, other former British colonies, India, Jamaica, or South Africa, for example, failed to produce the unique combination of strong and stable representative government with individual liberty found in the United States. In Latin America, meanwhile, each effort by former Spanish colonies such as Mexico, Gran Colombia, and Brazil to replicate our democratic model met with failure.

Thus, by the early nineteenth century, three hundred years of colonialism had divided the New World into two huge contending cultural groups, the Anglo-Saxon and the Spanish-Latin, with smaller groups of Portuguese, Dutch, French, and Caribbean English colonies. The colonists of the two dominant societies had inexorably undergone a transformation. They were no longer English or Spaniards. They were now Anglo-Americans and Latin Americans. They had adapted their religion, political and economic views, their speech, their music, and their food to the new land. They had built an uneasy intertwined identity with the natives they conquered and the Africans they brought as slaves. Latin America became a land of social inclusion and political exclusion. English America welcomed all political and religious beliefs but remained deeply intolerant in its social and racial attitudes. Latin America, subsumed by the force of its Indian and African majority, became a land of spirit, song, and suffering among its masses, its elite living a parasitic existence on immense estates. North America's white settlers, segregated from the races over which they held sway, developed a dual and contradictory identity and worldview: on the one hand, a spirit of will, work, and unwavering optimism among its small farmer masses; on the other, a predilection among its elite for cutthroat enterprise, land speculation, and domination of the weak and of non-Europeans.

The conquest of America profoundly challenged and transformed the beliefs of settlers, natives, and enslaved people alike, while it raised troubling questions for Europeans back home: Were all people God's children? What was savagery and what was civilization? Would the New World's racial mixing create a new cosmic race of men and women? Was church, king, or state the ultimate arbiter of society, or were individuals free to create their own destiny? The answers they chose—and the conflicts between those answers—molded the two main New World cultures that arose. Why the Spanish colonies, so rich in resources at the dawn of their nineteenth-century independence, stagnated and declined while the young North American republic flourished is the subject of our next chapter.

2

THE SPANISH BORDERLANDS
AND THE MAKING OF
AN EMPIRE
(1810–1898)

However our present interests may restrain us within our
limits, it is impossible not to look forward to distant times,
when our rapid multiplication will expand beyond those limits, and cover the whole northern if not the southern continent.

—THOMAS JEFFERSON, 1801

When they embarked on the road to independence in 1810,
Spain's American colonies were far richer in resources, territory, and population than the infant United States. Over the next
few decades, however, the four Spanish viceroyalties—New Spain,
New Granada, Peru, and Río Plata—fragmented into more than a
dozen separate nations, most of them crippled by internal strife, by
economic stagnation, by foreign debt, and by outside domination.
The United States, on the other hand, expanded dramatically in
territory and population, fashioned a stable and prosperous democracy, and warded off foreign control.

Why such a staggering difference in development? Historians in
this country usually attribute it to the legacies of English and Spanish colonialism. The austere Protestant democracy of Anglo-Saxon

farmers and merchants, they say, was ideally suited for carving prosperity from a virgin frontier in a way that the Catholic tyrannical societies of Latin America were not.[1]

That perspective, however, ignores the discordant and unequal relationship that emerged between the United States and Latin America from the first days of independence. It masks how a good deal of nineteenth-century U.S. growth flowed directly from the Anglo conquest of Spanish-speaking America. That conquest, how it unfolded and how it set the basis for the modern Latino presence in the United States, is the subject of this chapter.

Our nation's territorial expansion during the 1800s is well documented, but less attention has been given to how that expansion undermined and deformed the young republics to the south, especially those closest to the ever-changing U.S. borders. Annexation of the Spanish-speaking borderlands evolved in three distinct phases: Florida and the Southeast by 1820; Texas, California, and the Southwest by 1855; and, finally, Central America and the Caribbean during the second half of the century, a phase that culminated with the Spanish-American War of 1898. Those annexations transformed an isolated yeoman's democracy into a major world empire. In the process, Mexico lost half of its territory and three-quarters of its mineral resources, the Caribbean Basin was reduced to a permanent target for Yankee exploitation and intervention, and Latin Americans were made into a steady source of cheap labor for the first U.S. multinational corporations.

Popular history depicts that nineteenth-century movement as a heroic epic of humble farmers heading west in covered wagons to fight off savage Indians and tame a virgin land. Rarely do those accounts examine the movement's other face—the relentless incursions of Anglo settlers into Latin American territory.

Ahead of the settlers came the traders and merchants—men like Charles Stillman, Mifflin Kenedy, and Richard King in Texas; Cornelius Vanderbilt, George Law, and Minor Keith in Central America; William Safford, H. O. Havemeyer, and John Leamy in the Antilles; and John Craig in Venezuela—all of whom amassed huge fortunes in Latin American lands and products. The merchants were joined by adventurers and mercenaries like John McIntosh (Florida), Davy Crockett (Texas), and William Walker (Nicaragua), who swore allegiance to inexperienced or weak Latin American governments, then forcibly overthrew them in the name of freedom.

Most U.S. presidents backed the taking of Latin America's land.

CANADA
(BRITISH)

UNITED STATES
1776

MEXICO
1821

**NEW AMERICAN STATES
IN 1825**

Atlantic
Ocean

BAHAMAS (Br.)
CUBA (Sp.)
HAITI
(1804)
BRITISH
HONDURAS
(Sp.)
SANTO DOMINGO (1821)
PUERTO RICO (Sp.)
JAMAICA (Br.)

CENTRAL
AMERICA
1821

VENEZUELA
1811

GUIANAS
Br. Du. Fr.

COLOMBIA
1819

Pacific Ocean

ECUADOR
1822

BRAZIL
1822

PERU
1824

BOLIVIA
1825

CHILE
1824

PARAGUAY
1811

ARGENTINA
1816

URUGUAY
1825

☐ Independent nations

▨ European colonial
possessions

Jefferson, Jackson, and Teddy Roosevelt all regarded our country's domination of the region as ordained by nature. The main proponents and beneficiaries of empire building, however, were speculators, plantation owners, bankers, and merchants.[2] They fostered popular support for it by promising cheap land to the waves of European immigrants who kept arriving on our shores, and they bankrolled an endless string of armed rebellions in those Spanish-speaking lands by white settlers. To justify it all, our leaders popularized such pivotal notions as America for the Americans and Manifest Destiny, the latter term emerging as the nineteenth-century code for racial supremacy.

But along with the conquered lands came unwanted peoples: Native Americans, who were pushed farther west, then herded onto reservations, and several million Mexicans, Cubans, Filipinos, and Puerto Ricans, who were placed under U.S. sovereignty. Even when Congress officially declared some of the conquered peoples U.S. citizens, the newly arrived Anglo settlers routinely seized their properties, and those seizures were then upheld by the English-speaking courts the settlers installed. The Mexican Americans of the Southwest were transformed into a foreign minority in the land of their birth. Spanish-speaking, Catholic, and largely mestizo, they were rapidly relegated to a lower-caste status alongside Indians and Blacks. Cubans and Filipinos eventually won their independence but found their nations under the thumb of Washington for decades afterward, while Puerto Rico remains to this day a colony of second-class citizens.

THE REVOLUTIONARY YEARS: FROM INSPIRATION TO BETRAYAL

At the beginning of the 1800s, few Latin Americans could have foretold how the United States would treat them. The U.S. War of Independence, after all, was an enormous inspiration to intellectuals throughout the Spanish colonies. Some Latin Americans even fought alongside George Washington's rebel army. Bernardo de Gálvez, the Spanish governor of Louisiana, opened a second front against the English when he invaded British-controlled West Florida, defeated the garrison there, and reclaimed the peninsula as a Spanish colony. Merchants in Havana, meanwhile, supplied critical loans and supplies to Washington.

After the Revolution triumphed, Latin American patriots emulated the Founding Fathers. Fray Servando de Mier, a leading propagandist of Mexican independence, traveled to Philadelphia during Jefferson's presidency and often quoted Thomas Paine in his own polemics against monarchy.[3] In 1794, Antonio Nariño, a wealthy Bogotá intellectual and admirer of Benjamin Franklin's, translated and secretly published the French assembly's Declaration of the Rights of Man. José Antonio Rojas, the prominent Chilean revolutionary, met Franklin in Europe and later shipped numerous crates of Guillaume Raynal's writings about the North American revolution to Chile. In 1776, Rojas penned his own list of Chilean grievances against the Spanish monarchy. Simón Bolívar, the great Liberator of South America, traveled throughout the United States in 1806. Inspired by its accomplishments, he launched Venezuela's independence uprising a few years later.[4]

Perhaps the best example of the close ties between revolutionaries of the north and south was Francisco de Miranda, the "Morning Star" of Latin American independence. Born in 1750 into a prosperous merchant family in Caracas, Miranda joined the Spanish army at seventeen. He later traveled to North America, where he served first with Gálvez's Spanish troops in Florida, then with French general Comte de Rochambeau's troops. Handsome, erudite, and charismatic, Miranda was befriended by several U.S. leaders, including Alexander Hamilton and Robert Morris, and he met with President Washington. After a long personal odyssey through Europe, where he served as both a decorated general in Napoleon's army and a lover of Russia's Catherine the Great, Miranda returned to the United States and sought to win our government's backing for a campaign to liberate the Spanish colonies.[5]

Like all the well-known patriots of Latin America, however, Miranda was a *criollo* from the upper class. That limited his ability to win a mass following for independence among his own countrymen, for the criollos, unlike the Anglo-American revolutionaries, were a distinct minority within their own society. Of 13.5 million people living in the Spanish colonies in 1800, fewer than 3 million were white, and only 200,000 of those were *peninsulares*, that is, born in Spain.[6] Latin American rebels lived in constant fear of the 80 percent of the population that was Indian, Black, and mixed race, and that apprehension intensified during the final years of the U.S. Revolutionary War, when several major uprisings broke out among the Indians of South America.[7]

The specter of those uprisings made the criollos content at first to demand from Spain simply better treatment, not full-blown independence. They railed against high taxation, for more autonomy, and against the restrictions the Crown imposed on trade outside the empire. They condemned Spain's discrimination against them, how the Crown granted only *peninsulares* a monopoly on overseas trade, how it excluded criollos from top posts in the colonial government, and how it confined them only to mining and agriculture.[8] But no matter how much they might complain, the criollos dared not risk open rebellion for fear of unleashing revolt from the multitudes they had always oppressed.

In the end, the spark for Latin America's revolution came not from within the colonies but from Europe.[9] In 1808, Napoleon invaded Spain and installed his brother Joseph as king, setting off a chain of events that would lead to the breakup of the entire Spanish colonial empire. The Spanish people rejected the French invaders, formed local resistance juntas throughout the country, and initiated a guerrilla war to return their imprisoned king to the throne. When they heard of the events in Europe, criollo leaders in the colonies followed the lead of the Spanish resistance. They formed juntas of their own in all the major American cities and assumed control of their local affairs in the name of the king.

The rebel juntas in Spain soon convened a new Cortes (Spanish parliament), and that Cortes promulgated a liberal constitution, one that granted full citizenship to colonial subjects in the American colonies for the first time. But the Cortes stopped short of full equality when it refused to permit the colonies, whose population far outnumbered Spain's, a proportionate share of delegates. That refusal angered the most radical criollo leaders, who decided to break with the new Spanish government and declare their independence.

From then on, the Latin American revolution charted its own course. Even Napoleon's defeat at Waterloo and the ousting of the French from Spain failed to bring the shattered empire back together. King Ferdinand, who was restored to the throne after Napoleon's defeat, refused to accept the loss of his colonies and sent his army to subdue the upstart Latin Americans. A series of wars ensued throughout the continent between loyalists and rebels, and in several regions between the patriotic leaders themselves. The conflicts differed from country to country, yet everywhere the human toll was immense. The mammoth size of the colonies made for an epic, disordered, and bloody canvas. Mexico's independence wars, for instance, began in 1810 after parish priest Miguel Hidalgo led an uprising of thousands of Indian peasants and miners in the town of Dolores in the rich Bajió region northwest of Mexico City, using a statue of the Indian Virgen de Guadalupe to rally his followers. By the time the wars ended in 1821, more than six hundred thousand were dead, 10 percent of the country's population.[10] Venezuela had lost half of its nearly one million inhabitants.[11] Overall, the Latin American wars lasted much longer and proved far more destructive to the region's inhabitants than the U.S. War of Independence, which claimed only twenty-five thousand lives.

Despite their turbulent and debilitating fight for independence, the Latin American patriots always looked to the United States for their example. Several of the new nations modeled their constitutions on ours. During their wars, they pleaded for military aid from us, and after their victory, they sought friendship and assistance for their postwar reconstruction.[12]

Most U.S. leaders, however, coveted the Spanish colonies as targets for the nation's own expansion and held little regard for the abilities of the Latin American patriots. "However our present interests may restrain us within our limits," Jefferson wrote to James Monroe in 1801, "it is impossible not to look forward to distant times, when our rapid multiplication will expand beyond those limits, and cover the whole northern if not the southern continent."[13] Democracy no better suited Spanish America, John Adams said, than "the birds, beasts or fishes."

Miranda was the first to be surprised by the U.S. attitude. In 1806, after securing £12,000 from the British government for an expedition to liberate Venezuela, he rushed to the United States in expectation of further help, but President Jefferson and Secretary of State Madison rebuffed his appeals. Despite their refusal, Miranda managed to put together a rebel force from Anglo volunteers he recruited along the Eastern Seaboard. Once the expedition landed in Venezuela, however, Miranda's countrymen mistook it for a contingent of British soldiers. Instead of heeding his call for a revolt, the Venezuelans sided with the Spanish army, which quickly routed the rebels. Miranda barely managed to avoid capture and flee the country.

A decade later, with independence fever sweeping South America and the liberation armies battling fiercely against a powerful Spanish force, the United States rebuffed Bolívar as strongly as it had Miranda. Monroe, first as Madison's secretary of state and then as president, insisted on neutrality toward the South American wars. Like Jefferson before him, Monroe hoped to keep Spain friendly enough so it would eventually sell its Cuba and Florida colonies to the United States, a feeling shared by most of our nation's leaders. "We have no concern with South America," Edward Everett, editor of the influential *North American Review*, wrote at the time. "We can have no well-founded political sympathy with them. We are sprung from different stocks."[14]

Latin American freedom, however, did have support among many ordinary Americans, even a few in high places, who opposed our neutrality. Among those was Henry Marie Brackenridge, whom Monroe sent to the region to assess the situation in 1817 as part of a U.S. commission. "The patriots . . . complain that our government is cold towards them, as if ashamed to own them," Brackenridge reported back.[15] By then, the Latin Americans were becoming increasingly suspicious of U.S. intentions. That suspicion turned to bitterness after an incident that year involving two merchant ships, the *Tiger* and the *Liberty*. Soldiers from Bolívar's Republic of Gran Colombia seized the ships near the Orinoco River in Venezuela after discovering that their hulls were filled with military supplies for the Spanish army. The White House demanded that Colombia release the ships and indemnify their owners. Bolívar responded by condemning the two-faced U.S. policy. In a series of angry diplomatic letters, he reminded the White House that the U.S. Navy had intercepted and captured several merchant ships, even British ships, laden with supplies for his revolutionary army. So why were North Americans now supplying his enemy?[16]

Unknown to Bolívar, this peculiar brand of neutrality was about to pay off handsomely. The Adams-Onís Treaty of 1819 ceded Florida to the United States, but as part of those negotiations Monroe promised Spain that our country would continue denying aid to the Latin American patriots.[17] The Latin American leaders, unaware of the secret agreement, could not believe how the United States kept turning its back on them. Bolívar, who had once praised our country as a "model of political virtues and moral enlightenment unique in the history of mankind," had turned increasingly antagonistic to it by 1819. That year, he remarked: "In ten years of struggle and travail that beggar description, in ten years of suffering almost beyond human endurance, we have witnessed the indifference with which all Europe and even our brothers of the north have remained but passive spectators of our anguish."[18]

But there were deeper reasons behind the U.S. reluctance to see the Latin Americans succeed. Always foremost in the minds of southern planters and their congressional delegates was the issue of slavery. The planters watched with alarm as Latin America's independence wars dragged on, how Creole leaders like Bolívar were enlisting thousands of *pardos*, mestizos, Indians, and slaves in their armies, repaying the castes with greater social mobility and the enslaved with their freedom.

Our slave owners were well aware that after Bolívar's second defeat by the Spanish army, Haiti's president, Alexandre Pétion, had helped finance his return to South America in 1815, outfitting seven ships and six thousand men with weapons and ammunition on condition that Bolívar emancipate Venezuela's enslaved population.[19] The Liberator's subsequent public condemnations of slavery enraged planters in this country. "Slavery is the negation of all law, and any law which should perpetuate it would be a sacrilege," he proclaimed at the founding congress of Bolivia in 1826.[20] Clearly, plantation owners here feared that emancipation fervor would spread from Latin America into the United States—by 1850, all the former Spanish colonies that had won their independence had abolished slavery—and that fear turned them into implacable foes of Latin American liberation.[21]

Disregarded by the U.S. government from their inception, reviled by the conservative monarchies of Europe, the Latin American republics concluded that their only reliable ally was England. Some six thousand English, Scotch, and Irish, most of them unemployed veterans from the British wars against Napoleon, signed up for Bolívar's army in 1817–1819. Among those volunteers was Daniel O'Leary, who went on to serve as Bolívar's top secretary.[22] That British aid, together with the daring battlefield strategies of Bolívar, José de San Martín, Bernardo O'Higgins, Francisco de Paula Santander, and the other great generals, succeeded by 1826 in routing the last of the Spanish armies on the continent.

All of Spain's vast empire except Cuba and Puerto Rico was now free. That year, Bolívar convened the first Pan American Congress, where he elaborated his dream for a hemispheric confederation. His plan for uniting the revolutionary nations so worried U.S. leaders that Congress delayed sending representatives until the gathering had adjourned, and afterward, our government made clear to Bolívar that it was adamantly opposed to any expedition to liberate Cuba and Puerto Rico.

FREEDOM, FILIBUSTERS, AND MANIFEST DESTINY

If the South American liberators found policy makers in Washington aloof, Latinos living near the U.S. borderlands found their Anglo neighbors downright hostile. The gobbling up of chunks of Florida between 1810 and 1819 set the pattern for U.S. expansion across the Spanish borderlands. Jefferson's Louisiana Purchase in 1803 had brought the first group of Spanish-speaking people under the U.S. flag. But our nation did not "purchase" Florida in the same way it purchased Louisiana. The Adams-Onís Treaty was more akin to a street corner holdup. It culminated two decades of unceasing pressure by southern expansionists on Spain to relinquish the territory, an area which was then much larger in size than the current state, stretching along the Gulf Coast all the way to the towns of Natchez and Baton Rouge.

The few thousand Spaniards inhabiting Florida's fortified Gulf Coast towns had made great strides, since the Franciscan missions of the sixteenth century, in building ties with the Indians of the Southeast. For nearly two centuries, the Creek, Choctaw, Cherokee, and Chickasaw had formed a buffer between Spanish Florida and Anglo settlers in Georgia and Kentucky. Known as the "civilized tribes" because they readily adopted European dress, tools, and farming methods, they numbered about forty-five thousand in the year 1800. The Florida colony, however, was an irritant to the Anglos in so far as it provided refuge both to Indians on the warpath and to escaped slaves from the southern plantations.[23] Moreover, the plantation owners regarded with dismay the racial mixing between fugitive slaves and Indians that was commonplace among the Seminoles.

By the early 1800s, so many Anglo settlers were moving into Florida that Spanish soldiers in its thinly populated garrison towns could no longer control the territory. In a gamble aimed at reasserting that control, Spain agreed to legalize the newcomers, but in return the settlers had to pledge loyalty to the Crown, raise their children as Catholics, and refrain from land speculation or political assembly.[24] The policy backfired because it made it easier for settlers to immigrate and only postponed Spain's loss of the colony.[25]

In 1810, a group of settlers in West Florida launched a direct challenge to that authority. They resorted to a form of rebellion that eventually turned into a hallmark of Anglo adventurers and buccaneers throughout the Spanish borderlands: a band of newcomers or mercenaries simply occupied a town or territory and proclaimed their own republic. The Spanish called them *filibusteros* (freebooters), and the uprisings were known as filibusters. In one of the earliest attempts, a group of Anglo settlers seized the Spanish garrison at Baton Rouge on September 23, 1810, and declared their independence. The rebellion prompted President Madison to send in federal troops to occupy the surrounding territory, and Congress later incorporated the area into the new state of Louisiana.[26] The rest of West Florida fell into U.S. hands during the War of 1812, after General James Wilkinson, head of the U.S. Army and a master at filibustering, overran the Spanish garrison at Mobile in 1813 and Andrew Jackson captured Pensacola in 1814. Spain's government, still paralyzed by the Napoleonic Wars, was in no condition to resist any of the incursions.

Other filibuster revolts soon spread to East Florida (see table 1). Most of the revolts garnered backing from political leaders in the South who were eager to expand slave territories and to speculate in Florida land. One of those leaders, Andrew Jackson, had engaged in repeated speculation throughout his life. In 1796, for instance, Jackson bought a half interest in five thousand acres of the Chickasaw Bluffs in Mississippi for $100. He immediately sold a portion for a sizable profit. Twenty years later, as a U.S. Army commander, Jackson forced the Chickasaw to negotiate a treaty opening the territory to white settlers. He promptly sold the remaining part of his investment for $5,000.[27] But the parcel of land that always fired Old Hickory's imagination most was Florida. His soldiers invaded East Florida several times on the pretext of hunting down Seminole bands. Thanks to Jackson's repeated forays and to the filibuster revolts of Anglo settlers there, Spain gradually concluded that the U.S. thirst for Florida would never be quenched; the Adams-Onís Treaty was the result. In it, Spain ceded to the United States an area larger than Belgium, Denmark, the Netherlands, and Switzerland for a mere $5 million. Spain hoped that by giving up Florida it would salvage the remainder of its tottering empire, especially the province of Tejas, which had already been the scene of four separate filibuster revolts by bands of Anglos between 1801 and 1819.[28] As its only concession in the treaty, Washington officially renounced all other claims on Spanish lands and accepted the Sabine River as its border with Spain's Texas colony.

Such was the situation in 1822, when President Monroe, who for years had refused to aid the Latin American revolution, suddenly did an about-face and became the first world leader to recognize Mexico's independence. Monroe followed that up the next year with an even more audacious act. He declared the Americas off-limits to any new European colonization with his famous Monroe Doctrine. Actually, Monroe issued the warning quite reluctantly, and only after much British prodding. The British pressure was brought on by the defeat of Napoleon and the subsequent decision of Europe's Holy Alliance to back an attempt by Ferdinand VII to recover Spain's Latin American colonies. England was already ensconced as Latin America's biggest trading partner, and British foreign minister George Canning feared that any recolonization of the region would close off that commerce. So Canning urged Monroe to join him in warning the European powers to stay out of America. Canning, however, wanted reciprocity for his alliance. He wanted Monroe to renounce any plans to colonize Texas or Cuba, something Monroe would not do.[29]

Table 1

The Filibustering Record

(Invasions by U.S. Citizens into Spain's Colonies or the Latin American Republics during the 1800s)

1801—Philip Nolan crosses into Texas with a band of armed men; he is caught and shot by Spanish soldiers.

1809—General James Wilkinson's "volunteers" occupy parts of West Florida.

1810—Anglo settlers declare a republic in Baton Rouge, West Florida. Federal troops occupy the area and Congress annexes it into Louisiana.

1812—John McIntosh captures Amelia Island and Fernandina, declaring the Republic of Fernandina. Spanish troops defeat him.

1812—Former U.S. lieutenant Augustus Magee, Mexican Bernardo Gutiérrez, and a group of Americans invade East Texas and are routed.

1813—General James Wilkinson seizes Mobile in West Florida.

1817—Henry Perry invades Texas and marches on La Bahía.

1819—Mississippi merchant James Long invades Texas but fails to establish the Republic of Texas.

1826—Haden and Benjamin Edwards seize Nacogdoches and proclaim the Republic of Fredonia. Mexican soldiers defeat them with help from Stephen Austin.

1835—General Ignacio Mejía and two hundred Americans raid Río Panuco in Tamaulipas. His defeat prompts Mexico to ban American immigration.

1836—Sam Houston and Texas rebels, along with a small number of *tejano* federalists, revolt against General Antonio López de Santa Anna's rule. They defeat Santa Anna at San Jacinto and proclaim the Republic of Texas.

1839—Antonio Canales, a Mexican federalist, S. W. Jordan, and five hundred Americans declare the Republic of the Rio Grande. They become divided and are defeated by Mexican troops.

1849—Former Spanish army officer Narciso López, backed by publisher William O'Sullivan, attempts to invade Cuba, but U. S. authorities foil the plot.

1850—López invades at Cárdenas but is routed. Of his six hundred men, all but five are North American.

1851—López invades a second time, at Bahía Honda. Once again, North Americans are a majority of his four hundred volunteers. Spanish troops capture and execute him.

1853—William Walker invades Mexico and declares the Republic of Sonora. Mexican troops chase him back across the border.

1855—Walker arrives in Nicaragua, seizes power, and rules as dictator for two years until he is routed by the combined armies of Central America and Cornelius Vanderbilt.

1858—Walker invades Nicaragua again and is routed a second time.

1860—Walker invades Honduras, is seized, tried, and executed.

~~~~~~

Seeking to maneuver between the geopolitical schemes of England and the Holy Alliance, Monroe chose instead to act alone. After years of refusing support to the Latin American revolution, he suddenly reversed course. On December 2, 1823, during his annual address to Congress, he issued the most important policy statement in hemispheric history, announcing that the Latin American countries were "henceforth not to be considered as subjects for future colonization by any European powers ... it is impossible that the allied powers should extend their political system to any portion of [the continent] without endangering our peace and happiness."[30]

The new policy was hailed at first by Latin American leaders. At last, they thought, U.S. neutrality toward their struggle would end. "An act worthy of the classic land of liberty," said Colombia's president Santander. The European monarchies, of course, were more worried about the guns of the powerful British navy than the threats of the upstart North American republic. Nonetheless, with England and the United States as nominal protectors of Latin American independence, the new countries of the region at least managed to avert the catastrophes that befell much of Africa and Asia when the European powers divided those areas between them during the great colonial partitions of the late nineteenth century.

Notwithstanding the Monroe Doctrine's strong language, European governments successfully pursued more than a dozen major interventions into Latin America during the rest of the century, and numerous minor ones, with only occasional U.S. opposition.[31] Worse than the many U.S. failures to honor its own policy was how subsequent presidents turned the doctrine into its opposite. Latin America, especially the Caribbean Basin, was turned into a virtual U.S. sphere of influence. Bolívar, weary of the growing arrogance from North Americans, declared before his death that the United States seemed "destined by Providence to plague America with torments in the name of freedom."[32] During the twentieth century, a succession of presidents used Monroe's words to justify repeated military occupations of Latin American nations. This duel interpretation of the doctrine's provisions continues to this day. It underscores an unresolved contradiction of U.S. history—between our ideals of freedom and our predilection for conquest.

The earliest example of that contradiction came during the next phase of borderlands expansion, the repeated annexations of Mexican territory between 1836 and 1853. Prior to those annexations, the United States of Mexico, as the new country called itself, and the United States of America were eerily similar in territory and population. In 1824, Mexico comprised 1.7 million square miles and contained 6 million people, while the United States stretched for

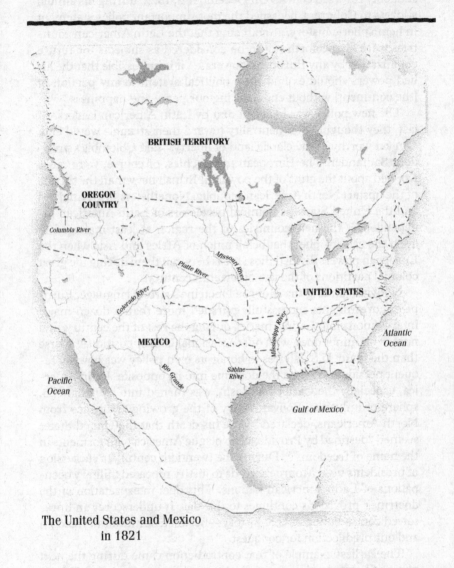

The United States and Mexico
in 1821

1.8 million square miles and had 9.6 million people. That equivalence was radically transformed over the next three decades as Anglo settlers poured onto Mexican land.

The settlements began with Moses and Stephen Austin and the town of San Felipe de Austin. Moses, who had lived in Missouri when Spain controlled the Louisiana territory, secured permission from the Spanish crown in 1820 to found a town of Anglo families in the province of Tejas. Within a year, Austin died and Mexico won its independence, but his son Stephen chose to carry out his father's plan. The new Mexican government honored Spain's grant so long as Austin's settlers took an oath of allegiance to Mexico and converted to Catholicism. San Felipe was so successful that dozens of other Anglo colonies in Texas soon followed.[33]

Farther south, at the mouth of the Rio Grande, Connecticut merchant Francis Stillman landed by ship near Matamoros with a cargo of hay and oats in 1825. Impressed by the demand for his goods, Stillman sent his son Charles to the area to set up a branch of the family business.[34] Charles, or Don Carlos as the Mexicans referred to him, proved to be a wizard at trade. Before long, he was the biggest merchant and landowner in the region. By 1832, three hundred foreigners were living in Matamoros, most of them North Americans.[35] Among them was James Power, who married Dolores de la Portilla, an heiress of the rich De la Garza landowning family. Power thus initiated a form of land acquisition that hundreds of Anglo adventurers in the Southwest copied—he married into the Mexican elite and thereby acquired a *mayorazgo*.[36] Across the river from Matamoros, Don Carlos Stillman founded the town of Brownsville, where his son James Stillman was born in 1850. That son would grow up to be a titan of American finance as the president of First National City Bank and as the notorious ally of robber barons John D. Rockefeller and J. P. Morgan.

Far to the north of the Rio Grande, Anglo settlers had started moving into East Texas in the 1820s. Many were illegal squatters drawn by fraudulent sales of land at one to ten cents an acre from speculators who had no legal title.[37] Some of those squatters soon took to filibustering.[38] The Haden Edwards revolt, in particular, prompted the Mexican government to bar further immigration by U.S. citizens. It even abolished slavery in 1829 in hopes of cutting off economic incentives for southerners to emigrate.

But it was too late. By then, Anglo settlers far outnumbered the Mexicans in Tejas. "Where others send invading armies," warned

Mexican secretary of state Lucas Alaman, in an eerie precursor to
our modern immigration debate, "[the Americans] send their colonists. . . . Texas will be lost for this Republic if adequate measures to
save it are not taken."[39] Local Mexican authorities, unlike the government in Mexico City, welcomed the economic boom that accompanied the influx of foreigners, just as today Anglo businessmen
routinely welcome Mexicans who have crossed illegally into the
country and are willing to work for low wages.

When General Santa Anna seized power in Mexico City in 1833,
one of his first acts was to abolish the exemptions from taxes and
antislavery laws that prior Mexican governments had granted the
Texans, giving them the excuse they needed to break from Mexico
City's "tyranny."

Few incidents in U.S. history so directly confront our cultural
identity as does the Texas War of Independence and its legendary
Battle of the Alamo. For more than a century and a half, the fort's
siege has been a part of American mythology. Its 187 martyred defenders, among them William Barret Travis, Jim Bowie, and Davy
Crockett, have been immortalized as American heroes despite the
fact that they openly defended slavery, that they were usurping the
land of others, and that they were not even American citizens. Tech-
nically, they were Mexican citizens rebelling to found the Republic
of Texas.

Most of the Anglo settlers had been in the province less than two
years. Many were adventurers, vagabonds, and land speculators.[40]
Travis had abandoned his family and escaped to Texas after killing
a man in the United States. Bowie, a slave trader, had wandered into
the Mexican province looking to make a fortune in mining. Sam
Houston, commander of the victorious rebels, and Crockett had
both served under Andrew Jackson in the grisly Creek War, and
they shared Old Hickory's racist and expansionist outlook toward
Latin America.

Houston, a onetime governor of Tennessee, was part of Jackson's
White House kitchen cabinet before moving to Texas in 1832. While
Houston plotted the rebellion, Jackson offered unsuccessfully to pur-
chase Texas outright from Mexico. The two men were so close that
Jackson's enemies, among them former president John Quincy
Adams, accused Houston of being Jackson's secret agent in Texas. Al-
though historians have found no documentary proof of this, Jackson
certainly was aware of his disciple's plans for the Mexican province.[41]

After the Alamo defeat, Houston's rebel army won the war's

decisive conflict at the Battle of San Jacinto, captured Santa Anna, and forced him to sign a treaty recognizing Texas independence in exchange for his freedom. But the Mexican government refused to sanction the treaty, and the precise boundaries of Texas remained in dispute for some time. The territory remained nominally independent until its annexation in 1845 only because northern congressmen kept blocking its admission to the union as a slave state. While the debate raged, cotton farming took hold in the Texas Republic, and its leaders allowed the territory to be turned into a major transit point for smuggling slaves from Cuba into the southern states.[42]

Texas annexation touched off a fever for even more westward expansion. The slogan of the Monroe Doctrine, America for the Americans, was barely two decades old when a new battle cry suddenly replaced it in the popular imagination—Manifest Destiny. John O'Sullivan coined the term in July 1845 in his *United States Magazine and Democratic Review*. O'Sullivan, a publicist for the Democratic Party and friend of several presidents, counted Poe, Longfellow, and Whittier among the contributors to his influential magazine and was a steadfast advocate of expansion into Latin America, especially Cuba, where he personally financed several filibuster expeditions.

Proponents of Manifest Destiny saw Latin Americans as inferior in cultural makeup and bereft of democratic institutions. Our country's Calvinist beliefs reinforced those territorial ambitions perfectly. Americans could point to the nation's prosperity, to its amazing new networks of canals, steamboats, and railroads, as proof of their God-given destiny to conquer the frontier. Newspapers and magazines of the day were replete with articles by noted phrenologists like Dr. George Caldwell and Dr. Josiah C. Nott, who propounded the superiority of white Europeans over Indians, Blacks, and Mexicans.

"To the Caucasian race is the world indebted for all the great and important discoveries, inventions, and improvements, that have been made in science and the arts," Caldwell wrote in his influential *Thoughts on the Original Unity of the Human Race*. Nott, one of the South's best-known surgeons, took Caldwell's notions one step further. He urged the need for eugenics to keep the white race pure. "Wherever in the history of the world the inferior races have been conquered and mixed in with the Caucasian, the latter have sunk into barbarism," Nott proclaimed in a speech in 1844.

The phrenologists were not some marginal intellectual sect. By 1850, their ideas were part of mainstream thought in this country.

Proponents traveled from town to town, carrying casts of skulls and detailed charts of the brain, giving speeches and distributing free books, and charging money to read heads. World-famous scholars such as Samuel George Morton, the Philadelphia ethnologist who possessed the largest collection of human skulls on earth, buttressed their conclusions with "scientific" studies on the relative size, capacity, and composition of the brains of different races. Morton, according to Nott, "has established the fact, that the capacity of the crania of the Mongol, Indian, and Negro, and all dark-skinned races, is smaller than that of the pure white man." Nott even extended those differences to single out other Caucasians or "mixed-breeds." Contrasting whites in the United States "with the dark-skinned Spaniards," he wrote, "It is clear that the dark-skinned Celts are fading away before the superior race, and that they must eventually be absorbed."[43]

With southern planters pressing to increase their proslavery votes in Congress, and many northerners captivated by the racialist theories of Manifest Destiny, the national outcry to annex more Mexican land became overwhelming. To no one's surprise, the entry of Texas into the union precipitated war with Mexico. It was a conflict that even the last president of the Texas Republic, Anson James, regarded as shameful. James blasted President Polk and war hero General Zachary Taylor for their attempts "to induce me to aid them in their unholy and execrable design of manufacturing a war with Mexico."[44] More than one hundred thousand U.S. soldiers served in the war, and nearly fourteen thousand perished, the highest mortality rate of any war in our history.[45] Their advance into Mexico produced horrifying incidents of brutality and racism by U.S. troops. A few even drew the public condemnation of generals Grant and Meade. Grant later admitted the war was "one of the most unjust ever waged by a stronger against a weaker nation."[46]

As the army advanced toward Mexico City, however, those same theories of Mexican inferiority sparked a national debate over how much of Mexico the United States should claim. By taking too much land, some argued, the country would be absorbing millions of racially mixed Mexicans, which in the long run might threaten the Anglo-Saxon majority. The Treaty of Guadalupe Hidalgo eventually forced Mexico to relinquish the half of its territory that was the least densely populated and that included the present-day states of New Mexico, California, Nevada, parts of Arizona, Utah, and the disputed sections of present-day Texas. Five years later, the United

States added an additional strip of land in Sonora, the Gadsden Purchase.[47]

Also included in the 1848 treaty was the crucial 150-mile-wide Nueces Strip, between the Rio Grande and Nueces Rivers. The U.S. negotiators demanded its inclusion as part of Texas despite the fact that Spain, and later Mexico, considered the strip part of Coahuila Province. The Nueces, which is equal in size to present-day Massachusetts, Connecticut, and New Jersey combined, was especially important because it included the fertile Lower Rio Grande valley and because the plains north of that valley were teeming with wild horses and cattle. The herds, introduced by Spanish settlers in the early 1700s, numbered more than three million head by 1830.[48] Securing control of those herds, and of the original Spanish land grants in the region, soon produced vast fortunes for early Anglo settlers like Charles Stillman, Richard King, and Mifflin Kenedy.

Out of those Mexican lands, the U.S. cattle industry was born, even though the majority of ranch hands in the industry's early decades were anything but Anglo. The vaqueros, or cowboys, were generally mestizos or *mulatos*, sometimes even Blacks or Indians. Certainly this was true on the famous King Ranch below Corpus Christi, which eventually grew to nearly one million acres. So dominant was the Mexican vaquero in the industry that Anglo cowboys copied virtually all the culture of the range from them. As historian Carey McWilliams has noted, the cowboy got from the vaquero:

> his lasso or lariat, cinch, halter, *mecate* or horsehair rope, "chaps" or *chaparejos*, "taps" or stirrup tips (*lapaderas*), the chin strap for his hat (*barboquejo*), the feedbag for his horse (*morral*) and his rope halter or *bosal*. Even his famous "ten gallon hat" comes from a mistranslation of a phrase in a Spanish-Mexican *corrido* "*su sombrero gallonado*," which referred to a festooned or "gallooned" sombrero.

The Nueces Strip and the northern part of New Mexico were the only regions where the original Mexican inhabitants remained a palpable majority over the Anglos even after annexation. As a result, the language of the range, even that used by Anglo-Americans, is derived mostly from Spanish words, among them bronco, buckaroo, burro, mesa, canyon, rodeo, corral, loco, lariat. Yet the cowboy myth in popular folklore, the one Hollywood has propagated around the world, is of a lone white Anglo sitting tall in the saddle, with

Mexicans of the Old West invariably portrayed either as bandits or doltish peasants riding donkeys.[49]

Texas, however, was not the richest prize of the war with Mexico— California was. From the early 1800s, New England sea captains who reached the Pacific sent back glowing reports of that far-off Spanish colony. Despite those reports, few Anglos had settled in the far West before the Mexican War because of the long and grueling overland passage through Indian country necessary to get there. Then, two weeks before the Treaty of Guadalupe Hidalgo was signed, gold was discovered at Sutter's Mill on the American River. The news touched off an overnight stampede. Prospectors streamed into the territory from the East, Mexico, and South America, even from Hawaii and Australia. Within a year, California's non-Indian population rocketed from twenty thousand to one hundred thousand, overwhelming the original Mexican inhabitants, who numbered only about thirteen thousand, and the territory's several hundred thousand Indians.

The first Mexican and South American prospectors to reach the California fields had a distinct advantage, for they drew on a tradition of gold and silver mining that dated back to the conquistadores. Not surprisingly, they had more initial success than the inexperienced Anglos from back East. That success frustrated the white prospectors and soon led to physical assaults, even lynchings, of Mexicans. In 1850, the state imposed a foreign miners tax to give Anglos a better edge.

Even though the gold fields petered out within a few years, the California discoveries provided immediate dividends to the entire country, just as Aztec gold and silver had for sixteenth-century Spain. The mines turned out more than a quarter billion dollars in ore during their first four years. Their revenues spawned a generation of new bankers who rapidly turned to financing myriad other ventures throughout the West. Eventually, the Anglo immigrants shifted their attention to the state's more enduring wealth, its soil. Thousands seized or squatted on the large estates of the native *californios*. Within two decades of the Sutter's Mill discovery, most Mexicans in the state had been driven off their land.

Just as Texas became the country's cotton and cattle center after the war, and California and Nevada its source for gold and silver mining, Arizona and New Mexico gave birth to two other critical U.S. industries—copper and wool.

New Mexico had served as a nexus for sheep raising from early colonial times, the first herds arriving with conquistador Juan de Oñate in 1598. By then, Spain already boasted the oldest and most advanced sheep culture in Europe. Its herdsmen introduced the churro and merino breeds to North America. The churro, a small, scrubby animal ideally suited to the arid Southwest, made possible the existence of many far-flung and remote Spanish outposts in the region. Sheep provided not only food and clothing to settlers and soldiers but also were a main source of cash. Over the centuries, New Mexicans evolved an intricate tradition of sheep raising, with formally defined rights, ranks, privileges, and even organizations among the sheepherding workforce. As cattle did for South Texas, sheep raising defined much of the culture of New Mexico, Colorado, and parts of California. But the sheep did more than provide culture; they created enormous wealth. Two years after New Mexico became a U.S. territory, southwestern herders were clipping a mere thirty-two thousand pounds of wool annually. By 1880, the number of pounds had zoomed to four million.[50]

What sheepherding was for New Mexico, copper became for Arizona. The Spaniards opened their first silver and copper mine, the Santa Rita, in western New Mexico in the early 1800s. That was followed by the Heintzelman mine in Tubac, Arizona, which employed eight hundred men by 1859. Then came the famous Clifton and Bisbee mines in the 1870s. Between 1838 and 1940, Arizona mines produced $3 billion in metal, most of it copper. Workers in the mines were overwhelmingly Mexicans, either natives to the territory or migrants recruited from across the border by labor contractors. "By the mid-1880s," writes Chicano historian Rudy Acuña, "Chihuahuan farmers, after planting their crops, traveled to eastern Arizona and local mines, working for day wages, returning home at harvest time."[51]

But the Mexican contribution to American prosperity didn't stop there. Before the coming of the railroads, Mexican workers provided the main teamster workforce in the Southwest, moving goods across the territory in long mule caravans. And after the railroads arrived, they were the section hands and track workers (*traqueros*) who maintained the fast-growing network of rail lines. One historian has estimated that between 1880 and 1930, Mexican *traqueros* composed nearly two-thirds of the track labor force that U.S. companies employed throughout the Southwest, Central Plains, and Midwest.[52] The Mexican population of the ceded territories was only 116,000 in 1848, but it grew steadily after the war as hundreds

of thousands more came and went between Mexico and the United
States as migrant laborers, which meant that Mexican influence on
the region was far greater than the early population figures might
suggest.

The combination of mineral and animal wealth the Anglos found
on the annexed Mexican lands, plus the Mexican laborers Anglo
businessmen recruited to extract it, provided the underpinnings of twentieth-century western prosperity. That combination
made possible the vast expansion of our country's electrical, cattle,
sheep, mining, and railroad industries.[53] Yet this historic Mexican
contribution has been virtually obliterated from popular frontier history, replaced by the enduring myth of the lazy, shiftless Mexican.

ANGLO SETTLERS HEAD
SOUTH OF THE BORDER

The Mexican annexations of 1836 to 1853, however, were not sufficient to satisfy the expansionist schemes of Manifest Destiny proponents. Some called for seizing more of Mexico's mineral-laden
northern territory. Southern planters especially coveted the tropical
Central America isthmus, where a half dozen fledgling republics
seemed ripe for conquest.

Perhaps the foremost representative of those expansionists was
William Walker. A Tennessee-born lawyer and journalist, Walker
hardly fit the image of the swashbuckling mercenary dictator he
would become. Originally trained as a doctor, he was soft-spoken, a
mere five feet, five inches tall, and weighed a paltry 120 pounds.
After a stint as a reporter in San Francisco, Walker appeared in November 1853 in Baja California with a small band of armed followers. From there, he instigated an uprising in Mexico's Sonora
Province, proclaimed the Republic of Sonora, and named himself its
president. Within a few weeks, Mexican troops chased him and his
ragtag followers back to the United States, where federal agents arrested him for violating U.S. neutrality laws. His audacious uprising
made him an instant folk hero of the expansionist press, and all the
newspapers reported extensively on his trial and eventual acquittal.

After the trial, Walker shifted his attention farther south, to the
little-known isthmus of Central America that had broken away
from Mexico in 1823 and formed a loose confederation called the
United Provinces of Central America. A few British and North

American businessmen, fired by dreams of building a canal across the isthmus to link the Atlantic and Pacific Oceans, had started visiting the region shortly after its independence.[54] In 1838, the confederation splintered into five independent countries, and the leaders of those countries were soon locked in intermittent shooting wars with one another. By then, the U.S. government, already concerned about a future canal, reached agreement with Colombia on the need to build that waterway through Panama, which was then a Colombian province. That agreement, cemented in a treaty in 1846, stipulated that the United States would guarantee the neutrality of any future canal.[55]

The California Gold Rush, however, created an instant demand for a faster route to the Pacific coast. The only sea route at the time, from New York to San Francisco around Cape Horn, took four months, and the narrow Central American isthmus offered the best bet for cutting that time dramatically.

Two competing New York merchant groups had recently secured contracts from Congress to carry mail between California and the East Coast by steamship lines and then overland through Panama. The U.S. Mail Steamship Company, operated by George Law and Marshall O. Roberts, had the Atlantic portion of the route, while William H. Aspinwall's Pacific Mail Steamship Company had the western portion. Using a generous $900,000 annual subsidy Congress allotted them for the mail, the companies decided to transport people as well. Unfortunately, the part of the trip that involved an arduous fifty-mile trek by mule train across Panama's jungle was too forbidding for the average person heading for California. So Aspinwall negotiated a deal with the Colombian government to build a railroad across the isthmus. His Panama Railroad took six years and $2 million to build, and it claimed four thousand lives, most of them West Indian and Chinese laborers whom Aspinwall imported. Once completed, however, the line paid for itself three times over within the first few years of operation.[56]

While Aspinwall was building his line in Panama, Cornelius Vanderbilt, perhaps the most ruthless tycoon of his age, moved to carve out a quicker competing route through Nicaragua. Vanderbilt and Joseph L. White, a former congressman, founded the Nicaragua Accessory Transit Company, a combination steamship and railroad line that began operation sooner than Aspinwall's railroad. The Nicaragua company grossed $5 million the first year, with profits of between 20 and 40 percent.[57]

Aspinwall's railroad and Vanderbilt's steamship line, however, were inadequate for U.S. merchants who wanted a canal through which their goods could travel on ships. Most engineers and politicians in the country favored a canal route through Nicaragua. While a Panama route was shorter, Nicaragua's was easier to build, they argued, since it could incorporate the natural waterways of the San Juan River and giant Lake Managua.

As a result, Nicaragua started to draw increasing attention from both Washington politicians and Anglo fortune hunters. In 1853, U.S. sailors went ashore to defend Vanderbilt's company in a dispute with the local government, and in 1854, the navy bombarded and destroyed the town of San Juan/Greytown over another financial dispute between a U.S. company and local authorities.[58]

Colonel Henry L. Kinney, a land speculator and founder of the Texas Rangers, arrived in 1854. Kinney immediately purchased twenty-two million acres of Nicaraguan land from trader Samuel H. Shepherd, who claimed he had been "granted" the land in 1839 by the Miskito king. The Nicaraguan government, as might be expected, refused to recognize Kinney's claim to 70 percent of its territory. Shareholders in Kinney's Central American Land and Mint Company included U.S. attorney general Caleb Cushing and Warren Faben, President Pierce's commercial agent in San Juan/Greytown.[59]

A *New York Times* correspondent who lauded Kinney's colonization scheme back then wrote, "Central America is destined to occupy an influential position in the family of nations, if her advantages of location, climate and soil are availed of by a race of 'Northmen' who shall supplant the tainted, mongrel and decaying race which now curses it so fearfully."[60]

To enforce his dubious claim, Kinney armed some followers and declared a revolt against the government, but he was forced to flee after Vanderbilt, anxious that the land dispute not affect his own investments, pressured the British and U.S. governments to oppose his claims.

Despite Kinney's setback, Yankee influence in Nicaragua kept growing. More than six hundred North Americans were living in the country by 1855.[61] By then, England, still the most powerful nation in the world, made clear that it would challenge any U.S. plans to dominate a transoceanic canal project. That year, the two nations negotiated the Clayton-Bulwer Treaty, in which they agreed to jointly guarantee the neutrality of any future canal, and to refrain from occupying or controlling any of the Central American countries. Neither nation, of course, bothered to consult any of the governments in the region affected by the treaty.

But politicians and merchants weren't the only ones suddenly eyeing Nicaragua. Walker, undaunted by his Mexican fiasco, set sail from San Francisco in 1855 with a band of fifty-six mercenaries he had recruited, supposedly to fight for a faction in Nicaragua's continuing civil war. Shortly after arriving, Walker rebelled against the faction that employed him, seized control of the country, and in one of the most bizarre episodes of Latin American history, declared himself president.

During his time in office, Walker reinstituted slavery, declared English a coequal language with Spanish, and required all lands to be registered. The latter decree facilitated passing many land titles into the hands of Anglo-American settlers.[62] Both Walker and the Nicaraguans, however, were actually pawns in a nefarious high-stakes contest for control of the region's commerce by competing groups of U.S. investors. A group of Transit Company officials who had temporarily wrested control of the shipping line from Vanderbilt helped finance Walker's army, while George Law, owner of the U.S. steamship line in Panama and Vanderbilt's chief competitor, supplied Walker with guns. In order to defeat his economic rivals, Vanderbilt bankrolled the allied armies of Costa Rica, El Salvador, and Honduras, which defeated and routed Walker in 1857.

Some have attempted to dismiss the Walker adventure as a minor footnote of American history. But during his two years of psychotic and racist rule, more than eleven thousand North Americans settled in Nicaragua, equal to one-third of the total white population in that country at the time.[63] Most of those immigrants were Walker supporters and anywhere from three thousand to five thousand joined his occupying army. In this country, thousands rallied in the major cities to cheer Walker as a hero. A Broadway musical based on his exploits became an overnight hit; the Pierce administration sanctioned his outright aggression by recognizing his government; and the Democratic Party convention of 1856, influenced by Walker's actions, nominated James Buchanan, a more rabid proponent of Manifest Destiny, over his opponent Pierce. As president, Buchanan proceeded to welcome Walker to the White House after his expulsion from Nicaragua. By then, a thousand U.S. citizens had been killed in Walker's war—a death toll greater than that of the Persian Gulf wars.[64] Walker made two more unsuccessful attempts

to return to power in Nicaragua. On his final try in 1860, he landed
in Honduras, where a British naval force captured him and handed
him over to local Honduran soldiers, who promptly executed him.[65]

By then, Manifest Destiny and the fervor for expansion were
being rapidly eclipsed by the conflict over slavery and the war between the North and South. Following the end of the Civil War, the
triumphant northern industrialists turned their attention to buying
up the western frontier and building a railroad system to connect
that frontier to the rest of the country. While a few U.S. policy makers still dreamed of a Central American canal route, the region's
leaders, bitter over the Walker episode, refused to consider the project for decades. The memory of Walker assured that Colombia and
Nicaragua would balk at any project that involved American control
over their territory.

So Central America turned to Europe instead. In 1880, Frenchman Ferdinand de Lesseps, seeking to replicate his triumph in
building the Suez Canal, secured Colombia's permission to begin
work on a Panama waterway. Like Vanderbilt's line through Nicaragua and the Panama railroad, the Lesseps project opted to use West
Indian Blacks as imported laborers. The French transported fifty
thousand Blacks to work on the project, but Lesseps's company collapsed in 1889, engulfing Europe in the biggest financial scandal in
history. When all work on the half-finished canal abruptly ended, the
West Indian workers were left stranded. As a result, West Indian colonies suddenly sprouted in the towns of Colón and Panama City.[66]

Lesseps's failure left the U.S.-owned Panama Railroad as the only
means of transportation across Central America. Throughout the
nineteenth century, the railroad remained the single largest U.S. investment in Latin America and the Colombian government's prime
source of revenue. The trip by ocean steamer and the Panama Railroad continued to be the fastest means of transport between the two
American coasts until 1869, when the first transcontinental railroad
began operating. The Panama line also became a constant source of
conflict, as U.S. troops intervened more than a dozen times before
1900 to enforce American control or to protect the line from warring Colombian factions.[67]

For the rest of the nineteenth century, railroads and banana
growing became the prime interest of the Anglo merchants who settled on the isthmus. In 1870, Charles Frank, a steward on the Pacific
Mail Steamship Line, began growing bananas on land the Panama

Railroad owned. During the same decade, Santo Oteri and the Macheca brothers, Italian immigrants from New Orleans, set up banana plantations along the coast of Honduras and Guatemala. Their firm eventually became the Standard Fruit Company.[68] In 1871, Costa Rica's president granted tycoon Henry Meiggs Keith the contract to build a railroad from the capital of San José to the country's undeveloped Atlantic coast. Keith, like others before him, imported thousands of West Indian and Chinese laborers for construction. He and his nephew, Minor Keith, eventually branched out into fruit growing. By 1886, their Tropical Trading and Transport Company was shipping twenty thousand tons of bananas annually to the United States.[69]

Far more important than Central America, however, was Mexico. Today, when many conservative U.S. politicians routinely heap scorn on Mexican migrants, accusing them of being conveyors of drugs and crime into our country, most Americans have virtually no knowledge of the immense wealth that thousands of U.S. investors— including some of the most storied families in our nation's history— systematically extracted from Mexico during the late nineteenth and early twentieth centuries. And it was not just a handful of Texas cattle barons, such as Charles Stillman, father of future National City Bank chief James Stillman. By the 1850s, Don Carlos, as Stillman was known, had already expanded south of the border, where he purchased a textile mill in Monterrey as well as iron, lead, silver, and copper mines in Nuevo Leon and Tamaulipas. Soon after the Civil War several major U.S. businessmen, including William E. Dodge and Anson Phelps of the Phelps Dodge Corporation, John Jacob Astor, William Aspinwall of the Pacific Mail Steamship Company, and New York newspaper publisher William C. Bryant, organized loans from Wall Street firms and arms shipments for President Benito Juárez to finance his war to end French occupation of Mexico. Other well-known business titans who sold discounted bonds to Juárez included J. P. Morgan, Moses Taylor of National City Bank, Cyrus W. Field, and Russell Sage of the Union Pacific Railroad. When the Juárez government defaulted on those loans—and any reasonable financial analyst should have known Mexico could not repay its growing debt— the bondholders sought other means of being made whole, either through awards of privatized Mexican land or through railroad concessions.[70] By then, several key American financiers were advocating that the United States seize more portions of northern Mexico. In

1868, a *New York Times* editorial noted: "The Territory, rich in minerals and agricultural resources, lies between us and the Pacific Coast, and it is requisite for our own prosperity that we should be permitted, when so inclined to conduct commercial and other pursuits there in undisturbed tranquility."[71] Most political leaders in Washington, however, balked at annexing land with such a large Spanish-speaking and racially mixed population.

The reign of dictator Porfirio Díaz (1876–1911) turned Mexico into a foreign investors' paradise. After Juárez died in 1872, Díaz, who had attempted previous unsuccessful uprisings, plunged into yet another revolt against Juárez's legally chosen successor, Sebastián Lerdo de Tejada. The latter was moving to cancel many concessions granted by the Juárez administration to foreign capitalists. Díaz, in contrast, was regarded as friendly to U.S. business interests, so much so that when he crossed from Texas into Mexico in 1876 with his initial rebel army of 1,600, half of his soldiers were Americans, and the financing and weapons for his rebel force came from the same circle of railroad magnates and bondholders from New York, Philadelphia, and Boston, as well as cattle barons from South Texas who were unhappy over Lerdo de Tejada's policies.[72]

Once he occupied Mexico City and seized power, Díaz insisted that his nation could only modernize by welcoming foreign capital. He systematically privatized the cooperative and communal pueblos of the country's indigenous and poor peasants—a policy that, in fairness, had started slowly under Juárez and the Liberal Party— and he fostered instead the amassing of colossal estates by foreigners and the Mexican elite. At the same time, his government doled out lucrative railroad, mining, smelting, oil, and agribusiness concessions to European and American entrepreneurs. Over the next few decades, the vast Mexican countryside evolved into an unprecedented laboratory for the spread of U.S. economic control over a foreign country. Mexico became, in effect, the incubator of the future American colonial empire. By the time a revolution erupted against the Díaz regime in 1910, U.S. investment in Mexico had surpassed $1.5 billion. By then, as one study would later note, "American capital owned 78 percent of the country's mines, 72 percent of the smelters, 58 percent of the oil, and 68 percent of the rubber business. American interests not only owned more holdings than all other foreign capitalists combined, they owned more than the Mexicans themselves."[73]

And it was not just a handful of industrial titans who were

involved in extracting Mexico's wealth: the Rockefellers, the Guggenheims, E. H. Harriman, J. P. Morgan, Cyrus McCormick, Peter W. Grace, and Joseph Headley Dulles (the great grandfather of John Foster Dulles). As historian John Mason Hart has meticulously documented, by 1910 there were more than 40,000 Americans living in Mexico. Of those, 15,000 had acquired land, and their holdings amounted to more that 130 million acres, or 27 percent of the country's entire surface area. The biggest of those owners, some 160 individuals and companies, each controlled 100,000 acres or more. There was, for instance Texas rancher Edwin Jessop Marshall's 2.5 million acre Las Polomas ranch in the state of Chihuahua, and William C. Greene's 2.5 million acre Cananea Cattle and Consolidated Copper Company in the state of Sonora, and the American Chicle Development Company's 3 million acres in Yucatán and Quintana Roo that supplied chewing gum to millions of Americans.[74] The Hearst family, whose newspapers and magazines routinely lauded Díaz, owned as many as 7 million acres themselves, with just one ranch in Chihuahua boasting a million cattle. U.S. trade with Mexico, which amounted to only $7 million in 1860, had jumped tenfold by 1908. By then, the United States was consuming 80 percent of Mexico's exports and supplying 66 percent of its imports. The massive exploitation of Mexican labor by foreign-owned enterprises became routine, with debt peonage in agriculture commonplace, and with scandalous gaps emerging between what was paid to Americans and to Mexicans in the same industries. In the mines of Guanajuato, for example, wages for American foremen averaged $1,500 per year, while those for Mexican laborers were $75 per year—a ratio of twenty to one.[75]

THE LURE OF THE GREATER ANTILLES

The same quest for trade, commerce, and conquest that propelled Americans into Mexico and Central America brought them to the Greater Antilles. As early as 1809, Thomas Jefferson had been eyeing Cuba.[76] "The annexation of Cuba to our federal republic will be indispensable to the continuance and integrity of the Union itself," wrote John Quincy Adams in 1823.[77] But U.S. leaders were unwilling to risk a war with the British navy over the island. They preferred allowing a weak Spain to keep control of Cuba rather than see it independent or under the sovereignty of another nation.[78] As

Martin Van Buren expressed it, "No attempt should be made in that island to throw off the yoke of Spanish independence, the first effect of which would be the sudden emancipation of a numerous slave population, the result of which could not be very sensibly felt upon the adjacent shores of the United States."[79]

Spain, after all, permitted North Americans to invest in Cuban property, and that was the most important matter. By 1823, as many as fifty North Americans owned plantations valued at $3 million just in the province of Matanzas.[80] Those planters soon joined with Cuban criollos and Spanish landlords to seek annexation to the United States. Planter D. B. Woodbury and merchant William F. Safford founded the city of Cárdenas in 1828 as a port to export sugar. So many U.S. citizens moved there that sections became virtual North American enclaves. "Our language is more common there than in any other Cuban city," wrote a visitor to Matanzas in 1859.[81] As early as 1848, President Polk offered Spain $100 million outright for the island. Four years later, President Pierce upped the offer to $130 million, without success.

While U.S. presidents sought to buy Cuba, American adventurers sought to obtain it with guns, just as they did with Florida, Texas, and Nicaragua. Between 1848 and 1851, three filibustering expeditions invaded the island. Each was led by Narciso López, a rich former Spanish army officer who favored annexation to the United States, and in all three attempts, North Americans made up most of the combatants. Of six hundred who assailed Cárdenas in 1849, for instance, only five were Cuban.[82]

Railroad construction in the late 1850s brought thousands of Anglo engineers and mechanics to the island.[83] This flow of immigrant labor from the North did not slow until the early 1870s, when the first Cuban War of Independence, known as the Ten Years' War, forced thousands of native Cubans and Yankee settlers to flee.

The North Americans returned as soon as the war ended, however. They rapidly dominated sugar production and established beachheads in other island industries. Bethlehem Steel Corporation and Pennsylvania Steel Company started iron, manganese, and nickel subsidiaries, and U.S. investments had grown to more than $50 million by 1890. By then, 94 percent of Cuba's sugar exports were going to the United States.[84] Among the new arrivals was Lorenzo Dow Baker, a Massachusetts captain who had initiated a steady trade of bananas from Jamaica to the United States. Baker joined Boston shipping agent Andrew Preston in 1885 to form a

new company, the Boston Fruit Company. Their firm was importing sixteen million bunches of bananas annually before the turn of
the century.[85]

So important did Cuba become to the United States that by the
1880s it had already accounted for nearly one-fourth of our nation's
world commerce.[86] On the eve of the Spanish-American War, the
island was a Spanish colony in name only.

A similar pattern developed in the Dominican Republic. After
Haiti's independence in 1804, Haitian armies invaded the eastern
end of Hispaniola and freed the enslaved Blacks there, but they also
oppressed the local elite. The occupation eventually sparked a popular rebellion that drove out the Haitians and led to the founding of
the Dominican Republic in 1844. The first emissary from Washington, John Hogan, arrived the following year. Hogan immediately
fixed his sights on the military potential of spectacular Samaná Bay
in the northeast. Samaná, he reported back home, is "capable of
providing protection to all the navies of the world."[87] Dominican
president Pedro Santana negotiated an initial deal to provide the bay
as a coal refueling station to the U.S. Navy. Santana even broached
the idea of the United States annexing his country, but opposition in
both nations quickly scuttled the scheme.

Next to arrive was William L. Cazneau, who had been involved
in Texas secession and later backed Walker in Nicaragua. Cazneau,
a fervent expansionist, resurrected the annexation scheme. He won
over William Seward, the secretary of state for both Andrew Johnson and Ulysses S. Grant.[88] At Seward's suggestion, Grant publicly
announced he favored it, and the white Dominican elite, who were
desperate to safeguard against another Haitian invasion, welcomed
his offer.

The rest of the Caribbean, however, was too alive with revolutionary ferment to accept annexation quietly. Puerto Rican and Cuban
patriots were locked in battle against Spanish rule, while popular
movements were in open rebellion against conservative oligarchies
in Haiti and the Dominican Republic. When the Haitian rebels triumphed in 1869, they offered their capital of Port-au-Prince as a safe
haven to all Caribbean democrats. Among those who accepted the
offer were Puerto Rico's Ramón Emeterio Betances and Dominican
generals Gregorio Luperón and José Cabral.[89]

In the midst of all this ferment, Grant signed his annexation
treaty with Dominican dictator Buenaventura Báez. Grant's idea
was to turn the Caribbean country into a colonizing venture for any

American Blacks who were dissatisfied with the post–Civil War South. The treaty outraged patriots throughout the Antilles, who saw it as the beginning of direct American control of their islands.[90] When he learned of it, Luperón prepared to invade his homeland from Haiti to overthrow Báez. The dictator appealed for U.S. help, and Grant instructed the navy to "to resist any effort to invade Dominican territory by land or sea."[91] Grant's navy may have been all-powerful in the Caribbean, but the president had overestimated his strength at home. The Senate, still dominated by post–Civil War Reconstruction radicals, did not share his dreams for a Caribbean empire. Led by Massachusetts abolitionist Charles Sumner, chair of the Foreign Relations Committee, it defeated Grant's treaty in 1870.[92]

The treaty's failure, however, did not deter American planters, who had suddenly discovered another weak, underdeveloped Latin American country that was ripe for exploiting. Before 1850, the bulk of Dominican trade had been with Europe, largely exports of tobacco, cocoa, and coffee.[93] That changed rapidly after three thousand Cuban and Spanish planters relocated to the country during the first Cuban War of Independence. The newcomers, with their advanced steam-driven mill technology, turned sugar into the leading Dominican crop almost overnight. Not far behind the transplanted Cubans were British, Italian, and North American planters. Americans Alexander Bass and his son William first acquired the Consuelo Mill in San Pedro de Macorís in the late 1880s. Then, in 1893, the family established the Central Romana, which would become one of the largest plantations in the Western Hemisphere.[94] As the sugar crop expanded, so did the importance of the American market. By 1882, less than forty years after independence, half of all Dominican trade was with the United States. The arriving Americans found a ready benefactor and ally in General Ulises Heureaux, the country's dictator from 1886 until 1899, when he was assassinated by Liberal Party rebels. During his reign, Heureaux reduced tariffs for U.S. imports, concluded numerous secret deals that benefited U.S. sugar growers, borrowed heavily abroad, first from Dutch financiers and later from Wall Street bankers, and filled his jails with anyone who opposed his policies.[95] By the time of his death, his nation had become another economic captive of the United States.

The pattern in U.S.-Latin American relations by now was unmistakable. During the first seventy-five years of their independence, Latin America's leaders had watched incredulously as their northern neighbor annexed first the Floridas, then Texas, then another huge chunk of Mexico. They followed with consternation the exploits of Walker in Nicaragua, of López and his mercenaries in Cuba; they were aghast at the arrogant way North American leaders treated them in diplomatic circles, at the racist labels those leaders used to describe Latin Americans in the U.S. popular press; they watched fearfully as annexation schemes gave way to massive economic penetration, so that by century's end, the Dominican Republic, Mexico, Spain's Cuban and Puerto Rican colonies, and much of Central America had become economic satellites of an expanding U.S. empire.

Anglo-Americans, on the other hand, saw a radically different and more benign canvas. Their image of the country's growth was perhaps best captured by historian Frederick Jackson Turner, who saw in the conquest of the frontier the essence of North American democracy, individualism, and progress. "American social development," Turner said in a famous speech in 1893, "has been continually beginning over again on the frontier." That frontier was for Turner the "meeting point between savagery and civilization." He believed that "this fluidity of American life, this expansion westward with its new opportunities, its continuous touch with the simplicity of primitive society, furnish the forces dominating American character." Turner, however, focused exclusively on how European settlers confronted Native Americans and a virgin land. His analysis mentioned nothing of Mexicans and other Latin Americans encountered on the frontier, either as settlers or immigrant laborers, or of their contribution to shaping our national character.

Moreover, this belief in the frontier as a democratizing element obscures how western expansion permitted violence to flourish against outsiders as a remedy for political problems. Whenever a politician such as Sam Houston or Davy Crockett found his rise barred by opponents at home, he simply packed his bags, conquered some new territory, and created a state where he and his allies could dominate. The frontier thus became an outlet for violence and corruption, for those within American society who wanted the fewest rules and least control.

U.S. territorial expansion did not climax with the closing of the western frontier; rather, it reached its culmination with the Spanish-American War of 1898. The mysterious explosion of the USS *Maine*, together with the prowar fever created by Hearst and other expansionist publishers, persuaded President McKinley to seek a declaration of war from Congress. But McKinley balked at recognizing the Cuban rebel army's provisional government as a partner in that war. "Such recognition," McKinley told Congress, "is not necessary in order to enable the United States to intervene and pacify the Island."[96]

Cuban patriots, who were on the verge of victory after thirty years of pro-independence struggle, had other ideas. "If intervention shall take place on that basis, and the United States shall land an armed force on Cuban soil," warned Horatio S. Rubens, a lawyer for the Cuban resistance, "we shall treat that force as an enemy to be opposed."[97]

Aware that the Cubans had a combat-hardened army of thirty thousand, Congress rebuffed McKinley and opposed any intervention that did not recognize Cuba's right to independence. Led by Senator Henry M. Teller of Colorado, Congress adopted a final joint war declaration that renounced any U.S. "intention to exercise sovereignty, jurisdiction, or control over said island except for the pacification there of."[98] Thanks to the Teller Amendment, the Cuban rebels welcomed the U.S. invasion and provided critical support to General William R. Shafter's U.S. troops. But once on Cuban soil, Shafter and his solders, mostly southern white volunteers, treated the Black Cuban soldiers with contempt. "Those people are no more fit for self-government than gunpowder is for hell," Shafter would say.[99] After the seizure of Santiago in the key battle of the war, Shafter barred Cuban soldiers from the city, refused to allow their general, Calixto García, to attend the Spanish surrender, and permitted the old Spanish colonial authorities to remain in charge of civilian government.[100]

A long line of historians, beginning with Julius W. Pratt in his 1934 study, *American Business and the Spanish American War*, have since insisted that McKinley and the U.S. business establishment were dragged unwillingly into the war and into a colonial empire by Hearst and by proexpansion intellectuals like Theodore Roosevelt, Henry Cabot Lodge, Alfred T. Mahan, and Henry Adams. In *The Rise of Modern America*, Arthur M. Schlesinger asserts that Wall Street actually favored peace with Spain over war. Those historians somehow divorce the war from the entire story of nineteenth-century U.S. expansionism in Latin America. Others, such as Martin Sklar, Walter LaFeber, and Philip Foner, offer less idealized accounts. They demonstrate that key sections of American business were demanding rapid expansion into the markets of Asia and Latin America. Foner, in particular, points to how corporate titans Astor,

Rockefeller, and Morgan all turned avidly prowar in the months preceding Congress's declaration.[101] Spain, a teetering, stagnant power, was never a match for the rising United States. Its defeat finally achieved what Jefferson, John Quincy Adams, and the other Founding Fathers had long sought: plopping Cuba, the juiciest plum of the Caribbean, into U.S. palms, and securing Anglo-American domination over Latin America for the next century. The Treaty of Paris that formally ended the war gave the United States direct control not only of Cuba but also over Puerto Rico, Guam, and the Philippines.

The end of the war brought a new wave of Yankee companies. On March 30, 1899, banana merchants Baker and Preston merged their Boston Fruit Company with Minor Keith's Central American holdings. They called the combined firm the United Fruit Company. At its inception, United Fruit owned more than 230,000 acres throughout the region and 112 miles of railroad.[102] More than any other U.S. company, United Fruit was to become the twentieth-century symbol of U.S. imperialism. It would evolve into a corporate octopus, controlling the livelihood of hundreds of thousands in Costa Rica, Honduras, Guatemala, Colombia, and Cuba, and toppling governments at will.

The Spanish borderlands had been brought to their knees. The next century would reveal the price of that conquest.

3

BANANA REPUBLICS
AND BONDS:
Taming the Empire's Backyard
(1898–1950)

Laborers are wanted in Hawaii to work in the sugar fields,
and in Cuba for the iron mines. Good wages are offered, and
many are persuaded to emigrate.

— CHARLES ALLEN, GOVERNOR OF PUERTO RICO,
1900–1901

Victory in the Spanish-American War and the sudden acquisition of overseas colonies made the nation uneasy at first. True,
Frederick Jackson Turner and others were espousing the stance that
territorial expansion and Anglo-American freedom were insepara-
ble, and most Americans believed that, but occupying foreign lands
and lording over their peoples seemed to contradict the very liberties
for which the nation had fought its own revolution. Not surprisingly,
the war with Spain led to our first anti-imperialist movement—
against suppression of the Filipino independence movement.

On the whole, outright territorial annexations ceased after 1898.
Wars of conquest, the sanctioning of armed invasions by filibuster
groups, the purchase of territories, gave way to gunboat diplomacy
and to a more disguised yet far more extensive system of financial
domination. Economic conquest replaced outright political annexation, as the region evolved into the incubator for the multinational

American corporation. By 1924, Latin America accounted for nearly half of all foreign U.S. investment, according to one U.S. Department of Commerce estimate (see table 2).

How that gunboat diplomacy and economic penetration deformed the Caribbean region's economy and paved the way for the huge influx of Latino immigrants during the second half of the twentieth century is the subject of this chapter.

Table 2

U.S. Direct Investment, 1924[1]

	(Millions)
Europe	$1,000
Asia and Oceania	$690
Latin America	$4,040
Canada and Newfoundland	$2,460

As we shall see, a series of military occupations early in the century—sometimes brief, sometimes lasting decades, but always for the most spurious of reasons—allowed U.S. banks and corporations to gain control over key industries in every country. Latin American ventures sprang up on Wall Street overnight as sugar, fruit, railroad, mining, gas, and electric company executives raced south on the heels of the marines. Thanks to the aid of pliant local elites and of U.S. diplomats or military commanders who often ended up as partners or managers of the new firms, the newcomers quickly corralled lucrative concessions while the host countries fell deeper into debt and dependence.

Whenever conflict erupted with a recalcitrant nationalist leader, the foreign companies simply called on Washington to intervene. The pretext was usually to save U.S. citizens or to prevent anarchy near our borders. To justify those interventions, our diplomats told people back home the Latin Americans were incapable of responsible government. Journalists, novelists, and film producers reinforced that message. They fashioned and perpetuated the image of El Jefe, the swarthy, ruthless dictator with slick black hair, a scarcely literate broken-English accent, dark sunglasses, and a sadistic personality, who ruled by fiat over a banana republic. Yet even as they propagated that image, our bankers and politicians kept peddling unsound loans at usurious rates to those very dictators.

Critical details of how the dictators rose to power and terrorized their people with Washington's help, or how their regimes provided a "friendly" business climate for North American firms, remained hidden deep in diplomatic correspondences. As U.S.-owned plantations spread rapidly into Mexico, Cuba, Puerto Rico, the Dominican Republic, Honduras, and Guatemala, millions of peasants were forced from their lands. Some were even displaced from their native countries when some of those same firms initiated cross-border labor recruitment efforts to meet the shifting needs of their far-flung subsidiaries. At first, the migratory labor streams flowed largely *between* the subject countries. West Indians, for instance, were recruited to build the Panama Canal, Haitians to cut sugar in the Dominican Republic, Puerto Ricans for the cane fields of Hawaii. But beginning with World War II, which shut down the supply of European labor, North American industrialists initiated massive contracting of Latin Americans for the domestic labor front. Thus began a migration process whose long-term results would transform twentieth-century America.

PUERTO RICO

Nowhere did the new U.S. policy leave such a profound legacy as in Puerto Rico. When General Nelson Miles landed in the town of Guánica on July 25, 1898, in the midst of the Spanish-American War, most Puerto Ricans greeted his arrival and rejoiced at his promise to end Spanish colonialism. "Our purpose is not to interfere with the existing laws and customs which are beneficial for your people," Miles declared in a proclamation.[2] Few imagined then that the island would remain a U.S. possession for the entire twentieth century, or that it would become the most important colony in our own country's history. Two years after the occupation started, Congress passed the Foraker Act, which declared the island a U.S. territory and authorized the president to appoint its civilian governor and top administrators. The new law permitted islanders their own House of Delegates, but it reserved for Congress the right to annul any laws those delegates passed. It assigned trade, treaty, postal, sanitary, and military powers to the federal government and it gave the island only one nonvoting delegate in Congress.[3] In many ways, the Foraker Act gave Puerto Ricans less self-government than they had enjoyed under Spain. Throughout most of the nineteenth century, after all, Puerto Ricans had been citizens of Spain and island voters had sent as many as sixteen voting delegates to the Spanish Cortes. And, in 1897, Spain had promulgated a new Charter of Autonomy, which gave the island virtual sovereignty.[4]

The Foraker Act, though, went beyond disenfranchising Puerto Ricans. It forbade the island from making commercial treaties with other countries and it replaced the Puerto Rican peso with the American dollar, while devaluing the peso.[5] This made it easier for U.S. sugar companies to gobble up Puerto Rican–owned lands. As a result, thousands of former independent coffee farmers joined the ranks of the mushrooming agricultural proletariat.

Legal challenges to the new law quickly led to several precedent-setting cases before the Supreme Court. Known as the Insular Cases, they have provided the principal legal backing for this country's holding of colonies to the present day. They are the equivalent for Puerto Ricans of the *Plessy v. Ferguson* decision for African Americans, sanctioning a separate but unequal status for overseas territories. The pivotal decision was *Downes v. Bidwell* in 1901, where the court ruled in a narrow 5–4 decision that "the Island of Porto Rico is a territory appurtenant and belonging to the United States, but not a part of the United States within the revenue clauses of the Constitution."[6] Given that the island was not an incorporated territory of the United States, as the frontier territories had been, the court ruled that the Constitution did not automatically apply in Puerto Rico unless Congress specifically granted Puerto Ricans citizenship.[7] In a stirring dissent, Justice John Marshall Harlan warned of the horrendous implications of the decision: "The idea that this country may acquire territories anywhere upon the earth, by conquest or treaty, and hold them as mere colonies or provinces, the people inhabiting them to enjoy only such rights as Congress chooses to accord to them, is wholly inconsistent with the spirit and genius as well as with the words of the Constitution."[8]

Despite the Foraker Act and the Insular Cases, many Puerto Ricans continued to back the U.S. occupation. Labor leaders who had suffered persecution under Spain, and big landowners who saw statehood as opening the U.S. market to their products, especially welcomed it. Trade union leaders never forgot that General Miles's soldiers freed from a Spanish jail the island's legendary labor figure, Santiago Iglesias. Iglesias and his Socialist Party turned into relentless advocates for statehood.[9] So was Luisa Capetillo, the feminist and anarchist popularly known as the first woman in Puerto Rico to wear pants in public. Capetillo reviled those who called for independence as "egotists, exploiters and aristocrats" who were trying to divide Puerto Rican and American workers.[10]

After the Foraker Act's passage, U.S. sugar growers flocked to the island. They not only set up plantations but also began recruiting Puerto Rican cane cutters to work in their overseas subsidiaries. Charles Allen, island governor from 1900 to 1901, noted that Anglo emigration agents

> penetrated the rural districts and offered golden inducements to these simple folk to travel and see foreign lands. Laborers are wanted in Hawaii to work in the sugar fields and in Cuba for the iron mines. Good wages are offered, and many are persuaded to emigrate. They crowd the seaport towns of Ponce, Mayaguez and Guanica. Very few embark at San Juan. . . . Most of them have gone to Honolulu, some thousands have gone to Cuba, and a few to Santo Domingo.[11]

Between 1900 and 1901, more than five thousand Puerto Ricans were transported to Hawaii in a dozen shiploads under contract to the Hawaii Sugar Planters Association.[12] It was a traumatic odyssey, first by ship to New Orleans, then by train to San Francisco, then by ship again to Honolulu, and scores escaped along the way from the harsh treatment they received.[13] The bulk of the migrants eventually settled on Oahu, where they founded the first major Puerto Rican community outside their homeland.

Back in Washington, Congress repeatedly turned down petitions by Puerto Rican leaders for full self-rule and eventual statehood for the island, angering even the most avidly proannexation leaders, like Dr. Julio Henna and José Celso Barbosa. By 1914, the full Puerto Rican House of Delegates, frustrated by this intransigence, asked Washington to cede the island its independence. Congress responded instead with the Jones-Shafroth Act in 1917, imposing U.S. citizenship on all Puerto Ricans over the unanimous objection of their House of Delegates.

"The Congress of the United States," declared Minnesota representative Clarence Miller, "says to the people of Porto Rico, once and for all, that they are part of the United States domain and will always remain there; that the legislation for independence in Porto Rico must come to a decided and permanent end."[14]

For the next thirty years, the island remained a direct colony, its Anglo governors appointed by the president, its population virtually ignored by Congress, and U.S. policy toward it controlled by a handful of American sugar companies. The companies so exploited their workers that in the 1930s and 1940s, Puerto Rico became notorious as the poorhouse of the Caribbean and as a hotbed for strikes and anti-American violence. Not until 1948, in response to a growing nationalist movement and to pressure from the United Nations to end colonialism, did Congress allow Puerto Ricans to elect their own governor. Four years later, the United States approved a form of limited self-rule, the Commonwealth of Puerto Rico, which exists to this day.

In fashioning this new political relationship, the Roosevelt and Truman administrations found an able ally in Luis Muñoz Marín, perhaps the most influential figure in the island's modern history. A socialist and *independentista* as a young man, Muñoz became an admirer of Roosevelt's and founded the Popular Democratic Party as a New Deal vehicle for the island. Once he gained control of the island's legislature, he pioneered a rapid industrialization program, Operation Bootstrap, which he turned into an economic model for underdeveloped countries. He lured foreign investment to the island, invariably U.S. companies, by offering them low wages, a tax-free environment to set up their factories, and duty-free export to the mainland.

Flushed by his early economic success, Muñoz deserted the pro-independence majority within his own party and opted instead for a form of local autonomy that would keep the island tied to the U.S. economy. That autonomy, Muñoz promised, would only be a transition stage to independence, and in the meantime, Puerto Ricans would retain their own language and culture. The voters, buoyed by the island's postwar prosperity, approved his commonwealth model in 1952. His opponents dismissed the referendum as a fraud, given that it offered a choice only between the existing colony or commonwealth, and neither independence nor statehood was on the ballot.

After the commonwealth vote, Washington began proudly pointing to Puerto Rico in international circles as a "showcase of the Caribbean," both politically and economically. True, by the 1950s the island was boasting one of the highest average incomes in Latin America, but the glowing statistics masked another reality. Every year, the number of people quitting the countryside for Puerto Rico's cities far outnumbered the new jobs the economy was creating. To thwart renewed unrest, Muñoz and officials in Washington started to encourage emigration to the north. By the early 1950s, their policy was sparking the largest flight of Latin Americans to the United States that the hemisphere had ever seen (see chapter 4).

CUBA

The U.S. occupation of Cuba followed a far different path. Much richer in resources than Puerto Rico, with a developed native land-owning class and a battle-tested independence army, Cuba was not easily subdued. During the initial occupation, U.S. officials turned the island into a protectorate by forcing the Platt Amendment into the Cuban constitution.

The first occupation government improved roads and health care and opened many new schools. It also presided over a rush of foreign investment. Cuban landowners, crushed by the debt and property destruction of the independence war, fell prey to American fortune hunters. "Nowhere else in the world are there such chances . . . for the man of moderate means, as well as for the capitalist as Cuba of-fers today,"[15] boasted an investor of the period. "A poor man's para-dise and the rich man's Mecca," said the *Commercial and Financial World* in describing the island. Percival Farquhar, for example, ar-rived in 1898 and soon controlled an electrification project and a railroad from Havana to Santiago. Minor Keith's United Fruit Com-pany acquired 200,000 acres for a pittance.[16] By 1902, the new To-bacco Trust in the United States controlled 90 percent of the export trade in Havana cigars. All told, U.S. investments nearly doubled, to $100 million, between 1895 and 1902, and they proceeded to mush-room tenfold by 1924, to more than $1.2 billion.[17]

The Cuban elite, led by Tomás Estrada Palma, a naturalized U.S. citizen whom the United States installed as the country's first presi-dent, welcomed the Americans at first, in return for a slice of the growing economic pie. Estrada Palma, like many well-to-do Cu-bans, favored eventual U.S. annexation. His reelection bid in 1905, however, was marred by widespread voter fraud that provoked vio-lent protests. U.S. troops returned in 1906, installed a provisional government, and stayed for three years.

This second occupation, headed by General Charles E. Magoon, ended up looting the country. When Magoon arrived, Cuba's national treasury had a $13 million surplus; when he left, it had a $12 million deficit. Public works projects he authorized routinely turned into boondoggles that lined the pockets of U.S. contractors. The plum of those concessions went to Frank Steinhart, who had arrived in Cuba as an army sergeant during the first occupation government and then landed appointment as American consul general in Havana after the troops left. Steinhart then lobbied Washington for a second military occupation and provided valuable intelligence to the U.S. troops. To reward him, General Magoon gave Steinhart the lucrative concession for expanding the Havana Electric Railway, Light and Power Company. Magoon also permitted him, as financial representative for Wall Street's Speyer and Company, to broker a $16.5 million loan to Cuba in 1909 for Havana sewage construction. By 1921, Havana Electric was reporting profits of $5 million a year, and the public was calling Steinhart Cuba's Rockefeller.[18]

U.S. soldiers returned for a third time in 1912 to put down a racially charged revolt by Black sugar workers. By then, nearly ten thousand Americans were living on the island: they ran the railroads, public utilities, mining and manufacturing companies, sugar and tobacco plantations, shipping and banking concerns, and held much of the government's debt.[19] More than three-fourths of the land was owned by foreigners.[20] Government employment and managerial jobs with foreign companies became the main source of income for the native upper class, and public corruption its primary source of wealth.[21] In 1917, President Wilson dispatched troops for a fourth time to help put down a rebellion against Conservative leader Mario García Menocal, the U.S.-backed candidate who had been reelected president in yet another fraud-tainted vote.

Soaring unemployment in the early 1920s forced many Cuban workers to follow in the tracks of their countrymen who had migrated to the United States during the nineteenth century. The new wave of immigrants settled in New Orleans, New York, Key West, and especially Tampa, where Spanish, Cuban, and Italian cigar makers had established a thriving industry.[22] At home, the crisis led to frequent labor strikes, and out of that unrest emerged Gerardo Machado, the country's first modern dictator. President Machado made Cuba hospitable for uneasy foreign investors by repressing or co-opting the rebellious labor movement. He enjoyed strong support from the directors of National City Bank, J. P. Morgan and Company, and Chase, who showered his government with loans. With each new loan, however, the bankers exacted more control over his government's spending. As the years passed and Machado's reign of terror grew, so did popular resistance.

After one such uprising paralyzed the country in 1933, President Franklin Roosevelt concluded that Machado had to go. Roosevelt sent veteran emissary Sumner Welles to quell the unrest by forcing the dictator's resignation, but Welles arrived too late. A nationwide general strike toppled both Machado and a U.S.-backed transitional government and brought to power a provisional revolutionary government, one that Welles could not control. The new government, led by Ramón Grau San Martín, embarked on a radical transformation of the country. It abolished the Platt Amendment, gave women the right to vote, and decreed a minimum wage and an eight-hour day. The liberal revolution spearheaded by Grau, however, lasted a mere one hundred days.

Welles was horrified by the new government's threat to U.S. interests. Although he considered himself a liberal, Welles, like most U.S. emissaries to Latin America, insisted on local leaders following dictates from Washington. When Grau refused to heed his warnings, Welles urged Fulgencio Batista, the new commander of the Cuban army, to stage a coup. In January 1934, Batista, whom Welles would laud as an "extraordinarily brilliant and able figure," did just that.[23] Batista's soldiers unleashed a bloody repression that crushed the Grau movement, killing or jailing most of its leaders and scattering the rest into exile abroad. From 1934 to 1944, whether as army strongman or president, Batista became Cuba's unquestioned ruler. To the United States, he offered welcome stability for foreign investors. To the Cuban people, he offered social reforms aimed at improving conditions among the poor. He accomplished the latter by cleverly co-opting the program of the Grau movement he had just destroyed. Batista even legalized the Communist Party in exchange for its guaranteeing him the support of Cuba's trade unions. And, in 1940, he oversaw the writing of the most democratic and progressive constitution in Cuba's history. Those reforms were made easier by temporary economic prosperity that bolstered Batista's standing, a prosperity brought about by World War II, and by the expanded demand for Cuban agricultural products in the United States. Despite that prosperity, Grau San Martín, who still had a big popular following, won the presidential elections in 1944, and his party stayed in power for the next eight years. Grau's Auténtico Party, however, proved to be the most corrupt in Cuban history. So many officials robbed the treasury that Batista staged another coup in 1952 and easily returned to power. His second period as maximum leader (1952–1958) was even more ruthless than the first. Once again, he jailed or simply eliminated his opponents, but this time he failed to produce any economic miracles. This time, Cuba's economy, by now a total appendage of the U.S. market, started unraveling. Unemployment skyrocketed, incomes dropped, and government corruption burgeoned, while Batista grew increasingly dependent for his power on a bizarre alliance of Wall Street investors, mobsters, and the Cuban managers of U.S. corporations.[24] The Batista dictatorship finally collapsed when the guerrillas of Fidel Castro's Twenty-sixth of July Movement marched into Havana on January 1, 1959.

PANAMA

After Cuba and Puerto Rico, the single largest U.S. expansion into Latin America was the Panama Canal, a project so ambitious, so grandiose, and so critical to the U.S. quest for economic power in the world that President Teddy Roosevelt devised a whole new nation just to house it. As mentioned in chapter 2, commercial groups in the United States had been calling for a Central American canal since the 1850s, with rival groups backing either a project through the mosquito-infested jungle of Colombia's Darién Province, or the route along Vanderbilt's old steamship and stagecoach line in Nicaragua. Nicaragua had the widest initial support among most engineers who had studied the project. But Ohio senator Mark Hanna, the powerful chairman of the national Republican Party, had other ideas. Hanna's close friend, New York lawyer William Nelson Cromwell, was an investor in the Panama route. A $60,000 donation by Cromwell to the Republicans in the midst of the debate seems to have strengthened Hanna's resolve and enabled him to secure a congressional majority for the Panama route.[25]

Colombia's president at the time was José Manuel Marroquín. As luck would have it, Marroquín had just come through a costly three-year civil war and was seeking a quick infusion of cash to bolster his exhausted treasury. So he offered President Teddy Roosevelt precisely what Nicaragua's president at the time, José Santos Zelaya, was refusing to give the United States—sovereignty over a ten-kilometer zone on both sides of the canal route. The result was the Hay-Herrán Treaty of 1903. But the treaty hit a snag at the last moment when Marroquín's opponents in the Colombian congress rejected the ten-kilometer provision as a violation of national sovereignty.

Their rejection enraged Roosevelt, who was not about to permit

some petty feud among inferior Latin Americans—he even referred
to the Colombian leaders as "foolish and homicidal corruptionists"—
to stop the greatest engineering project in U.S. history. Roosevelt
countered by backing a revolt aimed at the province's armed secession. Cromwell, along with Frenchman Philippe Bunau-Varilla and
Panamanian Manuel Amador, both investors in the Panama project,
prepared a blueprint for the uprising during a series of meetings in
September and October 1903, at Bunau-Varilla's room in New York's
Waldorf-Astoria. During his stay there, Bunau-Varilla traveled to
Washington, where he met on separate occasions with both Roosevelt and Secretary of State Hay, and came away from those meetings
convinced that the White House was already dispatching troops to
the Panamanian isthmus and would back an independence revolt.
On November 3, 1903, Amador led a rebel band that captured the
port towns of Panama City and Colón. While U.S. sailors dispatched
by Roosevelt assured the revolt's success by blocking the entry of
Colombian troops into Colón's harbor, Amador proclaimed Panama's independence. The new Panamanian government promptly
named Bunau-Varilla its new ambassador to the United States, and
he lost no time in signing the now renamed Hay–Bunau-Varilla
Treaty. So embarrassing was the "independence" revolt that Congress was forced to hold hearings in which Roosevelt's role as the
Panamanian godfather was revealed.[26]

It took ten long years (1904 to 1914) and 35,000 workers for the
U.S. Panama Canal Company to complete the project. Most of the
workers were English-speaking West Indians recruited by the company. If you include the families of those workers, more than
150,000 West Indians migrated to Panama during construction.
This enormous migration, which equaled more than a third of Panama's Spanish and Indian population of 400,000, transformed
every aspect of the new country's life.[27]

While press accounts praised the marvelous North American engineering feat through some of the world's thickest jungle, they
rarely mentioned the critical role immigrant Black workers played,
or their disproportionate sacrifice. During the first ten months of
1906, for instance, the death rate for white canal employees was seventeen per thousand, while among West Indians, it was fifty-nine
per thousand.[28]

The canal's opening led to enormous expansion of transoceanic
trade for the United States, and the waterway became an indispensable military resource for the country during both World War I and

World War II. The Canal Zone itself soon evolved into a miniature separate country within Panama, with several U.S. military bases and thousands of troops permanently assigned to guard it. Many of the West Indian laborers could not afford to return home when the main construction was complete, so they stayed on as maintenance workers. Canal Zone administrators and military commanders, many of them white southerners, soon replicated the same racial apartheid system that had existed for centuries in the American South. They established separate "gold" payrolls for American citizens and much lower "silver" ones for the noncitizen West Indians. Native Panamanians, meanwhile, were excluded from any jobs in the Zone. Blacks lived in squalid segregated company towns, while the whites resided in more opulent Zone communities, where everything from housing to health care to vacations were subsidized by the federal government.[29] For decades afterward, West Indians and Panamanians clashed with one another and with the Zone's Anglo-American minority over the discriminatory conditions (see chapter 9).

But the checkered story of U.S. control in Panama, Puerto Rico, and Cuba pales beside the bloody sagas of the Dominican Republic and Nicaragua, where long U.S. military occupations provoked costly guerrilla wars.

THE DOMINICAN REPUBLIC

The U.S. presence in the Dominican Republic, as we have noted in chapter 2, began with nineteenth-century dictator Ulises Heureaux, who saddled his country with massive foreign debt. To stave off bankruptcy, he hatched a refinancing plan in 1892 with the country's Dutch creditors and some New York investors. As part of the scheme, the Dutch sold their debt to a newly formed U.S. firm, the Santo Domingo Improvement Company, one of whose officers was a member of President Benjamin Harrison's cabinet. The new firm paid off the Dutch bonds and secretly gave Heureaux millions of dollars in new loans. Heureaux, in turn, gave the firm control of the national bank and one of the country's two railroads.

Only after Heureaux's assassination in 1896 did the new Dominican government discover that the former president had racked up $34 million in debt, the bulk of it to foreign creditors. The country's annual customs revenue, its main source of income at the time, was a mere $2 million. A good portion of the debt, it turned out, had been fraudulently marketed by the Improvement Company to un-suspecting Catholic farmers in Europe who thought they were lend-ing money to the Dominican religious order, not the Dominican Republic![30]

When a financial crisis hit in 1905, and customs revenues tum-bled, the new government suspended debt payments, prompting several European powers to threaten intervention. President Roos-evelt, worried that sea lanes to his unfinished Panama Canal might be imperiled by a European occupation, stepped in and offered to consolidate the Dominican debt with a new loan from a New York bank. Roosevelt insisted, however, that the Dominicans turn over all customs revenues to a U.S.-appointed agent and earmark the li-on's share of it for debt service. No longer would they be able to raise government spending or increase taxes without U.S. consent.

From that point on, the country was effectively a financial pro-tectorate. Once Roosevelt's overseers arrived, they jump-started ad-ditional legal reforms to benefit foreign investors. In 1906, for instance, they pressured the government to grant tax exemptions to all sugar produced for export. In 1911, they persuaded it to permit the division of communally owned lands, making it easier for sugar growers to enlarge their holdings. Each time Dominican officials balked at some new demand from Washington, Yankee warships appeared offshore to force their submission.

Defenders of the protectorate justified it by pointing to the coun-try's history of political violence and instability—in the first seventy-two years of independence, Dominicans had experienced twenty-nine coups and forty-eight presidents. Some of the very people who ridi-culed Dominican instability, however, conveniently overlooked that foreigners had financed much of the fighting. By 1915, a decade after Washington's protectorate commenced, political violence had not di-minished. Rather than reassess its methods, Washington chose to tighten its hold on the country's purse strings.

By then, war was looming in Europe, and President Woodrow Wilson had a new worry, that a major faction in Dominican politics might try to ally their country with Germany. To avert that possibil-ity, he demanded from the president, Juan Isidro Jiménez, the right to appoint U.S. citizens to key posts in the Dominican government and to replace the country's army with a new U.S.-trained National Guard. For a nation that had fought so long against Spanish, Haitian, and French occupation, these new conditions were unacceptable.

Even Jiménez, who had been installed by the United States, rejected them. Wilson retaliated by freezing the government's customs revenues. Still, the population refused to back down; thousands of government employees rallied behind their leaders and worked for months without pay.

In May 1916, Wilson sent in the marines, dissolved the legislature, imposed martial law and press censorship, and jailed hundreds of opponents. The occupation would last eight long years. It prompted widespread protests against the United States throughout Latin America, created deep bitterness in the Dominican population, and radically altered every sphere of Dominican society.

Supporters of the occupation point to the many improvements the marines brought about—supervising construction of the Caribbean's most modern highway system, reforming government financing, building hundreds of public schools, and carrying out successful public health campaigns against malaria and venereal and intestinal diseases. But the building program was financed with more foreign borrowing and by new taxes on property, alcohol, and other domestic manufacturing. And much of the early prosperity the country enjoyed was due to the war in Europe, which drove up the demand for sugar, tobacco, and other Dominican agricultural products. And no matter how the economy fared, Dominicans chafed under successive martial law governors who ruled them arrogantly in their own country. Even the elite in the cities refused to cooperate with the occupation army.

In the eastern part of the country, around the sugar plantation region of San Pedro de Macorís and Romana, a half dozen peasant bands mounted sporadic guerrilla resistance. The guerrillas, led by Martín Peguero, Ramón Natera, and Vicente Evangelista, proved adept at frustrating the Americans. Marines dispatched to the area committed so many atrocities against the local population that they drove most civilians to the side of the guerrillas.[31]

The infrastructure and health improvements the marines ushered in did not compare with the profound economic and military changes they set in motion. Those changes left the country irreversibly dependent on the United States. In 1919, for instance, a customs law opened the country to imports by declaring 245 U.S. products duty-free, while it sharply lowered tariffs on 700 others. The surge of imports that ensued drove many local Dominican producers out of business.

New property tax and land registration acts followed. The land law, in particular, created tremendous upheaval. Like all former Spanish colonies, the Dominican Republic's land tenure system had revolved for centuries around family-owned *mayorazgos*. The holdings of individuals were rarely demarcated from the rest of the family; informal agreements on land use predominated. The first land speculators and planters from the United States found the system an obstacle to the quick buying and selling of property. So, just as in Texas, California, and other former Spanish territories, they quickly set about rewriting the land laws. The sugar companies made the first try in 1911, but Dominicans were slow to implement the changes, and massive forging of titles and poor records doomed the effort. But the occupation government was more efficient. The marines decreed the immediate registration, surveying, and division of all communal lands and created a new land court to arbitrate disputes and administer the law.

As might be expected, the sugar companies hired the best lawyers and quickly bamboozled or bested thousands of illiterate peasants in the new land courts. Take the case of the New York–based Barahona Company, which was organized in 1916, the year of the invasion. By 1925, it had amassed 49,400 acres, largely from buying communal holdings, and was the second-largest plantation in the country. The Central Romana mushroomed in size from 3,000 acres in 1912 to 155,000 acres in 1925.[32] By 1924, twenty-one sugar companies controlled 438,000 acres—a quarter of the country's arable land. More than 80 percent of it belonged to twelve U.S. companies.[33] As land for subsistence farming diminished, staples had to be imported from the United States and the prices of food skyrocketed.[34]

But the sugar boom did not lead to higher wages. Instead of increasing what they paid their Spanish-speaking workers, the growers shifted to bringing in English-speaking Blacks from Jamaica, the Virgin Islands, and Turks and Caicos, whom they regarded as more docile and better suited to their needs than the Dominicans, Cubans, or Puerto Ricans. At some Dominican sugar mills, the entire workforce became English-speaking. Many of those migrants settled in the country after the harvest season, and their descendants inhabit areas around the old mills to this day. Local residents, angry at how the immigrant Blacks siphoned jobs away from natives, took to labeling them *cocolos*, a racial pejorative that still persists in the Caribbean.[35] Finally, the American planters at Central Romana and other giant mills turned to Haitian laborers.

Nearly half of twenty-two thousand contract workers officially imported in 1920 were Haitians, but some estimates put the number of
legal and illegal Haitians during the harvest season as high as one
hundred thousand.

Appalled by the greed of the sugar companies, military governor
Harry S. Knapp protested to the secretary of the navy in 1917: "I
would greatly prefer to see the Dominican, and especially the poorer
classes, brought to the point where they can work a small plot of
land on their own account and leaving the fruits of their labors in
Santo Domingo, than to see great companies come here and exploit
the country, taking out of it immense sums in the form of their profits."[36] Knapp's complaints were ignored.

The occupation's other lasting legacy was the national police. As
soon as they landed, the marines set about building a modern force
that could control the population permanently. Unfortunately,
once the marines left, that force copied the same arbitrary methods
of the occupation army. One of the early recruits to the new police
force was a former security guard for one of the sugar companies,
Rafael Leónidas Trujillo. American commanders, impressed with
the young man's intelligence and leadership ability, promoted him
rapidly through the ranks.

In 1920, Republican Warren Harding captured the White House,
and the new president dispatched Sumner Welles, the same diplo-
mat who would later engineer Batista's coup, to arrange a U.S. withdrawal from Santo Domingo. Welles antagonized most Dominican
leaders with his heavy-handed meddling in their plans for a post-
evacuation government while he was simultaneously lobbying for
business contracts for his friends in the United States. Those contracts saddled the country with even greater debt than before the
occupation.[37] It was not until 1924 that Welles finally arranged the
withdrawal of the marines. Once they were gone, Trujillo, who was
notorious for his corruption and ruthlessness, rose rapidly to commander of the rechristened national army, then was elected president in 1930 during a campaign in which his soldiers terrorized all
opponents. At first, Washington was cold to him, but American
diplomats eventually decided his stern methods were preferable to
continued instability.

For the next thirty years, either as president or through handpicked successors, Trujillo perfected the most notorious dictatorship in the hemisphere, running the country as a private fiefdom for
his family and friends. Known throughout the country as El Jefe, or

The Boss, his atrocities became legendary. He routinely kidnapped and raped Dominican women, even the wives and daughters of his subordinates.[38] He tortured, jailed, or executed thousands, including eighteen thousand Haitians massacred by his army in October 1937. His spies even tracked down and murdered his opponents in exile. His psychotic cruelty was immortalized in Gabriel García Márquez's haunting novel, *The Autumn of the Patriarch*. Only when he tried to assassinate the president of Venezuela in 1960 did the U.S. government, hoping to foil any repeat of Batista's overthrow in Cuba, begin to work for El Jefe's ouster. In May 1961, a group of his own officers assassinated him with the support of the CIA (see chapter 7).

NICARAGUA

Nicaraguans, meanwhile, were living through their own reign of *los jefes*. In their case, it was the rule of Anastasio Somoza García and his family. The Somozas' reign, like Trujillo's and Batista's, had its origins in an American occupation. Despite the debacle of the Walker wars, Nicaragua was a stable and prosperous country at the dawn of the twentieth century, thanks to José Santos Zelaya, the popular Liberal who served as president from 1893 to 1909. On the surface, Zelaya provided the kind of forward-looking, well-managed government other Latin American nations lacked. He even welcomed outside investment and paid the foreign debt on time. But he was also a nationalist, one who handed out lucrative commercial monopolies to favored Nicaraguans while refusing special treatment for foreigners. That brought him into conflict with the handful of U.S. executives who owned extensive banana, mahogany, and mining concessions in the country.

The concessions, all unregulated and untaxed, had been granted by Miskito leaders in the English-speaking Bluefields section along the Atlantic coast before Zelaya came to power. The foreign managers often quarreled with the central government over new taxes, and in both 1894 and 1899 they fomented unsuccessful anti-Zelaya revolts. Each time, the U.S. Navy intervened to protect their properties from confiscation.[39]

Zelaya's dispute with the Bluefields companies was just the beginning of his troubles. As we have seen, he lost the transoceanic canal project at the turn of the century because he would not give the United States sovereignty over the transitway. Then, in 1907, war broke out between Nicaragua and a coalition of Honduras, Guatemala, and El Salvador. Zelaya's army won several quick victories and occupied Honduras. With Nicaraguan troops advancing rapidly, the North American banana companies there persuaded President Roosevelt to dispatch marines to protect their plantations. U.S. troops were on the verge of confronting Zelaya's army when U.S. secretary of state Elihu Root and Mexican president Porfirio Díaz persuaded the Nicaraguan leader to withdraw. Their peace talks ended with the establishment of a Central American Court of Justice to arbitrate future conflicts.[40] The war, however, had raised Zelaya's stature considerably. He was now an indisputable regional power—much to the discomfort of U.S. officials.

After William Howard Taft succeeded Roosevelt, Taft's secretary of state, Philander Chase Knox, fashioned a new policy for the Caribbean that came to be known as dollar diplomacy. Knox, one of the best corporate lawyers of his day, was no stranger to Latin America. He had spent time in Panama and Cuba, and his former law firm represented the Fletcher family of Pittsburgh, which owned two major Nicaraguan firms, the United States and Nicaragua Company, and La Luz and Los Angeles Mining Company.

Knox's idea of financial reform was to set up customs receiverships in the region, and to replace European investment bankers, who held most of Central America's debt, with U.S. companies. To accomplish those ends, Knox did not scoff at calling in the marines.[41] He immediately decided Zelaya was an obstacle. After losing the canal project, Zelaya had embarked on his own vision for a transit route across Nicaragua—a railroad that would unite the West Coast to the isolated Atlantic region. He cut a deal with a German firm to build the railway and secured a $1.2 million loan from a British-French syndicate. Such financial independence irked not only Knox but also the banking houses of Brown Brothers, J. W. Seligman, and J. P. Morgan and Company, all of which were seeking a slice of the Central American loan business. In 1909, Juan Estrada, a Nicaraguan army officer, and Conservative Emiliano Chamorro rebelled against Zelaya. By then, sensational American newspaper accounts had begun vilifying the charismatic president as a butcher and tyrant, creating the first El Jefe stereotype among the American public.[42]

The Estrada rebellion against Zelaya, like that of Amador and Bunau-Varilla in Panama, was hardly homegrown. It was planned in

New Orleans and financed by U.S. companies through Alfonso Díaz, an executive of the Fletchers' Los Angeles Mining Company.[43] Scores of Anglo soldiers of fortune joined the rebels as advisers, in a throwback to the old filibuster revolts of the nineteenth century. Among the mercenaries were Godfrey Fowler, an active-duty captain in the Texas National Guard; Leonard Groce, who had been mining in Central America for years; and Virginia-born businessman Lee Roy Canon. Shortly after the rebellion started, Nicaraguan troops captured Canon and Groce as they were trying to dynamite a troop boat. Zelaya had them court-martialed and sentenced to death. That was all the excuse Taft needed to break diplomatic relations and unleash a campaign for Zelaya's ouster. The U.S. pressure quickly forced his resignation, but the crisis ended only when Estrada, Chamorro, and Díaz, Washington's choices, gained power in 1910 in a revolt against Zelaya's chosen successor, José Mádriz. The rebels had been on the verge of defeat in the country's Bluefields area by soldiers loyal to Mádriz when a U.S. gunboat appeared off the coast and decreed there could be no interference with local commerce, thus allowing the Estrada/Díaz forces to be resupplied with arms. A top aide to Knox at the time, Francis M. Huntington-Wilson would later describe in his memoirs the aim of U.S. policy in more stark and racial terms, noting "There was an educated, property-owning and civilized small minority [in Nicaragua] that . . . made up the Conservative Party. . . . A lower stratum . . . made up the Liberal Party. The aim of policy, thought I, should be to protect the small group of the best people from being over-whelmed, through Liberal politicians, by the Negro and Indian elements."[44]

The Estrada forces soon turned the tide and deposed Mádriz, then dutifully carried out all the "reforms" Knox wanted. They refinanced Zelaya's old English-French debt through Brown Brothers and Seligman, they installed a U.S. overseer to collect customs duties, and they invited American troops into the country. In the process, they also looted the treasury.[45] By the middle of 1912, the two Wall Street firms controlled the new National Bank of Nicaragua (chartered in Connecticut), and the Pacific Railroad (incorporated in Maine). Zelaya's own dream of uniting eastern and western Nicaragua by a rail line died with his ouster.[46] For the next thirteen years, a small force of marines remained in the country as Washington and Wall Street dictated the country's financial affairs.

The marines left in 1925 but were forced to return the following year when a new civil war erupted. This time, General Chamorro was trying to reinstall Díaz to power over Liberal Juan Sacasa, who had won the previous year's election. The marines claimed neutrality but threw their support to Díaz after peasants in the countryside took up arms to bring the popular Sacasa back to power. The peasant revolt lasted seven years, and it turned rebel leader Augusto César Sandino into a legend. As a young man, Sandino had witnessed firsthand the impact of U.S. multinationals on Central America's labor force, having worked at various times during the 1920s as a mechanic in Honduras for the Vaccaro Brothers, in Guatemala for United Fruit, and in Tampico, Mexico, for a subsidiary of Standard Oil, where he was deeply influenced by the Mexican revolution.[47] Hundreds of volunteers from other countries eventually joined Sandino's army, as it repeatedly eluded both government forces and the six thousand marines sent by Washington. When those soldiers bombed and machine-gunned to death some three hundred unarmed men, women, and children in a massacre at Ocotal in July 1927, public sentiment in the United States turned against the war.[48] The marines hung on until the Nicaraguans elected Sacasa president once again in 1932, whereupon public protests forced their withdrawal.

Sandino then rode triumphantly into Managua and embraced Sacasa at the presidential palace. It was the first time the United States had faced defeat in Latin America, and our leaders would not forget it. Before departing, the marines managed to train a new National Guard and install its English-speaking commander, Anastasio Somoza García. Somoza's soldiers ambushed and executed Sandino two years later. The assassination, according to several historians, had the secret backing of Ambassador Arthur Bliss Lane.[49] Somoza wasted little time in ousting Sacasa and turning Nicaragua into his personal fiefdom. After Somoza, his two sons succeeded him as the country's strongmen, assuring Somoza family control right up to the Sandinista revolution in 1979.

What propelled our government to assume this role of regional policeman throughout the Caribbean and Central America in the early twentieth century? Some historians argue that prior to World War I, our leaders genuinely feared that the Germans or other Europeans would establish beachheads near U.S. shores. But even after World War I ended and left the United States an unrivaled power in the Caribbean, the interventions continued.

Others point to the string of U.S. bankers and businessmen who loaned money to Latin American governments, much of it on unsound ventures. National City Bank opened the first Latin American branch of a U.S. bank in Argentina in November 1914; five years later, it had established forty-two branches.[50] U.S. firms floated some $2 billion in Latin American government bonds during the 1920s, most of it in Mexico, Central America, and the Caribbean. Once those loans were made, the bankers expected the marines to protect their investment.[51] But then came the Wall Street crash. Beginning with Bolivia in 1931, every Latin American country except Haiti defaulted on its loans. U.S. investors retreated from the region throughout the Depression years.

Whatever the reason for those early interventions, Franklin D. Roosevelt's election to the presidency brought a new approach to Latin America. Overt bullying from Washington and military occupations largely ended. Instead, American diplomats in the region sought to control events through pliant pro-U.S. dictators who were expected to maintain order. The mid-1930s and the 1940s thus became the heyday of *los jefes*. Except for a few, their names are almost unknown to the U.S. public. But to their countrymen, they represent lost decades so filled with horror and darkness that some nations are only now recovering.[52] Such was the period not only of Trujillo, Batista, and the Somozas, but of Guatemala's Jorge Ubico Castañeda, El Salvador's Maximiliano Hernández Martínez, and Honduras's Tiburcio Carías Andino. What seemed to unite them all was their ability to curry favor with Uncle Sam, first as allies against fascism during World War II, then as dependable anti-Communists in the late 1940s and 1950s.

Following the war, North American companies that resumed investment in the region invariably saw *los jefes* as dependable strongmen who offered welcome stability after decades of unrest. Direct U.S. investments tripled in Latin America between 1955 and 1969, mostly from mining, petroleum, and manufacturing, and profit margins skyrocketed.[53] Between 1950 and 1967, for instance, new U.S. investment in Latin America totaled less than $4 billion, but profits were nearly $13 billion.[54]

This soaring commerce and the rise of a Communist bloc in Europe and Asia brought with it a renewed determination by Washington to control its Latin American backyard. Wherever social democratic or radical leftist regimes came to power and threatened the business climate for U.S. companies, Washington responded by backing right-wing opponents to overthrow them. In 1954, the CIA helped oust the liberal reform government of Jacobo Arbenz in Guatemala.[55] In 1961, the agency organized the failed Bay of Pigs invasion of Cuba. Four years later, the marines invaded the Dominican Republic again, just as rebels loyal to the democratically elected president Juan Bosch were about to defeat a group of generals who had ousted Bosch in a coup two years before. Similar scenarios emerged in Chile under Salvador Allende, in Peru under Juan Velasco Alvarado in the 1970s, and in Nicaragua under Sandinista leader Daniel Ortega in the 1980s. When all else failed, our leaders resorted to direct invasion, as with Grenada in 1983 and Panama in 1989.

But as U.S. capital increasingly penetrated Latin America during the century, something else began to happen: Latin American labor headed north. More than a million people, one-tenth of Mexico's population, migrated to the Southwest between 1900 and 1930.[56] Some fled the chaos and repression of the 1910 revolution, but many were recruited as cheap labor for the railroads, mines, and cotton and fruit farms out west.

The Santa Fe and Southern Pacific, for instance, enlisted sixteen thousand Mexicans in 1908 for their lines. Henry Ford brought several hundred Mexicans in 1918 as student workers to Detroit, so that by 1928, there were fifteen thousand Mexicans living in the Motor City.[57] In 1923, Bethlehem Steel contracted a thousand Mexicans to work in its Pennsylvania mill. That same year, National Tube Company brought thirteen hundred migrants from Texas to work in its plant at Lorain, Ohio.[58] Great Western Sugar Beet Company brought more than thirty thousand Mexicans to the Colorado beet fields in the 1920s and 1930s. The Minnesota Sugar Company offered transportation, housing, and credit to Mexicans to migrate to that state. By 1912, there was a Mexican *colonia* in Saint Paul.[59] Similar contracting occurred in Michigan and Kansas.

After World War II, the trickle of migrants became a torrent, beginning with the Puerto Ricans in the 1950s, and followed by the Cubans and Dominicans in the 1960s, the Colombians in the 1970s, and the Central Americans in the 1980s. The migrations came from the same Caribbean countries our soldiers and businessmen had already penetrated, cowed, and transformed. But each country's diaspora, as we shall see, was markedly different. Different in class

makeup. Different in customs. Different in where and how they
settled, and in how America responded to them. Their separate
odysseys were as rich in experience and as varied as those of the
English, Irish, Italians, and Poles who came before them. Yet they
shared one bond that other waves of immigrants had not—a common language.

Toward the end of the twentieth century, those Latin American
newcomers started to transform this country in ways no one had expected. Anglo conquest had boomeranged back to U.S. shores.

PART II

Branches

(Las Ramas)

4

PUERTO RICANS:
Citizens Yet Foreigners

Marcantonio lost the election. They're jumping every Spic they can find.

—NEW YORK CITY COP, 1950

Until World War II, Mexican farmworkers were the most familiar Latin Americans in this country. True, a Latino might occasionally turn up in a Hollywood film role, or leading a band in a New York nightclub, or as the fancy fielder of some professional baseball team, but outside the Southwest, Anglo-Americans rarely saw Hispanics in everyday life and knew almost nothing about them.

Then the Puerto Ricans came.

More than 40,000 migrated from the Caribbean to New York City in 1946 alone. Actually, a small Puerto Rican enclave had existed in that city since World War I, and that *colonia* grew to 135,000 by the end of World War II, but the year 1946 saw an amazing growth in Puerto Rican arrivals, one that continued without letup for the next fifteen years. By 1960, more than 1 million were in the country, part of what one sociologist dubbed "the greatest airborne migration in history."[1] That population continued to expand to the point that, by 2017, far more Puerto Ricans were residing in the fifty states, some 5.8 million—than on the island, 3.2 million, according to Census Bureau estimates.[2]

My family was part of that 1946 wave. My parents, Juan and Florinda González, arrived on one of the first regular Pan American

Airline flights from San Juan. Along with the Mexican *braceros* out west, they were pioneers of the modern Latino diaspora.

Puerto Ricans were uniquely suited for a pioneer role. To this day, only we among all Latin Americans arrive here as U.S. citizens, without the need of a visa or resident alien card. But this unique advantage, a direct result of Puerto Rico's colonial status, has also led to unexpected obstacles. Despite our de jure citizenship, the average North American, whether white or Black, continues to regard Puerto Ricans as de facto foreigners. Even the Supreme Court, as we have seen, has had difficulty explaining the Puerto Rican condition. The contradiction of being at once citizens and foreigners, when joined with the reality that ours was a racially mixed population, has made the Puerto Rican migrant experience in America profoundly schizophrenic, more similar in some ways to that of African Americans or Native Americans than to any other Latino group.

To comprehend that schizophrenia, we would do well to examine the forces that shaped the Puerto Rican worldview: Why did the migrants leave their homeland in such numbers? What happened when they arrived here? How did others regard them? How did they cope with and survive in their new conditions? Why did so many get stuck in poverty, unable to climb the immigrant ladder? Hopefully, my family's story, one very typical of that early migration, will provide some insight.

WHY WE CAME

One morning in May 1932, road workers found chief engineer, my grandfather Teófilo González, feverish and delirious at their work camp on Puerto Rico's southwest coast. He died a few days later of pneumonia, and his death immediately plunged his young wife, María González Toledo, and their six children into abject poverty.[3]

My grandmother had married Teófilo in 1914 in the mountain town of Lares. She was sixteen at the time, an orphan, illiterate, and desperate to escape from her Spanish-born godmother, who had raised her as a virtual servant. Her new husband was thirty-four, well educated, and the eldest son of a prosperous coffee grower whose own parents had migrated to Lares from the Spanish island of Mallorca in the late 1850s.

Puerto Rican criollos resented the Mallorcan *peninsulares* who quickly bought up most of the businesses in Lares and rarely employed the town's native-born residents.[4] The Mallorcans were loyal to the Spanish Crown, while Lares was a hotbed of separatist and abolitionist sentiment. On September 23, 1868, El Grito de Lares erupted. It was the most significant independence revolt in island history. My grandfather's parents, Teófilo González Sr. and Aurelia Levi, were only teenagers then, but they cheered the Spanish soldiers, who quickly quashed the rebellion. To quell further unrest, Spain's Cortes abolished slavery on the island in 1873, but my great-grandparents, like many of the small coffee farmers in the region, circumvented the emancipation decree and illegally kept a few Black laborers on their farm as semislaves. This infuriated their youngest son, Onofre, who soon turned into a political dissident opposed to Spanish rule.

According to family legend, my great-grandparents scoffed at Onofre and called him a crazed idealist. They were still ridiculing him when the Spanish-American War erupted, and U.S. soldiers landed at Guánica. Soon after, Onofre stole several of his father's horses and rode south to volunteer his services to the Yankee invaders. He returned after a few weeks, proudly galloping into Lares as the lead scout for a column of U.S. soldiers.[5]

That early military occupation, as we have seen, quickly disillusioned even its Puerto Rican supporters. It wrecked the small coffee and tobacco growers who were the backbone of the island's economy. U.S. sugar companies gobbled up the land and created a vast agricultural proletariat whose members only worked a few months of the year. For the multitudes of poor, life became unbearable. "I have stopped at farm after farm, where lean, underfed women and sickly men repeated again and again the same story—little food and no opportunity to get more,"[6] wrote Theodore Roosevelt Jr., a former governor of the island and son of Teddy Roosevelt, in 1929.

During those desperate years, María and Teófilo González lost five of their eleven children to disease. Still, they were in better shape than most, thanks to his job building roads for the government. After her husband's death in 1932, though, the family's fortunes sank. María sold the big house they owned in the southern coastal city of Ponce and moved to a squalid shack in El Ligao, the worst section of the Mayor Cantera slum high in the hills of town. She found work as an aide in Ponce's Tricoche Hospital and occasionally as a coffee bean picker in the fields near Lares.

But the odd jobs could not provide enough money to support a large family, so she reluctantly gave several of her children away to friends in hopes of saving them from starvation. Her oldest daughter, my aunt Graciela, she placed with neighbors who owned a local store, and there the girl worked behind the counter in return for food and board. She sent another girl, my aunt Ana, to live with a neighbor as a housekeeper. She dispatched one son, my uncle Sergio, to live with a childless schoolteacher.

But her two youngest, my aunt Pura and my father, Pepe, were too young to be useful to anyone, so she placed six-year-old Pepe in an orphanage. The day she left him with the nuns at the orphanage, his terrified wails almost crushed her heart. Her guilt was so great that after a few years she reclaimed him from the nuns and sent him to live with another childless teacher. But the teacher sexually abused Pepe for years, turning him into a sullen and explosive alcoholic. Throughout the rest of his life there was such aimless rage buried inside him that whenever he drank heavily, he would always recite the story of how his mother had abandoned him.

Pura, the only one left at home, became her mother's constant companion—the other children were permitted to visit their mother only a few Sundays a month. María dragged the little girl with her everywhere. She hid her under the sink in the hospital whenever the supervisors appeared; in the fields, she would tie a can around Pura's neck and show her how to pluck the coffee beans with her tiny fingers. The psychological scars left in all of them by their long childhood separation were so deep that decades later, after they'd all been reunited and the family had moved to New York City, the González brothers and sisters never spoke openly of those times.

The 1930s were the most turbulent in Puerto Rico's modern history, and Ponce, where my family had settled, was the center of the storm. The Depression turned the island into a social inferno even more wretched than Haiti today. As one visitor described it:

> Slow, and sometimes rapid, starvation was found everywhere. If one drove a car over the country roads, one was delayed again and again by sorrowing funeral processions carrying the caskets of dead infants.
>
> Most of the cities were infested with "wolf gangs" of children ranging in ages from six to sixteen, many of whom had no idea who their parents were. They pilfered and robbed; they "protected" parked automobiles, and if the drivers didn't want to pay for such protection, they siphoned gasoline out of tanks, stole hub caps, slashed tires. They slept where they could—in parks, in hallways, in alleys.[7]

Ponce's hilltop El Ligao was notorious for its violence and crime. Neighbors often feuded and brutal killings in machete or knife fights were commonplace. One day, Pura González watched in horror as a young resident named Saro, who sold ice in a small pushcart, was dragged bleeding through the dirt street in front of her house by four men who brazenly hanged him from a tree, stabbed and castrated him. Saro, she discovered, was a numbers runner. An important town official had placed a bet with him, but when the number hit and the official came to collect his money, he discovered Saro had blown it all on liquor. As a lesson to El Ligao, the official ordered Saro's public execution.

Ponce was, at the same time, Puerto Rico's most prosperous and cultured city. It was the center of the island's Nationalist movement, whose president was Pedro Albizu Campos. Albizu graduated from Harvard in 1916, served in the U.S. Navy, and spent years traveling throughout Latin America. In 1932, he returned to his homeland and assumed the party's leadership. A charismatic speaker and devout Catholic, Albizu wasted no time tapping into the country's long-felt frustration over U.S. control, and soon took to propagating an almost mystical brand of anti-Yankee, anti-Protestant nationalism.

By the time of Albizu's return from abroad, the greed of the U.S. sugar plantations had created a social tinderbox. Wages for cane cutters, which had been sixty-three cents for a twelve-hour day in 1917, were down to fifty cents by 1932. Forty percent of the workforce was unemployed, yet company profits remained high.[8] During the last six months of 1933 alone, eighty-five strikes and protests erupted, several of them directed against the colonial government. In one of those strikes, thousands of sugar workers demanding an eight-hour day rebuffed their own ineffectual leaders and called on Albizu Campos and the Nationalists for help. For the first time, the Nationalists and the labor movement were becoming united. In other parts of the country, picket line violence during walkouts by needleworkers in Lares and Mayagüez left two dead and seventy injured.[9]

To stem the anti-Yankee violence, federal agents arrested Albizu Campos and several of the party's leaders on sedition charges in 1936. While they were in jail, the youth brigade of the party, the Cadets, scheduled a peaceful march in Ponce to press for their release. Governor Blanton Winship refused at the last moment to issue them a permit, but the Nationalists decided to march anyway.

The day was Palm Sunday, March 21, 1937. My aunt Graciela was sixteen and caught up in the Nationalist fervor at the time. Luckily, she decided to skip the march that day and go on a picnic with her sisters, Ana and Pura. They all trekked up to El Vigía, the magnificent hilltop estate of the Serralles family, owners of the Don Q rum distillery. From the rolling castle grounds you can look down on all of Ponce. Pura, the youngest of them, recalls that shortly after the Nationalists gathered, the church bells began to ring, and when she looked down the mountain toward the plaza, she saw people scattering in all directions. A young woman they knew ran up to them, screaming, "There's a massacre in town. The Nationalists and the soldiers are fighting. The hospital is full of wounded." When the smoke had cleared, 21 people were dead and 150 were wounded. A human rights commission would later report that all had been gunned down by police. It was the biggest massacre in Puerto Rican history.[10]

After the Palm Sunday Massacre, hysteria and near civil war swept the island. Nationalists were hunted and arrested on sight. Some headed for exile in New York City or Havana. Graciela, our family's only Nationalist Party member, decided that nothing could be won by fighting the Americans. With Albizu Campos in jail and the Nationalist ranks decimated, she quit the party.

By the early 1940s, my grandmother María had managed to re-unite the family. Her children were grown up by then, and the out-break of World War II had made jobs more plentiful. My father, Pepe, enlisted in the all–Puerto Rican Sixty-fifth Infantry and served with the regiment in North Africa, France, and Germany. His brothers, Sergio and Tomás, were drafted a year later.

The Puerto Ricans of the Sixty-fifth were segregated from the other American soldiers throughout the war and assigned largely to support work for combat units. Given that they spoke no English, they found themselves frequently ridiculed by their fellow GIs. Be-yond the prejudice they faced, they were deeply shaken by the devastated countryside of southern France and Germany, which re-minded them of the lush green hills of Puerto Rico. Displaced French farmers became haunting reminders of their own destitute *jíbaro* countrymen. The war transformed not only the González brothers, but also every Puerto Rican who participated in it. For the first time, a large group of Puerto Ricans had left home and traveled the world. Many of them were exposed to ethnic prejudice for the first time. And for the first time they had fought in defense of a country they knew nothing about. Nonetheless, they returned home believing, like their Mexican American counterparts, that they had earned a place at the American table; for the first time, they felt like citizens.

While María González's three sons were away at war, their army paychecks pulled the family out of poverty. But the returning González brothers found the island nearly as destitute as they'd left it. As soon as he got back, Pepe married my mother, Florinda, an orphan whose own mother had died giving birth to her, and whose father had gone off one day to work in the sugar plantations of the Dominican Republic and never returned, leaving her and her older brothers to be raised by their grandmother.

The postwar period, however, brought rapid change. In 1946, President Truman appointed the first Puerto Rican governor of the island, Jesús Piñero. Soon afterward, on December 15, 1947, Pedro Albizu Campos returned home after serving ten years in federal custody for his sedition conviction. Thousands of Nationalists greeted him at the airport as a returning hero. "The hour of decision has arrived," Albizu Campos warned his followers.[11] As the Nationalist Party and the U.S. government hurtled toward a final bloody confrontation, the González family and thousands of others packed their bags and headed for New York.

EARLY LIFE IN NEW YORK CITY'S EL BARRIO

They settled in the tenements of El Barrio in northern Manhattan, and there they encountered both helping hands and hostility. My uncle Tomás was the first to arrive in 1946. A fellow migrant found him a job serving coffee at the Copacabana, the most famous nightclub in New York at the time. Tomás immediately sent for his brothers, Sergio and Pepe, and landed them jobs at the Copa as dishwashers. Even though mobster Frank Costello ran the place then, politicians and police inspectors, high-priced lawyers, and professional ballplayers all flocked to the club to listen to performances by the era's biggest entertainers. The Filipino waiters and Puerto Rican kitchen workers reveled in the club's glamour and intrigue and enjoyed boasting about the famous people they routinely served.

My parents settled in a cold-water tenement flat on East 112th Street, near First Avenue. The block was part of East Harlem's

Italian section. The neighborhood's Sicilian elders would gather
each day inside unmarked storefront social clubs. At night, the men,
most of them garment workers and many of them members of the
anarchist or socialist movements, would play dominoes outdoors
while they debated the future of the union movement. By the late
1940s, many of the Italian immigrants' sons were joining neighborhood street gangs. The gang members, who were determined to
keep their tidy ghetto off-limits to outsiders, would patrol the big
city-owned Jefferson Pool and the string of bars along First and
Second Avenues, chasing off any Blacks or Puerto Ricans who wandered into the neighborhood.

Ethnic tensions stayed under control as long as Vito Marcantonio
was the local congressman. Marcantonio, an old-style socialist,
managed to fashion a unique coalition of East Harlem's ethnic and
racial groups, one that had kept him in the House of Representatives from 1934 to 1950. Marcantonio could always be found advocating for the poor, whether it was unemployed workers being
evicted from their homes or families with no food to eat. For years,
he was the lone critic in Washington of U.S. rule in Puerto Rico. In
1937, he helped elect this country's first Puerto Rican to political office. His protégé, Oscar García Rivera, won an assembly seat that
year as the candidate of both the Republican and American Labor
parties.[12] The city's political establishment, on the other hand, abhorred Marcantonio and his radical notions. In 1950, his enemies
finally beat him in an election and ousted him from Congress, but
even then it took an unprecedented alliance of the Republican,
Democratic, and Liberal Party bosses to unite behind one candidate.

With Marcantonio gone, East Harlem lost its main voice for
working-class unity. Racial tensions flared up immediately, with
some Italians blaming Puerto Ricans for his defeat. The elders of
our family still recall the terrible election night in November 1950
when the ethnic war began. That night, Eugenio Morales, a one-
time neighbor from Ponce's El Ligao, was visiting my grandmother
María and her grown daughters, Graciela and Pura. A handsome,
dark-skinned, humorous man, Morales delighted the women with a
stream of hilarious reminiscences about life in Puerto Rico. Around
ten p.m., as Morales got up to leave, Pura heard the radio blaring the
news about Marcantonio's losing his election, but no one was paying
much attention.

"Be careful out on those streets," my grandmother told him.

"The Italians on this block know us, but you're a stranger." She didn't say what she was thinking, that the González family was so light-skinned most of us could easily pass for Italian, but not Eugenio with his chocolate complexion.

"Don't worry, Doña María," he said with a shrug and a smile. "I can take care of myself." Then he walked out. A few minutes later, there was a loud banging at the door. Graciela rushed to open it and Eugenio collapsed at the entrance, blood spurting from his head, mouth, and chest. The bones on one side of his face had collapsed and fragments were piercing the skin. An ambulance rushed him to Metropolitan Hospital, where a few minutes later medics wheeled in a bloodied man named Casanova, a Puerto Rican amateur boxer. Casanova, Eugenio later learned, had been beaten and stabbed by Italians. Half an hour later, another battered Puerto Rican was admitted. Eugenio overheard a young Irish cop whisper to one of the nurses in the emergency room, "Marcantonio lost the election. They're jumping every Spic they can find."[13] Eugenio Morales never visited our family in East Harlem again, nor did any other of our dark-skinned relatives or friends. To keep from being run out of the neighborhood by the racist attacks, Puerto Ricans started organizing their own street gangs, groups like the Viceroys and Dragons, and soon the city's major newspapers were depicting a city terrorized by Puerto Rican and Black gangs. As the years passed, however, the new migrants became too numerous to frighten off, and the street gangs had faded in importance by the 1970s, at least in Puerto Rican communities.

Despite the bitter 1950s gang war era, common work experiences and the bond of the Catholic religion gradually drew Puerto Ricans, Italians, and Irish together—as neighbors, as friends, sometimes even as family. My aunt Pura, for instance, married Bing Morrone, an Italian American whose parents owned the only grocery store on our block, and their children, my cousins Anthony, María, and Julie, all grew up as both Puerto Rican and Italian.

This was still the era when working with your hands was considered the most honorable of professions, when downtown white-collar workers were relatively few in number. It was the era before the welfare system turned into an economic crutch, chaining countless Puerto Rican families into dependence on government. Jobs were still plentiful, mostly the kind that threatened to puncture or amputate your limbs with needles, presses, or blades, those mechanical contraptions of some entrepreneur who'd already made your dream of wealth his reality, but those jobs in postwar America, the chance to provide something better for your kids with enough ten- and twelve-hour sweat-filled days, made it possible to endure everything else.

My mother and aunts had their pick of employers when they arrived. Aunt Graciela, who had been a skilled seamstress in garment plants in Puerto Rico, could command a salary as high as thirty dollars a week, a tidy sum in those days. "Sometimes we would go out and in one day try out three or four different factories until we found one that we liked," she recalled.

The González brothers moved on from the Copa to better-paying union jobs in the meatpacking, restaurant, and taxi industries. By the mid-1950s, our family, along with many other Puerto Ricans, had started moving into public housing projects the federal government was building all over the city for the working poor. As we left East Harlem, however, we said goodbye to that close-knit network of Puerto Rican pioneers.

Meanwhile, new Puerto Rican communities were cropping up in Chicago, Philadelphia, and sections of Ohio, as both the U.S. and Puerto Rican governments encouraged emigration as a safety valve to impede further social unrest on the island.[14] Labor recruiters wound through the poorest neighborhoods, loudspeakers mounted atop their cars, offering jobs in the United States and the travel fare to get there. In Lorain, Ohio, for instance, the National Tube Company, a U.S. Steel subsidiary booming with military contracts, recruited 500 Puerto Ricans from the island to work in the company's steel mill in 1947–1948. Carnegie-Illinois Steel of Gary, Indiana, recruited 500 to work in its mill in 1948. And, in 1951, the Ohio Employment Service brought 1,524 Puerto Ricans to Youngstown and Cleveland.

Much of the hiring was contracted to the Philadelphia-based S.G. Friedman Labor Agency. (The president of the agency was the son of a Spanish-American War veteran who settled in Puerto Rico and organized the island's police department.) Once the migrants arrived in the mills, they sent for their families, while others came on their own after hearing stories about all the jobs in the steel, rubber, and auto industries of the Midwest.[15]

More than a million Puerto Ricans were living in the United States by the mid-1960s, most of them in New York City. But they were still largely invisible to Anglo society. They quietly pushed carts in the city's garment center, cleaned bedpans in the hospitals,

washed dishes in hotels and restaurants, performed maintenance
for the big apartment buildings, or they worked on factory assembly lines, or drove unlicensed cabs, or operated bodegas. By then,
however, the migration had spilled all over the Northeast and
Midwest. Farms in Connecticut, eastern Pennsylvania, Upstate
New York, Ohio, and South Jersey recruited Puerto Ricans to pick
the crops. When the harvest ended, the migrants settled in nearby
towns, and thus sprouted the Puerto Rican barrios of Haverstraw,
New York; Vineland, New Jersey; Hartford, Connecticut; and Ken-
nett Square, Pennsylvania.

THE SECOND GENERATION

As the children of those migrants started attending public schools in
the 1950s, they—I should say, we—entered a society accustomed to
thinking only in Black and white. It didn't take long for the white
English-speaking majority to start casting uneasy glances at the
growing number of brown-skinned, Spanish-speaking teenagers
who didn't seem to fit into any established racial group. New York
tabloids took to portraying young Puerto Rican criminals as savages. The most notorious of them were Salvador "Cape Man" Agron
and Frank Santana.[16] Despite the obvious working-class character
of the Puerto Rican migration, Hollywood created the enduring
image of Puerto Ricans as knife wielders prone to violence and ad-
dicted to drugs in such films as *Cry Tough* (1959), *The Young Savages*
(1961), and *West Side Story* (1961).[17]

Most of us became products of a sink-or-swim public school philosophy, immersed in English-language instruction from our first
day in class and actively discouraged from retaining our native
tongue. "Your name isn't Juan," the young teacher told me in first
grade at P.S. 87 in East Harlem. "In this country it's John. Shall I
call you John?" Confused and afraid, but sensing this as some fateful
decision, I timidly said no. But most children could not summon the
courage, so school officials routinely anglicized their names. Though
I had spoken only Spanish before I entered kindergarten, the teachers were amazed at how quickly I mastered English. From then on,
each time a new child from Puerto Rico was placed in any of my
classes, the teachers would sit him beside me so I could interpret the
lessons. Bewildered, terrified, and ashamed, the new kids grappled
with my clumsy attempts to decipher the teacher's strange words.

Inevitably, when the school year ended, they were forced to repeat the grade, sometimes more than once, all because they hadn't mastered English. Even now, more than sixty years later, the faces of those children are still fresh in my mind. They make today's debates on bilingual education so much more poignant, and the current push toward total English immersion so much more frightening (see chapter 12).

Our parents' generation rarely protested the way we were treated in school, which is understandable. After the terrible poverty they'd faced in Puerto Rico, they believed that an education—any education—was their children's only hope for progress. And if that meant putting up with a few psychological scars from Americanization, then so be it. My grandmother, who was illiterate, drove that into my father, who was barely literate himself, and he pushed my sister, Elena, and me to study with a frenzy that bordered on cruelty. It was not unusual for him to beat us mercilessly with a leather strap for bringing home a poor report card. These days, he'd probably be thrown in jail for child abuse.

As time passed, the González family became a melting-pot success story by anyone's measure. One by one, each of us completed high school and joined the first college-educated generation in the family's history. My uncle Sergio and aunt Catin produced a college instructor in Greek and Latin, another son who rose to be an official in the Nixon and Reagan administrations, and a South Bronx social worker. I went to Ivy League Columbia College and eventually on to a career in journalism; my sister became a public school teacher and later a college instructor; another cousin became a doctor; another a psychiatric social worker; another a police detective.

But we in that second generation—smart, urban, English dominant—remained acutely aware that the broader Anglo society still regarded Puerto Ricans as less than full Americans. We studied the history and culture of Europe in our classes, but nothing about Puerto Rico or Latin America, not even an inkling that our tiny homeland possessed any history and culture worthy of study. After the Vatican II reforms ushered in vernacular Catholic Masses, even the church relegated Puerto Ricans and Latinos to the basements of most parishes, despite our being its fastest-growing membership.

The country's ingrained racial traditions meant that Black or dark-skinned Puerto Ricans faced even greater prejudice. The lighter-skinned among us tended to settle in more stable Italian or Irish neighborhoods, and to pass for white. The darker-skinned ones, unable to find housing in the white neighborhoods, formed all–Puerto Rican enclaves or moved into Black neighborhoods. In many cities, our communities emerged as buffer zones between Blacks and whites. In Philadelphia, for instance, the Puerto Rican community evolved into a narrow north–south corridor on either side of Fifth Street, which ran almost the entire length of the city, separating the white eastern neighborhoods of town from the Black western ones.

While de facto segregation has been a pernicious part of this society since the end of slavery, in our case it became an unbearable assault on our family bonds. *"¿Y tu abuela, dónde está?"* ("And your grandmother, where is she?") is a familiar Puerto Rican refrain and the title of a popular poem by Fortunato Vizcarrondo. The phrase reminds us that Black blood runs through all Puerto Rican families. Puerto Ricans resisted the sharp racial demarcations so prevalent in this country, and their implicit diminishment of our human worth. But gradually, almost imperceptibly, I watched my aunts and uncles begin to adopt anti-Black attitudes, as if this were some rite of passage to becoming authentic Americans. "A hostile posture toward resident blacks must be struck at the Americanizing door before it will open," is how writer Toni Morrison so aptly describes it.[18]

The social imperative to *choose a racial identity*, and then only in purely Black-and-white terms, impelled those of us in the second generation at first to jettison our native language and culture, to assimilate into either the white or the Black world. My uncle Sergio and aunt Catin were my family's exception. They were the only ones who never left East Harlem. There they fiercely clung to the culture of the island. In their home, *aguinaldos*, the music of Puerto Rican *jíbaros*, could always be heard, a dominoes hand was always in the offing, weekend family *fiestas* were routine, and the neighbors, whether Puerto Rican or Anglo, Black or white, were always welcome.

Not surprisingly, one of the first expressions of community organization in the 1950s was an event that celebrated cultural pride— the annual Puerto Rican Day Parade. As the Puerto Rican population grew, the parade became the largest of the city's many ethnic celebrations. By 2019, more than two million people were estimated to attend it.

In the midst of the high tide of Puerto Rican migration, something else happened—African Americans rose up against racial segregation, unmasking the chasm that still existed between

Black-and-white society. We Puerto Ricans found ourselves having common ground with both sides, yet fitting in with neither. We simply had not been a part of the congenital birth defect of this country, the Anglo-Saxon slave system and its Jim Crow aftermath.

In 1964, the Reverend Milton Galamison, Malcolm X, and other Black leaders led a boycott of New York City public school parents against racial discrimination. A handful of Puerto Rican community leaders from the prewar migrant generation joined the boycott. Among them were Frank Espada, Evelina Antonetty, and Gilberto Gerena Valentín. Espada, a community organizer before joining Republican mayor John Lindsay's administration, would later develop a career as a brilliant photographer chronicling the Puerto Rican diaspora. Antonetty went on to found United Bronx Parents, the seminal parent advocacy group for Puerto Ricans in education. Gerena Valentín, a nationalist and labor organizer, was ousted from the hotel workers union during the 1950s anti-Communist hysteria for refusing to sign an affidavit denying any Communist Party membership. He would later create an influential federation of Puerto Rican hometown clubs, social clubs that proliferated in various New York City neighborhoods and that were named after the various towns on the island from which their members came, such as Arecibo, Caguas, Lares, Jayuya. Those clubs formed the political base with which Gerena captured a city council seat in the 1970s.[19] They, and others like them, composed the first postwar leadership of the emerging Puerto Rican community in New York.

That wave of leaders, however, was soon eclipsed by an even more radical group. The assassinations of Malcolm X (1965) and Martin Luther King Jr. (1968) sparked mass urban riots among Blacks and polarized the Civil Rights Movement and many of us who were influenced by those events found greater affinity with the Black power wing of the movement than with the integration wing. That identification intensified as thousands of Puerto Ricans went off to fight in the Vietnam War, only to return, like the veterans of World War II, to a country that still misunderstood and mistrusted them as foreigners.

As we came of age, we responded to that mistrust and misunderstanding with open rebellion. A slew of new nationalist and left-wing organizations sprang up among Puerto Ricans. Some were inspired by the old Nationalist Party in Puerto Rico or by the Black Panther Party here. The most influential was the Young Lords, an organization I helped to found in 1969. During its apogee (1969–1972), the Lords galvanized thousands of young Latinos into radical politics, and an amazing portion of the group's members later became influential leaders of the community (see chapter 10).[20]

Fueled by that political awakening, a cultural renaissance emerged among Puerto Rican artists. Writers Piri Thomas and Nicolasa Mohr, poets Pedro Pietri and José Angel Figueroa, playwrights Miguel Piñeiro and Miguel Algarín caught the public's attention as vibrant voices of the Puerto Rican migrant experience. Even Latin music experienced a resurgence as Eddie and Charlie Palmieri, Ray Barretto, and Willie Colón began producing politically charged lyrics that celebrated the new sense of emerging Puerto Rican power.[21]

The essence of that new movement was a sudden realization of who we were, economic refugees from the last major colony of the United States. That realization caused us to reject the path of our immigrant predecessors from Europe: the first generation accepting decades of second-class status while it established a foothold, the second securing an education and assimilating quietly, and the third emerging as 100 percent melting-pot American.

Puerto Ricans, we concluded, were in a different position from Italians or Swedes or Poles. Our homeland had been invaded and was still occupied, its wealth exploited, its patriots persecuted and jailed, by the very country to which we had migrated. Our experience was closer to Algerians in France before independence.[22] For decades, textbooks made in the United States had taught island schoolchildren our homeland was incapable of self-government and would perish economically without Uncle Sam. But in the early 1970s, a new generation of independent Puerto Rican scholars arose to challenge that premise. They confirmed for the second generation that Puerto Rico was as capable of being a prosperous independent nation as Israel or Taiwan or Switzerland, but that its history had been suppressed to encourage a sense of dependence among Puerto Ricans.

Our parents instinctively sympathized with this new awakening. Unlike white America, where New Left activism divided father and son, mother and daughter, the new nationalism brought the two Puerto Rican generations closer together. It inspired the young to reclaim and study our language. It helped us understand the suffering our parents had endured. And it transformed our psychological outlook. Never again would a Puerto Rican quietly accept an Anglo's

barking, "Speak English, you're in America now!" or the rote admo-
nition, "If you don't like it here, go back where you came from."

By the mid-1970s, however, economic recession struck, and new
groups of Latinos began arriving in the nation's cities. Competition
soared for a diminishing number of unskilled jobs, and the class nature of the Puerto Rican migration radically changed. Many college
graduates and professionals from the island, unable to find jobs
there, relocated to the United States, as did many of the poorest and
least skilled urban slum dwellers. At the same time, the first generation of migrants, the former factory workers and bodega owners,
having accumulated substantial savings, started returning to the island to retire or to fill jobs in the booming tourist industry, where a
good command of English was required. So many Puerto Ricans
left this country that the decade witnessed net migration back to the
island.

Thus, the Puerto Rican migrant community became dominated
during the 1980s by two very different social classes, both highly
dependent on government. At the top was a small but growing number of intelligentsia and white-collar professionals, many employed
in social programs or the educational system, and at the bottom a
large and fast-growing caste of low-paid, unskilled workers, alongside an underclass of long-term unemployed and welfare recipients.
Missing in any significant numbers were two critical groups: the
private business class whose members provide any ethnic group's
capital formation and self-reliant outlook, and the skilled technical
workers who provide stability and role models for those on the bottom to emulate.

Meanwhile, life in many of America's big cities by the early 1980s
was verging on chaos. A dwindling tax base, brought about by the
flight of industry and skilled white workers to the suburbs, massive
disinvestment by government in public schools and infrastructure,
and the epidemics of drug and alcohol abuse, all tore at the quality
of city life. As might be expected, the crisis took its heaviest toll
on the African American and Puerto Rican migrant communities
of those cities.

The third generation of Puerto Ricans, those who came of age in
the late 1980s and early 1990s, found themselves crippled by inferior schools, a lack of jobs, and underfunded social services. They
found their neighborhoods inundated with drugs and violence.
They grew up devoid, for the most part, of self-image, national
identity, or cultural awareness. They became the lost generation.

But the schism over identity and the quandary over language and heritage soon turned into problems not just for the Puerto Ricans. As Latin American immigration exploded, many Anglos started to worry that America's social fabric was disintegrating. The biggest source of that worry, as we shall see, was the nation's growing Mexican population.

5

MEXICANS:
Pioneers of a Different Type

The whole race of Mexicans here is becoming a useless commodity, becoming cheap, dog cheap. Eleven Mexicans, it is stated, have been found along the Nueces in a *hung up* condition.

—*Galveston Weekly News*, 1855

The Mexican diaspora is at the core of our country's Latino heritage. Not only are two of every three Latinos in the United States of Mexican origin, but only Mexicans can claim to be both early settlers on U.S. soil *and* the largest group of new arrivals. So many Mexicans have come since 1820 that they are now the largest immigrant nationality in our history. No Hispanic group has contributed more to the nation's prosperity than Mexicans, yet none makes white America more uneasy about the future.

Most troubling are the descendants of the Mexican pioneers, for once you admit Mexicans' long history on U.S. soil, you must necessarily accept Hispanic culture and the Spanish language as integral components of our own national saga.

Mexicans, in fact, have lived "here" since before there was a Mexico or a United States. And they have been coming to this country almost from its inception. Since 1820, when the federal government started keeping immigration records, Mexico has sent more people here than any other nation.

Whether or not Mexican immigration continues to surpass all

others, as it has in recent decades, depends largely on what happens *below* the Rio Grande. We often forget that Mexico is the most populous Spanish-speaking country in the world. In 2020, it had 129 million residents, a high birth rate, and desperate poverty.[1] A disturbing portion of its national wealth flows outside its borders each day and into the pockets of Wall Street shareholders. So much of that wealth has been siphoned off in recent years that the Mexican economy finds it increasingly difficult to feed and clothe its population. If these conditions do not change, Mexico will remain an inexhaustible source of migrants to the United States, which is why Americans need to pay more attention to our southern neighbor than to what is happening in, say, Israel or Palestine, Iraq or Afghanistan.

Table 3

**Top Sources of Legal Immigration
to the United States by Country
Fiscal Years 1820–2019[2]**

All Countries	85,990,168
Mexico	9,146,827
Germany	7,346,459
United Kingdom	5,562,696
Italy	5,494,369
Canada	4,892,056
Ireland	4,812,273
Austria-Hungary	4,428,561

Mexican Americans, meanwhile, face a frustrating identity problem similar to that of Puerto Ricans. They are both native-born and immigrants, pioneers and aliens, patriots and rebels; no matter how far back some may trace their ancestry on our soil, they are still battling to emerge from the obscure margins of official U.S. history, still clamoring to be fully recognized and understood, as we will see in the following story of one pioneer Mexican American family, the Canales clan of South Texas.

José Francisco Canales came to the New World in the 1640s from Reus, Spain. He settled in Monterrey, in what is now northeastern Mexico, and by 1660 he owned one of six stores in the town. His grandson, Blas Canales, was born in 1675 in Cerralvo, just north of Monterrey. Both towns had been founded by Christianized Jews trying to escape the Spanish Inquisition and had become flourishing mining centers on the northern frontier.[3]

In the late 1740s, the viceroy of New Spain authorized José de Escandón, a young army captain from Querétaro, to explore and colonize the region above Tampico all the way up to the Nueces River. The territory was then home to the Lipan Apache in the west, Comanche in the north, the Coahuiltecan along the Río Bravo, and the Karankawa along the Gulf Coast.[4]

After some initial exploration, Escandón set out in 1749 with several hundred criollo, mestizo, and Indian families from central Mexico, all drawn by promises of free land. He quickly established a string of settlements stretching up the Rio Grande, and along the river itself he founded the present-day cities of Camargo and Reynosa.[5] One of Escandón's chief aides was Captain Blas de la Garza Falcón, a Canales family member by marriage.[6]

Over the next few years, Escandón returned to start several more settlements, the last of which was the town of Laredo in 1755, thus capping one of the most successful colonizing ventures in the New World.[7] Altogether, the young captain is credited with establishing twenty towns and eighteen missions in less than ten years, all but one of which still exist. The missions he founded logged three thousand Indian converts in their first few years, far more than the Puritans accomplished in their first half century.

Escandón called his colony Nuevo Santander. Tightly linked through the family connections of its original land-grant settlers, and isolated from the rest of the colonial Spanish world by barren scrub plains and hostile Indians on either side of the valley, Nuevo Santander became a uniquely self-sufficient and self-contained pastoral community. The colony's life and the commerce of its towns revolved around and were unified by the river. The settlers used the fertile lands closest to the river for crops, and those at the edges of the river valley for livestock.[8] North of the Rio Grande, an immense dry plain stretched to the Nueces River 150 miles away. Thick grass grew year-round on that plain, and the countryside was dotted with chaparral and mesquite, ebony and huisache trees. The settlers' herds multiplied so rapidly that within two years the one hundred families in the towns of Camargo and Reynosa owned thirty-six thousand head of cattle, horses, and sheep.[9]

Several Canales family members traveled with Escandón's colonizing expedition. They settled first in Mier, on the southern side of the Río Bravo, but by the early 1800s, one of them, José Antonio Canales Salinas, secured a royal land grant on the northern banks of the river, in present-day Starr County, Texas. His land, which covered about ten thousand acres, was called the Sacatosa Grant and, later, the Buenavista Ranch. Like most of the original land grantees, the Canales family prospered and became members of the region's nineteenth-century elite. José Antonio Tiburcio Canales, for example, was one of the original signers of Mexico's declaration of independence.[10]

By the 1820s, however, immigrants from the United States, Ireland, and Germany began settling in the region, especially farther to the north, and the Mexicans along the Río Bravo felt increasingly threatened as the Anglos started to dispute their ownership of the grazing land south of the Nueces. It was over the Nueces Strip, in fact, that President Polk engineered the Mexican War. In early 1846, after Texas had joined the union, General Zachary Taylor's army crossed into the disputed territory, provoking a confrontation with Mexican army that led to war between the two countries.

One Canales descendant, General José Antonio Rosillo Canales, emerged a hero of the conflict, adopting guerrilla tactics against General Taylor's army with devastating results. During February 1847, his band inflicted more than 150 casualties on the Americans, who soon dubbed him the Chaparral Fox. By the war's conclusion, Canales had become so famous he was elected governor of Tamaulipas.[11]

Once the Treaty of Guadalupe Hidalgo relinquished the Nueces Strip to the United States, however, the inhabitants of Nuevo Santander were shocked to see the very river that had bound them together for a hundred years suddenly turned into its opposite—a dividing line between two hostile nations. The Anglos even changed the river's name, from Río Bravo to Rio Grande. Those Canales family members who lived below the river in Mier were now under different sovereignty than those living on the Buenavista Ranch and other small properties on the U.S. side. With the new sovereignty came a host of new laws, especially for land registration, tax, and inheritance. The new codes were promulgated and administered in English—a language the *mexicano* majority did not understand—and by lawyers,

sheriffs, and judges who could always count on the U.S. Army to enforce an Anglo's interpretation whenever a dispute arose.

Mifflin Kenedy, a Florida riverboat captain, arrived in the area in
the summer of 1846. The army had recruited him to operate a fleet
of boats up the Rio Grande. Kenedy sent for his longtime pilot, New
York–born Richard King, and after the war the two men purchased
some of the boats at army auction, so they could transport the
swarms of prospectors passing through on their way to the California gold fields.[12] To secure a monopoly of the river transport,
Kenedy and King decided to form an alliance with Charles Stillman. The cartel they created was blessed with the friendly assistance of Brevet Major W. W. Chapman, the local army commander,
who arranged lucrative army supply contracts for them.[13]

Meanwhile, farther to the north, another Anglo rancher had discovered his own way of cashing in on the fighting. H. L. Kinney, a
notorious smuggler south of the Nueces, secured an appointment as
a colonel and quartermaster for General Winfield Scott's troops and
turned his ranch into a boomtown of two thousand people. After the
war, Kinney founded the city of Corpus Christi on the site of his
ranch.[14]

From the start, the Anglo settlers saw the Mexicans in South
Texas as an obstacle to progress, and routinely cheated them out of
their land. Often it was seized at sheriffs' sales and auctioned for
pennies an acre for failure to pay taxes.

"Many [Mexicans] didn't know how to read or write," said Santos
Molina, a Canales family descendant who lives in Brownsville.
"They didn't understand their rights and those of their grandparents. Anybody could tell them, 'your grandfather lost his land, sold
it,' and they couldn't prove otherwise."[15]

Violence against Mexicans became commonplace. "The whole
race of Mexicans here is becoming a useless commodity, becoming
cheap, dog cheap," wrote the Corpus Christi correspondent for the
Galveston Weekly News in 1855. "Eleven Mexicans, it is stated, have
been found along the Nueces, in a *hung up* condition. Better so than
to be left on the ground for the howling lobos to tear in pieces, and
then howl the more for the red peppers that burn his insides raw."[16]
Lynching of Mexicans continued into the early 1900s, with Canales
family members witnessing one as late as 1917.[17]

Whole communities were driven from the towns of Austin,
Seguin, and Uvalde. A scant six years after Texas independence,
13 Anglos had gobbled up 1.3 million acres in "legal" sales from

358 Mexican landowners.[18] Among them was Scottish immigrant John Young, who opened a general store in Brownsville after the war and married Salome Ballí, member of a prominent Mexican land-grant family, thus gaining control of her family's estate. Edinburg, seat of Texas's Hidalgo County, is named after Young's native city in Scotland (though spelled differently). After Young died in 1859, his widow married his clerk, John McAllen. By the 1890s, the McAllen and Young ranches measured 160,000 acres, and the one-time clerk, following in the footsteps of his old boss, had his own town, McAllen.[19]

Merchants Stillman, King, and Kenedy soon joined the land rush as well. Stillman gained control of the giant Espíritu Santo Land Grant by buying up fraudulent squatters' titles and outlasting the real Mexican owners in the courts. He founded Brownsville on part of the estate and turned it into the region's gambling, saloon, and prostitution center.[20] While Stillman concentrated on the land around Brownsville, his steamboat partners King and Kenedy turned their attention to cobbling together cattle empires in the northern countryside. Stephen Powers, the sharpest land lawyer in the region, was their able assistant in that effort. Like Young and McAllen, Kenedy got his start by marrying a wealthy Mexican. In his case, her name was Petra Vela de Vidal.[21] The Kenedy Ranch, La Para, eventually stretched to 325,000 acres and employed three hundred ranch hands, virtually all of them Mexican.[22] As for King, by the time he died in 1885, his ranch encompassed 500,000 acres, employed more than five hundred people, and even contained its own town, Santa Gertrudis.

"The Santa Gertrudis ranch house," recalled former Texas Ranger George Durham in a chilling insight into life on the Nueces Strip, "was more like an army arsenal inside. In one big room there were eighty stands of Henry repeating rifles and maybe a hundred boxes of shells. Two men stood in the lookout tower day and night, and there was always a man at the ready for each of those rifles."[23]

That arsenal was there for a reason. Many of the new land barons rustled cattle from one another and from the herds of the *tejanos*. Richard King, an infamous cattle thief, was said to have turned the Texas Rangers into his own private security force. "His neighbors mysteriously vanish whilst his territory extends over entire counties," wrote a newspaper correspondent for the *Corpus Christi World* about King in 1878. "Fifty cents a head is paid to Mexicans for branding cattle on the plains with the King monogram, and somehow no one's herds can be induced to increase but those of the future cattle king."[24]

Mexicans who dared challenge the Anglo encroachment were often branded as bandits and outlaws. The most famous "bandit" of them all, Juan "Cheno" Cortina, was another Canales ancestor. In July 1859, Cortina, whose mother owned the Rancho del Carmen, shot a Brownsville marshal after witnessing him whip a drunken Mexican. He then rode into town with fifty followers, raised the Mexican flag, and shot to death the local jailer and four other whites who had been terrorizing Mexicans. The town's whites dispatched a militia and a company of Texas Rangers to capture him, but Cortina raised an army of twelve hundred Mexicans and routed them. He then declared a war against the Anglo settler minority.

For the next two decades, Cortina's band initiated sporadic guerrilla raids into Texas from safe havens on the Mexican side. Neither the Rangers nor a contingent of federal troops dispatched to the territory, and commanded by Colonel Robert E. Lee, was able to capture him. Accused of cattle rustling and indicted for treason, Cortina became the most feared Mexican American in Texas. Mere rumors that he was in the vicinity panicked whole towns.[25] The only respite from his raids occurred between 1862 and 1867, when Cortina declared a truce with the United States and turned his guns on the French army, after it occupied Mexico and installed the Austrian archduke Maximilian as emperor. One of Cortina's top officers during the resistance to France was Servando Canales, a veteran of the Mexican-American war and son of General José Antonio Canales. Like his father, Servando Canales went on to serve as governor of Tamaulipas. Cortina, however, remained the most powerful politician in the region until he was arrested in 1875 by President Porfirio Díaz at the request of the United States and thrown into jail in Mexico City.

The Cortina wars slowed but did not stop the Anglo expropriation of Mexican wealth. In 1850, property in Texas had been pretty evenly divided between the two groups. That year, according to the U.S. census, *tejanos* composed 32.4 percent of the workers in the state and owned 33 percent of its wealth. Over the next twenty years, however, things changed drastically. By 1870, *tejanos* were 47.6 percent of the workforce but possessed only 10.6 percent of the wealth.[26]

In South Texas, where Mexicans remained the overwhelming majority, one-third of the ranches and all the large estates were in

Anglo hands by 1900. Only the smaller *tejano* farmers clung to their titles. Among the diehards was Luciano Canales, who ran the family's Buenavista Ranch. As a result of Luciano's determination, Fiacro Salazaar, his great-grandson, still retains title to two hundred acres of the old ranch. "They had to protect it with guns," Salazaar, a San Antonio army engineer, recalled in a 1992 interview. "Any poor fellow who didn't, lost it."[27] Even as thousands lost their land, though, other Mexicans kept migrating into the Southwest. More than a million arrived in the region between 1900 and 1930.[28]

By the 1920s, the Rio Grande Valley was as segregated as apartheid South Africa. Mexicans composed more than 90 percent of its population, but the white minority controlled most of the land and all the political power. Imelda Garza, a retired public school teacher who was born in the town of Benavides in 1923 to Gervasio and Manuelita Canales, never met an Anglo until she was thirteen. "I met a black person for the first time when I moved to Kingsville to teach at Herrel Elementary School, she told me in 1992."

Her brother-in-law, Santos Molina, admits to "having seen Anglos around" during his childhood in Brownsville, "but I only got to meet them when I went to Oiltown high school."[29]

The first organized attempt to break down that segregation came in 1929, when seven Mexican organizations met in Corpus Christi to found the League of United Latin American Citizens. LULAC's goal from its inception was the complete assimilation of Mexicans and their acceptance as equal citizens by Anglo society. To accomplish that, LULAC made its chief goal teaching Mexicans to master English.[30]

Once the Great Depression hit and unemployment surged among whites, though, not even Mexicans who spoke fluent English escaped the anti-immigrant hysteria. More than five hundred thousand were forcibly deported during the 1930s, among them many who were U.S. citizens. One of the few areas of the country spared the hysteria was the Rio Grande Valley, where Mexicans were able to find safety in numbers.

"There were no jobs, but the land took good care of us," recalled Canales family member Santos Molina, now a San Antonio high school teacher. "We planted corn and grain and watermelons, calabazos and beans. We had four or five milk cows. We hunted rabbits and deer. Goats would cost you about a dollar then, so we had plenty to eat."[31]

The onset of World War II brought yet another reversal in U.S. policy toward Mexican immigrants. Three months after President Roosevelt declared war on the Axis powers, the United States and Mexico reached agreement on a new program to import Mexican workers. As many as one hundred thousand Mexicans a year were soon being contracted to work here. It was called the *bracero* program, and it would last in one form or another until 1965. While it did, it brought millions of migrants into the country for seasonal work, and each year after the harvest a good portion of them found a way to stay in the country illegally. Not that most Americans cared. Until the 1960s, few paid attention to the human traffic along the border, least of all the inhabitants of the area, for whom the international demarcation line was more a concoction of politicians in Washington than an everyday reality.[32]

But World War II did something else. It transformed the thinking of a whole generation of Mexican American men who served in it, just as it did to Puerto Ricans. As many as five hundred thousand Mexican Americans saw active duty in the U.S. armed forces, many in critical combat roles. From Texas alone, five *mexicanos* were awarded the Congressional Medal of Honor. In the Battle of Bataan, a quarter of the wounded were Mexican American.[33]

Santos Molina and Manuel Garza were two Canales family members who served in combat, in the same army so many of their ancestors had fought against. Molina enlisted in 1940 and was assigned to an airborne unit of the Seventh Infantry Division, where he led a squad onto Normandy beach on the second day of the Allied invasion of France. Nearly all his men were killed or wounded that day, and while Molina survived unscathed, he was severely wounded by machine gun fire later in Germany.

When the war ended, the Mexican American veterans returned home to much of the same discrimination and racism they had left behind, only this time they refused to accept it.

Manuel Garza, who served in a field artillery unit with the Special Forces in Europe, returned home to Kingsville, the nerve center of the King family ranch and one of the most racist towns in South Texas. "In town, the White Kitchens chain had cooks and busboys who were Mexicans, but they wouldn't let the Mexicans come in to eat," Garza recalled. "One day a bunch of us in uniform just walked in and forced them to serve us. The same thing with Kings Inn. It was in a neighborhood of pure Germans. Those people never let us in there. When we came out of the army, we started making a whole lot of noise and they let us eat. Today, they have more Mexican customers in Kings Inn than anything else."

Similar protests erupted throughout the Southwest. When Brownsville's Congressional Medal of Honor winner, Sergeant José Mendoza López, was denied service at a local restaurant, it touched off a furor among *mexicanos*. Middle-class organizations like LULAC and the newly formed American GI Forum pointed with pride to the war records of their members and demanded equal treatment.[34]

For the first time, the Mexicans even dared to challenge the Anglo minority's monopoly of political power. While working as a Kingsville truant officer in the 1950s, Nerio Garza, Manuel Garza's brother, became so angry at the Anglos' racism he decided to run for office. He roused the town's Mexican population against the lack of paved streets and lights and sewers on their side of town, and handily won his first race for town commissioner, where he remained for most of the next thirty years.

Despite Garza's victory in Kingsville, and a few others in Los Angeles and San Antonio, the cry for equality and respect from the generation of World War II went largely unheard, and segregationist policies against Mexicans persisted into the 1960s.

"The first time I was made to sit on the sidewalk for speaking Spanish I was six years old," recalled Sandra Garza, the daughter of Imelda and Manuel Garza. "I got caught because I was speaking to the janitor. He was *mexicano* and my next-door neighbor."[35]

By the 1960s, the majority of students at nearby Texas A&M were Mexican Americans. For the first time, they ran a slate that won control of the student government. They began calling themselves Chicanos, turning the slang word that had always been used among the poor in the Southwest to describe those born north of the Rio Grande into a badge of pride. The moniker became a way for young people to connect culturally with the Mexican homeland, in much the same way that the change from *Negro* to *Black* had affected the Civil Rights Movement in the South.

Some Chicanos even started referring to the Southwest as Aztlán, the name Aztec historians in the *Codex Ramírez* (1583–1587) gave to the area north of Mexico from which their ancestors had come. Reacting to the decades of Anglo racism, they now quixotically saw

Aztlán as a historic homeland in which Mexicans would eventually become the majority again, recovering their land from the white settlers.

South Texas was emerging as the center of Chicano unrest. When a slate of five working-class Mexican Americans won control of the Crystal City council in the Rio Grande Valley in 1963, the victory electrified Chicanos throughout the Southwest. Shortly afterward, a strike at La Casita Farms by Cesar Chavez's United Farm Workers union stirred young Chicanos with visions of recapturing majority rule—at least in South Texas.

One of the most influential groups to arise during the period was the Mexican American Youth Organization (MAYO), founded in San Antonio by a handful of local youths, including Willie Velasquez, a young community organizer for the Catholic Bishop's Committee on the Spanish Speaking, and Crystal City's José Angel Gutiérrez. Gutiérrez and Velasquez, both sons of Mexican immigrants, would end up symbolizing two trends within the new movement. Gutiérrez, whose father fought with Pancho Villa in the Mexican revolution, was a charismatic college-educated radical. He proselytized throughout the Southwest for an independent political party of Chicanos to counter the Democratic and Republican Parties, both of which he saw as racist.

Willie Velasquez, whose family also fled Mexico during the revolution, was more pragmatic. His parents had grown up in the Chicano barrio on the West Side of San Antonio, where his father became a meatpacking worker after returning from World War II.[36] One of Willie's classmates at St. Mary's College in San Antonio was a tall, gangly Chicano named Henry Cisneros. Velasquez was never comfortable with the more revolutionary ideas of Gutiérrez, believing instead that genuine social justice for Mexican Americans would come through the Democratic Party. This may have been due in part to his Catholic education or to the influence of Congressman Henry Gonzáles, the local hero who paved the road to power for Mexican Americans through mainstream electoral politics, or to his longtime friendship with Cisneros. Whatever the reason, Gutiérrez and Velasquez eventually parted ways.[37] Gutiérrez went on to found the militant Raza Unida Party, while Velasquez started the far less confrontational Southwest Voter Registration and Education Project and turned into the foremost advocate of Hispanic voting rights in the country.

Gutiérrez's new group, however, caught fire much more with the young Chicanos. It won a series of election victories in 1969 in a bunch of small Texas towns, including Crystal City and Kingsville. In Kingsville, a Raza Unida slate led by the party's state chairman, Carlos Guerra, and aided by Chicano students from Texas A&M, sought to capture control of the city council. Their slate challenged both the white ranchers and the older generation of established *tejanos*, among them Nerio Garza. Many of the militants regarded Garza as too accommodating to the white establishment. Their campaign against him divided entire families, including the Canales, and the bitterness engendered by those battles remains to this day. Sandra Garza joined the militants against her uncle Nerio, while Nerio's daughter, Diane Garza, defended him.[38]

"We had shitheads like that Guerra," recalled Diane Garza, a longtime administrator in the Brownsville public schools, during an interview decades later. "They came here and instilled all this drop-out-of-school bit, but their radical ways were not in the best interests of the town."[39]

The conflict even turned violent. "I was teaching here in Brownsville," recalled Diane Garza, "and I received a phone call that they were planning on lynching my dad. I still remember the night vividly. I call them 'La Raza Sumida.' They had gasoline cans in their hands. We had to call not only the highway patrol but the Texas Rangers. They couldn't even begin to break the crowd of idiots. We had locked my dad in the house. They were saying things like 'Nerio is a coconut.' But at gut level everyone knew who Nerio Garza was. He stood up to the ranch, to the big guys and the little ones, it didn't make any difference."

Carlos Guerra's group, some of its supporters conceded years later, pitted Mexicans against one another unnecessarily. "They thought my uncle was a *vendido*," recalled Sandra Garza. "But it was just the old blood not understanding the new. If you look at it now, they could have worked well together."

After the Kingsville election, Sandra Garza, who never forgot her parents' accounts of the Canales family legacy, or their stories of the land the *gringos* had taken from them, threw herself into the Chicano *movimiento*. For the next decade, she moved from town to town in the West and Southwest, as a teacher and community organizer, trying to reclaim those lost lands and that cultural tradition. She worked in Colorado with Corky González's Crusade for Justice, in northern New Mexico with Reies López Tijerina's Alianza Federal de Pueblos Libres (Federal Alliance of Free Towns), then in California and

Texas with labor unions organizing Latino workers. When I first interviewed her in 1992, Garza was a staff organizer in El Paso, Texas, with the Union of Industrial Needle Trade Employees (UNITE).

The Canales story has been repeated over and over in the Southwest by other Chicano families. It is sometimes difficult for white Americans to understand how deep the roots of Mexican Americans are in that part of the country. Most whites who live in the region, after all, only arrived there during the last hundred years. At best, their migration story goes back a few generations, hardly comparable to that of the old Mexicans. Farmworker leader Cesar Chavez's family, for instance, moved to Arizona in 1880, long before it was a state. The family owned land there until the Great Depression bankrupted them and forced them to move to California as migrant laborers. López Tijerina, who was born in Texas in 1926, often recounted the story of how his great-grandfather was killed by Anglos who stole the family's land.

Even many recently arrived Mexican immigrants can usually point to long historical ties to the Southwest. In a study of the old Mexican neighborhood of Lemon Grove in San Diego, for instance, ethnographer Robert Alvarez documents nearly two hundred years of a migratory circuit between Mexico's Baja California and our own state of California by the same extended families of miners and farmers. Family members would travel back and forth between the two territories in response to economic conditions. The two Californias, Alvarez maintains, have historically been one in geography, economics, and culture. Only in the last sixty years did the border become a barrier to those ties. Furthermore, Mexican family networks and solidarity were actually strengthened through the migratory circuit as individual family members relied increasingly on the remittances of distant relatives for survival.[40]

Mexican labor. The Mexican market. Mexican music and food. Mexican television and radio. Mexican names of cities, states, rivers, and mountains. Anglo America continues to deny how much the social, cultural, political, and economic reality of the West and Southwest has been shaped by Mexicans. They have been part of its creation and they will form an even bigger part of its future. That undeniable Mexican heritage will haunt the rest of us until we accept it as our own.

6

CUBANS:
Special Refugees

Few immigrant groups have commenced their economic
adaptation to American life from a position of such relative
advantage.

—ALEJANDRO PORTES[1]

During the summer of 1994, thousands of Cubans appeared off
the Florida coast in a flotilla of wooden rowboats, makeshift
rafts, and automobile tires lashed together with rope. Each day that
summer, the U.S. Coast Guard reported staggering jumps in the
number of Cuban *balseros* trying to reach our shores. The exodus
quickly overwhelmed Florida's immigration centers, which were already straining to cope with a stream of desperate Haitian boat people, and it fueled a growing national debate over immigration.

President Clinton reacted by doing what no U.S. president had
ever done—he ordered a halt to the special treatment of Cuban refugees. For more than thirty years, a succession of presidents had
dispensed unprecedented financial aid to those fleeing Cuba. During that time, Congress had financed numerous efforts by the refugees to topple Fidel Castro's Communist regime, and the CIA had
employed many of them as trusty Cold War foot soldiers. Neither
Dominicans fleeing the civil war of 1965 nor Haitians fleeing the
terror of Papa Doc Duvalier and a string of Haitian military juntas
got comparable treatment. Washington routinely rejected asylum
requests from Haitians picked up at sea while it invariably granted

asylum to the far smaller numbers of Cuban *balseros*. Under Clinton, many Haitians were even forcibly returned to their country.

But in 1994, the Cuban red carpet was pulled. By then, American fixation with the Cold War was over. Fear of immigrant hordes was replacing dread of Communist guerrillas. Henceforth, Clinton said, Cubans trying to reach the United States illegally would be detained and denied automatic entry just like any other immigrants. By the time he made his announcement, more than one million Cubans were living in the United States.

The *balseros* of 1994 were actually the fifth major wave of Cubans to land on our shores since thousands of tobacco workers migrated here during Cuba's independence wars in the nineteenth century. While middle-class Cubans continued to visit the United States throughout the first half of the twentieth century, few took up permanent residence until after the 1959 revolution of Fidel Castro reignited massive emigration. In the forty years since then, four major waves of Cubans have left. Each has been so distinctive in its social composition and political outlook that the Cuban diaspora is perhaps the most complex of all Latino immigrant sagas.

The refugees of the 1960s and 1970s were largely from the upper and middle classes and brought with them enormous technical skills. Those advantages, together with the massive aid the federal government dispensed to them, turned Cubans into this country's most prosperous Hispanic immigrants. Beginning with the Mariel boat wave in 1980, however, the Cubans who came were generally poorer and darker skinned. *Los marielitos*, as they were called, confronted a nativist backlash among white Americans and burgeoning class and racial conflicts within their own refugee community, making their experience more comparable to that of other Latino immigrants.

As a result of the tremendous disparities in class, education, and race among the various waves, there is no typical Cuban refugee, and some observers even dispute whether the terms *refugees* and *exiles* remain appropriate descriptions for today's Cuban immigrant community. I have chosen to focus on the experience of one Cuban family, the Del Rosarios of Miami, who seem to me representative of a significant but understudied segment of the community. Some of the family members arrived in 1994 with the *balseros*, while others have been in this country much longer. Luis Del Rosario, the family's most articulate spokesman, arrived here in 1979. Quiet, razor thin, nearly bald, and in his midforties, Luis was a former political prisoner in Cuba who, after settling in Miami, became active with Brothers to the Rescue, a militant exile group known for flying small planes over the Florida Straits to assist *balseros*.

I met him in the summer of 1994, while I was reporting on the *balseros*. Luis had just learned that one of his brothers, his sister-in-law, and their children had left Cuba on a raft and were lost somewhere at sea. Over the next few weeks, finding them became his personal obsession. The more we talked during those frantic days, the more I realized that the Del Rosario family could help illuminate key aspects of the Cuban diaspora.

THE EARLY MIGRANTS

The first Cuban migration to the United States is nearly forgotten these days. It occurred during the late nineteenth century, when more than one hundred thousand people, 10 percent of Cuba's population, fled abroad to escape the upheavals of the independence wars. The majority were unemployed tobacco workers who sought jobs in the new cigar factories that Spanish and Cuban manufacturers were setting up in Key West, Tampa, New Orleans, and New York City.

In 1885, Vicente Martínez Ybor and Ignacio Haya purchased forty acres of swamp near Tampa, drained the land, and set about building a company town. That town would become known as Ybor City. Martínez Ybor promptly set up a steamship line between Havana, Key West, and Tampa, ensuring himself a steady supply of workers and turning his new town into the cigar capital of the country. By 1900, there were 129 cigar factories in the town and fifteen thousand residents.

The steam line and the flourishing cigar industry created flesh-and-blood ties between Cuba and the United States. By the early twentieth century, as many as fifty thousand to one hundred thousand people traveled annually between Havana, Key West, and Tampa—so many that Cubans typically did not have to pass through customs or immigration.[2] While Cuba's millions of poor suffered under the turbulent regimes of Machado and then Batista, the small Cuban elite tied to U.S. companies basked in luxury. Its members invested their money on Wall Street. They sent their children to U.S. colleges. They went for treatment at U.S. hospitals. They vacationed in Saratoga Springs and other society resorts. Many even became U.S. citizens.

The 1959 revolution, however, sparked immediate flight. Some 215,000 left for the United States in the first four years. Thousands more went to Spain and Latin America.[3] That first wave was composed of the most wealthy: managers of U.S. corporations, the officers of dictator Batista's army and police, doctors, lawyers, scientists, and their families.[4] Metropolitan Miami's Hispanic population skyrocketed from a mere 50,000 in 1960 to more than 580,000 in 1980.[5]

"Few immigrant groups have commenced their economic adaptation to American life from a position of such relative advantage," wrote sociologist Alejandro Portes in a study of Cubans and Miami. The U.S. government provided a shelf full of government assistance programs under the 1966 Cuban Adjustment Act, programs that Mexicans, Puerto Ricans, and other Latinos never received. The refugees became instantly eligible for public assistance, Medicaid, food stamps, free English courses, scholarships, and low-interest college loans. They could secure immediate business credit and start-up loans. The state of Florida went even further—it provided direct cash allotments for Cuban families. Dade County opened civil service lists to noncitizens. The University of Miami Medical School even started special programs to help Cubans meet licensing requirements.[6]

Many of the refugees found additional assistance from covert programs of the Central Intelligence Agency. In those early days, both President John Kennedy and the exiles were confident Castro's revolution would be quickly overthrown. Their outlook was not dampened by the defeat of the CIA-sponsored Bay of Pigs invasion in 1961, and the capture of thousands of exiles from the expeditionary force, known as Brigada 2506. By 1962, the CIA station at the University of Miami was the biggest in the world next to the agency's Virginia headquarters. The agency had so many Cubans on its payroll that it became one of Miami's largest employers.[7] Those CIA paychecks provided many of the exiles a standard of living far beyond the imagination of any immigrants before them.

The refugees, in addition, brought with them extensive technical skills and perhaps the highest educational levels of any Hispanic immigrant group in U.S. history. At a time when only 4 percent of Cubans on the island had reached the twelfth grade, more than 36 percent of the refugees had college degrees, or at least some college education.[8]

Thanks to the unique combination of their own skills and federal largesse, the early exiles set about creating the Cuban miracle in

Miami. Within a few short years, the sleepy resort along Biscayne Bay was transformed into a commercial boomtown and a nexus for international trade. Cuban entrepreneurs who started their new life in this country with a small grocery or jewelry store quickly moved into banking, construction, and garment manufacturing. Some went to work for major U.S. firms and extended those firms into the Latin American market. Others served as real estate or banking agents in the United States for rich South Americans.[9]

At the same time, the refugees developed an intensely loyal internal market among their own. More than any other Hispanic immigrants, Cubans hired workers and purchased goods from within their own community.[10] Those who managed to get loan officer positions at small Miami banks made sure to lend start-up funds to fellow refugees who could not secure credit from Anglo lenders. They did so by pioneering the "character loan." An exile who didn't have collateral or credit could get a business loan based on his background or standing in Cuba. The borrowers proved to be impeccable risks and the loan policy turned many Cuban bank officers into millionaires.

Exiles who were barred from joining unions by the racist father-and-son policies of the building trades turned instead to pickup construction jobs among their own people. As the community grew, so did the mom-and-pop building partnerships. By 1979, half of the major construction companies in Dade County were Cuban owned.

At the same time, New York factory owners who felt their profits being squeezed by that city's garment unions jumped at the opportunity in the 1960s to forsake the North and set up production in Miami. In the decade before 1973, those relocations tripled the number of garment jobs in South Florida to twenty-four thousand. The new factories provided work for Cuban refugee women, many of whom ended up as contractors to the owners.[11] By 1987, there were sixty-one thousand Hispanic-owned firms in Miami with gross receipts of $3.8 billion, the largest by far of any city in the United States.[12]

The Cuban refugees were warmly welcomed during the 1960s and 1970s by a nation caught up in the fever of the Cold War. But that welcome changed almost overnight in 1980, as television news started to broadcast pictures of the Mariel boat people, an exodus named for the Cuban harbor from which the refugees embarked. More than 125,000 Cubans entered the country during the four months of the Mariel exodus. The new refugees, America realized, were no longer from the island's white elite. They were disproportionately single, young men, mostly blue-collar workers, a far greater percentage were Black than in previous waves, and a significant number were mentally ill or felons. Fidel Castro, according to some reports, took the opportunity to rid himself not just of dissidents but of criminals as well.[13]

For the first time, Cuban arrivals found a hostile reception and were dispersed to a half-dozen detention centers and army bases scattered about the country. Racial attitudes thus combined with economic fears—the sight of so many new refugees entering the country at a time of high unemployment angered many Americans. That anger grew when the refugees, frustrated with the cold treatment they were receiving, mounted noisy protests at several detention centers.

I recall visiting one refugee-processing center as a newspaper reporter that year and finding my own image of Cubans radically challenged. That image had been shaped by years of interaction on the streets of New York with the 1960s wave of refugees. Due to that experience, I had grown up believing that Cubans were usually white, well educated, and somewhat arrogant toward Puerto Ricans. Over the years, a certain enmity had developed between the two communities. We Puerto Ricans were resentful that many barrio businesses and the better-paying jobs in Spanish-language media had been gobbled up by the new Cuban arrivals both here and in our homeland—more than sixty thousand Cubans settled in Puerto Rico during the 1960s. So you can imagine my surprise when I encountered, behind the barbed wire of Fort Indiantown Gap, Pennsylvania, several thousand Cubans, almost all of them Black, all speaking in the same rapid-fire colloquial Spanish and with the same unaffected humility I had known among Puerto Ricans in East Harlem.

Mariel had repercussions far beyond the Cuban or Puerto Rican community. It came only months before a national election in which Republican candidate Ronald Reagan made an election issue out of President Carter's failure to control immigration, an issue that helped Reagan capture the White House. Similarly, the little-known governor of Arkansas at the time, Bill Clinton, attributed his defeat in a reelection effort that year to the voters' anger over his accepting so many Mariel refugees into Arkansas's Fort Chaffee. As we shall see later, Mariel marked the beginning of a major shift in how Americans regarded immigration (see chapter 11).

THE DEL ROSARIOS AND LIFE
UNDER THE REVOLUTION

Luis Del Rosario arrived in this country in the summer of 1979, a year before Mariel, as a pardoned political prisoner. His family is originally from a rice-growing area in Camagüey Province in the center of the island. His grandparents migrated there from the Canary Islands in the 1890s, when Spain, desperate to counter the growing independence sentiment among criollos, encouraged *peninsulares* to settle on the island. His parents were poor farmers—they rented land from a more prosperous relative—so they did not suffer the extreme misery that dogged Cuba's masses: the plantation workers, sharecroppers, and urban poor who formed the base of support for Castro's revolution.

Several Del Rosarios, in fact, had minor jobs with the Batista government. Luis's uncle, Chilo, served as a railroad policeman in Havana. Another uncle, Antolín, was a cop in Matanzas. The immediate family was a big one, seven boys and three girls. In the years before the revolution triumphed, Luis recalls, guerrilla leader Camilo Cienfuegos commanded a detachment of fighters from Fidel's Twenty-sixth of July Movement in their province. Cienfuegos's band arrived at their farm one day and asked permission to camp on the land, and Luis's father, though he was a Batista supporter, dared not refuse.

Luis was only ten when Castro's guerrilla army marched into Havana in January 1959. His parents sought at first to live in peace with the new regime. They even prospered from some of its early reforms. The government, for instance, built new houses for everyone in the region. All of the houses had cement floors, plywood walls, and zinc roofs—a step up from the dirt-floor hovels that were commonplace.[14] The new Del Rosario house had three bedrooms. The seven boys slept in one room, the girls in the second, and their parents in the third.

The government also built new schools and initiated extensive baseball and soccer programs for the region's youth. "The baseball uniforms were really important to us," Luis recalls. "We had gloves and bats and competed against other towns. I played for years, both in school and in the Little Leagues. Because of that kind of thing, I'd say ninety percent of the people supported Fidel at first." Numerous foreign studies of Cuban attitudes in the early days of the revolution confirm that view.[15]

But by the mid-1960s, euphoria for the revolution had waned. Young people started to quit their government-assigned jobs and move to Havana in search of better work. Luis heard the first real antigovernment sentiment around that time. After the death of his father in 1964, he moved to the capital and joined his brothers in a house in upper Havana, and together they started a small foundry in the back of the house. They would take old motors and discarded metal parts, then melt and recycle them into copper, bronze, or iron for the government. Nearly all of the dozen or so employees were family members. Luis tended the single antiquated oven and his brother Wenceslao served as the plant's main molder. Family foundries like theirs became critical to Cuba's survival after the U.S. embargo cut off access to spare parts for the many American-made cars and industrial machines in the country.

"It was a rustic operation," Luis recalls. "We had no technology and we used to burn ourselves a lot. Molten metal would spill pretty often and set off explosions. But we worked hard and the foundry made us a good living. If we had been allowed to grow, the country would be free today."

That never happened. In 1968, the government began nationalizing even small enterprises. "Some officials came and told us our foundry would become the property of the people," Luis recalled. "I got so angry I busted up our machines before we left."

Despite the bitter experience with the foundry, Luis still dreamed of prospering under socialism. He went to work as a postal clerk and later as a truck driver transporting food to the state-owned stores that dispensed all consumer goods under the country's system of rationing. It was during his daily trips around the Cuban countryside that Luis began to see firsthand how conditions were unraveling.

"Everything was going backward. If I tried to defend the revolution, others would tell me, 'How can you say that? Fidel only throws dirt at us.'" One day, a notice arrived from the government ordering him to report for military service, but he simply moved and decided to dodge the draft. Things were so disorganized in Cuba by then that the government never prosecuted him. Two of his other brothers did enlist, however, and one, Augusto, earned a rapid promotion to sergeant.

Luis passed the next few years managing several state stores in Havana. The stores were routinely bedeviled by long lines and shortages of goods, and they invariably turned into centers for both public discontent and private corruption. Seeing that some products always remained in abundance after ration cards were redeemed, store managers took to bartering or selling their surplus—five pounds of rice, say, for five pounds of meat.

"Many of us lived practically from robbing the government," Luis said. "The rationing system just didn't work."

By the early 1970s, Luis had come to hate the revolution. He and several brothers joined a clandestine group, the National Liberation Movement of October 10th. They were just amateur conspirators, he admitted, who would meet to plan grandiose sabotage operations but never carry them out. Eventually, an informant alerted the army, and soldiers arrested two of Luis's brothers, Gustavo and Wenceslao, outside an airport near Camagüey, as they were preparing to hijack a plane to the United States. A few months later, police arrested Luis for subversion. Convicted in a quick trial, he was sentenced to twelve years in jail but ended up serving only six and a half.

Unknown to Luis, a new group of anti-Castro Cuban Americans who were intent on normalizing U.S.-Cuba relations had traveled to Havana to meet with Fidel Castro. The group called itself the Committee of Seventy-five. It was immediately condemned by old-line anti-Castro groups in Miami as a front for Communist sympathizers. But the committee managed to persuade Castro to pardon more than a thousand political prisoners on condition that all the prisoners leave Cuba immediately.[16] Among those freed was Luis Del Rosario. On June 6, 1979, more than twenty years after Fidel marched out of the Sierra Maestra, Del Rosario, his wife, and two children boarded a Boeing 727 at José Martí Airport in Havana and flew to Miami. The rest of their relatives remained behind.

Luis quickly found work in a construction firm owned by another refugee, availed himself of all the federal programs, put a down payment on a house, and enrolled his children in Catholic schools. Several years later, after allowing his son Ismael to join the Civil Air Patrol, he developed an interest in flying, obtained his own pilot's license, and started flying air charters out of the Miami area. Meanwhile, he kept finding ways to get the rest of his family out of Cuba.

In the early 1990s, he joined Brothers to the Rescue, a group with historical ties to the CIA, and through the organization he came into contact with the aging chiefs of Miami's refugee community, a cadre of political bosses obsessed with returning to power in Cuba, who have made a lifelong, in some cases lucrative, career of stoking anti-Castro passions among their countrymen and the general U.S. population.

"They are a bunch of old men who just want Fidel out so that they can replace him," Del Rosario said of those leaders. Many of the working-class refugees who arrived in recent years share his perspective, he said, but few voice it publicly, for they fear ostracism as Communist sympathizers or physical assault by the anti-Castro underground. These most recent immigrants are the moderate side of the Cuban immigrant community most Americans never see. They oppose Castro's revolution, while at the same time not disputing that its early years brought much actual progress to Cuba's poor majority. They agree that many of the Batista backers who fled in the early days of the revolution to Miami were indeed criminals and exploiters of the nation. They do not seek to recover confiscated estates and fortunes they never possessed. They long for a Cuba free of violence, terror, and one-party rule, but they wish the unrelenting U.S. embargo against Cuba would end so they can freely visit the island and assist those relatives still there.

Two years after the boat exodus, I talked with Del Rosario again. His brother and family had been picked up at sea by the Coast Guard, kept in Guantánamo for more than a year, then quietly paroled into the United States. With new national elections approaching, President Clinton's policy of closing the doors to Cuban boat people had been just as quietly shelved. "This country doesn't care about Cubans," Rosario told me. "We're just pawns of politics."

7

DOMINICANS:
From the Duarte to the
George Washington Bridge

No man could know whether his neighbor, or his lifelong
friends, or even his brother or son or wife, might inform
against him. . . . Everyone feared. No one trusted anyone.

—JOHN BARTLOW MARTIN, FORMER AMBASSADOR
TO THE DOMINICAN REPUBLIC

During the weekend of July 4, 1992, hundreds of Dominican immigrants rioted in the Washington Heights area of New York City after rumors spread that a white policeman had fatally shot a young Dominican in the back. For several days, neighborhood youths torched cars, looted Korean- and white-owned businesses, and hurled rocks and bottles at police. City officials, fearing a repeat of the Los Angeles riot that had broken out two months earlier, rushed to calm residents with promises of an investigation. Although a Manhattan grand jury later concluded that the policeman had acted in self-defense against a known drug dealer, and that the alleged witnesses to the shooting had fabricated their stories, the first Dominican riot on U.S. soil had suddenly thrust a national spotlight on a new Latino immigrant group.

Between 1961 and 1986, more than 400,000 people legally immigrated to the United States from the Dominican Republic, and another 44,000 moved to Puerto Rico, while thousands more entered both places illegally. By 1990, more than 300,000 Dominicans lived in New York City alone. During the quarter century that followed, the Dominican immigrant population of the United States tripled, and by 2017 the number of Dominicans in the country, both foreign and U.S.-born, had surpassed two million.[1]

Much like the Puerto Ricans of the 1950s, Dominicans went largely unnoticed at first. New Yorkers tended to mistake them for Blacks who happened to speak Spanish. By the 1990s, however, they had become the second-largest Hispanic group in the Northeast, and by 2019 had even surpassed Puerto Ricans as the biggest Latino ethnic group in New York City.[2] As mainstream newspaper accounts of Dominicans involved in violent crime or drug trafficking became commonplace, some whites started to react with anger and blamed the new immigrants for the city's decline.

Rarely did the postriot news reports, however, seek to explain why so many Dominicans came to the United States in the first place. Few explored the new immigrants' enormous success in neighborhood commerce or their high enrollment in the public university system. And none of the reports clarified what was distinct about the Dominican diaspora from that of earlier European or even from other Latino immigrants.

The Dominican exodus, unlike that of Puerto Ricans and Mexicans, began largely as a refugee flight in the mid-1960s. Much of it followed a popular uprising in April 1965 that sought to restore to power the country's first democratically elected president, Juan Bosch. President Lyndon Johnson, fearing the revolt would lead to a Castro-style revolution, dispatched twenty-six thousand troops to invade the country, and those soldiers sided with the Dominican army in its efforts to crush the revolt. The U.S. occupation then paved the way for Joaquín Balaguer, a longtime aide of assassinated dictator Trujillo, to capture power during elections that followed in 1966. Those elections, despite supervision by U.S. and international observers, were plagued by right-wing violence against Bosch supporters. To diffuse the postelection crisis, U.S. officials hastily facilitated the mass exodus to the United States of the very revolutionaries our government had helped crush.[3]

For the next thirty years, Dominican political life was dominated by the same personalities and unresolved conflicts of the April 1965 revolution. Bloody political repression against Bosch's followers lasted for more than a decade. More than three thousand were killed between 1966 and 1974 alone. Thousands of others suffered imprisonment and torture.[4] Due to that right-wing repression, those who fled the country in the late 1960s and the 1970s were typically from the political left. Washington, however, refused to classify the Dominicans as refugees, as it did the Cubans who were fleeing Fidel Castro at the same time, so Dominicans received no federal assistance on arrival. Not until the 1980s, after the reign of terror ended back home, did Dominican immigration assume more an economic than a political character.

Those Dominicans who came here, whether in the early or later waves, were generally better educated, more urbanized, and more politically active than the average Mexican or Puerto Rican migrant. They also proved more adept at business enterprise, starting thousands of bodegas, supermarkets, and consumer goods stores in New York City, just as Cubans were doing in Miami. Manhattan's Washington Heights became their El Barrio and their Little Havana. The newcomers, though, were largely *mulato* and Black, and they quickly encountered racial discrimination even from other Hispanics.

Estela Vázquez was one of those Dominican pioneers. She arrived here as a teenager in August 1965, accompanied by her mother, her younger brother, and her sister. Her family's experiences typify those of the Dominican diaspora. They provide some insight into the obstacles the early immigrants faced, the organizations and networks they formed, and the unique identity they created.

THE LUCIANOS—THE EARLY YEARS

For Estela Vázquez Luciano, as for most Dominicans, modern existence began on May 30, 1961, when El Jefe, General Rafael Leónidas Trujillo, was assassinated by fellow officers after thirty-one years of wielding absolute power. President Kennedy and the CIA, the world would later learn, had decided to oust Trujillo even though previous U.S. governments had groomed and backed him.[5] Four turbulent years followed Trujillo's death. During that time, the country staged its first democratic election for president, and Juan Bosch, a populist reformer and intellectual, won the vote in a landslide. But Bosch's attempts at land reform and his refusal to repress the country's Communist movement placed him in immediate conflict with the sugar

growers and the U.S. government. Only seven months after his inauguration, he was overthrown by the army and forced into exile in
Puerto Rico.

Bosch remained popular even in exile, however, and two years
after his ouster, on April 24, 1965, a charismatic young follower of
his, Colonel Francisco Caamaño, led a revolt of young army officers
to restore him to power. From the moment the revolt began, the
people of Santo Domingo poured into the streets to reclaim their
democracy from the generals. Estela Vázquez, who was seventeen at
the time, immediately bolted from her grandmother's house and
followed the giant crowds toward the Duarte Bridge in the middle
of downtown to confront the soldiers who had overthrown Bosch.

That she ran from the house that day seemed somehow fated for
Estela, descended as she is from a line of poor but fiercely independent women. Her grandmother Ramona Luciano was a peasant
from Baní, near the country's western border with Haiti. As a young
woman, Ramona Luciano had fallen in love with Juan Mejías, a rich
local landowner who kept her as one of his many *queridas* for years.
Their long relationship produced seven children, one of them being
Ana María Luciano, Estela's mother, who was born in 1920.[6]

Ramona left Baní in the 1930s and moved with her children to
Santo Domingo, where she enrolled her daughter Ana María in one
of the many seamstress schools dictator Trujillo had created for
women. By 1938, Ana María had married Alcibiades Vilchez, the
owner of a small *pulpería* (grocery store), with whom she had three
children. The eldest, Estela, was born in 1948. The family was relatively privileged, thanks to minor connections they had to Trujillo
officials. One of Ana María's many brothers, Joaquín Mejías, who
was also fathered out of wedlock by the same rich Baní landowner,
was a top assistant to Trujillo confidant Manuel Moja López. Rafael
Sención, another brother, was a chauffeur to Moja López. In a
country where everything was accomplished by personal ties, the
lowly chauffeur, Uncle Rafael, eventually became *padrino* of the
whole family.

When Trujillo named Moja López ambassador to Washington in
1958, Uncle Rafael moved to the United States as his driver. He thus
became the first Luciano family member to leave for El Norte. Back
then, a Dominican traveling abroad was unheard-of except for the
very rich and famous. In early 1961, Uncle Rafael secured a passport
for one of his sisters, Esperanza, to work as a servant in Washington.
That same year, another sister, Consuelo, emigrated to New York.

Even then, three months before Trujillo's death, acquiring passports was virtually impossible without the dictator's approval. Consuelo, for example, had to produce twenty-four photos and take one to each police precinct in the capital so the authorities could check if she was a prostitute or known political dissident.

Not all of Ana María's family avoided the Trujillo terror. Another of her brothers, Juan Mejías, once made the mistake of publicly criticizing El Jefe. He was promptly arrested and thrown naked into La Cuarenta, a notorious prison on the outskirts of the capital. There he was tortured so badly that when he finally emerged, he had been driven insane and had lost all hearing. For the rest of his life he wandered the streets of the capital, homeless because no family member dared give him shelter.

The absolute power Trujillo wielded is almost unimaginable today. A former U.S. ambassador to the country recalled in his memoirs that "telephones were tapped, hotel rooms were wired with microphones. Mail was opened, cables scrutinized. Worst of all, as the dictator's secret informers seeped throughout the land, no man could know whether his neighbor, or his lifelong friends, or even his brother or son or wife, might inform against him. . . . Everyone feared. No one trusted anyone."[7]

"If the police were looking for you," recalled Dr. Arnulfo Reyes, a survivor of the repression, "you dared not run away. If you did, they would come and kill all the members of your family. So people just sat in their houses and waited for the police to come."[8]

Estela was still in junior high school when Trujillo was assassinated. At first, along with everyone else in the family, she mourned the death of the only leader most Dominicans had ever known. But those feelings of loss rapidly gave way to outrage as victims of the Trujillo years returned from exile abroad, and the stories those exiles revealed about the tortures they had endured under his depraved rule, stories that were all widely disseminated in the country's revived free press, jolted Dominican society from its thirty-year slumber. Soon, students began marching by the thousands to demand democratic elections and an end to the series of caretaker juntas that kept jockeying to fill the vacuum left by Trujillo's death. Radical newspapers and books proliferated. Leaders of the leftist June Fourteenth Movement became instant folk heroes. Estela, like most young Dominicans, was swept up by the political whirlwind.

In May 1963, with the country in upheaval, with jobs scarce, and with her husband too sick to work, Ana María Luciano decided to leave her children in the care of her mother and head to New York City to look for a job. She moved in with her sister Consuelo in the Bronx and landed work at a coat factory on Lower Broadway in Manhattan, which enabled her to send money back home each month to her husband and children. Soon after she arrived, she received word that her husband had died. She paid for the burial but could not afford to fly back for the funeral.

One night in June 1965, when Ana María arrived home from work, she found a telegram waiting for her: SOLDIERS ARRESTED ESTELA. SHE'S IN LA VICTORIA, the message from her mother read. Ana María grabbed the first flight back to Santo Domingo.

Most Americans still recall exactly what they were doing the day they heard the news that John Kennedy had been shot. So it is with Dominicans, who recall every detail of the afternoon of April 24, 1965, the day the Dominican revolution began. Estela Vázquez was sitting in her grandmother's house listening to the radio show of velvet-voiced commentator Francisco Peña Gómez.

Every Saturday, Peña Gómez, the youth leader of Juan Bosch's Dominican Revolutionary Party (PRD), would host a weekly show. It was called *Tribuna Democrática* (*Democratic Tribune*), and it was especially popular among poor, darker-skinned Dominicans who all knew that Peña Gómez was one of the few Blacks to hold a prominent political post in the country.

Listeners who tuned in that day were startled when they heard Peña Gómez announce that young officers in the army had embarked on a rebellion to bring President Bosch back to power. They were led, Peña told his listeners, by Colonel Caamaño, son of an infamous Trujillo-era general.[9] Estela rushed with her boyfriend and several of her cousins to Avenida Mella, one of Santo Domingo's big commercial streets, then down to the Duarte Bridge, the narrow span that controlled access to the heart of the city's colonial downtown area. As day turned to night, the people built barricades and constructed a makeshift encampment to hinder government soldiers stationed at the city's outskirts from entering town. Those who supported the return of Bosch called themselves the Constitutionalists; their opponents were dubbed the Loyalists. Few in the crowd had any idea whether Caamaño and the pro-Bosch rebel soldiers had managed to seize power, but still they cheered an endless string of civilian speakers proclaiming a people's victory.

On the second night of the uprising, military planes began

dropping bombs on the downtown area. In response, Bosch supporters, led by cadres of the June Fourteenth Movement, ambushed
and occupied several police stations. Estela, who was too young to
participate in the precinct assaults, carried weapons and ammunition for the rebels instead.

On the third morning of the revolt, the air force resumed an all-
out offensive on the Duarte Bridge. More than fifty people were
killed and a hundred wounded, but the Constitutionalists, reinforced
by Caamaño and his rebel soldiers, managed to hold the critical gate-
way to the city.[10] After that victory at the bridge, civilian support for
the rebels mushroomed, government soldiers began deserting their
posts, and it appeared that the generals were on the verge of surren-
dering. But President Johnson and his emissaries were determined
not to allow it. On April 28, Johnson sent in the marines as U.S. officials leaked exaggerated claims to the press that Communists were
in control of the rebellion and that American lives were in danger.
The White House called the intervention "neutral," but federal documents declassified since then leave no doubt that U.S. officials cooperated with and encouraged the ruling junta's effort to stamp out
the pro-Bosch forces.[11] Caamaño's rebels, several thousand strong,
retreated to the heart of the capital, where they were soon contained
inside fifty-four square blocks of the colonial city known as Ciudad
Nueva. There, cut off from the rest of the Dominican people by a
U.S.-enforced security corridor, the rebels remained in control of
the nerve center of the country—the presidential palace, the ports,
the telephone company, the main post office, and the radio and television stations.

In that rebel area, Estela lived for a month until a patrol of soldiers arrested her one afternoon in May as she slipped out to visit
her grandmother. The soldiers took the teenager to her grandmother's house to be identified. "Here, take this rope and hang her," her
grandmother Ramona told them, an old picture of dictator Trujillo
still on the wall. "I don't want any Communists in my family."

Ana María Luciano arrived in the capital in June and tried to secure her daughter's release. She appealed to every old political connection of the Lucianos, and finally secured a meeting with Colonel
Benoit, head of the new military junta.

"My family have always been supporters of Trujillo," she told the
busy colonel. "We are not Communists. We don't know about politics. My daughter is only a child."

"Señora Luciano, I can't release her," the soft-spoken colonel

said. "You don't know your own daughter. She'll run right back to
the Zona Prohibida [Prohibited Zone] and take up with those Communists again."

"Sir, I promise you, I won't allow it. She's leaving with me for
New York. She won't come back."

By August, Ana María's persistence had paid off. Colonel Benoit
authorized Estela's release—and her immediate deportation. Soldiers escorted her from prison to the airport, where her mother, her
younger sister, Doraliza, and her six-year-old brother, Rafael Leónidas, were waiting. At the age of seventeen, Estela Vázquez had become a political exile.

BUILDING A NEW LIFE IN NEW YORK CITY

Ana María Luciano returned to her old factory on Broadway, but
the supervisor refused at first to rehire her. Puerto Rican Eva Es-
trella, one of the factory's veteran seamstresses, was furious. "Ana
María didn't go to Santo Domingo to party and dance," Eva told the
boss. "She went there to save her children. If she doesn't come back
to work, all of us go on strike."

The next day, Ana María was back at her machine, and as soon as
she could, she found Estela a job in a small sweatshop nearby on
Astor Place. Her first week on the job, Estela was stuck for hours on
a New York subway when the Northeast was paralyzed by the greatest power blackout in U.S. history. In less than one year Estela had
lived through a fierce revolution, three months in a dank prison cell,
dislocation to a strange new country, the shock of becoming a teenage factory worker, and a blackout in a New York City subway
tunnel.

The following year, she married a young Puerto Rican coworker
of one of her cousins, and their marriage produced two children,
Evelyn and Alejandro. For a while, they all lived with Estela's mother
and younger brother and sister—seven people crammed into a two-
bedroom basement apartment that never saw sunlight and seldom
had heat in winter. To ward off the cold, they slept most nights in
their overcoats, wearing plastic fur-lined boots Ana María brought
home from the factory.

The lives of the Dominican pioneers, just as those of the Puerto
Ricans before them, were dominated by the search for work and the
day-to-day battle for survival. Both had come from islands where

unemployment compensation was nonexistent and the acceptance of charity frowned upon. Ana María Luciano, who stayed at the same factory for twenty-one years until it closed in 1984, always boasted even in retirement that she had never taken charity from anyone, especially the government. But those in the second generation found it harder to reconcile old values with their new reality. Estela's husband, for instance, abandoned her in 1973 for one of his mistresses, which forced her to resort to welfare along with her two young children. She kept struggling as a single parent, though, eventually learning English, getting her high school equivalency diploma, leaving the factory, enrolling in a community college, and finally landing a job she could be proud of—as an organizer at Mount Sinai Hospital in East Harlem with Local 1199, the health care workers' union.

THE NEW *COLONIA* IN NEW YORK

Dominicans who arrived in the 1960s typically settled near established Puerto Rican communities, the most popular being on the Upper West Side of Manhattan. Those early arrivals had expected to go home once the Balaguer terror ended, but as the years passed, the new society they'd found gradually altered their expectations and reconfigured their dreams.

The first organizations the immigrants formed were social clubs and sports associations that were meant to keep alive their sense of community. The more well-known were Club María Trinidad Sánchez, on Broadway near 104th Street, and the Thirtieth of March and the Twenty-seventh of February clubs, both named after important dates in Dominican history. The Centro Educacional Caribe, one of the first civic associations, was founded in the early 1970s by Alfredo White, a one-time leader of the sugarcane workers in San Pedro de Macorís. There, the immigrants learned English and began to study the American political system.

The new arrivals were generally better educated than either Puerto Rican migrants or Dominicans back home.[12] One 1980 study revealed that 41 percent of New York City's Dominican immigrants had completed ten years of school or better, nearly twice the average of city dwellers in the Dominican Republic.[13] On the whole, they were also more aware of politics than the average Puerto Rican or Mexican. The upheavals of the post-Trujillo era had turned

Dominicans into the most radical group of Spanish-speaking immigrants in U.S. history, akin to the Russian workers who reached the United States after the failed 1905 revolution, or the Italian anarcho-syndicalist immigrants of the 1920s. Many joined branches of political parties opposed to the Balaguer regime as soon as they arrived.

From the West Side, the community shifted at first to the area around City College, at 135th Street and Broadway, and as more immigrants arrived, it spread farther north to Washington Heights, which eventually became its center. At City College of New York (CCNY), the first organizations of Dominican students were formed in the late 1970s. Out of those groups emerged a core of teachers, doctors, and lawyers who would become the community's principal leaders. Guillermo Linares, the first Dominican-born city councilman, was a founder of one of those first groups. After graduation, he taught in the public schools and together with Fernando Lescaille, another fellow CCNY alumnus, he founded the Association of Progressive Dominicans (ACDP), the first social action group in Washington Heights. By the mid-1980s, ACDP members had won control of the local school and community boards, and those victories provided the springboard for Linares's election.

The surge in Dominican migration soon strained the traditional close ties between Dominicans and Puerto Ricans, ties that date back to the nineteenth century and early twentieth century, when many Puerto Ricans left their island to find work in the sugar plantations of the more prosperous Dominican Republic. Cultural interchange and intermarriage between the two groups were common back then. Both former Dominican president Joaquín Balaguer and his archenemy, Juan Bosch, for instance, claimed Puerto Rican ancestry on their mothers' side. And many Puerto Ricans assisted Dominican migrants in the 1960s to navigate the hostile and inscrutable Anglo world the newcomers found. But by the 1990s, sharp tension emerged between the groups, both here and in Puerto Rico.

Much of that tension resulted from undocumented Dominican immigration to Puerto Rico. In 1990 alone, the Immigration and Naturalization Service (INS) deported more than 13,200 Dominicans who entered Puerto Rico illegally.[14] Every night, smugglers launched *yolas* filled with Dominicans from eastern coastal towns and set sail across the Mona Passage to Puerto Rico. No one knows how many have drowned after paying *coyotes* to take them across the treacherous passage, but Puerto Rico newspapers are still

periodically filled with stories of dead Dominicans washing up on-
shore.[15]

Those who make it land near the western towns of Aguadilla,
Mayagüez, and Arecibo, then travel to the San Juan area and on to
New York or Miami. In as much as Puerto Rico is U.S. territory, it
has no mandatory immigration or customs checkpoints for the
scores of U.S.-bound flights that leave each day. But Dominicans,
lured by the island's climate, common language, and culture, and by
its greater prosperity, often decide to stay. The island's Dominican
population is still hotly debated. Some estimate it as high as 200,000,
though officials peg it much lower. The 2010 U.S. census, for example, reported 68,000 Dominicans living in Puerto Rico, while a
more recent Census Bureau estimate in 2017 of all non–Puerto
Rican Hispanic residents of the island (overwhelmingly Dominican)
was 104,000.[16] With island unemployment stubbornly high, an anti-
immigrant backlash was inevitable. Puerto Ricans, echoing the
fears of Americans here, perceive Dominicans as taking scarce jobs
away from natives. At the same time, island press reports typically
portray Dominicans as shiftless and prone to crime and drug trafficking. In urban neighborhoods such as Santurce's Barrio Obrero
and Villa Palmeras, whose populations are now overwhelmingly
Dominican, that resentment has turned increasingly racial.

Exaggerated accounts of the Dominican influx to the island were
routinely passed on to Puerto Rican relatives in the United States,
where competition over jobs and business opportunities sparked increasing rivalry during the 1990s between the two immigrant communities in the Northeast, one that echoed the growing tension
between Mexican Americans and the newer Central American immigrant communities in the far West.

The Puerto Rican–Dominican rivalry moved from one barrio industry to another. Whereas neighborhood bodegas were owned
largely by Puerto Ricans in the 1960s and 1970s, they became largely
Dominican owned toward the turn of the century. The same was
true of the livery taxi cab industry that operated in the outer bor-
oughs of New York. Initially dominated by Puerto Ricans and African Americans, it became largely owned by Dominicans and
Jamaicans. At Latin nightclubs and on Spanish-language radio,
where Puerto Rican salsa once reigned, merengues and bachatas
from the Dominican Republic were more likely to be heard. Some
Puerto Ricans even blamed Dominicans for the 1980s epidemic of
cocaine and crack trade in northeastern cities. Thus, we see some of

the same immigrant conflicts developing within the Latino community as existed between early arriving Latinos and Anglo-Americans.

Yet side by side with the poverty, drugs, and low-wage labor among Dominicans, immigrant success stories abound. Enrollment at jammed Hostos Community College in the South Bronx, originally created out of the educational battles of the 1960s as a school for Puerto Rican adult workers, was nearly 60 percent Hispanic by 2016—with at least half of those students being of Dominican ethnicity. Moreover, the various colleges that compose the sprawling City University of New York counted more than 22,500 undergraduates of Dominican descent and another 1,500 graduate students, amounting to more than 8.7 percent of the university's entire enrollment.[17]

Not only have Dominicans spawned a thriving mom-and-pop business community, they are also increasingly breaking into the medium-sized food and retailing industry. Several independent New York supermarkets—the Pioneer, Associated, and CTown chains—are now dominated by Dominican owners. By the early 1990s, the National Association of Supermarkets had become the richest economic bloc of Dominicans in the country. Even banks and factories owned and operated by Dominican immigrants have sprouted in recent years.

From designer Oscar de la Renta to jazz pianist Michel Camilo, to the novelists Julia Alvarez and Junot Díaz, from actress Zoe Saldana to rapper and songwriter Cardi B (Belcalis Marlenis Almánzar), Dominican contributions to U.S. culture are increasingly gaining national attention. And the amazing continuing dominance of Dominican athletes in Major League Baseball has been a source of enduring national pride to the immigrant community. From Sammy Sosa to Juan Samuel to George Bell, from Pedro Guerrero and Tony Fernández to Juan Guzmán, from Vladimir Guerrero to Robinson Cano, from David Ortiz to Albert Pujols, the list of Dominican baseball stars seems endless. Many come from the same section of the country, San Pedro de Macorís, where giant sugarcane plantations once dominated the landscape and U.S. Marines once hunted down guerrillas.

Often forgotten in the stereotypes, however, is the incredible mass poverty that drives young Dominicans to this country. The Dominican standard of living slumped throughout the 1980s and early 1990s. A government doctor there earned the equivalent of $160 a month in 1991. A public school teacher earned about $70.[18] And while the early years of the twenty-first century witnessed some of the most impressive economic growth for the Dominican Republic of any nation in the region, an estimated 23 percent of its people were still living in poverty in 2020.[19] As long as a Dominican doctor can earn more money washing dishes in Manhattan than performing surgery back home, how can he be expected to resist emigration?

In the United States, the smartest child in the family aspires to be an investment banker, an internet venture capitalist, a doctor. In the shantytowns of Santo Domingo and the Caribbean, the brightest and the best dream of reaching the United States to pull their family out of poverty. Today there is hardly an urban household in the Dominican Republic that does not have some family member living in the United States and sending occasional financial help back home.[20]

During the first three decades after the Lucianos arrived, other family members followed. All dreamed at first of returning. In 1979, Estela did go back. It was her first visit since her exile fourteen years earlier. By then, the Balaguer repression had ended and Antonio Guzmán, a member of Juan Bosch's old party, was the new president, so the New York exiles felt safe in returning. But the Guzmán government proved to be as corrupt as Balaguer's. Estela encountered a nation mired in poverty she had never imagined. The mushrooming population was straining all urban infrastructure. Electrical blackouts were commonplace. Drinking water was polluted. Shantytowns dotted the capital. Roads were in disrepair and unemployment was higher than ever.

That was when she realized she could not live back home.

Given the history of U.S. exploitation and bullying of the Dominican Republic, and the tremendous economic gap that exploitation has created, it seems unlikely that massive emigration will abate in the twenty-first century. Like Estela Vázquez, many Dominicans will continue being patriots from afar, in love with their homeland but unable to live there.

"I think if the U.S. offered more visas," she admitted one day in 1993, "everyone would leave the country. That's how bad things are."

8

CENTRAL AMERICANS:
Intervention Comes Home to Roost

> So many were tortured to death that if the army took you into
> custody and you survived, those in your circle would suspect
> you as a traitor. Women who were raped were too ashamed to
> return to their homes. Families and communities just disin-
> tegrated.
>
> —MARIO GONZÁLEZ, GUATEMALAN IMMIGRANT
> PSYCHOLOGIST, 1998

Although a few Salvadorans lived in San Francisco's Mission District and the Pico-Union area of Los Angeles as far back as 1970, and a tiny Guatemalan enclave took shape in Chicago's Humboldt Park area around the same time, Central Americans were a negligible presence in the United States until the final decades of the twentieth century. The U.S. census counted 94,000 Salvadoran-born inhabitants in the entire country in 1980. That figure had skyrocketed to 701,000 ten years later—an eightfold increase. By 2017, there were more than 2.3 million people of Salvadoran descent residing in this country, equal to nearly 40 percent of their homeland's population that year.[1] Similar astonishing jumps occurred during the 1980s for Guatemalans (from 71,642 to 226,000) and Nicaraguans (from 25,000 to 125,000). As of 2017, the census estimated 1.4 million Guatemalans were in the United States, with the total Central American population in this country surpassing 5.5 million.[2]

This sudden exodus did not originate with some newfound collective desire for the material benefits of U.S. society; rather, vicious civil wars and the social chaos those wars engendered forced the region's people to flee, and in each case the origins and spiraling intensity of those wars were a direct result of military and economic intervention by our own government.

As it had done with earlier Cuban and Dominican arrivals, Washington pursued a dual and discriminatory policy toward the new immigrants: the Immigration and Naturalization Service welcomed the Nicaraguans but intercepted and interned the Guatemalans and Salvadorans. By routinely denying refugee status to the latter two groups, our government condemned Salvadorans and Guatemalans who managed to sneak across the border to a precarious and illegal existence at the margins of Anglo society. They became the preferred gardeners, cooks, and nannies of a vast underground economy that mushroomed in the 1980s to service middle-class America.

Despite those obstacles, the new immigrants showed amazing resilience and a dogged work ethic. They rapidly established vibrant immigrant networks and self-help organizations; they mounted vigorous court challenges and lobbying campaigns to reform federal immigration policies; they emerged as a critical source of economic aid to their destitute homelands through the billions of dollars in annual remittances they sent home to relatives; and gradually, as their numbers multiplied, they transformed and reconfigured the Latino population of the United States.

To comprehend this new Latino wave, we must have a rudimentary sense of what the immigrants left behind. Simply put, the vast majority of Central Americans today live in persistent misery alongside tiny elites that enjoy unparalled prosperity. By the 1990s, the average cat in our country ate more beef than the average Central American. In Nicaragua, 42 percent of the people had no access to safe drinking water as recently as 2015, while in Guatemala it was 39 percent. More than six in ten Hondurans lived in poverty in 2017, and nearly as many did in Guatemala. Nearly three in ten rural residents of Honduras had no access to electricity, while in both Nicaragua and Guatemala, some 40 percent still did not have access to safe drinking water.[3] Guatemala has sharply reduced illiteracy since the late 1980s, when more than half of the country's adults could not read, down to 10 percent. But a 2011 study found that that country's illiteracy rate was much higher among adult women (24 percent) and most especially among indigenous women (51 percent). Moreover, it reported that only one-fifth of Guatemala's population had been able to acquire any secondary school education.[4]

The region's plight was made worse by the "lost decade" of the 1980s, when the Latin American debt crisis and the periodic devaluations of the region's currencies against the U.S. dollar drove down the real value of wages while driving up the cost of American imports. In every Central American country except Costa Rica, the per capita domestic product shrank between 1980 to 1996 (see table 4).

While the economic stagnation was regionwide, the immigration flow was not. The bulk of emigrants came from three war-torn countries. Fatalities from those wars had passed a quarter of a million by 1989—five times the U.S. death toll in Vietnam. More than 140,000 died in Guatemala, 70,000 in El Salvador, 60,000 in Nicaragua—unimaginable devastation for a such a small region.[5]

Table 4

Gross Domestic Product Per Capita 1980–1996
(IN 1990 U.S. DOLLARS)[6]

Country	1980	1990	1996
Costa Rica	$1,986	$1,865	$2,016
El Salvador	$1,219	$1,026	$1,171
Guatemala	$1,044	$857	$915
Honduras	$636	$585	$596
Nicaragua	$979	$645	$637

Central America's victims perished mostly at the hands of their own soldiers or from right-wing death squads, and invariably from weapons made in the U.S.A., given that in each country our government provided massive military aid to the side doing most of the killing. Even though international human rights groups repeatedly documented government-sponsored terror in the region, including several infamous assassinations of U.S. citizens and Catholic clergy, the Reagan and Bush administrations, obsessed with stopping Communism in the region, refused to assist the thousands streaming across the Mexican border to escape that terror. Between 1983 and 1990, the INS granted only 2.6 percent of political asylum requests from Salvadorans, 1.8 percent from Guatemalans, and 2.0 percent from Hondurans, yet it granted 25.2 percent of those from Nicaraguans, whose Sandinista government Washington was seeking to over-throw.[7] Even when the INS denied asylum to a Nicaraguan, the agency rarely sent that person home—of 31,000 denied between 1981 and 1989, only 750 were actually deported.[8]

Unfortunately, public knowledge about the wars in Central America was so scant that most Americans, when asked, could not even tell what side our government was backing in which country.[9] Leaders in Washington sought to portray the region as pivotal to the worldwide battle between democracy and Communism. Such simplistic justifi-cations obscured long-festering divisions between rich and poor in the region, and they ignored our own government's historic com-plicity in exacerbating those divisions.

NICARAGUA:
FROM SOMOZA TO THE SANDINISTAS

In Nicaragua, as we have seen, Washington backed the Somoza family's dictatorial rule and tolerated its pillaging of the country for more than forty years. During that time, more Nicaraguan military officers received training at the U.S. Army's School of the Americas in Panama than from any other country in Latin America.[10]

Most Nicaraguans had had enough of the Somozas by the mid-1970s. The turning point came with the massive earthquake that razed much of the capital of Managua in 1972 and left thousands dead. While their countrymen were digging out of the rubble, the ruling Liberal-Conservative junta led by President Anastasio So-moza Debayle and his cronies stole millions of dollars' worth of des-perately needed international relief supplies, sparking an outcry from the public. From then on, even the Catholic hierarchy and the members of the elite, many of whom had benefited from the Somoza era, turned against the regime.

A new generation of revolutionaries arose. They called them-selves the Sandinista National Liberation Front, after the country's legendary martyred leader, Augusto Sandino, and the guerrilla army they formed spread rapidly through the countryside. But even as the guerrillas advanced, and public sentiment turned heavily against the Somozas, the White House and Congress continued to back the regime. By the time the Carter administration finally decided to arrange a peaceful removal of Somoza in 1979, it was too late. A nationwide popular uprising toppled the clan and brought the Sandinistas to power.

At first, the Carter White House tried to work with the Sandinista revolutionaries, but that all changed when Ronald Reagan was elected president the following year. Reagan immediately authorized the CIA to arm, train, and finance many of the former Somoza soldiers and henchmen into the infamous Contra army. For the rest of the 1980s, the Contras and their CIA directors pursued a hit-and-run war of sabotage and terror aimed at destabilizing the new government. The covert war was overseen from the Reagan White House by Lieutenant Colonel Oliver North and was conducted from bases in Honduras and Costa Rica. While the Reagan and then the Bush administrations intensified the war and sought to isolate the Sandinista government internationally, the number of Nicaraguans fleeing their country kept growing.

EL SALVADOR—FROM *LA MATANZA* TO THE KILLING FIELDS

A similar pattern emerged in the Salvadoran civil war, whose origins go back to another almost-forgotten North American henchman, General Maximiliano Hernández Martínez. In 1932, shortly after seizing power in a military coup, Hernández masterminded the slaughter of as many as 30,000 Pipil Indians. The Pipil, impoverished peasants from the country's Izalco region, had rebelled against the local landlords and had sought help in organizing the revolt from the country's small Communist Party. Party leader Augustín Farabundo Martí was executed during the fighting, and the army's bloodletting against the peasants, known in Salvadoran history as *La Matanza*, was so widespread that it succeeded in stamping out popular opposition for the next forty years and suppressed all traces of Indian culture from El Salvador.

With U.S. approval, Hernández banned all unions and ruled the country with an iron fist from 1932 to 1944, until disgruntled army subordinates engineered his ouster. From then on, members of the tiny Salvadoran oligarchy, known as the fourteen families, alternated control of the government with the generals, while intermittent coups between factions of the elite became a way of life.[11]

In the Salvadoran countryside, the coffee oligarchy gobbled up so many farms that the number of landless peasants quadrupled between 1961 and 1975, and more than 300,000 Salvadorans were forced to migrate to thinly populated Honduras to work in that country's banana plantations. The Honduran government, overwhelmed by the migrants, responded with mass deportations, a policy that only exacerbated tensions along the border, and those tensions soon escalated into a shooting war in 1969 between the two countries. The outside world derisively labeled it the Soccer War, and while the conflict lasted only one week, it destabilized the entire region by effectively terminating Honduras's role as a safety valve for Salvador's unemployed. By the time the war ended, more than 130,000 Salvadoran migrants had been forced back home, the rest fleeing to Mexico and the United States. Those who arrived in this country eventually found their way to San Francisco and Los Angeles, where they created the first Salvadoran *colonias* in the United States.

Those migrants repatriated to El Salvador posed an immediate social problem for the government. Unable to find jobs or land to till, they resorted to mass demonstrations; many started squatting on properties controlled by the oligarchy. The government responded, as it had in Hernández's time, by calling out the army and allowing right-wing death squads to butcher the protesters. The most notorious of the paramilitary groups was ORDEN (the Democratic Nationalist Organization); it had been founded in 1968 by National Guard chief General José Alberto Medrano, who supplemented his government job by moonlighting for the CIA.[12]

There was one important force in Central America, however, that had changed substantially since the days of Sandino and Farabundo Martí—the Catholic Church. The church historically had been a bulwark of Latin America's oligarchies, but by the late 1960s it was assuming a new role. Scores of parish priests, nuns, and missionaries, responding to the social call of the Second Vatican Council, threw themselves into social action among the region's poor. They organized a raft of new civic groups, turning their churches and missions into centers for democratic dissent.[13]

The grassroots awakening proved an unexpected challenge to the Salvadoran oligarchy, as it aroused thousands of peasants, urban slum dwellers, and trade union members to use the country's ballot box for the first time. So strong did the new movement become that its opposition candidates were on the verge of winning national elections twice in the 1970s. To head off those victories, the National Guard instituted coups in both 1972 and 1977. The stronger the popular movement grew, the more blatantly the oligarchy rigged election results, so that after a while many Salvadorans started losing hope of any peaceful reform.[14]

In 1979, another army coup aborted the results of a democratic election, but this time the country erupted into civil war. Over the next two years, with right-wing death squads hunting down dissidents, more than eight thousand trade union leaders were murdered, wounded, abducted, or disappeared. The ferocious repression prompted many young Salvadorans to respond in kind. By 1980, five separate opposition guerrilla groups were operating in the countryside, and they soon banded together to form the Farabundo Martí National Liberation Front, named after the martyred leader of the 1932 uprising.[15]

That same year, a right-wing death squad assassinated San Salvador's archbishop Oscar Romero, a fierce critic of the Salvadoran junta, and several months later, four American Catholic nuns and lay workers were raped and killed by government soldiers. Those killings signaled to the outside world that the violence in El Salvador had spiraled out of control. Instead of denouncing a government that would permit such atrocities, the Bush and Reagan administrations, believing that the country's oligarchy was the only reliable anti-Communist force, rewarded that government. Washington quickly turned El Salvador into the biggest recipient of American military aid in Latin America. Seventy percent of the record $3.7 billion the United States pumped into El Salvador from 1981 to 1989 went for weapons and war assistance.[16] As the number of weapons in the country escalated, so did the numbers of Salvadorans fleeing the devastation those weapons caused.

GUATEMALA: BANANAS AND BODIES

In similar fashion, the violence that engulfed Guatemala during the late twentieth century was due in no small measure to U.S. foreign policy. A garrison state for more than forty years, Guatemala was home to the longest and bloodiest civil war in Central American history. The roots of that war go back to an almost-forgotten

CIA-sponsored coup in 1954, which overthrew a democratically elected president.

Throughout the early part of the century, Guatemalan presidents faithfully protected the interests of one landowner above all others, the United Fruit Company (UFCO). President Jorge Ubico, who ruled the country from 1931 to 1944, surpassed all his predecessors in the favors he bestowed on UFCO. By the time Ubico left office, the company owned more than a million acres of banana fields in Central America; it had a bigger annual budget than any nation in the region; its fleet of eighty-five ships carried most of the region's outside trade; it owned fourteen hundred miles of rail, including the largest line between Mexico and Panama. In Guatemala, UFCO and its affiliate, International Railways of Central America (IRCA), were the country's two largest employers, with twenty thousand people on their payrolls.[17]

In a country whose coffee-growing elite was largely German descended, President Ubico was somewhat of a fascist sympathizer. Nonetheless, he curried favor with Washington during World War II by interning German nationals, confiscating their plantations, and opening his economy further to U.S. investors. Those policies brought Guatemala considerable prosperity while the war lasted and enabled Ubico to finance an ambitious public works program, including the best highway system in Central America. The progress came at a cost, however. Ubico forced Guatemala's huge population of landless Maya to work on government projects in lieu of paying taxes. He made all Indians carry passbooks and used vagrancy laws to compel them to work for the big landowners.[18] As for Ubico's penchant for jailing opponents and stamping out dissent, Washington simply ignored it so long as U.S. investment in the country flourished.

Like all the region's dictators, Ubico eventually aroused the population against him. In 1944, a coalition of middle-class professionals, teachers, and junior officers, many of them inspired by Franklin D. Roosevelt's New Deal liberalism, initiated a democracy movement. The movement won the backing of the country's growing trade unions and rapidly turned into a popular uprising that forced Ubico to resign.

The first democratic election in Guatemalan history followed in 1945, and voters chose as president Juan José Arévalo, a university philosophy professor and author who had been living in exile in Argentina. Tall, handsome, and heavily built, Arévalo was a spellbinding orator. From the moment he returned home to commence his campaign, he became an almost messianic figure to Guatemala's impoverished masses.

Arévalo promised his countrymen a peaceful revolution, one that would take as its inspiration neither the mechanical materialism of the Communists nor the rapacious capitalism of Ubico and the old guard. He called it spiritual socialism, and once in office, he pressed forward with an ambitious program of reform. He abolished Ubico's hated vagrancy laws, recognized labor rights, established the country's first social security and rural education programs, and offered government loans to small farmers. Quite predictably, his reforms sparked resistance from United Fruit and from the Guatemalan upper classes. In an effort to counterbalance that resistance, Arévalo, even though he was personally opposed to Communism, ended up depending on the country's small but well-organized group of Communists and the trade unions they controlled to marshal public support for his program.[19]

After six years in office, Arévalo was succeeded by Jacobo Arbenz Guzmán, a young military officer and Arévalo disciple. Arbenz swept to victory in the 1951 elections and vowed to take Arévalo's peaceful revolution a step further by redistributing all idle lands to the peasants. Arbenz knew that in a country with no industry to speak of, with more than 70 percent of the population illiterate, and with 80 percent barely eking out survival in the countryside, ownership and control of land was Guatemala's fundamental economic issue. The country's soil was immensely fertile, but only 2 percent of the landholders owned 72 percent of the arable land, and only a tiny part of those holdings were under cultivation.[20]

The following year, Arbenz got the Guatemalan Congress to pass Decree 900. The new law required the expropriation of all property that was larger than six hundred acres and not in cultivation. The confiscated lands were to be divided among the landless. The owners were to receive compensation based on the land's assessed tax value, and they were to be paid with twenty-five-year government bonds, while the peasants would get low-interest loans from the government to buy their plots. As land reform programs go, it was by no means a radical one when you consider it affected only large estates. Of 341,000 landowners, only 1,700 holdings came under its provisions. But those holdings represented half the private land in the country. Most important, it covered the vast holdings of the United Fruit Company, which owned some six hundred thousand acres—most of it unused.

Arbenz shocked UFCO officials even more when he actually confiscated a huge chunk of the company's land and offered $1.2 million as compensation, a figure that was based on the tax value the company's own accountants had declared before Decree 900 was passed. United Fruit and the U.S. State Department countered with a demand for $16 million. When Arbenz refused, Secretary of State John Foster Dulles and CIA director Allen Dulles convinced President Eisenhower that Arbenz had to go. The Dulles brothers, of course, were hardly neutral parties. Both were former partners of United Fruit's main law firm in Washington. On their advice, Eisenhower authorized the CIA to organize Operation Success, a plan for the armed overthrow of Arbenz, which took place in June 1954. The agency selected Guatemalan colonel Carlos Castillo Armas to lead the coup, it financed and trained Castillo's rebels in Somoza's Nicaragua, and it backed up the invasion with CIA-piloted planes. During and after the coup, more than nine thousand Guatemalan supporters of Arbenz were arrested.

Despite the violent and illegal manner by which Castillo's government came to power, Washington promptly recognized it and showered it with foreign aid. Castillo lost no time in repaying his sponsors. He quickly outlawed more than five hundred trade unions and returned more than 1.5 million acres to United Fruit and the country's other big landowners. Guatemala's brief experiment with democracy was over. For the next four decades, its people suffered from government terror without equal in the modern history of Latin America. As one American observer described it, "In Guatemala City, unlicensed vans full of heavily armed men pull to a stop and in broad daylight kidnap another death squad victim. Mutilated bodies are dropped from helicopters on crowded stadiums to keep the population terrified . . . those who dare ask about 'disappeared' loved ones have their tongues cut out."[21]

Within a few years of the Arbenz overthrow, most Guatemalans lost hope that peaceful change and democratic elections would return. Inspired by Fidel Castro's Cuban revolution, radical students and intellectuals took to the hills in 1960, where they formed several guerrilla groups to resist the dictatorship. To hunt them down, the government responded with scorched-earth campaigns, pacification programs, and paramilitary death squads, often with assistance from U.S. Special Forces advisers. By 1976, more than twenty thousand people had been killed. While the slaughter expanded in the countryside, a series of army strongmen wielded power in the government, and sham elections alternated with military coups as the elite disputed among themselves the best way to crush the guerrillas. One of those strongmen was Carlos Arana Osorio, a colonel who rose to head of state in 1970. Arana had earned the name Butcher of Zacapa for all the massacres that took place while he directed the counterinsurgency campaign in the late 1960s. "If it is necessary to turn the country into a cemetery in order to pacify it," Arana once boasted, "I will not hesitate to do so."

The dead and disappeared reached 75,000 by 1985; another 150,000, most of them Indians, had fled by then into Mexico. But Guatemala's dirty war barely raised eyebrows in Washington. Lawmakers and the press were far more concerned with El Salvador, where the murders of priests and nuns had sparked outrage among U.S. Catholics, and with Nicaragua, where the Reagan administration had drawn its line in the sand against Communism.

THE EXODUS TO EL NORTE

By the early 1980s, Guatemala, El Salvador, and Nicaragua were all engulfed in wars for which our own government bore much responsibility. In El Salvador alone, human rights groups estimated that five hundred people a month were being massacred by the death squads. The carnage caused so many refugees to stream across the Mexican border that five hundred thousand Salvadorans had arrived in the United States by 1984.[22] Their presence raised an unsettling question: Why were so many people fleeing a government our country supported?

For nearly thirty years, U.S. law, as expressed in the Immigration and Nationality Act of 1952, had granted refugee status only to people escaping Communist regimes. But the Central American exodus—and the public outcry that resulted—changed all that. In the final year of the Carter administration, Congress enacted Public Law 96-212, the 1980 Refugee Act. The new law declared anyone eligible for political asylum who had suffered persecution or who had a "well-founded fear of persecution based on race, religion, nationality, membership in a particular social group, or political opinion." It no longer mattered what kind of regime was in power in the refugee's homeland.

Before the law could take effect, Ronald Reagan assumed the presidency and reasserted the fight against Central America's "Communists" as a linchpin of his foreign policy. As part of that policy, Attorney General William French Smith directed in 1981 that all undocumented immigrants applying for political asylum from Central America be held in INS detention centers. Within months, the country's immigration jails filled to overflowing, and the INS hastily erected makeshift detention camps to hold the excess. Still, the Salvadorans and Guatemalans kept coming. Those who managed to get past the Border Patrol opted for the uncertainty of hiding out illegally in this country over the risk of perishing at the hands of death squads or guerrillas back home.[23]

The Salvadoran community of Los Angeles, which numbered a mere thirty thousand in 1979, mushroomed within four years to three hundred thousand, mostly in the neighborhoods of Pico-Union, East L.A., and South Central. Others settled in Adams Morgan in Washington, D.C., and the suburban towns of Long Island, New York, or Maryland. So many Salvadorans settled in a series of apartment complexes in Alexandria, Virginia—all of them from the same hometown of Chirilagua—that the immigrants eventually pooled their resources together, purchased the complex, and changed its name to Chirilandria.[24]

The Guatemalans carved out similar new communities in Los Angeles, northwest Chicago, and Houston, but they differed from the Salvadorans in several respects. For the most part, the Guatemalans were Indian peasants from that nation's underdeveloped highlands, whereas the Salvadorans were largely mestizos from the cities and towns of a country that was far more densely populated and much more cosmopolitan. Many of the Salvadorans even had previous experience as migrant workers in Honduras and thus were quicker to adapt to a new country than the Guatemalans. The Salvadorans who settled in the Washington area went to work in the local hotel and restaurant industry, and, perhaps because of their country's extensive tradition of trade unionism, they soon became mainstays of the city's organized labor movement. A good number of Guatemalans, on the other hand, chose to settle outside the major cities, gravitating instead to the farm belts and small industrial towns of California, Florida, and North Carolina.

By the time the Central Americans arrived, the Latino immigrants of prior years had built stable ethnic enclaves, had perfected their ill

English-speaking abilities, and even boasted an embryonic professional class with a basic grasp of its civil rights. The average Central American, on the other hand, spoke no English, was undocumented, unskilled, and desperate for any kind of work.

Take the Guatemalans of Houston, for example. They were largely highland Maya from El Quiché and Totonicapán who were drawn to that city through kinship ties with earlier pioneers. They settled in the scores of low-rise and low-rent apartment complexes in Gulfton, a working-class neighborhood on Houston's southwest side that had been virtually emptied of whites during the oil bust period, and there they set about re-creating their old kinship-based society and Maya customs. By 1990, two-thirds of Gulfton's forty thousand people were Latino, most of them Guatemalan.[25] Along with the Hondurans, the Guatemalans soon filled the ranks of the maintenance force in the city's downtown office buildings, and a considerable number found work with the Randall's supermarket chain.[26]

Around 1982, Maya fleeing the scorched-earth policies of the Guatemalan military started to arrive in the Florida Everglades, where they gravitated to jobs in the tomato fields. Many settled in Indiantown and Immokalee near Lake Okeechobee, or in the area around Lake Worth on the East Coast, so that by the mid-1990s more than twenty-five thousand Guatemalan Indians were living in South Florida.[27]

Meanwhile, back in the Southwest, a modern version of the Underground Railroad was taking shape inside scores of U.S. churches whose members opposed our government's Central American policy. Church leaders called it the Sanctuary movement, and they date its official beginnings from March 1982, when the Reverend John Fife, minister of the Southside Presbyterian Church in Tucson, wrote a letter to the Justice Department. Fife's congregation, the letter said, had concluded that the federal government was violating the 1980 Refugee Act by jailing and deporting Central American refugees. Church members, Fife said, would begin using their building as a sanctuary for Central Americans. The protest movement spread quickly across the country. Within a few years, more than two hundred other churches had enlisted and were openly defying the government.

Although the Sanctuary movement appeared to be led by American priests and ministers, its inspiration and direction actually came from the refugees themselves, especially those who had been political opposition leaders back home. Carlos Vaquerano, for example, fled to the United States from El Salvador in November 1980, after one of his brothers was killed by a right-wing death squad. Vaquerano had been a university student leader from the town of Apastepeque in the department of San Vicente and sympathized with the left-wing guerrillas of the FMLN (Farabundo Martí National Liberation Front). Once he arrived in Los Angeles, he brought together fellow Salvadorans to educate North Americans about the war in hopes of bringing about a change in U.S. policies.[28] A network of Salvadoran groups, most of them organized in secret, arose in the refugee community. Members of those groups fanned out across the country, speaking to church, university, and labor organizations about the conditions in El Salvador, and it was from those exchanges that the Sanctuary movement arose.

The sanctuaries, in turn, provided the basis for the first publicly known Central American organizations. Casa Maryland, for instance, was founded in 1983 as a sanctuary in the basement of a Presbyterian church in Takoma, Maryland. It soon became the largest Salvadoran community agency in the region. That same year, Salvadoran Aquiles Magaña and other refugees in Los Angeles founded the Central American Refugee Center, popularly known as CARECEN. Staffed by Salvadorans who worked in tandem with progressive white American lawyers, the center offered valuable legal assistance, food pantries, and counseling to fellow immigrants. More CARECENs began to sprout up in Chicago, Washington, D.C., and Long Island.[29]

In 1983, a formal national congress of Sanctuary delegates in Chicago elected the movement's first coordinating body, which was composed of six North Americans, three Salvadorans, and three Guatemalans. The three Guatemalans, in turn, set about organizing their own subnetwork, which they christened La Red Atanasio Tzul (the Atanasio Tzul Network), after the leader of an early nineteenth-century Maya independence revolt against Spain.

Mario González, one of Atanasio Tzul's founders, is a Guatemalan psychologist who fled his homeland in the late 1970s. González was passing through Chicago on his way to study at the University of Berlin when a small circle of Guatemalan refugees living in the city persuaded him to stay and organize the network. Those early refugees, like González, were mostly middle-class urban professionals or skilled workers who at first could find jobs only as laborers in Chicago factories. As more of their countrymen arrived in the 1980s, the

Guatemalan *colonia* in that city began to take shape. At first, fearing deportation back home, most of the early migrants avoided any kind of civic involvement and sought to lose themselves among other Latinos.

"Those who lived in the Puerto Rican neighborhoods started acting and talking like Puerto Ricans, even claiming they were Puerto Rican," González recalls. "And those who lived in the Mexican neighborhoods swore they were Mexican."[30] The only exception to that anonymity was in sports, where the Guatemalans organized dozens of soccer leagues. Other than those soccer leagues, the new *colonia*'s first real organization in Chicago was the Guatemalan Civic Society, which was founded in the late 1970s, but which was confined mostly to the tiny professional sector and thus had only minimal impact on immigrant life.

Guatemalans in Florida likewise got their first impetus to organize from the Atanasio Tzul Network. Gerónimo Campo Seco, a founding member of the network, is a Kanjobal Indian and former schoolteacher who fled northwestern Guatemala in 1980. He was one of the first from his country to be granted political asylum in the United States. Four years later, he moved to South Florida, where hundreds of Maya were already living as farmworkers. There he met Nancy Couch, the director of the Catholic Committee for Justice and Peace in Palm Beach County.[31]

"I was in Indiantown working with the migrants, and Gerónimo came up to me and asked if I could help him with his people," Couch recalled. She started by assisting Campo Seco with asylum applications and soon turned into a tireless advocate for the Guatemalans. Indiantown's three thousand residents included whites, Haitians, American Blacks, and Mexican Americans, but each winter, when the harvest came, the population ballooned by as many as fifteen hundred Maya.

In 1986, Congress succumbed to growing anti-immigrant sentiment by passing the Immigration Reform and Control Act (IRCA). The bill was intended to curb illegal immigration, but it produced unintended consequences. The bill's amnesty provision for longtime illegal residents, for instance, paved the way for Central American pioneers such as González to quickly legalize their status. Once those pioneers had a "green card," some were free to sneak a visit back home to relatives without fear of being unable to return. Most important, they were free to advocate openly for the rights of the new arrivals. After 1986, the Atanasio Tzul Network gradually separated itself from the underground Sanctuary movement and turned into a full-fledged Guatemalan organization.

Despite the efforts of the Reagan and Bush administrations, many Anglo-Americans refused to endorse U.S. policy in Central America. Unflagging advocacy for the region's refugees by a combination of groups—from the Catholic Church and the Sanctuary movement, to civil rights lawyers, to left-wing political organizations like the Committee in Support of the People of El Salvador (CISPES)—finally culminated in two historic breakthroughs toward the end of 1990. That November, Congress yielded to public pressure and granted Salvadorans a suspension of deportation—temporary protected status (TPS)—and subsequently extended it to Guatemalans and Nicaraguans as well.

Then, in December, a U.S. district court judge approved a consent decree in a pivotal class-action suit, *American Baptist Churches v. Thornburgh* (the ABC decision), which struck down as discriminatory the INS policy of deporting Salvadorans and Guatemalans. The decree overturned one hundred thousand cases in which the INS had denied asylum requests, the largest number of federal judicial decisions ever negated by a single court case. Both the ABC decision and the TPS law proved to be stunning victories for human rights. Along with IRCA's amnesty provision, they permitted Central Americans a respite from the limbo of illegality they faced.

FROM UNWANTED REFUGEES TO IMMIGRANT VOTING BLOC

With the threat of immediate deportation removed, immigrant leaders turned their attention to putting down roots in their new society. González, for instance, helped found Casa Guatemala, an uptown Chicago group that sought to solve the day-to-day needs of the new arrivals. By the late 1990s, his full-time job was clinical director at Chicago's Kobler Center for the Treatment of Survivors of Torture, where he and his staff counsel hundreds of Guatemalans who were subjected to rape, beatings, and electroshock during the four-decade civil war.

"The terror in my country created a psychosocial disaster," González told me. "So many were tortured to death that if the army took you into custody and you survived, those in your circle would suspect you as a traitor. Women who were raped were too ashamed

to return to their homes. Families and communities just disintegrated. Even though we live in this country, most Guatemalans still
dare not organize themselves in public."

In South Florida, a similar transition from clandestine to legal
existence took place among the Maya. As their settlement took
root, Campo Seco formed two organizations in the early 1990s:
CORN Maya, an activist group in Indiantown, and the Guatemalan
Center in Lake Worth. The efforts of all the Guatemalan immigrant
leaders received a huge boost in 1992 when fellow Maya Rigoberta
Menchú was awarded the Nobel Peace Prize.[32]

The post-ABC period also saw the stirrings of a civil and labor
rights movement among both Salvadorans and Guatemalans. At
first, that movement took a chaotic and violent form. Three urban
riots erupted in the early 1990s in which Latinos played a significant
role, and two of those involved Central American neighborhoods. In
May 1991, several hundred Latinos rampaged and looted a four-
square block of the Mount Pleasant area of Northwest Washington,
D.C., after a police officer shot a Latino. In the days following the
disturbances, Hispanic leaders complained of racism and insensi-
tivity by the District's police and government officials. Reaction
from the mostly Black political leadership was sharply divided.
"After listening to the Hispanic young people I went home and told
my wife it was like listening to myself 20 years ago," said Councilman John Wilson, a former member of the Student Nonviolent
Coordinating Committee. "If they [Hispanics] don't appreciate
our country, get out," said another Black councilman, H. R. Crawford.[33]

A year later, the acquittal of four cops who had beaten Black mo-
torist Rodney King touched off the Los Angeles riot, and thousands
of Hispanics, most of them Central American, joined in the four
days of arson and looting. Two centers of the rioting, South Central
Los Angeles and Pico-Union, were largely immigrant communities.
There were actually more Latinos among the twelve thousand arrested during the riot than there were African Americans, and police identified the most deadly street gang involved in the rioting as
the Mara Salvatrucha, a Salvadoran group. During the week I spent
covering that riot, I was amazed that the older Mexican American
neighborhoods, like East Los Angeles and Echo Park, experienced
no problems. A middle-aged Mexican American and Vietnam War
veteran, whom I met while he was standing armed guard over the
photo store he owned to protect it from looters, explained to me, "A

community only riots once. When you realize it takes twenty years to recover, you never want to see that again." The other major civil disturbance involving Latinos was the riot mentioned previously that occurred in the Washington Heights section of New York City in July 1992, among another immigrant community—Dominicans.

Those early lawless eruptions by angry youths, however, soon gave way to more orderly demands for justice. In 1990, Ana Sol Gutiérrez became the first Salvadoran-born elected official in U.S. history when she won a seat on the school board of Montgomery County, Maryland. Ironically, Montgomery County is one of the richest counties in the United States, Gutiérrez was not a war refugee, and her victory did not depend on Latino voters. The daughter of a former Salvadoran ambassador to the United States, she came to this country in 1948 at the age of three. Her father, a founder of the World Bank, also worked for the Organization of American States during the Kennedy years. His diplomatic assignments kept the family traveling back and forth between San Salvador and Washington, so that Gutiérrez grew up largely in suburban Chevy Chase and attended American schools, where she graduated with degrees in both chemistry and engineering.

Her election to the school board, she said in an interview, had "more to do with my credentials than being Salvadoran; the voter realized I was totally into math and science." Nonetheless, her victory signaled the beginning of Central American empowerment. As she went door-to-door in suburban Montgomery County soliciting votes, Gutiérrez was astounded to discover that many of those answering her knocks were Salvadorans who had settled in the county almost invisibly after moving there from cramped apartments in Washington, D.C.[34]

The earliest Salvadorans in the nation's capital, Gutiérrez noted, arrived as domestic workers for Latin American diplomats and other Latinos in the federal government. "I've had three housekeepers from El Salvador over the years, all of whom are now citizens and residents in this area," she said. With eruption of the civil war, however, the legal residents brought as many of their relatives into the country as they could. The first types of immigrant organization in the Washington area, as in almost every U.S. city, were soccer leagues—there were more than fifty by the late 1990s. After the soccer teams came a local CARECEN center in the Adams Morgan area.

Once she got elected, Gutiérrez became the most prominent

advocate for Central Americans in the metropolitan area. She founded the Hispanic Alliance, the first Salvadoran group aimed at influencing domestic policy and education issues, a group that initially drew its membership from more middle-class Salvadorans. Gutiérrez soon realized, however, that the community's future would be determined by its far greater number of working-class immigrants.

"There is a real thirst to participate, an eagerness to become citizens among all the immigrants," insisted Gutiérrez, who would go on to win election in 2002 to the Maryland General Assembly, the first Hispanic to do so, where she served until 2019. Those who migrated from her homeland during the early 1980s, who worked hard and managed to become legal residents after IRCA passed in 1986, began moving to the suburbs and buying their own homes ten years later, so that Salvadorans emerged as the largest immigrant group by far in Maryland, composing 13 percent of the state's 911,000 foreign-born residents in 2015, and that's without even counting the growing number of U.S.-born children of Salvadoran descent.[35]

Casa Maryland, for which Gutiérrez served as board president for several years, reflects the Salvadoran community's shifting emphasis to domestic issues. The agency has developed a sophisticated array of services for the Latino community. Among the first of those services was a day laborer program that responded to local concerns that many Salvadorans were congregating on street corners in several county towns while they waited for contractors to hire them for a day's work. White residents saw the clusters of foreigners on their streets as a potential source of crime, and some of the immigrants became targets of racially motivated beatings. Those who did manage to land work were often cheated out of wages by unscrupulous employers but had no place to go to complain. Nowadays, Casa staff organize and supervise specific locations where the employers can hire their help and where the workers can obtain legal counseling. The program proved so successful that the agency plunged into training programs in carpentry, drywall, and asbestos removal to improve the immigrants' skills and earning power. Subsequently, the agency branched out into adult education, English and computer classes; and even initiated a program to challenge housing discrimination.

Perhaps nothing characterizes the Central Americans so much as their dedication to hard work. The labor force participation rate of Salvadorans and Guatemalans is among the highest of any ethnic group, whether immigrant or native-born.[36] And once on the job, even when confined to the lowest-paying work, they have shown a remarkable ability to organize for better conditions. In Los Angeles, for instance, Salvadoran and Guatemalan janitors became the mainstay of the Justice for Janitors Campaign, a union drive that recruited thousands of new members into the Service Employees International Union.

Guatemalan workers at a poultry plant in Morganton, North Carolina, electrified the labor movement in 1996 and 1997 with their militant campaign for union recognition. Officials at the chicken plant, Case Farms, had begun in 1990 to offer Guatemalan migrants from South Florida higher pay and free transportation to Morganton. Five years later, 85 percent of the plant's 450 workers were Guatemalan. Once they arrived, however, the new workers found lower pay rates than promised and working conditions so terrible that they attempted to bring in the Laborers International Union. Despite fierce company opposition, the workers mounted repeated strikes, picketed company plants in other states, and even demonstrated outside the Wall Street offices of the firm's biggest lender, the Bank of New York. Their persistent campaign caught the attention of the new AFL-CIO leaders in Washington, who pointed to the Case Farms battle as symbolic of the increasing influence Central American immigrants are poised to exert on the U.S. labor movement.[37]

Throughout the rest of the country, major manufacturers took to recruiting undocumented Central Americans in the 1990s. They did so by ignoring the employer sanction provisions of IRCA, secure in the knowledge that the federal government was unlikely to monitor their plants or to penalize them too harshly if they were caught. Many of those employers believed the Central Americans would be more docile than native African Americans or earlier groups of Latino immigrants. But those corporate policies, propelled by the constant search for lower wage costs, have brought unexpected consequences to the heartland of America, as white communities that had never known any Latinos suddenly had to cope with a fast-growing Hispanic presence. Even the smallest towns in most states now have a burgeoning Latino population while only a few decades ago residents in those places were either Black or white. In 2017, for instance, Latinos were an estimated 50 percent of the residents of Dalton, Georgia; 62 percent of Lexington, Nebraska; and 61 percent of Dodge City, Kansas. Meanwhile, North Carolina's Latino population grew to 9.1 by 2017; Arkansas's to 7.2; and Tennessee's to 5.2 percent.[38]

The last of the Central American civil wars had come to an end by 1996. But the full extent of U.S. involvement in the human carnage there was not publicly acknowledged until 1999. On February 25 of that year, a stunning report was issued by an international truth commission that had been set up as part of the U.S.-supervised peace accord in Guatemala.

The commission, which spent eighteen months reviewing Guatemalan and U.S. government declassified records, accused the Guatemalan military of "acts of genocide" and "massive extermination of defenseless Mayan communities" during that country's thirty-six-year war. Furthermore, the commission reported, the United States, "through its constituent structures, including the Central Intelligence Agency, lent direct and indirect support" to many of those "illegal state operations."

Some two hundred thousand Guatemalans died during the civil war, the commission estimated. In 90 percent of the twenty-nine thousand deaths it had directly investigated, the commission found that the government and its allies were responsible. One month later, during a visit to several Central American countries, President Clinton publicly apologized to the Guatemalan people for past U.S. support of repressive governments in the region.[39]

But the changes wrought on both the sending and receiving nations by the massive Central American exodus of the 1980s have become irreversible. Today, the Salvadoran populations of Los Angeles and Washington, D.C., are bigger than any place except San Salvador itself. Guatemalans and Hondurans have forever altered the ethnic panorama of Houston, Chicago, and the Florida farm belt, as have the Nicaraguans of Miami. The Central Americans have had enormous influence on the older Latino groups by upending the tribal battles and divisions that once existed between Mexicans, Cubans, and Puerto Ricans. Their arrival, in short, began forcing a gradual amalgamation of the various Hispanic immigrant groups into a broader Latino mosaic, where each ethnic group maintains its separate ethnic identity, but all of them together comprise a new linguistic subset within the complex reality of twenty-first-century American society.

9

COLOMBIANS
AND PANAMANIANS:
Overcoming Division and Disdain

Cartoons in the newspapers depicted the canal being dug by
cheerful white Americans with picks and shovels . . . in truth,
the color line, of which almost nothing was said in print, cut
through every facet of life in the Zone, as clearly drawn and
as closely observed as anywhere in the Deep South or the
most rigid colonial enclaves of Africa.

—DAVID MCCULLOUGH, *The Path Between the Seas*

Colombians and Panamanians seem unusual migrants to consider in the same breath—at least until you delve into their
history.

Panamanians started arriving in the United States during the
1950s, most of them settling in Brooklyn, New York. By 1965, they
numbered between fifteen thousand and thirty thousand, yet they
went virtually unnoticed by the white society. Most were descendants of West Indian canal workers, and they assimilated rapidly
into New York's African American neighborhoods.[1]

Colombian immigration came a little later but proved far more
extensive and durable. More than 72,000 arrived during the 1960s,
another 77,000 the following decade, and 122,000 in the 1980s.[2]
Thousands more came here illegally. Typically, Colombians would
fly into New York or Miami on tourist visas and simply overstay

their allotted time. By 2020, more than 1.2 million Colombians resided in our country, mostly in metropolitan New York and South Florida.[3]

Unlike Cubans and Dominicans, Colombians were not fleeing political persecution, nor were they contract laborers or migrant farmers as were so many Puerto Ricans and Mexicans, and, unlike the Panamanians, most were middle-class professionals, skilled workers, and white.

But what made the Panamanians and Colombians emigrate in the 1960s and 1970s? And why to the United States, not to some other country? What was distinct about their experience from that of other Latinos? Once they arrived here, where did they settle? How did they relate to African Americans, to other Latinos, and to Anglo-Americans? As with these other groups, we begin our search for answers by tracing how U.S. policy affected both Colombia and Panama. The modern history of both nations, after all, began in 1903, when Teddy Roosevelt paved the way for building his transoceanic canal by fomenting the creation of an "independent" Panama, one that was severed from Colombian territory.

The following accounts of some early Colombian and Panamanian migrants, the White and Méndez families, may supply some insights and some answers.

THE WHITE FAMILY, WORKING ON THE CANAL

McKenzie White and his wife, Wilhemina, were both born in the Virgin Islands in the 1880s, but migrated to the Dominican Republic after the turn of the century when White signed on as a contract laborer to cut sugarcane for a U.S.-owned Dominican plantation.[4] While in the Dominican Republic, the young couple, unable to conceive a child, adopted a baby girl whom they named Monica. A decade or so later, they migrated again. This time, McKenzie took his wife and daughter to Panama, where he landed a job with the dredging division of the U.S. canal project that was then nearing completion.

The Panama Canal has long been acknowledged as one of the technical marvels of the twentieth century, a triumph of Yankee vision, audacity, and engineering that enabled a massive expansion of oceanic commerce and helped to unite North American society by sharply reducing the time needed for the transit of people, goods, and information between the Pacific and Atlantic coasts.

But the canal also led to profound fissures in the lives of the Panamanian people. West Indian migrants, as we have noted, provided the bulk of the canal workers and suffered the greatest casualties during its construction. Canal administrators preferred the West Indians because they spoke English and because it was believed they could better withstand the tropical heat. Yet those same West Indians were virtually forgotten when it came to chronicling the almost mythical saga of the canal. As one historian who tried to set the record straight noted, "To judge by the many published accounts, the whole enormous black underside of the caste system simply did not exist. Cartoons in the newspapers depicted the canal being dug by cheerful white Americans with picks and shovels and many came to Panama expecting to see just that" only to learn of "the awful gulf that separates the sacred white American from the rest of the Canal Zone world."[5]

Blacks were the canal's overwhelming labor force, more than three-fourths of the forty-five thousand to fifty thousand employees in the last years of construction. They were so numerous that, according to historian David McCullough,

> [visitors] could not help but be amazed, even astounded, at the degree to which the entire system, not simply the construction, depended on black labor. There were not only thousands of West Indians down amid the turmoil of Culebra Cut or at the lock sites but black waiters in every hotel, black stevedores, teamsters, porters, hospital orderlies, cooks, laundresses, nursemaids, janitors, delivery boys, coachmen, icemen, garbage men, yardmen, mail clerks, police, plumbers, house painters, gravediggers. A black man walking along spraying oil on still water, a metal tank on his back, was one of the most familiar of all sights in the Canal Zone. Whenever a mosquito was seen in a white household, the Sanitary Department was notified and immediately a black man came with chloroform and a glass vial to catch the insect and take it back to a laboratory for analysis.[6]

From the first days of construction, the white American supervisors created a racial apartheid system that dominated canal life for half a century. The centerpieces of that system were separate racially based payrolls, a "gold" category for white American citizens and a "silver" one for the West Indians. All benefits were segregated according to those rolls—housing, commissaries, clubhouses, health care, schools for children of workers.[7]

Black workers were shunted into segregated company towns or into slums in the cities of Colón and Panama City, while whites lived surrounded by tropical opulence in planned communities like Pedro Miguel, Cristóbal, and Gamboa, with everything from housing to health care to vacations subsidized for them by the federal government.

"For black children, our schools stopped at the eighth grade," recalled Monica White Manderson, daughter of Wilhemina and McKenzie White. "We only had black teachers and we didn't get top priority for many things." The separate Black schools kept the West Indians isolated from their new Panamanian homeland, teaching the students only in English and the same subject matter taught in U.S. public schools.[8]

By the time it opened in 1914, however, the canal had turned into a cauldron of labor unrest. West Indians, unhappy over their pay and working conditions, and offended by the racism of the U.S. soldiers and administrators, erupted in several militant strikes, each of which ended with massive evictions of strikers from the Zone. Periodic layoffs forced thousands of others to move into Panama's cities in search of work, and as they did so, their relations with native Panamanians rapidly deteriorated.[9]

"The Panamanians were prejudiced against the West Indians," Monica White recalled. "They were determined to get us out of their country, back where we came from. It was like there were two countries, one was Panama and the other was the Canal Zone." Actually there were three, because the Zone itself contained separate and unequal white and Black worlds.

Panamanians, meanwhile, felt discriminated against in their own country. They resented how canal authorities employed only West Indians on construction and maintenance, jobs that invariably paid higher wages than most others in Panama. In response, a succession of Panamanian governments attempted to ban further West Indian immigration, or at least to prevent the immigrants' children from attaining Panamanian citizenship. After 1928, West Indian children born in Panama had to wait until age twenty-one to be naturalized. Even then, the government required them to pass a test demonstrating their competency in Spanish and in Panamanian history.

The new naturalization law prompted Monica White to move out of the Canal Zone soon after her son, Vicente, was born, so he could be educated in Panamanian schools and get his citizenship. By then, she was separated from Vicente's father, and she opened a beauty salon in Panama City in 1935. A few years later, she married another West Indian, Ernest Manderson.

Not until the early 1940s did Washington lawmakers finally begin to rethink the Canal Zone's Jim Crow segregation system. President Franklin D. Roosevelt issued an executive order in 1941 ending discrimination in the defense industries and he specified the Canal Zone in that order. But canal administrators, most of them white southerners, resisted any change. Fearful that integration of their gold and silver rolls would undermine labor control, they persisted with the "apartheid" system well into the 1950s.[10]

"Even the toilets and water fountains were segregated," recalled Vicente White. "You walked in a building and you saw a sign: gold, silver. Gold toilets were clean and their drinking fountains always had cold water. The silver ones were dirty and the water was always warm."[11]

By the mid-1950s, Monica Manderson and many other West Indians found themselves caught in the middle between the demands of Latin Panamanians for more control over the canal—the country's most vital resource—and recalcitrant Zone officials who were determined to impede integration.

Ironically, it was a key victory by the U.S. Civil Rights Movement that ended up forcing many Black Panamanians to emigrate. In 1954, after the Supreme Court's ruling in *Brown v. Board of Education* outlawed separate but equal public schools throughout the nation, the federal government instructed Canal Zone authorities to integrate their schools as well. To avoid that, the canal's governor changed the language of instruction in the Black schools to Spanish and forcibly relocated many Blacks out of the Zone, thus shifting the onerous of housing and educating their children onto the Panamanian government.[12] A new canal treaty in 1955 made matters even worse for the West Indians—it required them for the first time to pay Panamanian taxes.

After four decades in Panama, Monica Manderson decided she was fed up with the racism from both white Anglo-Americans and Spanish-speaking Panamanians. Like many West Indians, she was proud of her Anglo-Caribbean culture. She wanted to retain her

English tongue and her involvement in the Protestant church and benevolent societies that formed the core of her heritage. But she couldn't do it in Panama. So in 1957 she left for the United States.

THE PANAMANIAN ENCLAVE IN BROOKLYN

Monica Manderson was not alone. From the mid-1950s to the mid-1960s, an estimated thirty thousand West Indians from Panama immigrated to the United States, about three-quarters of them settling in New York City. While not a huge migration compared with the Puerto Ricans and Cubans who came around the same time, it represented, according to prominent West Indian leader George Westerman, the most talented of Panama's Black community.[13]

Until she got settled in the United States, Manderson left her son, Vicente, with his father in Panama. She moved into an apartment on Schenectady Avenue in the Bedford-Stuyvesant section of Brooklyn, which was the first *colonia* for the new immigrants. For the next twenty years, until her retirement in 1974, she worked at a variety of low-paying jobs—laundry worker, school aide, home care attendant—and she devoted herself to the many church and civic groups that sprang up to minister to the needs of the Panamanian enclave. Among those groups was Las Servidoras (the Servants), a women's group that provided college scholarships to needy Panamanian youths.

Initially, the immigrants had trouble fitting into either the Latin American or African American communities, so they founded their own hometown social clubs. One of the first, the Pabsco Club, was located at Schenectady Avenue and Sterling Place. It became the gathering place for expatriates to unwind on weekends, dance to their own *cumbia* and *guaracha* music, and organize group excursions to their homeland.

The Panamanians' mastery of English made their transition easier than that of other Latin Americans. It facilitated their finding better-paying jobs, especially in government civil service, and it eased their assimilation into the city's larger Black community. "Gradually, the white people started moving out of Bedford-Stuyvesant," Manderson recalled, but new tension arose. "The American blacks were always jealous of us West Indians," she said. "We were trying to better our jobs and better ourselves, and they hated that."

Vicente, who followed his mother to New York a few years later, has a different opinion. "Some Jamaicans and Barbadians believe that stuff and begin to feel superior to American blacks," he said. "And some blacks, only a few, fall for that, too. They say, 'Here you come, banana boy, taking our jobs.'"

Vicente's stance reflects the third generation of West Indians. Due to his mother enrolling him in Panama City schools, he grew up not only writing and speaking Spanish but also feeling more a part of Panamanian than of West Indian society. As a boy, he and the neighborhood children would play in a park near the National Assembly in Panama City. Behind the huge building ran a street that divided Panamanian territory from the Canal Zone.

"On the other side of the street stood a row of giant mango trees," White recalled. "We Panamanian kids would cross over to pick mangoes, and each time the Zone police would chase and beat us." Decades later, he still recalled with bitterness the foreigners who forbade him as a boy to pick fruit in his own country.

Ironically, after he finished high school, White ended up a policeman in the Canal Zone.

"I worked in the jails in Gamboa," he said. "When they had no prisoners the white officers would tell the troops, 'Go and bring me some damn Panamanians so we can get some maintenance here.' We would have to go out in the Zone and arrest any Panamanian walking around and charge them with loitering. *Holgazaneando*, that's the term we used. By six in the morning, from an empty jail, you'd have twelve people. I became disgusted with it."

In 1959, the first signs of Panamanian resentment against U.S. control erupted. That year, students rioted after U.S. soldiers stopped them from hoisting the Panamanian flag beside the American flag in the Zone. White, a cop in the Balboa garrison at the time, followed the orders of his North American commanders to chase down and arrest the protesters. The shame that overcame him during the following weeks over what he'd done to his own countrymen sealed his decision to leave Panama.[14]

His father died a few months later. White, who was newly married, migrated to New York with his bride, and moved into his mother's apartment in Brooklyn. Shortly afterward, he enlisted in the air force. In view of his Canal Zone experience, he was assigned to the military police and stationed in Fairbanks, Alaska. That's where he was still stationed in January 1964, when he heard the news that protests had broken out again over Panamanians hoisting their national flag in the Canal Zone. This time, though, U.S. soldiers fired on the young demonstrators, killing twenty-four and wounding hundreds. The killings sparked an uproar in Panama and throughout Latin America.

"I thought right away that the riot was just," White recalled. "There was too much abuse by Americans in the Canal Zone. But being in the service, I kept to myself and said nothing."

In the aftermath of the riot, President Johnson concluded that unless he granted Panamanians a voice in the running of the canal, he would risk another Cuban-style revolution, so he authorized negotiations that culminated in the Carter-Torrijos Treaty of 1977. As a result of that treaty, U.S. troops were gradually withdrawn, Panama regained sovereignty over the Zone, and nearly a century after Roosevelt's machinations, Panamanians regained complete control over the vital waterway.

White resigned from the air force after the 1964 riot and returned to New York. There he took a job as an undercover investigator with the state attorney general, eventually moving on to the Brooklyn district attorney's office, which is where I met him during one of New York's most infamous racial-bias trials. It was called the Yusuf Hawkins case. Hawkins, a Black sixteen-year-old, had wandered into the all-white neighborhood of Bensonhurst, where he was assaulted and killed by a gang of neighborhood whites. I was covering the trial for the *New York Daily News*, and White, who had fled Panama to get away from racism, was an investigator assigned to the prosecution team.

Most white Americans, White reminded me as we talked about his homeland one day in court, have no idea about the racially segregated system our leaders permitted there for so long. As for the antagonism his mother and the older generation of West Indians feel for the Latin Panamanians, White believes they became unwitting dupes of white Canal Zone administrators and the *rabiblancos*, the Panamanian term for the tiny compliant white elite who traditionally ran politics there. "It was the U.S. who tried to paint the Panamanians as antiblack, anti–West Indians, and antiwhite," he said. "I never had a problem with Hispanics," White continued. "Once, I was down in Miami picking up a prisoner and went into a Cuban restaurant with a black partner. At first, they were standoffish, like they didn't want to serve us. But then I started speaking Spanish and right away they changed. The language, it's a bonding thing between Hispanics."

THE MÉNDEZ FAMILY AND COLOMBIA'S CYCLE OF VIOLENCE

Héctor and Pedro Méndez were born in the countryside of Colombia's western department of Tolima, into a typically large peasant family of eighteen children. Their father was Lázaro Méndez, a prosperous mestizo landowner descended from the Piajo tribe of that area. Pedro was born in 1940 and Héctor five years later. At the time, Colombia was relatively prosperous and peaceful, and the mountainous region around Tolima and neighboring Antioquía—of which Medellín is the capital—was a veritable "democracy of small farmers," according to one account.[15]

That tranquility ruptured on April 9, 1948, with the assassination of the charismatic Liberal Party leader Jorge Eliécer Gaitán. The murder so enraged his supporters that mobs ransacked and burned Bogotá in the worst urban riot in Latin American history, leaving 2,000 dead and millions of dollars in property damage. That touched off ten years of brutal civil war between Liberals and Conservatives, a bloodletting so horrific that all Colombians simply refer to it as La Violencia. No one knows how many died. Estimates range from 180,000 to more than 200,000, making it far more devastating, given Colombia's size, than the U.S. Civil War. Death squads, called *pájaros*, roamed the countryside on orders of the landed oligarchy, butchering any farmer suspected of being a Liberal, while guerrilla bands of Liberal Party supporters targeted the biggest landowners.[16] Every family was torn apart by the conflict, but those living in Tolima and Antioquía suffered the brunt of the killing. Lázaro Méndez's relatives were all Liberals, those of his wife Conservatives. Once the conflict erupted, the Méndez children were never again permitted to see their mother's family. "To this day, we've never known what happened to them," Héctor Méndez acknowledged in 1995.

The civil war destroyed agricultural production and emptied the countryside as millions fled to the cities. Ibagué, Bogotá, and Cali, which had been sleepy towns until La Violencia began, turned into sprawling metropolises overnight, brimming with dislocated farmers and landless peasants. The Méndez family fled to Cali in 1953. Lázaro and his wife purchased a plot of land in a mountainous area on the city's outskirts and he embarked on a new career as a moneylender. The family's house was so isolated the children had to walk more than a mile down the mountain to the nearest bus stop to get downtown. Their parents sent Héctor and Pedro to a school run by Salesian priests, and because the priests required all the students to learn a trade, Héctor became a linotypist and Pedro a pressman.

La Violencia ended in 1957 after Liberal and Conservative leaders reached an agreement to alternate power. But the years of bloodshed had uprooted and permanently disfigured much of Colombian society. The sons and daughters of the peasants who had fled the countryside when the fighting began were now urban dwellers and no longer tied to tradition. Many finished their studies during the 1960s only to find there were no jobs. Héctor Méndez was luckier than most. He found work as a linotypist at *El País*, one of Cali's big daily newspapers. The pay was good by Colombian standards—he was earning 4,500 pesos a month when the minimum wage was 350—but it was far inferior to printers' salaries in other parts of the world. Nearly all of Héctor's coworkers at *El País* started leaving for Australia when that country's publishers dangled offers of all-expense-paid travel, free housing, and top pay to any Colombian who would emigrate. Others accepted similar offers from Venezuela.

Violence, meanwhile, emerged as an accepted Colombian way of settling disputes, not just in the countryside where the civil war had raged but in the cities and shantytowns created by the war's refugees. Disaffected youths from those slums became easy recruits for new left-wing guerrilla groups, such as M-19, while the FARC (Armed Forces of the Colombian Revolution) and other revolutionary organizations wrested control of whole rural regions from the government. Several of the new revolutionary groups were started by former Liberal Party members who did not accept the power-sharing truce that ended La Violencia, while others were newly inspired by the Cuban revolution. In its effort to wipe out the guerrillas, the army killed or jailed dissidents of every kind. In 1964, soldiers quashed the independent republic of Marquetalia, one of several peasant secessionist movements in Colombian history. But the repression against left-wing groups left behind thousands of leaderless slum youths whom the guerrillas had trained.

In the late 1970s, when drug lords from Cali and Medellín coalesced into competing cartels that battled each other for control of the world's cocaine market, they recruited thousands of those same youths as their foot soldiers, using them as *mulas* (drug couriers) and *sicarios* (assassins).[17] Medellín, long the nation's industrial center, was mired in crisis-level unemployment at the time so it was easy for the drug lords to recruit with promises of fast money.[18] Meanwhile, in the countryside the Colombian army, unable to stamp out the guerrillas, began a "dirty war" against their supporters. Thousands were abducted, killed, or jailed by both soldiers and right-wing paramilitary groups on the slightest suspicion that they were sympathetic to the guerrillas.[19] The result was a second low-intensity civil war that lasted for more than fifty years and produced a murder rate in Colombia unparalleled in the rest of the world. One Bogotá newspaper reported in 1987 that "43 people were killed on the streets of Bogotá, Cali and Medellín, the three largest cities, assassinated by armed hoodlums who indiscriminately gunned down women, children, beggars, and garbage collectors for fun and target practice."[20] In 1997 alone, 31,000 people were killed in Colombia, approximately equal to the U.S. murder toll that year, although our population is seven times larger.[21]

One by one, the Méndez brothers decided to emigrate. They chose the United States because it seemed more stable and peaceful than the rest of Latin America and because they knew there was already a large number of Hispanics living there. First to leave was their eldest brother, Gregorio, who arrived in 1964 with a legal resident's visa and went to work in the accounting department of a major bank. Pedro Méndez, his wife, Aurora, and his brother Héctor arrived in the early 1970s and quickly secured their legal residency permits.

A COLOMBIAN ENCLAVE
IN QUEENS, NEW YORK

Unlike Puerto Ricans and Dominicans, who found mainly low-paying jobs in restaurants and the garment industry, many of the early Colombians were skilled and middle-class. They commanded excellent salaries from the start and prospered rapidly. Before long, the printing industry and major newspaper linotype shops in many U.S. cities were filled with journeyman printers from Colombia.

Carlos Malagón, a friend of the Méndez brothers, arrived in this country in 1967 at the age of thirty-five. He left behind a thriving hairstyling shop in downtown Bogotá and headed for New York City, he recalls, "on a whim, to seek out adventure."[22] A former Malagón employee who had visited the United States convinced him he could spend three to five years in El Norte, strike it rich, and return home. Malagón went to work for a German barber in Wood-side, Queens. After only eight months, he had enough money to open his own shop. It was situated a block away from the giant Bulova watch company, where hundreds of newly arrived Colombians worked, and before long they all became Malagón's customers. Thirty years later, his Granada Hair Stylist was an immigrant landmark and Malagón a respected elder of the Colombian diaspora.

Those who came illegally faced greater obstacles. The Uribe sisters, for instance—Gloria, Norelia, and Beatrice—grew up in middle-class comfort in Medellín. Their mother, who owned a small garment factory, sent all seven of her daughters to private school but also trained them in needlework so they would have a marketable skill.[23] Norelia emigrated first. In 1970, a Jewish textile owner for whom she worked helped find her a job in New York. The next year, her sister Gloria, pining from the breakup of a marriage, followed.[24] Then Beatrice, who owned a delicatessen in Medellín, visited New York on vacation and decided to stay. All three moved in with another Colombian woman, into a one-bedroom apartment on Queens Boulevard, and from there they landed factory jobs in the industrial parks of Long Island City. By the late 1970s, young Colombian women were being recruited avidly by factory managers in Queens due to their reputation for industriousness. But given that most were in the country illegally and their bosses knew it, the women were often forced to endure low wages and constant sexual harassment by their supervisors.

Their greatest fear was being caught and deported by INS agents. "That was the panic in everyone," Beatrice recalled. "You never went to the movies because of rumors immigration was waiting there. We never took the subways since we heard agents might check your papers—only the buses."

By the late 1970s, smugglers were moving as many as five hundred Colombians a week illegally into the United States by way of Bimini and the Bahamas, charging their clients as much as $6,000 apiece. Typically, the *coyote* would take off from a South Florida airport in a small private plane on a purported domestic flight, then scamper over to one of the Caribbean islands by flying under U.S. radar, where he would pick up the Colombians. Once he was back in Florida, he would land on a deserted road in the Everglades where a van would be waiting to take the clients to Miami or straight to New York City. Many of the smugglers later realized that bringing in kilos of cocaine instead of people was far more lucrative, so they graduated to drug trafficking.[25]

Eventually, as a way to obtain legal residency, each of the Uribe sisters paid for so-called marriages of convenience to strangers who were U.S. citizens. In 1984, for instance, Beatrice married a Puerto Rican she barely knew—the union had been arranged through a professional marriage broker—and she became a U.S. citizen nine years later.

The first attempt at civic organizing by the Colombian pioneers was in the late 1960s, when a small group of professionals who called themselves *Colombianos en el Exterior* (Colombians Abroad) began meeting at the Colombian consulate in Manhattan. Their fledgling effort collapsed in 1971 due to political feuds between those allied with the opposing political parties back home.

The next attempt was *El Comité 20 de Julio* (The 20th of July Committee, the date of Colombian independence), of which barber Carlos Malagón served as secretary-treasurer for several years. That group began the tradition of having hundreds of Colombian children march in New York's annual Día de La Raza Parade. The *Comité* grew to as many as four hundred members and held regular meetings at Club Millonario, a nightclub partly owned by the famous Colombian orchestra leader Arti Bastias, but internal squabbling eventually brought on its demise.

The Méndez brothers, meanwhile, were prospering. They opened their printing shop, the first Colombian-owned business on the Roosevelt Avenue shopping strip in Jackson Heights, in 1980. That same year, the first permanent émigré organization in the United States, the Colombian Civic Center, was founded by expatriate members of the Conservative Party. The immigrants called it Centro Cívico. Despite its politically connected origins, the organization, located in a small building in Jackson Heights, flourished as a nonpartisan gathering place for the whole community. Both Malagón and the Méndez brothers were among its early leaders. In the decade after it was founded, Colombian businesses and restaurants mushroomed all along Roosevelt Avenue.

Meanwhile, back home, the cycle of violence in Colombian society was throwing the country into virtual anarchy. Shooting wars between the drug cartels, between the cartels and the government, between the guerrillas and the cartels, and between the guerrillas and the government led to constant outbreaks of bombings, kidnappings, hijackings, and assassinations, as well as complex and labyrinthine alliances between those responsible. As drug trafficking pumped more than $3 billion a year into Colombia during the 1980s, virtually any figure in the country became susceptible to corruption, including police, prosecutors, generals, and politicians. So large was the influx of drug money that Colombia was the only country in Latin America to maintain positive economic growth during that decade. The boom allowed the country to maintain a first-rate infrastructure of roads, public utilities, and all the accoutrements of a modern consumer society—glistening skyscrapers, sprawling suburban shopping malls, and a glittering nightlife. Hundreds of U.S. firms, especially chemical companies, fueled the boom by setting up operations there despite the escalating violence.

Those Colombians who refused the cartels' bribes were simply terrorized into submission or killed. No one was safe. During the 1980s alone, nearly fifty judges, numerous journalists, and several presidential candidates were assassinated. Violence escalated to the point that in the early 1990s more than two thousand members of the leftist Patriotic Union were killed by right-wing assassins. Most of the right-wing groups were financed by the country's richest landowners with tacit army approval.[26] In August 1989, after Liberal Party leader Luis Carlos Galán was gunned down on orders of drug lord Pablo Escobar, the Colombian government declared all-out war on Escobar's Medellín cartel, the most violent of the two drug mobs. Hundreds of midlevel Medellín traffickers and *sicarios* fled the country and hid in the Colombian communities of New York City and Miami. As they did so, turf wars escalated between the Cali and Medellín networks for control of the wholesale cocaine trade in America's cities. The war led to an explosion of both laundered drug money and bullet-ridden bodies in the Colombian immigrant neighborhoods.[27]

"Jackson Heights became a boomtown overnight," Héctor Méndez recalls. "That's when migrants of low quality began arriving. Many of the businesses that sprang up, you wondered if they weren't from drugs. People like us, who used to be so proud of having studied and worked hard to make it, began to encounter this new type of immigrant, [and we] knew they didn't have the money or education to come themselves. We called them *los nuevos ricos* [the nouveau riche]. They looked at the rest of us like we were garbage."

"You would go to the beauty parlor and all you'd hear about were drugs," recalled another early immigrant.

In the Centro Cívico, Héctor Méndez started classes to provide guidance to new immigrants who wanted to set up businesses. But everywhere the Méndez brothers went they began to notice how suspected drug traffickers were trying to legitimize themselves by infiltrating the few honest organizations, the Centro Cívico, the Liberal Party, the Conservative Party, the Colombian Merchants Association, even local community newspapers.

"Everyone started to lose trust in every one else," Méndez said. "You never knew if the person you were talking to was involved in that business."

In the summer of 1991, Pedro Méndez accused one of the new immigrants who had joined the Centro Cívico, Juan Manuel Ortíz Alvear, of using a false identity in the United States to hide a criminal record back home. At the time, Ortíz was the publisher of *El Universal*, a local Queens Spanish-language newspaper, and he was trying to control the Centro's board of directors. Ortíz had been a controversial fixture in the community since his arrival from Cali in 1985. Many were accustomed to seeing him speeding around the neighborhood in his white Mercedes and spending huge sums of money night after night at a half dozen Queens nightclubs. Usually he was accompanied by a group of armed bodyguards who sometimes abducted and raped women at gunpoint from those clubs, yet they were never arrested. He and his band had the entire neighborhood living in fear.

After Méndez's public accusation, the leaders of the Centro Cívico expelled Ortíz. Enraged by their action, Ortíz, who insisted he was a legitimate businessman, initiated a campaign in his newspaper against the group. Soon, Pedro Méndez began receiving telephoned death threats, and a few months later, on August 6, 1991, as he was returning home one night from his printing shop, Méndez was shot to death. The next day, none of the city's daily English-language newspapers mentioned the murder of one of the Colombian community's most respected businessmen. Queens homicide detectives, overwhelmed by the rash of unsolved killings in Jackson Heights, hardly paid much more attention. The murder remains unsolved.

Seven months later came a second and even bigger murder. On March 11, 1992, Manuel de Dios Unanue, a Cuban-born journalist and former editor of *El Diario–La Prensa*, New York's oldest Spanish-language newspaper, was shot to death by a hooded assassin in a Jackson Heights restaurant. At the time of his death, de Dios had been publishing two muckraking magazines in whose pages he gave considerable space to exposing the inner workings and the hierarchy of the Medellín and Cali networks in this country. Organizational charts; names and photos of traffickers who were posing as legitimate Queens businessmen; narratives of drug conspiracies culled from federal indictments; even gossip about gangsters who were not yet indicted—de Dios published them all in detail, something no mainstream English-language publication had done until then. What police did not know at the time was that a few Colombian pioneers in Queens who were fed up with the growing influence of the drug traffickers in their community had been feeding de Dios information.

The murders of Méndez and de Dios, two such prominent Hispanics, were signals that Colombia's uncontrolled violence was reaching into the United States. A few courageous Colombians, aided by Latino political leaders and journalists from around the city, kept pressure on the Police Department and federal agencies to solve the murders. Several immigrants took enormous risks by joining public marches in the community in memory of de Dios. One of those was the son of Beatrice Uribe, William Acosta, one of the first Colombian-born members of the New York Police Department. Acosta, who had worked in both U.S. military intelligence and with U.S. Customs before becoming a cop, had far better knowledge of what was going on among Colombian drug dealers in New York than most of the veteran Drug Enforcement Administration agents in the city. But like many Latino cops in law enforcement, his information and even his loyalty were often doubted, and his attempts to volunteer in solving the Manuel de Dios and Pedro Méndez murders were repeatedly rebuffed. After nearly ten frustrating years in the NYPD, Acosta resigned in the late 1990s and sued the department for discrimination.[28]

Public pressure and dogged work by several Latino detectives eventually solved the de Dios murder. Six people were convicted in federal court of arranging and carrying out the assassination on orders of José Santa Cruz Londoño, a leader of the Cali cartel who was subsequently killed by Colombian police. And while the Méndez murder was never solved, Ortíz Alvear, the man who had waged a campaign against him, was later convicted of drug trafficking and money laundering for the Cali cartel as well as of the attempted murder of another Colombian immigrant, and was sentenced to long prison terms for each conviction.

The jailing of Ortíz and the solving of the de Dios murder went a long way toward breaking the stranglehold of the cartels over the immigrant Colombian community. Drug trafficking did not end, but attempts by the drug bosses to terrorize and intimidate the hardworking majority were drastically reduced. From that point on, Colombians in this country could breathe a little easier, and the Colombian diaspora ceased being an aberration within the wider Latino immigrant saga.

As for the political violence and civil war back home, it was not until June 2016 that the Colombian government and the FARC, the main guerilla group, finally signed a cease-fire that brought an end to the fighting.

PART III

Harvest

(La Cosecha)

10

THE RETURN OF JUAN SEGUÍN:
Latinos and the Remaking of American Politics

> At every hour of the day and night my countrymen ran to me
> for protection against the assaults or exaction of those adven-
> turers. Sometimes, by persuasion, I prevailed on them to de-
> sist; sometimes, also, force had to be resorted to. How could
> I have done otherwise? Could I leave them defenseless, ex-
> posed to the assaults of foreigners who, on the pretext that
> they were Mexicans, treated them worse than brutes?
>
> —JUAN SEGUÍN[1]

Most Americans recognize the name Davy Crockett, the frontier legend who died defending the Alamo; but Juan Seguín,
who fought with Crockett and survived, is virtually unknown.

Seguín's ancestors settled present-day San Antonio fifty years
before the American Revolution. A rich landowner and federalist
opposed to Mexican president Santa Anna, Seguín was part of the
small group of Mexicans who joined the Texas rebels at the Alamo,
but he was dispatched from the fort with a message to Sam Houston
before the siege began and thus escaped the massacre. Seguín went
on to fight with Houston's army at the Battle of San Jacinto, was
later elected a senator of the Texas Republic, and served several
terms as mayor of San Antonio. Then, in 1842, Anglo newcomers
chased him from office at gunpoint, seized his land, and forced him

to flee to Mexico, making him the last Hispanic mayor of San Antonio until Henry Cisneros took office 140 years later.[2]

Seguín is the forgotten father of Latino politics in the United States. The story of his life and career has left Mexican Americans with a somewhat different political legacy from the one that Washington, Jefferson, and the Founding Fathers bequeathed to white Americans, or that Nat Turner, Sojourner Truth, and W. E. B. Du Bois symbolize for Black Americans. How our nation comes to terms with that legacy will determine much of American politics during the twenty-first century.

The reason is simple. The political influence of Hispanic Americans has grown at breakneck speed. Between 1976 and 2016 the number of Hispanics registered to vote climbed by more than 500 percent—from 2.5 million to 15.2 million—while for the nation as a whole voter registration grew by just 61 percent.[3]

In a mushrooming democratic revolution that is echoing what African Americans accomplished in the 1970s and 1980s, Latinos have been gaining majority control of school boards and rural governments throughout the Southwest, while the South, the Northeast, and the Midwest are experiencing similar upheavals. During the first two decades of the new century, Latino candidates captured a record number of top elected posts around the country, including the governorships of New Mexico and Nevada, and the mayoralties of cities such as Los Angeles, Tucson, and Hartford, Connecticut, though some of those mayors were subsequently succeeded by non-Latinos. But the biggest symbol of progress came in 2009, with the appointment by President Obama of the first Hispanic U.S. Supreme Court justice, Sonia Sotomayor. Then, in 2016, Catherine Cortez Masto (D-NV) and Ted Cruz (R-TX) won election to the U.S. Senate, making a record number of four Hispanics in that body. Two years later, a twenty-nine-year-old unknown and complete novice to politics, Alexandria Ocasio-Cortez, shocked the political world by toppling one of the most powerful Democratic members of Congress, Joseph Crowley, the U.S. representative from Queens, New York. As a self-proclaimed democratic socialist and the youngest woman ever elected to the House of Representatives, Ocasio-Cortez instantly became a leader of the Democratic Party's progressive wing and the most-often quoted of the record thirty-six Latino members of the House in 2019. Given these recent gains, it is entirely likely that over the next decade Latino candidates will win the governorships of California, Florida, and even Texas, additional U.S.

Senate seats in California and Arizona, along with the mayoralties of major cities such as Chicago, New York, and Houston.

This political revolution will not be halted by the rise of anti-Hispanic sentiment among some white and Black Americans, nor by the federal government spending billions of dollars for a wall along the Mexican border, nor by renewed efforts at mass deportation of undocumented immigrants. It will not be turned back by Supreme Court decisions that negated as "racial gerrymandering" a handful of congressional districts redrawn after the 1990 census, and that subsequently struck down provisions of the 1965 Voting Rights Act—a law which had provided federal oversight of any redistricting proposals in Southern states and big cities with a history of abridging the voting rights of racial minorities. The anti-Hispanic backlash—most symbolized by the English-only and anti-immigration movements of the 1980s and 1990s—turned even fiercer after 2016, when Donald Trump captured the White House, pressed to complete construction of a wall along the Mexican border, and targeted undocumented migrants with "zero tolerance" policies like family separation, mass detention, and deportations. But that backlash has only heightened the clamor of Latinos for full political equality.

Several new factors have fueled the spread of this peaceful revolution:

1. *A rush to citizenship.* Legal Hispanic immigrants, fearing threats from federal and local initiatives that targeted all immigrants or denied them social services and other legal protections, moved in record numbers over the past thirty years to acquire full citizenship. Among the most controversial measures that fueled this rush to naturalize were California's Proposition 187 in 1994; the 1996 Immigration and Terrorism Act; the proposed Sensenbrenner bill in 2006; state and municipal laws empowering local law enforcement to arrest the undocumented, such as Arizona's "show me your papers" law that was passed in 2010; and the targeting of Latino migrants for stepped up deportations during both the Obama and Trump administrations.

2. *Demographics.* With a median age far younger than the rest of the U.S. population, Hispanics are rapidly increasing their portion of the U.S. electorate, a trend that will continue throughout the first half of this century regardless of changes in future immigration levels.

3. *The consolidation of a cohesive national Latino lobby.* Historically disparate Hispanic ethnic groups have begun to master the art of building intra-Latino coalitions to affect the policies of Washington lawmakers.

4. *The emergence of a socially oriented Hispanic middle class.* During the 1980s, a significant Latino professional and business class arose that—perhaps with the unique exception of the Cuban American wing—still identifies both its roots and its future with the masses of blue-collar Latinos. Those Latino professionals, marginalized for years by white critics who kept labeling them the inferior products of affirmative action, have now spent decades accumulating wealth and technical skills, and have matured into a burgeoning middle class that is insisting on accountability to the Latino population by both government and other institutions within society.

5. *The rise of the Latino Third Force.* Latino leaders and voters began to function during the last decade of the twentieth century as an unpredictable "swing factor" in the nation's political landscape—refusing to be taken for granted by either the Democratic or Republican parties, or by those who see all politics in the country through the flawed prism of a white-Black racial divide. As anti-immigrant sentiment surged in the early 2000s, however, and as Republicans in Congress kept blocking comprehensive reform of a broken immigration system (see chapter 11), a significant number of Latinos, especially among the youth, gravitated toward mass protests, and toward more progressive and radical political ideas, while an overwhelming majority of the Latino community has remained a bulwark of the Democratic Party base.

6. *Puerto Rico's emergence as a national political issue.* U.S. leaders and the national media have rarely paid much attention to events in Puerto Rico, except for mass protests that erupted in 1999 against the navy's bombing practice on the island of Vieques, which eventually forced the Pentagon to halt such maneuvers. But that traditional neglect started changing in 2015 with the financial collapse of the island's government in what became the biggest local government bankruptcy in U.S. history. The financial meltdown was soon followed by federal imposition of a control board over island affairs, by a spate of austerity measures and privatization of public services on the island, and by endless legal battles between Wall Street banks and

bondholders seeking to recover the money owed to them. Then came horrific devastation in September 2017 from one of the worst hurricanes in Puerto Rico's history, a botched federal relief effort that left nearly three thousand dead in the hurricane's aftermath, and the subsequent flight of some two hundred thousand Puerto Rican climate refugees to the continental United States. Less than two years later, massive protests erupted against the island's corrupt political elite, which culminated in the toppling of Puerto Rico's governor. This series of crises kept Puerto Rico in the national news, forcing leaders in Washington to repeatedly grapple with the undeniable failure of the island's sixty-year-old model of commonwealth government, and it posed the vexing issue: What is to be done with this nation's last major colonial possession? (See chapter 14.)

Seventy years ago, Latino registered voters in the United States could be counted in the thousands; by 2018 they numbered more than 15 million. Seventy years ago, no presidential candidate bothered to worry about issues affecting Hispanics. Today, both major parties bankroll sophisticated efforts to track, court, and influence Latino voters.

This revolution did not happen overnight. It has been building since the end of World War II and has passed through several stages during that time. The way those stages unfolded has been largely ignored by most political observers, given that few systematic studies of Latino politics in the United States have been produced until recent decades.[4]

In this chapter, I identify and analyze each stage of the modern Latino political movement: the people, organizations, ideas, and methods that dominated each stage, and the important lessons each generation carried forward from one stage to another. Hopefully, my effort will prod others to produce more comprehensive studies. While this classification system does not apply uniformly to each Latino group, the parallels among them are far more striking than the differences. I have divided the past seventy years into six major periods:

- The Integration Period: 1950–1964

- The Radical Nationalist Period: 1965–1974

- The Voting Rights Period: 1975–1984

- The Rainbow Period: 1985–1994

- The Third Force Period: 1995–2005
- The Immigrant Rights Period: 2006 to the present

THE INTEGRATION PERIOD: 1950–1964

The most decisive influence on Latino politics this century was
World War II. Thousands of Mexican Americans and Puerto Ricans who served their country in that war—and in the Korean War
a few years later—returned from the battlefield with a new confidence regarding their rights as Americans. These veterans refused
to accept the blatant anti-Hispanic segregation that had been the
rule for generations, especially in the Southwest. In 1949, for instance, when a funeral home in Three Rivers, Texas, refused to
bury war veteran Felix Longoria, civic leaders such as Dr. Hector
García, attorney Gus García, and other veterans founded the American GI Forum, a civil rights and veterans advocacy group that won
a wide following among Mexican Americans.[5] The Longoria incident, much like the controversy over Sergeant José Mendoza, the
Congressional Medal of Honor winner from Brownsville, galvanized Mexican American anger throughout the nation.

The veterans not only threw themselves into organizations like
the Forum and the older League of United Latin American Citizens, but they also turned to politics and began to challenge the historic exclusion of Mexicans from the voting booth. The infamous
Texas poll tax and other measures to restrict ballot access (such as
the all-white primary and annual voter registration months before
an election) had been rammed through the Texas legislature at the
beginning of the century by the Democratic Party's white elite to
counter the growth of the Populist movement among Blacks, Mexicans, and poor whites. At the height of the People's Party in 1896,
for instance, its candidate for governor of Texas carried 44 percent
of the vote, with an amazing 88 percent of voting-age adults going
to the polls. But after the poll tax became law, turnout in Texas elections tumbled by as much as two-thirds, and it failed to reach higher
than 40 percent for the first half of the twentieth century. Poor
whites, Blacks, and Mexicans simply could not afford to pay a tax
that in some cases equaled almost 30 percent of the average weekly
factory wage in the South.[6] The tax remained in effect until 1966,
when a federal judge declared it unconstitutional. Its elimination

made it possible for Blacks and Mexican Americans to finally return to the voting rolls in large numbers.

Before World War II, only New Mexico could claim any tradition of Mexican Americans holding federal elected office. Benigno Hernández, for instance, represented the state in the U.S. House of Representatives from 1915 to 1917, while Dennis Chávez served in the U.S. Senate from 1935 to 1962. But few Hispanics held public office anywhere else in the country. Puerto Rican Oscar García Rivera, the only example in New York, was elected to the state assembly in 1937. After the war, the giant barrios of Los Angeles and San Antonio emerged as the centers of Hispanic political power. In San Antonio, Henry B. González, a war veteran and former juvenile probation officer, began organizing the *tejanos* of the West Side through his Pan American Progressive Association, while in Los Angeles, social worker Edward Roybal, another war veteran, rallied *mexicanos* to register and vote. They were the first Latino councilmen in their respective cities since the mid-nineteenth century—Roybal in 1949 and González in 1953.[7]

John F. Kennedy's nomination as the Democratic Party's presidential candidate in 1960 was the watershed moment of the Integration Period. Until then, Mexican Americans had backed liberal candidates in state elections but had made no visible impact on a national election. In Texas, for instance, Mexicans were loyal backers of populist Democratic senators Ralph Yarborough and Lyndon B. Johnson. But the campaign of Kennedy, a charismatic, liberal Catholic, gave Roybal, González, and the other World War II veterans the opportunity to show the growing clout of Latinos. They formed Viva Kennedy clubs throughout the Southwest to back the young Massachusetts senator against Vice President Richard Nixon.

In a close election, Kennedy swept 91 percent of the 200,000 Mexican votes in Texas, which helped him carry the state. And while he managed only a minority of the white vote in neighboring New Mexico, he garnered 70 percent of the Mexican vote, enough for a razor-thin margin there. Nationwide, he amassed 85 percent of the Mexican vote. Kennedy, in turn, threw his support to González in his victorious run for Congress in a special election the following year; and he provided similar support to Roybal in 1962, enabling him to win a congressional seat from a district that was only 9 percent *mexicano*. Then, in the Democratic landslide that propelled Lyndon Johnson to victory over Barry Goldwater in 1964, Eligio "Kika" de la Garza won a second Texas congressional seat and

Joseph Montoya, the congressman from New Mexico, secured a U.S. Senate seat.

That handful of victories during the early 1960s opened the gates for the modern Hispanic political movement. For decades afterward, it was common to find Mexican homes in the Southwest where a faded photo of John Kennedy was displayed prominently near one of the Virgin of Guadalupe—a testament to Kennedy's role as the first U.S. president to address the concerns of Latinos. At the time De la Garza was elected, however, *tejanos* held only 31 of 3,300 elected positions in the state and only 5 of 11,800 appointed posts. By 1994, just three decades later, the number of Texas Hispanic officeholders had skyrocketed to 2,215, and it grew to 2,753 by 2018.[8]

Those early political gains, however, were largely confined to Mexican Americans. Although nearly a million Puerto Ricans had settled in the United States by the late 1950s, they were concentrated in New York City and more concerned with political events on the island than with those on the mainland. In August 1936, for instance, more than ten thousand people joined a march for Puerto Rican independence organized by radical East Harlem congressman Vito Marcantonio, and throughout the 1950s the debate over the status of Puerto Rico dominated the barrios of New York.[9]

After Marcantonio's ouster, the few Puerto Ricans who won elective office in that city were all handpicked by the Tammany Hall machine. None had the pioneering zeal exhibited by Mexican Americans González and Roybal at the other end of the country. Among those machine candidates were Felipe Torres, who snared a Bronx state assembly seat in 1954, and J. López Ramos, who went to the assembly from East Harlem in 1958.[10] The first citywide Puerto Rican civic associations, the Puerto Rican Forum, the Puerto Rican Family Institute, and the Puerto Rican Association for Community Affairs, were founded around that time. The machine's grip on Puerto Rican voters was not challenged until 1965, when Herman Badillo won the borough presidency of the Bronx as a candidate of the Democratic Party's reform wing, thus becoming the first Puerto Rican to hold a major municipal post. Badillo's victory, however, depended largely on liberal Jewish and Black voters instead of Puerto Ricans, who remained a tiny electoral force.

During the 1960s, the Johnson administration, under pressure from a rising civil rights movement, pushed a series of landmark bills through Congress. Those laws, the Civil Rights Act of 1964, the

Voting Rights Act of 1965, and the Fair Housing Act of 1968, toppled the legal underpinnings of discrimination against both Blacks
and Hispanics. Some conservatives challenged the inclusion of Hispanics under those laws, claiming that "Hispanics had never been
subject to the same denial of their basic right to vote that blacks had
suffered."[11] Such assertions somehow disregarded the genuine obstacles to political representation Mexicans faced as a result of the
caste system in place since the days of Juan Seguín.

In 1954, two weeks before its *Brown v. Board of Education* decision, the Supreme Court decided a seminal case affecting Mexican
Americans. In *Peter Hernandez v. Texas*, the court ruled that Mexicans were "a distinct class" who could claim protection from discrimination. The court found that of six thousand jurors called in
the previous twenty-five years in Jackson County, Texas, none had
been Mexican, even though Mexicans composed 14 percent of the
county's population. To attribute that to "mere chance," wrote Chief
Justice Earl Warren for the court's majority, "taxes our credulity."
Instead, the court found ample proof that the political system of the
county discriminated against Mexicans as a class distinct from either whites or Blacks.

A restaurant in town, Warren noted, had signs saying: NO MEX-
ICANS SERVED; toilets in the local courthouse were segregated,
with one men's door marked COLORED MEN and HOMBRES AQUI
(MEN HERE); and "until very recent times, children of Mexican descent were required to attend a segregated school for the first four
grades."

The court thus reversed the murder conviction of plaintiff Peter
Hernandez because of the systematic exclusion of Mexicans from
juries in the county. In doing so, the court's majority noted that "the
Fourteenth Amendment is not directed solely against discrimination due to a 'two-class theory'—that is, based upon differences between 'white' and Negro."[12] Three years later, in *Hernandez et al.
v. Driscol Consolidated Independent School System*, a federal district
court outlawed segregated schools for Mexicans, which the court
said had been a fact of life in Texas since the Anglo settlers first arrived.[13]

While new laws and federal court decisions during the Kennedy-
Johnson era spurred Latino political involvement by eliminating
legal discrimination, they did little to alter the economic and social
inequities that had accumulated from both the Mexican caste system
and Jim Crow segregation. Meanwhile, the pervasive new influence

of television—whether in transmitting stories of dilapidated Harlem tenements or the shacks of migrant workers, Bull Connor's dogs or the Watts riot—suddenly made social inequity more glaring. The 1965 Watts uprising signaled the end of the incremental Integration Period. Along with everyone else in America, Hispanics entered a new psychological and political era—one of rebellion and social polarization.

THE RADICAL NATIONALIST PERIOD: 1965–1974

Watts sparked the greatest period of civil unrest in the United States during the twentieth century. For several years, riots became an annual reality in urban America, and as they did, many white Americans began to regard protests by Blacks and Hispanics as a threat to the nation's stability. At the same time, African American and Latino youth concluded that their parents' attempt at integration within the political system had failed. Only through massive protests, disruptive boycotts, and strikes or even riots, the new generation decided, could qualitative (some called it revolutionary) change be accomplished.

Within a few years, a whole gamut of new organizations arose to compete with the more established groups such as LULAC, the GI Forum, and the Puerto Rican Forum. The brash new groups—the Brown Berets, La Raza Unida, La Alianza, the United Farm Workers, the Young Lords, El Comité, Los Siete de La Raza, the Crusade for Justice, CASA (Centro de Acción Social Autonomo), Movimiento Pro Independencia (later renamed the Puerto Rican Socialist Party), MECHA, the August Twenty-ninth Movement—were invariably more radical, their membership younger and usually from lower-class origins, than the established civic organizations. They saw the older organizations as too tied to the status quo, too concerned with appearing to be respectable and reasonable to Anglo society.

The radical groups sprang up almost overnight in every urban barrio and Southwest farm community, rarely with much organizational connection. Inspired by the Black power and anti–Vietnam War movement at home and by the anticolonial revolutions in the Third World, especially the Cuban revolution, most offered a utopian, vaguely socialist vision of changing America, and all of them called for a reinterpretation of the Latino's place in history, for a new narrative about the evolution of the Latino community. They insisted that both Puerto Ricans and Mexicans were descendants of conquered peoples who had been forcibly subjugated when the United States annexed their territories during its expansion. Due to those annexations, the rebels insisted, Puerto Ricans and Mexicans were more comparable to the Native Americans and the African Americans than to Scotch, German, Irish, or Italian immigrants.

This was also the period when the Latino community itself became more ethnically diverse. Dominican and Cuban refugees arrived in massive numbers in New York and Florida in the late 1960s, followed by Colombians, Salvadorans, Guatemalans, and Nicaraguans in succeeding decades. Meanwhile, Puerto Ricans and Mexican immigrants—both those who were here legally and those who were undocumented—spread beyond their original enclaves in the Northeast and the Southwest.

The Mexican Americans and Puerto Ricans tended to form nationalist groups with left-wing outlooks, while the Cubans typically maintained anti-Communist stances aimed at ousting Fidel Castro from power in their homeland. For the latter group, the failed Bay of Pigs invasion in 1961 became a defining event. Many blamed lack of support from the Kennedy administration for its failure. That resentment resulted in Cuban leaders allying themselves with the Republican Party.

For the next two decades, the overriding goal of Cuban immigrants was returning to a homeland free from Castro and Communism. That obsession gave them more the character of an exile group than of a traditional immigrant community.[14] The organizations they formed reflected that preoccupation. They had names like Omega 7, Alpha 66, Comando Zero, Acción Cubana, and at one time they even formed a grand coalition called the Bloque Revolucionario. Their threats, bombings, and assassinations of those within the exile community whom they considered traitors, or those in the broader society whom they perceived as agents of Communism, had enormous impact in forcing near unanimity in the right-wing outlook of the exile community.[15]

It did not take long for Cubans to make their presence felt in local politics. Thanks to Public Law 89-732, which Congress passed in 1966, Cubans found it easier to secure U.S. visas and did not have to wait the normal five years for citizenship. An instant surge of Cuban naturalizations followed, and with it an explosion of Cuban voting power.[16] By the early 1970s—only a decade after their immigration started—Cuban Americans had won their first seats on the Miami Board of Education, the city governments of Miami and Hialeah, and the Dade County judicial system. By contrast, Dominicans took until 1991—twenty-five years after their mass migration to the United States began—to elect their first city council members, Guillermo Linares in New York City and Kay Palacios in Englewood Cliffs, New Jersey, and it was not until 1996 that the first Colombian American was elected to office, Juan Carlos Zapata, who landed a seat in the Community Council of West Kendall, Florida.[17]

The Hispanic population was growing rapidly, but by the mid-1970s only Mexican Americans in the Southwest, Puerto Ricans in New York, and the Cubans of South Florida boasted a sufficient number of voters to draw the attention of Anglo politicians. Because the three groups were concentrated in separate regions of the country, a tense competition arose between their leaders when it came to influencing national policy, with each group's spokesmen fearing that their specific interests or power would be sacrificed under the broader banners of Hispanic or Latino.

As the civil rights and anti–Vietnam War movements deepened, however, divisions took root among the Latino radicals as well. The Young Lords, Los Siete de La Raza, the August Twenty-ninth, and the Brown Berets refused to participate in the traditional electoral process and sought alliances instead with revolutionary groups outside the Latino community, such as the Black Panther Party, Students for a Democratic Society, and other New Left organizations.

Eventually, those coalitions splintered and evolved into scores of fringe Marxist factions, and in the case of Puerto Ricans, those splinters included several clandestine urban groups that resorted to terrorist bombings, such as the FALN (Fuerzas Armadas de Liberación Nacional) and Los Macheteros. In the Cuban community, the most extreme anti-Castro activists began working jointly with other non-Cuban anti-Communist movements in the United States and Latin America, often with CIA sponsorship.[18] These radical factions, whether from the left or from the right, became increasingly divorced not only from one another but from the everyday reality that Latinos were facing. All failed to understand that despite the inequality and stubborn racism Latinos faced in the United States, conditions here, even for the most destitute, were substantially better than in the Latin American nations from which they'd emigrated, a reality that to this day has relegated revolutionary Marxist movements in this country to tiny followings.

A second trend was represented by Rodolfo "Corky" Gonzáles's Crusade for Justice in Colorado, by Reies Tijerina's Alianza de los Pueblos, and by La Raza Unida Party in Colorado and Texas. While their rhetoric mirrored the militant nationalism of the Marxists, these groups opted for working within the American electoral system. But they rejected the Democratic and Republican parties as bankrupt and sought instead to build independent Chicano organizations that would try to win elected office in what the movement called Aztlán, the original Aztec homeland that encompassed the old territory ceded by the Treaty of Guadalupe Hidalgo. As we have seen, the party they formed, La Raza Unida, made some impressive showings in small towns in South Texas, but it proved unable to spark widespread Mexican American desertions from the Democratic Party.

A third trend was represented by Cesar Chavez's United Farm Workers Organizing Committee, by the National Council of La Raza (NCLR), and by Puerto Rican civic leaders like Gilberto Gerena Valentín. Members of that trend concentrated on winning the basic rights that *mexicanos* and Puerto Ricans had as American citizens—the right to unionize, the right to vote, the right to basic government services like schools, public housing, sewers, and drinking water. Chavez, the foremost representative of that trend, eventually became the most admired Hispanic leader in the country.

Out of NCLR's work emerged two pivotal organizations, the Mexican American Legal Defense and Education Fund (MALDEF), formed in 1967 by Pete Tijerina and Gregory Luna, and the Southwest Voter Registration Education Project (SVREP), whose founder was San Antonio's Willie Velasquez. While NCLR became the main lobbying group for Hispanic issues in Washington, MALDEF and SVREP concentrated in the Southwest, where they provided Mexican Americans at the grassroots level the legal and organizational tools to enter the third period of Hispanic political development.

Meanwhile, Puerto Ricans in several Northeast cities were founding similar new civil rights groups. Gilberto Gerena Valentín, the longtime labor leader, united the various island hometown social clubs into a loose federation that pressured city government for better services; educator Antonia Pantoja founded ASPIRA, an educational organization to train a new generation of leaders; John Olivero,

César Perales, and Luis Alvarez founded the Puerto Rican Legal
Defense and Education Fund. Where *puertorriqueños* lagged behind
mexicanos was in failing to involve themselves significantly in electoral politics, the major exception being Herman Badillo, who in
1969 became the first Puerto Rican elected to Congress.

THE VOTING RIGHTS PERIOD: 1975–1984

After 1975, Latino involvement with revolutionary organizations
and nationalistic independent politics waned. Most leaders returned
to integrationist and reformist goals, a stage I have labeled the Voting
Rights Period. Once again, the movement reverted to political equality as a primary goal, only now it was infused with the cultural and
ethnic pride awakened by 1960s radicalism. Admittedly, the militancy was more muted, for America as a whole had changed. The
reforms the federal government conceded to the civil rights, feminist, and peace movements during the Vietnam War era had in turn
spawned a New Right backlash. That backlash began in 1964 with
Barry Goldwater, gathered force with George Wallace's presidential
campaign in 1968, and spread with the aid of Protestant fundamen-
talist sects into a nationwide conservative populist movement.

Meanwhile, on the economic front, U.S. companies in search of
cheap labor began relocating industrial jobs to the Global South.
White workers, frustrated at rising unemployment and a declining
standard of living, sought someone to blame, and African Americans and Hispanics became convenient scapegoats. The issues minority community leaders were raising—equal housing opportunity,
school busing for desegregation, affirmative action, equal political
representation, bilingual education—were all blamed for subverting
established values and principles of fairness in American society.
The nation entered a conservative period wherein millions of whites
called for restoring American traditions, yet few stopped to consider
how some of those traditions had been based on the subjugation and
exclusion of others.

In this new climate, the second generation of postwar Latino
leaders jettisoned any thought of overthrowing political power and
sought instead a proportional share of it. But theirs was not simply a
replay of the earlier Integration Period, for each generation, consciously or not, absorbs lessons from its predecessors. Several new
factors distinguished the Voting Rights Period: first, Latino leaders

filed an unprecedented number of federal civil rights lawsuits; second, they formed the first durable national coalitions across ethnic and racial lines; third, they expanded their movement beyond just middle-class professionals into poor Latino communities by combining 1960s-style mass protests with voter registration and election campaigns.

On the legal front, the Southwest Voter Registration Education Project, the Mexican American Legal Defense and Education Fund, and, some years later, the Midwest Voter Registration Education Project filed and won numerous voting rights suits against at-large election systems that prevailed in many municipalities. Those systems had effectively shut out Mexican Americans from office for decades. In as much as Latinos were historically segregated into barrios, they could best increase representation by electing candidates from compact geographic districts, not at-large ones.

Those court victories, together with massive voter registration drives pioneered by SVREP in Mexican American towns and counties of South Texas, produced a virtual revolution in that state's politics, one best symbolized by the 1982 election of Henry Cisneros as mayor of San Antonio.[19]

At the other end of the country, Puerto Ricans renewed their own efforts at building civil rights or advocacy groups. By then, their *colonias* had spread to many Rust Belt cities and farming counties. New groups arose that devoted considerably more attention to voter registration and lobbying than previous ones had. Among that new generation of organizations were the National Puerto Rican Coalition (formed by Luis Alvarez, Louis Núñez, and Amalia Betanzos in 1973 with seed money from the Ford Foundation), the Coalition in Defense of Puerto Rican and Hispanic Rights (founded in New York City in the late 1970s by lawyer Ramón Jiménez, Manuel Ortíz, and others), the National Congress for Puerto Rican Rights (founded in 1981 by scores of former Young Lords and other 1960s radicals, including me), and the Institute for Puerto Rican Policy (a research and public policy think tank founded by political scientist Angelo Falcón).

The new groups worked closely with the Puerto Rican Legal Defense and Education Fund on several voting rights suits. As a result, in both New York and Chicago, federal judges ruled in the early 1980s that apportionment of municipal districts had discriminated against Hispanics and African Americans. In Chicago, that led to the creation of seven new aldermanic districts—three with majority

Black populations and four majority Hispanic. A special election in
1984 resulted in the number of Hispanic aldermen increasing from
one to four: Miguel Santiago (the only incumbent), Jesús García,
Juan Soliz, and Luis Gutiérrez. The Gutiérrez victory rocked the
city because it gave a one-vote majority in the city council to Chicago's new Black mayor, Harold Washington, and thus symbolized
the potential of a developing African American and Hispanic alliance.[20]

In New York, the Puerto Rican Legal Defense and Education
Fund (PRLDEF) was able to halt the 1981 municipal elections and
get the federal courts to eliminate at-large council seats.[21] The redrawn council districts opened the way for increases in Puerto
Rican representation on the council. In so far as New York has always been the trendsetter for Puerto Ricans, the battle sparked a
new awareness of voting rights throughout the East Coast. As a result of both this new activism and other voting rights court victories,
by the mid-1980s New York had a new, more independent group of
Puerto Rican officials, such as city councilman José Rivera and state
assemblymen José Serrano and Israel Ruiz. Similar victories occurred in other eastern and midwestern cities.[22] Usually, the victories resulted from alliances the Hispanic candidates struck with a
strong African American electoral campaign. Such was the case
with Gutiérrez in Chicago, with Angel Ortiz in Philadelphia, who
won an at-large city council seat as part of Wilson Goode's victorious 1983 mayoral campaign, and with Nelson Merced, the first Hispanic elected to the Massachusetts House of Representatives—from
a predominantly Black Boston district.

The climax of the Voting Rights Period came in 1983, with the
stunning mayoral victories of Harold Washington in Chicago and
Wilson Goode in Philadelphia. Suddenly, the nation awoke to a new
reality. Power in the Democratic Party's urban areas had slipped
from organizations of white politicians and their ethnic constituen-
cies to coalitions of African Americans and Hispanics. In both Chicago and Philadelphia, Hispanic voters, who until then had been
ignored by political candidates, demonstrated a newfound ability to
tip an election by registering and voting in unprecedented numbers.
Washington, who had received only 25 percent of the Hispanic vote
in a hard-fought Democratic primary, went on to accumulate 74
percent of that vote in the general election against conservative Republican Bernard Epton.[23]

Likewise, in Philadelphia, Goode eked out a victory in a close

Democratic primary against former mayor Frank Rizzo, thanks to a Black-Hispanic liberal alliance; then he routed a weak Republican opponent. In both cases, Hispanic voters, mostly Puerto Rican, opted for Goode by more than two to one.

In South Florida, meanwhile, Cuban exile leaders, who at first had limited their political goals almost exclusively to ousting Castro and returning to Cuba, began a drastic change in the mid-1970s, one that was sharply influenced by the new generation of Cubans who had been born or raised in this country. Between 1973 and 1979, according to one study, those who said they planned to return to Cuba if Castro should be overthrown dropped from 60 to 22 percent.[24] This shifting attitude by Cuban émigrés was reflected in politics. By 1974, some two hundred thousand Cubans in South Florida had become citizens, and many were voting regularly. After several unsuccessful attempts, the first two Cubans were elected to office in 1973—Manolo Reboso to the Miami City Commission and Alfredo Durán to the Dade County School Board.[25] Not surprisingly, both were Bay of Pigs veterans. Then, in late 1975, Cuban professionals, aided by Hispanic media personalities, established a citizenship campaign. The following year more than twenty-six thousand exiles were naturalized. By 1980, more than 55 percent of the exiles had become citizens, double the percentage in 1970.[26]

They quickly made their presence felt, though at first it was largely in symbolic ways. On April 15, 1973, the Metro Dade County Commission, which had no Hispanics among its nine members, bowed to Cuban pressure and declared the county "officially bilingual." But that symbolism quickly turned real. In 1978, Jorge Valdés became the country's first Cuban American mayor, in Sweetwater, followed by Raul Martínez in Hialeah.[27]

This growth of Cuban voting power, together with the new wave of immigrants brought by the Mariel exodus, soon touched off a backlash among whites in Dade County, who struck back with a 1980 referendum to nullify their commission's earlier bilingual declaration. They introduced a referendum to prohibit "the expenditure of county funds for the purpose of utilizing any language other than English, or promoting any culture other than that of the United States." It passed handily, with the vote polarized almost exclusively along ethnic lines—71 percent of non-Hispanic whites voted for it and 85 percent of Latinos voted against.[28] While they found growing resistance from whites on their domestic agenda, Cuban politicians had great success in pushing their anti-Communist initiatives. The

Miami City Commission passed twenty-eight resolutions or ordi-
nances against Communism in Latin America during one sixteen-
month period before May 1983.[29]

The anti-Cuban backlash, however, prompted some soul-searching
by first- and second-generation immigrant leaders, who decided
to counter the negative image of their community in the English-
speaking press. In 1980, civic leaders founded both the Spanish
American League Against Discrimination (SALAD) and the Cuban
American National Foundation (CANF); and two years later they
started Facts About Cuban Exiles (FACE).[30]

Ronald Reagan's election as president in 1980 signaled a new era
for Cuban Americans. With a friend like Reagan in the White
House, powerful Miami groups like CANF and the Latin American
Builders Association perfected a well-funded behind-the-scenes
lobby in Washington for their special projects—Radio Martí, TV
Martí, and aid to the Nicaraguan Contras. At the same time, they
adopted a new pragmatism in public, focusing less on controversial
issues like bilingual education.[31]

Cuban voters diverged from Puerto Ricans and Mexican Americans in another crucial way—their posture toward the Black community. While *mexicanos*, and especially Puerto Ricans, managed to
build tenuous alliances with Blacks in several major cities, Cuban
Americans and African Americans in Dade County turned into bitter enemies, especially as the much older Black community of
Miami watched the newer Cuban immigrants catapult over them
economically. During the early 1970s, a Puerto Rican, Mauricio
Ferré, the blond, blue-eyed scion of one of the island's richest families, had won the Miami mayoralty by building an alliance of the
Black and liberal Jewish community to stave off the burgeoning
conservative Cuban political movement.

Sporadic riots erupted in Miami's Black communities during the
1970s and 1980s, and allegations by Black residents of mistreatment
by Cubans were usually raised as underlying factors. By the mid-
1980s, Cuban immigrants had turned South Florida into the center
of Hispanic conservative power throughout the country. Nothing
reflected that more than the election of the first Cuban American to
Congress in 1989. Ileana Ros-Lehtinen, a conservative Republican,
narrowly won the race despite her Democratic opponent's getting
88 percent of the Anglo vote and 94 percent of the Black vote. Ros-
Lehtinen's margin of victory was made possible by a Latino turnout
of nearly 60 percent.[32]

THE RAINBOW PERIOD: 1985–1994

When Jesse Jackson began his first campaign for the Democratic nomination for president in 1984 by calling for a new "Rainbow Coalition," Washington experts dubbed his effort a meaningless protest. He promptly shocked all the experts by winning the majority of African American votes and a substantial minority of Latino and white votes. Jackson, who had witnessed the power of a Black–Latino liberal white coalition in both Chicago and Philadelphia, was determined to replicate it at the national level. Four years later, he harnessed widespread support from Black and Latino politicians who had not supported him in 1984, and garnered 7 million votes against the eventual Democratic presidential candidate, Michael Dukakis. In places like New York and Connecticut, Jackson won the majority of Latino votes, while in California, Texas, and elsewhere in the Southwest, he improved his showing but remained below 50 percent.[33]

The 1984 and 1988 Jackson campaigns brought millions of first-time voters to the polls in the South and the northern ghettos, and those same voters sent Blacks and Hispanics to Congress in record numbers. In some states, Blacks showed higher election turnouts than white voters for the first time, and candidates who identified themselves as part of Jackson's Rainbow Coalition won isolated local elections. In Hartford, Connecticut, for instance, a Rainbow alliance gained control of the city council in the late 1980s and elected that city's first Black mayor.

Then in 1989 came the most electrifying of local victories for the Rainbow movement. David Dinkins won the mayoralty of New York City—the first African American to hold the post—and he did so by capturing 88 percent of the Black vote, 64 percent of the Hispanic vote, and nearly 35 percent of the white vote.[34] But even as African Americans and Hispanics gained greater influence within the Democratic Party, white middle-class and suburban voters kept deserting the party.

The Rainbow's revolutionary potential came from its appeal to those sectors of the nation's voting-age population that had remained alienated and disenfranchised throughout most of the twentieth century—African Americans, Hispanics, the young, and the poor. Our country has had for decades one of the lowest voter turnout rates of any industrial democracy, assuring that those elected to office, from either the Democratic or Republican Party, represent only a

minority of voting-age adults. In 1972, for instance, 77 percent of
middle-class property owners voted compared with 52 percent
of working-class Americans. And well-educated Americans usually
vote at twice the rate of less educated citizens.[35] Jackson's Rainbow
movement, by contrast, placed prime importance not only on registering new voters but on removing legal obstacles in many states to
simple and universal voter registration. But in both the 1988 and
1992 elections, Democratic presidential candidates chose to continue competing with the Republicans for the same small number of
already registered voters who had fled the Democrats—the so-called
Reagan Democrats—in the hope of getting them to "swing" back.
They dismissed Jackson's strategy of recruiting millions of new voters from the lower classes onto the rolls to fashion the basis of a new
political majority.

After that initial breakthrough of the late 1980s, however, the
Rainbow Coalition stalled due to its own internal divisions. Jackson
and many of the veteran Black officeholders around him started
treating the white, Hispanic, and Asian members of the Coalition as
permanent junior partners who could be mobilized as allies but who
would not be permitted autonomy or opportunity to shape organizational strategy and policy. At the same time, a few Black and Hispanic leaders started promoting ethnic competition for jobs and
elected posts in a variety of cities. "The Blacks want everything for
themselves," was a common phrase of some Hispanic leaders, and
"Latinos just want to ride to power on our coattails" was a refrain of
many of their Black counterparts.

While the Rainbow leaders argued, their followers clashed over
government contracts and patronage jobs. The steady rise in the
number of Hispanics elected to office, for instance, was not reflected
by a rise in the number appointed to jobs in local governments, as
had happened with the Irish, Italian, and African American urban
political coalitions of the past. After the urban rebellions of the
1960s, federal and municipal government employment had turned
into a prime vehicle for many African Americans to rise into the
middle class. But Hispanics, perhaps in part because of the language
barrier some had to overcome, did not witness similar progress. The
few who did land government jobs invariably perceived Blacks who
were in supervisory positions over them as reluctant to aid their
progress.

Differences in attitude toward race also tore at the Coalition. Jackson portrayed the Rainbow as a "common ground" for all Americans

seeking economic justice; he urged an inclusive approach toward all minorities. Many African Americans, however, believe Latinos aspire to be considered white, while many Hispanics regard Blacks as obsessed with race; and a good number even harbor anti-Black bias themselves. In reality, Latinos simply regard race relations from a historically different perspective. Rather than experiencing a stark white-Black dichotomy in the country, many Latinos see national origin or ethnicity as shaping their lives. This dynamic is mirrored by the physical locations of many Latino communities in U.S. cities; often, they have emerged as buffer areas between Black and white neighborhoods. Rather than airing these differences and resolving them through debate and education, the Rainbow swept them under the rug, thus undermining its own unity.

The sudden death of Chicago mayor Harold Washington in 1987 was the first signal that keeping the Rainbow Coalition together would be even harder than constructing it. Within a few years, some of the very Latino leaders who had backed Washington deserted his splintered movement and forged a new alliance with the old Democratic Party machine, now headed by Richard Daley, son of the legendary former mayor. Among those was Luis Gutiérrez, an activist in the Puerto Rican independence movement.[36] As a result of his switch, Gutiérrez would later win Daley's support for a new congressional seat created by reapportionment in 1991. At the same time, in New York City, Puerto Rican leader Nydia Velázquez fought to keep the Rainbow Coalition together, winning key support from both Jackson and the Reverend Al Sharpton in a race for a new congressional seat. In 1992, Gutiérrez and Velázquez became the second and third Puerto Rican voting members of Congress, yet they swept into office through distinct electoral alliances.

In Philadelphia, the Black-Latino alliance started to rupture in 1991. Of those Puerto Ricans who had supported Wilson Goode throughout his two terms, some backed a liberal Black Democratic leader who attempted to succeed him, John White Jr., while others backed the more moderate white Democrat and eventual winner, Ed Rendell.

Finally, in 1993, the coalition of African Americans and Latinos in New York City foundered during the reelection campaign of David Dinkins. While Dinkins retained a majority of Latino votes, his percentage had declined, as had voter turnout in the Latino community, enabling Republican Rudy Giuliani to squeak to victory with a very slim margin. Thus, by 1995, the mayoralty in four of the country's largest cities—New York, Los Angeles, Chicago, and Philadelphia—had passed from a liberal or moderate Black incumbent to a more conservative white leader. In each case, Hispanic voters shifted in significant percentages from the previous Black mayor to the new white candidate, and each time the argument of those who switched sounded the same: "We weren't treated as equal by the Black leaders." Meanwhile, the failure of Jesse Jackson to expand his Rainbow Coalition through a third presidential campaign in 1992 left the movement organizationally adrift at the national level. Even as the number of Black and Hispanic leaders in Congress reached a record number, the cohesiveness of the alliance fractured, especially as Black voters along with whites grew increasingly uneasy about the country's population of Latinos and Asians. In November of 1994, for instance, a sizable portion of Black Californians voted for Proposition 187 to cut off all public benefits to unauthorized immigrants.[37] Thus, the Rainbow Coalition was dead as a vehicle for a new progressive alliance by early 1995, even though Jackson never officially declared its demise but simply folded it into his old Operation PUSH organization.

THE THIRD FORCE PERIOD, 1995–2005

Following the disintegration of the Rainbow, Latinos entered a new stage, one that I have dubbed the Third Force Period. The hallmarks of this period were a massive rush to citizenship by Hispanic immigrants, a huge increase in voter participation levels, and a newfound independence by Latino leaders from urban Democratic Party machines.

Between 1994 and 1997, citizenship applications nearly tripled from 543,353 to 1,411,981, the overwhelming majority of them from Hispanics. In the years after that, new applications remained at about 700,000 annually, even though Immigration and Customs Enforcement (ICE, formerly the INS) sharply raised fees for processing them and the number rejected grew to more than 100,000 a year.[38] More than half of the one million immigrants sworn in as U.S. citizens in 2008 were from Latin America.[39] This stampede to citizenship was caused by several factors. First and most important was the spate of restrictive immigration laws that began with Proposition 187 in California and then spread across the country. Until then, Mexicans had the lowest naturalization rates of any immigrant group. One study showed that only 3 percent of Mexicans admitted into the country in 1970 had become citizens by 1979. Similar trends prevailed in later years, though not as pronounced. By 2010, for instance, Mexicans still had the lowest naturalization rate (25.1 percent) of any migrant nationality in the United States, with Hondurans, Salvadorans, and Guatemalans all exhibiting similar low rates.[40] Many Mexicans who had lived and worked in this country for years invariably expected to return home someday, so they rarely sought citizenship. Likewise, the Central Americans who fled civil wars in the 1980s expected to return once those wars ended.

But the new immigration laws sparked a Latino backlash. Of the 3 million undocumented immigrants who became legal U.S. residents under the amnesty provisions of the Immigration Reform and Control Act of 1986 (IRCA), for instance, 2.6 million were from Latin America, and as soon as they were eligible for citizenship in 1992, most opted to apply for it.[41] In addition, the Republican-sponsored ban in 1996 on federal benefits for legal permanent residents (later partially repealed) prompted hundreds of thousands who were here legally to seek naturalization. As soon as they were sworn in, those new citizens registered to vote.

The second factor in the rush to citizenship was the peace accords in Nicaragua, El Salvador, and Guatemala, which ended the fighting but not the economic chaos in those countries. Once the wars ended, the Central American refugees suddenly turned into the main source of economic aid to their beleaguered countries through the billions of dollars in remittances they sent home each year. As a result, both the immigrants and their home governments resisted their repatriation, and many chose to become U.S. citizens.

A third factor was the transformation of citizenship laws in Latin America, with governments there increasingly adopting dual citizenship provisions that allowed their nationals to retain home country rights even if they became U.S. citizens. Between 1991 and 2003, twelve Latin American countries passed regulations recognizing dual citizenship, among them Colombia (1991), the Dominican Republic (1994), Brazil (1996), Mexico (1998), Guatemala (1999), and Honduras (2003).[42]

The combination of all those factors turned the dormant potential of Latino politics into reality starting in 1996, when the Hispanic vote astounded political experts with both its explosive growth and its unpredictability.[43] More than five million Latinos went to the polls that year, a remarkable 20 percent increase over 1992.[44]

And turnout was higher in the new immigrant neighborhoods than in more established Latino areas. In New York City, for instance, overall Latino turnout was 48 percent of registered voters, but it reached 63 percent in the Dominican area of Washington Heights, and 60 percent in the Colombian section of Jackson Heights.[45]

Those who went to the polls in 1996 voted overwhelmingly for Bill Clinton and the Democratic Party. Clinton garnered 72 percent of the Latino vote compared with 61 percent in 1992.[46] Even in Florida, where Cubans had always voted solidly Republican, he captured 44 percent to Bob Dole's 46 percent.[47] The seismic shift was best exemplified in California, where a relative unknown, Loretta Sánchez, narrowly defeated right-wing congressman Robert Dornan in Orange County, a historically conservative Republican stronghold.

The following year, local elections in many cities repeated the same pattern of high Hispanic turnout but also showed that the Latino vote was becoming less predictable than in the past. In the New York and Los Angeles mayoral races, for instance, not only did the number of Latino votes exceed that of Blacks for the first time, but Latinos gave substantial backing to victorious Republican incumbents—45 percent to New York's Rudy Giuliani and 48 percent to L.A.'s Richard Riordan—while Blacks voted heavily against both.[48]

The first decade of the new century provided vivid evidence that the movement for greater representation in government that was launched by disparate Latino ethnic groups in distinct parts of the country during the 1950s and 1960s has begun to mature into a cohesive force. Mexican, Puerto Rican, Cuban, and other Latin American communities are increasingly responding to ethnic and racial discrimination from the dominant white society by seeking common ground—strength in numbers—with one another. In the process, they have given birth to a new imagined "Latino" community within American society, and to a new hybrid ethnic/racial pole in U.S. politics.

In key local and statewide elections around the country, Hispanic voters moved from being virtually ignored by the political establishment to being feverishly courted as major factors in electoral victories, while Latino politicians have won major municipal, state, and federal elections in the past decade.

Perhaps the best known during the final years of the "Third Force" period was Bill Richardson, the moderate Democrat who had served as Bill Clinton's United Nations ambassador and then energy secretary, and who became for several years the most sought-after Latino leader in the country, especially after Henry Cisneros, the charismatic former mayor of San Antonio and one-time secretary of Housing and Urban Development, was forced out of politics due to a personal scandal. In 2002, Richardson was elected governor of New Mexico—only the fourth Hispanic chief executive in that state's history. He quickly won praise for his effective management of state government and was easily reelected four years later. He then became in 2008 the first Latino to mount a serious run for the Democratic presidential nomination, eventually throwing his support to Barack Obama's insurgent campaign over Hillary Clinton, the first choice of most Hispanic voters. In return, President-elect Obama later nominated Richardson for commerce secretary. But the New Mexico governor was quickly caught up in a scandal of his own over the awarding of public pension investments in his state and ended up withdrawing from the cabinet post before his confirmation hearing.

By then, the U.S. Senate had witnessed an increase in Latino representation. In 2004, Florida Republican Mel Martinez, a descendant of the early nineteenth-century Cuban immigrants to Ybor City, won election to one of his state's Senate seats. That same year, Mexican American Ken Salazar, a conservative Democrat, won a second Senate seat in Colorado. And in 2005, New Jersey's newly elected governor, John Corzine, appointed U.S. representative Robert Menendez, a fellow Democrat and a Cuban American, to fill the Senate seat Corzine had just vacated. Thus, by mid-decade, a record three Latinos were sitting in the Senate, all of them moderate or conservative in their political outlook.

The remarkable situation did not last very long, however, for while Menendez handily won reelection to his seat in 2006, Florida's Martinez subsequently retired and Salazar resigned in 2009 to become interior secretary under President Obama.

THE NEW CALIFORNIA VOTE

Perhaps no area of the country has reflected the growth of Latino political power more during the past few decades than California, where 39.3 percent of the state's nearly forty million residents in 2018 were Hispanic. Democrats seized control of the California legislature in 1996, in part because of Latino turnout at the polls after Republican governor Pete Wilson supported the infamous anti-immigrant Proposition 187. That year, Cruz Bustamante, an assemblyman from Fresno, became the first Hispanic speaker of the legislature. Between then and 2020, five of California's nine assembly speakers were Latino, and all were Democrats.

Bustamante went on to serve two terms as lieutenant governor. His successor as speaker, Antonio Villaraigosa, subsequently engineered a pivotal electoral victory among Latinos nationwide. A one-time Chicano student activist at UCLA and former labor organizer, Villaraigosa ran for mayor of Los Angeles in 2001 against fellow Democrat James Hahn, the son of Kenneth Hahn, a former ten-time Los Angeles County supervisor who was one of the city's most beloved politicians. His father's liberal record on civil rights engendered so much support for James Hahn's candidacy in the city's Black community that he was the early favorite to win the race.

After a close and hard-fought runoff election, Hahn prevailed, but he enraged many Latino leaders when he resorted to last-minute campaign commercials that evoked the infamous "Willie Horton" ads used by George H. W. Bush in his 1988 presidential race against Michael Dukakis. The Hahn commercials highlighted Villaraigosa's support of a pardon for a Latino convicted drug dealer and they openly played on fears among some whites of rising crime in the Latino community.

Four years later, Villaraigosa ran against Hahn a second time. By then, the mayor had lost significant support among Black voters for his refusal to reappoint the city's African American police commissioner, Bernard Parks. Meanwhile, Villaraigosa had spent the intervening years building ties with the city's Black leaders, and he enjoyed the support of the city's most powerful Black member of Congress, Maxine Waters. He swept to a landslide victory against Hahn to become the first Latino mayor of Los Angeles since the 1870s.

Villaraigosa enjoyed enormous popularity during his first term and easily won reelection in 2009. But that popularity soon became tainted by a personal scandal over an extramarital affair with a news reporter, and by allegations that he was too cozy with real estate developers and spent too much time traveling out of town. His political career did not recover in subsequent years.[49]

MAYORAL ELECTIONS
IN HARTFORD AND NEW YORK CITY

At the same time, mayoral races in Hartford, Connecticut, and New York City evinced the growing strength of the Latino vote on the East Coast. Puerto Rican–born Eddie Perez, a former community organizer, won election as the first Latino mayor of Hartford in 2001. Perez benefited from a strong, independent grassroots movement that arose in that city during the 1980s, and he won reelection as mayor two more times. But in 2009, during his third term, he was arrested on state bribery charges, found guilty a year later, and sentenced to three years in prison.

In New York, Puerto Rican Fernando Ferrer, the borough president of the Bronx, lost a bitterly fought primary election runoff in 2001 to fellow Democrat Mark Green for the Democratic mayoral nomination. Given that New York voters are overwhelmingly Democratic, Green was expected to romp to victory in the general election against a little-known Republican billionaire, Michael Bloomberg. But Bloomberg eked out an upset victory, with Green's defeat due in part to the defection of many Latino voters. Ferrer supporters became angry that Green, like Hahn in Los Angeles, had used racially charged flyers and last-minute automated phone calls to stir up white voters against Ferrer and his key ally in the Black community, the Reverend Al Sharpton.

Four years later, Ferrer ran for mayor again. This time he sought to build an alliance of Latino and African American voters with middle-class whites. He prevailed in the Democratic primary only to be trounced in the general election by Bloomberg, who, despite enjoying the power of incumbency, spent a record $79 million of his own money on the campaign. But while Ferrer failed in both his campaigns for mayor, his emergence as a viable candidate signaled that even in the country's biggest and most important city, the political establishment could no longer ignore the growing number of Latino voters.

IMMIGRANT RIGHTS PERIOD—
2006 TO THE PRESENT

Beginning in 2006, a sequence of extraordinary events unfolded that marked yet a new stage for Latino politics in the United States.

They began with several tumultuous weeks of unprecedented immigration protests during the spring of that year (see chapter 11). They were followed soon after by the Great Recession of 2007–2009, which virtually obliterated much of the little wealth that the nation's Latinos had managed to accumulate. Then in the midst of that economic meltdown came the improbable victory of Barack Obama in his race for the White House in November 2008. These three distinct phenomena combined to propel a new generation of young Latinos into political activism. Many of those youths, at least those who had been brought to this country as children by their undocumented parents and who had attended college here, were suddenly confronting the real threat that they or their family members could be deported. They came to be known as Dreamers, and they soon joined with many Latino citizen youth to give birth to a grassroots movement that took a more militant path than the activists of the previous Third Force period, echoing instead the militancy of the 1960s and 1970s. Some of the new movement's most visible leaders not only won political office but did so while publicly declaring themselves democratic socialists in the vein of Vermont senator Bernie Sanders, among them U.S. representative Alexandria Ocasio-Cortez of New York, Chicago City Council members Carlos Ramirez-Rosa and Rosanna Rodríguez-Sánchez, and New York State senator from Brooklyn Julia Salazar.

Many others, while not quite as radical as this latter group, nonetheless aligned themselves with the resurgent progressive wing of the Democratic Party. At the same time, leaders from Latino ethnic groups that in the past had lacked any representation began to win political office. They included the first member of Congress to have emigrated from the Dominican Republic, Adriano Espaillat (New York City, 2016); from Ecuador, Debbie Jessika Mucarsel-Powell (South Florida, 2018); and from Guatemala, Norma Torres (Los Angeles, 2014); also, the first Salvadoran American member of the California State Assembly, Wendy Carillo (Los Angeles, 2017); and the first Colombian American member of the Dade County Board of Commissioners, Juan C. Zapata (2012).[50]

Following Barack Obama's 2008 victory, many Latinos harbored high expectations for major improvement in their lives, but those hopes were soon dashed, especially when Obama failed to adopt an immediate plan to assist the millions of homeowners who had defaulted on their mortgages. The catastrophic loss of wealth for people of color that accompanied the mortgage crisis cannot be overstated, and this was especially true for Latinos. In 2005, for instance, U.S. Latino households had a median net worth of just $18,359, largely as a result of home equity. That was far below the median net worth for white ($134,992) or Asian ($168,103) households, and it was slightly higher than that of Black households ($12,124). But by 2009, net worth for Latinos had slumped to just $6,325—a drop of 66 percent, while African American and Asian households had registered slightly smaller declines of 53 percent and 54 percent, respectively, and white median wealth had dropped by just 16 percent.[51]

The Obama administration, however, opted not to hold the nation's biggest banks criminally accountable for their role in packaging and peddling billions of dollars of unsound and even fraudulent mortgage securities, while its efforts to assist distressed homeowners turned into a glaring failure. For the brief period from 2009 to 2011 during which Democrats controlled the White House and both houses of Congress, homeowner relief was relegated to a back burner. So was Obama's campaign promise to sign during his first year as president a comprehensive immigration reform law with a path to citizenship for the nation's eleven million undocumented migrants. His top aides focused instead on implementing a massive federal infrastructure spending plan to pull the country out of the Great Recession, and on passing health care reform, the Affordable Care Act (Obamacare). But any hope for immigration reform faded after Republicans regained control of the House following the midterm election of 2010. Despite the president's repeated expressions of support for such legislation, he ended up ramping up the number of deportations of undocumented persons to record levels, some four hundred thousand annually, a feat that prompted some immigrant rights advocates to label him the "deporter-in-chief."[52]

SAN ANTONIO AND THE "GREAT LATINO HOPE"

Texas, the state with the most Latino elected officials, began pointing the way in the early 2000s for a more moderate generation of Latino leaders, especially in San Antonio, which boasted the highest proportion of Latinos—61 percent—of any major city. After Henry Cisneros left the San Antonio mayoralty in 1989, no local Hispanic leader emerged to follow in his shoes until city council member Ed Garza prevailed in the mayoral race in 2001. Garza served two

two-year terms, only to opt afterward for a career in private business. Councilman Julián Castro, then a thirty-one-year-old graduate of Stanford and Harvard Law School, attempted in 2005 to
succeed Garza. Despite his youth and inexperience, Castro narrowly
lost a runoff to retired judge Phil Hardberger. He returned in 2009
for a second attempt. Assisted by the extensive political network that
his mother, Rosie Castro, a 1970s leader of the nationalist Raza
Unida Party, had built over the years, Castro won a landslide victory,
thus becoming the youngest mayor of a major city in the country.

Political experts in the mainstream media immediately christened Castro the first "post-Hispanic" Hispanic candidate. He did
not rely on the narrow ethnic pride used by old-style politicians to
win votes, those experts said. Like Barack Obama or Cory Booker,
who was at the time Newark, New Jersey's mayor, Castro was young,
charismatic, articulate, and most of all, a political moderate, one who
emphasized technocratic skills and his first-class education to achieve
cross-ethnic and cross-racial appeal. Able to move easily between the
barrio and the boardroom and to not appear threatening to white
voters, Castro was already being dubbed the "Great Latino Hope,"
with the potential to one day reach the White House. Such quick labels, of course, have been accorded other young Latino leaders in the
past. Another Harvard graduate, Cisneros, was so anointed in the
1980s. So was Yale graduate Mauricio Ferre, the one-time mayor of
Miami; as well as Linda Chavez, former White House assistant to
President Reagan, and former Denver mayor Federico Peña. It is
part of a recurrent effort by the political establishment to ordain and
groom nonthreatening minority political leaders, an effort that is
likely to increase as the Latino vote grows in influence.[53]

Most young Latinos involved in politics at the grassroots level,
however, are suspicious of such attempts by others to choose their
leaders. At the same time, they have become increasingly frustrated
by the disturbing number of Latino leaders who initially won election through ethnic appeals to Hispanic voters only to become corrupted by their time in power, or who self-destructed through
personal scandals. In New York City alone, more than a half dozen
Hispanic officials were convicted of malfeasance in the early 2000s.[54]

As for Castro, he was tapped during President Obama's second
term to serve as secretary of Housing and Urban Development, and
when the Democratic Party leaders elevated him to their national
convention keynote speaker in 2012, his future as a national leader
seemed bright. His only signature accomplishment while at HUD,

however, was to finally implement a long-stalled provision of the Fair Housing Act of 1968—one which requires thousands of state and local governments that receive HUD funds to affirmatively determine whether their local planning and zoning regulations function as barriers against fair and affordable housing. Castro nonetheless faced relentless criticism from affordable housing advocates for overseeing a fire sale of millions of distressed homes whose mortgages had fallen in default. One 2014 study found that during the first two years of the program's existence, 97 percent of HUD sales of foreclosed properties went to for-profit companies, including private equity firms like Blackstone, while only 3 percent resulted in the original owners keeping their homes.[55]

A HISPANIC JUSTICE
OF THE SUPREME COURT

No single event of this century's first decade more conspicuously symbolized the political progress of the Latino community than did President Obama's nomination of Sonia Sotomayor in May 2009 to replace retiring justice David Souter on the U.S. Supreme Court.

The president's announcement instantly catapulted the little-known fifty-four-year-old federal appeals court judge from New York City into the national spotlight as the first Hispanic American—and only the third woman—named to the high court. The process of her confirmation brought unprecedented media attention to all Latinos and it sparked a surprising public examination of Sotomayor's relationship to her heritage and her community, with the term *wise Latina* suddenly becoming part of the national lexicon.[56]

The Nuyorican daughter of Puerto Rican workers who had migrated to the United States during World War II and eventually settled in a Bronx public housing project, Sotomayor rose from humble beginnings, much as Obama had in his journey to the White House. Like the president, she had attended Ivy League schools—in her case, Princeton and Yale—and had graduated with top honors. Like him, she had excelled as editor of her school's law review.

But Sotomayor's story differed from Obama's in several key ways. For one thing, she had spent nearly twenty years as a U.S. district and federal appeals judge. She also had a record before she became a judge of involvement in organizations and issues that affected the Latino community. As a Princeton undergraduate, for example, she had joined and become cochair of Acción Puertorriqueña, a student organization that eventually filed a complaint with the federal Department of Health, Education, and Welfare, accusing the school of discrimination in hiring and admission. At both Princeton and Yale, she wrote student theses and law review articles that examined the unequal relationship between Puerto Rico and the United States. And in the early 1980s, she joined the board of directors of the Puerto Rican Legal Defense and Education Fund, which was then spearheading voting rights and housing discrimination lawsuits.[57]

White conservative talk show hosts quickly seized on her previous social activism to condemn her nomination. Most often cited was a 2001 speech at the University of California, Berkeley, where Sotomayor told a group of students she hoped "a wise Latina woman with the richness of her experiences would more often than not reach a better conclusion than a white male who hasn't lived that life."

With Democrats holding a substantial majority in the Senate, Sotomayor was confirmed on August 6, 2009, by a 68–31 vote as the 111th Supreme Court justice. For millions of Latinos in this country, and especially for millions of Hispanic women, her confirmation marked a historic milestone. And within ten years of her confirmation, some analysts concluded she had become the most outspoken and eloquent member of the high court's liberal minority.[58]

REPUBLICAN PARTY INROADS AMONG LATINOS IN THE 2010 ELECTION

When Republicans regained control of the House of Representatives in 2010, one aspect of the party's resurgence that received scant attention was a sudden increase in what had always been a tiny number of Latino Republican officials. Two Hispanic Republicans, for example, won election as governors that year, while the number of Hispanics in Congress doubled.

In New Mexico, Susana Martinez, the district attorney of Doña Ana County, became the first female Hispanic governor of a state, succeeding Democrat Bill Richardson, who was term limited. Endorsed by former Alaska Republican governor and vice presidential candidate Sarah Palin, Martinez campaigned on a staunch conservative platform. She opposed abortion and same-sex marriage, advocated a crackdown on illegal immigration, defended gun owners' rights, and pressed for balanced budgets. Despite those positions, she made significant inroads into the state's large group of Hispanic and mostly Democratic voters. Meanwhile, in neighboring Nevada, Brian Sandoval, a former state attorney general and U.S. district judge, became the state's first Latino governor.

Even more startling changes occurred in the far Northwest, where Republican Jaime Herrera, a Washington State representative, won a congressional seat there, as did businessman Raul Labrador in Idaho. Both Herrera and Labrador were the first Hispanics to represent their states in Congress, and both won in overwhelmingly white districts.

In Florida, Tea Party favorite Marco Rubio prevailed in one of that state's U.S. Senate races. The only other Hispanic serving in the Senate at that point was Democrat Bob Menendez of New Jersey. In addition to Rubio, the number of Republican Hispanics in the House of Representatives jumped from three to seven.

But the Democratic Party felt the impact of Latino voters as well. A big turnout of Hispanics in Nevada is generally credited with assuring Senate majority leader Harry Reid's victory over Tea Party Republican Sharron Angle, while the victories of Jerry Brown in California's gubernatorial race and Barbara Boxer in the that state's Senate race were in large measure a result of strong Hispanic support.[59]

OBAMA, THE DREAMERS, AND THE SECOND FAILURE OF IMMIGRATION REFORM

During the waning months of his first term, President Obama came under dogged pressure from Latino activists to curtail the federal government's mass deportations and to take executive action on immigration, especially after Republicans in the Senate, joined by a handful of centrist Democrats, managed to defeat even the least controversial legislation on the issue, the Development, Relief, and Education for Alien Minors (DREAM) Act, which offered legal status for undocumented migrants who had been brought to this country as children. Early on the morning of December 18, 2010, despite protests, sit-ins, and hunger strikes across the country, the Senate failed to achieve the required 60 votes needed to end a filibuster, even though a majority of senators (55-41) favored the bill. Among the activist groups that advocated for the bill were United We Dream, a national network cofounded by Julieta Garibay and Cristina

Jiménez, both of whom had been brought to the country by their parents as undocumented children; the DREAM Action Coalition (DRM), cofounded by former congressional staffer and Arizona immigrant rights advocate Erika Andiola; and the National Immigrant Youth Alliance (NIYA). Much of the pressure among lawmakers on immigration reform was spearheaded by U.S. representative Luis Gutiérrez (D-IL). A native of Puerto Rico and thus a U.S. citizen by birth, Gutiérrez seemed at first an unlikely champion on this issue; nonetheless he soon took to barnstorming the country, urging comprehensive immigration reform at town hall meetings far from his Chicago district, and personally urging Obama on several occasions to decree some form of presidential protection from deportation for the Dreamers, given that the United States was the only country most of them had ever known.

Meanwhile, many Latinos were especially angered by the administration's expansion of the Secure Communities program, through which the federal government collected fingerprints from local law enforcement agencies to identify and deport immigrants with criminal records, often people with minor offenses. Before long the activists embarked on a coordinated campaign to disrupt the president's public events, while more established Latino leaders reviled his failure to act. As they did so, Obama chafed at their criticism, his aides insisting that his tough stance on illegal immigration was part of an effort to persuade Republicans in Congress to support comprehensive immigration reform.[60]

In June 2012, only five months before his reelection contest against Republican challenger Mitt Romney, Obama finally responded to the mounting pressure from the Hispanic community by issuing an executive order that he labeled Deferred Action for Childhood Arrivals (DACA). This new program, the president said, was a "temporary stopgap measure" to suspend deportations and issue work permits for undocumented Dreamers pending a vote by Congress on more permanent immigration legislation. DACA eventually provided protection to some seven hundred thousand youths, more than 90 percent of whom were from Latin American countries, and it likely played a significant role in propelling greater numbers of Latinos to cast ballots for Obama that November. As voter exit polls from the 2012 election found, the president garnered the support of 71 percent of Latinos who cast ballots in that race, a significant increase from the 67 percent he had won four years earlier. Moreover, he received 74 percent of the votes of

eighteen-to-twenty-nine-year-old Hispanics, compared with only
60 percent among all youth.[61]

Throughout his second term, however, Obama failed to get Congress to fix the country's broken immigration system, his most dramatic defeat being the so-called Gang of Eight compromise bill of
2013, an effort that passed the Senate by a wide margin but failed in
the Republican-controlled House of Representatives (see chapter 11).
After that defeat, Obama pivoted once again to an executive order,
announcing in a prime-time televised speech to the nation in November 2014 the creation of Deferred Action for Parents of Americans and Lawful Permanent Residents (DAPA), a program aimed at
granting temporary three-year work permits and lawful status for
nearly half of the nation's undocumented population, and he finally
ordered an end to the Secure Communities program. DAPA, however, was blocked by federal court injunctions in early 2015 after several states sued the federal government, and it was subsequently
overturned by a U.S. circuit court, a ruling which was then upheld
when the Supreme Court deadlocked 4–4 on an appeal of the case.[62]

DONALD TRUMP'S WAR ON IMMIGRANTS

From the moment he announced his unlikely run for president in
June 2015, real estate mogul and reality-TV star Donald Trump
turned immigration into a central issue of his campaign. As we have
seen, public debate over the nation's broken immigration system had
been simmering for decades, yet Congress had failed in repeated attempts to craft a comprehensive solution. Trump railed against what
he labeled an uncontrolled "invasion" of Mexican migrants and
vowed to seal the nation's southern border. "When Mexico sends its
people, they're not sending their best," he declared when he initiated
his presidential campaign. "They're sending people that have lots of
problems, and they're bringing those problems with us. They're
bringing drugs. They're bringing crime. They're rapists. And some,
I assume, are good people." As for the border wall that Washington
politicians had been talking about for years, Trump boasted, "I will
build a great, great wall on our southern border. And I will have
Mexico pay for that wall. Mark my words."[63]

But once in office Trump quickly made it evident his aim would be
not only to reduce the flow of undocumented migrants through
militarization of the border, mass detentions, and separation of

families—or simply reverse actions his predecessor Obama had taken to legalize the status of some migrants—but rather his broader goal was to radically restructure the U.S. immigration system by sharply reducing the number of newcomers of any type who could be admitted annually, including refugees, asylum seekers, and legal migrants from Muslim countries. By doing away with family reunification policies that have been a bedrock of federal immigration policy for more than fifty years—Trump labeled it "chain migration"—he vowed to shift instead to a visa system based on "merit" that would give priority to foreign applicants who were well educated or well-off financially. In short, Trump sought to turn back the clock on more than fifty years of U.S. immigration policy, harkening back to the days of racially infused immigration restriction (see chapter 11).

The Extraordinary Growth of the Latino Vote

The number of Latinos who reported voting in presidential elections increased from 2.1 million in 1976 to 12.6 million in 2016, a 500 percent jump, while barely rising (28 percent) among non-Hispanic whites (see table 5). By comparison, the number of African Americans who reported voting grew by 138 percent during the same period. Just in the eight years between the election of Barack Obama in 2008 and the victory of Donald Trump in 2016, 3 million more Latinos reported voting, while among African Americans, the increase was just 1 million.

Table 5

Votes Cast in 1976, 2008, and 2016 Presidential Elections by Race and Hispanic Origin

(IN MILLIONS)[64]

Group	1976	2008	2016	Percent Increase, 1976–2016
White	78.8*	109.1	100.8	28%
Black	7.2	17.1	17.1	138%
Hispanic	2.1	9.7	12.6	500%

*Includes both non-Hispanic whites and Hispanics who identified themselves as white.

Even more noteworthy was what occurred in the midterm election of 2018, when nearly as many Latinos cast ballots as had done so for the presidential contest between Trump and Hillary Clinton. In midterm elections going back as far as the 1970s, the Latino turnout had always been far lower than in presidential voting years, reaching a high point of only 6.8 million in 2014. But according to the U.S. census, *11.7 million Latinos reported voting in 2018, nearly double the number of 2014.* This unexpectedly high Latino turnout helped Democrats recapture control of the House of Representatives. And while it was most likely driven by the constant scapegoating of Latinos and immigrants by the Trump administration and Republicans in Congress, it nonetheless signaled that Latino voters were placing as much emphasis on who controlled the Congress as on who sat in the White House.[65]

As we shall see, the extraordinary rise in Latino voter participation accelerated further in the 2020 presidential election, and it is almost certain to continue for decades. The 12.6 million who cast ballots in 2016, for example, represented barely a third of the 38.9 million Hispanics in the country who were over the age of eighteen at that point. Only about two-thirds of those 38.9 million were already U.S. citizens and thus eligible to cast a ballot. The rest were either legal residents or undocumented migrants. But most of the legal residents will become citizens someday and turn into eligible voters, and if Congress eventually approves some sort of path for legalizing the undocumented, so will many of those who are currently in the country unlawfully.[66]

And no matter what happens with Latino adults, there is still a huge cohort of Latino children who will eventually reach voting age. In 2019, for instance, 30.8 percent of the country's Hispanic population was under the age of eighteen, compared with only 18.6 percent of white Americans. Thus, the inescapable fact is that the Hispanic electorate will continue to mushroom.[67]

Some political leaders, fearing that trend, stepped up efforts in recent years to suppress the growth of the minority vote. From 2003 to 2006, state legislatures and ballot initiatives in Florida, Ohio, New Mexico, and Arizona successfully sought to make voter registration more arduous. Such laws were a reaction in part to supposed abuses in registration efforts by organizations like Association of Community Organizations for Reform Now (ACORN) and in part to a xenophobic effort to stem alleged "illegal-alien voter fraud." They were implemented despite any significant proof that either voter registration or actual ballot fraud by minority voters had occurred.[68] A 2005 study by a commission headed by former president Jimmy Carter and former secretary of state James Baker concluded that "while election fraud occurs, it is difficult to measure." The commission noted that "noncitizens have registered to vote in several recent elections," including a disputed 1996 congressional election in California "where 784 invalid votes were cast by individuals who had registered illegally," and a 2004 election in Harris County, Texas, where "at least 35 foreign citizens applied for or received voter cards." But the commission found no evidence that such abuses were widespread.[69]

"It is more likely an individual will be struck by lightning than that he will engage in voter fraud," concluded the Brennan Center for Justice, after its own exhaustive study of voter irregularities. Far more common than actual incidents of noncitizens voting, the Brennan Center found, are "allegations of noncitizen voting that prove wholly unfounded."[70]

VOTER SUPPRESSION IN THE POST-OBAMA YEARS

In the wake of historic voter participation levels among Hispanics and African Americans that helped produce the Obama presidential victories of 2008 and 2012, the extreme conservative wing of the Republican Party grew increasingly worried about the prospect of a growing Democratic majority at the national level. Leaders of that wing redoubled their efforts to suppress and restrict voter turnout. Between 2010 and 2018, twenty-four states enacted new restrictions on voting. That strategy received an immeasurable boost from a 2013 Supreme Court decision, *Shelby County v. Holder*, that gutted federal enforcement of the 1965 Voting Rights Act. In a narrow 5–4 vote, the court effectively ended the requirement that any city or state with a history of racial discrimination apply for preclearance from the Justice Department for changes to local voting laws or practices. After the *Shelby* decision, efforts soared to gerrymander election districts, to purge voter rolls, to reduce the number of polling places in minority neighborhoods, and to expand ID requirements for voting, to the point that the Brennan Center for Justice warned in a 2018 report that "the range of voter suppression efforts has been more widespread, intense, and brazen this cycle than in any other since the modern-day assault on voting began."[71]

The rise of Donald Trump saw an escalation in such efforts. Although he won the electoral college vote handily against his opponent, Democrat Hillary Clinton, Trump was bedeviled by the fact that Clinton had won the popular vote nationwide by 2.9 million. His response was to claim that three to five million noncitizens had illegally cast ballots in the November 2016 election, even though there was no evidence of such massive fraud. Trump even appointed the Presidential Advisory Commission on Election Integrity in May 2017 to investigate such fraud, naming Vice President Mike Pence as its chair and Kansas secretary of state Kris Kobach as vice chair and administrator. Civil liberties groups, legal scholars, and many media editorial boards condemned it as a vehicle for voter suppression, and Trump abruptly disbanded his commission in January 2018, with no indication that it had found the kind of massive voter fraud he'd alleged.[72]

A NEW GENERATION COMES OF AGE

Even as anti-Latino rhetoric, anti-immigrant policies, and mass deportations surged across the country throughout the Obama and Trump administrations, a very different dynamic was taking root within the Hispanic community: more young Latinos began joining grassroots social movements to advocate for their communities, and more of them than ever began to run for and win political office at the local level or to gain top positions within mainstream private and professional groups—positions that Latinos had not previously held. And more of them, as we have seen, started to vote.

This new generation of Latino political leaders did not emerge, as others had in the past, by working loyally within the established political parties until the hierarchy of those parties judged them ready for promotion. Instead, they often mounted dissident challenges to that hierarchy and managed to oust entrenched officials. Gregorio Casar was a typical example. Thin in build, with a neatly trimmed beard and dark, piercing eyes, Casar is the son of Mexican immigrants. As a teenager he joined the 2006 immigrant rights protests that swept through his hometown of Houston, Texas, and two years later, while studying at the University of Virginia, he volunteered for

Barack Obama's presidential campaign. After college, he moved to Austin, Texas, and took a job as an organizer for the Workers Defense Project, an advocacy group for low-wage and mostly immigrant workers. There he joined a grassroots coalition against downtown business groups, and in 2014, at the age of twenty-five, Casar, who proclaimed himself a democratic socialist, became the youngest person ever elected to the Austin City Council. The following year, civil rights attorney Lorena González won election to the Seattle City Council, the first Hispanic to do so. González's parents came to the United States from Mexico as undocumented migrants in the 1960s and were farmworkers in Washington state, where she was born, before they eventually acquired American citizenship. Then there was Adriano Espaillat, the Dominican-born community leader from the Washington Heights section of Manhattan who had himself been undocumented for many years before legalizing his status and becoming a citizen. In 2016, after serving several terms in the New York State Legislature, Espaillat bucked his party's established leaders and won the Harlem congressional seat that had previously been held for more than half a century by two legendary African American politicians, first Adam Clayton Powell Jr., and then Charles Rangel.

Even small-town America and states rarely seen as affected by migration began to feel the impact of a rising Latino population. In 2015, for instance, Wilder, Idaho, a town of just 1,500 residents in a farming area near that state's western border, drew national attention when it elected an all-Latino city council. Among the four council members was Ismael Fernández, a nineteen-year-old freshman at the College of Idaho, who became one of the youngest politicians in Idaho's history, and Alicia Almazan, then fifty-one, whose family had lived in Wilder for more than forty years. By then, nearly 75 percent of the town's population was Hispanic, as was 25 percent of surrounding Canyon County. More than three hundred miles to the northwest, in Yakima, Washington, a city of 95,000 people, more than 40 percent Latino, a similar political earthquake took place. Following a successful voting rights lawsuit by the American Civil Liberties Union, the structure of Yakima's city council elections changed from an at-large to a district system. The result was the election of the first three council members (out of seven) in the city's history who were Hispanic—all of them women.[73]

But no political novice from the Latino community sparked more national attention in the new century than New York's Alexandria Ocasio-Cortez with her surprise victory over U.S. representative Joe

Crowley in a 2018 Democratic primary. At the time, Crowley was not only the fourth-ranking leader among House Democrats, he was also the powerful head of the Queens County Democratic Party. Ocasio-Cortez, who was quickly dubbed AOC, soon joined several radical and progressive young women of color in the "Squad," all of whom had staged similar upsets of Democratic incumbents that same year. Their group sent a signal to established leaders of both the Democratic and Republican parties that democratic socialist ideals had made significant inroads among Latinos and other racial minorities. The Squad's unabashed support of Medicare for All, a Green New Deal, a fifteen-dollar-an-hour federal minimum wage, universal free prekindergarten, and national rent control quickly garnered nonstop press attention. It won AOC millions of followers on social media, and led President Trump to target her periodically for criticism.[74]

THE 2020 ELECTION AND CLAIMS OF A LATINO SHIFT TOWARD TRUMP

The 2020 presidential contest between Donald Trump and Democratic challenger Joe Biden took place in the midst of the COVID-19 worldwide pandemic and deep economic hardship throughout the country, yet it produced record voter participation. Nearly 159 million people cast ballots, the highest percentage turnout in a century—and a dramatic 15.9 percent increase over the 2016 election—with Biden securing a 7 million margin in the popular vote, and a 306–232 majority of the all-important electoral college vote.

Within hours of the polls closing, however, a cascade of media accounts asserted that Latino voters—and to some extent African American men—had shifted significantly, and surprisingly, toward supporting Trump, with Biden capturing "only" 65 percent of Latino votes to Trump's 32 percent, a smaller margin than Hillary Clinton had achieved four years earlier. Such results, according to that narrative, were somehow proof that Latinos are more conservative than many Americans realize, even that there is no such thing as a cohesive "Latino vote."[75]

That narrative, however, was a misleading one. Erected on flawed data from an early national exit poll and on incomplete vote returns, it failed to highlight one of the biggest lessons of the 2020 race: an unprecedented turnout by Latino voters. It would take months, until April 2021, for the Census Bureau to release its own postelection survey, which indicated that at least 16.4 million Latinos had reported casting ballots in the presidential contest, nearly 4 million more than in 2016, an astounding increase of 30.1 percent, the largest single four-year jump ever recorded in the Latino vote. It also signified that Latinos achieved nearly double the historic jump in turnout among all voters of 15.9 percent.[76]

Meanwhile, the main narrative of a dramatic shift toward Trump among Latinos was, in fact, not that dramatic at all.[77] It was generally within the ballpark of how Republican presidential candidates have historically fared among Latinos—and was actually at the low end. Even if you accept the results of the much-criticized Edison Research exit poll's estimate that Trump garnered 32 percent of the Hispanic vote, some Republican presidential candidates have achieved far better results. George W. Bush did so twice (a high of 40 percent in 2004) and Ronald Reagan twice (a high of 37 percent in 1984), while John McCain (31 percent in 2008) and George H. W. Bush (30 percent in 1988) achieved results similar to those of Trump in losing efforts.[78] Researchers at UCLA's Latino Policy and Politics Initiative concluded that Biden won 70 percent of Latino voters nationwide to 27 percent for Trump. Yes, they acknowledged, there was a small increase in the percentage of Latinos who voted for Trump from four years earlier, but the main story, they insisted, was the unprecedented increase in Latino voters, which helped ensure Biden's victory in key battleground states, among them, Arizona, Pennsylvania, and Wisconsin, in each of which Biden garnered more than 70 percent of Latino votes.[79]

LATINO VOTERS IN THE TWENTY-FIRST CENTURY

Some studies claim the Latino electorate is conservative at heart, but I would urge caution before accepting such conclusions. True, wherever Hispanic communities achieve relative prosperity—in places like Miami and Orlando, northern New Mexico, Contra Costa County, California—they inevitably become more moderate in their voting patterns. But Hispanics remain overwhelmingly concentrated among the country's working-class and lower-middle-class sectors. The economic quest of that majority to improve its standard of living necessarily brings it into conflict with corporate America's drive to achieve maximum profit from fewer and fewer workers. Moreover, Latinos are constantly influenced by news of how people in their homelands are struggling to survive within the new global economy. Those economic realities, together with the anti-Hispanic bias they confront each day in the United States, continually force them, no matter their family's nation of origin, to bind together to defend their interests. Furthermore, Latin American immigrants are more politically sophisticated than most of us realize. They come from countries where civil wars and political strife have forced them to pay attention to politics.

Most experts argue that the new Latino electorate will never function in nearly the unified manner that African Americans have historically. The terms *Hispanic* or *Latino*, they note, are umbrella categories masking huge ethnic differences, and given those differences, Latinos will gradually adopt voting patterns closer to the old European immigrants. While the first conclusion is certainly true, the second fails to appreciate the emergence during the last several decades of a rich new Latinx identity on U.S. soil. From what was at first largely a Mexican American population in the Southwest and a Puerto Rican enclave in New York City, the different Hispanic groups have undergone, and continue to undergo, cultural amalgamation among themselves—through intermarriage, through shared knowledge of one another's music, food, and traditions, through common language, through a common experience of combating anti-Hispanic prejudice and being shunted into the same segregated neighborhoods. No longer do a handful of Mexican American or Puerto Rican or Cuban groups dominate the national political debate on Hispanics; rather, the leaders of once disparate groups are now speaking with a more unified voice through organizations like the National Association of Latino Elected and Appointed Officials, the National Hispanic Agenda, the National Hispanic Chamber of Commerce, the Labor Council for Latin American Advancement, and the National Hispanic Political Action Committee.

In early 2021, nearly seventy years after Ed Roybal pioneered modern Latino politics, there were more than 6,800 Latino elected officials in the nation, including a record 6 in the U.S. Senate: Catherine Cortez Masto (D-NV), Ted Cruz (R-TX), Bob Menendez (D-NJ), Ben Ray Luján (D–NM), Alex Padilla (D-CA), and Marco Rubio (R-FL). Yet those 6,800 still represented slightly more than 1 percent of all elected officials, at a time when Latinos composed 18.7 percent of the total population.[80]

Given the continuing economic crisis in Latin America, more

immigrants will keep coming, and given the maturing of this inter-ethnic Hispanic identity here, I have no doubt that the twenty-first century will lead to a full awakening of the voting power of Latinos. During the next few decades Hispanic Americans will continue to register and vote in record numbers, energized by the historic sense that "our time has come." The enormous impact of the Latinx population's growth is increasingly evident. The 2020 census, for example, revealed there were thirteen states in which Latinos amounted to more than 15 percent of the total population (see table 6). That included six contiguous states—California, Nevada, Colorado, Arizona, New Mexico, and Texas—whose combined population was more than 35 percent Latino, an unmistakable sign that a new "Brown Belt" has begun to emerge precisely in the portion of the U.S. Southwest that was once a part of Mexico.

Table 6

States with More than 15 Percent Hispanic Population in 2020[81]

	Hispanic/Latino/Latinx Percentage of Population
New Mexico	47.7%
California	39.4%
Texas	39.3%
Arizona	30.7%
Nevada	28.7%
Florida	26.5%
Colorado	21.9%
New Jersey	21.6%
New York	19.5%
Illinois	18.2%
Connecticut	17.3%
Rhode Island	16.6%
Utah	15.1%

Hispanic political leaders who fully heed this demographic transformation, and who refuse to be subsumed into the ever-recurring Black-white divide on racial issues or to be taken for granted as a preserve of the centrist wing of the Democratic Party, will succeed in turning the Hispanic voter, along with the growing number of Asian American voters, into the basis of a new interracial coalition, or "Third Force," in American political life. Such a Third Force movement would seek to build a genuinely multiracial, multiethnic civic majority. Its aim would be not just getting more people to vote, but getting them to participate actively in social and civic institutions, creating space and voice for citizens of all races and ethnic groups to achieve an end to racial injustice. Because such a coalition would reach out to those who so far have been alienated and disenfranchised, it would necessarily change the terms of national debate, providing an alternative to the corporate-conservative minority that has financed and run both major political parties throughout our nation's modern history.

By building such a coalition to renew American politics, the descendants of Juan Seguín will not merely reclaim their role in American history, they will rewrite it.

11

IMMIGRANTS OLD AND NEW:
Closing Borders of the Mind

For fifteen centuries they were the backbone of a continent,
unchanging while all about them radical changes again and
again recast the civilization in which they lived.

—OSCAR HANDLIN, *The Uprooted*

Immigration policy has provoked fierce public debate in the United
States for more than thirty years. Repeated boom-to-bust periods
of the nation's economy—the latest being the Great Recession of
2008–2009 and the COVID-19 pandemic of 2020–2021—have left
millions of ordinary Americans reeling from prolonged stagnation
in their standard of living, loss of good-paying factory jobs to offshore production, skyrocketing housing costs, and lack of affordable
health insurance. Frustration with the gyrations of global capitalism
and growing income inequality prompted many to direct their anger
at undocumented immigrants as a source of the nation's economic
woes, particularly those from Latin America. This was especially
true during the presidencies of George W. Bush and Barack Obama,
when mass deportations of migrants reached record levels. But the
presidential campaign of Donald Trump and the ensuing Trump
presidency marked a qualitative escalation of hostility against immigrants, as the White House itself championed racist hysteria, and as
the federal government embarked on an unprecedented assault on
migrants through mass detentions and separation of families arriving at the border, through draconian restrictions on legal migration,

and through overt threats against the Mexican and Central American governments, including sharp cuts in foreign aid, all aimed at forcing those governments to shut down migrant flows.[1]

Many Americans, however, were stunned in 2018 at the impact of the Trump policies, especially a "zero tolerance" order to criminally prosecute all migrants apprehended crossing the border, which under federal law is a misdemeanor for first-time offenders.[2] Those policies soon produced heartrending images of thousands of migrants being housed by Customs and Border Protection (CBP) agents inside chain-link cages at overcrowded detention camps, with parents forcibly separated from their children, some of them only infants and toddlers. During fiscal year 2019–2020, the astounding number of nearly seventy thousand migrant children were held in U.S. detention without their parents, according to an investigation by the Associated Press and PBS's *Frontline*—a 42 percent increase over the previous year. Even more shocking were the rash of child deaths, such as Jakelin Caal Maquin, a seven-year-old Guatemalan girl who fell ill and died after she and her father were detained by CBP while crossing the border. They were only a small part of the thousands of migrants—estimates range from seven thousand to ten thousand—who have perished while attempting to cross the border since the 1990s. Yet by late 2020, nearly fourteen years after Congress first attempted to overhaul the nation's immigration laws, no major progress had occurred in Washington.[3]

Anti-immigrant backlashes, however, are not new in U.S. history. Each major wave of newcomers to our shores has provoked consternation among previous settlers, who then justified periodic clampdowns with allegations against the migrants that were very similar to those heard today. This most recent nativist backlash is the third major eruption since the country's founding, though there have been several smaller ones. It began in the late 1980s, as Americans were increasingly told by advocates of restrictionist policies that the new Latino immigrants were *different* from the past waves of Europeans. They were clinging to their native language, refusing to assimilate, draining public services, and producing a disturbing share of criminals. Television news and radio talk shows stoked such fears, depicting immigration agents at our borders and airports as overwhelmed by the massive influx of illegal foreigners. As the panic spread, a gamut of conservative politicians, moderate academics, and even liberal environmentalists demanded a crackdown. The nation's way of life, its very identity, was under siege, they said.

California struck the first major blow in 1994 when its voters overwhelmingly approved Proposition 187, banning all public services for unauthorized immigrants, a measure that was subsequently overturned by the courts. Then, in 1996, Congress enacted and President Clinton signed a series of draconian new laws meant to sharply reduce both legal and illegal immigration and to speed up deportation of those the government deemed undesirable. Following the devastating terror attacks on the World Trade Center in 2001, the newly created Department of Homeland Security redoubled the federal government's effort to control the nation's borders and deport undocumented immigrants.

On December 6, 2005, James Sensenbrenner, a conservative Republican from Milwaukee, introduced a new bill in the U.S. House of Representatives, the Border Protection, Antiterrorism, and Illegal Immigration Control Act, which sought to make it a felony for any foreigner to reside in the country illegally or for others to hire or assist such undocumented immigrants. Historically, it has been a civil violation for any immigrant to be in the country unlawfully. Whenever immigration authorities apprehended such persons, they detained them and began deportation proceedings. The Sensenbrenner bill sought to change that by turning all illegal immigrants into felons, along with any citizen or legal immigrant who hired an undocumented worker, or any family member, social service worker, or religious minister who housed or provided assistance to one. In addition, the bill sought to step up the militarization of the U.S.-Mexico border.

Many Americans were understandably concerned that foreign terrorists would take advantage of porous borders to unleash another assault. But to many Latino leaders, the post-9/11 immigration crackdown hearkened back to the massive repatriation campaign launched by President Hoover during the early 1930s or to President Eisenhower's "Operation Wetback" in 1954, both of which targeted Mexican migrants.

Sensenbrenner's proposal flew through several committees in record time with virtually no hearing. On December 16, ten days after the bill was introduced, the House of Representatives passed it in a 239–182 vote. Its adoption hit immigrant rights advocates like a thunderbolt. With the Senate scheduled to take up its own version of the legislation in the spring of 2006, those advocates feverishly rushed to stop the bill's final passage and began pressing Congress to overhaul immigration laws completely. They also decided to organize protests in the spring that would highlight the need to legalize millions of undocumented immigrants. Thus began perhaps the biggest protest movement in our nation's history up to that time, a movement that merits deeper analysis for its long-term significance.

THE MEGA MARCHES BEGIN

The first sign that something unprecedented was afoot came on Friday, March 10, 2006, in Chicago, when a crowd estimated by local police at more than one hundred thousand assembled at Union Park and paraded to Federal Plaza in the downtown Loop. These marchers were not the usual activists commonly seen at antiwar or labor protests. Although it included sizable contingents of Polish, Irish, and Chinese immigrants, the crowd was largely composed of young Latinos, a sector of Chicago's population that had been almost invisible to the city's elite until then.[4]

The Chicago event was followed by a March 23 rally of more than ten thousand people at Zeidler Park in Sensenbrenner's own city of Milwaukee. The next day, an estimated twenty-five thousand Latinos gathered in front of the Phoenix office of Republican U.S. senator John Kyle, a supporter of the bill, in one of the largest protests ever seen in Arizona.[5]

Then on March 25, the streets of downtown Los Angeles were jammed by yet another protest, one that stretched for miles. Its size far exceeded the most optimistic expectations of its leaders. One of the chief organizers, Victor Narro of the UCLA Labor Center, originally secured a police permit for five thousand people to trudge from Olympic Boulevard and Broadway to Los Angeles City Hall. In the week before the event, Narro revised that number to fifty thousand. On the day of the rally at least half a million people showed up, according to official police estimates; organizers claimed the turnout was closer to one million. Both sides agreed, however, that the event was historic even by California standards. "I've been on the force thirty-eight years, and I've never seen a rally this big," police commander Louis Gray Jr., who supervised the event, told the Associated Press.[6]

Part of the reason the huge rallies caught establishment leaders and even protest organizers by surprise was the powerful impact of the Spanish-language press and radio DJs. In Los Angeles, for instance, many demonstrators were inspired to act by Spanish-language public-affairs shows such as *Here We Are with Alfredo Gutierrez*, on Radio Campesina, KNAI-FM (88.3), and Elias Bermudez's *Let's Talk*, on KIDR-AM (740). Others had learned of the protests by tuning in to *Piolín por la Mañana*, a popular syndicated Spanish-language morning show broadcast locally on KHOT-FM (105.9). The show's host, Eddie "Piolín" Sotelo, urged his listeners to participate, to wear white to symbolize peace, and to march peacefully.[7]

The same day of the Los Angeles event, more than fifty thousand Latinos gathered in Denver's Civic Center Park, while five thousand rallied in Charlotte, North Carolina. Over the following days, a dizzying string of similar actions occurred in Detroit (fifty thousand), Nashville (eight thousand), and Columbus, Ohio (seven thousand). Increasingly, the rallies were accompanied by spontaneous walkouts of hundreds and even thousands of Latino students from high schools and colleges throughout the Southwest.[8]

But March was only the prelude to a second and more widespread wave of protests the following month. On April 9 and 10, between 1.3 and 1.7 million people joined rallies in more than one hundred towns and cities. In Dallas, more than 350,000 participated on Sunday, April 9, in perhaps the largest social protest in the history of Texas.[9] The following day, Phoenix, New York, and Washington, D.C., all drew crowds of more than 100,000 each. The sheer number of rallies over those two days was astounding, especially on April 10, which was a weekday. Among the most striking of the smaller events was in Albertville, Alabama, where a crowd of Latinos estimated at between 2,000 and 5,000 paraded through town. The turnout represented from a tenth to a quarter of Albertville's entire population.

More protests continued intermittently throughout April. But by then many of the movement's key organizers had started to focus their attention on a third wave of nationwide actions that were scheduled for May 1, International Workers' Day.

This final wave would become the new movement's most controversial and most startling effort. May Day immigrant rights rallies had been organized for years in a handful of U.S. cities by radical migrant worker groups from Central and South America, where International Workers' Day is a traditional holiday and day of protest. But such events in the United States had typically attracted only tiny followings. All of that changed in the aftermath of the March and April events. The new coalition's more radical community-based organizations insisted that the only way to achieve comprehensive immigration reform in Congress was through a vivid demonstration of the importance of Latinos and other immigrants to the U.S. economy. It was time to go beyond simple rallies, they said, and May Day was the perfect time to mount a one-day national boycott and work stoppage by immigrant workers. They called it the Great American Boycott, while others dubbed it A Day Without Immigrants.

The call for the boycott splintered the national alliance. The more moderate establishment wing, which included the Catholic Church, major labor organizations like the Service Employees International Union, the big Washington-based immigration lobbying groups, and the Democratic Party, openly condemned any work stoppage. Such aggressive action would anger white Americans and harden opposition to reform among conservative Republicans in Congress, they warned.

By then, however, established leaders had lost effective control of the millions of Latinos awakened to action by the huge March and April protests. In Chicago, Los Angeles, Seattle, Denver, and dozens of other cities, May Day rallies drew even more overwhelming crowds than earlier events that spring.

The tactic of a work stoppage/boycott proved more effective than anyone had imagined. In California, 90 percent of the truckers at the Port of Los Angeles stayed home on May 1. Attendance in the city's public schools that day dropped by 27 percent. Farms came to a halt throughout the fertile Central and Imperial valleys in the biggest agricultural work stoppage in California history. In other parts of the country, major corporations like Tyson Foods, Perdue, and Swift gave their workers the day off rather than risk widespread disruption of their production. In New York City, major immigrant neighborhoods such as Washington Heights and Brooklyn's Sunset Park turned into virtual ghost towns as thousands of Latino- and Korean-owned businesses shuttered their doors for the day.[10]

How did scores of little-known Latino activists manage to organize such unprecedented nationwide protests even though they were scattered across the country, possessed few financial resources, and had to overcome stiff opposition to their tactics from their allies in the political establishment? To fully comprehend their historic accomplishment, one must first dispel the notion that the leaders of the Mega Marches were some ragtag collection of inexperienced community activists or that Washington's liberal politicians and union leaders orchestrated their moves. In reality, they represented the culmination of grassroots political organizing by three generations of Latino leaders. Many of those leaders were seasoned organizers from trade union and farmworker organizations in the United States or in their native Latin American homelands.

The oldest generation of those leaders had first become active during the Chicano and Puerto Rican nationalist upsurges of the 1960s and 1970s, according to a study by political scientist Alfonso Gonzales. In Los Angeles, for instance, key organizers like Javier Rodríguez, a media strategist for the March 25th Coalition, and Nativo Lopez, president of the Mexican American Political Association, had both been members of CASA (Centro de Acción Social Autónoma), a radical Latino labor organization founded decades earlier by Bert Corona, the legendary Chicano organizer of Mexican migrant workers. Others, like Armando Navarro and Carlos Montes, had originally emerged from the Raza Unida Party and Brown Beret movements of the 1970s.[11]

A second, younger generation had drawn vital experience during the 1980s from involvement in the immigration amnesty and Central American sanctuary movements. Guatemalan-born Juan José Gutiérrez, executive director of Latino Movement USA, for example, and Mexican American Gloria Saucedo, director of the Hermandad Mexicana Nacional of the San Fernando Valley, had both worked on amnesty efforts that led to the Immigration Reform and Control Act of 1986. Gutiérrez became one of the most visible spokespeople for the 2006 protests.

The long and brutal character of the wars in El Salvador, Guatemala, and Nicaragua meant that political activists who survived those conflicts and fled to the United States as refugees were often far more experienced and resourceful organizers than the Chicanos and Puerto Ricans who had grown up here.

The third and youngest generation of leaders came from the ranks of former Latino college students who had become active in campaigns against Proposition 187 and other anti-immigrant initiatives during the 1990s. They included Ron Gochez, a founder of the Coordinadora Estudiantil de La Raza, and Esther Portillo, who, after finishing her education, became an organizer of Salvadoran immigrant women in Los Angeles.

The personal histories of the protest organizers in Los Angeles were not unique. Hundreds of Latino community leaders in scores of cities had quietly spent decades accumulating knowledge and experience in the workings of the American political system. By coming together in the spring of 2006 to demand respect for their fellow Hispanic immigrants, they unleashed an unprecedented movement and turned their actions into a seminal moment in the history of U.S. Latinos.

The movement so stunned the nation that our leaders in Washington quickly shelved the Sensenbrenner bill. But the angry backlash from conservative Americans grew so strong that in 2007 it derailed any efforts to achieve the immigration advocates' main goal—comprehensive immigration reform. Meanwhile, the movement itself soon fractured in disputes between the big national organizations and the grassroots groups. The Washington groups urged compromise with Republicans: tougher new penalties for the undocumented, a new guest worker program, and militarization of the border in exchange for some form of drawn-out legalization program. The more grassroots organizations insisted on a less restrictive path toward citizenship and opposed further militarization of the border.

Some of what the current nativists say is undoubtedly true. The latest immigration to the United States has been markedly different from previous waves. Fifty-nine million foreigners settled in the United States between 1965 and 2015, with each decade marking an increase in arrivals over the previous one. This immigration wave thus surpasses in number any fifty-year period in the country's history, the previous high having been the 37.2 million who came between 1880 and 1930, though the population of the country was much smaller back then. Unlike earlier waves, half the new immigrants this time have been from Latin America and the Caribbean, and another quarter have come from Asia and Africa. The sheer size of the migration from those regions has permanently transformed the long-held image of the United States as a nation of transplanted Europeans.[12]

And some of those new immigrants do differ from the Europeans who came before them—even from today's Asian immigrants—but not due to some innate propensity to fall into crime and poverty or some conscious and stubborn refusal to learn English and enter the American mainstream. Rather, the Latin American and Caribbean immigrants confronted specific external factors in the nature and the timing of their migration that greatly influenced their integration—or lack of integration—into our national life. Unlike the Europeans and Asians, Latin Americans moved from the backyard of the U.S. empire to its heartland, from one part of the New World to another. Given that their countries of origin were so much closer to the United States, in both geographical and political terms, Latin American migration has historically been more fluid and uncontainable than that of Europeans and Asians, involving more travel back and forth, more communication and physical connection between the migrants and their homelands, and that in turn has led to far stronger ties between them and their old cultures than previous migrants experienced.

In addition, because they came from countries that have been long dominated by the United States, the attitude of Latin American migrants toward North American society was invariably more ambivalent, certainly more critical, than those of newcomers from other parts of the world. Finally, the timing of their arrival, as the United States was entering a postindustrial information-based economy, had enormous impact on the ability of Latin American migrants to assimilate in the same manner their European counterparts did in previous eras. No matter what restrictions are placed on it, however, Latin American immigration seems sure to continue at historically high levels deep into this new century, for it is fueled by political, economic, and demographic forces beyond the control of any set of immigration "reforms." Among those forces are:

1. Periodic economic crises in Latin America that continue to deepen the region's wealth divide and push migrants here;

2. Corporate globalization, which inexorably *pulls* Latin Americans here;

3. A declining birth rate and aging of the white population of the United States, which assures a continued *demand* for low-paid Latin American labor.

FROM BACKLASH TO BACKLASH

In 1729, Pennsylvania's Quakers, having concluded that the newly arrived Scotch-Irish immigrants were an unworthy and crime-prone lot, passed a law to penalize those who brought them in.[13]

Shortly after the War of Independence, the descendants of the original colonists assumed the label "native" Americans to distinguish themselves from those who arrived later. It didn't take long for an influx of newcomers to alarm them. During the 1840s, Irish escaping the Great Famine and German workers and intellectuals fleeing the repression that followed the failed revolutions of 1848 began arriving in large numbers. These immigrants were Catholics, which worried the older settlers, and they quickly established their voice and strength at the voting booth. They built formidable urban political machines that openly challenged Protestant power by opposing public schools and temperance laws. Their rising influence led to anti-Catholic bigotry and provoked the founding of a new anti-immigrant party, the Know-Nothings, or American Party. The Know-Nothings accused the pope and his followers of subverting this country's Protestant origins. The party grew rapidly in influence, and its leaders soon advocated banning the immigration of paupers or criminals, a twenty-one-year wait for citizenship, the mandatory use of the Protestant Bible in all public schools, and a ban on immigrants holding office or receiving federal land grants.[14]

"Their Catholicism and their atheism produce a pest wherever they go," said one Boston Know-Nothing newspaper of the Irish and Germans.[15] One modern sociologist's review of crime convictions by ethnic group in New York City for the year 1859 unmistakably indicates which group was considered the greatest "threat" to society (see table 7).

Table 7

**New York City Crime Convictions
by Ethnic Group (1859)[16]**

Canadians	80
Scotch	118
English	666
Germans	1,403
Irish	11,305

The nativists found intellectual support for their prejudices from a growing school of eugenicists, such as Edward Jarvis, who published studies showing high rates of lunacy among the new immigrants. In

1855, deadly riots erupted between Know-Nothings and German immigrants in Cincinnati, Columbus, and Louisville. By then, the Know-Nothings were so entrenched that they controlled the governorships or legislatures of seven states. Publisher Horace Greeley, their fiercest opponent, estimated that seventy-five congressmen were associated with the party.[17] Only the bitter debate between North and South over slavery finally eclipsed the burgeoning nativist movement; the Know-Nothings became so divided over that issue that they ruptured in 1857 and disappeared from sight.

Another major nativist surge began in the 1870s against the Chinese. That was followed by an even bigger wave in the 1890s that targeted southern and eastern Europeans—Italians, Slovaks, and Jews from Poland and Russia—and which lasted more than thirty years. Racist theories found renewed support among older settlers, as yet another generation of eugenicists, purporting to base themselves on social Darwinism, once again proclaimed immigrants and Blacks as inferior. Among them was Dr. Harry Laughlin, who was appointed a consultant to the House Committee on Immigration and Naturalization in 1922. To buttress his anti-immigrant beliefs, Laughlin reported to Congress that the foreign born in federal and state hospitals had three times the insanity rate of American natives.[18]

"The European governments took the opportunity to unload upon careless, wealthy and hospitable America the sweepings of their jails and asylums," charged a typical writer of the period.

> The result was the new immigration . . . [which] contained a large and increasing number of the weak, the broken and the mentally crippled of all races drawn from the lowest stratum of the Mediterranean basin and the Balkans, together with hordes of the wretched, submerged populations of the Polish ghettos. Our jails, insane asylums and almshouses are filled with this human flotsam and the whole tone of American life, social, moral and political, has been lowered and vulgarized by them.[19]

Bowing to this public outcry, Congress passed the most restrictive immigration law in U.S. history, with a nationality-based national quota system. This nativism found particular popularity in the Ku Klux Klan, which swelled to six million members in the 1920s while championing anti-Black racism and rejecting modernism and urbanization. Jim Crow laws were enacted throughout the South by then. In 1919 alone, seventy-four Blacks were lynched.[20]

A century later, our nation is in the midst of another nativist tide, one that has ebbed and flowed since the 1970s. In 1980, *Time* magazine startled middle America with its proclamation that the eighties would be the "Decade of the Hispanic," while *Foreign Affairs* warned its influential readers that "50 percent or more of legal and illegal immigrants to the United States have come from a single foreign-language group [Spanish-speaking]" from 1968 to 1977.[21]

Five years later, former Colorado governor Richard Lamm endorsed a movement against Hispanic immigration in a much-publicized book, *The Immigration Time Bomb*. "Most of us would not want the United States to be unrecognizably different from the way it is today," Lamm wrote. "But if you don't believe that unassimilated immigrants have the power to change America, go to Miami, in Dade County, Florida." There, he said, white English-speaking Americans were fleeing and Black Americans had become victims of the "culture clash, the feeling of being a foreigner within one's own country."[22] Lamm was among the first prominent U.S. leaders to charge that the new immigrants, unlike prior waves, were responsible for a rise in crime and were resisting assimilation.

Soon after Lamm's book appeared, Congress passed the first federal attempt to clamp down on contemporary immigration, the 1986 Immigration Reform and Control Act (IRCA), sponsored by Wyoming senator Alan Simpson. IRCA coupled an amnesty program for long-term undocumented immigrants with stiff fines against employers who hired unauthorized migrants. While it led to the legalization of 2.6 million people who were already in the country, IRCA failed to stem the tide of illegal entries.

Much of that failure was the government's fault. While federal officials beefed up border interdiction programs, they were slow to crack down on employers who knowingly broke the law by recruiting and hiring undocumented workers. Between 1989 and 1994, as part of President Reagan's policy to reduce the size of government, the Immigration and Naturalization Service (INS) cut in half the number of agents assigned to enforce employer sanctions. Predictably, the number of fines issued dropped by the same amount. By 1994, INS was completing fewer than two thousand investigations annually and had a backlog of thirty-six thousand cases.[23]

In reaction to IRCA's inadequacy, whites near the Mexican border began to dramatize their frustration at uncontrolled immigration. Citizens in Southern California formed vigilante movements like Light Up the Border, which gathered at night to shine their car headlights across the border and stop Mexicans from crossing illegally. In some cases, armed groups of white supremacists took to violence against immigrants.[24]

As alien menace stories proliferated, politicians responded.[25] Pat Buchanan became the first major presidential candidate since World War II to run on an anti-immigrant platform in the 1992 Republican primary. Two years later, Republicans incorporated his stance into their Contract with America. By 1995, another much-ballyhooed book, Peter Brimelow's *Alien Nation*, staked out an even more radical stand. Our "white nation," Brimelow warned, was being subverted by uncontrolled Third World immigration. "There is no precedent for a sovereign country undergoing such a rapid and radical transformation of its ethnic character in the entire history of the world," he alleged.[26] Along with other populist conservatives, Brimelow blamed the liberal Democrats in Congress for opening the floodgates to nonwhite migrants through the Immigration and Naturalization Act of 1965. He called for a 1920s-like retrenchment, a near-total moratorium on immigration to save white America from social and racial degeneration.

Notions like Brimelow's and Buchanan's, fueled by right-wing talk radio hosts, resonated across the heartland. The result was a rash of 1996 immigration laws that have led to a virtual militarization of our border with Mexico, sharp reductions in legal immigration quotas, skyrocketing fees and other economic obstacles for those applying for legal residency or citizenship, and accelerated deportation procedures for noncitizens convicted of even the most minimal of crimes.

In the aftermath of the huge immigration protests of 2006, the Bush administration activated the most extensive government campaign of roundups and deportations of undocumented immigrants since the days of Operation Wetback. Nearly nine hundred thousand people were deported by Immigration and Customs Enforcement from 2006 to 2008—nearly three times the number removed from 2001 to 2003.

Military-style raids by ICE agents became so prevalent at many low-wage factories and in poor Latino neighborhoods that the news media soon ceased to chronicle all but the biggest ones. The dragnets at big-name factories usually drew the greatest attention, but more shocking and terrifying were the thousands of invisible pre-dawn invasions of homes by teams of armed ICE agents searching for "criminal aliens," and the lockdowns of entire neighborhoods in an effort to seize violent gang members.

THE CAMPAIGN OF WORKPLACE RAIDS

Between 2002 and 2006, workplace arrests of undocumented immigrants skyrocketed by 750 percent, going from 485 to 3,667. They continued climbing, to 4,077 in 2007 and then to 5,184 in 2008.[27] In many of the early raids, hundreds of immigrant parents were summarily removed to distant federal detention centers without any chance to call schools or family members to arrange for the care of their children. That practice provoked such a public outcry that ICE officials began outfitting detained mothers of young children with electronic ankle bracelets and releasing them temporarily on humanitarian grounds until their deportation hearings. Still, thousands of children, many of them U.S. citizens, have ended up separated for months or even permanently from their undocumented parents who were jailed and subsequently deported.

In several cases, local officials, having received no warning beforehand about the raids, publicly condemned the terror ICE actions were sowing in local immigrant communities. Following scores of arrests at a Swift and Company meat plant in Marshalltown, Iowa, in December 2006, for instance, Iowa governor Tom Vilsack warned Homeland Security secretary Michael Chertoff that the raid had "created undue hardship for many not at fault, and led to resentment and further mistrust of government."

Among the most spectacular raids were:

- December 16, 2006: Hundreds of ICE agents set up cordons around six Swift meatpacking plants—in Worthington, Minnesota; Greeley, Colorado; Cactus, Texas; Grand Island, Nebraska; Hyrum, Utah; and Marshalltown, Iowa—in an action they dubbed Operation Wagon Train. The agents locked down the plants, interrogated all employees, and eventually detained 1,282 on immigration violations. Those arrested included workers from Mexico, Guatemala, Honduras, El Salvador, Peru, Laos, Sudan, and Ethiopia. Sixty-five were slapped with felony charges related to identity theft.[28]

- January 24, 2007: Agents arrested twenty-one workers at the Smithfield plant in Tar Heel, North Carolina, and in the surrounding neighborhood, after which hundreds of workers on other shifts abandoned their jobs and fled the town for fear of being detained.[29]

♦ March 6, 2007: More than 360 mostly women workers were arrested at the Michael Bianco factory in New Bedford, Massachusetts, a manufacturer of backpacks and gear for the military. The workers were charged with immigration violations.

♦ May 23, 2007: More than one hundred employees at George's Processing, a poultry plant in Butterfield, Missouri, were detained and jailed for deportation.[30]

♦ June 12, 2007: More than 165 at the Fresh Del Monte produce plant in Portland, Oregon, were arrested. Three were charged with criminal identity fraud, while the others were sent to immigration detention pending deportation.[31]

♦ April 16, 2008: Agents conducted simultaneous raids on five Pilgrim's Pride poultry plants—in Batesville, Arkansas; Live Oak, Florida; Chattanooga, Tennessee; Mount Pleasant, Texas; and Moorefield, West Virginia—and arrested four hundred for immigration violations.[32]

♦ May 12, 2008: More than 390 workers at the Agriprocessors kosher meatpacking plant in Postville, Iowa, were held, pending their deportation.

♦ August 25, 2008: In the largest workplace raid in U.S. history, ICE agents surrounded and entered the Howard Industries transformer plant in Laurel, Mississippi. They rounded up 595 of the company's 800 employees, almost all of them Latinos. Of those detained, only 9 were charged in federal court with identity theft. Some 100 mothers, sole caregivers of young children, were later fitted with electronic bracelets and released on humanitarian grounds pending deportation, while about 475 workers were shipped to a federal detention center in Jena, Louisiana.[33]

A GROWING TERROR
IN LATINO NEIGHBORHOODS

The more pervasive aspect of the extraordinary federal crackdown were predawn raids conducted by teams of heavily armed federal agents. Acting under two little-known Homeland Security initiatives,

Operation Community Shield and the National Fugitive Operations Program, ICE agents cordoned off entire streets in scores of residential Latino communities throughout the country, often forcing their way into private homes without displaying warrants. The ostensible aim of these raids was to arrest criminal aliens, either dangerous felons, gang members, or sex offenders.

Under the Fugitive Operations Program, for example, more than ninety-six thousand people were apprehended between 2003 and 2008. But a study by the Migration Policy Institute found that 73 percent of those people had no criminal conviction. In 2007, 40 percent of those seized under the program were merely "ordinary status violators," the study concluded. In other words, a program designed by Congress to go after dangerous fugitives had turned, in large part, into a way for ICE agents to raid individual homes and seize undocumented immigrants.[34]

In addition, the flagrant constitutional abuses that agents too often committed against both immigrants and U.S. citizens caught up in these raids enraged Latino leaders and civil rights advocates. Researchers at the Cardozo School of Law analyzed immigration arrest records in the New York and New Jersey area and court cases around the country and found an "unacceptable level of illegal entries by ICE agents during home raid operations in violation of the Fourth Amendment."[35]

"There is story after story," the report noted, "of ICE agents, armed with only an administrative warrant, yelling and banging on doors and then forcing their way into homes in the pre-dawn hours by pushing their way in if residents unlock their doors, and otherwise climbing through windows or kicking in doors. Some residents report being awakened by the presence of armed ICE officers in their bedrooms who illegally gained entry through an unlocked door."

In one case in early 2009 in Arizona, Jimmy Slaughter, himself a former Homeland Security officer, filed suit against ICE. In an affidavit, Slaughter claimed: "I was at home with my wife when the door bell rang. I opened the door and noticed approximately 7 uniformed ICE agents with vests and guns standing at my door. . . . I opened the door to look at the paperwork and five agents entered my house. The agents then told my wife to stand in the center of 'OUR' living room. Not once did anyone say they had a warrant."[36]

In more than half of the one thousand New York and New Jersey arrest records the Cardozo researchers examined, agents never obtained consent to enter the homes. New Jersey ICE agents were "either fabricating consent in their reports or misunderstanding the legal requirement of consent," the researchers concluded. In one example, an agent from the Newark Fugitive Operations team reported that they "gained access" to an apartment "by way of knocking, thus the door was opened from the intensity of the banging."[37]

Moreover, in two-thirds of the arrests, the people apprehended were not the criminal aliens the agents were seeking. Most were civil immigration violators who had been swept up in the process. More than 90 percent of those collateral arrestees were Latino, even though Latinos represented just 66 percent of the targets of the raids, which suggests that Hispanics were being disproportionately targeted.[38]

Following a March 2007 immigration raid in San Rafael, a suburban community north of San Francisco, town mayor Al Boro wrote to U.S. senator Dianne Feinstein to complain that ICE agents had left his residents "in turmoil." Boro warned that "waking people up in the dark of night, at 5 a.m., in their homes seems more like a scare tactic than a law enforcement necessity."[39]

The federal crackdowns had even more severe effects in parts of the country where zealous local officials adopted their own laws and policies to target illegal immigrants. In July 2007, for instance, the town of Hazleton, Pennsylvania, adopted an ordinance to penalize local businesses that employed "unauthorized aliens" and another to require "proof of legal citizenship or residency" for anyone seeking to rent an apartment in the town. Hazleton mayor Lou Barletta publicly declared it an effort to drive out illegal immigrants. Even though a federal judge overturned the law a few months later, Barletta became a media celebrity and a hero among right-wing talk show hosts for his tough stance on immigration.

An even bigger folk hero on Fox News and other conservative media was Joe Arpaio, the sheriff of Maricopa County, Arizona, which covers Phoenix and its sprawling suburbs. Arpaio dubbed himself America's Toughest Sheriff, and his draconian treatment of prisoners and many dragnets into immigrant communities quickly endeared him to contemporary nativists.

But even the conservative Goldwater Institute condemned Arpaio's policies. In a scathing policy report issued in December 2008, the institute concluded that Arpaio's "massive diversion of resources into policing illegal immigration—largely in communities such as Phoenix and Mesa that have police departments—coincides with growing rates of violent crimes, plummeting arrest rates, and increased response time to citizens' calls for help."[40]

Shortly after the Goldwater Institute issued its report, a *New York Times* editorial blog labeled Arpaio "a genuine public menace with a long and well-documented trail of inmate abuses, unjustified arrests, racial profiling, brutal and inept policing and wasteful spending."[41]

In 2010, the Arizona legislature adopted aspects of the Arpaio approach by approving Senate Bill 1070, known as the "show me your papers" law. It authorized local law enforcement officers to stop and grill any individual whom officers had a "reasonable suspicion" was in the country illegally, to request proof of the person's legal status, and to arrest the person if he or she had no proof. Like the Sensenbrenner bill of 2005, the new Arizona law ignited a firestorm among Latinos across the country. But this time the opposition came as well from many African American and even moderate white leaders, who saw it as a new version of racial profiling. With millions of Latinos in the country who are already U.S. citizens, opponents argued, what would constitute "reasonable suspicion" that a person was illegally in the country? In July 2010, a U.S. district judge issued a preliminary injunction against key provisions of the law. Two years later the Supreme Court upheld the provision requiring immigration checks but struck down three other provisions.[42] In the process, Arpaio and Arizona became national symbols of intolerance toward Latinos in much the same way that Selma's sheriff Bull Connor and the state of Alabama were in the 1960s toward African Americans.

Many Latino leaders initially expected President Obama to reverse the worst aspects of the immigration raids that flourished under President Bush. During his campaign for the White House, Obama had repeatedly condemned such crackdowns and had promised Latino leaders he would seek comprehensive immigration reform in his first year in office. But in March 2010, frustrated Latino leaders publicly blasted the new administration's immigration policy. They noted that during Obama's first year in office a record 387,000 people were removed from the country, more than the 369,000 removed in Bush's last year.

"These are the same enforcement practices that we marched against during the Bush administration," said Angelica Salas, director of the Coalition for Humane Immigrant Rights of Los Angeles. On any given day, she noted, thirty-two thousand people were being held in immigration detention facilities under Obama.[43]

IMMIGRATION REFORM DEFEATED AGAIN

Shortly after the new Congress took office in 2013, the Senate, which was then controlled by the Democrats, attempted to tackle immigration reform through a bill that was initially crafted in secret talks by a bipartisan group of senators dubbed the Gang of Eight.[44] President Obama's reelection victory in 2012 had convinced some mainstream conservatives, those more closely allied with the Bush family's wing of the Republican Party, that the party needed to stem its growing alienation from the Latino community. In June, the bipartisan effort, the Border Security, Economic Opportunity, and Immigration Modernization Act of 2013, passed the Senate by a 68–32 margin. But just as had happened in 2007 during the George W. Bush administration, this new bill sparked furious resistance among immigration restrictionists who mobilized to foil its passage in the House.[45]

The key individuals who spearheaded the bill's defeat were Jeff Sessions, the Republican senator from Alabama whom Donald Trump would later name as his first attorney general, and Stephen Miller, an aide to Sessions, who would go on to serve as Trump's first speechwriter and then as a senior White House adviser. During his time in the Senate, Sessions was known as that body's chief proponent of immigration restriction, while Miller was closely allied with the right-wing internet site *Breitbart News*, and with a network of think tanks and lobbying groups that for decades had stoked public fears of a "brown tide" of immigrants. Those groups included the Center for Immigration Studies, the Federation for American Immigration Reform (FAIR), and NumbersUSA. All three were heavily bankrolled by Cordelia Scaife May, the reclusive billionaire philanthropist and heiress of the Mellon-Scaife family fortune. May, who died in 2005, believed the country was "being invaded on all fronts" by foreigners who "breed like hamsters" and who were exhausting natural resources. A 2019 *New York Times* investigation found that May had been for decades the behind-the-scenes godmother of the nation's modern anti-immigrant movement by donating more than $180 million to groups seeking to militarize the border, cap legal immigration, reduce public benefits for immigrants, and end family reunification policies—precisely the agenda Trump adopted as president. Several of the restrictionist groups had been founded by Dr. John Tanton, an advocate of racist eugenicist theories, which led mainstream Republicans to dismiss them as fringe organizations. But Miller utilized the support of that network to mount the campaign in 2013 that defeated the Gang of Eight's immigration reform bill. His victory over immigration moderates within the Republican Party pushed the party even further toward right-wing populism, thus paving the way for the rise of Trump.[46]

Meanwhile, the controversial Joe Arpaio, who had become a lightning rod of national immigration debate, continued to openly flout court orders against racial profiling by his deputies. His bravado drew profuse praise from presidential candidate Trump, who even invited him to speak at the 2016 Republican national convention. Later that year, however, Arpaio was voted out of office, and an Arizona federal judge subsequently convicted him in July 2017 of contempt of court and sentenced him to six months in jail. That sentence was nullified two months later, however, when President Trump pardoned him.[47]

THE NEW MIGRANT SURGE FROM CENTRAL AMERICA

Restrictionists in the United States have long regarded immigration from Mexico as the gravest threat to the country's future. Throughout the latter half of the twentieth century, Mexico was the main sending nation for both legal and unauthorized migrants to this country. As recently as 2000, Mexican nationals composed 98 percent of more than 1.6 million apprehensions made at the border.[48] But that is no longer true. The overall number of people seeking to cross the southern border began dropping significantly in the first decade of this century, the result of both stepped up enforcement by the federal government and a sharp decline in demand for cheap labor due to the Great Recession. Border Patrol apprehensions fell by 2007 to a historic low of 327,000, and they stayed that way for the next decade, only rising significantly in 2017, before climbing again to 857,000 in 2019.[49]

But this time, a dramatic shift had taken place in the composition of the migrants. The number of people coming from Mexico plunged while it surged steadily from Central America's Northern Triangle nations. In fiscal year 2016–2017, for instance, the U.S. Border Patrol recorded more apprehensions at the Southwest border of migrants from El Salvador, Guatemala, and Honduras (199,000) than of Mexicans (188,000). Since then, the difference has grown astronomically, with 607,000 apprehensions of Northern Triangle nationals in FY 2019–2020, compared with just 166,000 of Mexicans, even though the combined population of those three countries barely totals a quarter of that of Mexico's.[50] Not since the civil wars that devastated Central America during the 1980s have so many from that region fled to this country. For Honduras alone, the more than 253,000 migrants apprehended at the border in 2019 represented nearly 2.8 percent of that tiny country's entire population. Even more important, while earlier migrant apprehensions had been largely of single males, those in recent years have been increasingly of families or unaccompanied minors. The latter represented nearly 500,000 apprehensions in 2019.

Why such a marked increase in the migrant flow? Mass media reports and immigrant rights advocates rightly point to phenomenal crime rates and gang violence in the Northern Triangle countries as a key reason so many flee. But other equally significant factors have garnered far less public attention. They include natural disasters (fueled in part by climate change), growing political repression by local elites, and a deepening economic crisis. All of these, including the gang violence, can be traced in no small measure to U.S. government policies toward the region.

Perhaps least understood is the impact of natural disasters and climate change. Few Americans even recall that the deadliest Atlantic storm of the twentieth century struck Central America on October 26, 1998. Hurricane Mitch, a Category 5 storm, killed more than ten thousand people, displaced another 1.5 million from their homes, and destroyed 70 percent of the agricultural infrastructure of Honduras. One of every five inhabitants of Honduras, Nicaragua, El Salvador, and Guatemala was affected. Less than three years later, a series of earthquakes ravaged El Salvador, the most powerful of which erupted on January 13, 2001, and registered 7.6 on the Richter scale. Over the next month, three thousand aftershocks and another large quake followed. By the time the tremors had subsided, more than 1,200 people were dead, nearly 9,000 injured, and some three hundred thousand homes had been damaged or destroyed, along with 75 percent of the country's potable water system. More recently, extreme weather has brought unprecedented drought conditions to Central America's "dry corridor," which stretches through 58 percent of El Salvador, 38 percent of Guatemala, and 21 percent of Honduras. Years with little rainfall since 2014 have brought "levels of food insecurity [that] have not been previously seen in the region," noted a United Nations World Food Program report—this in an area already among the most vulnerable on the planet for natural disasters. Central American migrants, in other words, along with Puerto Ricans who fled the aftermath of Hurricane María, may be the first waves of climate change refugees to arrive in this country.[51]

GANG VIOLENCE: BORN IN THE USA

Donald Trump repeatedly claimed during both his campaign for president and throughout his years in office that the United States was facing an "invasion" of illegal immigrants, especially of criminals from violence-prone Central American gangs such as MS-13. In his January 2017 inauguration speech, for example, Trump railed against "the crime and the gangs and the drugs that have stolen too many lives and robbed our country of so much unrealized potential," and he vowed that "this American carnage stops right here and stops right now." He uttered those words despite U.S. crime rates being at their lowest point since the 1970s.[52] In his first prime-time address to the nation from the Oval Office in January 2019—in the midst of a federal government shutdown he precipitated to force Congress to provide more funding for his border wall—Trump said:

> In Maryland, MS-13 gang members who arrived in the United States as unaccompanied minors were arrested and charged last year after viciously stabbing and beating a 16-year-old girl. Over the last several years, I've met with dozens of families whose loved ones were stolen by illegal immigration. . . . How much more American blood must we shed before Congress does its job?[53]

These apocalyptic descriptions of the Central American gang threat were bogus in multiple ways, obscuring the reality that the United States has been exporting its crime problems to that region for years. Mara Salvatrucha (MS-13) and 18th Street (or M-18), the two gangs repeatedly cited by Trump, *were organizations born and developed right here in the United States*, according to numerous studies by federal and international officials and by crime experts, one of whom labeled them "originally an American phenomenon." A 2007 Congressional Research Service report notes:

> The 18th Street gang was formed by Mexican youth in the Rampart section of Los Angeles in the 1960s who were not accepted into

existing Hispanic gangs. It was the first Hispanic gang to accept members from all races and to recruit members from other states. MS-13 was created during the 1980s by Salvadorans in Los Angeles who had fled the country's civil conflict.[54]

Moreover, while the gangs eventually spread from Southern California across the United States, their initial appearance in Central America was a direct result of specific federal policies. In 1996, two laws passed by Congress and signed by President Clinton, the Illegal Immigration Reform and Immigrant Responsibility Act and the Antiterrorism and Effective Death Penalty Act, expanded the definition of "aggravated felony" to encompass numerous less serious transgressions while also eliminating many recourses immigrants convicted of crimes previously could utilize to challenge their removal from the country. The result was a massive program of deportation of "criminal aliens." Between 2010 and 2017, immigration authorities shipped 1.3 million noncitizens previously convicted of such "aggravated felonies" in the United States back to their homelands. The bulk of them—from 50 to 60 percent per year, according to the Department of Homeland Security's own data—were actually convicted of minor infractions related to immigration, drugs, or traffic-related offenses (such as DUI or hit-and-run), while only a small percentage had actually been guilty of violent crimes. Amazingly, 93 percent of those deported were from just four countries, Mexico, Guatemala, Honduras, and El Salvador, while just 7 percent were from all the other nations of the world combined—such a disproportionate percentage that the entire U.S. deportation system appears aimed at America's closest southern neighbors.[55]

In total, federal officials repatriated some three hundred thousand noncitizens with criminal records to the Northern Triangle nations between 1998 and 2014. Most were young men who had come to the United States as children, grown up here, and spoke little, if any, Spanish. Only a small portion had actually been gang members in the States, and those few had largely joined as a way to feel included and protected in the hostile barrios of urban America. But once shipped back to countries they barely knew and where they had few family connections, the deportees often faced ostracism, most could not find jobs, and they were hounded and abused by local police. Ramped up military and police aid from Washington encouraged the region's governments to target them for repression. Aid to El Salvador, for example, skyrocketed from just $700,000 in 1996 to more than $18 million in 2006. With that money, the right-wing ARENA government of President Francisco Flores commenced its own zero tolerance policy known as Plan *Mano Dura* ("Strong Hand"), with police jailing many youths not for any crime but for just having tattoos associated with gangs. The country's prison population boomed from just seven thousand in 2000 to more than twenty-four thousand a decade later. In neighboring Honduras, President Ricardo Maduro embarked on his own Mano Dura campaign. Local prisons filled up beyond capacity and inmate riots became commonplace. Instead of discouraging gang proliferation, the police abuse and mass jailings fueled it, as the inmates reassembled their networks behind bars. They swiftly founded local *clicas*, or chapters, of the U.S. gangs in Central America's barrios; in turn, these *clicas* rapidly attracted local youths and either supplanted or absorbed existing *pandillas* [local gangs]. And in each of the Northern Triangle countries the *maras* responded to the government's heavy hand by turning even more violent. Estimates of membership in the region's gangs ranged from seventy thousand to one hundred thousand by 2005. Such growth, however, was not inevitable. As political scientist Alfonso Gonzales convincingly argues, by exporting disaffected youths from U.S. cities and then funding a war on gangs and drugs in Central America, U.S. policy makers made "the gang problem and criminal deportees the rationale for [an] emergent transnational system of migration control."[56]

These gangs, moreover, are hardly well-oiled criminal operations involved in significant cross-border drug trafficking into the United States, as President Trump has claimed. "The *maras* (MS-13 and M-18) play very little role in transnational cocaine trafficking," one United Nations report found, and even though their members exist in several countries, this "should not be mistaken for evidence that they operate transnationally, or that they all respond to some international chain of command." Rather, they are essentially street thugs who focus on extorting local businesses, especially in the transport sector, on petty crimes, on kidnapping for ransom, on turf wars among themselves, and on terrorizing into submission residents of communities under their control. In Honduras alone, for example, more than 1,500 people working in transportation have been murdered since 2010.[57]

VIOLENT CRIME FUELS MIGRATION

It is precisely the horrifying level of death and mayhem the *maras* routinely produce that many Central American migrants cite as their reason for fleeing to the United States. The region's murder rates are almost beyond comprehension. At 82 murders per 100,000 residents in 2010, Honduras was the homicide capital of the world, with its rate increasing even more the following year to 92 per 100,000. El Salvador's, meanwhile, skyrocketed to 103 per 100,000 in 2015, among the highest ever recorded. By comparison, the homicide rate in the United Kingdom that year was 1 per 100,000, while it was 4.9 in the United States. In major Central American cities the toll is even more astounding; San Salvador, for example, registered 190 homicides per 100,000 residents in 2015. And while the numbers have diminished in recent years, the region remains among the deadliest on earth. The U.S. policy of mass deportations, according to one 2018 quantitative study, had a "strong and robust effect" on homicide rates in Latin America and the Caribbean, with "the deportation of an additional ten individuals with a criminal record per 100,000 persons in the homeland increase[ing] that country's expected homicide rates by two to three per 100,000 persons." Another study looked at unaccompanied minors apprehended at the U.S.-Mexico border between 2011 and 2016—a staggering 170,000 in total, who represented 8 percent of all the seventeen-year-olds in the region during that period. Analyzing murders in the cities from which the minors came, the researchers concluded that, on average, one additional homicide per year during that six-year span had caused 3.7 more unaccompanied minors to appear at the U.S. border.[58]

There is yet another way U.S. policies have made refugee flight worse: the export of guns. Central America is literally awash in firearms, with an estimated 2.2 million registered weapons and another 2.8 million unregistered, enough to arm one of every three men in the region. Most of those weapons were manufactured in the United States. Enormous caches remain from military aid supplied to the region by Washington and its allies during the civil wars of the 1980s. In El Salvador alone, an estimated 360,000 military-style weapons were never recovered after that country's armed conflict ended, and most remain in private hands. In addition, U.S. arms exports to Mexico and the Northern Triangle have more than doubled over the past decade. Existing stocks are steadily augmented by tens of thousands of handguns that are purchased each year in the United States and smuggled into Mexico and Central America. The result should be no surprise. In 2010, 84 percent of homicides in Guatemala were committed with guns; in Honduras, 82 percent. That's far higher than the 68 percent of murders in the United States committed with guns.[59]

Other factors apart from climate change, gangs, and gun violence have also spurred the refugee exodus, but they are rarely discussed in the current immigration debate. These include rampant political repression, crushing poverty, and systemic government corruption, all of which have led to virtual failed states throughout the region (see chapter 13).

THE IMMIGRATION-INDUSTRIAL
COMPLEX AND THE RISE
OF SANCTUARY CITIES

The resources devoted to migration enforcement by the federal government in recent years are staggering. They have spawned an entire new wing of the existing prison-industrial complex, geared exclusively to preventing noncitizens from entering the country and to prosecuting, imprisoning, and deporting them, even if they previously enjoyed legal status. In 2012, for example, the federal government spent more money on immigration enforcement ($18 billion) than it did on its five main federal enforcement agencies—the FBI, the Drug Enforcement Administration (DEA), the Secret Service, the U.S. Marshals Service, and the Bureau of Alcohol, Tobacco, Firearms and Explosives (ATF), whose combined budgets were $14.4 billion.[60]

A review of Department of Justice statistics over the past thirty years makes obvious the dramatic shift by federal law enforcement agencies to pursuing and criminalizing immigrants. Back in 1998, two-thirds of all federal arrests were of U.S. citizens, but twenty years later that proportion had been reversed: *two-thirds of those arrested in 2018 were noncitizens*, even though the latter composed just 7 percent of the nation's total population. In raw numbers, arrests of noncitizens leaped by more than 50,000 in just one year—from 73,022 in 2017 to 125,027 in 2018. That year, federal agents arrested more Mexican citizens in this country on criminal charges than they did U.S. citizens. Not surprisingly, the number of noncitizens in immigration detention swelled; the average daily population went from 7,000 in 1998 to 52,000 by the spring of 2019.[61]

This unprecedented system of mass detention, prosecutions, and deportations, together with President Trump's continued push to build a complete border wall with Mexico, have generated billions of dollars in government contracts for a slew of private companies. An entire industry has arisen to transport, house, and feed detainees, to care for children removed from their parents, to design and operate drones and the latest surveillance equipment, to track migrants digitally with ever-expanding databases and facial recognition software, to erect walls over rugged deserts and mountains. At the same time, media reports have increasingly spotlighted the huge profits of major contractors, many of whose top executives are also big donors to the Republican Party.[62]

Yet even as the federal government keeps criminalizing the undocumented, hundreds of municipalities across the country have joined a growing resistance, known as sanctuary cities. By early 2018, 760 counties (24 percent of the nation's total number) were declining to hold migrants in their county jails following a detainer request from ICE, and that number has been steadily growing. Such detainers, several federal district courts have ruled, are not legal warrants, and cities that execute them are violating the Fourth Amendment. A smaller, but significant number of counties prohibit other forms of cooperation with ICE, while only 4 percent of them actually had signed contracts with ICE to detain immigrants or enforce immigration law, as did Arizona's Maricopa County under Joe Arpaio. The areas with the biggest number of rebellious counties include virtually all of California, Oregon, Vermont, much of New Mexico, and most of the country's largest cities. Only five days after taking office, Trump issued an executive order declaring undocumented immigration a "clear and present danger" to the country, and he attempted to suppress the sanctuary city movement by ordering suspension of federal funds to them. But the U.S. Court of Appeals for the Ninth Circuit in California later ruled his order unconstitutional.[63]

LEGAL IMMIGRATION ASSAILED

The Trump administration, as mentioned previously, did not merely target unauthorized migrants; it also endeavored to dramatically reverse the historic role of the United States as a haven for the poor and dispossessed, for political or religious refugees from other parts of the world, thus making every effort to radically redefine who can seek U.S. citizenship in the twenty-first century. While a detailed examination of the many changes devised by Trump and his chief immigration adviser, Stephen Miller, is beyond the scope of this book, some of those policies included:

♦ **Dismantling the asylum and refugee system in place since 1980.** By 2020, the federal government had reduced the annual cap on refugee resettlements from 110,000 during the final year of the Obama administration to a mere 18,000 in FY 2019–2020.[64] To hinder Central American asylum seekers from reaching U.S. ports of entry, officials began deeming them ineligible for asylum if they failed to make their request first to a designated "safe third country" through which they passed on their way to the United States. By the end of 2019, the White House had also extracted agreements from the governments of El Salvador, Guatemala, and Honduras to accept deportations of their nationals who had not abided by the safe country requirement.[65]

♦ **Ending the Temporary Protected Status Program.** Trump put an end to TPS, which had allowed nearly three hundred thousand migrants from a half dozen countries, including El Salvador, Honduras, Haiti, and Sudan, to live and work in the United States. The president's order was temporarily blocked in October 2019 by California U.S. District Court Judge Edward Chen, who concluded that a legal challenge against the cancellation had "raised serious questions whether the actions [were] based on animus against non-white, non-European immigrants in violation of Equal Protection guaranteed by the Constitution." Chen ordered a stay pending a trial on the merits of the challenge.[66]

♦ **Expanding the "public charge" rule for legal immigrants.** The administration announced plans to deny green cards to immigrants who use basic public benefits, such as SNAP (food stamps), Medicaid, and public housing assistance, by deeming them likely to become dependent on government at any point in their lives. Scheduled to take effect in October 2019, the new rules were initially blocked by federal judges in New York, California, and Washington, then stayed by appellate courts pending a Supreme Court review. In March 2021, however, the high court dismissed all litigation at the request of the new Biden administration, and President Biden then issued a new executive order rescinding the public charge rule. Also, in May 2019 the Department of Housing and Urban Development announced plans for new rules that would require families in federally assisted public housing to be evicted if even one member of a family is undocumented. In the past, mixed-status families had been allowed to remain in public housing at a reduced subsidy. But with the new rule, local public housing officials estimated that more than one hundred thousand people would have to be evicted, including fifty-five thousand children. Trump left office before the rules took effect, and Biden immediately revoked all such plans.[67]

♦ **Seeking to end family reunification policies.** Trump sought to abandon family reunification policies of the past fifty years—what he and other immigration restrictionists call "chain migration"— and move toward open preferences for more wealthy and well-educated immigrants.

And all of his happened while the president himself consistently issued xenophobic tweets and racist references in his public pronouncements about migrants from Latin America, Africa, and Asia.

SOME MYTHS AND REALITIES

This latest targeting of Latin Americans for mass deportation should come as no surprise given the way nativists and eugenicists have whipped up anti-Latino fervor with recycled myths and stereotypes.

Myth #1: Latin Americans come to this country to get on welfare.

Reality: The labor force participation rate—the percentage of those working or actively seeking a job—is far higher for Latin

American immigrants than for native-born Americans, and often higher than for other immigrants (see table 8).

Table 8

Labor Force Participation Rates for Selected Immigrant Groups, 2010[68]

Country of Birth	Percentage in U.S. Labor Force
Japan	54.3%
Canada	58.0%
United Kingdom	59.9%
United States	64.5%
Dominican Republic	67.8%
Mexico	70.6%
India	71.5%
Ecuador	74.4%
Nicaragua	74.7%
Honduras	77.3%
Guatemala	78.3%
El Salvador	79.2%

Not only are Latino immigrants more prone to work than native-born Americans, but a California study found that half of all immigrants from western Mexico, whether they are in the United States legally or illegally, return home within two years, and fewer than one-third stay for ten years.[69] Mexicans, remember, constitute nearly 60 percent of all Hispanic immigrants.

Myth #2: Immigrants bring more crime to this country. According to a 2019 Gallup Poll, 42 percent of Americans believed migrants worsened the crime situation.

Reality: Crime rates are lower among immigrants, both those who are naturalized U.S. citizens as well as those who are either legal residents or undocumented, than they are among native-born Americans. A 2017 study by the conservative Cato Institute, for example, found that legal immigrants in the United States were 69 percent less likely to be incarcerated than native-born Americans, and undocumented immigrants 44 percent less likely. Meanwhile, a comprehensive study by four universities that analyzed crime data in two hundred metropolitan areas over several decades found that even as the immigrant population in those cities surged, crime rates dropped or remained stable.[70]

Myth #3: Latino immigrants drain public resources such as education and government services.

Reality: Numerous studies demonstrate that immigrants in this country make enormous contributions to U.S. society in taxes and Social Security. The major problem is that those contributions are *unevenly distributed* between federal and local governments.

In New York State, for instance, immigrants, the bulk of them Latinos, made up 17.7 percent of the population in 1995, earned 17.3 percent of total state personal income, and paid 16.4 percent of total taxes. The problem was that 69 percent of those taxes went to the federal government (in Social Security and income taxes), while only 31 percent remained in local coffers, where municipal and state governments incurred the biggest expenses for services to immigrant residents. A similar study in 1990–1991 of undocumented immigrants in Los Angeles County overwhelmingly showed that they contributed $3 billion in taxes, but 56 percent of the money went to Washington, while the local costs of dispensing health care, education, law enforcement, and social services to the county's undocumented population far surpassed the immigrants' contributions.

In essence, young immigrant workers today are helping to fund the federal budget and Social Security benefits of native workers while local governments are being saddled with paying the social costs of services to those immigrants, and in the case of those who are undocumented, the states rarely receive the proportionate share of federal aid to pay those expenses, because many of the immigrants do not qualify for such aid or are not even officially counted.[71]

Two areas where both unauthorized and legal immigrants do utilize government services extensively are public schools and the health care system, and these areas have become the focus of the allegations that immigrants drain the nation's resources. Proponents of this theory rarely mention that most of the twenty million foreign-born residents of the United States in 1990 came here during the prime working years of their lives. The cost of their education was thus borne by the governments of their homelands, yet the sending countries lost the benefits of that investment in human capital when many of their brightest, most ambitious, and resourceful citizens immigrated to the United States. Meanwhile, the United States gained young workers in whose education it did not have to invest any money. As for the children of those immigrants, *all children*, whether from immigrant families or native ones, are a drain on the resources of a country. Only when those children grow up and become productive citizens is the investment made by that society then repaid. So, logically, any calculation of the cost of educating immigrant children should include calculations of their future productivity to the general society.

Myth #4: Latino immigrants take jobs away from U.S. citizens.

Reality: While some studies do indicate that skilled Asian or West Indian immigrants have had a negative impact on white and Black employment in some industries, Latino immigrants, especially those in the country illegally, have actually improved local economies for whites, according to several studies, given that their willingness to work for lower wages has rejuvenated the profitability of ailing industries and thus prevented further job losses.[72] (How many big-city restaurants and service establishments, how many construction and landscaping businesses, for instance, could afford to stay in operation if they had to pay their immigrant workers wages comparable to those of native-born Americans?)

WHY LATINO IMMIGRATION WILL CONTINUE INTO THE TWENTY-FIRST CENTURY

Rupturing immigrant stereotypes is one thing. Harder to grasp is what makes Latino immigration distinct, and the forces that propel it. Consider these factors:

1. *The catastrophic economic crisis in Latin America.*

Latin America's population continues to grow more rapidly than that of the United States, and the conditions its people face are more dire.[73] As recently as 1950, the populations of the United States and Latin America were roughly equal. Since then, Latin America's has multiplied at nearly three times our rate, while a substantial portion of the U.S. increase has been of Latin Americans who migrated here (see table 9).

Table 9

Estimated Population of the United States and Latin America and the Caribbean[74]

	1950	2019	Increase
United States	150,000,000	329,000,000	119%
Latin America and the Caribbean	167,000,000	648,000,000	288%

Meanwhile, living conditions in Latin America have steadily deteriorated, especially during the 1980s and 1990s. More than 40 percent lived in poverty in 1990, according to the United Nations Economic Commission for Latin America.[75] The region's per capita gross domestic product actually declined over that period.[76] Millions of peasants, forced off the land by competition from American agribusiness, have fled to the major cities, where enormous shantytowns have sprouted.

At the same time, a tiny elite benefits from an economic boom brought about in large measure by the selling of public assets and the opening of the region's labor market to multinational corporate investment. More of Latin America's wealth is being siphoned to El Norte each day. The region's total foreign debt, which stood at $575 billion in 1995, had risen to nearly $2.5 trillion by 2021, equaling 79 percent of total domestic product, thus making Latin America and the Caribbean the most indebted region in the developing world, with most of the interest on that debt flowing to the United States and Europe. The COVID-19 pandemic, in particular, caused the biggest economic decline in the region's history and was likely, according to one United Nations report, to "sink per capita GDP to 2010 levels and poverty rates to figures not seen since 2006." That same report noted that the region had suffered 28.7 percent of global COVID fatalities by early 2021 even though it contained only 8.4 percent of the world's population.[77]

Among many Latin American families, emigration is no longer simply an issue of better opportunity; it is a matter of survival. In some villages and urban neighborhoods of the Caribbean, Mexico, and Central America, almost every family has someone working up north and sending money back home to feed those left behind.

Between 2001 and 2008, immigrant remittances to just five Latin American countries—Colombia, the Dominican Republic, El Salvador, Guatemala, and Mexico—nearly tripled in size, from $14.9 billion to $41.2 billion annually, most of it coming from migrants in the United States, according to one recent study. The inflow of money from expatriates working abroad now represents a significant portion of the gross domestic product of several Latin American countries. For Honduras, it was 20 percent of GDP in 2018; for El Salvador, 21 percent; for Nicaragua, 11 percent; for Guatemala, 12 percent. Total remittances from Latino workers in the United States to their native countries set a record of $47.6 billion in 2008. That year, Latinos in the United States sent more money home than the U.S. government dispatched in total foreign aid to all the nations of the world. And those cash remittances did not include the value of consumer goods and clothing the migrants regularly shipped home or took back as gifts when they visited. In 2009, however, remittances dropped sharply to $44.3 billion, largely because the deep U.S. recession created a sharp increase in unemployment among Latino immigrants. By 2017, however, the Pew Center estimated that remittances from the United States to the region were once again at a record high of $57.3 billion.[78]

Latin American immigrants, in short, are preventing the total collapse of their homelands. The only way to keep more of them from leaving for the United States is through economic policies that ensure that a greater portion of the wealth their countries produce stays home.

2. *Latino immigration is a movement of urban workers within the New World, not a rural movement of peasants, as was the old European and much of the modern Asian influx.*

The Europeans who came here at the beginning of the century were mostly poor farmers. They left their homelands prepared to sever their ties with the Old World and remake their lives in the New. As Oscar Handlin, the consummate chronicler of their exodus, wrote, "From the westernmost reaches of Europe, in Ireland, to Russia in the east, the peasant masses had maintained an imperturbable sameness; for fifteen centuries they were the backbone of a continent, unchanging while all about them radical changes again and again recast the civilization in which they lived."[79]

Latin American immigration, on the other hand, is a movement of people from the New World's impoverished southern,

Spanish-speaking periphery to its more prosperous northern, English-speaking hub. The cultural traditions and national identities of both regions—no matter how immutable some may claim them to be—are still relatively young and in a constant process of change.

Precisely as a result of their geographic proximity to the United States and their long historical relationship to it, Latin Americans do not come here planning to stay, or planning to integrate into a new, more modern society. Rather, they come looking to survive, to find a better-paying job. Within every migrant heart beats the hope of returning home someday. Some do, as often as once a year, laden with holiday gifts for relatives. Those who cannot afford the trip keep in regular touch with loved ones by telephone, text messages, and video chats.

This has meant a new fluidity in the migration process unknown among Europeans, one that finds numerous expressions. A son falls into drugs or gangs in South Central Los Angeles, so the immigrant mother sends him back home to live with a relative in Guatemala or Honduras for a few years. A young woman gets pregnant out of wedlock or is abandoned by her husband in the Dominican Republic, so she leaves for the United States to escape the shame or to find a job to support herself and her child. A Mexican travels back and forth each year from a small farm in Sonora to work in the grape fields of California at harvest time. A Dominican livery cabdriver in New York City spends the summers driving fares around Manhattan, then spends the winters relaxing in the new house he's built back home in El Cibao.

To a far greater extent than most people realize, this constant movement back and forth—itself a reflection of the removal of restraints to both capital and labor in our new global economy—serves to both reinforce and undermine aspects of the cultures of the sending and receiving countries alike. Just as corporations pride themselves on their ability to move about the world with ever-increasing rapidity, migrant labor has become increasingly mobile, and Latin American labor the most mobile of all.

Latin Americans, moreover, can hardly be considered peasants from an unchanging countryside, as were the early Europeans. They are, with the exception of indigenous migrants from Mexico, Guatemala, and Peru, largely city dwellers, a reflection of the fact that since World War II, Latin America has been transformed into the planet's largest urban ghetto. While in 1930 more than two-thirds of its people lived in the countryside, now more than eight in ten inhabit its cities. In 2019, four of the world's twenty largest metropolises were located in the region—São Paulo, Mexico City, Buenos Aires, and Rio de Janeiro—each with more than thirteen million inhabitants. Sixty-five additional Latin American cities contained more than one million residents in 2018. By comparison, the United States had only ten cities in 2018 with more than one million population. The Latin American city is usually a gleaming downtown core whose infrastructure is bursting at the seams and is enveloped by sprawling megaslums of cardboard and corrugated tin.

Before they ever head north, Latin Americans have been exposed to years of social conditioning about the dream life that awaits them. Hollywood films, U.S. programs on local television, Anglo music on local radio, outdoor billboards plastered with Madison Avenue fashion models, and Spanish translations of U.S. magazines all combine to create a thirst for a lifestyle beyond anything that could be satisfied at home.

Moreover, Latin American immigrants, while generally less educated than migrants from other regions, are usually better educated than their compatriots who stay behind. Studies during the 1990s of undocumented Mexican immigrants, for instance, showed that from 3 percent to 10 percent were illiterate, whereas the illiteracy rate in Mexico then was at 22 percent. More recent data show that unauthorized migrants from Latin America are more likely to have college degrees (nearly a third did in 2016) than in previous years, though the lowest rates for college completion were among undocumented Mexicans (6 percent), Salvadorans (7 percent), and Guatemalans (7 percent).[80] Many Latin American migrants have worked for years for an American firm in one of the free trade zones, have studied English, and have thus been socialized into American methods before arriving. In short, they are far more urbanized, educated, and socially prepared to adapt to postindustrial U.S. society than were the Europeans who came here at the beginning of the century. What they lack, and what their European predecessors found plentiful in the automobile, steel, rubber, and coal factories of the early twentieth century, is a sufficient number of semiskilled jobs that pay a decent wage and provide some measure of job security.

3. *Mexicans, the largest of Latino immigrant groups, have historically been "pulled" here only to be treated as easily deportable labor.*

As we have seen, Mexicans were recruited between the 1880s and the 1930s to work on the railroads and in the fields of the southwestern and midwestern United States. More than a million crossed the border between 1920 and 1930 alone.[81] Then the Depression hit, domestic unemployment skyrocketed, and the migrant laborers found they were no longer welcomed. During the 1930s, an estimated half million Mexicans were forcibly deported back home.[82]

When World War II closed off European and Asian immigration, however, our corporations persuaded the federal government to renew the massive importation of Mexican and Latin American labor. Thus began the wartime *bracero* program in 1942. In its first year, it brought in 52,000 Mexicans to work in railroad maintenance and agriculture, and after the war, the program became a regular feature of American life, for the Southwest was growing rapidly and agribusiness needed more low-wage workers. In 1950 alone, 450,000 people passed through Mexico's three main *bracero* recruitment centers, and hundreds of thousands more entered the United States illegally to look for work.

Almost as soon as it was reopened, however, the door was slammed shut once again after the Korean War, when a new recession led to anti-Mexican protests by unemployed Anglos. In July 1954, as previously mentioned, the federal government unleashed one of the darkest periods in immigrant history—Operation Wetback. Brutal dragnets were conducted in hundreds of Mexican neighborhoods as migrants were summarily thrown into jails, herded into trucks or trains, then shipped back to Mexico. Many of those abducted were American citizens of Mexican descent. The government, ignoring all due process, deported approximately one million people in a few short months. As soon as the recession ended, however, the demand for Mexican labor picked up again and the *bracero* program was resuscitated.

And so it was that the United States perfected two contradictory— some would say hypocritical—policies toward Mexican immigration: while southwestern businesses welcomed cheap Mexican labor and lobbied Congress to allow more migrants in, the federal government, reacting to periodic outbursts of public frustration over the boom-and-bust cycles of our capitalist economy, conducted periodic dragnets to throw them out.

By 1960, thanks in large measure to the "pull" aspect of the *bracero* program, one-quarter of the workforce in the Southwest consisted of immigrant labor from Mexico.[83] President Johnson finally ended the program in 1964, but agribusiness merely supplanted it with a scaled-down version called the H-2 guest worker program. Finally, American manufacturers and the Mexican government came up with a new strategy: instead of bringing Mexicans to work here, they would shift production to Mexico. And so the border industrialization program began in 1966 (see chapter 13).

But the pull factor is not just a reality with Mexicans. Immigration to the United States has always served first and foremost the labor needs of capitalist expansion and contraction. The ever-changing religious, ethnic, and racial composition of the various immigrant waves has historically made it easier for farmers and manufacturers to thwart the inevitable demands of their workers for better wages and working conditions simply by pitting one group of native-born employees against another of newly hired immigrants.

4. The United States, faced with an aging white population, will need an increasing number of Latin American workers to fill unskilled jobs.

Along with all the other major powers that fought World War II, the United States confronts a looming demographic crisis in the first half of the twenty-first century—a shortage of young workers. The country's white population is growing inexorably older. The median age among whites was 34.0 years in 1992, but it climbed to 43.6 by 2018. For Hispanics, however, it grew only slightly, from 26.0 in 1992 to 30.0 in 2018. At the same time, births to Hispanic women remained higher than for white women. In 2017, Latinos composed 17.8 percent of the population but nearly a quarter (23 percent) of all U.S. births.[84]

By the time most baby boomers retire, 20 percent of the population will be over sixty-five. This demographic reality not only threatens the viability of the Social Security system, but it will also create a huge demand for workers in the health and social service fields, especially for unskilled workers who can take care of an aging population. "Retiring baby boomers need people who can contribute more in taxes than they consume in services," noted one conservative writer.[85] Because Latin America contains the closest pool of such ready labor, workers who are easiest to repatriate when they are no longer needed, it will continue to function as a labor reserve for the United States, no matter how loudly the classical conservatives may roar.

In summary, the more that U.S. corporations, U.S. culture, and the U.S. dollar penetrate into Latin America, the more that laborers from that region will be pulled here, and the more that deteriorating conditions in their own homelands will push migrants here. This push-and-pull phenomenon creates an irresistible force, and a constant stream of migrants heading north. Whether we regard this human stream as bane or boon does not matter, for it is the harvest of empire and it will not be stopped until the empire's expansion is redirected and its prosperity more equitably shared.

12

SPEAK SPANISH, YOU'RE IN AMERICA!:
El Huracán over Language and Culture

It matters not that they be cultivated men
Or rude, wild, barbarous, and gross,
For 'tis enough, and more, to know that they are men
And know that, except for the Fiend himself,
They all are the worst beast, when they do wish,
Of all the ones that God created . . .

—GASPAR PÉREZ DE VILLAGRÁ,
Historia de la Nueva México, 1610

On August 28, 1995, during a child-custody hearing in a divorce case in Amarillo, Texas, state district judge Samuel Kiser directed Martha Laureano, a U.S. citizen of Mexican descent, to speak English at home to her five-year-old daughter. "[You are] abusing that child and relegating her to the position of a housemaid," the judge told Laureano after she acknowledged that she spoke only Spanish to the girl. "It's not in her best interest to be ignorant," Kiser said, threatening to end Laureano's custody unless she changed her method of communicating. Newspaper reports of the courtroom exchange rocked Latino households around the country and sparked an outcry from community leaders. While the judge toned down his order and issued a partial apology a few days later, he was only echoing what many white Americans have believed for years.[1]

No issue so clearly puts Hispanic Americans at odds with English-speaking white and Black Americans as the issue of language. Backers of a constitutional amendment that would make English our official language say that the rising number of immigrants, especially the flood of Latin Americans during the past few decades, is threatening to Balkanize the nation into warring linguistic groups, to make English speakers strangers in their own land.

This debate over language, of course, is not unique to the United States. Virtually every modern nation-state confronts linguistic minorities within its borders. But with forty-one million residents who spoke Spanish at home in 2018, we are in the unique position of being not only the largest English-speaking country in the world, but also the fifth-largest Spanish-speaking one, surpassed only by Mexico, Spain, Argentina, and Colombia. By another measure, we are already second in the world only to Mexico in Spanish speakers, if you add an estimated eleven million U.S. residents who identify as speaking some degree of Spanish.[2]

In this country, the squabble over language has been intertwined for years with the even deeper discord over how we interpret and teach the American experience. Language, after all, is at the heart of an individual's social identity. It is the vehicle through which the songs, folklore, and customs of any group are preserved and transmitted to its descendants. Given the vast ethnic diversity of this country's immigrant populations throughout its history, our leaders have long perceived English as a critical thread in the national fabric, one that not only provides common means of communication but that also helps to bind the different immigrant groups into one American tapestry.

In his 1992 polemic, *The Disuniting of America*, historian Arthur Schlesinger Jr. railed against the rising "cult of ethnicity" or "compensatory history" by contemporary advocates of multiculturalism and bilingualism. In the process, Schlesinger served up his version of the creation story of America: "Having cleared most of North America of their French, Spanish, and Dutch rivals, the British were free to set the mold. The language of the new nation, its laws, its institutions, its political ideas, its literature, its customs, its precepts, its prayers, primarily derived from Britain."[3]

Unfortunately, whether the mythmaking comes from Bible Belt conservatives or renowned liberal historians, it suffers from the same flaw—a refusal to recognize that the quest for empire, fueled as it was by the racialist theory of Manifest Destiny, divided and deformed the course of ethnic relations from our nation's inception, repeatedly fragmenting and subverting any quest for a single "national language" and "national culture."

Few of us would disagree that English is the *common* language of the country. Yet the very process of territorial expansion—not just immigration—created repeated battles throughout U.S. history over whether English should be the *only* recognized tongue. Many ethnic groups attempted to preserve their native languages at the same time they adopted English, while our government, especially at the federal level, sought just as strenuously to suppress efforts at bilingualism.

Those language battles from prior eras do not all fall under one neat category—rather, a close examination of them reveals three main trends, and the qualitative differences between those trends too often get lost in the rhetoric of the current debate. The first category includes the millions of immigrants who came here from Europe and Asia voluntarily seeking American citizenship, and who, by doing so, were cutting ties with their homelands, adopting the language of their new country and accepting a subsidiary status, if any, for their native tongues.

The second category was made up of those from dozens of African nations who were brought here in chains, forced from the start to give up their various mother tongues, and not permitted even to acquire a reading or writing knowledge of English so that the slave owners could more easily control and dominate them.

The third category, and the one least understood, encompasses those people who were already living in the New World when their lands were either conquered or acquired by the United States: Native Americans, French Creoles of Louisiana, Mexicans, and Puerto Ricans. These latter groups became American citizens by force. Congress declared them so without any vote or petition on their part; it did not care what language they spoke nor did it seek their public oath of allegiance.

In so far as a new sovereignty was imposed on them while they were still residing on their old lands, these "annexed" Americans could hardly consider themselves foreigners. This turned them into persistent defenders of the right to use their own language, and the new Anglo authorities who assumed the administration of territories in which they resided occasionally understood that outlook and accommodated their wishes. The federal government, on the other hand, typically reacted with hostility to any linguistic diversity.

Throughout the past two centuries, Anglo historians consistently relegated the languages of these conquered nationalities to the margins of the American experience, dismissing their cultures as either primitive or nonexistent. Despite that marginalization, Latinos in particular managed to preserve their language and traditions by fashioning a parallel subterranean storehouse of music, dance, theater, journalism, literature, and folklore—in English, as well as Spanish. Over time, the cultures of Mexicans, Puerto Ricans, Cubans, and other Latinos who resided here gradually fused while continuing to receive nourishment from subsequent waves of newcomers from Latin America. At the same time, this emerging U.S.-Latino culture combined with and reshaped aspects of African American and Euro-American music, dance, and theater, creating in the process a dazzling array of hybrid forms that are today uniquely American, and that are most evident in musical genres such as Tex-Mex, Cubop, Latin jazz, Latin rock, bugaloo, salsa, rap, and even country rock, but that have spread to other areas of the arts as well. Only through the phenomenal growth of Latino immigration has this underground cultural stream finally surfaced and begun to sweep away the melting-pot myth of the United States. Despite that resurgence, Latinos remained invisible to mainstream chronicles of American culture and, until only recently, they were virtually absent from the culture's most influential contemporary media, Hollywood movies and television.

THE EARLY BATTLES OVER LANGUAGE

From the very beginning, the thirteen colonies confronted a quandary over language. Before independence, German was virtually the only tongue spoken throughout fifteen thousand square miles of eastern Pennsylvania, while Dutch was widely used in the Hudson River Valley. Between 1732 and 1800, at least thirty-eight German-language newspapers were published in the Pennsylvania colony, and the University of Pennsylvania established a program in German bilingual education as early as 1780. So widespread was the use of German that the first U.S. census reported that 8.7 percent of Americans spoke it as their first language, almost identical to the proportion of Hispanics in our country in 1990.[4]

The prevalence of a German linguistic minority continued into the twentieth century. By 1900, as many as six hundred thousand children in American public and parochial schools were being taught in German, nearly 4 percent of the country's school population.[5] Only with the Americanization policy that accompanied World War I was German finally eliminated as a language of instruction.

The experience of European immigrants, however, is not as relevant to the modern-day language debate as that of the annexed nationalities. When Louisiana became a state in 1812, for instance, the majority of its residents spoke French. As a result, until the 1920s, all laws and public documents in the state were published in French and English. The courts, the public schools, even the state legislature operated in two languages. Louisiana's second governor, Jacques Villeré, spoke no English and always addressed the legislature in French. As more settlers moved in, and English speakers became the majority during the 1840s, the use of French diminished, but it did so through the evolution of the population, not through government fiat, and the rights of French-speaking children continued to be recognized in the public schools.[6]

The Treaty of Guadalupe Hidalgo imposed U.S. citizenship on the Mexicans inhabiting the annexed territories, with those who chose to retain their Mexican citizenship required to register their refusal to U.S. authorities. Congress did not, however, require its new subjects to swear allegiance to their new nation or adopt a new language, and most *mexicanos* continued their lives pretty much as before. Native Americans within the territories, however, were excluded from citizenship, even though Spain had recognized them as such since 1812.[7] As late as the 1870s, more than a quarter century after annexation, New Mexico's legislature operated mostly in Spanish. By then, only two of fourteen counties had switched to jury trials in English, thirty-three of thirty-nine school commissioners were *mexicanos*, and two-thirds of the public schools conducted their instruction solely in Spanish. Even as late as 1890, 65 percent of Mexicans over the age of ten could not speak English.[8] This did not mean they resisted learning the language, only that their opportunities to be exposed to it were minimal in isolated rural communities where they composed the overwhelming majority. Due to that, New Mexico was one of the last territories to become a state, in 1912, but only after European and Anglo-American settlers composed a majority of its population.[9] A similar dynamic over language evolved in the Rio Grande Valley of Texas, only there *mexicanos* have remained the overwhelming majority for more than 250 years, with most residents still retaining the use of Spanish while also being fluent in English.

Then there is the language experience of some Native Americans. Oklahoma's Cherokee built a public school system in the 1850s in which 90 percent of the children were taught in their native language while also learning English. So successful was the effort that Cherokee children of that era registered higher levels of English literacy than white children in the neighboring states of Texas and Arkansas. But in the late 1800s, the federal government initiated a policy of Americanization. It forcibly removed thousands of Indian children from their families and shipped them to boarding schools to learn English. The disastrous result, as documented by repeated studies during the second half of the twentieth century, was that 40 percent of Cherokee children became *illiterate in any language* and 75 percent dropped out of school.[10]

Finally, there is Puerto Rico's forgotten language saga. Shortly after the U.S. occupation of the island in 1898, Congress declared the territory officially bilingual, even though its population had spoken Spanish for four hundred years and almost no one spoke English. Military governor Guy Henry promptly required all public school teachers to become fluent in the language of their new country, even instituting an English-proficiency test for high school graduation. Despite widespread resistance from island politicians, educators, and students, the territory's Anglo administrators declared English the language of instruction in all island schools. The result was a near-total collapse of the education system as thousands of students stopped attending classes, and those who stayed struggled to learn academic subjects in a language they did not understand.

Efforts to force Puerto Ricans to learn English persisted unsuccessfully for nearly half a century, with only a brief reversion to Spanish instruction in the 1930s when José Padin, the island's education commissioner, tried to reintroduce Spanish. But President Roosevelt promptly fired Padin on the advice of Secretary of the Interior Harold Ickes and brought back the English-only policy. A few years later, after Governor Rexford Tugwell and then President Truman vetoed a bill that had passed overwhelmingly in Puerto Rico's legislature to bring back Spanish as the language of instruction, massive island protests erupted and more than one hundred thousand university and high school students went out on strike in November 1946. Several scholars have argued, in fact, that popular resistance to the imposition of English during the 1940s became a pivotal means for Puerto Ricans to preserve their national identity under colonial rule.[11] Not until 1949 did the island's first elected governor, Luis Muñoz Marín, finally end the hated policy of language suppression. Even though Muñoz and the local legislature reinstituted Spanish as the language of instruction, they nonetheless required pupils to learn English as a second language. The Popular Democrats took their reforms one step further in 1965: they brought back Spanish as the official language of the island's local courts. Congress, however, insisted that English remain as the language of the federal courts on the island.[12]

The mere existence of an entire U.S. territory whose residents speak Spanish has created enormous problems for theorists of a monolingual U.S. nation. In 1917, the same year Congress established a literacy test for all foreigners applying for citizenship, it declared Puerto Ricans citizens without requiring them to demonstrate any English proficiency! Once Puerto Ricans began moving to the United States in big numbers after World War II, this contradiction was exacerbated. It produced such a dilemma that Congress had to include a special "Puerto Rican" provision in the Voting Rights Act of 1965. That act, which suspended literacy tests in southern states where such tests had been used to prevent Blacks from voting, also featured a section, introduced by New York senator Robert Kennedy, that prohibited states that had education requirements for voters—such as New York State, which had a sixth-grade education requirement for voters at the time—from denying the vote to any citizen whose education had been in an American-flag school where "predominant classroom instruction was other than English." Through that provision, Congress acknowledged that, at least in the case of Puerto Ricans, U.S. territorial expansion had created Spanish-speaking citizens with a claim to certain linguistic rights.

The Mexican, Puerto Rican, French Creole, and Native American language experiences, then, are markedly different from that of European immigrants, who, as Schlesinger notes, "stayed for a season with their old language" before the next generation adopted English.[13] Spanish, Cajun, and the surviving Native American languages are not "foreign." They are the tongues of long-settled linguistic minorities who were absorbed by an expanding state.

FEDERAL LAW AND LANGUAGE
DISCRIMINATION

International law has long recognized that linguistic minorities within a multiethnic state like ours have a right to protection against discrimination. Article 53 of the United Nations Charter, for example, urges member states to promote "universal respect for and observance of human rights and fundamental freedom for all without distinction as to race, sex, *language* or religion" (my emphasis). Similar descriptions can be found in the United Nations Universal Declaration of Human Rights and in proclamations of the European and inter-American states.[14]

Those principles, however, are routinely violated in this country, where federal courts prohibit discrimination because of a person's race, religion, or national origin, but in some cases continue to permit language discrimination. A classic example occurred in Texas in the case of *García v. Gloor.* Héctor García, the plaintiff in the case, was a twenty-four-year-old native-born Texan who attended public schools in Brownsville and who spoke both English and Spanish. His parents, however, were Mexican immigrants, and the family always spoke Spanish at home, so he felt more comfortable in Spanish.

García was hired as a salesman by Gloor Lumber and Supply, Co., Inc., specifically because he could speak Spanish to its customers, but the company had a policy that employees could not speak Spanish *to one another* on the job, though they were free to speak whatever language they wanted off the job. In June 1975, García was dismissed after violating the company rule several times, whereupon he filed a federal discrimination complaint. At the trial, the U.S. district court found that seven of the eight salesmen Gloor employed, and thirty-one of its thirty-nine employees, were Hispanic, that 75 percent of the customers in the Brownsville business area also were Hispanic, and that many of them wished to be waited on by salesmen who spoke Spanish. Alton Gloor, an officer and stockholder, testified that there were business reasons for the Spanish ban, among them that his English-speaking customers objected to communications between employees that they could not understand; pamphlets and trade literature were only in English, so employees needed to improve their English skills; and supervisors who did not speak Spanish could better oversee their subordinates. The court ruled in Gloor's favor, finding no discrimination.

The case eventually went to the U.S. Court of Appeals for the Fifth Circuit, which acknowledged in a May 1980 decision that "Mr. Garcia's use of Spanish was a significant factor" in his firing. The court concluded, however, that García had not suffered national discrimination, even though he presented an expert witness who testified that the "Spanish language is the most important aspect of ethnic identification for Mexican Americans," and even though he was backed in his contention by the Equal Employment Opportunity Commission. The court's decision went on to say:

> Mr. Garcia was fully bilingual. He chose deliberately to speak Spanish instead of English while actually at work. . . . Let us assume, as contended by Mr. Garcia, there was no genuine business need for the rule and that its adoption by Gloor was arbitrary. The EEO Act does not prohibit all arbitrary employment practices. . . . It is directed only at specific impermissible bases of discrimination, race, color, religion, sex, or national origin. National origin must not be confused with ethnic or sociocultural traits or an unrelated status, such as citizenship or alienage . . . a hiring policy that distinguishes on some other ground, such as grooming codes or how to run his business, is related more closely to the employer's choice of how to run his business than to equality of employment.

In other words, because García was bilingual, he had lost any right to speak his language—the language for which he was hired and the majority language in the community—at work. Spanish was a "preference" of his, the court said, and an employer could legally ban it just as he could ban "persons born under a certain sign of the zodiac or persons having long hair or short hair or no hair at all."[15] The court thus performed a Solomon-like miracle—severing García's nationality or ethnic origin from his language.

In the years since *García v. Gloor*, the federal Equal Employment Opportunity Commission (EEOC) has received thousands of language-discrimination complaints alleging violations of the "national origin" protections of the 1964 Civil Rights Act, and has generally been more willing to consider them. The agency's regulations have maintained since 1980 a broad definition of national origin discrimination to include "denial of equal employment opportunity because of an individual's, or his or her ancestor's, place of origin; or because an individual has the physical, cultural or linguistic characteristics of a national origin group," even noting that a person's primary language "is often an essential national origin characteristic."[16] In 2002 alone, the commission handled 228 complaints that challenged English-only policies by employers.

Federal court reviews of such cases in various parts of the country, however, have resulted in contradictory rulings. In 2000, for example, the U.S. District Court for the North District of Texas upheld a class-action language-discrimination charge brought by the EEOC against Premier Operator Services. The firm, a long-distance telephone operator, had specifically hired bilingual employees to service Spanish-speaking customers. It subsequently prohibited those same employees from speaking Spanish except when they were servicing customers, and it fired thirteen who protested the policy. Such English-only rules, the court ruled, "disproportionately burden national origin minorities because they preclude many members of these groups from speaking the language in which they are best able to communicate." The court awarded $709,000 in damages and back pay to the thirteen employees.[17]

But a key decision by the Ninth Circuit Court of Appeals in the case of *Garcia v. Spun Steak* rejected an EEOC complaint of language-based "national origin" discrimination. That case involved a San Francisco meat plant that instituted an English-only policy for its largely Latino workforce in the early 1990s. The policy applied only to work hours, with employees free to speak Spanish during their breaks or lunch periods. It was not consistently enforced, though two plaintiffs were disciplined for speaking Spanish during work hours. The court concluded that English-only policies were not, on their face, discriminatory and could be applied to truly bilingual employees because those individuals do not suffer adverse impact.[18]

The EEOC, however, has continued to pursue language discrimination issues with occasional success. The manufacturer Wisconsin Plastics, for instance, acceded in 2017 to paying $475,000 in a federal court consent decree to settle an EEOC complaint that the company had committed national origin discrimination when it fired twenty-two Hispanic and Hmong immigrant workers at its plant in Green Bay, claiming they lacked sufficient English-language skills, even though they did not need English to do their jobs.[19]

Given the conflicts between federal court decisions in various parts of the country, the Supreme Court will eventually be forced to tackle the issue of language discrimination. This is especially true with the spread of English-only laws at the state level (twenty-nine states currently have English-only provisions for local government, with some states, such as Tennessee and Illinois, adopting contradictory laws on whether private firms may prohibit employees from speaking a particular language).[20] Until the high court acts, however, our nation will remain one of the few advanced countries that does not fully recognize the rights of linguistic minorities.

In Europe, for instance, the European Charter for Regional or Minority Languages specifies that "the right to use a regional or minority language in private and public life is an inalienable right." Since the treaty's adoption in 1992, more than twenty countries, including Germany, Spain, the United Kingdom, Austria, Denmark, Poland, and Sweden, have formally ratified it.[21]

THE CULTURE OF THE CONQUERED

The language debate is a nagging reminder that the conquest and annexation of a territory by force does not ensure the assimilation of that territory's original inhabitants. Nor does the passing of a few generations ensure the gradual disappearance of the culture of those inhabitants. For if conquered people perceive themselves to be oppressed, they inevitably turn their language and culture into weapons of resistance, into tools with which they demand full equality within the conquering society. This is precisely what happened with Latinos in America toward the end of the twentieth century.

Unfortunately, even some of the best Anglo historians have misread that movement as one that extols backwardness and seeks separation rather than inclusion. "It may be too bad that dead white European males have played so large a role in shaping our culture," Schlesinger declared in *The Disuniting of America*. "But that's the way it is. One cannot erase history."

Schlesinger wrote those words in 1992, but nearly twenty years later the Arizona legislature sought to codify his outlook. Only weeks after approving the nation's toughest immigration law, Arizona lawmakers decreed in May 2010 that the teaching of ethnic studies in its public schools would be curtailed. Under the new measure they approved, any school district providing courses that were designed for a particular ethnic group, or that promoted ethnic solidarity or resentment of a race or class, would lose 10 percent of its state education aid.

Arizona's education commissioner, Tom Horne, championed the law, aiming it especially at Mexican American Studies courses in Tucson's school system. "They are teaching a radical ideology in Raza, including that Arizona and other states were stolen from Mexico and should be given back," Horne said. "My point of view is that these kids' parents and grandparents came, mostly legally, because this is the land of opportunity, and we should teach them that if they work hard, they can accomplish anything."[22]

Those ethnic studies programs, however, sought to undo damage from centuries of what literary critic and social activist Edward Said called cultural imperialism. A culture's music, song, fiction, theater, and popular lore, in Said's view, together with specialized disciplines—sociology, literary history, ethnography, and the like—compose the narratives by which a people understand the best of themselves, their place in the world, their identity. But over the course of civilization, culture became attached to specific nations and states, and at least since the time of the Greeks, those attachments have led to classifications, often antagonistic notions of "us" and "them," of superior and inferior societies, thus turning culture into another weapon by which the strong dominate the weak. As Said expressed it:

The main battle in imperialism is over land, of course; but when it came to who owned the land, who had the right to settle and work on it, who kept it going, who won it back, and who now plans its future—these issues were reflected, contested, and even for a time decided in narrative [culture] . . . the power to narrate, or to block other narratives from forming and emerging, is very important to culture and imperialism and constitutes one of the main connections between them.[23]

In the United States, the nexus between culture and empire has been harder to grasp, partly because our heterogeneous immigrant society has made even the definition of a "dominant" culture more difficult to distill, but that link is just as strong as it was between the former European powers and their colonies, Said claimed.

Before we can agree what the American identity is made of, we have to concede that as an immigrant settler society superimposed on the ruins of considerable native presence, American identity is too varied to be a unitary and homogeneous thing; indeed the battle within it is between advocates of a unitary identity and those who see the whole as a complex but not reductively unified one. . . .

Partly because of empire, all cultures are involved in one another; none is single and pure, all are hybrid, heterogeneous, extraordinarily differentiated, and unmonolithic. This, I believe, is as true of the contemporary United States as it is of the modern Arab world.[24]

In his pioneering literary analysis, *Culture and Imperialism*, Said demonstrated how many of the West's greatest fiction writers all unconsciously promoted in their works the imperial ambitions of their own nations, while they ignored or overlooked the intrinsic value of the colonial cultures their novels depicted.

Much the same has happened in this country with both classical and popular traditions and culture. During the nineteenth century, Anglo settlers in the Southwest readily adapted the Spanish hacienda styles of architecture, Spanish names for cities, rivers, and even states, Mexican food, the vaquero life of the Mexican rancho, or the hunting, camping, and solitary worship of nature so prevalent among Native Americans, while they refused to regard the Mexicans or Indians among them as equals. The job of justifying that frontier conquest fell to the dime-store novelists of frontier life, to the travel writers, and to the journalists.

THE MEDIA WAR OVER IMAGE AND REALITY

During the twentieth century, Hollywood films and television replaced newspapers and novels as the primary tools for banishing Hispanics to the shadows of American culture. A half dozen major surveys over several decades documented the virtual absence of Hispanics on television.

In *Watching America*, a study of thirty years of television programming from 1955 to 1986, the Center for Media and Public Affairs (CMPA) found that Hispanics averaged barely 2 percent of all characters. Worse, the CMPA discovered that the percentage steadily decreased, from 3 percent in the 1950s to 1 percent in the 1980s, even as the Hispanic population grew. A survey by the Annenberg School for Communication found that Hispanics averaged 1.1 percent of prime-time characters on television from 1982 to

1992, compared with 10.8 percent for African Americans. Given that Hispanics composed at least 9 percent of the population in 1990, that means they were nine times less likely to appear on your living room television than in real life.

The few Latino characters who did make it to the screen were disproportionately unsavory. The Center for Media and Public Affairs analyzed 620 fictional television shows from 1955 to 1986 and found that 41 percent of Hispanic characters were portrayed negatively, substantially more than whites (31 percent) or Blacks (24 percent). A review of twenty-one thousand television characters over a twenty-year period by the Annenberg School for Communication revealed seventy-five Hispanic villains for every one hundred "good" Hispanic characters, compared with thirty-nine white villains for every one hundred "good" white characters.[25]

In Hollywood films, Latinos actually received more prominent leading roles and a wider variety of parts during the 1940s and 1950s than later in the century. Part of that was due to the fact that during and after World War II, Latin Americans were regarded as "Good Neighbors," as important allies against Fascism, so there was pressure to portray them more sympathetically than in the past. In addition, the war cut off the European market for the United States, so studios scrambled to make up for lost revenues by boosting their sales in Latin America. Among the great Latino parts in those years were Anthony Quinn as the daring vaquero in *The Ox-Bow Incident* (1943); Ricardo Montalban as the heroic Mexican government official in *Border Incident* (1949); José Ferrer in the Oscar-winning *Cyrano de Bergerac* (1950); Katy Jurado as the savvy businesswoman in *High Noon* (1952); a whole Mexican community in the labor classic *Salt of the Earth* (1953); Cesar Romero and Gilbert Roland, both of whom starred in the *Cisco Kid* television series; and perhaps the most famous of all, Desi Arnaz as the charming, hot-tempered Latin husband in *I Love Lucy*.

Once those golden years ended, few identifiably Hispanic actors were able to find work beyond stereotypical and unflattering roles. One major exception was Rita Moreno, who played a Hungarian in *She Loves Me*, a midwestern WASP in *Gentry*, and an Irishwoman in *The Miracle Worker*. There were, of course, those actors the public rarely recognized as Hispanic and who thus encountered more opportunities and a richer variety of roles, among them Quinn, Rita Hayworth, Raquel Welch, and Linda Carter.

By the 1970s, the rash of films portraying Latinos as criminals, drug addicts, or welfare dependents became endless: *Dirty Harry* and *The French Connection* (1971), *The New Centurions* (1972), *The Seven-Ups, Badge 373, Magnum Force* (1973), *Death Wish* (1974), *Boardwalk* (1979), *The Exterminator* (1980), *Fort Apache: The Bronx* (1981), *Colors* (1988), and *Falling Down* (1993).[26]

Whether Hollywood producers realized what they were doing or not is irrelevant. The fact remains that the stunted images and unsympathetic portrayals of Latinos produced by the industry during the 1970s and 1980s had a devastating impact. To a generation of young Hispanics, they glorified a violent, outlaw, marginal identity. To white Americans, they reinforced prejudices that have accumulated in white folklore since the days of Manifest Destiny. For both groups, they created the "us" and "them" cultural construct Said identified as a critical part of imperialist cultural domination. Nowhere to be found in any of these films by Anglo producers and directors was any inkling that Latinos have been a positive force in U.S. society, that they possessed a culture of any value before they were conquered or that they contributed to or expanded the culture of this nation.

The first two decades of the new century revealed little progress in film and television images. Only 5.8 percent of some eleven thousand speaking roles in major Hollywood movies, cable, and television series during 2014–2015 went to Latinx actors, according to one recent study, even though Hispanics composed 17.6 percent of the nation's population by then. In comparison, African Americans, who composed 13.2 percent of the population, were also underrepresented but to a far less extent, garnering 12.5 percent of speaking roles.[27] A subsequent study found Latino actors held a mere 2.7 percent of Hollywood film roles in 2016—a smaller percentage than in the 1950s—even though Hispanic consumers today purchase more than 24 percent of all U.S. movie tickets.[28] Yet even those appalling figures mask how wide the chasm in media representation has actually become when it comes to U.S. Latinos. As Los Angeles movie critic Carlos Aguilar noted, many of today's most celebrated Hispanic figures in American film and television are foreign nationals from Latin America or Spain whose formative years were not part of the U.S. Latino experience, including such figures as Oscar-winning directors Alfonso Cuarón and Guillermo del Toro, and actors Antonio Banderas, Salma Hayek, Javier Bardem, and Penelope Cruz.[29]

U.S. LATINO CULTURE—
NOTES ON AN UNTOLD STORY

Latino literary heritage in this country dates back to 1610, when
Gaspar Pérez de Villagrá penned the first epic poem in U.S. history,
Historia de la Nueva México. A Mexican-born criollo, Pérez de Villagrá accompanied the expedition of conquistador Juan de Oñate,
who colonized New Mexico and stamped out the resistance of the
Pueblo Indians in 1599. The poem, written fourteen years before
Captain John Smith's *General History of Virginia*, is an account of
that expedition and of the conquest of the Pueblos of Acoma.[30] A
Spanish court subsequently convicted Oñate of atrocities against
the natives and banished him from New Mexico, thus removing
him from the pantheon of the conquistadores of his age.[31]

Pérez de Villagrá's epic, however, survived as a definitive narrative
of that conflict. It is written in the classical canto style of Spain's
Golden Age, using hendecasyllabic verse (metrical lines of eleven syl-
lables each), and while much of it gets bogged down in a mundane
recounting of events, occasional passages rival in their vividness
those found in the *Iliad* or *Paradise Lost*. Yet few American-literature
students have even heard of the poem.

Some of that is understandable, given that Pérez de Villagrá wrote
in Spanish, and this epic dates back four hundred years, but the same
cannot be said of Felix Varela's work less than two hundred years ago.
Perhaps no single Latino left a greater imprint on nineteenth-
century American culture than Varela, the father of the Catholic
press in the United States. A Cuban-born priest, philosophy professor, and revolutionary, Varela fled to the United States in 1823 to
avoid arrest by the Spanish Crown and settled in Philadelphia. There
he published Cuba's first pro-independence journal, *El Habanero*,
and dedicated himself to translating important English works into
Spanish, including Thomas Jefferson's *Manual of Parliamentary
Practice* and Sir Humphry Davy's *Elements of Agricultural Chemistry*.

He was eventually appointed pastor of his own church in New
York City, where he garnered a legendary reputation for his work
among New York's Irish immigrants, creating dozens of schools
and social service organizations for the city's poor and even founding the New York Catholic Temperance Association in 1840, and
where he rose to become vicar-general of the New York Archdiocese. But it was in the realms of theology and literature that Varela
left his most important legacy. Among the pioneering publications

he edited and helped to found were *The Protestant's Abridger and Annotator* (1830), the country's first ecclesiastical review; the weekly *Catholic Observer* (1836–1939); and the first two literary and theological Catholic journals, *The Catholic Expositor and Literary Magazine* (1841–1843) and the *Catholic Expositor* (1843–1844). Even as he juggled his amazing workload, Varela found time to inspire and mentor a generation of patriots back in his homeland, where he is still revered as the greatest Cuban thinker of his time. He died in 1853 in Saint Augustine, Florida, without ever getting to see his Cuba free of Spanish rule.[32]

The *mexicanos* living in the annexed territories of the Southwest saw their cultural ties with Mexico become stronger after 1848, given that many of them traveled back and forth across the border and drew consistent nourishment from Mexico's well-established theater, music, art, and folklore traditions.

The first Latino-owned theater in this country was in Los Angeles, where *mexicano* theatrical companies had been mounting professional performances since the early 1820s. Antonio Coronel, a wealthy *californio* who served for a time as the city's mayor, opened his three-hundred-seat Coronel Theater in 1848. Perhaps because of the influence of his Anglo wife, Mariana Williamson, Coronel staged his plays in both Spanish and English. By the late 1850s, his theater faced competition from several others, including Vicente Guerrero's Union Theater, Abel Stearn's Arcadia Hall, and Juan Temple's Temple Theater, all of which staged performances in Spanish. The state's Spanish-theater movement became so well-known that by the 1860s a few top performing groups from Latin America relocated there.[33]

The heyday of Mexican American theater, however, was the 1920s, when the Mexican revolution sparked an artistic renaissance in Los Angeles that spread to the *mexicano* communities of the Southwest. Those communities had expanded in size during World War I with migrants who came north to work in American factories. After the war, thousands of Mexican Americans returned home from the European battlefields. Those veterans had acquired a broader view of the world and enough money in their pockets to support the Latino entertainment industry in places like Los Angeles.

Something else had occurred below the border at the turn of the century. A new generation of Latin American writers and artists began to define a literary and social vision that was distinct from both

Europeans and Anglo-Americans. This new philosophy, the *modernista* movement, was a form of Pan–Latin Americanism that drew on the unique mixture of African, Indian, mestizo, and *mulato* traditions of the region. In 1900, Uruguayan positivist José Enrique Rodó published *Ariel*, one of the seminal works of Latin American literature. In it Rodó claimed the United States had sacrificed the idealism of its founders and succumbed to materialist pursuits. It was now up to Latin America to preserve the idealism that the New World represented, he argued. Rodó and Nicaraguan poet Rubén Darío were the most celebrated of the modernists. Gabriela Mistral's publication in 1914 of *Sonetos de la Muerte* (*Sonnets of Death*) inspired the modern era of Chilean poetry. She would become in 1945 the first Latin American writer awarded the Nobel Prize in Literature. Six years before Rodó's *Ariel*, José Martí published his electrifying "Our America" essay. Latin American artists, intellectuals, and political leaders, Martí argued, needed to draw inspiration from their own traditions and stop importing the teachings and customs of Europe and the Old World.

"The European university must bow to the American university," Martí declared. "The history of America, from the Incas to the present, must be taught in clear detail and to the letter, even if the archons of Greece are overlooked. Our Greece must take priority over the Greece which is not ours. . . . Let the world be grafted onto our republics, but the trunk must be our own."[34]

In response to the new modernism here and below the border, playwrights like Esteban Escalante, Gabriel Navarro, Adalberto Elías González, and Brigido Caro created the first theatrical works depicting Mexican life in this country rather than using themes from Spain. Stylistically, the new playwrights experimented with a variety of forms, from old Spanish *zarzuelas* to *bufos cubanos* to *revistas* to *comedias*. Caro's classic *Joaquín Murieta*, for instance, told the tragic story of the heroic California rebel most white Americans knew only as a bandit. Similar experiments flourished in San Antonio and Tucson as well. And this Latino renaissance was not confined just to Mexicans, for whites often attended theater performances as well.[35]

In the East, Cuban, Spanish, and Puerto Rican actors and playwrights created a thriving theater movement in New York City and Tampa. Cuban Alberto O'Farrill was the master of *bufos cubanos*, perfecting the classic role of a poor, Afro-Cuban comic in 1920s New York. During the same decade, Puerto Rican actor Erasmo Vando and playwrights Juan Nadal and Gonzalo O'Neill garnered a wide following from the city's small but growing Hispanic community. O'Neill's 1928 play, *Bajo una sola bandera*, electrified theatergoers with its daring advocacy of Puerto Rican independence from the United States.

But the greatest influence of Latino culture on American life, the area in which Latinos most intermingled with, borrowed from, and transformed popular expression, has been in music. Critic John Storm Roberts, in his brilliant book *The Latin Tinge: The Impact of Latin American Music on the United States*, traces the origins of that influence to two places, South Texas and New Orleans. Along the Rio Grande Valley, Mexican settlers developed *corrido* music, folk ballads that were sung to the polka, waltz, or march music, and whose lyrics chronicled real events of the day, from gun battles and wars, to crimes and love affairs, to cattle drives and the coming of the railroads. The average *corrido* was usually so filled with dates, names, and factual details that it functioned not only as entertainment but also as a news report, historical narrative, and commentary for the mass of Mexicans who were still illiterate. One of the earliest U.S. *corridos* told the story of General José Antonio Canales and his guerrilla strikes against the U.S. Army in the Mexican-American War; another related the life and times of Juan Cortina; while others recounted the atrocities of the Texas Rangers and the exploits of Mexican outlaws. Some of the most popular *corridos* were of Gregorio Cortez, the early twentieth-century figure falsely accused of being a horse thief.

On the southwestern frontier, it was not unusual for wagon trains of Mexicans and Anglo cowhands to cross paths, camp together for the night, and start a friendly campfire competition between *corrido* singers and Anglo ballad singers, thus initiating some of the earliest musical exchanges between the two cultures.[36]

In New Orleans, one of the first piano virtuosos in the United States, Louis Moreau Gottschalk (1829–1869), started introducing Cuban elements into his classical American compositions in the 1850s, creating such works as "Ojos Criollos" and *Escenas Campestres Cubanas*, an orchestra suite, as well as "Marche des Gibaros," which was based on a Puerto Rican folk song. New Orleans emerged as a center for more than just the fusion of classical music themes. By the end of the nineteenth century Mexican and Cuban musicians, together with descendants of the original Spanish residents of Louisiana, were playing major roles in the flourishing ragtime scene of the city's Latin Quarter. "Latin rhythms have been absorbed into Black American styles far more consistently than into white popular music, despite Latin music's popularity among whites," Roberts notes.[37] Perlops Nuñez, for instance, ran one of the city's first Black bands in the 1880s, and Jimmy "Spriggs" Palau played with famous jazzman Buddy Bolden. As New Orleans ragtime and then jazz evolved, they drew considerable inspiration from Mexican, Cuban, and later Brazilian music.

During the early twentieth century, a succession of Latin music forms captivated the American public. In 1913, Vernon and Irene Castle, a husband-and-wife dance team, performed their first tango at New York's Knickerbocker Theater, touching off a nationwide tango craze. Then, in the late 1920s, the Hurtado Brothers of Guatemala started recording and performing the marimba music of Guatemala; soon a half dozen marimba bands were touring the country before enthusiastic crowds. The Cuban composer Ernesto Lecuona became popular with Broadway composers, who soon took to imitating Lecuona's habanera songs. George Gershwin's "Argentina" and Richard Rodgers's "Havana" are only two examples from that decade.[38]

By the late 1920s, immigrant musicians from the Caribbean were fusing their arrangements with the ragtime and jazz greats of New York City. Writer Ruth Glasser has reconstructed the little-known saga of how a group of talented Puerto Rican musicians, all products of a rich tradition of classical training on the island, migrated to New York and initiated collaborations with African American musicians that reshaped the musical history of the city.

That collaboration was sparked by Lieutenant James Reese Europe, the composer and bandleader who conducted the most famous musical group of World War I, the 369th Infantry's Hellfighters Band. While he was putting together the band, Europe persuaded his commander, Colonel William Hayward, to let him travel to Puerto Rico in 1917 to recruit some wind instrument players. Europe had heard that Puerto Rico was brimming with talented musicians, thanks to a long tradition of army and municipal marching bands under the Spaniards. Better yet, all the Puerto Ricans could read sheet music—and they usually played more than one instrument. During a quick trip to the island, Europe recruited eighteen young men, among them Rafael Hernández, who would become Puerto Rico's greatest composer; Hernández's brother, Jesús; and clarinetist Rafael Duchesne, the scion of an illustrious family of composers and conductors.

After the war, Hernández and the other Puerto Ricans moved to

New York. Several of them ended up playing for Broadway pit bands or in top jazz orchestras of the day. Their success prompted more Puerto Rican and Cuban musicians to leave home for New York's bright lights. Puerto Rican trombonist Francisco Tizol, for instance, played for the 1922 show *Shuffle Along*, and both he and fellow trombonist Fernando Arbelo were regulars in Fletcher Henderson's band; tuba player Ralph Escudero worked in the orchestra of *Chocolate Dandies* in 1928; and clarinetist Ramón "Moncho" Usera worked in *Blackbirds*.[39]

In 1929, Cuban Mario Bauza, already a veteran of Havana's symphony orchestra, arrived in New York. He spent the next ten years playing for the greatest bandleaders of the era, among them Noble Sissle, Don Redman, Cab Calloway, and Chick Webb. While in Calloway's band, Bauza played alongside another young trumpet player, Dizzy Gillespie. Likewise, Augusto Coen, the Ponce-born son of an American Jew and Afro–Puerto Rican mother, arrived in New York in the 1920s. A virtuoso with the guitar, trumpet, and several other instruments, Coen went on to perform with Sissle, Duke Ellington, Henderson, and others.

The tango rage of the 1920s was followed by the rumba craze of the 1930s, a sound pioneered by Cuban big-band leaders like Don Azpiazú, Xavier Cugat, and later, Desi Arnaz. In its first Broadway performance in 1930, Azpiazú's orchestra introduced what would become the most famous Cuban tune in U.S. history, *"El Manicero"* ("The Peanut Vendor"). Those early bands exposed American audiences for the first time to the powerful and exotic combination of Cuban instruments—maracas, claves, guiros, bongos, congas, and timbales—many of which would later be adopted by countless white and Black musical groups. By adopting English lyrics to their tunes, and often by featuring American women as vocalists, Azpiazú, Cugat, and Arnaz pioneered the first successful commercial crossover bands. Throughout the 1940s, Hollywood produced dozens of movies with Latin tunes and themes and made bandleaders like Cugat (*Holiday in Mexico, The Three Caballeros*) and Arnaz (*Cuban Pete*) stars in the process. Bing Crosby and Bob Hope starred in *Road to Rio* (1947), and Groucho Marx and Carmen Miranda were paired in *Copacabana*.

But for serious lovers of music, the most exciting experiments were happening in Harlem and in the jazz clubs of Manhattan, where the great Afro-Cuban and Afro–Puerto Rican musicians, still ignored by a race-conscious country, were exploring new forms with the great

African American bands. By the 1940s, some of those Cubans and Puerto Ricans, Bauza, Coen, Frank "Machito" Grillo, and Alberto Socarrías, began to form their own orchestras. Their groups fused the big-band sound of American music—with its clarinet, saxophone, and trumpet sections—with island instruments such as *panderetas*, maracas, guiros, and bongos; they adapted the Cuban *guarachas* and *son* and the Puerto Rican *danzas* and *plenas* to lyrics of their new American reality, and out of all that came new hybrid musical genres.

No major musician in the country, whether on Broadway, in Hollywood, at the major recording studios, or in the concert halls, escaped the influence of the new Latin music they created. Glenn Miller, Cab Calloway, Charlie Parker, Woody Herman—all of them experimented with fusing jazz and Cuban music—and later the Brazilian samba. Nat King Cole recorded his first Latin-inspired album, *Rumba à la King*, in Cuba in 1946 with Alfredo "Chocolate" Armenteros, one of the greatest of Cuban trumpet players. Out of those experiments, two distinct but interrelated musical styles had emerged by the 1950s, the mambo, which was popularized by musicians like Perez Prado, Tito Puente, and Tito Rodriguez, and Cubop or Afro-Cuban jazz, whose creative founders were Machito, Stan Kenton, Dizzy Gillespie, Chano Pozo, Puente, and others.

Meanwhile, British pianist George Shearing, who had been experimenting with Latin music for a decade, organized a new quintet in 1953 to play Latin-oriented jazz in California. The musicians Shearing recruited would became a virtual musical hall of fame decades later. They included Cubans Mongo Santamaria on conga and Armando Peraza on bongo, Puerto Rican Willie Bobo on timbales, and Swedish American Cal Tjader on vibraphones.[40]

A simultaneous but distinct fusion of Latin and Euro-American music occurred in South Texas, where the *norteño* music of Mexico gave rise to conjunto, or Tex-Mex. The development of conjunto is explored in Manuel Peña's incisive study, *The Texas-Mexican Conjunto: History of a Working-Class Music*. Peña traces how the accordion, a European instrument, was adopted into Mexican music as early as the 1850s. But it was not until 1928, when Narciso Martinez, a South Texas master of the Chicano accordion style, teamed with Santiago Almedia, who played the Mexican *bajo sexto*, that the main instrumental components of conjunto were created. The other major conjunto musician of the 1930s was Santiago "Flaco" Jimenez Sr.[41] The ranchera, *corrido*, and conjunto forms gradually spread beyond the Mexican border towns and seeped into American country music.

In the Southwest, John Roberts notes, country music "took both guitar techniques and songs from Mexican sources. The 'Spanish Two-
Step' has been suggested as the origin of 'San Antonio Rose,' and 'El
Rancho Grande' was played by almost all western swing bands and
has become a 'standard' in country music."[42]

The Chicano influence on American music, especially on rock
and country, continued from the 1950s on, from the Latin rock of
Carlos Santana to the country rock of Linda Ronstadt, to the wild
Tex-Mex rock and roll of Freddy Fender, to the fusion style of "Lit-
tle Joe" Hernandez and La Familia, and finally, to the pop Tex-Mex
of Selena Quintanilla. The past three decades have seen a raft
of Latino crossover musicians propel to megastar status among
English-speaking audiences. They include Cuban American Gloria
Estefan; Puerto Ricans Ricky Martin, Marc Anthony, and Jennifer
Lopez; Colombian-born Shakira; and Spaniard Enrique Iglesias.
But perhaps the most pervasive influence of Latino performers has
been by hip-hop and reggaeton artists among the country's youth.
The list of the Latinx hip-hop icons since the early 1990s is too long
to list here, but it includes Big Pun (Christopher Rios), Fat Joe (Jo-
seph Cartagena), and Cardi B (Belcalis Marlenis Almánzar), all
from the South Bronx; Pitbull (Armando Christian Pérez) from
Miami; as well as reggaeton king Daddy Yankee (Ramón Luis Ayala
Rodriguez) and Bad Bunny (Benito Antonio Martínez) from Puerto
Rico. Los Angeles, meanwhile, has produced Becky G (Becky Gomez)
and Akwid (brothers Sergio and Francisco Gomez), born in Mexico
and raised in the United States, who fused hip-hop with traditional
Mexican regional music; and Jae-P (Juan Pablo Huerta), also born in
Mexico and raised in the States. Jae-P's hit debut album in 2003 was
appropriately titled *Ni De Aquí, Ni De Allá* (*Neither From Here Nor
There*). More recently, Calle 13, the eclectic urban music band
founded by Puerto Rican stepbrothers René Pérez Joglar (*Residente*)
and Eduardo José Cabra Martínez (*Visitante*), with its trademark politically radical lyrics, has become a worldwide sensation and captured a record twenty-one Latin Grammy awards.[43]

If the period between World Wars I and II marked the rise of Latino
theater and music, the 1960s saw the rise of Latino literature,
marked by classics such as José Antonio Villareal's *Pocho* (1959), Piri
Thomas's *Down These Mean Streets* (1967), and Rudolfo Anaya's

coming-of-age classic, *Bless Me, Ultima* (1972). The long delay in the rise of English-language Latino literature should come as no surprise. It is one thing to learn a new language, quite another to develop a literary tradition in that language.

Since then, we have witnessed a surge of Latino creativity—from the novels and stories of Nicolasa Mohr, John Rechy, Sandra Cisneros, Esmeralda Santiago, Oscar Hijuelos, Cristina García, Julia Alvarez, Ana Castillo, Junot Díaz, and Isabel Allende to the poetry and essays of Pedro Pietri, Tato Laviera, Martín Espada, Cherie Moraga, and Gloria Anzaldúa, to the films and theatrical works of Luis Valdéz, Edward James Olmos, Moctesuma Esparza, Dolores Prida, Josefina Lopez, and Lin-Manuel Miranda.

The Mariel exodus, in addition, brought some of Cuba's finest writers and artists to the United States. Refugees Reinaldo Arenas, author of the classic *Hallucinating World*, Juan Abreu, Carlos Alfonzo, Victor Gómez, and Andrés Valerio sparked a revival of the arts in the émigré community soon after their arrival, and with it, a renewal of pride in Cuban culture.[44]

No single Latinx artist had as significant an impact on American culture, however, as did playwright Lin-Manuel Miranda with his successive Broadway musical hits *In the Heights* (2005) and *Hamilton* (2015). *Hamilton*, in particular, garnered eleven Tony Awards, a Grammy, and a Pulitzer Prize for drama, and it virtually transformed American theater from a traditional arena for the elite into a venue for a more popular and diverse cultural storytelling, prompting scholars, educators, politicians, and ordinary Americans to reimagine the nation's history. It even provoked Oskar Eustis, artistic director of New York's Public Theater, to compare Miranda to a young Shakespeare. "Shakespeare told England's national story to the audience at the Globe," Eustis said, "and helped make England England—helped give it its self-consciousness. That is exactly what Lin is doing with *Hamilton*. By telling the story of the founding of the country through the eyes of a bastard, immigrant orphan, told entirely by people of color, he is saying, "This is our country. We get to lay claim to it."[45]

In summary, Latino artists accomplished several simultaneous fusion movements, whether in theater, music, literature, or film. They borrowed and absorbed lessons from one another's separate national experiences; they found reinforcement and new approaches from the artistic traditions of Latin America; and they explored and adapted the styles and content of African American and

Anglo-American artists. Out of all these fusion efforts, they created a vibrant and kaleidoscopic Latino branch of American culture. Yet with the exception of Miranda's breakthrough efforts during the past decade, few of their accomplishments show up in high school texts, Hollywood films, or network television shows.

BILINGUALISM AND THE HUNGER TO FORGET LANGUAGE

Most of the debate around language policy in the United States has centered on the "threat" of bilingualism, even though virtually all studies have repeatedly shown that most Latinos believe that mastery of English is critical for their progress in this country. They believe it so fervently that 75 percent of Hispanic immigrants are speaking English on a daily basis by the time they have lived in the United States for fifteen years, and 70 percent of the children of those immigrants become dominant in or only speak English.[46]

Even in the nineteenth century, Spanish-language newspapers rejected a separatist linguistic philosophy and embraced the need to learn English. Francisco Ramirez's newspaper, *El Clamor Público*, the first of its kind in California, added a page in the 1850s to help its readers learn the language. But those early *mexicanos* also rejected the notion that Spanish was a "foreign" tongue, and they defended use of their native language. A major goal of LULAC, the nation's oldest Hispanic civil rights group, since its founding early in the twentieth century, has been to teach English to all immigrants. *El Independiente*, of Las Vegas, Nevada, for instance, urged its readers back in the late nineteenth century to learn English while not allowing Spanish "to be trampled underfoot." The use of "Spanglish," in fact, dates back to that era. The college-educated children of General Mariano Vallejo, the prominent *californio* leader, for example, often wrote back home to their parents in English mixed with Spanish. As Rosina Lozano notes of one exchange she unearthed from the family archives:

> Fluent in spoken Spanish, they peppered their correspondence with Spanish phrases and sometimes combined the two languages. 'Si puede—compreme a little box of drawing pencils si puede,' Maria Vallejo exclaimed to her father.[47]

In his 1982 bestselling autobiography, *Hunger of Memory*, writer Richard Rodriguez recounted how he immersed himself in the English language from his earliest years in school as a way of willing himself to become "a middle-class American man. Assimilated."[48]

Those 1950s English immersion programs did succeed in one sense. They turned Rodriguez and thousands of others from our generation into skillful users of the English language. But what of the many who faltered and were left back in school again and again, only to end up illiterate in two languages? Or who were tracked into special education or vocational programs only because they could not master English and ended up dropping out of school?

Those childhood memories of sink-or-swim immersion programs turned me into a consistent advocate of bilingual education. By that, I do not mean the most extreme form, the "maintenance model," which seeks to maintain Spanish literacy at times to the detriment of rapid English acquisition, and which too often leads to government-subsidized cultural enclaves, but the "transitional" model instead.

The bilingual education movement, in fact, was born not among poor Hispanic immigrants but among upper-class Cuban refugees who arrived in Miami in the 1960s. Initially financed by the federal government, the program sought to make what was then considered a temporary stay by the refugees as easy as possible. Over the years, the policy turned into a vast jobs program, first for Cuban professionals and then for other middle-class Latin Americans who were recruited from abroad to teach in the bilingual programs that proliferated across the country.

Had most schools adopted the "transitional" bilingual model, which instructs in the native language for a limited amount of time—two to four years—while the child masters English, or the dual language model, where all students receive instruction in two languages, the acrimony of the current debate might have been mitigated. But extreme positions on both sides drew the most media attention. In a climate of "Americanization," proponents of total immersion gained momentum. Under this system, children are placed in intensive English-language courses until they gain a basic knowledge of the language, which means they fall behind in their other subjects. It also means their knowledge of Spanish is treated as a handicap, not as an asset.

Critics of bilingual education correctly point to the excesses of a bilingual bureaucracy that began to feed on itself.[49] They point to

New York City, for instance, where studies show that twenty-five thousand students were kept in bilingual programs for four or more years. But changing a child's language is not as simple as learning to dress differently. It involves a complex switching of cultural markers that, if not handled properly, can lead to years of psychological repercussions. The older a child is when he or she begins the transition, the more grueling it becomes to achieve mastery in the new language. In the case of Puerto Ricans and Mexican Americans who are born and raised as American citizens in households where Spanish has been a part of family life for generations, language becomes integral to a sense of who one is.

Native language retention is no doubt higher among Hispanics than other immigrants, but that is caused by very real factors—proximity to the cultural influence of Latin America and seventy years of continued massive immigration. Throughout the Mexican border region, for example, broadcasts from television and radio stations in Mexico can be picked up on the American side (just as broadcasts from the U.S. side can be heard in Mexico). In a small city like El Paso, Texas, which sits across the Rio Grande from the far larger Mexican metropolis of Ciudad Juárez, it should surprise no one that the Spanish language and Mexican culture exercise a dominant influence.

The fear of some Americans that English will soon be replaced as the country's language is not only contrary to the facts, it borders on paranoia. If anything, the global reach of American commerce and communications is accomplishing the opposite. Throughout Latin America, English is virtually the second language of all public schools, the main language of many private academies, and the principal language on the internet. It is everywhere in the mass media and in advertising. It is already the lingua franca of empire. At night, in cities throughout the southern half of the hemisphere, hundreds of thousands of young Latin Americans eagerly pack private schools to learn it. Young Latinos who are raised in this country are proud of their English and often recoil with greater disgust than white students at the idea of having to study Spanish in high school. In a strange way, those Latino students have internalized the broader society's scorn of Spanish, as if admitting that speaking a language different from that of the majority relegates you to a status of less than American.

It behooves all Americans to recognize how essential Latino culture and the Spanish language have been to our own history and traditions. Our schools should be dissecting and analyzing the new hybrid cultural trends that emerged in the twentieth century from the amalgamations and fusions of Latino, African American, and Anglo-American arts. From Tex-Mex, bugaloo, and mambo to Latin jazz, reggae, rap, and hip-hop, these new musical genres are our best examples of cultural bridges. History is filled with examples of other great nations that sought to stamp out "differences" of race, religion, and language, only to end up destroying themselves. We fool ourselves in thinking our fate would be any different.

As Pérez de Villagrá, the first poet on American soil, wrote more than four hundred years ago as he described the battle at Acoma between the Spanish and the Pueblos:

> It matters not that they be cultivated men
> Or rude, wild, barbarous, and gross,
> For 'tis enough, and more, to know that they are men
> And know that, except for the Fiend himself,
> They all are the worst beast, when they do wish,
> Of all the ones that God created . . .[50]

13

FREE TRADE:
The Final Conquest of Latin America

After two centuries, England has found it convenient to adopt free trade *because* it thinks that protection can no longer offer it anything . . . my knowledge of our country leads me to believe that within two hundred years, when America has gotten out of protection all that it can offer, it too will adopt free trade.

—ULYSSES S. GRANT

Latin America was where neoliberal globalization assumed its most pernicious form . . . with an unprecedented concentration of wealth and power into the hands of a small minority.

—XIMENA DE LA BARRA,
Latin America after the Neoliberal Debacle

During the second half of the twentieth century a momentous shift occurred in American economic life. U.S. transnational firms searching for cheap labor and maximum profit shifted much of their manufacturing to Third World countries, especially to Latin America. As part of the shift, the U.S. government led a worldwide campaign for "free trade." It pressed developing nations to lower tariffs on imported goods and to create new export-oriented manufacturing zones, largely to serve the needs of foreign firms.

But the U.S. version of free trade, as we shall see in this chapter, deeply distorted many Latin American economies. It became a key pillar starting in the 1980s for a new neoliberal economic strategy. Sometimes dubbed the Washington Consensus, that strategy also included the mass sell-off of public assets, the privatization of basic government services, and the submission of national governments to the financial and trade dictates of agencies like the International Monetary Fund, the World Bank, and the World Trade Organization.[1]

While foreign investors and a domestic elite prospered from the boom in expanded trade, the Latin American nations that rushed to adopt the neoliberal model soon discovered it did not produce the miracle progress for ordinary people its proponents had predicted. By the late 1990s, wealth disparity had grown so rapidly that the region was reporting the biggest income gaps in the world between rich and poor. Ironically, Latin America, which historically had been a major destination for millions of migrants from around the world, was transformed into a giant exporter of its own people—and the bulk of those migrants headed for the United States.[2]

Perhaps nowhere was the free trade model more enthusiastically embraced than in neighboring Mexico, which formally entered a permanent economic union with the United States and Canada through the North American Free Trade Agreement (NAFTA) in 1994. NAFTA set off a stampede by U.S. and other foreign investors to gobble up key portions of Mexico's manufacturing, agricultural, and banking industries. The sudden infusion of foreign capital, however, drove so many small Mexican manufacturers and farmers out of business that millions of people were dislocated and unemployment mushroomed. Thus, instead of reducing the pressure on Mexicans to migrate, NAFTA fueled it.

A big part of Donald Trump's appeal to working-class Americans during the 2016 election was his condemnation of NAFTA and the free trade policies so long espoused by key sectors of both the Republican and Democratic parties, yet his replacement of NAFTA with the U.S.-Mexico-Canada Agreement (USMCA), which Congress ratified at the end of 2019, marked only minor tinkering with what remains a fundamentally unequal trade relationship with Mexico.

By the late 1990s, the deepening crisis of poverty throughout Latin America ignited a firestorm of popular discontent. One after another, local governments that had espoused neoliberalism were toppled from power by massive protest movements, or they were routed in national elections. The new leaders who came to office invariably sought a more socially conscious road to economic growth, one more independent of U.S. control. Their governments swept to power thanks to complex alliances between traditional left-wing politicians and labor leaders and newer civil society organizations. Many of those civic groups were based in sectors long ignored by the established political parties and economic elite of Latin America: indigenous peoples, poor farmers, urban slum dwellers, racial minorities, and lower-level civil servants.

With the elections of Hugo Chávez in Venezuela in 1998, Brazil's Luis Inácio "Lula" da Silva in 2002, Argentina's Néstor Kirchner in 2003, and Evo Morales as Bolivia's first indigenous president in 2005, Latin American leaders began to chart foreign and domestic policies that could no longer be dictated by the United States. Over the next decade, the region turned into a worldwide center for mass participation in democracy, for new economic alliances between neighboring nations, and for new social initiatives by governments at home, a phenomenon soon referred to as the pink tide movement. Several countries in the region began to show remarkable progress in reducing their domestic income gap and reducing poverty.

These new governments, however, faced economic hostility from both Republican and Democratic administrations in Washington, which sought to destabilize them or to back overt armed rebellions to overthrow them, starting with the failed coup against Venezuela's Chávez in 2002.[3] The new leaders responded by inaugurating their own regional economic blocs and seeking new sources of international investment and financing. The People's Republic of China, the world's second-largest economy, soon proved eager to fill the void, especially as the United States was preoccupied with wars in the Middle East. Beijing quickly offered Latin American governments massive low-interest loans and outright development grants, with the goal of capturing a greater share of the region's commodity exports, just as it was already doing in Africa. This rise of Chinese influence in Latin America represents a significant geopolitical shift for a region long seen as the backyard of the U.S. empire.

But the progressive upsurge did not last for long. Starting with the overthrow of President José Manuel Zelaya of Honduras in 2009, the wave of left-wing presidents was gradually eclipsed. They were either driven from power in right-wing coups or forced out by corruption probes, several of which rested on scant real evidence but were widely amplified by media companies tied to local elites—a practice known as lawfare—or they were unseated in regular elections by resurgent conservative opponents who relied on social media to whip up public fury. From Chile and Argentina in the south to Honduras and Guatemala at the region's northern end, neoliberal governments returned to office, once again espousing an unfettered free market and free trade politics.[4] Only Mexico managed to buck the overall trend, with the victory in 2018 of Andrés Manuel López Obrador and his MORENA Party.

Within a year, however, the COVID-19 pandemic that swept across the globe struck Latin America especially hard, killing more than 1.3 million people by late 2021 and tossing tens of millions more out of work. In the process, the pandemic laid bare the abysmal public health and social safety net that had resulted from resurgent neoliberal policies, and in country after county voters began propelling new left-wing political movements back into power.[5] Nonetheless, decades of U.S. free trade policies have left a lasting imprint on both Latin America and Latino migration to this country. Which is why the current Latino presence in the United States cannot be understood without first grasping the deep imprint our government's free trade policies have produced in the region.

THE RISE OF FREE TRADE ZONES

As we have seen, North Americans at first ventured into Mexico, the Caribbean, and Central America during the nineteenth century to buy up land and build massive transportation projects: Vanderbilt's Nicaraguan Transit Company, Minor Keith's Central American Railroad, Aspinwall's Panama Railroad, for example. By the early twentieth century, the main methods of exploitation had shifted to extracting raw materials—bananas, sugar, coffee, oil—and to financing the operations of Latin American governments. The region grew to be so important that by 1914 U.S. companies had $416 million in direct investments in Mexico alone, the highest of any country, and Latin America overall accounted for nearly half of all U.S. foreign investment in the world.[6]

The period after World War II brought a third shift, as U.S.

apparel, then electronics, plastics, and chemical companies, started closing down factories at home and reopening them abroad. That offshore production is at the heart of the free trade model the United States has promoted and perfected in Latin America. It is a model that has so far developed in four main stages:

1. Panama and Puerto Rico (1947)
2. Mexico's border industrialization program (1965)
3. The Caribbean Basin Initiative (1985)
4. NAFTA (1994)

As quickly as industrial plants were shuttered in the Northeast and Midwest, scores of shiny new industrial parks and factory towns, usually called free trade zones (FTZs) or export processing zones (EPZs), sprang up south of the border. By 1992, there were more than two hundred of these zones in Mexico and the Caribbean Basin. They housed more than three thousand assembly plants, employed 735,000 workers, and produced $14 billion in annual exports to the United States.[7]

These FTZs were allowed to operate as virtual sovereign enclaves within the host countries, routinely exempted from the few local labor and environmental laws that existed. Inside the zones, child labor was reborn and the most basic rights of workers trampled. As agricultural production in many Latin American countries fell under the sway of foreign agribusiness, millions of Latin America's young people fled the countryside to find work in or near the zones. But the cities to which the migrants flocked lacked sufficient infrastructure of roads, sewage systems, housing, and schools to sustain the sudden surge in population. Giant shantytowns sprang up almost overnight. The makeshift slums and the new factories around which they developed led to a public health nightmare of industrial pollution, untreated human waste, and disease.

Thus, FTZs, which were meant to stabilize the economies of the countries that established them, only led to more drastic and unexpected problems. While the new factories they spawned did provide a certain number of low-wage jobs for the host nations, they also fueled even more massive Latin American immigration to the United States.

Typically, young Latin American workers from the countryside migrated to the local city in their country and found work in a free trade zone factory, commonly known as *maquiladoras* or *maquilas*. There workers learned rudimentary industrial skills—the rigors of assembly production, the discipline of time, the necessity for obedience to instructions. At night, many began studying English in the scores of private language schools that abounded in the new urban environment. They became immersed in American shows on newly bought televisions. In 1993, *maquila* workers in Honduras were more likely to own a television (67 percent) than non-*maquila* workers (60 percent); in fact, they were more likely to own a television than a stove (49 percent) or a refrigerator (24 percent).[8] Each day, they were able to devour the Spanish-language magazines and newspapers that were easily available in the cities and that glorified life in the United States. They quickly discovered they could earn ten times their salary in the *maquila* doing the same job in a factory across the border. Eventually, filled with a new consciousness and disgusted with a dead-end shantytown existence, workers saved enough money to pay a *coyote* and risk the trip to El Norte, or to visit the United States as a tourist and then overstay their visa.

DO AS I SAY, NOT AS I DO

The term *free trade* seems innocuous at first glance. Who could be against the idea that nations should seek the maximum freedom to trade with one another? Or that increased trade will bring with it greater prosperity? Unfortunately, the history of most major industrialized nations is just the opposite. None of them practiced free trade during their early period of economic growth. Instead, they used high tariffs to protect their domestic industries from foreign competition, often engaging in tariff wars against rivals.

"In the early days, when British industry was still at a disadvantage, an English man caught exporting raw wool was sentenced to lose his right hand, and if he repeated the sin he was hanged," Uruguayan journalist Eduardo Galeano reminds us.[9]

Only when England gained a decided advantage over all other countries in world commerce did its government begin advocating free trade in the nineteenth century. During the early days of Latin American independence, England used the slogan to justify bullying the new criollo governments. In the 1850s, for instance, British and French warships sailed up the Río Paraná to force the protectionist government of Argentine leader Juan Manuel de Rosas to open his country's prospering market to British bankers and traders.[10] Eventually, the British concentrated on controlling the South American market, ceding control over most of the Caribbean region to the United States.

In our own country, Congress pursued protectionist policies throughout the post–Civil War period, an era of extraordinary industrial growth for the nation. "In every year from 1862 to 1911, the average [U.S.] duty on all imports exceeded 20 percent . . . [and] in forty-six of those fifty years . . . [it] exceeded 40 percent," notes economist Alfred Eckes, who served on the International Trade Commission under President Reagan.[11] Germany pursued a similar protectionist policy during its nineteenth-century industrial expansion. Not surprisingly, both the German and the U.S. economies experienced higher growth rates during that century than did England, the era's main proponent of free trade.

Despite the historical record, most neoliberal economists in the advanced industrial nations continue to praise the fall of tariffs and the growth of free trade during the past few decades. They contrast the new open global marketplace to the "bad old days" of the 1970s, when governments in underdeveloped countries resorted to high tariffs to protect their own fledgling industries, a strategy called import substitution.

But does expanded world commerce automatically spur an increase in wealth, as the free traders say? And just who are the main beneficiaries of today's surge in international trading?

Free trade proponents would have us believe this unfettered commerce is occurring between millions of businessmen in scores of countries and that the money changing hands is creating more and better-paid workers, who then have more money to spend, which in turn means that markets expand. But the reality is quite different. As much as two-thirds of all the trade in the world today is between multinational corporations, and one-third of it represents multinational corporations trading with their own foreign subsidiaries! Those trends are even more pronounced in this country, with 42 percent of all U.S. trade in 2016 occurring between multinationals headquartered here and their "related party" firms abroad. A General Motors plant in Matamoros, for example, moves parts and finished cars between itself and the parent company in the

United States; or General Electric ships goods to one of its seven-teen assembly plants in Mexico. Between 1982 and 1995, exports of U.S. multinational corporations more than doubled, but the portion of those exports that represented intracompany trading more than tripled. As a result of this enormous expansion of multinationals, the largest private traders and employers in Mexico today are not Mexican firms but U.S. corporations.[12]

Furthermore, if free trade leads to greater prosperity, as its pro-ponents claim, why has economic inequality soared and poverty deepened in virtually every underdeveloped country that adopted neoliberal free trade policies? According to the United Nations, in 1997 the 225 richest people in the world had a net worth equal to the income of 2.5 billion people, or 47 percent of the world's population. That wealth chasm kept widening in subsequent years, so that by 2018 just 26 billionaires owned as much in assets as 50 percent of the world's population.[13]

Before the 1980s, Latin Americans generally protected their domes-tic industries through heavy government ownership, high tariffs, and import substitution. Mexico pursued that policy from 1940 to 1980, and during that time it averaged annual growth rates of more than 6 percent, with both manufacturing output and real wages for indus-trial workers growing consistently. But then came the debt crisis of the 1980s. Along with other Latin American countries, Mexico was gradually pressured by U.S.-controlled international financial insti-tutions to adopt neoliberal free trade policies. Those policies included selling public assets and increasing exports to pay down its debt. Be-tween 1982 and 1992, the Mexican government sold off 1,100 of 1,500 state-owned companies and privatized more than eighteen banks. This fire sale, instead of bringing prosperity, only deepened the chasm between rich and poor, as a new crop of Mexican billion-aires emerged, real wages crashed, and two hundred thousand Mex-icans lost their jobs.[14]

Mexico, however, was not the birthplace of Latin America's free trade model; it started even earlier in two territories the United States directly controlled.

THE FIRST EXPERIMENTS—PUERTO RICO AND PANAMA

The first attempts by American corporations to operate offshore factories on any grand scale started in the late 1940s in the Panama Canal Zone and Puerto Rico, where pliant local governments cooperated in setting up corporate oases that had no tariffs or local taxes but included super-low wages; minimal enforcement of environmental and labor laws; financial incentives from Washington for companies to relocate there; and federal tax exemption for the repatriated income of those companies. By the 1980s, six hundred firms had factories operating in the Colón Free Zone on the Atlantic coast, where they could take advantage of Panama's seventy-five-cents-an-hour wages.[15]

Puerto Rico's experiment was even more extensive. The whole island was turned into a virtual free trade zone, thanks to a little-known loophole in the Internal Revenue Service Code—called Section 936 in its last incarnation—which exempted from federal taxes the income of U.S. subsidiaries.[16]

First to arrive was Textron, which relocated to the island in 1947 after shutting six of its U.S. mills and laying off 3,500 workers. By the early 1950s, more than one new factory a week was being inaugurated. But the boom proved ephemeral. As more U.S. companies opened up, Puerto Rican–owned factories, unable to compete, were driven out of business. During the first ten years of the program, new U.S. factories created 37,300 island jobs, but the job losses among Puerto Rican manufacturers totaled 16,600.[17]

The new jobs the factories created were not sufficient to dent the soaring unemployment in the countryside caused by the rapid mechanization of agriculture and the flight of people to the cities. As a result, both the U.S. and Puerto Rican governments actively encouraged migration to the mainland as a safety valve to hinder social unrest. They offered cheap airfares and facilitated large-scale labor contracting by American companies through a network of offices of the Commonwealth of Puerto Rico, which were established in several U.S. cities.[18] The result was that at the height of the new U.S. investment, the greatest number of Puerto Ricans in history migrated to the United States (see chapter 14).

Puerto Rico set the mold for a trend that then repeated itself throughout the Caribbean region for two generations: American corporations moved in and set up low-wage factories, the factories drew laborers to the cities from the impoverished countryside, the migrants came in greater numbers than the jobs available, and the surplus workers began leaving for the United States, either as contract laborers or as unauthorized immigrants.

Puerto Rico had one wrinkle that set it apart, however—it was still a U.S. territory. That meant federal labor and environmental laws protected factory workers' health and safety and their right to unionize. By the 1960s, as the island's labor movement became increasingly militant, it began demanding wages and working conditions closer to U.S. levels, prompting many U.S. firms to sour on the "Puerto Rican miracle." The firms started moving to other Caribbean countries willing to offer lower labor costs and more lax environmental and safety laws. The shift away from Puerto Rican production, however, failed initially to address one important cost area—tariffs. Once they left U.S. territory, manufacturers could not count on duty-free entry to the American market. To replicate their Puerto Rican oasis, therefore, American industrialists needed steep tariff reductions wherever they were going next.

THE RISE OF THE *MAQUILAS*

Beginning in 1965, the manufacturing scene shifted to Mexico. That country's new border industrialization program (BIP) spawned the "miracle" of the *maquiladoras*, a swath of industrial parks all along the U.S. border.

In colonial Mexico, *maquiladora* denoted the share of grain a miller would charge a farmer for processing his harvest. Over time, the word came to represent a step in a larger operation that occurred elsewhere.[19] As envisioned in the original BIP legislation, the first *maquilas* were supposed to be "twin plants," each with a partner factory on the U.S. side. The Mexican plant would assemble a product from components imported from its twin plant in the United States, then ship the finished product back across the border for sale in the American market; and when the product crossed the border, only the value added by the Mexican labor would be subject to a tariff.

Given that this was a very specific and limited form of tariff reduction, the Mexican government initially permitted it only in areas near the border. That way, supporters argued, jobs would be created on both sides of the border, and the *maquilas* would reduce immigration because Mexicans would choose to stay and work in their own country with the new North American subsidiaries.

But the BIP turned instead into a way for corporations to evade U.S. labor and environmental laws while manufacturing hundreds of yards from our own country. From Tijuana on the Pacific coast to Matamoros near the Texas Gulf, the *maquiladora* zone emerged as a giant industrial strip all along that border.

Too often, the twin plant on this side of the border became nothing more than a warehouse, providing jobs to only a few people.[20] The General Electric Company, which opened its first *maquiladora* in 1971, had eight Mexican plants within a decade, where 8,500 workers made circuit breakers, motors, coils, and pumps.[21] In one year alone, General Motors opened twelve new *maquilas* while closing eleven factories in the United States and laying off 29,000 people. By the early 1990s, GM was the biggest private employer in Mexico, with fifty *maquila* plants and 50,000 workers.[22] On the eve of Congress's approval of the North American Free Trade Agreement in late 1993, more than two thousand *maquila* factories were employing 550,000 Mexicans. At the time, the total number of manufacturing jobs in the United States stood at 16.7 million, but it would plummet by 5 million that were lost between 2000 and 2014.[23] In little more than two decades, the industrial heartland of North America was unceremoniously uprooted from America's Midwest to Mexico's northern border.

Unlike the old U.S. factories that largely employed men, the *maquilas* took to recruiting young Mexican women, who traditionally had not been part of Mexico's labor force. Their U.S. managers considered Mexican men tougher to control and hired as few as possible.[24] Thus, Mexico's unemployment problem, which had always been more severe for its men, was barely dented by the *maquila* program. Drawing so many young women from the countryside to the border factories disrupted social organization in rural villages, where women historically provided critical unpaid labor. Even though young men had no job prospects, they ended up following the women to the cities, and once they arrived at the border towns, many decided to head for the United States. As sociologist Saskia Sassen notes: "People first uprooted from traditional ways of life, then left unemployed and unemployable as export firms hire younger workers or move production to other countries, may see few options but emigration—especially if export-led strategies have sapped the country's domestic economy."[25]

Those who managed to find jobs in the *maquilas* soon discovered that their meager wages bought less and less each day. Real wages in the industry crashed when measured against the U.S. dollar. They dropped 68 percent between 1980 and 1992 even though *maquila* productivity rose by 41 percent. Most of the drop resulted from two successive devaluations of the Mexican peso in the 1980s—and all that was before the huge December 1994 devaluation, where the peso lost an additional 50 percent value.

Contrary to the glowing predictions of our government and business leaders, the explosion of *maquiladoras* has done nothing to slow Mexican emigration. Instead, emigration has escalated side by side with *maquila* growth—exactly as happened with Puerto Rico (see table 10).

Table 10

Legal Mexican Immigration to the United States

(BY FISCAL YEAR)[26]

1960–1969	441,824
1970–1979	621,218
1980–1989	1,009,586
1990–1999	2,757,418
2000–2009	1,701,166
2010–2019	1,506,738

The biggest jump in Mexican migration to the United States, in fact, occurred during the years following passage of NAFTA, increasing from 430,000 annually in 1993 to 770,000 by 2000.[27] The miracle prosperity that lower trade barriers were supposed to bring never reached the majority of Mexicans outside the *maquilas* either. Per capita domestic product for the whole country dropped from $2,421 annually in 1980 to $2,284 in 1994.[28] While factory wages in East Asia rose throughout the 1980s, Mexican wages slipped, making the country and the whole Caribbean region the most desirable place in the world for U.S. direct investment.[29]

Meanwhile, Mexico's government, thanks to its tight control over national unions, assured foreign investors that no one would challenge the super-low wage structures of the *maquilas*. In most free trade zones along the border, only government unions were allowed to operate. In those rare cases where independent unions gained a foothold, such as the northeastern state of Tamaulipas, the workers saw immediate benefit. *Maquila* workers there earned 30 percent more than their counterparts in other Mexican states for a forty-hour week, while workers in other states were required to work forty-eight hours.

NIGHTMARE ON THE BORDER

The other side of Mexico's industrial transformation is the social and environmental disaster created by unrestrained growth.

Sleepy border towns have been catapulted helter-skelter into the industrial age. Just across the Rio Grande from El Paso, for instance, is Ciudad Juárez, whose population, just 250,000 in 1960, jumped to 1.5 million by 2020.[30] Reynosa, across the river from McAllen, Texas, zoomed from 4,800 inhabitants in 1930, to 280,000 in 1990, to 899,000 in 2020. So frenetic has been the pace of growth that by the 1990s, 60 percent of Reynosa's *maquila* workers had lived in the city less than five years, and 20 percent less than a year.[31]

The same population explosion has been replicated in the border cities of Tijuana, Mexicali, Nogales, Nuevo Laredo, and Matamoros. As thousands flocked to the farrago of *maquiladoras* in search of work, the border towns became overwhelmed by the lack of roads, housing, electrical power, schools, even clean drinking water for the new migrants. The result was urban anarchy on a scale almost unimaginable to Americans. In Reynosa, one researcher counted two hundred shantytowns in 1992, most without cement roads. More than a third of the city's population had no indoor plumbing and 15 percent no electricity.[32] Not until after the passage of NAFTA did any major city along the border boast a fully operational sewage treatment plant. Nuevo Laredo, population 635,000, opened one in 1997 with subsidies from the International Boundary and Water Commission, a joint effort of the United States and Mexico. Tijuana opened a plant west of San Ysidro the following year with similar subsidies, followed by Ciudad Juárez in 2014 and Matamoros in 2018. But the Nuevo Laredo system is already dilapidated and in need of $55 million in upgrades. Its pipes currently dump more than six million gallons of raw sewage per day into the Rio Grande—the same river that supplies the city's drinking water. Meanwhile, the population of Mexico's border cities continues to skyrocket. Wastewater from Tijuana's 1.8 million residents overwhelm its treatment system on a daily basis, spewing millions of gallons of raw sewage daily into the Tijuana River, which drains northward into the Pacific, periodically polluting beaches in Southern California. And much the same is true all along the border.[33]

Added to the human waste and garbage created by the population surge has been the pollution released from the unprecedented concentration of factories. The most cursory summary of the worst contamination episodes from these works would fill scores of pages. Among them are the repeated escapes of deadly toxic gas clouds from Dupont's Quimica Flor plant in a densely populated neighborhood of Matamoros; the eighty thousand tons of lead sulfate found illegally dumped in 1992 outside Tijuana by Los Angeles–based Alco Pacific, which ran a lead-processing plant there for more than a decade; the discharges of xylene—a highly toxic industrial solvent—by the General Motors Rimir plant into the sewers of Matamoros, where a Boston-based environmental group found xylene at 6,300 times the level permitted by U.S. drinking water standards.[34]

The human impact of so much toxic pollution is inescapable:

+ In the mid-1980s, Mexican health professionals in Matamoros discovered that deformities in many of the city's children might be traced to one of the first *maquiladoras*, Mallory Mexicana S.A., an Indiana-based plant that had produced capacitors for televisions during its early years and in the process exposed employees to various toxic chemicals, including PCBs.

  At least 70 severely disabled Mallory children had been identified in 1992 when I first visited Matamoros. The number climbed in subsequent years to 120. All the children were born between 1970 and 1977 to mothers who had worked on the assembly line while pregnant. By the time the mothers realized the source of their problem, the plant had closed and the company had been repeatedly sold in a string of deals involving several U.S. firms.[35] Many of those children, when I saw them as adults in the early 1990s, still wore diapers; others moved and talked normally but possessed the minds of seven-year-olds. Their facial features were flat and listless and some communicated in bone-chilling shrieks, their spindly arms and legs constantly convulsing. On August 27, 1995, more than a half dozen *maquiladora* firms consented to pay $17 million to settle a lawsuit by twenty-seven of the families, though the companies insisted no proof had been established of any environmental cause.[36]

♦ In 1993, American Rivers, a national conservation group, concluded that the Rio Grande "poses a greater threat to human health than any other river system in North America." The report blamed industrial waste from *maquiladoras* for much of the problem.[37]

♦ From 1991 to 1993, childhood cancers in the Brownsville public schools increased 230 percent.[38]

♦ In the 1990s, abnormal clusters of anencephalic births were identified in Cameron County on the U.S. side of the border and in the adjacent state of Taumalipas on the Mexican side. Though a few studies by U.S. medical experts found no association to pollution, many residents and environmental activists remain convinced the birth defects were related to the toxins produced by the *maquilas*.[39]

♦ Gallbladder problems, liver cancer, and hepatitis rates are higher along the thirty-three Texas counties near the Rio Grande than in the rest of the state and the nation, and as recently as 2015 Hispanics in those counties suffered from far higher liver cancer rates than Hispanics anywhere else in the country.[40]

THE CARIBBEAN BACKYARD

By the mid-1980s, American industrialists had persuaded our federal government to replicate the Puerto Rico and Mexico experiments throughout the rest of the Caribbean and Central America. The Reagan administration called this next stage the Caribbean Basin Initiative (CBI). Under the program, Congress provided direct federal aid to countries in the Caribbean that established free trade zones and eliminated tariffs for manufactured goods entering the United States from those zones. Passage of the bill fueled an immediate expansion of offshore production. Many of the new manufacturers were direct subsidiaries of U.S. firms or were owned by Korean and Taiwanese middlemen who supplied the U.S. market.

But CBI went much further than the Mexico program. U.S. officials actually enticed U.S. companies to close down their U.S. factories and eliminate American jobs. The policy became public late in 1992 when a coalition of labor unions pulled off the first labor sting in American history. The sting, organized by the National Labor Committee, involved the creation of a fictitious firm, New Age Textiles. The "executives" of the fake firm attended textile industry trade shows, where they secretly filmed officials of the U.S. Agency for International Development and the U.S. Commerce Department urging their firm to locate production in the Caribbean region. The federal officials offered to arrange financing, feasibility studies, and site selection trips to the Caribbean free trade zones, and they even boasted how union activists were blacklisted and unions kept out of the zones.

When the sting was finally revealed on a network television news program, it turned out that the federal government had spent nearly $700 million since 1980 on projects aimed at promoting Caribbean *maquiladoras*.[41] The revelations, coming in the midst of a recession and just before the 1992 presidential elections, threw Washington into an uproar and persuaded Congress to enact new restrictions on economic aid under CBI. A decade after the program had been established, more than five hundred companies had utilized CBI incentives to set up their first production facilities in the region's FTZs, and another three hundred had expanded operations.[42]

By the time of my first trip to the Dominican Republic in 1992, that country already boasted twenty-three free trade zones, which employed 170,000 people. Few of those jobs had existed a decade earlier. The largest FTZ was in the southeastern city of San Pedro de Macorís. It contained ninety plants and was brimming with 40,000 workers, most of them teenagers and young women who worked ten- and twelve-hour shifts for as little as four dollars a day.

Once again, however, the staggering growth in jobs did nothing to stem emigration. The same decade that saw the most *maquila* jobs created in the Dominican Republic also saw the greatest Dominican exodus to the United States; from 1981 to 1990, 252,000 emigrated legally to this country and an unknown number illegally—more than in the previous two decades combined.

With *maquila* profits booming, you might expect some meager

prosperity to find its way to the average Dominican. Just the opposite occurred. Dominican gross national product decreased almost
every year between 1982 and 1992, and per capita consumption
dropped 22 percent during that time.[43]

Central Americans have not fared much better. At first, the civil
wars in the region dampened foreign investment interest, but since
the end of the fighting, Central America has joined the *maquila*
bandwagon, with free trade zones sprouting throughout the region.
By 1998, the Caribbean Basin had become the world's largest
supplier of clothing to the U.S. market, and while China would later
surpass it, the region still ranked in 2019 as the number two source
for U.S. imported clothes.[44] Name an American retailer whose
soaring profits made it a darling of Wall Street during the 1990s and
in all likelihood its garments were being produced by teenagers in
Central America. Average hourly wages in those zones began a spiraling race to the bottom. In 1992, they were forty-five cents for El
Salvador, thirty-nine cents for Honduras, twenty-six cents for Costa
Rica, and sixty-two cents for Guatemala.[45]

Among the U.S. firms that closed domestic plants and flocked to
the region were Farah, Haggar, GTE, Kellwood, Levi Strauss, Leslie Fay, Sara Lee, Oxford, and Arrow. In 1981, for instance, Kellwood Company, a St. Louis–based manufacturer of apparel and
home furnishings, employed 16,000 people in sixty-two U.S. plants
and it had no overseas production. Eleven years later, Kellwood had
closed fifty of those plants and eliminated 9,500 domestic jobs, replacing them with 8,900 new workers in the Dominican Republic,
Honduras, Haiti, and Costa Rica. By 1997, 58 percent of Kellwood's
workers were offshore, where they earned only a few dollars a day.[46]

The frenetic pace of factory expansion in the region was astounding. A 1993 U.S. AID study of the free trade zones in Honduras
reported that the number of Honduran *maquila* workers had skyrocketed by 43 percent in just one year, to more than twenty-two
thousand, and was expected to triple by 1996. Those Honduran
workers were overwhelmingly women (71 percent) and under twenty-
five years of age (83 percent), with nearly half of them teenagers.[47]

Claudia Leticia Molina was one of those teenagers. She was a
rail-thin sixteen-year-old who weighed ninety-three pounds when
she began working at a Honduran factory called Orion Apparel in
one of the zones outside San Pedro Sula. Her supervisors sometimes
forced Claudia to clock into work at 7:00 a.m. on a Friday, and she
would not leave the factory until 4:00 a.m. the next morning. Her

only rest was catching a few hours' sleep on the floor by her machine. A week of such work earned her forty-three dollars. In neighboring El Salvador, Judith Yanira Viera, eighteen, would work as
many as seventy hours per week at Mandarin International, a
Taiwanese-owned plant that produced shirts for such well-known
American retailers as Eddie Bauer, the Gap, and JCPenney. Her average pay was fifty-six cents an hour.[48]

Physical and sexual abuse against women in the zones is commonplace. In some factories, women are fired when they become
pregnant, and there have been documented instances of factory
owners requiring employees to take birth control pills each morning
as they reported to work.

In San Salvador, the Human Rights Office of the Catholic Archdiocese denounced an incident in which numerous female employees at Mandarin International were beaten with pistol butts on June
29, 1995, by a factory manager and a Salvadoran army colonel who
was a partner in the firm. At the time, the women were protesting
the firing of 350 of their coworkers for trying to organize a union.[49]
The outcry by church and labor groups in El Salvador and the
United States led to a boycott against the Gap, one of Mandarin's
principal customers. As the boycott appeared to gather steam,
image-conscious Gap officials offered to settle the dispute and get
the workers rehired. The Gap also consented to a pioneering set of
employee rights, which the firm pledged all its future contractors
would honor.

The growth of factories in the free trade zones became so great
that one federal study warned of a looming shortage of female workers. The report, compiled for the U.S. Agency for International Development by Price Waterhouse, noted that in Honduras, where 50
percent of young females in the Sula Valley were already working in
the factories, "it is likely that the female participation rate will level
off between 65 percent and 70 percent, so future labor force growth
will depend on vegetative population increase plus immigration."[50]

Unfortunately, the phenomenal profits being made by the multinational corporations and their middlemen producers did not
trickle down to the average Central American worker. While foreign investment in the free trade zones boomed, overall annual exports from the region to the United States dropped by more than
$1 billion from 1984 to 1991, and per capita income in the Carib-
bean Basin fell at a rate two and a half times faster than the rest of
Latin America. By then, the United Nations estimated that 60

percent of the people of Central America and the Caribbean were living below the poverty line.[51]

Just as in Puerto Rico, Mexico, and the Dominican Republic, *maquiladora* growth in Central America did not slow immigration. During the decade of the 1980s—at the height of the region's civil wars—468,000 Central Americans came to the United States legally and many more illegally. After the fighting stopped, however, the exodus continued. Between 1991 and 1996, another 344,000 arrived legally. And in the aftermath of the Great Recession, migration to the United States from Central America has reached near record levels. The conclusion is inescapable. The neoliberal free trade strategy has done little to improve basic conditions in the region. If anything, it only accelerated migration and rootlessness among the region's workers, who, once they have fled their villages for the *maquilas*, find it even easier to flee the *maquilas* for El Norte.

Nonetheless, leaders of both the Democratic and Republican parties pressed forward with an expansion of that strategy throughout the region. In the early morning hours of July 27, 2005, the House of Representatives approved a new Central American Free Trade Agreement by the slimmest of margins, 217 to 215. The measure, which eventually included the Dominican Republic as well as the United States and five Central American nations, prevailed only after an extraordinary fight on the House floor, during which Republican leaders kept the vote open for more than an hour as they brazenly strong-armed reluctant members and even offered pork barrel inducements to several of them in order to eke out a victory.[52]

NAFTA: WHERE DID ALL THE PROMISES GO?

None of the prior phases of this free trade juggernaut compared in scope with what happened after the U.S. Congress approved NAFTA. The treaty, which took effect on January 1, 1994, created a new common market whose aim was to remove all tariff barriers between Mexico, Canada, and the United States by 2010.[53]

During the bitter fight in Congress over the treaty, NAFTA's advocates promised a new era of prosperity for what they billed as the world's biggest economic bloc. President Clinton predicted 170,000 new jobs would be created for Americans from increased exports to Mexico just in NAFTA's first year.[54] During the initial ten years, some experts claimed, Mexico would gain more than one million new industrial jobs. Clinton and Vice President Al Gore lobbied fiercely for the treaty and they were joined by several former Republican and Democratic presidents. They all assured the public, just as previous leaders had with the border industrialization program, that the economic boom from NAFTA would benefit Americans and that it would slow the tide of illegal immigration.

The same day NAFTA took effect, Maya peasants in Chiapas erupted in the Zapatista insurrection. One of the demands of the rebels was for protection against NAFTA's expected impact on agriculture. The treaty's provisions, the Zapatistas and some American critics insisted, had the potential to devastate close to two million Mexican peasants who produced corn, the country's food staple, on small individual plots. By reducing agricultural tariffs, NAFTA would drive the farmers out of business because they would not be able to compete with the expected surge of American corn and wheat, crops whose harvests here are highly mechanized.[55]

The guerrilla uprising jolted world financial experts who had long trumpeted Mexico as an economic miracle and a model for Latin America.[56] What those experts refused to acknowledge was that Mexico remains a nation divided by immense disparities of wealth. In 1992, for instance, the top 10 percent of Mexicans took in 38 percent of total income, while the bottom half received only 18 percent.[57]

The Mexican leader most in tune with corporate America's desire for NAFTA, and the man who shepherded the treaty through the Mexican legislature, was former president Carlos Salinas. Throughout his presidency, Salinas fueled the Mexican miracle with risky gambits: high-interest short-term bonds sold to foreign investors and denominated in U.S. dollars. By 1995, Mexico owed $29 billion in those bonds. It needed another $9 billion a year just to service the interest on its regular long-term debt, already one of the biggest in the world. The combined debt, together with a ballooning trade deficit, had driven the country to the brink of insolvency by late 1993 and early 1994.

Both the Clinton and Salinas administrations, however, ignored the growing crisis. They were determined first to win passage for NAFTA in the U.S. Congress, then to salvage another victory for Salinas's chosen successor for president, Ernesto Zedillo, in the August 1994 election, so they dared not risk any belt-tightening financial reforms that would anger the Mexican electorate. Salinas's failure to act left Mexico's economy in such shambles that his successor was forced to order an open-ended devaluation of the peso only months after assuming the presidency. Zedillo's decision stunned world markets and propelled the country into economic free fall.

President Clinton hastily engineered a $50 billion international bailout, $20 billion of which he offered from the U.S. Treasury, so that Mexico could pay off its foreign creditors. The bailout was conditioned on the Zedillo government's ramming a severe austerity program onto its people. By midyear 1995, the Mexican peso had lost 50 percent of its value against the dollar, one million Mexicans had lost their jobs, and interest rates had skyrocketed to the point that Mexican consumers were paying as much as 100 percent interest for credit card loans. All predictions of immediate post-NAFTA prosperity vanished in the meltdown. Four years later, the average Mexican had still not regained their precrisis standard of living.

Many economists in this country attempted to detach the NAFTA accords from the Mexican financial meltdown. By doing so they overlooked the fundamental weakness of the common market the treaty created when it married Mexico, a developing country still torn by severe poverty and class conflict, to two of the richest economies in the world.

NAFTA'S IMPACT ON THE UNITED STATES AND CANADA

By the fifteenth anniversary of the new economic union in 2009, many of the original promises had dissipated. Even some of the strongest backers of the treaty had long since conceded that while trade had surged sharply between the United States, Canada, and Mexico, "the NAFTA deal has expanded U.S. gross domestic product (GDP) 'very slightly,' and has had a similar effect—both positive and small—on the Canadian and Mexican economies."[58]

Others painted a far more troubling picture. In Canada, which had initiated a bilateral predecessor agreement to NAFTA with the United States in 1989, unemployment rose to an average of 9.6 percent throughout the 1990s—the highest levels in that country since the Great Depression; meanwhile, income inequality increased. And even though over 870,000 new Canadian jobs were created between 1989 and 1997 by the surge in exports, an estimated 1,147,000 were lost from an even higher growth in imports.[59]

Here in the United States, the Department of Labor estimated that 214,000 factory layoffs between 1994 and 1998 were due to jobs transferred south of the border. Union leaders, however, insisted that the government's measuring standards were too narrow and that job losses were actually twice that figure. They claimed as well that industrial wages at home were kept artificially low because a growing number of U.S. manufacturing firms had responded to their workers' demands for more pay by threatening to move production to low-wage Mexico.

The U.S. trade deficit with its NAFTA partners, meanwhile, grew at a startling clip. In 1993, for example, this country enjoyed a $1.7 billion trade surplus with Mexico, but that surplus quickly evaporated, turning into an eye-popping $74.7 billion deficit by 2007, and while that figure shrank for a few years in the wake of the Great Recession, by 2020 the trade deficit with Mexico was once again at a historic high of $112 billion.[60]

As a result of spiraling trade deficits with Mexico and Canada, the United States endured a net loss of 1,015,290 trade-related jobs between NAFTA's inception and 2004, according to a report by the Economic Policy Institute, with Mexico accounting for about 560,000 of that net loss, and Canada for about 455,000.[61]

Those lost jobs, moreover, had paid on average $800 per week, considerably more than the manufacturing jobs that remained in the United States, the report concluded, adding:

> The average job in the rest of the economy paid only $683 per week, 16% to 19% less than trade-related jobs. Growing trade deficits with Mexico and Canada have pushed more than 1 million workers out of higher-wage jobs and into lower-wage positions in non-trade related industries. Thus, the displacement of 1 million jobs from traded to non-traded goods industries *reduced wage payments to U.S. workers by $7.6 billion in 2004 alone* (my emphasis).[62]

Overall, the U.S. economy lost nearly 3.8 million manufacturing sector jobs between 2001 and 2008, a 22 percent decline in less than a decade. A Congressional Budget Office report pointed to cheaply produced foreign imports as a major contributor. "Although many factors other than trade affect manufacturing employment," the report noted, "in recent years, the pattern of decline in employment across industries has been correlated with the rate of increase of import penetration."[63]

Only the strong growth of the U.S. economy during the 1990s and the early years of the new century obscured the seriousness of NAFTA's failure at home. Nothing, however, could hide what was happening in Mexico.

NAFTA AND THE REORDERING OF MEXICAN SOCIETY

It is not easy for Americans to appreciate the immense dislocation and fracturing of Mexican society that has resulted from NAFTA— harder still to imagine that our government's trade policies have actually accelerated the exodus of Mexican workers to our own country. Supporters of the trade accord, after all, promised it would bring general prosperity to the three partner nations and would reduce the flow of immigrants from below the Rio Grande.

At first, Mexico did attract a breathtaking amount of new foreign investment and jobs, but the employment growth proved to be temporary. Furthermore, it obscured profound transformations that were occurring simultaneously in Mexico's banking system, and most of all, in its agriculture, where the social cost was greater than even the Zapatistas and other NAFTA critics had warned.

The number of jobs in foreign-owned Mexican *maquiladoras* nearly tripled between 1993 and 2000, from about 546,000 to more than 1.3 million. This was due in part to the peso devaluation of 1995, which so lowered the cost of Mexican labor that foreign companies rushed to set up new factories. *Maquila* employment peaked in 2000 at nearly 1.3 million, but then it remained largely stagnant for several years, registering around 1.2 million in 2008. Thus, the first fifteen years of NAFTA produced a net job gain of only 660,000 in foreign-owned manufacturing plants. By then, however, official Mexican government reports had begun making significant changes to the method used to track *maquiladora* employment. The government's new method *added production by foreign-owned companies for domestic consumption and also expanded the data to cover mining and agricultural operations*. The result was a sharp statistical increase in the number of *maquiladora* workers to some 2.7 million by 2012, but it made any comparisons with data from the early years of NAFTA almost impossible.[64]

Mexico's own local industry, meanwhile, was languishing, largely due to the new foreign-owned companies that tended to utilize few domestic components for their export-oriented factories. By 2008, employment in the country's non-*maquila* industry had fallen to 1.24 million—159,000 *fewer jobs* than when NAFTA took effect. Not only did foreign firms by then produce as many jobs in Mexican manufacturing as the country's own domestic plants, but the net gain in manufacturing jobs from both foreign-controlled and domestic companies was just 500,000 for the entire period. To put that number in perspective, Mexico must produce 1 million new jobs *each year* just to keep pace with the number of people who enter its workforce.[65]

The labor picture became even more dismal once you factored in NAFTA's impact on the Mexican countryside. With government subsidies for sowing corn eliminated, small farmers simply could not compete with the mechanized output of U.S. agribusiness. Mexico's grain imports from the United States tripled from 1994 levels and now represent 40 percent of that country's food needs. Agricultural employment tumbled by nearly 20 percent between 1991 and 2007, from 10.6 million to 8.6 million. Many of those 2 million unemployed peasants were forced to either join the ranks of the country's huge informal economy or migrate to the United States.[66]

So instead of slowing down the exodus to the United States, NAFTA, with its extraordinary impact on Mexican agriculture, has sped it up. The Mexican-born population of the United States went from 4.5 million in 1990 to 9 million in 2000, and then to 12.7 million in 2008, with more than half of that population being undocumented. Rural dwellers represented 44 percent of those migrants even though only one-quarter of Mexico's people reside in the countryside.[67]

As a study by the Carnegie Foundation noted, "One of the paradoxes of NAFTA, which leaders promised would help Mexico 'export goods, not people,' is that Mexico now 'exports' more people than ever and more of them reside permanently in the United States without documents."[68]

Those Mexicans who have remained in their country have been forced to contend with a relentless downward pressure on wages and on the quality of life. A little-noticed consequence of the flood of processed imported U.S. foods has been an epidemic of obesity. The convenience store giant Oxxo, for example, a branch of Coca-Cola's Mexican subsidiary, operated fourteen thousand outlets throughout Mexico by 2015, making it the second-largest retail chain in the country after Walmart. Thanks to the flood of sugary drinks available at Oxxo and other retailers, Mexico became the world's second-largest consumer of sodas, and diabetes became the country's leading cause of death, claiming nearly eighty-thousand lives per year. More than 70 percent of the adult population was overweight in 2017, with 32 percent classified as obese.[69]

Only 10 percent of Mexican households have seen their incomes increase since 1994, while 90 percent have seen stagnation or a decline in incomes. As recently as 2018, only 269,000 Mexicans—just one-half of 1 percent of the country's 53.8 million workers—earned more than sixteen dollars per hour. The gap between U.S. and Mexican factory workers' wages has steadily widened. The average U.S. manufacturing wage in 1993 was 5.6 times higher than in Mexico; by 2007 it was 5.8 times higher; and by 2017 it had mushroomed to 9 times higher. The biggest beneficiaries of NAFTA have been U.S. and other international companies, with automobile products representing about a third of Mexico's manufacturing exports. As labor economist Harley Shaiken noted, eleven automobile assembly plants were built in North America between 2009 and 2017—eight of them in Mexico and three in the United States. By 2018, Mexico had nearly as many automobile jobs (763,000) as the United States did (780,000), yet wages for Mexican workers were about one-tenth those of their U.S. counterparts. Moreover, half the new jobs created in Mexico do not offer basic benefits that are mandated by that country's laws, such as social security and paid vacation time.[70]

The real value of Mexican wages increased by just 4.1 percent, when adjusted for inflation, from NAFTA's inception in 1994 to 2014, while the minimum wage actually had fallen by 19.3 percent as of 2015. Chiapas, birthplace of the Zapatista movement, had the country's highest poverty rate, at nearly 75 percent. And though the overall poverty rate dropped from 53 percent in 1994 to 43 percent in 2016, that was due largely to targeted antipoverty programs that the Mexican government was forced to develop to handle the lack of labor income. More than 18 percent of Mexican households were receiving government transfers in 2006 through its two main poverty programs, Procampo and Oportunidades (formerly called Progresa).[71]

Another factor contributing mightily to poverty reduction was the continued exodus of unemployed laborers to the United States and the money those migrants then send back to their families. By 2017, remittances to Mexico had jumped to $30 billion, more than seven times higher than pre-NAFTA levels.[72]

Meanwhile, the biggest beneficiaries of free trade with Mexico have been foreign multinational corporations, especially those from the United States. Between 1994 and 2004, American companies produced 67 percent of all new foreign direct investment in the country, making Mexico more dependent than ever on the ups and downs of the U.S. economy. Whereas in 1970, 70 percent of Mexican exports went to the United States, by 2017 that figure had climbed to nearly 80 percent. Not surprisingly, when the Great Recession caused a rapid contraction of the U.S. economy in 2008, Mexican workers were especially hard hit. Exports to the United States in 2009 dropped by more than 15 percent, from $215 billion to $176 billion.[73]

Mexico's banking system has been even more affected by NAFTA than its industry. The trade agreement combined with the country's financial crisis of 1994–1995 opened the floodgates for foreign banking operations. Citibank, for instance, had been the only non-Mexican company authorized to operate independently in Mexico, with all other outsiders limited to owning no more than a 30 percent share of major domestic banks. But between 1994 and 2004, a tsunami of foreign financial investment struck that was "unprecedented for an economy the size of Mexico," according to one economist. U.S., Canadian, and European banks poured in more than $30 billion and ended up seizing near total control of the country's financial sector. Whereas foreign firms had controlled just 16 percent of banking assets in 1997, that figure had soared to 82 percent by 2004. By then, eight of the country's ten largest banks were in the hands of outsiders. Just two of those banks, BBVA Bancomer (owned by Spain's Grupo BBVA) and Banamex (owned by Citigroup), controlled 48 percent of all banking assets.[74]

A public uproar ensued when the foreign banks started charging Mexican businesses and consumers service fees up to three times higher than they charged clients in other countries and when they made access to credit far more strenuous for ordinary Mexicans than had been the custom previously. In 2004, for instance, private sector lending by the country's banks affected only 15 percent of the economy, compared with 70 percent in the United States. So pervasive did the exorbitant fees and lending restrictions become that

President Vicente Fox and the Mexican legislature publicly rebuked the foreign banks and demanded a change in their policies. Nonetheless, the damage was done. Within ten years of NAFTA, most of the banking deposits of the Mexican people were under the control of American and European bankers, a level of financial domination that no developed country would tolerate.[75]

THE WAR ON DRUGS AND THREATS TO FOOD SUPPLY

Mexico has been beset for years by escalating violence connected to illicit drug trafficking and to efforts by Mexican and U.S. law enforcement to eradicate it. But while that violence has attracted growing attention from the U.S. news media and prompted huge increases in aid from Washington for heightened interdiction, few reports have analyzed the connection between NAFTA and the mushrooming narcotics trade.

The cross-border flow of money and guns into northern Mexico, and of marijuana, opium, and methamphetamines into the United States, gradually emerged into a lethal industry now estimated to generate $15 billion to $30 billion annually. The major cartels that control that trade turned so brazen that they have periodically assassinated police and government officials, gunned down civilians in broad daylight, and even instigated raids against law enforcement outposts. The country's murder rate has increased at an alarming rate since 2007, from an average of 20,000 per year during the presidency of Felipe Calderón (2006–2012), to an average of 30,000 annually under his successor, Enrique Peña Nieto (2012–2018), with a record of 35,964 murders recorded in Peña Nieto's final year in office. Peña Nieto's successor, Andrés Manuel López Obrador, managed only a slight reduction in homicides during his first two years in office. As many as one-third to one-half of all killings are thought to be connected to drug trafficking.[76]

Under the Mérida Initiative (also known as Plan Mexico), the U.S. government supplied more than $700 million in aid to Mexico between 2007 and 2009 for military equipment, training, and surveillance technology to ramp up the efforts of President Calderón against the drug trafficking organizations. Yet the drug trade continued to flourish and the murder rate spiraled.[77]

The U.S. State Department's annual survey of worldwide narcotics trafficking estimated that thirty-seven thousand acres of land in Mexico were cultivated with opium in 2009. That was more than double the amount from the previous year, and the "highest level of [opium] production ever estimated in all of Mexico and Latin America combined," the report concluded. In subsequent years, poppy production kept growing, so that by 2017 the United Nations estimated that some seventy-five thousand acres were being used for opium. Meanwhile, land use for marijuana cultivation was higher than at any time since 2002. In addition, Mexico produces 80 percent of the methamphetamines sold in this country and is the transit place for 90 percent of the U.S. cocaine supply.[78]

Some Mexican officials see a direct relation between drug trafficking, NAFTA, and the crisis in Mexican agriculture. They note that hundreds of thousands of the country's peasants can no longer make a living from growing beans and corn because of the competition from cheap U.S. grain imports that began with NAFTA. Drug traffickers are increasingly luring many of those farmers to cultivate illicit crops instead. As much as 30 percent of Mexico's farmland may currently be planted in part with marijuana and opium poppies, according to an estimate by Ricardo García Villalobos, head of one of the country's federal courts that handles agrarian issues. And with more than two million farm laborers out of work since NAFTA began, the northern cities of Mexico are teeming with an army of desperate, unemployed men. Many of those unemployed become easy to recruit for the operations of drug gangs. Finally, the massive volume of truck traffic crossing the U.S.-Mexico border each day to transport NAFTA-generated imports and exports makes it even more unfeasible for U.S. border agents to find and isolate drug contraband without at the same time interrupting the legal trade.[79]

Meanwhile, NAFTA's impact on food quality in the United States rarely gets mentioned by proponents of export-based free trade. Nearly 96 percent of all strawberries and 52 percent of all other fruits and vegetables consumed in the United States in 2000 came from Mexico. At the same time, the rates of food inspections on both sides of the border have fallen precipitously. In 1997, 270 people in five states were sickened by a strain of potentially fatal hepatitis A from frozen Mexican strawberries. The U.S. Food and Drug Administration (FDA) estimated in 2007 that it would conduct border inspections that year on less than 1 percent of the food that it regulates, largely vegetables, fruit, seafood, grains, dairy, and animal feed. That was down from an already low 8 percent prior to NAFTA. According to an investigation by Scripps News, more than 50,000 Americans got sick or died from something they ate between 2001 and 2004, but in two-thirds of food poisoning incidents, health officials failed even to diagnose the outbreak or pinpoint the source. The Centers for Disease Control and Prevention identified 196 outbreaks of food poisoning in the United States associated with imported products between 1996 and 2014, with the number of incidents escalating from an average of 3 annually in the earlier years to 18 more recently. Imports from Mexico represented the largest number of outbreaks, 42.[80]

LATIN AMERICA'S REVOLT AGAINST FREE TRADE

In the years after the creation of NAFTA, U.S. officials aggressively sought similar treaties with governments throughout Latin America, including the regional Caribbean Free Trade Agreement, the hemisphere-wide Free Trade Area of the Americas, and individual pacts with key nations like Chile and Colombia. But those efforts met increasing resistance from a wave of new populist governments that began to reject the Washington Consensus. Media reports in the United States tended to focus attention on the most confrontational of those leaders, Venezuela's Hugo Chávez and Bolivia's Evo Morales, but the reality was, the entire region was undergoing a transformation.

The reason for the new resistance was simple: two decades of neoliberalism had failed. Economic policies promoted by the United States had produced not prosperity but deeper economic misery throughout Latin America. Between 1990 and 2004, the official unemployment rate in the region rose from 6.9 percent to 10 percent. Seven out of every ten new jobs created during the period were in the informal sector, where workers enjoyed little security, few fringe benefits, and virtually no health and safety protection. By 2006, the International Labor Organization reported that 23 million Latin Americans were unemployed and another 103 million were "precariously" employed—more than half of the region's active workforce.[81]

In response to the crisis, new social movements arose that were unlike any others in the modern history of Latin America. Their leadership did not come from traditional opposition groups, the old social democratic and Communist parties or the petrified trade union hierarchy, nor was it inspired by the remnants of Marxist guerrilla bands, such as Peru's Shining Path or Colombia's FARC. Instead, the new movements emerged from the most impoverished sectors of their societies, long-ignored indigenous and Black populations: the peasant *cocalero* movements in Bolivia and Peru; the Zapatista rebels in Chiapas, Mexico; the factory takeover movement in Argentina; the Landless People's Movement of Brazil. These uprisings did not merely oppose their own governments and domestic elites, they increasingly directed their ire at the neoliberal agenda of international bodies like the International Monetary Fund, the World Bank, and the World Trade Organization.

In January 2003, on the tenth anniversary of NAFTA, a movement called *El Campo No Aguanta Más* (the Rural Sector Can't Take It Anymore) blocked the border bridge connecting Ciudad Juárez and El Paso, while more than one hundred thousand Mexican *campesinos* marched in Mexico City to condemn the dumping of low-cost U.S. corn and the massive displacement of Mexico's small farmers.[82]

Numerous protests erupted, as well, against the continued sell-off of government assets and services in the region:

• In Puerto Rico, more than half a million people joined a two-day general strike in 1998, shutting down hospitals, government offices, and commercial malls and barricading all roads to San Juan's international airport. Their aim was to stop the government's sale of the Puerto Rico Telephone Company to U.S.-based GTE. Even though polls showed 65 percent opposition to the sale among Puerto Ricans, the island's governor, Pedro Rosselló, proceeded with the deal. In 2010, university students paralyzed eleven campuses of the University of Puerto Rico for more than a month to protest government privatization and increased tuition.

• In Bolivia, tens of thousands of urban poor filled the streets of Cochabamba in 2000 in a successful rebellion against water privatization. Organized by the Coordinating Committee in Defense of Water and Life, the protesters were furious about huge price hikes instituted after the government sold the city's water supply to a subsidiary of the U.S. multinational giant Bechtel.

- In Costa Rica, thousands took to the streets in 2002 against the privatization of the nation's electricity.

- In El Salvador, doctors and public health workers went on strike for nine months in 2002 and 2003 and successfully stopped the privatization of that nation's health system.

- In Panama, two general strikes in late 2003 paralyzed the country. Both were aimed at stopping President Mireya Moscoso from privatizing that country's social security system. The unrest led to Moscoso's defeat in new elections the following year, though her successor, Martín Torrijos, then severely repressed the movement and proceeded with the social security reform.[83]

The new social movements soon began sweeping aside regimes whose leaders refused to heed their concerns. Between 1997 and 2007, seven presidents in four Latin American countries were forced from office by their people before finishing their terms: in Bolivia, Gonzalo Sánchez de Lozada (2003) and Carlos Mesa (2005); in Ecuador, Abdalá Bucaram (1997), Jamil Mahuad (2000), and Lucio Gutiérrez (2005); in Paraguay, Raúl Cubas Grau (1999); and in Peru, Alberto Fujimori (2000).[84]

The extraordinary political and economic changes in Latin America during those years are beyond the scope of this book to chronicle. It is no understatement to say, however, that most countries in the region began to chart policies for the first time in their history that were independent of Washington and Wall Street, in both their domestic and international affairs. Unfortunately, U.S. media accounts of the region sought to perpetuate the stereotypical image of El Jefe—by repeatedly spotlighting Hugo Chávez of Venezuela and Evo Morales of Bolivia, the most confrontational opponents of the old Washington Consensus—as a new Latin American "threat." But Chávez and Morales were only two of more than a dozen presidents in the region who began to contest U.S.-imposed economic remedies. The list of left-wing Latin American populist leaders democratically elected to office during that period was truly unprecedented.

Table 11

Presidents Elected in Latin America with Left-Wing Coalitions, 1998–2009

Hugo Chávez	Venezuela	December 1998*
Luis Inácio "Lula" da Silva	Brazil	October 2002
Néstor Kirchner	Argentina	May 2003
Tabaré Vázquez	Uruguay	October 2004
Evo Morales	Bolivia	December 2005
Michelle Bachelet	Chile	December 2005
Daniel Ortega	Nicaragua	November 2006
Rafael Correa	Ecuador	December 2006
Álvaro Colom	Guatemala	September 2007
Mauricio Funes	El Salvador	March 2009

*Chávez was reelected in 2000 and 2006. Cristina Fernández de Kirchner was elected to succeed her husband as Argentine president in October 2007.

Only Mexico and Colombia managed to elect conservative presidents allied to the United States. In the case of Mexico, however, the narrow victory of businessman Felipe Calderón in 2006 was marred by persistent accusations of voter fraud and by months of massive postelection protests from supporters of his opponent, left-wing populist Andrés Manuel López Obrador. The only other center-right candidate to emerge victorious in a presidential election in Latin America during the decade was Sebastián Piñera, whom Chilean voters chose in January 2010 to succeed Michelle Bachelet.

The region's new populist leaders, despite big differences in approach and style, reached considerable unity on a number of policies. All sought to end or restrict imperial domination of their countries by Europe and the United States through exercising greater control over the natural resources and renegotiating unequal arrangements with foreign multinational companies; using the power of their governments to reduce income inequality at home; building stronger economic integration within the region; and insisting on fair trade pacts with the major industrialized countries.

In their attempts to overcome Latin America's long history of Balkanization, the new leaders fell largely into two camps, the moderate "neodevelopmentalist" trend headed by Brazil and Argentina, and the more radical Bolivarian Alliance for the Peoples of Our America (ALBA) spearheaded by Venezuela and Cuba. In July 2004, Mercosur, the trade bloc founded in 1991 by Brazil, Argentina, Uruguay, and Paraguay, expanded its formal membership from four to ten nations, including Venezuela and Colombia. Then, in December 2004 at the Third South American Summit in Cuzco, Peru, twelve nations led by Brazil and Venezuela established the South American Community of Nations, a trading bloc of 361 million people.[85]

Meanwhile, Venezuela's Chávez used his country's immense oil wealth to negotiate more than a dozen bilateral trade pacts with neighboring countries for cheap oil, and as a result, his influence in the region skyrocketed. More important, Chávez and Morales both nurtured and encouraged nongovernment social movements in the region. Groups such as the Continental Social Alliance and the World Social Forum mobilized tens of thousands of people throughout Latin America to oppose U.S. initiatives like the Free Trade Area of the Americas (FTAA).

Originally envisioned as a further expansion of NAFTA, the FTAA was an attempt by the Bush administration to consolidate the hegemony of U.S. multinationals over the hemisphere by creating a single free trade bloc of thirty-four countries. The plan collapsed in November 2005 at the Summit of the Americas, when Brazil, Argentina, Cuba, Venezuela, and a half dozen other nations refused to join. The defeat followed by only a few years the 1999 street protests in Seattle that had derailed Washington's efforts to strengthen the World Trade Organization. But whereas the events in Seattle had largely featured opposition by a few thousand radical protesters, the rejection of the FTAA was a signal that an entire region of the world had turned against free trade agreements dictated by the rich countries. The new wave of Latin American leaders had effectively proclaimed their region's independence, or at least its autonomy, from the United States.[86]

Such independent policies gradually began to show concrete benefits for ordinary Latin Americans. Between 2002 and 2008, the region experienced a dramatic decline in its overall poverty rate, from 44 percent to 33 percent. Some of the biggest improvements occurred in those nations that most rejected neoliberal policies: Venezuela (from 48.6 percent to 27.6 percent); Argentina (from 45.4 percent to 21.0 percent), Ecuador (49.0 percent to 38.8 percent), Bolivia (62.4 percent to 54.0 percent), and Brazil (37.5

percent to 30.0 percent). The U.S. poverty rate, by contrast, increased from 12.4 percent in 2002 to 13.2 percent in 2008.[87]

COUNTERATTACK:
THE NEOLIBERALS RETURN TO POWER

As the first decade of the new century drew to a close, financial elites in both the United States and Latin America grew even bolder in their efforts to dislodge or overthrow the region's pink tide governments. As mentioned earlier, a U.S.-backed coup in 2002 against Venezuelan president Hugo Chávez had ended in failure when thousands of his Venezuelan supporters poured into the streets to support Chávez, and key sections of the military remained loyal to him. The same would not be true in Honduras, however. There the military arrested and successfully ousted that country's democratically elected president José Manuel "Mel" Zelaya on June 28, 2009, an action that, perhaps more than any other, signaled the start of a new counteroffensive by those elites.

Ironically, Zelaya was himself a member of the Honduran upper class. A rancher and longtime member of the Liberal Party—one of the two parties that had traditionally alternated control of the government—he had been elected president in 2006 on a center-right platform, but once in office, no doubt influenced by the region's new populist wave, he moved to stop the privatization of public services, reestablished land rights for small farmers, and even instituted in January 2009 a 60 percent increase in the country's minimum wage. As a result, income inequality in Honduras dropped throughout his time in office. Zelaya's political transformation has been described as "the first case in Latin America's post-democratization history of a candidate elected on a right-of-center platform switching to left-of-center policies after taking office," though there have been numerous examples of leaders switching in the opposite direction. Zelaya further alarmed both the Honduran oligarchy and the U.S. government when he initiated the entry of Honduras into the Venezuelan-led ALBA in 2008, making his nation the sixth to join the anti-neoliberal trading bloc.[88]

The coup, according to U.S. military and state department records that became public years later, had the advance knowledge and support of key Pentagon officers, with Secretary of State Hillary Clinton working behind the scenes to thwart Zelaya's reinstatement, and the Obama administration effectively endorsing the regime change.[89] The right-wing governments of Porfirio Lobo Sosa and Juan Orlando Hernández that succeeded Zelaya, and which were propped up by the Honduran military, sought to stamp out all opposition social movements. In the first three years following the coup, progovernment death squads routinely assassinated dissidents, while ten thousand complaints of abuse by police or the military went unaddressed, according to human rights groups. Historian Dana Frank estimates that nearly one hundred peasant leaders and their family members were murdered just in the country's Lower Aguán Valley between January 2010 and February 2013. The most prominent victim of the post-Zelaya repression was Berta Cáceres, an internationally known environmentalist and indigenous leader who was assassinated in her home in March 2016 by a death squad of former military officers. As for journalists, while only one had been killed during Zelaya's term in office, thirty-three were murdered during the term of Porfirio Lobo. Despite their record of human rights violations, the post-Zelaya Honduran administrations continued to receive support from both the Obama and Trump White Houses. That support continued even as top leaders, including President Hernández and his brother, Tony Hernández, a former congressman of the ruling National Party, were accused by Trump's own Justice Department of being involved in or receiving money from drug trafficking, with Tony Hernández even indicted and arrested. Given the litany of natural and man-made disasters Hondurans have endured in the past twenty years, the mass flight of that country's people northward should come as no surprise.[90]

AFTERMATH OF THE GREAT RECESSION

The economies of other Central American nations were further deformed during the first decade of the new century to meet the needs of foreign capital. On New Year's Day 2001, for example, El Salvador's citizens woke up with a new official currency, the U.S. dollar. The ARENA Party of President Francisco Flores and its conservative allies in the legislature had suddenly pushed through the change to supplant the country's historic currency, the *colon*, with virtually no public notice or hearings, making El Salvador one of only a handful of independent nations to switch to the dollar. Massive public protests ensued against the decision, but all opposition was cut

short a few days later by the deadly earthquake that ravaged the
country and claimed thousands of lives.

Meanwhile, outside investors to the region's free trade zones continued to find open arms from both conservative and even some
left-wing governments. The Zelaya administration, for one, exempted *maquiladora* owners from its 2009 decree that sharply increased the Honduran minimum wage, while the Sandinista party
in Nicaragua, after its leader Daniel Ortega won the presidency
again in 2007, also promoted the expansion of that country's free
trade zones, with Nicaragua boasting the lowest minimum wage of
any Central American country. Throughout the region, the minimum wage for *maquila* workers remains lower than for employees
of domestic industries, with the gap between the two growing in the
aftermath of the Great Recession, as local governments sought to
make their countries event more attractive to foreign investment.[91]
In each country except El Salvador, the *maquila* minimums are less
than half the national poverty line (see graph below). In Honduras,
for example, it was $297 per month in 2018, yet the income a Hon-
duran family needed to stay out of poverty was $763 per month.
One U.S. government study found that the monthly mean salary for
factory workers in Guatemala in 2015 was just $161 monthly, less
than half that country's legal minimum at the time.[92]

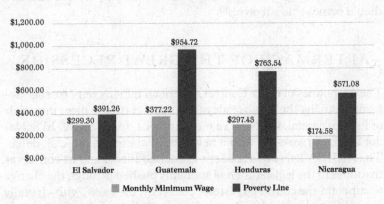

**Monthly Minimum Wage and Poverty Line
in Four Central American Countries,[93]
U.S. Dollars, 2018**

Source: Equipo de Investigaciones Laborales (EIL) / Red de solidaridad de la
Maquila (RSM), *Salarios de Maquila en Centro América 2018 e Iniciativas internacionales por un Salario Digno*, October 2018.

The Great Recession temporarily reduced employment in export-oriented *maquila* plants, but within a few years most countries in the region had surpassed prerecession employment levels, with *maquiladoras* in Nicaragua and the Northern Triangle countries employing more than 425,000 workers by 2019—a figure comparable with that of Mexico's *maquila* industry at the dawn of NAFTA. Two countries in particular, Honduras and Nicaragua, saw significant growth in recent years.[94] Not surprisingly, those two also have the lowest official minimum wage in Central America.

THE LÓPEZ OBRADOR REVOLUTION AND NAFTA 2.0

The victory of veteran leftist politician Andrés Manuel López Obrador (popularly known as AMLO) in Mexico's July 2018 presidential race proved a stunning exception to the trend of conservative and neoliberal parties ousting Latin America's pink tide leaders. It was especially important given that Mexico boasts the second-largest population in Latin America and is a major U.S. trading partner. In his inaugural address to the Mexican Congress, AMLO issued a fiery condemnation of the "failure of the neoliberal economic model" followed by Mexican governments since the 1980s. As a result, he noted, the very country that gave the world corn was now the biggest importer of corn. "Before neoliberalism, we produced and were self-sufficient in gasoline, diesel, natural gas and electricity" as well, he added. "Today we buy more than half [from others] of what we consume of these products." He vowed to turn back the privatization of education in the country, to preserve Mexico's oil and gas industry under government ownership, and to oppose natural gas fracking and genetically modified foods.[95]

The alliance led by López Obrador's National Regeneration Movement (MORENA), having won an ample majority in both houses of the Mexican congress, was thus free to carry out the new president's ambitious program, which he dubbed the Fourth Transformation of Mexico.[96] Within days, AMLO stripped past presidents of lifetime pensions, lowered the salaries of top government officials, including his own, put the presidential plane and sixty other government-owned aircraft up for sale, and refused to live in the luxurious presidential palace, turning it instead into a public museum. At the same time, he increased the minimum wage by 16 percent nationwide—even doubling it to nine dollars per day along Mexico's northern border, where most *maquiladoras* are located. He also increased government pensions for the elderly and disabled and instituted a new form of direct cash support for the poor, bypassing established government programs and civil society groups that had long functioned as extensions of the traditional political parties. Such bold policies made him hugely popular to most Mexicans during his first year in office. His conservative critics, on the other hand, accused AMLO of fostering a new authoritarianism, with Wall Street financiers and the Mexican elite blasting his tougher stance on foreign investment in Mexico's oil industry and his immediate cancellation of a costly new mega airport for Mexico City. Meanwhile, some on the left, including the Zapatistas in Chiapas, opposed his ambitious plan to build a nearly nine-hundred-mile train line through Maya areas of southeast Mexico to spur tourism and economic growth.[97]

Buoyed by López Obrador's promise of a new era, tens of thousands of Mexican *maquila* workers in the border city of Tamaulipas, most of them women relegated to a dollar-an-hour wage, started a series of wildcat strikes in January 2019. The walkouts were not initially supported by their union leaders, who had extensive ties to prior governments. Nonetheless, the strikers persevered and galvanized the nation with their bold slogan of "20/32" (a 20 percent increase in wages, plus a 32,000-peso annual bonus ($1,578 U.S.), echoing the fifteen-dollar-an-hour movement that had already spread throughout the United States. By February, forty-eight factories had accepted their demands.

Then on April 29, 2019, came perhaps the most significant reform to grassroots democracy in Mexico of the past hundred years— a wholesale revision of the nation's labor laws. The new reform required for the first time secret ballot elections by Mexico's workers on more than seven hundred thousand labor contracts, a process aimed at verifying that they had freely approved those contracts. It further mandated that all union bylaws be amended to institute direct election of union leaders, and it established new labor courts and an independent oversight agency to resolve labor disputes, with the government eventually earmarking nearly $70 million from its annual budget to implement the changes. In one fell swoop, the AMLO majority in Congress thus set about dismantling decades of notorious collusion (commonly known as "protection" agreements) between government-controlled unions and both foreign and domestic employers, fostering instead a new, independent labor movement.[98]

The new labor law achieved another purpose, however, when it came to President Trump's demands on U.S.-Mexico trade policy. While campaigning for the White House, Trump had vowed to pull out of NAFTA unless key provisions of the nearly twenty-five-year-old pact were rewritten. But the United States-Mexico-Canada Agreement (USMCA) his negotiators initially consented to in November 2018—just weeks prior to AMLO's inauguration—included only minor new safeguards to stem shipping of more manufacturing jobs to Mexico. Its fine print actually offered lucrative new intellectual property protections to the pharmaceutical and tech industries. Many progressives and U.S. labor union leaders were determined to derail the pact in Congress, especially after Democrats won a majority in the House in 2018. The López Obrador government responded to their concerns by touting Mexico's labor law reforms as a key part of a renegotiated trade deal, and by agreeing to accept monitoring of how Mexico implemented those reforms. Lifting Mexico's wages and worker protections would curtail the exporting of U.S. jobs south of the border. AMLO thus managed to win support for the pact from the AFL-CIO. House Speaker Nancy Pelosi also secured additional concessions from the Trump administration on changes to pharmaceutical provisions of the pact, thus persuading a surprising number of Democrats to join Republicans in December 2019 to ratify the pact. Still, several environmental groups, auto unions, and progressives like Vermont senator Bernie Sanders continued to condemn NAFTA 2.0 as only marginally better than its predecessor pact.[99]

But where López Obrador provoked most criticism was in his response to President Trump's "no tolerance" immigration crackdown. Many had expected a major showdown between him and Trump over the issue. In January 2019, however, AMLO suddenly reversed his initial humanitarian stance on Central American migration to the United States and his promises to address the economic roots of the problem. He acquiesced instead to a new policy Trump announced that required asylum seekers at the border to remain in Mexico while their applications were processed, forcing thousands to remain in makeshift camps for months. A few months later, Trump threatened to impose new tariffs on imports from Mexico unless it curtailed the number of migrants reaching the U.S. border. AMLO immediately moved to placate Trump. Having already secured the creation of a new national guard, which was ostensibly meant to halt drug trafficking and the country's epidemic of violence, he then directed that guard to seal off Mexico's southern border and to conduct stepped up deportations of Central Americans. In other words, even as Trump struggled in the United States to win funding from Congress to build a wall at the southern border, AMLO, Mexico's most left-wing president in nearly a century, was, ironically, turning Mexico itself into a wall against migrants and asylum seekers.[100]

CHINA'S RISING INFLUENCE IN LATIN AMERICA

After two hundred years of hegemony by U.S. capital over Latin America, the first decades of the twenty-first century marked the dramatic arrival to the region of a new world power—the People's Republic of China. Trade between Latin America and China skyrocketed from just $10 billion annually in 2000 to more than $270 billion in 2012. This spectacular growth was fueled by China's limitless thirst for raw materials and by its willingness to provide outright grants and long-term loans to the region, especially to the pink tide governments of South America, while at the same time refraining from any political pressures or demands that those governments adhere to any economic model. By 2018, Latin America was second only to Asia for Chinese investment abroad. Venezuela alone had accumulated $68 billion in debt to China; Brazil, $28 billion; Ecuador, $18 billion. "Given the choice between the onerous conditions of the neoliberal Washington Consensus and the no-strings-attached largesse of the Chinese, elevating relations with Beijing was a nobrainer," one report noted. China was by then the main trading partner for Brazil, Chile, and Peru. It was providing more loans to the region than the World Bank and the International Development Bank combined, and it was financing and building scores of breathtaking infrastructure projects—two hydroelectric dams on the Santa Cruz River in the Patagonia area of Argentina at a cost of $4.7 billion, a transcontinental railroad from Brazil to Peru, and a new interoceanic shipping canal across Nicaragua. Through such assistance, Chinese leaders provided the region's governments a viable alternative to Washington's demand that they return to neoliberal free trade policies. In short, China's arrival on the scene ensured that Latin America would no longer remain the empire's backyard.[101]

AFTER THE PINK TIDE

The death in March 2013 of Hugo Chávez marked the decisive halt to Latin America's leftward shift. With his charismatic personality, his defiance of U.S. hegemony, and his willingness to use Venezuela's immense oil reserves as a political weapon to reduce the region's glaring wealth disparities, Chávez had emerged during his fourteen years in office as the main symbol of Latin America's growing independence. Many of his supporters regarded his untimely death, at the relatively young age of fifty-eight, as suspicious.[102]

Both the Bush and Obama administrations, as we have seen, actively sought to defeat the spread of Chavismo. Following its tacit approval of a military coup against Zelaya in Honduras, the Obama White House also backed the suppression of Haiti's most popular political party, Fanmi Lavalas, during that country's 2010–2011 election, and it endorsed parliamentary coups in Paraguay against President Fernando Lugo in 2012 and against Brazil's president Dilma Rousseff in 2016.[103] It is beyond the scope of this book to delve into the many changes that occurred in each of the region's countries over the past decade. Suffice to say that several of the left-wing populist leaders sought to extend their stay in office by rewriting constitutions, or that others became ensnared in corruption scandals among their top aides. Meanwhile, in places where right-wing governments remained in power, such as Colombia, a fierce repression ensued against the left. U.S. policy toward Latin America during the Obama years sought to defuse longstanding conflicts, while also maintaining U.S. economic domination. Perhaps the single greatest accomplishment of the Obama era was its effort to normalize relations with the Cuban government after more than sixty years of economic boycott and efforts at regime change. But that effort was short-lived, as Obama's successor, Donald Trump, promptly rolled back those efforts.

Despite Latin America's improving situation in the new century, more than 184 million people remained mired in poverty in 2017, 30 percent of the region's population.[104] In the barrios, shantytowns, and villages where those poor reside, fifty years of neoliberal free trade policies have brought little of the prosperity proponents

promised. Instead, they produced a desperate exodus by millions to
El Norte in search of work. Those Latin American migrants, as previously noted, have assumed a pivotal role today in sustaining their
countrymen through the remittances they send back home each
month (see chapter 11). Ironically, the massive movement of labor
across national borders may have accomplished more to aid Latin
America than all the free trade policies espoused by the hemisphere's
financial elites.

14

PUERTO RICO, U.S.A.:
Possessed and Unwanted

Colonialism is not satisfied merely with holding a people in
its grip and emptying the native's brain of all form and content. By a kind of perverted logic, it turns to the past of the
oppressed people, and distorts, disfigures, and destroys it....
—FRANTZ FANON, *The Wretched of the Earth*

North Americans have known two contrasting images of Puerto
Rico for more than a century. One is the vacation paradise of
shady beaches, turquoise waters, and glittering casinos, a U.S. island that in the 1960s boasted Latin America's second highest standard of living. The other is of an impoverished and economically
dependent U.S. territory. Nearly 46 percent of Puerto Rican households had an annual income below the poverty level in 2017, with
median income just $19,775, a third of what it was for U.S. house-
holds. As a result, Puerto Ricans continue to receive ever-increasing
amounts of assistance from Washington. Net federal transfer payments to island residents totaled about $30 billion in 2020, about
triple what they were in 2000. Those costs are borne largely by U.S.
taxpayers because Puerto Ricans, even though they are American
citizens, have no voting representation in Congress and thus pay no
federal individual income taxes, though they do contribute to Social
Security and Medicare payroll taxes. Meanwhile, the island's homicide, drug addiction, and AIDS rates rival the worst of any state of
the union, and so many residents have had to emigrate that more

than 60 percent of all people of Puerto Rican descent were living in
the continental United States in 2018.[1]

Until recent years, little else was known about the island, given
that news outlets in this country rarely reported events there, except
for the periodic hurricanes that bedevil the tourist trade. But that
historic neglect began to change after the island's governor, Alejandro García Padilla, suddenly announced on June 29, 2015, that
Puerto Rico's enormous $72 billion in bond debt was "no longer
payable." The governor's declaration shocked the financial world
and set his government on a path to the largest bankruptcy by a local
government in American history. Over the next few years, Wall
Street investors, Washington politicians, and the U.S. media directed more attention to Puerto Rico than they ever had. Congress
grappled with what to do about the debt—it eventually totaled more
than $120 billion—before opting to impose a financial control board
to run Puerto Rico's affairs. The Puerto Rico Oversight, Management, and Economic Stability Act (PROMESA) that authorized the
board marked a new constitutive moment in Puerto Rican history,
effectively returning the island to direct U.S. colonial control, much
like that of the 1940s.

Just as the control board began implementing unpopular austerity measures, two Category 4 storms struck the island successively
on September 6 and 20, 2017. Hurricanes Irma and María left catastrophic damage to the island's housing and infrastructure and
months of unprecedented electrical blackouts. Rescue and recovery
efforts by the federal and commonwealth governments were so
inept, so delayed, and so tainted with corruption that the storm's
death toll eventually soared to at least three thousand, and it sparked
a further surge of thousands of Puerto Ricans fleeing to the United
States. Then, in the summer of 2019, a spontaneous grassroots protest movement erupted among island residents against Governor
Ricardo Rosselló, García Padilla's successor, and against the financial control board. Within two weeks the protests grew so large that
they galvanized public attention across the United States and forced
Rosselló to resign. For one rare instance in both Puerto Rican and
U.S. history, a sitting governor was forced to resign by popular
street protests. This series of remarkable events, each in its own way
unprecedented, thus signaled a new stage in the long and tortuous
relationship between Puerto Rico and the United States, one in
which the age-old neglect of island affairs by Washington and the
U.S. public was no longer viable.[2]

From the days of sociologist Oscar Lewis's bestselling *La Vida: A Puerto Rican Family in the Culture of Poverty—San Juan and New York*, a host of academics cultivated a grim portrait of Puerto Rican social life, both on the island and in the United States.[3] Former Reagan White House staff member Linda Chavez, for instance, wrote in her 1992 book, *Out of the Barrio*: "Puerto Ricans are not simply the poorest of all Hispanic groups; they experience the highest degree of social dysfunction of any Hispanic group and exceed that of blacks on some indicators."[4] Chavez attributed much of this "dysfunction" to the "self-inflicted" wounds of welfare dependency and out-of-wedlock childbirth. Both "vacation paradise" and "welfare sinkhole" are simplistic images and catchy sound bites, grossly inaccurate ones, for they mask a profound and disquieting reality: that Puerto Rico remains the biggest and oldest colony of the United States in an age when colonies were supposed to have disappeared.

As we shall see in this chapter, Puerto Rico has provided more wealth to the United States than perhaps any country in history. That wealth, together with the numerous American military bases to which the island was home for fifty years, and the enormous sacrifices made by thousands of Puerto Rican who have fought in this nation's wars, dwarfs the value of any federal aid its residents have received.

While the U.S. presence in Puerto Rico brought some undeniable benefits, it also deformed the island's economy and the psychology of its people, fostering the very dependent relationship for which Puerto Ricans were then blamed. Only a century after occupying the island did U.S. policy makers take some initial steps to rid themselves of their last major overseas possession. Yet decades of sporadic debate in Congress over bills to determine Puerto Rico's final status accomplished very little. Leaders in both Washington and San Juan remained sharply divided over the choices: statehood, independence, or a more autonomous form of the current commonwealth. They are divided because no matter the option—and all sides acknowledge the current relationship is unsatisfactory—any change will produce far-reaching repercussions for both Puerto Rico and the United States. Acquiring a colony, it turns out, is considerably easier than relinquishing it.

THE RICHEST COLONY
IN AMERICAN HISTORY

As an American territorial possession—belonging to the United States but not being a part of it—Puerto Rico has long held a unique position. Island residents are U.S. citizens at birth, but they do not have the same rights and protections or the same responsibilities as other Americans. They do not, for example, vote in federal elections, and thus are exempt from paying federal taxes. Trade between the island and the continental United States has always been exempt from import duties, so Puerto Rico's economy is wholly integrated into that of this country.

It is far more important, however, to unravel *how* the mechanisms of colonial control have evolved, and *why* they have managed to survive for so long. In that regard, it helps to demarcate the island's history under U.S. rule as divided into three distinct phases:

+ The Classic Colony: During the first fifty years after the Spanish-American War, the U.S. occupation was distinguished by an economic policy of resource extraction through agribusiness (largely North American sugar companies); by a cultural policy of stamping out the Spanish language and Puerto Rican heritage; and in politics, by the direct control of local affairs by North American governors and other top officials appointed directly by the White House, as well as by naked outright repression of pro-independence activists (see chapters 3 and 4).

+ The Industrialized "Autonomous" Colony: The next sixty years were marked by an economic strategy of rapid industrialization based on cheap labor and tax exemptions for U.S. multinationals (the first free trade zones); by the Pentagon's militarizing of the island as a U.S. Caribbean bastion during the Cold War; by vigorous New Deal reforms that included limited self-rule through commonwealth status, land reform, and aggressive state planning based on the creation of various government-owned corporations; and by a return to Spanish as the language of instruction in public schools, along with a revived movement to embrace Puerto Rico's cultural heritage.

+ The Postindustrial Neoliberal Colony: Since the early 2000s, as manufacturing jobs fled, finance capital became the dominant force in Puerto Rico. Government loans supplied by Wall Street investors emerged as the main way to keep the economy afloat, even as the Defense Department shuttered almost all of its military bases in the post–Cold War period. Local government services were systematically dismantled and privatized and public employment slashed, with even the professional classes increasingly opting to migrate. Those trends culminated in 2016 with the reimposition by Congress of direct rule over the island's affairs through the financial control board.

Federal tax exemption, as we saw in the previous chapter, created an irresistible draw for investment, with the arrival of hundreds of U.S. firms after World War II spurring an economic miracle that made Puerto Rico the envy of the developing world. As a result of industrialization, Governor Muñoz Marín built a first-class port, highway and communications systems, public schools for all, an advanced health care network, a huge tourist industry, and an imposing array of government-owned corporations, all of which helped create a model living standard for Latin America during the 1950s and 1960s.

But the miracle evaporated quickly. Annual economic growth rates dropped from an average of 6 percent in the 1950s to 4 percent in the 1970s, and they were stagnant throughout the 1980s.[5] Despite that stagnation, manufacturing continued to grow as a portion of the island's economic activity. By the 1970s, as the federal minimum wage gradually covered the island's workers, and as labor unions became better organized, many of the U.S. firms began fleeing to Mexico or the Dominican Republic in search of even cheaper labor.[6]

Those that remained tended to be larger multinational corporations involved in the manufacture of chemicals, pharmaceuticals, electronics, and scientific equipment. Companies in those sectors quickly realized that they could turn the loophole of the Section 936 federal tax exemption into a secret gold mine.[7]

The secret was simple. Firms with high research, development, and marketing expenses but low production costs farmed out factory production to wholly owned subsidiaries in Puerto Rico, then transferred the patents and trademarks from their U.S. headquarters to the subsidiaries as well, thus shielding all product revenue from federal taxes.[8] The tablets in that bottle of prescription pills from your local pharmacy, for example, may have cost only pennies apiece to manufacture in Puerto Rico, but the lion's share of the bottle's seventy-five-dollar price tag, which represents the sum of the research and marketing costs the firm spent in the United States, plus the production costs on the island, were all tax-exempt under Section 936 and its predecessor, Section 931. The loophole proved to be such a gravy train that by 1974 more than 110 of the Fortune 500 companies had Puerto Rico subsidiaries.[9]

Scores of pharmaceutical and medical plants opened on the out-skirts of virtually every small town on the island, employing more than one hundred thousand workers by the early 1990s. Between 1960 and 1976, tiny Puerto Rico catapulted from sixth to first in Latin America for total direct U.S. investment. With island workers registering some of the highest productivity levels in the world, the results were profit levels unheard of at home. By 1976, Puerto Rico accounted for 40 percent of all U.S. profit in Latin America—more than the combined earnings of all U.S. subsidiaries in Brazil, Mexico, and Venezuela.[10] So great were the windfall returns that several major multinationals reported that more than a quarter of their worldwide profits were coming from the island. In 1975, thirty-five pharmaceutical firms located on the island paid their employees an average of $10,000 in annual compensation while receiving $35,000 per worker in federal tax savings—three and a half times their labor cost. The biggest of those firms received $500,000 in tax benefits that year for every one of their Puerto Rico employees, according to one treasury department study.[11]

The tax credit bonanza continued for years despite repeated attempts by Congress to curb it, and despite improved wages for pharmaceutical employees. In 1986, for example, drug companies paid an average of $30,300 in salary and benefits to their Puerto Rican workers but received $85,600 per employee in federal tax benefits.[12] From its four thousand workers in Puerto Rico alone, pharmaceutical giant Johnson & Johnson saved $1 billion in federal taxes between 1980 and 1990. SmithKline Beecham saved $987 million; Merck & Co., $749 million; Bristol-Myers Squibb, $627 million.[13]

The cost in lost taxes to the federal treasury had mushroomed to more than $2 billion annually by 1992 as Puerto Rico rapidly turned into the number one source of profit in the world for U.S. companies. By 1986, the island's profitability had surpassed even industrial giants such as Germany, Canada, Japan, and the United Kingdom. That year, U.S. companies earned $5.8 billion from their Puerto Rican investments.[14]

A decade later, net income from direct investments of nonresidents in Puerto Rico (largely American corporations) had ballooned to $14.3 billion. This was greater than the income of all U.S. firms in the United Kingdom and nearly double that of any other country in the world. It was an extraordinary amount considering that Puerto Rico's population was less than 3.8 million in 1995, while the United Kingdom's was 58 million. The reason for such outsized (and little-known) profits from tiny Puerto Rico was simple: the island was not only a tax haven, it was among the most industrialized and most captive economies in the developing world. Eighty-five percent of its exports are manufactured goods. And despite attempts by the local government to diversify its foreign markets in recent years, 74.9 percent of those exports were still going to the United States in 2017.[15]

Table 12

Net Income from U.S. Direct Investment*
in Selected Countries, 1995

(IN MILLIONS OF DOLLARS)[16]

Puerto Rico	$14,339†
United Kingdom	$13,773
Ireland	$7,440
Germany	$5,271
Brazil	$4,579
Japan	$4,237
France	$4,077
Hong Kong	$3,005
Mexico	$916

*For majority-owned nonbank foreign affiliates.

†Because Puerto Rico is not considered a foreign country, figures
are for direct investments of nonresidents (overwhelmingly U.S.
corporations).

By the early 1990s, the Section 936 tax exemption had become such an obvious form of corporate welfare that it was creating a big furor in Congress. President Clinton sought to calm the controversy by simply reducing the benefit, but a Republican majority in Congress, with the help of a considerable number of Democrats, pushed through legislation in 1996 to phase it out entirely within ten years. By the time Section 936 ended in 2005, many U.S. companies had moved to reduce or end production in Puerto Rico. Manufacturing jobs on the island slumped by 35 percent between 2006 and 2016—from 112,000 to just 73,000.[17]

Pharmaceutical companies, however, continued to enjoy enormous profits from their Puerto Rican subsidiaries, given that the drug and chemical industry, together with the government of Puerto Rico, managed to devise a substitute loophole that allowed U.S.-owned firms on the island to continue escaping federal taxes. Their main vehicle for the new loophole was the controlled foreign corporation (CFC). This is a multinational firm that is incorporated in a third country (including Puerto Rico) but is majority owned by U.S. shareholders. Such companies pay federal taxes only on income they bring back to the United States—and in today's globalized economy multinational firms can easily divert funds to other foreign subsidiaries.[18]

The profits CFCs generate in Puerto Rico are truly unparalleled, especially for pharmaceutical companies. Even though they employed only about a fifth of all manufacturing workers on the island, drug companies' share of net manufacturing income went from 50 percent in 2002 to more than 70 percent in 2009.[19] One federal study concluded that each pharmaceutical worker in Puerto Rico produced $1.5 million in value for his or her employer in 2002—three times more than similar workers in the United States.[20]

Puerto Rico, in short, is the primary offshore tax haven for the American drug industry.

That's why the island still ranked as the seventh most profitable place in the world for U.S. firms in 2005, even after the Section 936 tax exemption had been eliminated. U.S. multinationals made more profit in Puerto Rico that year than they did in such Third World developing giants as China, Brazil, Mexico, or India.[21]

The foregone federal corporate income taxes from Puerto Rico pale in comparison to the massive tax breaks the island's own government provides to foreigners. The latter figure was not even publicly disclosed until 2019, when the island's treasury department issued a report on all local tax concessions. According to that report, individuals and corporations received more than $20 billion in tax breaks in 2017. The largest chunk—some $16 billion—went to corporations, and 98 percent of those firms were headquartered outside the island. The $20 billion figure represented more than twice the annual general fund budget of the government, and it equaled 20 percent of the national domestic product.[22]

Despite the Puerto Rican government's dual strategy of encouraging mass emigration while promoting tax-free industrialization, the unemployment rate remained persistently higher on the island than on the mainland. From 1976 to 2019, it never dipped below 10 percent and was often at depressionlike levels of more than 20 percent, declining in recent years only because of the upsurge of Puerto Ricans migrating to the United States. Another indicator of the profound inability of Puerto Rico's economy to produce sufficient jobs is the labor force participation rate, the percentage of adults either employed or looking for jobs. It has hovered below 50 percent for the past quarter century, dropping to 41 percent in 2019—one of the lowest rates in the world.[23]

Meanwhile, a distressing share of the income Puerto Ricans produce never touches Puerto Rican hands. In 2008, nearly four out of every ten dollars made on the island ended up in the bank accounts of U.S.-controlled firms. So much manufacturing income has been siphoned from the island's economy that the salaries of Puerto Rican factory workers now compose just a fraction of the actual value they produce. As recently as 1963, for example, factory salaries represented 63 percent of the island's total manufacturing income. They plunged to just 21 percent by 1995, then fell to a minuscule 8 percent by 2012. In other words, for every ten dollars Puerto Rican factory workers produced in income for their employers that year, they received just eighty cents in pay. By contrast, U.S. manufacturing workers, even after all the corporate downsizing and union busting of the past thirty years, still retained an average of 61 percent of their employers' income as salaries in 2012, while all U.S. workers retained an average of 56 percent. This vast discrepancy between what U.S. and Puerto Rican workers are permitted to keep from the wealth their labor produces reflects the day-to-day material essence of colonialism.[24]

Despite high worker productivity and historic profit levels for U.S. companies on the island, 45 percent of Puerto Ricans still live below the poverty level. While this is a marked improvement over the 60 percent rate that was prevalent in the late 1990s, it is still double the poverty level of Mississippi, the poorest of the fifty states. A huge portion of Puerto Rico's population, unable to find enough living-wage jobs to meet its basic needs, was forced to either migrate or to remain on the island and depend on a gamut of federal entitlements to survive. Those federal payments started escalating around 1975, just as the gap between the Puerto Rican workers' income and corporate income began to widen.[25]

In summary, the colonial status of Puerto Rico turned the island, with its combination of duty-free trade, low wages, and tax loopholes, into a corporate oasis unlike any other in the world. At the same time, the federal government was forced to spend billions annually in federal welfare and transfer payments to alleviate the island-wide poverty these very corporations perpetuated.[26]

But there are other examples of how Puerto Rico's colonial status has created unnecessary hardship for its people.

Among the most obvious are:

1. *Shipping.* Since its early days as a U.S. possession, Puerto Rico has been deemed by Congress to be under the coastal shipping laws of the United States, even though the island is more than a thousand miles from the North American coast and surrounded by several other island countries. The Jones Act (Merchant Marine Act of 1920) requires that all coastal trade between U.S. ports must be on U.S. flag ships that are made in the United States and manned largely by U.S. citizens, a provision devised in order to preserve an American merchant fleet in case of war.[27] The law extends to noncontiguous states and U.S. territories, though American Samoa, the Northern Mariana Islands, and the Virgin Islands are exempt. As a result, while the rest of the world transports much of its cargo on low-cost Panamanian- and Liberian-flag freighters, Puerto Rico residents end up paying as much as 25 percent higher prices for imported goods due to higher transport costs. Amazingly, the handful of private companies whose ships carry Jones Act cargo enjoy direct federal subsidies as well as preferences for shipping U.S. food aid and other military cargo overseas. In 2017, for example, every Jones Act ship received a $5 million annual subsidy from the Department of Defense, totaling direct government support to those companies of $300 million.[28] This loophole in maritime law has turned tiny Puerto Rico into the main subsidizer of the U.S. merchant fleet, along with two other distant states, Alaska and Hawaii. In 2004, Puerto Rican shipments represented 17.5 percent of the value of all U.S.-flag cargo, even though the

island's people made up less than 1.5 percent of the U.S. population. By 2018, the value of shipments by vessels between the United States and Puerto Rico totaled $36.9 billion. Yet bipartisan efforts in Congress to reform the Jones Act, or at least to create waivers for Puerto Rico similar to those for the Virgin Islands, have repeatedly failed due to pressure from both the maritime companies and the AFL-CIO, which is determined to protect a few thousand union jobs in the industry.[29]

2. *Trade.* As a Caribbean nation, Puerto Rico's trade and commerce needs are vastly different from those of the United States, yet the island has always been subject to the same commercial treaties and import tariffs as the fifty states. Congress has repeatedly rejected requests by the Puerto Rican government to negotiate its own trade or commercial agreements with other countries, a right Puerto Rico had already enjoyed as a possession of Spain back in 1897. Take air travel as an example. San Juan's Luis Muñoz Marín International Airport, which is regulated by the Federal Aviation Authority, was once a hub for international flights to the Caribbean. As recently as 2001, sixteen airlines from Asia, Europe, and Latin America had regular flights scheduled into and out of San Juan, often for passengers in transit to smaller Caribbean islands. But after the 9/11 terrorist attacks, the federal government sharply restricted such transit flights. As a result, international traffic to Puerto Rico has dropped by 50 percent and the island has lost $30 million annually in hotel and airport spending by tourists.[30]

In addition, Puerto Ricans are the largest per capita importers of U.S. goods in the world. One study found that trade between the two countries created 487,000 jobs in the United States and 322,000 jobs on the island. The United States not only gained one-third more jobs from the relationship, but American workers earned two to three times more income than the Puerto Ricans. Meanwhile, Puerto Rico's ability to expand exports to the rest of the world is often constrained by the needs of mainland industries.[31]

3. *Courts.* Spanish is the language of the island's local courts, but English is the language of the U.S. District Court for the District of Puerto Rico, in San Juan. This effectively excludes the majority of island residents who do not speak English from serving on federal juries. It also requires all litigants who file appeals of lower court decisions to the federal courts to switch language in midstream.

Furthermore, all appeals from the U.S. District Court for Puerto Rico are handled thousands of miles away in Boston, instead of at a closer jurisdiction, such as Atlanta or Washington, which would be less of a hardship for litigants.

4. *Federal programs.* In recent decades, Congress has attempted to reduce federal spending by capping scores of entitlement programs, such as Medicaid, public assistance, and federal aid to education, at lower levels for Puerto Rico than for the fifty states, while it has completely excluded the island from federal highway construction funds, Supplemental Security Income (SSI), revenue sharing, the earned income tax credit, or the Affordable Care Act. Federal Medicaid benefits, for example, were projected to average $2,144 per enrollee on the island in 2020, less than a third of the median benefit of $6,763 for enrollees in the fifty states. As for SSI, if Puerto Rico had been included in the program in 2011, it would have received from $1.5 billion to $1.8 billion in additional federal payments.[32] Those congressional restrictions have sent an unambiguous message to island residents that while they may be U.S. citizens, they are second-class citizens. Only by moving to the United States can they receive equal treatment from the federal government.

5. *Military.* Throughout the second half of the twentieth century, Puerto Rico was one of the major military bastions of the United States. At one point, twenty-five distinct army, navy, and air force facilities occupied up to 14 percent of the island's territory. But as local opposition to the excessive military presence became more pronounced, and especially after the Cold War ended, the federal government moved to close many of the bases. Public discontent climaxed in 1999 when a massive movement of civil disobedience erupted against decades of naval bombing practice on the tiny, inhabited island of Vieques. The federal government reluctantly bowed to that pressure and consented to leave Vieques in 2003, and the Pentagon shuttered the giant Roosevelt Roads Naval Base near Vieques the following year. Today, only one active military base remains, Fort Buchanan near San Juan.

Beyond the issue of bases is U.S. military service itself. Puerto Ricans were drafted or volunteered to fight in every U.S. war since the early years of the twentieth century (see table 13). In the Korean and Vietnam wars especially, Puerto Rican soldiers distinguished themselves repeatedly in combat. In Korea, they suffered the second-highest casualty rate (Hawaii had the highest), nearly 1 for every 600 soldiers, while in the rest of the United States, the rate was 1 for every 1,125. Yet the island's people have never had a vote in the Congress that declared any of those wars.[33]

Table 13

Military Service of Puerto Ricans in U.S. Wars[34]

	Number Who Served	Number Killed
World War I	18,000	1
World War II	65,000	23
Korea	61,000	750
Vietnam	48,000	342
Gulf War	10,000	4
Iraq/Afghanistan	25,000	80

HAVE WE EVER AMOUNTED TO ANYTHING?

A century of economic and political control has left a deep psychological imprint on all Puerto Ricans and has affected the way North Americans regard the island and its people. Such notions have turned markedly negative since Puerto Ricans began migrating here in large numbers after World War II.

Take, for instance, this article from *New York* magazine in 1972:

These people were "Spanish." They came in swarms like ants turning the sidewalks brown, and they settled in, multiplied, whole sections of the city fallen to their shiny black raincoats and chewing-gum speech. We called them "mee-dahs," because they were always shouting "mee-dah, mee-dah." . . .

I only knew they grew in numbers rather than stature, that they were neither white nor black but some indelicate tan, and that they were here, irrevocably; the best you could do to avoid contamination was to keep them out of mind.[35]

Or take Oxford University professor Raymond Carr, an expert
on Latin American studies, who wrote in 1984:

> Few Americans take seriously the claims of Puerto Rican culture.
> They arrive in an island where they are offered rum and Coca-Cola by
> English-speaking waiters and where they see book shops crammed
> with American paperbacks. Puerto Rican culture appears to them
> merely quaint folklore kept alive for the tourist trade.[36]

Or Linda Chavez in *Out of the Barrio*: "So long as significant
numbers of young Puerto Rican men remain alienated from the
work force, living by means of crime or charity, fathering children
toward whom they feel no responsibility, the prospects of Puerto
Ricans in the United States will dim."[37]

This theory that Puerto Ricans have allowed a culture of poverty
to take root, that whole sectors are eagerly dependent on government handouts, has made amazing inroads among many white
Americans. Dependency, however, has little to do with the specific
culture of any people and much to do with the exterior forces those
people confront. It is something that is taught, nurtured, and reinforced. Frantz Fanon, the psychiatrist and theorist of Algerian independence, best analyzed how colonial systems have historically
created a psychology of dependence in their subjects:

> Colonialism is not satisfied merely with holding a people in its grip and
> emptying the native's brain of all form and content. By a kind of per-
> verted logic, it turns to the past of the oppressed people, and distorts,
> disfigures, and destroys it. . . . The effect consciously sought by colo-
> nialism [is] to drive into the natives' heads the idea that if the settlers
> were to leave, they would at once fall back into barbarism, degrada-
> tion, and bestiality.[38]

To be independent, to stand on one's own, a person, a group, a
nation must first conceive of itself as whole, as separate and distinct
from others. Unlike other immigrants, even other Latin Americans,
Puerto Ricans have always suffered from deep ambivalence and insecurity when it comes to something as basic as who we are. Several
studies have claimed that Puerto Ricans suffer from disproportionately high rates of mental and personality disorders—three times
the U.S. average—and that schizophrenia is by far the most treated

psychosis. In a speech to the American Academy of Psychoanalysis in 1980, Dr. Hector R. Bird said:

> The present state of Puerto Rican society is one of identity diffusion and identity confusion.
>
> Numerous social indicators reflect the depth and breadth of the Puerto Rican crisis and suggest a collectivity in a state of psychosocial disintegration. Criminality is rampant, divorce rates are among the highest in the world, as are the rates of alcoholism and drug abuse and the high incidence of psychopathology and emotional malfunction. . . . We do not mean to imply that identity conflicts are the sole explanation for all of Puerto Rico's social ills. Such a highly complex situation is evidently multidetermined and a host of other factors contribute (such as overpopulation, the stresses of repeated uprootings in the pattern of back-and-forth migration, rapid social change, and so forth). But many of these factors are directly or indirectly related to the colonial status and to the absence of the aforementioned "mutually supportive psychosocial equilibrium" to which identity conflicts contribute.[39]

Generations of Puerto Ricans have learned only about Washington, Lincoln, and the Roosevelts, about Whitman and Hemingway and Poe. For the first fifty years of the U.S. occupation, public schools on the island sought to bury any memory of a culture and history that existed before the U.S. flag was planted. They even tried unsuccessfully to eliminate the most critical vehicle for preserving that history and culture, the island's language. In this country, meanwhile, few children in the public schools, including Puerto Rican children, are taught anything about Puerto Rico except for its geographical location and the fact that it "belongs" to the United States.

Given that century of cultural oppression, it is amazing that Puerto Ricans on the island have preserved *any* knowledge of their cultural heritage, from Alonso Ramírez's 1849 masterpiece, *El Jíbaro*, to the works of poets José Gautier Benítez (1851–1880) and Lola Rodríguez de Tió (1843–1924); to painters Francisco Oller (1833–1917) and Ramón Frade (1875–1956); to essayists and historians like Eugenio María de Hostos (1839–1903) and Salvador Brau (1842–1912).[40] Much of the credit for preserving that cultural legacy is owed to government organizations that developed under the

Popular Party toward the second half of the twentieth century, such as the Institute for Puerto Rican Culture, and to the research and writings of scores of scholars, many of them pro-independence, at the University of Puerto Rico.

At the popular level, island culture has shown special resilience in the fields of music and dance: from the classical *danzas* of Julio Arteaga (1867–1923) and Juan Morel Campos (1857–1896); the *plena*, with its hypnotic staccato beat; the early twentieth-century songs of Joselino "Bumbun" Oppenheimer (1884–1929), César Concepción and Rafael Hernández in the 1940s, and Rafael Cortijo and Ismael Rivera in the 1950s and 1960s; to the legions of first-class salsa and jazz musicians of today.

While Puerto Ricans on the island had to battle to preserve their culture from annihilation, those who resided in the United States were largely denied even the most rudimentary access to it, and thus grew up with virtually no understanding of our unique relationship to the United States.

"Citizenship, which should have enhanced Puerto Rican achievement," Chavez asserted, "may actually have hindered it by conferring entitlements, such as welfare, with no concomitant obligations."[41] As proof, Chavez pointed to the disproportionate level of welfare dependency among New York Hispanics (42 percent of all recipients of Aid to Families with Dependent Children in 1977, when Hispanics were only 12 percent of the population). No doubt, a dependent mentality toward government, pessimism about one's ability to change the future, self-hatred, and self-deprecation became ingrained in too many Puerto Ricans of that era. But these did not originate from the breakup of the family and the growth of out-of-wedlock births, as she and others claimed, including sociologist and future U.S. senator Daniel Patrick Moynihan in his controversial Moynihan Report.[42] Rather, they are symptoms of a more deep-rooted malady—the structure of colonialism itself. Moreover, rapid industrialization itself had a debilitating impact on the Puerto Rican family structure. U.S. firms chose to hire mainly Puerto Rican women for their island factories, perhaps seeing them as easier to control then than men. In 1980, women represented 36.5 percent of Puerto Rico's labor force but 48.3 percent of its factory workers. From the end of World War II to 1980, the labor force participation rate of the island's adult males dropped from 70.6 percent to 54.4 percent.[43] Those men who had trouble landing jobs at home found the U.S. migrant farm labor program eager and ready to transport them to the fields of New Jersey, New York, Connecticut, Massachusetts, Michigan, and Ohio, a process that detached them from their families for months out of every year and often led to permanent breakups of marriages.

Added to the strains of a migrant labor existence was the decline of industrial employment in this country. Deindustrialization took hold in the Northeast and Midwest shortly after Puerto Ricans migrated to those regions. In New York, for example, 60 percent of Puerto Rican workers in 1960 had factory jobs, so they were particularly vulnerable to economic insecurity over the succeeding decades as those jobs disappeared.[44] As the nature of work changed in urban America, Puerto Ricans also found themselves shut out of the growing areas of white-collar financial, professional, and government jobs. This was due not so much to their own volition as it was to language barriers, lack of education, and racial discrimination.

In addition, the ease by which Puerto Ricans move back and forth on the "air bridge" connecting the island and the mainland—an option other Latino immigrants lack—brought unique problems of instability. Those migrant pioneers who were successful in business found it easier just to pack up and return to Puerto Rico. Once there, with their modest savings and their newfound fluency in English, they joined the island middle class as employees in the fast-growing tourist industry, as managers of American companies, or just as comfortable retirees. Their return home, however, depleted the Puerto Rican barrios on the mainland of a developing middle class. As new waves of unskilled laborers moved up from the island, those barrios remained disproportionately filled with the unemployed and poor, and thus appeared to outsiders as unable to progress.

By the late 1970s, Puerto Rican professionals, unable to find work at home, started migrating here as well. But these new professionals often settled far from the old Puerto Rican barrios or in cities where Mexicans or Cubans predominated. A considerable number of island-trained engineers, for instance, went to work for NASA in Houston or the burgeoning computer industry in California (Orlando, Florida, now boasts the fastest-growing Puerto Rican community). The result of this back-and-forth migration has been a Puerto Rican middle class here that is less stable and less connected to institution building among the masses of poor people than in, say, the Mexican and Cuban immigrant communities.

The above factors indicate why Puerto Ricans, more than any other Latino group, feel such an intimate bond to their homeland,

and why they should be regarded by the rest of American society as one people. The experiences of the 5.8 million Puerto Ricans in this country cannot be separated from those of the 3.2 million on the island. All 9 million, after all, are legally U.S. citizens, and all continue to live with the effects—whether the rest of American society realizes it or not—of more than one hundred years of colonialism.[45]

THE HISTORIC VIEQUES CAMPAIGN OF 1999–2003

On April 19, 1999, David Sanes Rodríguez, a thirty-five-year-old civilian security guard, was on patrol near an observation post adjacent to the U.S. naval bombing range in Vieques, Puerto Rico, when a pair of U.S. F-18 jets on a routine training mission missed their targets and dropped two five-hundred-pound bombs near his post, killing Sanes and wounding four others. The tragic accident unleashed public resentment that had been building for decades over the navy's treatment of local residents and sparked a four-year protest movement against the navy's presence on the island. That movement soon turned Vieques into a worldwide symbol of resistance to colonialism while at the same time deepening a rift between Pentagon chiefs and the Clinton White House.

With its pristine beaches, crystal-clear azure waters, and lush vegetation, the fifty-five-square-mile island off the eastern coast of Puerto Rico is one of the most scenic and unspoiled spots in the Caribbean. During World War II, the navy appropriated more than two-thirds of its territory for a target range and weapons storage facilities and later developed an underwater submarine range just offshore. The combination of the submarine range, the large Vieques beaches suitable for large amphibious exercises, and the sprawling Roosevelt Roads Naval Base only six miles away soon turned the island into the crown jewel of naval training facilities. So popular was it with the Pentagon that U.S. commanders routinely rented it out to the navies of Latin America and our European allies for their own target practice.

Meanwhile, the original Vieques population of 16,000 dwindled to only about 9,400, all of them restricted by the navy to inhabiting a small enclave in the center of the island. Over the decades, those residents endured on an almost daily basis the thunderous explosions of bombs and naval artillery from the nearby range, the deafening roar of low-flying jets, and the relentless sound of small weapons fire. This incessant military activity stunted the growth of industry and tourism, left fishing as the only source of jobs for local residents, and turned the island into Puerto Rico's poorest and most isolated municipality.[46]

By the 1970s, Vieques residents began to complain of major health problems they suspected were caused by the military presence. The Puerto Rican government initially ignored their concerns. But several studies in the 1990s revealed that Vieques residents had a 27 percent higher cancer rate than the rest of Puerto Rico and a far higher incidence of heart disease. The cancer rate, the studies showed, was three times higher for Vieques children than for children on the main island. Local residents also suffered from higher rates of diabetes, respiratory disease, and epilepsy than did other Puerto Ricans.

It took the death of Sanes, however, for outsiders to pay serious attention to the unfolding public health catastrophe. In 2000, Puerto Rican epidemiologist Carmen Ortiz Roque discovered high levels of lead, mercury, and cadmium in forty-four of forty-nine residents she tested. Meanwhile, biologists at the University of Puerto Rico detected high concentrations of heavy metals in vegetation on Vieques. According to one peer-reviewed study, island samples had "up to 10 times more lead and 3 times more cadmium than samples from Puerto Rico itself," and the Vieques samples "exceeded safety standards." Other studies revealed contamination of air, groundwater, fish—even hair and urine samples of residents—with heavy metals and other toxic compounds, including uranium.[47]

Pentagon officials would later acknowledge that they had experimented with chemical weapons on the range and had dropped napalm, Agent Orange, and even some depleted uranium shells there. They conceded, as well, that the island was littered with more than eighteen thousand unexploded shells.[48]

Within weeks of the bombing accident, scores of Puerto Rican activists invaded the restricted area of the range and demanded that the navy leave. They then set up more than a dozen makeshift protest encampments on the beaches in a standoff that lasted for thirteen months, impeding further target practice during that time. As top aides in the Clinton White House debated how to respond, Pentagon officials insisted that the Vieques training facility was unique, irreplaceable, and essential to U.S. national defense.[49]

In January 2000, Clinton and Rosselló announced an agreement to hold a referendum in Víeques on the future presence of the navy. Clinton offered to provide $50 million in infrastructure and housing aid to the island if local residents accepted continued live-fire training. The plan was rejected by protesters in the camps and roundly criticized by most civic groups in Puerto Rico. Less than a month later, an estimated eighty thousand people filled the streets of San Juan to condemn both the navy and the Clinton-Rosselló plan.[50]

Thirteen months after the crisis began, FBI agents and federal marshals swept through the protest camps and arrested more than two hundred people. A few days later, the navy resumed bombing practice with inert munitions. But bands of bombing opponents continued to trespass onto the range and disrupt those exercises before being caught by federal agents and jailed. As news of the Vieques conflict spread around the world, human rights activists, politicians, and celebrities flocked to the island to show their support. In April 2001, the Reverend Al Sharpton; Robert F. Kennedy Jr.; actor Edward James Olmos; famed Puerto Rican singer Danny Rivera; and Jackie Jackson, the wife of the Reverend Jesse Jackson, were all arrested in Vieques. So were two Puerto Rican members of Congress, New York's Nydia Velázquez and Chicago's Luis Gutiérrez, while the third, New York's José Serrano, was similarly arrested in an antinavy protest in front of the White House. All told, federal agents arrested more than 1,400 people in Vieques between May 2000 and September 2001.[51]

When a new governor, the Popular Democratic Party's Sila Calderón, took office in January 2001, she immediately rejected the Clinton-Rosselló pact. In March, the navy notified Calderón that, as part of that agreement, it would soon resume inert bombing on Vieques. The governor promptly secured passage of a new Noise Prohibition Act, making such bombing illegal under Puerto Rican law. She then sued the navy unsuccessfully in federal court to hinder any further bombings, while also scheduling a November referendum on Vieques, one that included the option of immediate cessation of bombing. By then, the Bush administration was realizing that Puerto Rico's opposition to the navy could not be turned around. On June 14, 2001, Bush shocked the military and his own Republican leaders in Congress by announcing that all navy exercises on Vieques would end within two years. Even that huge concession, however, did not completely quiet the furor. In the Vieques referendum held that November, 68 percent of voters backed an immediate cessation of training.[52]

In retrospect, the Vieques movement and the navy's forced withdrawal from the island in May 2003 represented a remarkable human rights victory, one that was even more inspiring considering that it came about through nonviolent civil disobedience. Many Americans, nonetheless, could not understand why Puerto Ricans, being U.S. citizens, would so vehemently oppose the navy's presence. Similarly, Puerto Ricans, especially the inhabitants of Vieques, could not fathom why Washington politicians had permitted the navy to destroy their land, their health, and their livelihood for so many decades. Vieques, in other words, was the most vivid example of a colonial condition that had to end.

FREEDOM OF CHOICE
AND THE DEBATE OVER STATUS

For more than half a century, Congress had insisted that Puerto Ricans wanted that relationship, that island residents voluntarily chose to be a dressed-up colony, or commonwealth, and had voted accordingly in previous status referenda. That claim began to be unmasked in 1989 when the island's three major political parties jointly declared that Puerto Ricans had never really exercised their right of self-determination. That year, the Popular Democratic, the New Progressive, and the Puerto Rican Independence Party, jointly petitioned Congress for a new referendum to decide the island's final status.

As serious students of Puerto Rican history know, two prior referenda in 1952 and 1967 were so unfairly stacked for one option that they mocked the idea of free choice. The 1952 vote offered Puerto Ricans only the choice of remaining a direct colony or accepting the limited self-rule then represented by the commonwealth status. Neither statehood nor independence was put on the ballot by Congress. In fact, government repression of the independence movement was at its height at the time. Even peaceful advocates of separation were systematically blacklisted from government jobs. The infamous 1948 "gag law," passed by the precommonwealth legislature, made it a crime to publicly advocate violent opposition to the U.S. occupation, and nationalists could be arrested for even flying the Puerto Rican flag. After the failed Jayuya independence revolt of 1950, the gag law was invoked to declare virtual martial law and imprison thousands of nationalists and their sympathizers. Despite that repression, candidates of the pro-independence party garnered an amazing 20 percent of the vote in island elections in the 1950s, and they managed to keep the issue of Puerto Rico's colonial status alive at the United Nations.[53]

By the 1960s, however, as more African and Asian colonies secured their independence and joined the United Nations, the new member states began to demand answers from the U.S. delegation about Puerto Rico's status. The pressure prompted President Johnson in 1964 to appoint a blue-ribbon U.S.-Puerto Rico Status Commission. That commission recommended a new plebiscite in which, for the first time, independence, statehood, and commonwealth would all be offered as options of "equal dignity and equal status." The referendum was held on July 23, 1967. Governor Muñoz Marín campaigned strenuously for what he called "enhanced commonwealth," which he described as having greater autonomy than the federal government had approved in 1948.

While the choices were a vast improvement over those offered in 1952, they still suffered from fundamental flaws. First, Congress refused to commit itself before the vote to accept whatever decision the Puerto Rican people made, insisting instead on its sovereign right to decide the island's status. Second, Congress refused to clarify how the federal government would treat the island economically under a transition period to each of the three choices. As a result of those flaws, the Puerto Rican Independence Party and a section of the statehood party boycotted the referendum, thus assuring a 60 percent margin for "enhanced commonwealth."

Only years later was a third and even more serious flaw revealed— a conspiracy by federal officials to subvert the vote. FBI agents conducted a campaign of dirty tricks and harassment against the Puerto Rican Independence Party aimed at diminishing its support.[54] Even for Muñoz Marín and the Popular Democrats, however, the referendum proved to be a hollow victory, as Congress repeatedly rebuffed Muñoz's efforts to achieve the greater autonomy that Puerto Rico's voters had approved.

Shortly after Jimmy Carter became president in 1977, his Latin America experts privately counseled a reexamination of Puerto Rico. Not only was the island's status creating repeated embarrassment before the United Nations Decolonization Committee but its intractable poverty was becoming a drain on the federal treasury. Some advisers urged steering the island toward a form of sovereignty, but one that would preserve U.S. influence and control.[55]

Before a new presidential commission could complete its work, however, Carter lost the 1980 presidential election, and his two immediate successors, Ronald Reagan and George H. W. Bush, both endorsed statehood for the island. The Reagan-Bush vision of statehood differed markedly, however, from that of annexationist leaders on the island. Those leaders, such as former governor Carlos Romero Barceló, advocated *un estado criollo*, "a Creole state." For them, Spanish would remain the island's language even after it joined the union, and this was something conservatives in Congress refused to accept.[56] As a result, the 1980s passed without federal action when the White House and Congress couldn't concur.

It was their frustration over the zigzags in U.S. policy that thus prompted the three island parties to unite in 1989 and petition Washington for a new plebiscite. In response to that petition, U.S. lawmakers began crafting a "Puerto Rico Self-Determination Act" under the leadership of Louisiana senator J. Bennett Johnston. This time, Puerto Rican leaders demanded the specific definitions of each status, something that prior plebiscites had avoided. Those specifics, they argued, were the meat and potatoes of any real choices. How Congress spelled out the economic and cultural ramifications of each alternative would determine the voters' decision, they insisted.

The Senate committee drafting the bill, however, rejected most of the key requests of all sides. It dismissed statehooders' insistence that Spanish remain the language of instruction in the public schools and rejected any phase-in period for the paying of federal taxes, or any special tariffs to protect Puerto Rican coffee farmers from imports. Likewise, it spurned virtually all the "enhanced commonwealth" proposals as unconstitutional and a usurpation of U.S. sovereignty.

More important, the Senate insisted that whatever choice Puerto Ricans eventually made must cost the federal government no additional funds. When a Congressional Budget Office study revealed that statehood would require an additional $18 billion over nine years to equalize Medicaid and other benefits to the island, the Senate's reluctance to approve any bill increased. The most cost-effective alternative, the CBO concluded, was independence, since it would save the Treasury $1 billion annually.[57] Two years of dogged negotiations and contentious public hearings followed, with the Senate's Natural Resources Committee finally failing to approve the plebiscite bill by a 10–10 vote.

A second effort to pass a referendum bill failed in 1991. By then, conservative Republicans started voicing concerns that Puerto Rican statehood would lead to another Quebec.[58] Not lost on leaders of both parties was the reality that most of the pro-statehood and all the procommonwealth politicians on the island were affiliated with the Democratic Party. A Puerto Rican state was thus likely to elect two Democratic senators and six Democratic members of Congress. It might even fuel longstanding demands by African Americans for statehood for the District of Columbia. The whole issue, in short, threatened a major expansion of the voting franchise to millions of Latinos and African Americans and an almost certain realignment of federal political power.

Soon after the plebiscite bill's defeat, island elections swept the pro-statehood New Progressive Party into power. The new governor, Pedro Rosselló, decided to ignore Congress and immediately organize his own status referendum in November 1993. Even though the vote had no congressional sanction, Rosselló hoped it would keep the pressure on Washington for a final resolution, and he was confident that statehood would finally achieve a majority. But the final tally showed 48.4 percent for commonwealth, 46.25 percent for statehood, and 4.4 percent for independence. An astounding 80 percent of the electorate had turned out. For the third time in fifty years, commonwealth supporters had won a referendum, and once again, Washington simply ignored the island's vote.

The Republicans seized control of Congress the following year, and bitter battles over the federal budget temporarily relegated Puerto Rico's status to the political shadows. The new Republican majority subsequently rammed through a series of bills that were regarded as anti-immigrant, and which caused U.S. citizen Latinos to turn out in record numbers in the 1996 election, thus helping re-elect President Clinton. All the polls after that election confirmed that Republicans were losing support among Hispanics, the country's fastest-growing group of voters. Party consultants warned House Speaker Newt Gingrich that the slim Republican majority in Congress might slip away in the 1998 election unless the party got more Latino votes. So, against the wishes of the party's most conservative wing, Gingrich green-lighted a new Puerto Rico plebiscite bill for a vote in the full House. The Clinton administration, in an unusual display of bipartisanship, backed Gingrich's plan and marshaled all the Democrats it could in favor of the bill.

In the months leading up to that vote, Puerto Rican leaders

lobbied feverishly over the content of the legislation, while conservative groups seeking to head off statehood lobbied just as hard to kill it. The final version, sponsored by Alaska Republican Don Young, passed on March 4, 1998, by a razor-thin 209 to 208 margin. The Senate, however, shelved any action on the bill.

THE YOUNG BILL—THE FIRST ADMISSION THAT COLONIALISM MUST END

Even though the Young bill eventually died in the Senate, it was a major milestone in the century-long status debate. For example, the bill's preamble conceded that the United States has never allowed Puerto Ricans genuine self-determination. For the first time, Congress considered offering island voters a choice between commonwealth, statehood, and "separate sovereignty." It asserted that commonwealth was not a permanent panacea in the eyes of the United States, nor was the greater self-rule implied by "enhanced commonwealth" constitutional. According to the bill, should Puerto Ricans choose commonwealth, a new referendum would be held every ten years until a majority chose either statehood or "separate sovereignty."

The marathon twelve-hour debate that preceded the House vote was televised over C-Span in both Puerto Rico and the United States, which meant that the American people witnessed the first public debate by our leaders over what to do with the nation's most important colony. And this time the debate was led by four members of the House of Representatives who had been born in Puerto Rico. The four mirrored the same deep divisions and passion over status that exist among all Puerto Ricans. The rest of Congress was just as sharply divided as its Puerto Rican members. The close final vote reflected deep uncertainty over this country's continued relationship with the island. Some congressmen even asked why the matter of Puerto Rico was coming up for debate at all—as if the issue could be tabled for another hundred years.

Pro-statehood governor Pedro Rosselló, however, refused to be deterred by inaction in Congress. He scheduled yet another referendum on status for the end of 1998, the hundredth anniversary of the U.S. occupation, in hopes of pressuring Washington for action. He even rejected requests to postpone the referendum after Hurricane Georges plowed through the Caribbean that September and devastated Puerto Rico and a dozen other islands. Rosselló alienated voters further by excluding the "commonwealth" option favored by the Popular Democrats from the ballot. The result was a massive voter protest against the entire process, with more than 50 percent choosing "none of the above" and statehood getting just 46 percent. The bizarre tally only confounded Congress, permitting its members to postpone any new debate on the island.

For most of the next decade, procommonwealth governments—first under Governor Sila Calderón and then under her successor, Aníbal Acevedo Vilá—ignored the status issue. But after the pro-statehood party swept to power in 2008 in both the governor's mansion and the Puerto Rican legislature, its leaders began pressing Washington for another status referendum. If Congress did not authorize a new vote, statehooders warned, Puerto Rico would hold its own. Meanwhile, independence supporters kept urging United Nations intervention and the creation of a constituent assembly to achieve self-determination. In April 2010, the House of Representatives passed the Puerto Rico Democracy Act. The bill represented a dramatic departure from past congressional legislation. It authorized a two-stage referendum among all Puerto Ricans, both those residing on the island and those born there but living in the United States. In the first round, voters would decide whether to maintain the current status or change it. If the majority voted for change, a second round would offer four options: statehood, commonwealth, independence, or a free association "between sovereign nations."

The new bill, like prior efforts in the 1990s, failed to win approval in the Senate. But action by Congress could not be postponed indefinitely. Puerto Rico's colonial status was becoming increasingly unacceptable, with all leaders on the island demanding a change. Unfortunately, getting a majority in either Puerto Rico or the United States for one option has so far proved elusive. Public opinion polls show Puerto Ricans are against any choice that gives up either their American citizenship or their right to speak Spanish in island schools and courts. To most English-speaking Americans, those two "rights" are mutually exclusive, an insoluble paradox. But to Puerto Ricans, they are no less contradictory than the current position of Congress and the Supreme Court that Puerto Rico "belongs to but is not a part of the United States." No ethnic or territorial group, Puerto Ricans are now saying, can remain the "property" of another nation forever, and if the cost of ending that colonial relationship ends up inconveniencing the colonizing nation, perhaps forcing it to change its Constitution, then so be it.

But another factor was propelling Congress to act: the United States no longer needs Puerto Rico as a colony. Possessing a foreign territory inhabited by millions of people, after all, involves huge costs of upkeep that sooner or later become a burden on the colonial administrator. As we have noted, it is easier today for U.S. corporations to exploit laborers in the Dominican Republic or Mexico than in Puerto Rico, whose workers now enjoy the labor rights of other Americans, so the continued cost of possessing Puerto Rico can no longer be justified.

MASSIVE DEFAULT AND NO WAY TO FIX IT

When Governor García Padilla announced in 2015 that Puerto Rico's public sector debt was no longer payable, his government and its agencies owed more than $72 billion to bondholders. In addition, government pension funds for public employees were empty and faced some $50 billion in unfunded liabilities to current and retired workers. This overall debt of more than $120 billion, along with years of government operating deficits, a shrinking economy, and staggering population loss had by then combined to create a perfect storm that Puerto Rico could no longer withstand.

Some observers began to describe Puerto Rico as America's Greece. The island's economic collapse and financial crisis, they warned, was poised to threaten the larger American economy, of which it is such an integral part, by sparking instability and uncertainty in the huge municipal bond market.[59] Up to that point, the largest public debt default in U.S. history had occurred in Detroit, which owed just $18 billion in bond and pension liabilities. Puerto Rico's debt, by comparison, was nearly seven times larger. And while most economic experts publicly dismissed the notion of contagion, the bondholder groups nonetheless lobbied fiercely in Washington for more than a year to prevent a federal bailout or a major reduction of the island's debt while backing some sort of mechanism to restructure it.[60]

Unlike independent nations that have faced debt crises in modern times, Puerto Rico could not seek a bailout and restructure its debt through the International Monetary Fund. Nor could it use the federal restructuring mechanism that states employ for rare municipal defaults, known as Chapter 9 bankruptcy protection. Until 1984,

Congress had included all the territories and possessions of the United States under Chapter 9. But that year, a provision was inserted into federal law that specifically exempted Puerto Rico and its public authorities from using Chapter 9 to restructure their debt. No reason for the amendment was spelled out nor was it the subject of any debate. By a few simple phrases in the 1984 amendment, one in which Puerto Rico had no say, Congress thus laid the basis for the unique situation the island's government would confront in 2015: it was not only broke, there was no established legal recourse for it to get a federal judge to decide which creditors would be paid, and how much. Moreover, Puerto Rico's constitution required the government to pay its general obligation debt before any other expenditures, a guarantee that historically had always made Puerto Rico uncommonly attractive to Wall Street financiers.[61]

Even as Congress was debating how to handle the default crisis, the Supreme Court issued decisions in two pivotal cases that reaffirmed the limits to Puerto Rico's form of self-government. The first ruling, in *Puerto Rico v. Sanchez Valle*, came on June 9, 2016, just three weeks before the PROMESA law was enacted. That case centered on whether an accused criminal, Luis Sanchez Valle, could be tried on gun-selling charges by local prosecutors under Puerto Rican law and separately by federal prosecutors under U.S. law—in other words, whether Puerto Rico had the power, as do states and even tribal governments under the doctrine of "dual sovereignty," to prosecute individuals for the same offense separately from federal prosecutors. In a 6-to-2 decision, the court ruled that Puerto Rico has never had its own sovereignty. Justice Elena Kagan's majority opinion found that Congress was "the original source of power for Puerto Rico's prosecutors—as it is for the Federal Government's." In an eloquent dissent, Justice Stephen Breyer, joined by Justice Sonia Sotomayor, insisted that the federal government, by approving the creation of commonwealth status, had already recognized Puerto Rico's "freedom from control or interference by the Congress in respect to internal government and administration," and furthermore, that U.S. diplomats had even asserted to the United Nations back then that the island was self-governing.[62]

Only a few days after the *Sanchez* decision, the high court delivered a second blow, this time in *Puerto Rico v. California Franklin Tax-Free Trust*. At issue in that case was the bankruptcy law the island's legislature had approved in 2014 to remedy Puerto Rico's exclusion from full bankruptcy code protections that Congress had ordained back in 1984. A group of U.S. hedge funds and mutual fund managers who held a portion of the island's debt immediately sued to overturn the Puerto Rico law. In a 5-to-2 decision, the Supreme Court affirmed lower court rulings that such legislation was not permitted under federal law, with only Justices Sotomayor and Ginsburg dissenting. The outcomes in both *Sanchez Valle* and *California Franklin Tax-Free Trust* were further proof that Puerto Rico's status and laws have always been subject to the will of Congress.[63]

CONTROL BOARD BRINGS AUSTERITY BUT NO ACCOUNTABILITY

The prospect of financial chaos stemming from debt default eventually prompted the Republican-controlled Congress and the Obama administration to enact the PROMESA bill, creating a financial control board to restructure island finances. The law authorized the president to appoint the board's seven voting members, four from lists provided by majority leaders of the Senate and the House, two from lists provided by minority leaders of those bodies, with only one being freely chosen by the president. That assured Republican control of the board. In addition, only two appointees had to be residents or engaged in business primarily in Puerto Rico. This was a stark contrast from the District of Columbia oversight board that Republican House Speaker Newt Gingrich and the Clinton White House had created in 1995.[64] PROMESA, on the other hand, imposed control by non–Puerto Rican residents over the island; it required the government of Puerto Rico to pay all costs associated with the board; and it gave the new body sweeping powers over legislation and budgets—an overt return to early twentieth-century colonial rule.

Once the board began operating, in September 2016, it initiated a massive austerity program that included the closing of hundreds of public schools, the slashing of public employee benefits, cuts in government pensions of 10 percent, sharp reductions in spending for health care and police, a doubling of tuition at the public University of Puerto Rico while also ordering $550 million in cuts to the university's budget, and the privatization of the government-owned electric utility (PREPA).[65]

Left unanswered was the crucial question of how a territory as small as Puerto Rico had managed to incur such enormous debt in the first place. Congressional Republicans ascribed principal blame

to ineptness and corruption by island officials. The Obama administration's point person on the crisis, treasury official Antonio Weiss,
insisted it would take too long to sort out the actual causes, that immediate action was needed to stave off financial chaos and restructure the debt. Few asked why Wall Street bankers had peddled
massive loans for years to a government they knew was unlikely to
repay them. Facing a public outcry, the island legislature created a
commission in 2015 to audit the debt. That body never received sufficient funding to do its work, and once pro-statehood leader Ricky
Rosselló—son of former governor Pedro Rosselló—took office as
governor in 2017, he quickly disbanded the commission. One of its
subcommittees, however, managed to issue a damning preliminary report that identified several illegal practices in the issuing of
Puerto Rico bonds. Those practices included at least $30 billion
borrowed just to pay off government budget deficits, which was specifically prohibited by the island's constitution. A judge could inval-
idate such debts as illegally contracted and thus unpayable, the
report warned.[66]

Soon after the PROMESA board was installed, it commissioned
its own investigation into the origins of the financial crisis, hiring a
U.S. firm, Kobre & Kim, and granting it the power to subpoena records and witnesses. The six-hundred-page report produced by the
firm in August 2018 confirmed some startling information. Among
its findings:

+ 70 percent of $46 billion in bonds that Puerto Rico and its
  agencies issued between 2005 and 2014 had gone to pay off
  previous debt, while only 30 percent went to actual capital
  projects.

+ Between 2008 and 2014, the government and its public corporations lost more than $1 billion in "termination fees" to
  Wall Street banks to unwind lost bets on complex interest rate
  "swaps" that the island officials who approved them later acknowledged they could not even understand.

+ More than 10 percent of the island's overall bond debt of $74
  billion was in instruments called Capital Appreciation Bonds.
  These were virtual "pay-day loans" for which the lenders
  agreed to receive no interest and no principal for up to forty-
  seven years, but by the time the bonds matured, the balances
  owed were seven or eight times the original loans.[67]

The Kobre & Kim report confirmed that substantial portions of the debt appeared to have violated Puerto Rican law; nonetheless, it downplayed any potential criminal liability or fraud by government officials or private banks. Moreover, its investigators issued only a handful of subpoenas for records, none of them to U.S. firms such as Goldman Sachs, Morgan Stanley, and JPMorgan Chase, which had arranged much of the debt while collecting lucrative fees. Nor did the investigators require sworn testimony or even maintain transcripts of interviews. There was the case, for example, of one unidentified lead banker for Goldman Sachs who in 2005 had spearheaded lobbying for legislation in Puerto Rico to permit interest swaps—the very swaps through which his firm later landed $55 million in termination fees. He repeatedly told the Kobre & Kim investigators that he could not recall any involvement by himself or any other Goldman Sachs banker in either lobbying for the legislation or arranging any actual swaps. Faced with such absurd denials, the investigators opted not to subpoena that banker's emails or other correspondence, thus precluding any genuine attempt to uncover fraudulent or corrupt behavior by a major Wall Street bank.[68]

There are those, however, for whom Puerto Rico's financial collapse turned into an instant gold mine—bankruptcy professionals. By January of 2018, more than fifty law firms and financial advisers, most of them U.S.-based companies, had billed $400 million in fees and expenses connected to the Puerto Rico default litigation, with total legal and advisory costs projected to surpass $1.4 billion.[69]

HURRICANE MARÍA AND ITS AFTERMATH

When it roared over Puerto Rico on the morning of September 20, 2017, Hurricane María deluged the island with thirty-seven inches of rain and sustained winds of more than 150 miles per hour (just below a Category 5 storm). Nearly one million residents were already reeling from power outages caused by the glancing blow of another major storm, Hurricane Irma, two weeks earlier, but María's direct hit proceeded to cripple the country's entire electrical grid, half of its water supply, and nearly all cellphone service. The storm triggered more than forty thousand landslides, wrecked 160,000 homes, left 90 percent of Puerto Rico's roads impassable, damaged thirty-one million trees, and ravaged 80 percent of agricultural production, with early estimates of the physical destruction calculated at more than $90 billion.[70]

Even more shocking was the bungled and calamitous rescue and recovery effort from both Washington officials and Puerto Rico's central government. The electrical blackout turned into the longest in U.S. history, with twenty-two thousand customers still without power nearly seven months after the storm. Moreover, the Trump administration provided far less disaster assistance to Puerto Rico than it did that same year to Texas residents after Hurricane Harvey or to Florida residents after Hurricane Irma, and it dispatched far fewer federal disaster personnel to the island, even though the damage and lives lost on the island were far greater. "Within the first 9 days after the hurricanes hit, both Harvey and Irma survivors had already each received nearly US $100 million in FEMA dollars awarded to individuals and families, whereas Maria survivors had only received slightly over US $6 million in recovery aid," one study noted. Initial congressional appropriations to Puerto Rico came largely in loans and were highly restricted, whereas those to Texas and Florida were in grants and had fewer restrictions.[71]

The most-publicized scandal turned out to be the storm's official death count. During a brief visit to Puerto Rico less than two weeks after María struck, Trump touted how few people had been killed, even contrasting the toll to the 1,800 fatalities in New Orleans during Hurricane Katrina, and he lauded the rapid federal response. "You can be very proud of all of your people, all of our people working together," he said. "Sixteen [deaths] versus literally thousands of people. You can be very proud." A few weeks later, Governor Rosselló amended the death count to 64. But independent journalists and local political leaders kept insisting it was far greater. They noted that the continuing electrical blackout, impassable roads, and a crippled health system made it impossible for people with chronic health problems and a dearth of potable water to access medicines and vital medical equipment. As a result, hundreds had perished at home. Puerto Rico's Center for Investigative Journalism was the first to report that in the forty days after the storm hit nearly 1,000 more people had died on the island than had died during the same period in previous years. As more media organizations challenged the official count, Rosselló commissioned an independent study by George Washington University. That final report led the governor, nearly a year after the storm, to revise the official toll to 2,975, thus acknowledging María had been one of the deadliest storms in U.S. history.[72]

Meanwhile, federal funds for Puerto Rico's rebuilding quickly turned into a cesspool of corruption and waste that enriched politically connected U.S. firms. Among the startling examples:

- The two-employee Whitefish Energy firm from Montana that somehow landed a $300 million no-bid contract from the Puerto Rico Electric Authority to help restore power. Despite being paid more than $300 per hour for each utility line worker, it failed to hire sufficient staff, and the ensuing public outcry prompted Governor Rosselló to oust the firm, whose CEO, it turned out, was a neighbor and acquaintance of Trump's secretary of the interior, Ryan Zinke.[73]

- Cobra Acquisitions LLC, a firm with no previous experience in electrical infrastructure, won a $200 million contract from PREPA to rebuild the island's transmission lines with FEMA funds. Cobra had been incorporated only months before the storm by Oklahoma-based Mammoth Energy Services, and its contract soon ballooned to $1.4 billion. Federal prosecutors in Miami subsequently indicted Cobra's chief executive, Donald Ellison, and Ahsha Tribble, a top FEMA administrator for Puerto Rico and a former Homeland Security official under President Obama, for bribery and fraud. Tribble was charged with accepting bribes from Ellison in exchange for steering contracts to Cobra.[74]

- A one-woman company from Atlanta, Georgia, with no experience in disaster relief landed a $156 million contract from FEMA for emergency meals to Puerto Rico. Within a month, the company, Tribute Contracting LLC, had delivered only fifty thousand of the thirty million meals promised, and its contract was scrapped.[75]

THE PEOPLE RESPOND: ROSSELLÓ AND *EL VERANO BORICUA*

The four years from mid 2015 to 2019 emerged as the most tumultuous in Puerto Rico's modern history: the debt crisis and financial collapse, the imposition of the control board, massive cutbacks in government services, the devastation of Hurricane María, the appalling disaster response by the Trump administration, and repeated corruption scandals within Governor Rosselló's administration all combined to produce an unprecedented calamity, one that prompted tens of thousands to flee to the United States. Nothing seemed to deter the neoliberal push for more austerity—not the scores of isolated protests by university students and labor unions, nor the extraordinary examples of grassroots mutual aid efforts in the aftermath of the hurricane—until, in the summer of 2019, a sudden and historic fifteen-day popular uprising swiftly toppled Governor Ricky Rosselló from power. Island residents called it *El Verano Boricua*—the Puerto Rican summer (a reference to the island's original Taíno name, Borikén).

The protests erupted following the leak of nearly nine hundred pages of Telegram app messages between the governor and his closest male advisers, chats that were laced with sexist, homophobic, and vulgar references to other political leaders, especially women, and in which they even mocked the victims of Hurricane María. The revelations from Puerto Rico's Center for Investigative Journalism, coming only days after the FBI arrested two former top Rosselló officials for corruption, stunned the island and provoked massive protests, even a general strike, and within days Ricky Rosselló was forced to resign.[76]

Given the decades of controversy over Puerto Rico's status, why not end colonialism by welcoming the island territory as the fifty-first state, as the annexationists want? Haven't Puerto Ricans proved their loyalty by fighting in every major U.S. war this century? José Trías Monge, a former chief justice of the Supreme Court of Puerto Rico, insists that statehood was never intended by Congress for the island. In a book reviewing congressional law and Supreme Court decisions on Puerto Rico, Trías Monge notes that unlike Hawaii and Alaska, which Congress deemed incorporated territories and slated for annexation from the start, Puerto Rico was kept "unincorporated" specifically to avoid offering it statehood.

President Taft made that policy evident during his annual message to Congress in 1912, when he said:

I believe that the demand for citizenship is just, and that it is amply earned by the sustained loyalty on the part of the inhabitants of the

island. But it should be remembered that the demand must be, in the
minds of most Porto Ricans is, entirely dissociated from any thought
of statehood. I believe that no substantial public opinion in the United
States or in Puerto Rico contemplates statehood for the island as the
ultimate form of relation between us.[77]

How much truer Taft's words seem today. With our government
clamping down on the flood of Latin American immigrants, it is almost unthinkable that a congressional majority would be prepared to
admit an entire state whose people are racially mixed and who speak
Spanish as their main language. Hawaii petitioned Congress for
statehood for the first time in 1919. Its residents voted overwhelmingly for it in a plebiscite as early as 1940. Yet Congress denied that
plea for nineteen more years because the territory had a substantial
native and Asian population.[78] How much more challenging will
statehood be for Puerto Rico, when the population of Anglo-
Americans there is still tiny and not even a bare majority of islanders
is petitioning for statehood after a hundred years?

Well, then, what about independence? Any concept of a Puerto
Rican republic that fails to preserve U.S. citizenship for most island-
ers is doomed to fail in the foreseeable future. The reason is simple.
The United States is the richest and most powerful nation in the
world. At a time when millions of people in other countries will travel
any distance, make any sacrifice, overcome any obstacle to achieve
U.S. citizenship, or at least permanent residence here, a majority of
Puerto Ricans are unlikely to give theirs up voluntarily.

How, then, can a solution be found that meets the contradictory
needs of both the American and Puerto Rican people? A small but
highly influential group of island leaders has urged for years that the
only way out of this quagmire is a new status, one that incorporates
aspects of the three historic choices. They call it the associated republic, *república asociada*, an arrangement chosen in 1986 by the
Pacific Trust Territories of the United States. It is the equivalent in
the United Nations decolonization process to a "free associated
state."

The associated republic begins with the premise that Puerto
Rico is a distinct nation with the right to "sovereignty and self-
government." It posits that the people of the United States and of
Puerto Rico have chosen to maintain a "close and mutually beneficial
relationship in a voluntary association."

The inclusion of a "free association" option in the proposed

Puerto Rico Democracy Act of 2010 was a recognition, at long last, that some members of Congress were willing to consider this other option.

The main elements of that new union would be:

- Puerto Rico conducts its own international affairs, including its own treaties, customs duties, and participation in the United Nations and other international organizations.

- Dual American and Puerto Rican citizenship for those born on the island.

- A common market, common currency, and common postal system between the two nations.

- No immigration barriers to citizens of either country.

- U.S. "authority and responsibility for international security and defense" of the island, but requiring the consent of the Puerto Rican legislature to involve the island in a war.

- Negotiated use and adequate rent for U.S. military installations.

- Foreign investment incentives to replace the Section 936 tax exemption.

- Elimination of the U.S. maritime monopoly on Puerto Rican shipping.

- Block grants of foreign aid to replace current federal transfer payments.

- A twenty-five-year lifetime for the compact, after which it would be renegotiated.[79]

The associated republic option offers a new common ground. In many ways, it is the logical extension of Muñoz Marín's fifty-year-old dream of "enhanced commonwealth," but it does require U.S. leaders to recognize the obvious, that Puerto Rico is a distinct nation from the United States. At the same time, the new status would not sever all citizenship ties with this country, and it would not challenge the military's desire for a long-term presence on the island. It would provide some of the reforms sought by commonwealth supporters in customs and treaties and would eliminate the maritime monopoly. It would put an end to the second-class status abhorred by statehooders while maintaining the island's Spanish language and culture. By giving up the quest for statehood, Puerto Ricans could ease the fears of millions of Americans on the mainland that complete annexation of the island would further fragment the nation's cultural unity, and they would dispel concerns that Puerto Rico will remain an enclave of poverty laying annual claim to ever-larger doses of federal aid.

Puerto Ricans cannot be the only ones to make concessions, however. The American people should enthusiastically endorse long-term federal assistance to the island. Given the enormous sacrifices Puerto Ricans have made in this country's wars and the immense wealth U.S. corporations have secured from island labor, a free associated Puerto Rico deserves at least as much federal assistance as Israel or Egypt, nations with more distant and less enduring relationships to this country. Free association could pave the way for moving the world's oldest colony toward equality in the world of nations. To generations of Puerto Ricans, the psychological benefit that would follow the termination of colonial dependency would be incalculable. For Americans, it would wash away an old and ugly stain on this nation's most cherished ideals.

One hundred and twenty-four years, after all, is time enough to decide the fate of the last major U.S. colony.

Epilogue

The Chinese spent almost two thousand years perfecting their Great Wall, the Spanish endured eight centuries of foreign occupation before finally expelling the Moors, and the dazzling civilization of Teotihuacán flourished for seven centuries before suddenly disappearing, so the mere two centuries that have elapsed since the Americas broke away from European colonialism barely amount to a crawling stage on the road to nationhood.

The new American states were all unprecedented social experiments into which were amalgamated the cultures, races, and political traditions of both settlers and indigenous peoples. The societies that arose from those experiments are still in search of solid identities today, still extracting and refining the ore that will become their legacy to civilization. The United States is no exception. No matter what the leaders of this nation may claim about its immutable Anglo-Saxon character, fresh waves of immigrants arrive each year, flinging themselves and their customs into the mix, recombining and redefining, ever so slightly, the locus of shared memories that make up the definition of America. This process of growth and change, of cross-fertilization and amalgamation, is more likely to speed up in the twenty-first century than to slow down.

During those first two hundred years, the United States emerged as the world's only superpower and its richest nation. No empire, whether in ancient or modern times, ever saw its influence spread so far or determined the thoughts and actions of so many people around the world as our nation does today. That spectacular success was due in large measure to the unique brand of representative democracy, the spirit of bold enterprise, the respect for individual liberty, and the rugged devotion to hard work that characterized so many of the early American settlers. But there was another aspect to that success, as I have tried to show, the details of which most Americans knew nothing about, but which was always carried out in their name. It was a vicious and relentless drive for territorial expansion, conquest, and subjugation of others—Native Americans, enslaved Africans, and Latin Americans—one that our leaders justified as Manifest Destiny for us.

That expansion transformed the entire hemisphere into an economic satellite and sphere of influence of the United States. The empire that expansion created produced an unexpected harvest here at home toward the end of the twentieth century—massive Latin American immigration. As U.S. capital penetrated the region, it dislocated Latin Americans from their land, impoverished them, then recruited them into a ragtag army of low-priced labor wandering along carefully charted migratory circuits. The best wages in the hemisphere, and the lion's share of its wealth, remained in the United States, so the hardiest of those uprooted workers inevitably headed here, some drawn by corporate recruiters, others pushed by political repression.

By seeking a piece of our prosperity, however, Latin Americans were merely reliving our immigrant creation story. They came by the millions, desperate, unarmed, heads bowed, not dictating terms at gunpoint or declaring their independence in filibuster revolts as did the Anglo pioneers who ventured into Latin America before them, yet the peaceful transformation they have achieved has been just as inexorable. It is nothing less than Latinization of the United States from the bottom up. If current trends continue, Latinos, who numbered one of every ten Americans in 2000, will increase to one of every four by the year 2050.[1]

All attempts to stem this immigration explosion will fail as long as nothing is done to control the unfettered spread of U.S. corporate power below the Rio Grande. Those who keep trying to block immigration with exclusionary laws risk inciting the very ethnic

Balkanization and domestic civil strife they fear. In seeking to defend the "old America," they risk permanently damaging the current one.

It does not have to be this way. Profound change in our country's ethnic makeup need not undermine its deepest-held beliefs. Just as the abolition of slavery signaled a new beginning, a chance to make democracy more universal, so too can a policy of embracing the Latin American masses with whom U.S. history has always been so intertwined. White Anglo leaders must begin by rejecting cultural intolerance and marginalization of Latinx people. They must move quickly to reduce a growing alienation between Hispanic Americans and the rest of the nation. They must stop regarding them as a linguistic caste within the empire, as conquered peoples, and they must press for specific economic and social reforms that have gone ignored for too long.

Only radical change will bring about qualitative progress in Latino economic life. That change has little to do with the behavior-based panaceas of conservatives, with catchy slogans like "family values," "work ethic," or "personal responsibility," or with the Band-Aid remedies of liberals: bigger and better government social programs, school integration, affirmative action. The reforms I am suggesting may seem at first to belong more in the realm of foreign than domestic policy. Yet they are essential precisely because the Latino presence here is so directly connected to our nation's foreign conquest. Only by changing the nature of the American empire can Latino equality and assimilation become real. The following changes in national policy are the ones I consider essential for this new century.

1. *End the predatory dual labor market in cheap Mexican labor.* The only way to reduce the continued exploitation of millions of Mexicans, both in this country and across the Rio Grande, is with the complete mobility of labor between the two nations and the gradual equalizing of their respective environmental and labor laws. In 1994, NAFTA created a common market for goods but not a common market for people, and neither did its successor treaty in 2019, the USMCA. A common market for goods essentially benefits small elites in both countries, while one for people would be a boon to the majority of workers in both. A common labor market—perhaps even with cross-border labor unions or alliances such as the American-Canadian AFL-CIO unions already in existence—would reduce the

gap between wages and labor standards in the United States and
Mexico. As wages rise south of the border, Mexicans will consume
more U.S. goods and fewer of them will seek to emigrate north.
Abolishing the concept of "illegality" among Mexicans, who are
overwhelmingly the largest source of undocumented labor, would
drive up wages at the bottom of our society. How? Because U.S. employers would find it harder to exploit those who can freely organize
unions and petition the courts and government for their legal rights.
It is just that kind of free movement of labor that exists as a basic
right of all members of the European Union.

2. *End the colonial status of Puerto Rico.* Congress should immediately schedule a plebiscite on Puerto Rico's permanent status. It
should consent beforehand to implement whatever status Puerto
Ricans decide, whether that be a sovereign associated state, a fully
autonomous commonwealth, an independent nation, or the fifty-
first state. Should Puerto Ricans choose either free association or
independence, Congress, in recognition of the immense wealth islanders provided this country for one hundred years, and out of
gratitude for the thousands of Puerto Ricans who fought in U.S.
wars, should commit itself to provide transitional federal assistance,
the right of all islanders to retain dual U.S. citizenship, and a free
trade market with the United States. Should Puerto Ricans choose
statehood, Congress should not delay in granting it, one in which
English and Spanish become co-official languages. Only through
genuine decolonization can the second-class limbo Puerto Ricans
experience finally end.

3. *Recognize the rights of language minorities and promote the
widespread study of Spanish.* Unlike many nations in the world, the
United States has yet to recognize the right of language minorities
to protection against discrimination. Puerto Ricans, Cubans, and
Mexicans in this country are each ethnic minorities, but all Hispanics together compose a linguistic minority, one whose origins pre-
date the founding of the country. Spanish is not a foreign tongue in
the United States. It is the principal language of the Western Hemisphere and the second language of the United States, and should finally be recognized as such. Instead of passing anachronistic
English-only laws, our leaders should, at the minimum, be embracing bilingualism. American public schools, for instance, should foster the teaching of Spanish as a main secondary language, maybe

even requiring its study in those regions or states where Hispanics are a substantial minority. Doing so will not in any way reduce the pivotal role English performs as the country's main language. On the contrary, it will foster greater understanding among Americans of all races. As more whites and Blacks in this country learn Spanish, as they taste the greater cultural sophistication and intellectual power that comes from breaking out of an English monolingual ghetto, they will turn into bridge builders and healers within our own population.

4. *Reinvest in U.S. cities and public schools.* The bulk of Latinos live, work, and learn in urban America. Our future is tied to that of the cities. A federal program aimed at rebuilding urban America's infrastructure and at investing in its public schools would provide jobs and upward mobility into the middle class for many Latinos now caught at the economic margins, just as the building of the suburbs in the 1950s helped create the white middle class.

5. *End U.S. militarism in Latin America.* From the days of gunboat diplomacy to the era of the Jefes, from the secret wars of the CIA to the current war on drugs, the U.S. military has always sought to dictate the affairs of Latin America, installing or propping up unpopular leaders, defending rogue Yankee businessmen, or simply spurring sales of U.S. weapons to local governments and private paramilitary groups. Our government must renounce this militarism once and for all. Only such an about-face would begin to ameliorate the estrangement felt by Salvadoran, Guatemalan, Colombian, and Dominican immigrants, many of whom continue to harbor bitter feelings about this country's role in recent civil wars in their countries of origin.

6. *End the economic blockade of Cuba.* Given the flourishing economic and political relations our government has cultivated with socialist countries such as China and Vietnam in recent years, Washington's stubborn sixty-year blockade of Cuba remains a glaring example of how Uncle Sam still regards Latin America as its own backyard and refuses to tolerate dissent in the region. The blockade is almost universally condemned by the rest of the world. While the extraordinary government assistance provided to Cuban immigrants in the past has helped turn them into the most successful Latino group economically, it has also led to a dual standard in

immigration policy and resentment from all other Latinos. Ending
the blockade and normalizing relations would improve economic
conditions in Cuba and pave the way for an end to that dual standard.

These policy cures did not find receptive ears during the decades
that conservative and neoliberal views dominated Western policies,
as many government leaders preferred to search for the causes of
crime and poverty in the actions or inaction of those at the very bottom of society. The obscene transfers of wealth over the past forty
years from that bottom to a privileged few at the top—and from
much of the Global South to financial elites in the West—were all
excused as the natural evolution of the market, when, in fact, they
are products of unparalleled greed by those who dominate and direct that market. Only in recent years has the market and those
elites confronted sustained opposition.

That is why my solutions aim directly at that all-powerful and invisible market and the empire we have created in its name. Immigrant labor has always been critical to the market's prosperity. The
market recruits it, exploits it, abuses it, divides it, then ships it back
home when no longer needed. Only by reining in that market, by
challenging its relentless greed, by humbling its colossal power, can
Latinos in this country move from incremental to qualitative progress; only then can they shatter the caste system to which they have
been relegated. Only by taming the market can the people of the
Americas, north and south, move beyond our ethnic, racial, and linguistic divisions. Only then can we grasp our common humanity,
realize our common dreams.

America, after all, never did end at the Rio Grande.

Acknowledgments

Many thanks to my various editors at Penguin Putnam: Don Fehr, who originally guided me during the first few years in making the transition from newspapers to books, and whose meticulous analysis and uncanny sense of organization and structure turned my primitive and chaotic initial drafts into a coherent whole; Jane von Mehren, whose constant support and careful reviews of the manuscript helped frame my sense of audience; Sarah Baker, whose probing questions repeatedly exposed the weaknesses in my thinking and copy; and Matt Klise, who guided this revised and updated edition to completion. For improving the content, I am grateful to several people who read various drafts of chapters over the years and offered their suggestions: Tom Acosta, Stephen Handelman, and Dennis Rivera in New York; Gil Cedillo and David Sandoval in California; *New York Daily News* editors James "Hap" Hairston and Albor Ruiz; Greg Tarpinian of Labor Research Associates; Clara Rodríguez of Fordham University; Héctor Cordero Guzmán of the City University of New York Graduate Center; two of Puerto Rico's most brilliant journalists, Juan Manuel García-Passalacqua and Jesús Dávila; and Lilia Fernández, a wonderful scholar of U.S. urban and Latino history who also happens to be my wife.

I am especially indebted to my friend and agent for several decades, Frances Goldin, whose relentless defense of her writers was matched only by her untiring devotion to social justice, and to her successor Ellen Geiger.

Many thanks to Amilcar Tirado at the Center for Puerto Rican Studies Library at Hunter College in New York, to Yolanda González at the Arnulfo Oliveiras Memorial Library at the University of Texas at Brownsville, to Margo Gutiérrez at the Benson Latin American Collection of the University of Texas at Austin, and to Faigi Rosenthal, chief librarian at the *New York Daily News*, for their invaluable help in locating source material, and to my research assistants through various editions, Esther (Nequi) González, Jaisal Noor, Karen Yi, Genia Blaser, and Jennifer Natoli.

Countless Latinos in this country, as well as in Mexico, Central America, and the Caribbean, welcomed me into their homes and opened their hearts to me over the past few decades. Whether I was reporting for a newspaper or doing research for this book, they willingly recounted little-known family tales in hopes that the rest of America would more fully understand their story. Many of the best-known leaders of the Latino community—too many to mention here—have generously shared their thoughts with me over the years and thus helped to shape the views in this book.

But special thanks go to the lesser-known Latinos who facilitated my getting to know the families whose migration stories form the emotional core of the book. People like Domingo Gonzáles in Brownsville, Texas; Sandra Garza in El Paso; Estela Vázquez, Alfredo White, Héctor Méndez, and William Acosta in New York City; Luis Del Rosario in Miami; Mario González in Chicago; Ignacio Soto and Heraclio Rivera in the Dominican Republic; and Víctor Alfaro Clark in Mexico.

Finally, thanks to my own family—especially my mother, Florinda Guillén, and my deceased father, Juan González, for never letting me forget how far we've come.

Bibliography

Abramson, Michael. *Palante: Young Lords Party*. New York: McGraw-Hill, 1971.

Acosta, Ivonne. *La Mordaza: Puerto Rico, 1948–1957*. Río Piedras, PR: Editorial Edil, Inc., 1989.

Acosta-Belén, Edna, and Barbara R. Sjostrom. *The Hispanic Experience in the United States*. New York: Praeger, 1988.

Acuña, Rodolfo. *Occupied America: A History of Chicanos*. New York: Harper Collins, 1988.

Adams, John Quincy. *The Writings of John Quincy Adams*, vol. 7. Edited by Worthington C. Ford. New York: Macmillan, 1913–17.

Álvarez, Alberto Martín. *From Revolutionary War to Democratic Revolution: the Farabundo Martí National Liberation Front (FMLN) in El Salvador*. Edited by Véronique Dudouet and Hans J. Giessmann. Berlin: Berghof Transitions Series. Resistance/Liberation Movements and Transition to Politics, 2010.

Alvarez, Roberto R., Jr. *Familia: Migration and Adaptation in Baja and Alta California, 1800–1975*. Berkeley: University of California Press, 1991.

Ambrosius, Christian, and David Leblang. "Exporting Murder: US Deportations and the Spread of Violence." Free University of Berlin, School of Economics and Business, discussion paper, August 21, 2018.

American Civil Liberties Union. "The Trump Administration's Proposed 'Mixed-Status' Housing Rule Is Another Form of Family Separation," July 10, 2019.

American Friends Service Committee, Mexico-U.S. Border Program. *Sealing Our Borders: The Human Toll*. Philadelphia, February 1992.

American Immigration Council. "Immigrants in Maryland," Washington, D.C., 2017.

American Rivers. *Endangered Rivers of America: The Nation's Ten Endangered Rivers and Fifteen Most Threatened Rivers for 1993*. Washington, D.C., April 20, 1993.

Americas Watch Report. "Labor Rights in El Salvador," 1988.

Anderson, Carol, and Dick Durbin. *One Person, No Vote, How Voter Suppression Is Destroying Our Democracy*. New York: Bloomsbury, 2018.

Aptheker, Herbert. *The Colonial Era*. New York: International Publishers, 1959.

Arana, Ana. "How the Street Gangs Took Central America," *Foreign Affairs* 84, no. 3. (May-June 2005).

Arrigoitia, Delma S. *José De Diego, El Legislador: Su visión de Puerto Rico en la Historia, 1903–1918*. San Juan: Instituto de Cultura Puertorriqueña, 1991.

Auster, Laurence. "The Forbidden Topic." *National Review*, April 27, 1992.

Azicri, Max. "The Politics of Exile: Trends and Dynamics of Political Change Among Cuban-Americans." *Cuban Studies* 11. Pittsburgh: University of Pittsburgh Press, 1981.

Bailyn, Bernard. *The Peopling of British North America*. New York: Vintage Books, 1988.

Balderrama, Francisco E., and Raymond Rodríguez. *Decade of Betrayal: Mexican Repatriation in the 1930s*. Albuquerque: University of New Mexico Press, 1995.

Bannon, John Francis. *The Spanish Borderlands Frontier 1513–1821*. Albuquerque: University of New Mexico Press, 1974.

Barber, Willard F., and Neale Ronning. *Internal Security and Military Power: Counterinsurgency and Civic Action in Latin America*. Columbus: Ohio State University Press, 1966.

Barbier, Jacques, and Allan J. Kuethe, eds. *The North American Role in the Spanish Imperial Economy, 1760–1819*. Manchester: Manchester University Press, 1984.

Barnes, Robert. "Supreme Court Rejects Much of Arizona Immigration Law," *Washington Post*, June 25, 2012.

Barreto, Matt A., Tyler Reny, and Bryan Wilcox-Archuleta. "Survey Methodology and the Latina/o Vote: Why a Bilingual, Bicultural, Latino-Centered Approach Matters." *Aztlán* 42, no. 2 (2017): 211–17.

Barry, Tom, and Deb Preusch. *The Central America Fact Book*. New York: Grove Press, 1986.

Belanger, Maurice. "A Chronology of the Treatment of Central American War Refugees in the U.S." Washington, D.C.: National Immigration Forum, 1997.

Bell, Roger. *Last Among Equals: Hawaiian Statehood and American Politics*. Honolulu: University of Hawaii Press, 1984.

Berman, Ari. *Give Us the Ballot: The Modern Struggle for Voting Rights in America*. New York: Picador, Farrar, Straus and Giroux, 2016.

Bermann, Karl. *Under the Big Stick: Nicaragua and the United States Since 1848.* Boston: South End Press, 1986.

Bethell, Leslie, ed. *Colonial Spanish America.* New York: Cambridge University Press, 1987.

Bessette-Kirton, Erin K., et al. "Landslides Triggered by Hurricane María: Assessment of an Extreme Event in Puerto Rico." *GSA Today* 29, no. 6 (June 2019).

Bofill Valdés, Jaime. "Comportamiento de Diversas Variables Macro-Económicas de Puerto Rico y de la Trayectoria de Crecimiento entre Puerto Rico y Estados Unidos Durante 1950–94." *Boletín de Economía* 1, no. 1 (julio–septiembre 1995).

Bolick, Clint. "Mission Unaccomplished: The Misplaced Priorities of the Maricopa County Sheriff's Office," Goldwater Institute, December 2, 2008.

Bolívar, Simón. *Selected Writings of Bolívar. Vol. 1, 1810–1822.* Edited by Harold A. Bierck Jr. New York: Colonial Press, Inc., 1951.

Booth, John A., and Thomas Walker. *Understanding Central America.* Boulder, CO: Westview Press, 1993.

Boswell, Thomas D., and James R. Curtis. *The Cuban American Experience: Culture, Images and Perspectives.* Totowa, NJ: Rowman & Allanheld Publishers, 1984.

Botari, Mary. "Trade Deficit in Food Safety: Proposed NAFTA Expansions Replicate Limits on U.S. Food Safety Policy That Are Contributing to Unsafe Food Imports," Public Citizen, July 25, 2007.

Brackenridge, Henry Marie. "South America: A Letter on Present State of That Country to James Monroe." Washington, D.C.: Office of the National Register, October 15, 1817.

Bradford, William. *Of Plymouth Plantation, 1620–1647.* Edited by Samuel E. Morrison. New York: Random House, 1952.

Brigada, Anna-Catherine. "Nearly 60% of Migrants from Guatemala's Dry Corridor Cited Climate Change and Food Insecurity as Their Reason for Leaving," Univision, May 11, 2018.

Brimelow, Peter. *Alien Nation: Common Sense About America's Immigration Disaster.* New York: Random House, 1995.

Brooke-Eisen, Lauren. "America's Faulty Perception of Crime Rates," Brennan Center for Justice, March 16, 2015.

Brown, Charles H. *Agent of Manifest Destiny: The Lives and Times of the Filibusters.* Chapel Hill: University of North Carolina Press, 1980.

Brusi, Rima, and Isar Godreau. "Dismantling Public Education in Puerto Rico," in *Aftershocks of Disaster: Puerto Rico Before and After the Storm.* Edited by Yarimar Bonilla and Marisol Lebrón. Chicago: Haymarket Books, 2019.

Bunau-Varilla, Phillipe. *The Great Adventure of Panama.* New York: Doubleday, Page & Company, 1920.

Burgen, Stephen. "US Now Has More Spanish Speakers Than Spain—Only Mexico Has More." *The Guardian*, June 29, 2015.

Bush, Rod. *The New Black Vote: Politics and Power in Four American Cities.* San Francisco: Synthesis, 1984.

Cabeza de Vaca, Alvar Núñez. *Adventures in the Unknown Interior of America.* Translated and edited by Cyclone Covey. Albuquerque: University of New Mexico, 1990.

Cafferty, Pastora San Juan. "The Language Question: The Dilemma of Bilingual Education for Hispanics in America," in *Ethnic Relations in America: Immigration, the Cities, Lingualism, Ethnic Politics, Group Rights.* Edited by Lance Liebman. Englewood Cliffs, NJ: Prentice Hall, 1982.

Calder, Bruce J. *The Impact of Intervention: The Dominican Republic During the U.S. Occupation of 1916–1924.* Austin: University of Texas Press, 1984.

Calderón, Laura Y., Kimberly Heinle, Octavio Rodríguez Ferreira, and David A. Shirk. *Organized Crime and Violence in Mexico: Analysis Through 2018.* Justice in Mexico, Department of Political Science and International Relations, University of San Diego. San Diego: UCSD, April 2019.

Canales, Judge J. T. "Juan N. Cortina Presents His Motion for a New Trial." *Collected Papers of the Lower Rio Grande Valley Historical Society.* Vol. 1. Harlingen, Texas: 1949–1979.

Capps, Randy, Doris Meissner, Ariel G. Ruiz Soto, Jessica Bolter, and Sarah Pierce. "From Control to Crisis: Changing Trends and Policies Reshaping U.S.-Mexico Border Enforcement." Migration Policy Institute, August 2019.

Carr, Albert Z. *The World and William Walker.* New York: Harper & Row, 1963.

Carr, Norma. "The Puerto Ricans in Hawaii: 1900–1958." University of Michigan, doctoral dissertation, 1989.

Carr, Raymond. *Puerto Rico: A Colonial Experiment.* New York: Vintage Books, 1984.

Castañeda, Carlos. *The Mexican Side of the Texas Revolution.* Washington, D.C.: Documentary Publications, 1971.

———. *Our Heritage in Texas, 1519–1933.* Vol. 6. New York: Arno Press, 1976.

Castañeda, Jorge G. *The Mexican Shock: Its Meaning for the U.S.* New York: The New Press, 1995.

Castro Caycedo, Germán. *El Hueco: La entrada ilegal de colombianos a Estados Unidos por México, Bahamas y Haití.* Bogotá: Planeta Colombiana Editorial S.A., 1989.

Cavazo Garza, Israel. *Diccionario Biográfico de Nuevo León.* Tomo 1. Monterrey: Universidad Autónoma de Nuevo León, 1984.

Center on Extremism of the Anti-Defamation League. "Mainstreaming Hate: The Anti-Immigrant Movement in the U.S.," November 29, 2018.

Centers for Disease Control and Prevention. "Risk for COVID-19 Infection, Hospitalization and Death by Race/Ethnicity," March 12, 2021.

———. "Demographic Characteristics of People Receiving COVID-19 Vaccinations in the United States," March 15, 2021.

Centro de Estudios Fronterizos y de Promoción de los Derechos Humanos. *La Industria Maquiladora en Reynosa y Matamoros.* Tamaulipas, Mexico, 1992.

Centro de Estudios Puertorriqueños. *Documents of the Puerto Rican Migration.* Research Foundation of the City University of New York, 1977.

———. *Extended Roots: From Hawaii to New York, Migraciones Puertorriqueñas.* New York: CUNY, 1988.

Chávez, John. *The Lost Land: The Chicano Image of the Southwest.* Albuquerque: University of New Mexico Press, 1984.

Chavez, Linda. *Out of the Barrio: Toward a New Politics of Hispanic Assimilation.* New York: Basic Books, 1991.

Chicago Daily Law Bulletin. "John Marshall Marks a Century Since its First Latino Graduate," November 27, 2012.

Chisti, Muzaffa, Sara Pierce, and Jessica Bolter. "The Obama Record on Deportations: Deporter in Chief or Not." Migration Policy Institute, January 26, 2017.

Chomsky, Aviva. *West Indian Workers and the United Fruit Company in Costa Rica, 1870–1940.* Baton Rouge: Louisiana State University Press, 1996.

Clark, David D. "The Mariel Cuban Problem." New York Department of Correctional Services, Division of Program Planning, Research and Evaluation, April 1991.

Clemens, Michael A. "Violence, Development, and Migration Waves: Evidence from Central American Child Migrant Apprehensions," Center for Global Development, Working Paper 459, July 2017.

Cloward, Richard A., and Frances Fox Piven. *Why Americans Don't Vote.* New York: Pantheon Books, 1988.

Coaston, Jane, Peter Brimelow, and VDare. "The White Nationalist Website with Close Ties to the Right, Explained," *Vox,* September 24, 2018.

Cockcroft, James D. *Outlaws in the Promised Land: Mexican Immigrant Workers and America's Future.* New York: Grove Press, 1986.

Cohen, Felix. "Americanizing the White Man." *America Scholar* 21, no. 2 (1952).

Colby, Jason M. *The Business of Empire: United Fruit, Race, and U.S. Expansion in Central America.* Ithaca, NY: Cornell University Press, 2013.

Collier, Simon, Thomas E. Skidmore, and Harold Blakemore, eds. *The Cambridge Encyclopedia of Latin America.* New York: Cambridge University Press, 1992.

Collins, Shannon. "Puerto Ricans Represented Throughout U.S. Military History." *Department of Defense News*, October 14, 2016.

Colón, Jesús. *A Puerto Rican in New York and Other Sketches*. New York: Mainstream Publishers, 1961.

Comisionado Nacional de lo Derechos Humanos. *Informe Anual Sobre El Estado General de Los Derechos Humanos en Honduras, Año 2013*. Honduras: CONADEH, 2014.

Commager, Henry Steele. *The Empire of Reason: How Europe Imagined and America Realized the Enlightenment*. New York: Doubleday/Anchor, 1977.

———. *Documents of American History*. Vol. 1, *To 1899*. Englewood Cliffs, NJ: Prentice Hall, 1988.

Commonwealth of Puerto Rico, Department of Labor and Human Resources. *Puerto Rico Economic Analysis Report 2015–2016*. San Juan, 2016.

Congressional Research Service. "American War and Military Operations Casualties: Lists and Statistics," September 24, 2019.

———. "The Trump Administration's 'Zero Tolerance' Immigration Enforcement Policy," February 26, 2019.

———. "Central American Migration: Root Causes and U.S. Policy," June 13, 2019.

Connolly, Brian J. "Promise Unfulfilled? Zoning, Disparate Impact and Affirmatively Furthering Fair Housing," *Urban Lawyer*, Fall 2016, American Bar Association.

Conniff, Michael L. *Black Labor on a White Canal: Panama, 1904–1981*. Pittsburgh: University of Pittsburgh Press, 1985.

Corbett, Theodore G. "Migration to a Spanish Imperial Frontier in the Seventeenth and Eighteenth Centuries: St. Augustine." *Hispanic American Historical Review* 54, no. 3 (August 1974).

Cordero Guzmán, Héctor. "Some Contradictions of Dependent Development in Puerto Rico in the Context of Global Economy." Centro de Estudios Puertorriqueños, September 19, 1996.

Crawford, James. *Hold Your Tongue: Bilingualism and the Politics of "English Only."* Reading, MA: Addison-Wesley Publishing Company, 1992.

Crossa, Mateo. "Maquiladora Industry Wages in Central America Are Not Living Wages." Center for Economic and Policy Research, May 20, 2015.

Crow, John A. *The Epic of Latin America*. Berkeley: University of California Press, 1992.

Cruse, Harold. *Plural but Equal: Blacks and Minorities in America's Plural Society*. New York: William Morrow, 1987.

Cummings, William. "Federal Appeals Court Rules Trump's Sanctuary City Order Unconstitutional," *USA Today*, August 1, 2018.

Davidson, Ann J. "A Credit for All Reasons: The Ambivalent Role of Section 936." *University of Miami Inter-American Law Review* 19, no. 1 (October 1, 1987).

Davidson, Chandler. *Race and Class in Texas Politics*. Princeton, NJ: Princeton University Press, 1990.

Dávila Colón, Luis R. "The Blood Tax: The Puerto Rican Contribution to the United States War Effort." *Review of the Colegio de Abogados de Puerto Rico*, November 1979.

Davis, Julie Hirshfield, and Maggie Haberman. "Trump Pardons Joe Arpaio, Who Became Face of Crackdown on Illegal Immigration," *New York Times*, August 25, 2017.

De la Garza, Rodolfo, Manuel Orozco, and Miguel Baraona. *The Binational Impact of Latino Remittances*. Report of the Tomás Rivera Policy Institute. Claremont, CA, March 1997.

De la Garza Treviño, Ciro. *Historia de Tamaulipas: Anales y Efemérides*. Mexico City: Princeton University Press, 1956.

De las Casas, Bartolomé. *A Short Account of the Destruction of the Indies*. London: Penguin Classics, 1992.

De León, Arnoldo. *Tejanos and the Numbers Game: A Socio-Historical Interpretation from the Federal Censuses, 1850–1900*. Albuquerque: University of New Mexico Press, 1989.

De Nogales, Rafael. *The Looting of Nicaragua*. New York: Robert M. McBride & Company, 1928.

Deive, Carlos Esteban. *Las Emigraciones Dominicanas a Cuba (1795–1808)*. Santo Domingo: Fundación Cultural Dominicana, 1989.

Del Valle, Manuel. "Developing a Language-Based National Origin Discrimination Modality." *Journal of Hispanic Policy (1989–1990)*. John F. Kennedy School of Government, Harvard University, 1990.

Denevan, William M. *The Native Population of the Americas in 1492*. Madison: University of Wisconsin Press, 1992.

DeParle, Jason. "Shift Against Immigration Lifted a Young Firebrand: How a Movement Allowed Miller to Lead a Crusade from the White House," *New York Times*, August 18, 2019.

Díaz, Elba, and Arturo Massol-Deya. "Trace Element Composition in Forage Samples from a Military Target Range, Three Agricultural Areas, and One Natural Area in Puerto Rico." *Caribbean Journal of Science* 39, no. 2 (2003).

Díaz-Callejas, Apolinar. *Colombia–Estados Unidos: Entre la Autonomía y la Subordinación de la Independencia a Panamá*. Bogotá: Planeta Colombiana Editorial S.A., 1997.

Díaz del Castillo, Bernal. *The Conquest of New Spain*. London: Penguin Books, 1963.

Dietz, James L. *Economic History of Puerto Rico: Institutional Change and Capitalist Development*. Princeton, NJ: Princeton University Press, 1986.

Dietz, James L., and Emilio Pantojas-García. "Puerto Rico's New Role in the Caribbean: The High-Finance/Maquiladora Strategy," in *Colonial Dilemma: Critical Perspectives on Contemporary Puerto Rico.* Edited by Edwin Meléndez and Edgardo Meléndez. Boston: South End Press, 1993.

Diez Castillo, Luis A. *El Canal de Panamá y Su Gente.* Panamá: L. A. Diez Castillo, 1990.

Domínguez-Villegas, Rodrigo, et al. "Vote Choice of Latino Voters in the 2020 Presidential Election." UCLA Latino Politics and Policy Initiative, January 19, 2021.

Drake, Paul W., ed. *Money Doctors, Foreign Debts, and Economic Reforms in Latin America from the 1890s to the Present.* Wilmington, DE: Scholarly Resources, 1994.

Duany, Jorge. *Los Dominicanos en Puerto Rico: Migración en la Semi-Periferia.* Río Piedras, PR: Ediciones Huracán, 1990.

Dunn, Robert W. *American Foreign Investments.* New York: Viking Press, 1926.

Durham, George. *Taming the Nueces Strip: The Story of McNelly's Rangers.* Austin: University of Texas Press, 1962.

Dwyer, Augusta. *On the Line: Life on the US-Mexican Border.* London: Latin American Bureau, 1994.

Eckes, Alfred E., Jr. *Opening America's Market: U.S. Foreign Trade Policy Since 1776.* Chapel Hill: University of North Carolina Press, 1995.

Eisenhower, John S. D. *So Far from God: The U.S. War with Mexico, 1846–1848.* New York: Doubleday, 1989.

Elliot, J. H. *The Old World and the New.* New York: Cambridge University Press, 1970.

Elliot, Larry. "World's 26 Richest People Own as Much as Poorest 50%, Says Oxfam," *The Guardian*, January 20, 2019.

Elton, Geoffrey. *The English.* Cambridge, MA: Blackwell Publishers, 1995.

Engstrom, James D. "Industry and Immigration in Dalton, Georgia," in *Latino Workers in the Contemporary South.* Edited by Arthur D. Murphy et al. Athens: University of Georgia Press, 2001.

Epstein, Reid J. "NCLR Head: Obama 'Deporter-in-Chief,'" *Politico*, March 4, 2014.

Equipo de Investigaciones Laborales (EIL)/Red de Solidaridad de la Maquila (RSM). *Salarios de Maquilas en Centro América 2018 e Inciativas Internacionales por un Salario Digno.* Toronto: October 2018.

———. *Los Salarios Mínimos de Maquila y las Canastas Básicas de Alimento en Cuatro Países de Centroamérica 2019.* San Salvador, October 2019.

Ericson Eblen, Jack. *The First and Second United States Empires: Governors and Territorial Government, 1784–1912.* Pittsburgh: University of Pittsburgh Press, 1968.

Eschbach, Karl, Jacqueline Hagan, Nestor Rodriguez, Ruben Hernandez-Leon, and Stanley Bailey. "Death at the Border." *The International Migration Review* 33, no. 2 (Summer 1999).

Escobar, Cristina. "Extraterritorial Political Rights and Dual Citizenship in Latin America." *Latin American Research Review* 42, no. 3 (2007).

Esquenazi-Mayo, Roberto, ed. *El Padre Valera: Pensador, Sacerdote, Patriota.* Washington D.C.: Georgetown University Press, 1990.

Esquivel, Gerardo. "The Dynamics of Income Inequality in Mexico since NAFTA." *Economia* 12, no.1 (2011).

Esteva-Fabregat, Claudio. *Mestizaje in Ibero-America.* Translated by John Wheat. Tucson: University of Arizona Press, 1995.

Fagen, Richard R., Richard A. Brody, and Thomas J. O'Leary. *Cubans in Exile: Disaffection and Revolution.* Palo Alto: Stanford University Press, 1968.

Falcón, Angelo. "Beyond La Macarena: The New City Latino Vote." *Hispanic Link Weekly Report* 25 (November 1996).

Fanon, Frantz. *The Wretched of the Earth.* New York: Grove Press, 1963.

Farley, Robert. "Trump's Bogus Voter Fraud Claims Revisited," FactCheck .org, January 25, 2017.

Faulk, Odie B. *The Last Years of Spanish Texas, 1778–1821.* London: Mouton, 1964.

Fernández, Ronald. *The Disenchanted Island: Puerto Rico and the United States in the Twentieth Century.* New York: Praeger, 1992.

———. *Prisoner of Colonialism: The Struggle for Justice in Puerto Rico.* Monroe, ME: Common Courage Press, 1994.

———. *Cruising the Caribbean: U.S. Influence and Intervention in the Twentieth Century.* Monroe, ME: Common Courage Press, 1994.

Fernández Retamar, Roberto. *Caliban and Other Essays.* Translated by Edward Baker. Minneapolis: University of Minnesota Press, 1989.

Ferreras, Ramón Alberto. *Trujillo y sus Mujeres.* Santo Domingo: Editorial del Nordeste, 1982.

Field Institute. "California Opinion Index: A Summary Analysis of Voting in the 1994 General Election." San Francisco: Field Institute, 1995.

Figueroa, Loida. *Tres Puntos Claves: Lares, Idioma y Soberanía.* San Juan: Editorial Edil, 1972.

Financial Oversight and Management Board for Puerto Rico (FOMB). *Special Investigation Committee: Independent Investigator's Final Investigative Report.* San Juan, August 20, 2018.

Fisher, John. *Commercial Relations Between Spain and Spanish America in the Era of Free Trade, 1778–1796.* Liverpool: Centre for Latin American Studies, University of Liverpool, 1985.

Fitzpatrick, Joseph P. *Puerto Rican Americans: The Meaning of the Migration to the Mainland.* Englewood Cliffs, NJ: Prentice Hall, 1987.

——. *The Stranger Is Our Own: Reflections on the Journey of Puerto Rican Migrants*. Kansas City: Sheed & Ward, 1996.

Flagg, Anna. "The Myth of the Criminal Immigrant," *New York Times*, March 30, 2018.

Flores-Yeffal, Nadia Y., and Karen A. Pren. "Predicting Unauthorized Salvadoran Migrants' First Migration to the United States between 1965 and 2007." *Journal on Migration and Human Security* 1, no.14 (2018).

Folkman, David, Jr. *The Nicaragua Route*. Salt Lake City: University of Utah Press, 1972.

Foner, Laura, and Eugene D. Genovese, eds. *Slavery in the New World*. Englewood Cliffs, NJ: Prentice Hall, 1969.

Foner, Philip S. *The Spanish-Cuban-American War and the Birth of American Imperialism*. 2 vols. New York: Monthly Review Press, 1972.

——. *Labor and the American Revolution*. Westport, CT: Greenwood Press, 1976.

Frank, Dana. *The Long Honduran Night: Resistance, Terror, and the United States in the Aftermath of the Coup*. Chicago: Haymarket Books, 2018.

Free, Lloyd. "Attitudes of the Cuban People Toward the Castro Regime," Princeton, NJ: Institute for International Social Research, 1960.

Frost, Elsa Cecilia, et al. *Labor and Laborers Through Mexican History*. Tucson: University of Arizona Press, 1979.

Fuchs, Lawrence H. *Hawaii Pono: A Social History*. New York: Harcourt, Brace & World, 1996.

Funes, Freddy. "Removal of Central American Gang Members: How Immigration Laws Fail to Reflect Global Reality," *University of Miami Law Review*, October 1, 2008.

Galeano, Eduardo. *Open Veins of Latin America: Five Centuries of the Pillage of a Continent*. New York: Monthly Review Press, 1973.

Gallagher, Kevin P., and Margaret Meyers. "China-Latin America Finance Database." Washington, D.C.: InterAmerican Dialogue, 2019.

Gálvez, Alyshia. *Eating NAFTA: Trade, Food Policies, and the Destruction of Mexico*. Oakland: University of California Press, 2018.

García, Ignacio M. *United We Win: The Rise and Fall of La Raza Unida Party*. Tucson: Masrc, 1989.

García, María Cristina. *Havana USA: Cuban Exiles and Cuban Americans in South Florida, 1959–1994*. Berkeley: University of California Press, 1996.

García-Passalacqua, Juan Manuel. "The 1993 Plebiscite in Puerto Rico: A First Step to Decolonization." *Current History* 93, no. 581 (March 1994).

García-Passalacqua, Juan Manuel, and Carlos Rivera Lugo, eds. *Puerto Rico y los Estado Unidos: El Proceso de Consulta y Negociación de 1989 y 1990*. Vol. 2. Río Piedras, PR: Editorial de la Universidad de Puerto Rico, 1991.

Garcilazo, Jeffrey Marcos. *Traqueros: Mexican Railroad Workers in the United States 1870-1930*. Denton, TX: University of North Texas Press, 2012.

Gilbert, Alan. *The Latin American City*. London: Latin American Bureau, 1994.

Gimpel, James G. "Latino Voting in the 2006 Election: Realignment to the GOP Remains Distant," Center for Immigration Studies, March 2007.

Glasser, Ruth. *My Music Is My Flag: Puerto Rican Musicians and Their New York Communities, 1917-1940*. Berkeley: University of California Press, 1995.

Glazer, Nathan, and Daniel P. Moynihan. *Beyond the Melting Pot*. Cambridge, MA: MIT Press, 1963.

Gleijeses, Piero. *Shattered Hope: The Guatemalan Revolution and the United States, 1944-1954*. Princeton, NJ: Princeton University Press, 1991.

Globalm, Banyan. *USAID/Guatemala Gender Analysis Final Report 2018*. United States Agency for International Development, September 14, 2018.

Goldfinch, Charles W. "Juan N. Cortina, 1824-1892: A Re-Appraisal." University of Chicago, master's thesis, 1949.

Goldstein, Richard. "The Big Mango." *New York*, August 7, 1972.

Gomez, Alan. "The Six Countries 300,000 Must Return to with End of TPS Program," *USA Today*, October 15, 2018.

Gómez Quiñones, Juan. *Chicano Politics: Reality and Promise, 1940-1990*. Albuquerque: University of New Mexico Press, 1990.

Gonzales, Alfonso. *Reform Without Justice: Latino Migrant Politics and the Homeland Security State*. New York: Oxford University Press, 2014.

Gonzalez-Barrera, Angela, and Jens Manuel Krogstad. "What We Know About Illegal Migration from Mexico," Pew Research Center, June 28, 2019.

González, Juan. "The Turbulent Progress of Puerto Ricans in Philadelphia." *Bulletin of the Center for Puerto Rican Studies* 2, no. 2 (Winter 1987-1988).

Gore, Charles. "The Rise and Fall of the Washington Consensus as a Paradigm for Developing Countries." *World Development* 28, no. 5. (2000).

Gottfried, Robert S. *The Black Death*. New York: The Free Press, 1993.

Gould, L. Hannah, et al. "Outbreaks of Disease Associated with Food Imported into the United States, 1996-2014." *Emerging Infectious Diseases Journal* 23, no. 7 (March 2017).

Grabow, Colin. "New Reports Detail Jones Act's Cost to Puerto Rico," Cato Institute, February 25, 2019.

Gramlich, John, and Luis Noe-Bustamante. "What's Happening at the U.S.-Mexico Border in Five Charts," Pew Research Center, November 1, 2019.

Grant, Charles. *Democracy in the Connecticut Frontier Town of Kent*. New York: Columbia University Press, 1961.

Grant, Ulysses S. *Personal Memoirs of U. S. Grant*, vol. 1. New York: Charles A. Webster & Co., 1885.

Grasmuck, Sherri, and Patricia R. Pessar. *Between Two Islands: Dominican International Migration.* Berkeley: University of California Press, 1991.

Gregory, Desmond. *Brute New World: The Rediscovery of Latin America in the Early Nineteenth Century.* London: British Academic Press, 1992.

Grimaldi, Victor. *El Diario Secreto de la Intervención Norteamericana de 1965.* Santo Domingo: Amigo del Hogar, 1989.

Guerra y Sánchez, Ramiro. *La Expansión Territorial de los Estados Unidos: A Expensas de España y de los Países Hispanoamericanos.* La Habana: Editorial del Consejo Nacional de Universidades, 1964.

Gugliotta, Guy, and Jeff Leen. *Kings of Cocaine.* New York: Harper Paperbacks, 1990.

Gutiérrez, José Angel. *The Making of a Chicago Militant: Lessons from Cristal.* Madison: University of Wisconsin Press, 1998.

Hagan, Jacqueline Maria. *Deciding to Be Legal: A Maya Community in Houston.* Philadelphia: Temple University Press, 1994.

Halperin-Donghi, Tulio. *The Contemporary History of Latin America.* Durham, NC: Duke University Press, 1993.

Harper, Brian. "Get the Numbers: Immigration Enforcement in the Trump Era," *Americas Society/Council of the Americas,* August 14, 2018.

Harris, William Warner. *Puerto Rico's Fighting 65th U.S. Infantry: From San Juan to Chorwan.* San Rafael, CA: Presidio Press, 1980.

Harrison, Benjamin. "The United States and the 1909 Nicaragua Revolution," *Caribbean Quarterly* 41, no. 3/4 (September–December 1995).

Hart, John Mason. *Empire and Revolution: The Americans in Mexico Since the Civil War.* Berkeley: University of California Press, 2001.

Hazen, Don. *Facts and Fictions About "Free Trade."* New York: Institute for Alternative Journalism, 1993.

Healy, David. *Drive to Hegemony: The United States in the Caribbean, 1898-1917.* Madison: University of Wisconsin Press, 1988.

Hegeman, Roxana. "New Voter Get Notices Listing Wrong Dodge City Polling Site," Associated Press, October 25, 2018.

Hennessey-Fiske, Molly. "Six Migrant Children Have Died in U.S. Custody. Here's What We Know About Them," *Los Angeles Times,* May 24, 2019.

Herman, Edward S., and Frank Brodhead. *Demonstration Elections: U.S.-Staged Elections in the Dominican Republic, Vietnam, and El Salvador.* Boston: South End Press, 1984.

Hermann, Hamlet. *Francis Caamaño.* Santo Domingo: Editorial Alfa y Omega, 1983.

Hernández, Ramona, Francisco Rivera-Batiz, and Roberto Agodini. "Dominican New Yorkers: A Socioeconomic Profile." *Dominican Research Monographs.* New York: CUNY Dominican Studies Institute, 1995.

Hess, Abigail. "29-year-old Alexandria Ocasio-Cortez Makes History as the Youngest Woman Ever Elected to Congress," CNBC, November 7, 2018.

Hesson, Ted. "15 Companies that Profit from Border Security," ABC News, April 15, 2013.

Hesson, Ted, and Lorraine Woellert. "DHS and HHS Officials Blindsided by 'Zero Tolerance' Border Policy," *Politico*, October 24, 2018.

Holmes, Brian. "Wilder's All-Latino Leadership a First for Idaho," 7KTVB .com, February 10, 2016.

Horsman, Reginald. *Race and Manifest Destiny: The Origins of American Racial Anglo-Saxonism*. Cambridge, MA: Harvard University Press, 1981.

Hostos Community College. "Hostos Community College Student Profile," 2016.

Human Rights Watch. *Mexico, No Guarantees: Sex Discrimination in Mexico's Maquiladora Sector*. New York, August 1996.

———. *War Without Quarter: Colombia and International Humanitarian Law*. New York, 1998.

Humboldt, Alexander von. *Political Essay on the Kingdom of New Spain*. Norman: University of Oklahoma Press, 1988.

Hunt, Darnell, et al. *Hollywood Diversity Report 2018: Five Years of Progress and Missed Opportunities*. Los Angeles: UCLA College of Social Sciences, February, 2018.

Hurth, Salim. "Hired Labor's Share of Income Is Lowest in Puerto Rico." *The Heritage Foundation*. Issue Brief no. 4502, December 29, 2015.

Huseman, Jessica. "How the Case for Voter Fraud was Tested—and Utterly Failed," *ProPublica*, June 19, 2018.

Ibe, Peniel. "Trump's Attacks on Legal Immigration System Explained," American Friends Service Committee, October 3, 2019.

Immerman, Richard H. *The CIA in Guatemala: The Foreign Policy of Intervention*. Austin: University of Texas Press, 1982.

Immigrant Legal Resource Center. "The Rise of Sanctuary: Getting Local Officers Out of the Business of Deportations in the Trump Era," January 2018.

Institute for Criminal Policy Research. "World Prison Population List, Eleventh Edition," 2015.

Institute for Puerto Rican Policy. *The Puerto Rican and Latino Vote in the 1984 NYS Democratic Presidential Primary*. New York, April 5, 1984.

———. *Puerto Ricans and the 1988 Presidential Elections: Results from the National Puerto Rican Opinion Survey*. New York, November 7, 1988.

———. *The 1989 Mayoral Election and Charter Revision Vote in New York City: The Role of the Puerto Rican/Latino Voter*. New York, November, 1989.

———. *The Dinkins Administration and the Puerto Rican Community: Lessons From the Puerto Rican Experience with African-American Mayors in Chicago and Philadelphia*. New York, February 1990.

Instituto Nacional de Estadística, Geografía e Informática (INEGI). "Indicadores de Establecimientos Con Programa IMMEX, Cifras Durante Febrero de 2019." Mexico City, April 29, 2019.

———. "Síntesis Metodológica de la Estadística del Programa de la Industria Manufacturera, Maquiladora y Servicios de Exportación." Mexico City, 2015.

Inter-American Commission on Human Rights Report. "Preliminary Observations Concerning the Human Rights Situation in Honduras." Organization of American States, December 5, 2014.

Inter-American Development Bank. *Annual Report 1986*. Washington, D.C., 1987.

———. *Annual Report 1994*. Washington, D.C., 1995.

———. *Annual Report 1996*. Washington, D.C., 1997.

International Crisis Group. "El Salvador's Crisis of Perpetual Violence," Latin America Report, no. 64, December 19, 2017.

Jefferson, Thomas. *Notes on the State of Virginia*. Boston: H. Sprague, 1802.

Jennings, Francis. *The Invasion of America: Indians, Colonialism and the Cant of Conquest*. New York: W. W. Norton, 1976.

Jennings, James, and Monte Rivera. *Puerto Rican Politics in Urban America*. Westport, CT: Greenwood Press, 1984.

Johansen, Bruce E. *Forgotten Founders: How the American Indians Helped Shape Democracy*. Boston: Harvard Common Press, 1982.

Johnston, Jake, and Stephan Lefebvre. "Honduras Since the Coup: Economic and Social Outcomes." Center for Economic Policy and Research, November 2013.

Jones, Anson. *Memoranda and Official Correspondence Relating to the Republic of Texas, Its History and Annexation*. New York: Arno Press, 1973.

Josephy, Alvin, Jr. *The Indian Heritage of America*. Boston: Houghton Mifflin, 1991.

Kahn, Robert S. *Other People's Blood: U.S. Immigration Prisons in the Reagan Decade*. Boulder, CO: Westview Press, 1996.

Kamarck, Elaine, and Christine Stenglein. "How Many Undocumented Immigrants Are in the United States and Who Are They?" Brookings Institution, November 12, 2019.

Kanellos, Nicolas. *A History of Hispanic Theater in the U.S.: Origins to 1940*. Austin: University of Texas Press, 1990.

Karns, Thomas. *Tropical Enterprise: The Standard Fruit and Steamship Company in Latin America*. Baton Rouge: Louisiana State University Press, 1978.

Kearney, Milo. *More Studies in Brownsville History*. Brownsville, TX: Pan American University, 1989.

Keen, Benjamin. "The Black Legend Revisited." *Hispanic American Historical Review* 49 no. 4 (1969).

Kehoe, Alice B. *North American Indians: A Comprehensive Account*. Englewood Cliffs, NJ: Prentice Hall, 1992.

Keller, William F. *The Nation's Advocate: Henry Marie Brackenridge and Young America*. Pittsburgh: University of Pittsburgh, 1956.

Kelley, Pat. *River of Lost Dreams*. Lincoln: University of Nebraska Press, 1986.

Klein, Herbert S. *African Slavery in Latin America and the Caribbean*. Oxford, UK: Oxford University Press, 1986.

Kochhar, Rakesh, Richard Fry, and Paul Taylor. "Wealth Gaps Rise to Record Highs Between Whites, Blacks and Hispanics." Pew Hispanic Center, Social and Demographic Trends, July 26, 2011.

Krogstad, Jens Manuel, and Jynah Radford. "Education Levels of U.S. Immigrants Are on the Rise," Pew Research Center, September 14, 2018.

Kulish, Nicholas, and Mike McIntire. "An Heiress Intent on Closing America's Doors: How a Nature Lover Helped Fuel the Trump Immigration Agenda," *New York Times*, August 15, 2019.

LaFeber, Walter. *The Panama Canal: The Crisis in Historical Perspective*. New York: Oxford University Press, 1978.

———. *Inevitable Revolutions: The United States in Central America*. New York: W. W. Norton, 1993.

Lakatos, Csilla, and Fanziska Ohnsorge. "Arm's-Length Trade: A Source of Post-Crisis Trade Weakness," Policy Research Working Paper No. 8144. Washington, D.C.: World Bank, 2017.

Lamm, Richard D., and Gary Imhoff. *The Immigration Time Bomb: The Fragmenting of America*. New York: Truman Talley Books, 1985.

Landgrave, Michelangelo, and Alex Nowrasteh. "Criminal Immigrants: Their Numbers, Demographics, and Countries of Origin," Immigration and Policy Brief no. 1, Cato Institute, March 15, 2017.

Lane, James B., and Edward J. Escobar. *Forging a Community: The Latino Community in Northwest Indiana, 1919-1975*, Bloomington: Indiana University Press, 1987.

Lane, Wheaton J. *Commodore Vanderbilt: An Epic of the Steam Age*. New York: Alfred A. Knopf, 1942.

Langer, Erick, and Robert H. Jackson. *The New Latin American Mission in History*. Lincoln: University of Nebraska Press, 1995.

Langley, Lester D. *The United States and the Caribbean in the Twentieth Century*. Athens: University of Georgia Press, 1989.

———. *The Americas in the Age of Revolution, 1750–1850*. New Haven, CT: Yale University Press, 1996.

Larzelere, Alex. *Castro's Ploy—America's Dilemma: The 1980 Cuban Boatlift*. Washington, D.C.: National Defense University Press, 1980.

Latorre Cabal, Hugo. *The Revolution of the Latin American Church.* Translated by Frances K. Hendricks and Beatrice Berler. Norman: University of Oklahoma Press, 1978.

León-Portilla, Miguel. *The Broken Spears: The Aztec Account of the Conquest of Mexico.* Boston: Beacon Press, 1992.

Lewis, Oscar. *La Vida: A Puerto Rican Family in the Culture of Poverty—San Juan and New York.* New York: Random House, 1966.

Lewis, Sanford J. *Border Trouble: Rivers in Peril: A Report of Water Pollution Due to Industrial Development in Northern Mexico.* Boston: National Toxic Campaign Fund, 1991.

Lidin, Harold J. *History of the Puerto Rican Independence Movement.* Vol. 1, *19th Century.* Hato Rey: Master Typesetting of Puerto Rico, 1981.

Liebman, Lance, ed. *Ethnic Relations in America: Immigration, the Cities, Lingualism, Ethnic Politics, Group Rights.* Englewood Cliffs, NJ: Prentice Hall, 1982.

Lin, Annette. "AMLO's Crumbling Promise to Migrants," North American Congress on Latin America, July 24, 2019.

Lind, Dara. "'Immigrants are Coming Over the Border to Kill You' is the Only Speech Trump Knows How to Give,' *Vox,* January 9, 2019.

Linthicum, Kate. "Obama Ends Secure Communities Program as Part of Immigration Action," *Los Angeles Times,* November 21, 2014.

Lockward, Alfonso, Dr. *Documentos para la Historia de las Relaciones Dominico-Americanas.* Vol. 1, *1837–1860.* Santo Domingo: Editorial Corripio, 1987.

Lopez, Alfredo. *The Puerto Rican Papers: Notes on the Re-emergence of a Nation.* New York: Bobbs-Merrill, 1973.

Lopez, Mark Hugo, and Paul Taylor. "Latino Voters in the 2012 Election," Pew Research Center, Hispanic Trends, November 7, 2012.

Lozano, Rosina. *An American Language: The History of Spanish in the United States.* Oakland: University of California Press, 2018.

Lungo Uclés, Mario. *El Salvador in the Eighties: Counterinsurgency and Revolution.* Philadelphia: Temple University Press, 1996.

Luque de Sánchez, María Dolores. *La Ocupación Norteamericana y la Ley Foraker: La Opinión Pública Puertorriqueña, 1898–1904.* Río Piedras, PR: Editorial de la Universidad de Puerto Rico, 1986.

Lutz, Ellen L. *Human Rights in Mexico: A Policy of Impunity.* New York: America's Watch, June 1990.

Lynch, John, ed. *Latin American Revolutions, 1808–1826.* Norman: University of Oklahoma Press, 1994.

Mahler, Sarah J. *American Dreaming: Immigrant Life on the Margins.* Princeton, NJ: Princeton University Press, 1995.

Main, Alexander. "The Right Has Power in Latin America, but No Plan," *Jacobin,* August 3, 2019.

Malavet Vega, Pedro. *La Vellonera Está Directa: Felipe Rodríguez (La Voz) y los Años '50*. Republica Dominicana: Editorial Corripio, 1984.

Maldonado-Denis, Manuel. *The Emigration Dialectic: Puerto Rico and the USA*. New York: International Publisher, 1980.

Maquila Solidarity Network. "Catching Up on the Labour Reform #2: Mexico Budgets for the Transition," December 2019.

Marans, Daniel. "The Federal Government Failed Homeowners: How Much Blame Does Julián Castro Deserve?" *HuffPost*, April 22, 2019.

Marketwatch. "Here Are the Companies Poised to Profit From the Trump Wall," February 25, 2019.

Marte, Roberto. *Cuba y La República Dominicana: Transición Económica en el Caribe del Siglo XIX*. Santo Domingo: Editorial CENAPEC, 1988.

Martin, John Bartlow. *Overtaken by Events: The Dominican Crisis from the Fall of Trujillo to the Civil War*. New York: Doubleday, 1966.

Martínez-Alier, Verena. *Marriage, Class and Colour in Nineteenth Century Cuba: A Study of Racial Attitudes and Sexual Values in a Slave Society*. Ann Arbor: University of Michigan Press, 1989.

Mataloni, Raymond J., Jr. "U.S. Multinational Companies: Operations in 1995." *Survey of Current Business*, October 1995.

Matthews, T. J., and Brady E. Hamilton. "Total Fertility Rates by State and Race and Hispanic Origin, United States, 2017." *Centers for Disease Control National Vital Statistics Report* 68, no. 1 (January 10, 2019).

McCullough, David. *The Path Between the Seas: The Creation of the Panama Canal, 1870–1914*. New York: Simon & Schuster, 1977.

McDonald, Patrick Range. "Who Fixed Los Angeles? Not Former Mayor Antonio Villaraigosa, Say His Fiercest Critics," *Politico*, March 5, 2014.

McDougal, Topher, David A. Shirk, Robert Muggah, and John H. Patterson. "The Way of the Gun: Estimating Firearms Trafficking Across the US–Mexico Border," *Journal of Economic Geography* 15, no. 2 (2015).

McEwan, Bonnie G., ed. *The Spanish Missions of Florida*. Gainesville: University Press of Florida, 1993.

McFeely, William S. *Grant: A Biography*. New York: W. W. Norton, 1981.

McWilliams, Carey. *North from Mexico: The Spanish-Speaking People of the United States*. Edition updated by Matt S. Meier. New York: Praeger, 1990.

Mead, Rebecca. "All About the Hamiltons," *New Yorker*, February 9, 2015.

Meissner, Doris, Donald M. Kerwin, Muzaffar Chishti, and Claire Bergeron. "Immigration Enforcement in the United States: The Rise of a Formidable Machinery," Migration Policy Institute, January 2013.

Meléndez, Edwin, and Edgardo Meléndez, eds. *Colonial Dilemma: Critical Perspectives on Contemporary Puerto Rico*. Boston: South End Press, 1993.

Mendelson, Margot, Shayna Strom, and Michael Wishnie. "Collateral Damage: An Examination of ICE's Fugitive Operations Program," Migration Policy Institute, February 2009.

Merk, Frederick. *Slavery and the Annexation of Texas*. New York: Alfred A. Knopf, 1972.

Merling, Lara, and Jake Johnston. "Puerto Rico's New Fiscal Plan: Certain Pain, Uncertain Gain," Center for Economic Policy and Research, June 2018.

Merling, Lara, Kevin Cashman, Jake Johnston, and Mark Weisbrot. *Life After Debt in Puerto Rico: How Many More Lost Decades?* Washington, D.C.: Center for Economic and Policy Research, July 2017.

Merrill, Tim L. *Honduras: A Country Study*. 3rd edition, Washington, D.C.: Library of Congress, 1995.

Meyer, Gerald. *Vito Marcantonio: Radical Politician, 1902–1954*. Albany: State University of New York, 1989.

Minge, Ward Alan. *Acoma: Pueblo in the Sky*. Albuquerque: University of New Mexico Press, 1991.

Montecillo, Ian. "Yakima Elects First Latina City Council Members," *Oregon Public Broadcasting*, November 5, 2015.

Montejano, David. *Anglos and Mexicans in the Making of Texas, 1836–1986*. Austin: University of Texas Press, 1987.

Moody, Kim. *Workers in a Lean World: Unions in the International Economy*. New York: Verso, 1997.

Morales Carrión, Arturo. *Puerto Rico: A Political and Cultural History*. New York: W. W. Norton, 1983.

Morales-Moreno, Isidro. "Mexico's Agricultural Trade Policies: International Commitments and Domestic Pressure," in *Managing the Challenges of World Trade Organization Participation: 45 Case Studies*. Edited by Peter Gallagher, Patrick Low, and Andrew Stoller. Cambridge, UK: Cambridge University Press, 2005.

Moreno-Brid, Juan Carlos, Esteban Pérez Caldentey, and Pablo Ruíz Nápoles. "The Washington Consensus: A Latin American Perspective Fifteen Years Later." *Journal of Post Keynesian Economics* 27, no. 2 (2004–2005).

Mormino, Gary R., and George E. Pozzetta. *The Immigrant World of Ybor City: Italians and Their Latin Neighbors in Tampa, 1885–1985*. Urbana: University of Illinois Press, 1987.

Morris, Irwin L. "African American Voting on Proposition 187: Rethinking the Prevalence of Interminority Conflict." *Political Research Quarterly* 53, no. 1 (2000).

Morris, Lydia. "Women without Me: Domestic Organization and the Welfare State as Seen in a Coastal Community of Puerto Rico." *The British Journal of Sociology* 30, no. 3 (1979).

Morrison, Toni. "On the Backs of Blacks," *Time*, December 2, 1993.

Motivans, Mark. "Immigration, Citizenship, and the Federal Justice System, 1998-2018," U.S. Department of Justice, Bureau of Justice Statistics, August 2019.

Moya Pons, Frank. *The Dominican Republic: A National History.* New York: Hispaniola Books, 1995.

Moynihan, Daniel P. *The Negro Family: The Case for National Action.* Washington, D.C.: U.S. Department of Labor, 1965.

Munro, Dana. *Intervention and Dollar Diplomacy in the Caribbean, 1900–1921.* Princeton, NJ: Princeton University Press, 1964.

Myers, Gustavus. *History of the Great American Fortunes,* vol. 2. Chicago: C. H. Kerr, 1910.

NAFTA. *Broken Promises: The Border Betrayed.* Washington, D.C.: Public Citizen Publications, 1996.

Narea, Nicole. "The Trump Administration Just Inked Another Deal Making it Harder to Seek Asylum in the U.S.," *Vox,* September 25, 2019.

National Association of Latino Elected Officials. *1994 National Roster of Hispanic Elected Officials.* Los Angeles, 1995.

———. *1996 Latino Election Handbook.* Los Angeles, 1996.

———. *2018 National Directory of Latino Elected Officials.* Los Angeles, 2018.

National Labor Committee Education Fund. *Paying to Lose Our Jobs.* New York, September 1992.

———. *Free Trade's Hidden Secrets: Why We Are Losing Our Shirts.* New York, November 1993.

National Public Radio. "Federal Judges in 3 States Block Trump's 'Public Charge' Rule for Green Cards," October 11, 2019.

National World War II Museum. "Los Veteranos—Latinos in WWII," 2017.

Navarro, Armando. *La Raza Unida Party: A Chicano Challenge to the U.S. Two-Party Dictatorship.* Philadelphia: Temple University Press, 2000.

Nazario, Sonia. "Pay or Die," *New York Times,* July 28, 2019.

NBC News. "Why Immigration Reform Died in Congress," June 30, 2014.

Neal, Larry. *The Rise of Financial Capitalism: International Capital Markets in the Age of Reason.* Cambridge, UK: Cambridge University Press, 1990.

Nearing, Scott, and Joseph Freeman. *Dollar Diplomacy: A Study in American Imperialism.* New York: B. W. Huebsch, 1925.

Nelson Limerick, Patricia. *The Legacy of Conquest: The Unbroken Past of the American West.* New York: W. W. Norton, 1987.

Nerval, Gaston. *Autopsy of the Monroe Doctrine.* New York: Macmillan, 1934.

Neuman, William. "Dominican Candidates in New York Tout Their Pioneer Status, but History is Complicated," *New York Times,* June 27, 2016.

Newkirk, Vann R., II. "How *Shelby County v. Holder* Broke America," *Atlantic*, July 10, 2018.

———. "Puerto Rico Enters a New Age of Austerity," *Atlantic*, May 5, 2018.

Nguyen, Tiny. "Oops, GOP Docs Reveal Census Questions Were Designed to Help White Republicans," *Vanity Fair*, May 30, 2019.

Noé-Bustamante, Luis. "Key Facts about U.S. Hispanics and Their Diverse Heritage," Pew Research Center, September 16, 2019.

Noe-Bustamante, Luis, Lauren Mora, and Mark Hugo Lopez. "About One-in-Four U.S. Hispanics Have Heard of Latinx, but Just 3% Use It," Pew Research Center, August 11, 2020.

North, Anna. "How 4 Congresswomen Came to Be Known as 'The Squad,'" *Vox*, July 17, 2019.

Novak, Michael. *The Rise of the Unmeltable Ethnics: Politics and Culture in the Seventies.* New York: Macmillan, 1972.

Office of the Press Secretary. 67 "Remarks by the President on Immigration." The White House, June 15, 2012.

Office of the United States Trade Secretary. "U.S.-Mexico Trade Facts," July 23, 2009.

Organization for Economic Co-operation and Development. *Obesity Update 2017.* OECD, 2017.

O'Rourke, Ronald. "Vieques, Puerto Rico Naval Training Range: Background and Issues for Congress," Congressional Research Service, December 17, 2001.

Orozco, Manuel, and Marcela Valdivia. "Educational Challenges in Guatemala and Consequences for Human Capital and Development," *Inter-American Dialogue*, working paper, 2017.

Orozco, Manuel, Laura Porras, and Julia Yansura. "Remittances to Latin America and the Caribbean in 2018." *The Dialogue*, April 2019.

Orozco, Manuel, and Marcela Valdivia. "Educational Challenges in Guatemala and Consequences for Human Capital and Development," *Inter-American Dialogue*, working paper, 2017.

Ortega, Bob. "Border Patrol Failed to Count Hundreds of Migrant Deaths on US Soil," CNN, May 15, 2018.

Ortega Frier, José. *Memorandum Relativo a la Intervención de Sumner en la República Dominicana.* Santo Domingo: Ediciones de Taller, 1975.

Ortego y Gasca, Philip, and Arnoldo De León, eds. *The Tejano Yearbook: 1519–1978: A Selective Chronicle of the Hispanic Presence in Texas.* San Antonio: Caravel Press, 1978.

Ortiz Angleró, David. "Testimony Before the Co-Coordinators of the Interagency Working Group on Puerto Rico on the Future of Puerto Rico." Washington, D.C.: Cambio XXI, 1995.

Painter, William L., and Audrey Singer. "DHS Border Barrier Funding," Congressional Research Center, January 29, 2020.

Pantojas-García, Emilio. *Development Strategies as Ideology: Puerto Rico's Export-Led Industrialization Experience*. London: Lynne Rienner Publishers, 1990.

Parker Hanson, Earl. *Puerto Rico: Land of Wonders*. New York: Alfred A. Knopf, 1960.

Parsons, Chelsea, and Eugenio Weigand Vargas. "Beyond Our Borders: How Weak U.S. Guns Laws Contribute to Violent Crime Abroad," Center for American Progress, February 2, 2018.

Passel, Jeffrey S., and Rebecca L. Clark. *Immigrants in New York: Their Legal Status, Incomes, and Taxes*, executive summary. Washington, D.C.: Urban Institute, April 1998.

Passel, Jeffrey S., and D'Vera Cohn. "Mexicans Decline to Less Than Half of U.S. Unauthorized Immigrant Population for the First Time," Pew Research Center, June 12, 2019.

Pedraza Bailey, Silvia. "Cubans and Mexicans in the United States: The Functions of Political and Economic Migration." *Cuban Studies* 11. Pittsburgh: University of Pittsburgh Press, 1981.

———. "Los Marielitos of 1980: Race, Class, Gender and Sexuality," Association for the Study of the Cuban Economy, November 30, 2004.

Peña, Manuel H. *The Texas-Mexican Conjunto: History of a Working Class Music*. Austin: University of Texas Press, 1985.

Pérez, Louis A. *Cuba Under the Platt Amendment, 1902–1934*. Pittsburgh: University of Pittsburgh Press, 1986.

———. *Cuba and the United States: Ties of Singular Intimacy*. Athens: University of Georgia Press, 1990.

———. *Cuba Between Reform and Revolution*. New York: Oxford University Press, 1995.

Pérez, Richie. "From Assimilation to Annihilation: Puerto Rican Images in U.S. Films." *Center for Puerto Rican Studies Bulletin* 2, no. 8 (Spring 1990).

Perry, Nancy J. "What's Powering Mexico's Success." *Fortune*, February 10, 1992.

Petras, James, and Morris Morley. *Latin America in the Time of Cholera: Electoral Politics, Market Economics, and Permanent Crisis*. New York: Routledge, 1992.

Pew Research Center. "Dissecting the 2008 Electorate: Most Diverse in the U.S. History," April 30, 2009.

———. "Hispanics of Puerto Rican Origin in the United States, 2007," July 13, 2009.

———. "Modern Immigration Wave Brings 59 Million to U.S., Driving Population Growth and Change Through 2065," September 28, 2015.

———. "Remittance Flows Worldwide in 2017," April 3, 2019.

Piccone, Ted. "The Geopolitics of China's Rise in Latin America." Brookings Institution, *Geoeconomics and Global Issues,* Paper 2 (November 2016).

Plant, Roger. *Sugar and Modern Slavery: A Tale of Two Countries.* London: Zed Books, 1987.

Portes, Alejandro. "The Rise of Ethnicity: Determinants of Ethnic Perceptions Among Cuban Exiles in Miami." *American Sociological Review* 49, no. 3 (June 1984).

Portes, Alejandro, and Alex Stepick. *City on the Edge: The Transformation of Miami.* Berkeley: University of California Press, 1993.

Portes, Alejandro, Juan M. Clark, and Manuel M. López. "Six Years Later, the Process of Incorporation of Cuban Exiles in the United States: 1973–1979." *Cuban Studies,* July 1981–January 1982.

Portes, Alejandro, and Rubén G. Rumbaut. *Immigrant America: A Portrait,* 4th ed. Berkeley: University of California Press, 2014.

Pratt, Julius W. *Expansionists of 1898: The Acquisition of Hawaii and the Spanish Islands.* Chicago: Quadrangle Paperbacks, 1964.

Price Waterhouse. *Update of Baseline Study of Honduran Export Processing Zones. Report to United States Agency for International Development.* Washington, D.C., 1993.

Public Citizen. "Redo of USMCA Better Than Original NAFTA After Year-long Effort to Improve Trump's 2018 deal," December 10, 2019.

Puerto Rico Planning Board. *Economic Report to the Governor 1995.* San Juan, March 1996.

Putney, Bryant. "Protection of American Interests in Mexico," In *Editorial Research Reports 1938,* vol. I, Washington, D.C.: CQ Press, 1938.

Quintanilla, Luis. *A Latin American Speaks.* New York: Macmillan, 1943.

Rama, Carlos M. *La Idea de la Federación Antillana en los Independentistas Puertorriqueños del Siglo XIX.* Río Piedras, PR: Librería Internacional, 1971.

Rapoza, Kenneth. "Hugo Chavez Cancer Conspiracy Theories Resurface After Death," *Forbes,* March 6, 2013.

Ray, Rebecca, and Keehan Wang, *China-Latin America Economic Bulletin, 2019 Edition.* Boston: Boston University Global Development Policy Center, 2019.

Rayburn, John C., and Virginia Kemp Rayburn. *Century of Conflict, 1821–1913: Incidents in the Lives of Willian Neale and William A. Neale, Early Settlers in South Texas.* Waco, TX: Texian Press, 1966.

Research Institute for Cuba and the Caribbean Center for Advanced International Studies. "The Cuban Immigration 1959–1966 and Its Impact on Miami–Dade County, Florida." University of Miami, July 10, 1967.

Reuters. "Judge Finds Kansas' Kris Kobach in Contempt of Court," April 18, 2018.

Reyes, Belinda I. "Dynamics of Immigration: Return Migration to Western Mexico." Public Policy Institute of California, January 28, 1997.

Ribando, Clare M. "Gangs in Central America," Congressional Research Service Report for Congress, July 27, 2007.

Ríos, Palmira N. "Acercamiento al Conflicto Dominico-Boricua." *Center for Puerto Rican Studies Bulletin* 4, no. 2 (Spring 1992).

Rivera, Eugene. "The Puerto Rican Colony of Lorain, Ohio." *Center for Puerto Rican Studies Bulletin* 2, no. 1 (Spring 1987).

Rivera, Eugenio. "La Colonia de Lorain, Ohio." In *The Puerto Rican Diaspora: Historical Perspectives*. Edited by Carmen Whalen and Victor Vasquez. Philadelphia: Temple University Press, 2005.

Rivero, Angel. *Crónica de la Guerra Hispano Americana en Puerto Rico*. New York: Plus Ultra Educational Publishers, 1973.

Rivlin, Gary. *Fire on the Prairie: Chicago's Harold Washington and the Politics of Race*. New York: Henry Holt, 1992.

Roa, Jorge. *Los Estados Unidos y Europa en Hispano America: Interpretación Política y Económica de la Doctrina Monroe, 1823–1933*. Havana: Carasa, 1933.

Roberts, John Storm. *The Latin Tinge: The Impact of Latin American Music on the United States*. New York: Oxford University Press, 1999.

Roddick, Jackie. *The Dance of Millions: Latin America and the Debt Crisis*. London: Latin America Research Bureau, 1988.

Rodríguez, Clara. *Puerto Ricans: Born in the U.S.A.* Boston: Unwin Hyman, 1989.

———. *Latin Looks: Images of Latinas and Latinos in the U.S. Media*. Boulder, CO: Westview Press, 1997.

Rodríguez, Clara, and Héctor Cordero-Guzmán. "Placing Race in Context." *Ethnic and Racial Studies* 15, no. 4 (October 1992).

Rodríguez Demorizi, Emilio. *Luperón y Hostos*. Santo Domingo: Editorial Taller, 1975.

Rodriguez, Richard. *Hunger of Memory: The Education of Richard Rodriguez*. Toronto: Bantam Books, 1982.

Rodriguez-Fraticelli, Carlos, ed. *Gilberto Gerena Valentín, My Life As a Community Activist, Labor Organizer and Progressive Politician in New York City*. New York: Center for Puerto Rican Studies, Hunter College, 2013.

Rodrik, Dani. "Goodbye Washington Consensus, Hello Washington Confusion? A Review of the World Bank's Economic Growth in the 1990s: Learning from a Decade of Reform." *Journal of Economic Literature* 44, no. 4 (2006).

Rogin, Michael Paul. *Fathers and Children: Andrew Jackson and the Subjugation of the American Indian*. New York: Alfred A. Knopf, 1975.

Rohrbough, Malcolm. *The Land Office Business: The Settlement and Administration of American Public Lands, 1789–1837*. New York: Oxford University Press, 1968.

Rosen, Fred, and Deidre McFadyen, eds. *Free Trade and Economic Restructuring in Latin America*. New York: Monthly Review Press, 1995.

Ross, Zachary, and Wendy R. Reiser. "This Is the Worst Voter Suppression We've Seen in the Modern Era," Brennan Center for Justice, November 2, 2018.

Rubin, Nancy. *Isabella of Castile: The First Renaissance Queen*. New York: St. Martin's Press, 1991.

Ruiz, Angel L., and Fernando Zalacain. "The Economic Relation of the United States and the Puerto Rican Economies: An International Input-Output Approach." Unidad de Investigaciones Económicas, Universidad de Puerto Rico. *Boletín de Economía* 3, no. 1 (September 1997).

Said, Edward W. *Culture and Imperialism*. New York: Alfred A. Knopf, 1993.

Salazaar, Alonso. *Born to Die in Medellín*. New York: Monthly Review Press, 1990.

Saldivar, Gabriel. *Historia Compendida de Tamaulipas*. Mexico: Academia Nacional de Historia y Geografía, 1945.

Sanchez Korrol, Virginia. *From Colonia to Community: The History of Puerto Ricans in New York City, 1917–1948*. Westport, CT: Greenwood Press, 1983.

Santiago Ortíz, Nicolás. *Korea 1951, La Guerra Olvidada: El Orgullo de Haber Sobrevivido*. Río Piedras, PR: Emaco Printers, 1991.

Schaeffer, Katherine. "Racial, Ethnic Diversity Increases yet Again in the 117th Congress," Pew Research Center, January 28, 2021.

Scheips, Paul, ed. *The Panama Canal: Readings on Its History*. Wilmington, DE: Michael Glazier, 1979.

Schlesinger, Arthur M. *The Disuniting of America: Reflections on a Multicultural Society*. New York: W. W. Norton, 1992.

Schlesinger, Stephen, and Stephen Kinzer. *Bitter Fruit: The Untold Story of the American Coup in Guatemala*. New York: Doubleday, 1983.

Schulz, Heiner. "Foreign Banks in Mexico: New Conquistadors or Agents of Change?" Wharton Financial Institutions Center Working Paper no. 06-11, April 22, 2006.

Scott, Florence Johnson. *Historical Heritage of Lower Rio Grande*. San Antonio: Naylor, 1937.

———. *Royal Land Grants North of the Rio Grande, 1777–1821*. Rio Grande City, TX: La Retana Press, 1969.

Scott, Peter Dale, and Jonathan Marshall. *Cocaine Politics: Drugs, Armies, and the CIA in Central America*. Berkeley: University of California Press, 1991.

Scott, Robert E. "Manufacturing Job Loss: Trade, not Productivity, Is the Culprit," Economic Policy Institute, August 11, 2015.

Scott, Robert E., Carlos Salas, and Bruce Campbell. "Revisiting NAFTA: Still Not Working for North America's Workers," Economic Policy Institute, Briefing Paper no. 173, September 28, 2006.

Seguín, Juan N. *A Revolution Remembered: The Memoirs and Selected Correspondence of Juan N. Seguín*. Edited by Jesús De la Teja. Austin, TX: State House Press, 1991.

Seijo Bruno, Mini. *La Insurrección Nacionalista en Puerto Rico, 1950*. Río Piedras, PR: Editorial Edil, 1989.

Selser, Gregorio. *Sandino: General of the Free*. New York: Monthly Review Press, 1981.

———. *Cronología de las intervenciones extranjeras en América Latina*. Vol. 2, *1776–1848*. Mexico City: UNAM, 1994.

Shaiken, Harley. "Mexico's Labor Reform: Opportunities and Challenges for an Improved NAFTA." Testimony before the Subcommittee on Trade, Committee on Ways and Means, U.S. House of Representatives, June 25, 2019.

Shaxson, Nick. "Over a Third of World Trade Happens Inside Multinational Corporations," Tax Justice Network, April 9, 2019.

Shear, Michael D. "Obama, Daring Congress, Acts to Overhaul Immigration," *New York Times*, November 20, 2014.

Shear, Michael D, and Zolan Kanno-Youngs. "Trump Slashes Refugee Cap to 18,000, Curtailing U.S. Role as a Haven," *New York Times*, September 26, 2019.

Shelby County v. Holder, a Case Summary, Constitutional Accountability Center.

Sherman, Christopher, Martha Mendoza, and Garance Burke. "US Held Record Number of Migrant Children in Custody in 2019," Associated Press, November 12, 2019.

Shoichet, Catherine E. "Federal Judge Temporarily Blocks Trump Administration from Ending TPS," CNN, October 4, 2018.

Sinha, Anil K., and Shikah Srivastava. "Comparative Study on Recovery and Reconstruction: A Case for an International Platform," International Recovery Platform, 2003.

Slack, Jeremy, and Daniel E. Martínez. "The Geography of Migrant Death: Violence on the U.S.-Mexico Border," in *Handbook on Critical Geographies of Migration*. Edited by Katharyne Mitchell et al. Cheltenham, UK: Edward Elgar Publishing, 2019.

Smith, Adam. *The Wealth of Nations (1776)*, vol. 2. Edited by Edwin Cannan. London: University Paperbacks, 1996.

Smith, Carol, ed. *Guatemalan Indians and the State: 1540–1988*. Austin: University of Texas Press, 1992.

Smith, Stacy L., Marc Choueiti, and Katherine Pieper. "Inclusion or Invisibility? Comprehensive Annenberg Report on Diversity in Entertainment Media." Los Angeles: USC Annenberg, 2016.

Stack, John F., and Christopher L. Warren. "Ethnicity and the Politics of Symbolism in Miami's Cuban Community." *Cuban Studies* 20. Pittsburgh: University of Pittsburgh Press, 1990.

Stallings, Barbara. *Banker to the Third World: U.S. Portfolio Investment in Latin America, 1900–1986*. Berkeley: University of California Press, 1987.

State University of New York. *New York Public University Systems Embark on Multilateral Academic Collaborations with Dominican Republic Education Ministries*. December 7, 2018.

Stephens, Gena. "Changing Climate Forces Desperate Guatemalans to Flee," *National Geographic*, October 23, 2018.

Stillman, Chauncey Devereux. *Charles Stillman, 1810–1875*. New York: C. D. Stillman, 1956.

Stockwell, John. *In Search of Enemies: A CIA Story*. New York: W. W. Norton, 1978.

Suro, Roberto. *Strangers Among Us: How Latino Immigration Is Transforming America*. New York: Alfred A. Knopf, 1998.

Tackett, Michael, and Michael Wines. "Trump Disbands Commission on Voter Fraud," *New York Times*, January 3, 2018.

Tansil, Charles C. *The United States and Santo Domingo, 1798–1873: A Chapter on Caribbean Diplomacy*. Baltimore: Johns Hopkins University Press, 1983.

Taylor, Robert W., and Harry E. Vanden. "Defining Terrorism in El Salvador: "La Matanza." *Annals of the American Academy of Political and Social Science* 463 (1982).

Teitelbaum, Michael. "Right Versus Right: Immigration and Refugee Policy in the United States." *Foreign Affairs* 59, no. 1 (Fall 1980).

Teitelbaum, Michael S., and Myron Weiner, eds. *Threatened Peoples, Threatened Borders: World Migration and U.S. Policy*. New York: W. W. Norton, 1995.

Texas Department of Health. "An Investigation of Neural Tube Defects in Cameron County, Texas," July 1, 1992.

Texas Department of Health Services. "Liver and Intrahepatic Bile Duct Cancer in Texas," Texas Cancer Registry, November 2018.

Tienda, Marta. "Welfare and Work in Chicago's Inner City," *The American Economic Review* 80, no. 2 (February 1990).

Time. "Here's Donald Trump's Presidential Announcement Speech," June 16, 2015.

The Economist. "The World's Most Dangerous Cities," March 31, 2017.

The Field Institute. *California Opinion Index, A Summary Analysis of Voting in the 1994 General Election*. San Francisco: The Field Institute, 1995.

The Guardian. "Berta Cáceres: Seven Men Convicted of Murdering Honduran Environmentalist," November 29, 2018.

The New York Times. "All Presidents Are Deporters in Chief," July 14, 2019.

The Washington Post. "Trump's Voter-Fraud Commission Itself *Is* a Fraud," July 18, 2017.

Thomas, Hugh. *Conquest: Montezuma, Cortés, and the Fall of the Old Mexico*. New York: Simon & Schuster, 1993.

Torruella, Juan R. *The Supreme Court and Puerto Rico: The Doctrine of Separate and Equal*. Río Piedras, PR: Editorial de la Universidad de Puerto Rico, 1988.

Trías Monge, José. *Puerto Rico: The Trials of the Oldest Colony in the World*. New Haven, CT: Yale University Press, 1998.

Turner, John Kenneth. *Barbarous Mexico*. Chicago: C. H. Kerr, 1910.

Tzvetan, Todorov. *The Conquest of America*. New York: HarperCollins, 1984.

Uclés, Mario Lungo. *El Salvador in the Eighties: Counterinsurgency and Revolution*. Philadelphia: Temple University Press, 1996.

United Nations Conference on Trade and Development. *TNC's and World Development*. London, 1996.

United Nations Department of Economic and Social Affairs. "World Population Prospects 2019: Highlights."

United Nations Development Programme. *Human Development Report 1998*. New York: Oxford University Press, 1998.

United Nations Economic Commission for Latin America and the Caribbean. *Financing for Development in the Era of COVID-19 and Beyond: Priorities of Latin America and the Caribbean in Relation to the Financing for Development Global Policy Agenda*. CEPAL, March 11, 2021.

———. *Foreign Direct Investment in Latin America and the Caribbean*. CEPAL, August 2021.

United Nations Office on Drugs and Crime. "Transnational Organized Crime in Central America and the Caribbean: A Threat Assessment," September 2012.

United States Hispanic Leadership Institute. *Latino Electoral Potential 2000–2025*, Report no. 312. Chicago, 1998.

Urbi, Jaden. "Here's who's making money from immigration enforcement," CNBC, June 29, 2018.

U.S. Border Patrol. *Southwest Border Deaths by Fiscal Year*. March 2019.

U.S. Census Bureau. *1790 Census: Whole Number of Persons Within the Districts of the United States*. Washington, D.C.: U.S. Government Printing Office, 1790.

———. *2013-2017 American Community Survey 5-Year Estimates*. Washington, D.C.: U.S. Government Printing Office, 2017.

———. *Annual Estimates of the Resident Population by Sex, Single Year of Age, Race, and Hispanic Origin for the United States*. Washington, D.C.: U.S. Government Printing Office, 2018.

———. *Hispanic Americans Today: Current Population Reports, P23-183*. Washington, D.C.: U.S. Government Printing Office, 1993.

———. *Hispanic or Latino by Type in Puerto Rico: 2010*. Washington, D.C.: U.S. Government Printing Office, 2010.

———. *Hispanic or Latino Origin by Specific Origin Universe: Total Population, 2017*. Washington, D.C.: U.S. Government Printing Office, 2017.

———. *Language Spoken at Home: 2017*. Washington, D.C.: U.S. Government Printing Office, 2017.

———. *Statistical Abstract of the United States: 1997*. Washington, D.C.: U.S. Government Printing Office, 1997.

———. *Selected Population Profile in Puerto Rico: 2017*. Washington, D.C.: U.S. Government Printing Office, 2017.

———. *Trade in Goods with Mexico*. Washington, D.C.: U.S. Government Printing Office, 2010.

———. *U.S. Trade with Puerto Rico and U.S. Possessions, 2004*. Washington, D.C.: U.S. Government Printing Office, 2005.

———. *U.S. Trade with Puerto Rico and U.S. Possessions, 2018*. Washington, D.C.: U.S. Government Printing Office, 2019.

———. *Voting and Registration in the Election of November 2016*. Washington, D.C.: U.S. Government Printing Office, 2016.

———. *Voting and Registration in the Election of November 2018*. Washington, D.C.: U.S. Government Printing Office, 2019.

———. *Voting and Registration in the Election of 2020*. Washington, D.C.: U.S. Government Printing Office, April 2021.

U.S. Commission on Ocean Policy. *An Ocean Policy for the 21st Century, Final Report*. Washington, D.C.: U.S. Government Printing Office, 2004.

U.S. Congressional Budget Office. "Potential Economic Impacts of Changes in Puerto Rico Status Under S. 712." April 1990.

———. "The Effects of NAFTA on U.S.-Mexico Trade and GDP," May 2003.

U.S. Customs and Border Protection. "U.S. Border Patrol Apprehensions by Sector Fiscal Year 2019," October 29, 2019.

———. *Yearbook of Immigration Statistics: 2008*. Washington, D.C.: U.S. Government Printing Office, 2008.

———. *Yearbook of Immigration Statistics: 2017*. Washington, D.C.: U.S. Government Printing Office, 2017.

———. *Yearbook of Immigration Statistics: 2019*. Washington, D.C.: U.S. Government Printing Office, 2019.

U.S. Department of Justice. *1996 Statistical Yearbook of the Immigration and Naturalization Service*. Washington, D.C.: U.S. Government Printing Office, 1997.

———. "Attorney General Announces Zero-Tolerance Policy for Criminal Illegal Entry," April 6, 2018.

U.S. Department of Homeland Security. *Annual Report, Immigration Enforcement Actions: 2017*, March 2019.

U.S. General Accounting Office. *Pharmaceutical Industry Tax Benefits of Operating in Puerto Rico*. Washington, D.C.: May 1992.

———. *Puerto Rican Fiscal and Economic Trends*. Washington, D.C.: May 1997.

———. *Tax Policy: Puerto Rico and the Section 936 Tax Credit*. Washington, D.C.: June 1993.

U.S. Senate Joint Committee on Taxation. "An Overview of Special Tax Laws Related to Puerto Rico and an Analysis of the Tax and Economic

Policy Implications of Recent Legislative Options." Washington, D.C.: June 23, 2006.

U.S. State Department. "Report to Congress on Corruption in El Salvador, Guatemala, and Honduras," May 18, 2019.

U.S. White House. 53 "Remarks of President Donald J. Trump—As Prepared for Delivery," January 20, 2017.

Valentín, Luis J., and Carla Minet. "The 889 Pages of the Telegram Chat Between Rosselló Nevares and his Closest Aides," Centro de Periodismo Investigativo, July 13, 2019.

Valle Ferrer, Norma. *Luisa Capetillo: Historia de una Mujer Proscrita*. San Juan: Editorial Cultura, 1990.

Van Alstyne, R. W. *The Rising American Empire*. Chicago: Quadrangle Books, 1965.

Vanderpool, Tim. "The Festering Sanitation Crisis at Our Border," National Resources Defense Council, December 3, 2018.

Vargas, Zaragosa. *Proletarians of the North: A History of Mexican Industrial Workers in Detroit and the Midwest, 1917–1933*. Berkeley: University of California Press, 1993.

———. *Crucible of Struggle: A History of Mexican Americans from Colonial Times to the Present Era*. New York: Oxford University Press, 2011.

Vega, Bernardo. *Control y Represión en la Dictadora Trujillista*. Santo Domingo: Fundación Cultural Dominicana, 1986.

———. *Trujillo y el Control Financiereo Norteamericano*. Santo Domingo: Fundación Cultural Dominicana, 1990.

Veillette, Connie, and Susan B. Epstein. *State, Foreign Operations and Related Programs: FY 2008 Appropriations*. Congressional Research Service, December 14, 2007.

Villagrá, Gaspar Pérez de. *Historia de la Nueva México*, 1610. Translated and edited by Miguel Encinias, Alfred Rodríguez, and Joseph P. Sánchez. Albuquerque: University of New Mexico Press, 1992.

Villareal, M. Angeles. "USMCA and Mexico's New Labor Law," Congressional Research Service, May 22, 2019.

Wagenheim, Kal, and Olga Jiménez de Wagenheim. *The Puerto Ricans: A Documentary History*. Maplewood, NJ: Waterfront Press, 1998.

Wallsten, Peter. "President Obama Bristles When He is the Target of Activist Tactics He Once Used," *Washington Post*, June 10, 2012.

Weatherford, Jack. *Indian Givers: How the Indians of the Americas Transformed the World*. New York: Fawcett Columbine, 1988.

Weber, David J. *The Mexican Frontier, 1821–1846: The American Southwest Under Mexico*. Albuquerque: University of New Mexico Press, 1982.

———. *The Spanish Frontier in North America*. New Haven, CT: Yale University Press, 1992.

Weisbrot, Mark, Lara Merling, Vitor Mello, Stephan Lefebvre, and Joseph Sammut. *Did NAFTA Help Mexico? An Update After 23 Years.* Washington, D.C.: Center for Economic and Policy Research, March 2017.

Welles, Sumner. *The Time for Decision.* New York: Harper, 1944.

Weyr, Thomas. *Hispanic U.S.A.: Breaking the Melting Pot.* New York: Harper & Row, 1988.

Whitaker, Arthur Preston. *The Spanish-American Frontier: 1783–1795.* Lincoln: University of Nebraska Press, 1927.

Whitcomb, Dan. "Once Again, L.A. Pledges to End Police Brutality," Reuters, May 8, 2007.

White, Christopher M. *The History of El Salvador.* Westport, CT: Greenwood Publishing Group, 2009.

Whitney, Mike. "The Strange Death of Hugo Chávez: an Interview with Eva Golinger," *Counterpunch,* April 22, 2016.

Wilkins, Mira. *The Emergence of Multinational Enterprise: American Business Abroad from the Colonial Era to 1914.* Cambridge, MA: Harvard University Press, 1970.

Wilkinson, J. B. *Laredo and the Rio Bravo Frontier.* Austin, TX: Jenkins Publishing Company, 1975.

Williams, Eric. *From Columbus to Castro: The History of the Caribbean, 1492–1969.* New York: Vintage Books, 1984.

Williams, John Hoyt. *Sam Houston: A Biography of the Father of Texas.* New York: Simon & Schuster, 1993.

Willison, Charley E., et al. "Quantifying Inequities in US Federal Response to Hurricane Disaster in Texas and Florida Compared with Puerto Rico." *BMJ Global Health* 4, no. 1 (2019).

Wilson, Samuel. *Hispaniola: Caribbean Chiefdoms in the Age of Columbus.* Tuscaloosa: University of Alabama Press, 1990.

Wines, Michael. "Deceased GOP Strategist's Hard Drives Reveal New Details on the Census Citizenship Question," *New York Times,* May 30, 2019.

Wissler, Clark. *Indians of the United States: Four Centuries of Their History and Culture.* New York: Doubleday Doran, 1940.

Wittke, Carl. *Refugees of Revolution: The German Forty-eighters in America.* Philadelphia: University of Pennsylvania Press, 1952.

Wolf, Richard. "'The People's Justice': After Decade on Supreme Court, Sonia Sotomayor Is Most Outspoken on Bench and Off," *USA Today,* August 12, 2019.

Wong, Scott, and Shira Toeplitz. "DREAM Act Dies in Senate," *Politico,* December 18, 2010.

Wood, Conan T. "Cerralvo as the Mother City of the Lower Rio Bravo Valley." *Selected Documents of the Lower Rio Grande Historical Society: 1949–1979,* vol. 1. Harlingen, TX, 1980.

World Bank. "Country Profile: Mexico," 2021.

World Integrated Trade Solutions. "United States Clothing and Textile Imports by Country in U.S.$ Thousand in 2019," World Bank, 2019.

Yablon, Alex. "Trump is Sending Guns South as Migrants Flee North," *Foreign Policy*, March 8, 2019.

Young, Julia G. "Making America 1920s Again? Nativism and U.S. Immigration, Past and Present," *Journal on Migration and Human Security* 5, no. 1 (2017).

Zeigler, Karen, and Steve Camarota. "67.3 Million in the United States Spoke a Foreign Language at Home in 2018," Center for Immigration Studies, October 29, 2019.

Zeitlin, Maurice. "Economic Insecurity and Political Attitudes of Cuban Workers." *American Sociological Review* 31 (February 1996).

Zepeda, Eduardo, Timothy A. Wise, and Kevin P. Gallagher. "Rethinking Trade Policy for Development: Lessons from Mexico under NAFTA," Carnegie Endowment for International Peace, December 2009.

Zibechi, Raúl. "Regional Integration after the Collapse of the FTAA." Silver City, NM: International Relations Center, November 21, 2005.

Zong, Jie, and Jeanne Batalova. "Naturalization Trends in the United States," Migration Policy Institute, August 10, 2016.

Zorrilla, Luis G. *Historia de las Relaciones entre Mexico y los Estados Unidos de América 1800–1958*. Mexico: Editorial Porrua, 1995.

Interviews

The list below represents a small portion of the hundreds of interviews I conducted in the United States, Mexico, Central America, and the Caribbean for the first edition of this book.

William Acosta, New York City police officer, March, May, December 1992; November 1995.

Victor Alfaro Clark, attorney, Tijuana, Mexico, May 1992.

Beatrice Beaumont, Puerto Cortés, Honduras, March 1990.

Lalyce Beaumont, Puerto Cortés, Honduras, January 8, 1995.

Aquilino Boyd, Panama City, Panama, December 1989.

Rev. Greg Boyle, Los Angeles, April 1992.

Othal Brand, mayor of McAllen, Texas, June 1995.

Sila Calderón, mayor of San Juan, Puerto Rico, March 1999.

Rafael Callejas, president of Honduras, San Pedro Sula, Honduras, April 1990.

Gerónimo Campo Seco, former leader, Atanasio Tzul, August 1998.

Eduardo Canales, Canales family descendant, San Antonio, Texas, January 20, 1992.

Gil Cedillo, Los Angeles labor leader, April 1993.

Rafael Chinea, Korean War veteran, Guaynabo, Puerto Rico, August 22, 1992.

Daniel Dacreas, Panamanian pioneer, Brooklyn, New York, February 19, 1993.

Erna Dacreas, Brooklyn, New York, February 6, 1995.

Manuel de Dios Unanue, member of the Committee of Seventy-five, New York City, May 1990.

Luis Del Rosario, Cuban refugee, Miami, Florida, August 1994, May 1996.

Dorca Noemi Díaz, Honduran *maquila* worker, June 1994.

Carlos Julio Gaitan, consul of Colombia, November 1992.

José and Henrietta García, son killed in Los Angeles riot, April 1992.

Diane Garza, school administrator, Brownsville, Texas, January 19, 1992.

Imelda Garza, Canales family descendant, Kingsville, Texas, April 28, 1992.

Paula Gómez, Brownsville Community Health Center, Texas, June 1993.

Agapito González, Jr., labor leader, Matamoros, Mexico, June 1993.

Antonio González, Southwest Voter Registration and Education Project, San Antonio, Texas, May 11, 1992.

Domingo González, Coalition for Justice for the Maquiladora Workers, Brownsville, Texas, May 1992, June 1995.

Mario González, Kobler Center, Chicago, Illinois, August 1998.

Sergio González, González family, Cayey, Puerto Rico, August 14, 1992.

Eva Guadrón, Potrerillos, Honduras, April 1990.

Juan Guerra, district attorney, Raymondville, Texas, June 1995.

Ana Sol Gutiérrez, Montgomery County School Board member, August 18, 1998.

Juan Gutiérrez, Matamoros, Mexico, June 1993.

Jorge Hinojosa, U.S.–Mexico Border Program, American Friends Service Committee, San Diego, California, May 1992.

Carlos Ixuuiac, Guatemalan Support Center of Los Angeles, August 20, 1998.

Mayra Jiménez, *maquila* worker, San Pedro de Macorís, Dominican Republic, August 1991.

Benito Juárez, Guatemalan Support Network, Houston, Texas, August 1998.

Rafael Lantigua, Dominican pioneer, New York City, May 1994.

Guillermo Linares, New York City councilman, April 1996.

Rev. Héctor López Sierra, Santurce, Puerto Rico, August 28, 1992.

Jorge Giovanni López, San Pedro Sula, Honduras, April 1990.

Ana María Luciano, Luciano family, May 29, 1992.

Carlos Malagón, Colombian pioneer, Queens, New York, January 27, 1995.

Monica Manderson, Panamanian pioneer, Brooklyn, New York, January 21, 1995.

Roberto Martínez, U.S.–Mexico Border Program, American Friends Service Committee, San Diego, California, May 1992.

Patricia Maza-Pittsford, consul of Honduras, New York City, September 8, 1997.

Ana Meléndez and Charlie Meléndez, June 1993.

Héctor Méndez, Colombian pioneer, Queens, New York, January 20, 1995.

Luis Mojica, Federation of Provincial Workers of San Pedro de Macorís, San Pedro, Dominican Republic, August 1991.

Claudia Leticia Molina, Honduran *maquila* worker, New York City, July 1995.

Santos Molina, Canales family descendant, Brownsville, Texas, May 9, 1992.

Eugenio Morales, New York City, June 1992.

Pura Morrone, González family descendant, Bronx, New York, August 11, 1992.

Cecelia Muñoz, National Council of La Raza, Washington, D.C., July 1997.

Edward James Olmos, actor, Los Angeles, April 1993.

Eddie Palmieri, musician, New York City, May 12, 1990.

Mario Paredes, Catholic Archdiocese of New York, December 1997.

José Francisco Peña Gómez, Dominican Republic, September 2, 1992.

Tito Puente, musician, March 1998.

Graciela Ramos, González family descendant, New York City, August 8, 1992.

Dr. Arnulfo Reyes, victim of Trujillo dictatorship, Dominican Republic, September 5, 1992.

Silvestre Reyes, Border Patrol chief, McAllen Sector, June 1995.

Palmira Ríos, New York City, June 1994.

Heraclio "Pancho" Rivera, Santo Domingo, Dominican Republic, September 4, 1992.

Matias Rodríguez, Sixty-fifth Infantry veteran, Puerto Rico, August 20, 1992.

Carlos Romero Barceló, resident commissioner of Puerto Rico, March 1996.

Israel Roque Borrero, political dissident, Cojimar, Cuba, September 1994.

Albor Ruiz, member of Committee of Seventy-five, January 1998.

Alfonso Ruiz Fernández, director, Quimica Flour factory in *maquiladora* zone of Matamoros, Mexico, June 1991.

Emilio Ruiz, editor of *La Tribuna*, Long Island, New York, July 26, 1998.

Emilio Sagardía, Sixty-fifth Infantry veteran, Puerto Rico, August 20, 1992.

Fiacro Salazaar, Canales family descendant, San Antonio, Texas, January 20, 1992.

Angela Sambrano, CARECEN, Los Angeles, August 1998.

Gil Sánchez, labor leader, Los Angeles, October 1991.

David Sandoval, educator, Los Angeles, April 1992, June 1995.

Amparo Sención, Luciano family member, Dominican Republic, September 3, 1992.

Tony Sención, Luciano family member, Dominican Republic, September 2, 1992.

José Serrano, U.S. House of Representatives from New York City.

Harley Shaiken, professor of education, University of California, Berkeley.

Ignacio Soto, labor leader, Dominican Republic, August 1991.

Carlos Spector, immigration attorney, El Paso, Texas, May 1992.

Sandra Spector Garza, Canales family descendant, El Paso, Texas, May 6, 1992, June 1995.

Julio Sterling, legislator, Dominican Republic, September 5, 1992.

Esteban Torres, U.S. representative from Los Angeles, November 1996.

Beatrice Uribe, Queens, New York, February 4, 6, 1995.

Gloria Uribe, Queens, New York, August 1992.

Virtudes Uribe, Dominican Republic, August 1991.

Carlos Vaquerano, Los Angeles, August 1998.

Estela Vázquez, Luciano family descendant, New York City, April 10, April 18, August 7, October 24, 1992.

Mary Velasquez, mother of Willie Velasquez, San Antonio, Texas, May 12, 1992.

Nydia Velázquez, U.S. representative from New York City.

Vicente White, New York City, February 10, 1993, December 29, 1994, April 16, 1994, January 15, 1995.

Judith Yanira, Salvadoran *maquila* worker, New York City, July 1995.

Pedro Zamón Rodríguez, Cuban refugee, Key West, Florida, August 1994.

Notes

INTRODUCTION TO THE SECOND REVISED AND UPDATED EDITION

1. Nomaan Merchant, "Hundreds of Children Wait in Border Patrol facility in Texas," Associated Press, June 18, 2018, https://apnews.com/article/9794de32d39d4c6f89fbefaea3780769; Southern Poverty Law Center, "Family Separation under the Trump Administration—a Timeline," June 17, 2020, https://www.splcenter.org/news/2020/06/17/family-separation-under-trump-administration-timeline.

2. Patricia Sulbarán Lovera, "How Did Six Migrant Children die on the US Border?" BBC News, May 23, 2019, https://www.bbc.com/news/world-us-canada-48346228; Daniel Gonzalez, "628 Parents of Separated Children Are Still Missing. Here's Why Immigrant Advocates Can't Find Them," *USA Today*, December 11, 2020.

3. Jeffrey S. Passel and D'Vera Cohn, "Mexicans Decline to Less Than Half the U.S. Unauthorized Population for the First Time," Pew Research Center, June 12, 2019, https://www.pewresearch.org/fact-tank/2019/06/12/us-unauthorized-immigrant-population-2017/.

4. Lucy Rodgers and Dominic Bailey, "Trump Wall: How Much Has He Actually Built?" BBC News, October 31, 2020, https://www.bbc.com/news/world-us-canada-46824649; William L. Painter and Audrey Singer, "DHS Border Barrier Funding," Congressional Research Service, January 29, 2020, https://crsreports.congress.gov/product/pdf/R/R45888.

5. The senators included Alex Padilla (D-CA), who was appointed by Governor Gavin Newsom to fill the vacated seat of Vice President Kamala Harris; Ben Ray Lujan (D-NM), who won election in 2018; and four previously elected senators: Bob Menendez (D-NJ), Catherine Cortez Masto (D-NV), Ted Cruz (R-TX), and Marco Rubio (R-FL). See Katherine Schaeffer,

"Racial, Ethnic Diversity Increases yet Again in the 117th Congress," Pew Research Center, January 28, 2021, https://www.pewresearch.org/fact-tank/2021/01/28/racial-ethnic-diversity-increases-yet-again-with-the-117th-congress/.

6. Luis Noe-Bustamante, Lauren Mora, and Mark Hugo Lopez, "About One-in-Four U.S. Hispanics Have Heard of Latinx, but Just 3% Use It," Pew Research Center, Hispanic Trends, August 11, 2020, https://www.pewresearch.org/hispanic/2020/08/11/about-one-in-four-u-s-hispanics-have-heard-of-latinx-but-just-3-use-it/.

7. Centers for Disease Control and Prevention, "Risk for COVID-19 Infection, Hospitalization and Death by Race/Ethnicity," March 12, 2021, https://www.cdc.gov/coronavirus/2019-ncov/covid-data/investigations-discovery/hospitalization-death-by-race-ethnicity.html. For vaccination rates, see: Centers for Disease Control and Prevention, "Demographic Characteristics of People Receiving COVID-19 Vaccinations in the United States,"March 15, 2021,https://covid.cdc.gov/covid-data-tracker/#vaccination-demographic.

8. "Fatal Force: 1,004 People Have Been Shot and Killed by Police in the Past Year," *Washington Post*, March 11, 2021.

INTRODUCTION TO THE SECOND EDITION

1. Ascertaining crowd sizes in protest marches has historically been fraught with controversy, with government agencies typically underreporting the numbers and organizers usually exaggerating them. In recent years, many police authorities and local governments have refrained from issuing official estimates. The most systematic attempt to measure the size of the 2006 protests, based on local media reports from each city, concluded that 3.5 million to 5.1 million people participated in more than 165 cities. In many of the bigger cities, there were multiple events during that period. See Xóchitl Bada, Jonathan Fox, Elvia Zazueta, and Ingrid García, "Database: Immigrant Rights Marches, Spring 2006," Mexico Institute: Mexican Migrant Civic and Political Participation, Woodrow Wilson International Center for Scholars, 2007.

2. See "The Latino Electorate: An Analysis of the 2006 Election," Pew Hispanic Center fact sheet, July 24, 2007, https://www.pewresearch.org/hispanic/2007/07/24/the-latino-electorate-an-analysis-of-the-2006-election/; also James G. Gimpel, "Latino Voting in the 2006 Election: Realignment to the GOP Remains Distant," Center for Immigration Studies, March 2007, https://www.researchgate.net/publication/237478390_Latino_Voting_in_the_2006_Election_Realignment_to_the_GOP_Remains_Distant.

3. Pew Research Center, "Dissecting the 2008 Electorate: Most Diverse in the U.S. History," April 30, 2009, https://www.pewresearch.org/hispanic/2009/04/30/dissecting-the-2008-electorate-most-diverse-in-us-history/.

4. The National Association of Latino Elected Officials' (NALEO) annual tally of Hispanic officeholders placed the overall number in 2009 at 5,670, which at first glance indicates there has been little progress compared with the 5,459 Hispanic officials that NALEO reported back in 1994. But in 2002, NALEO

ceased to include in its annual tabulation those Latinos elected as members of the Chicago School Councils. The councils represent the largest local body of school board officials in the nation. Of the 7,700 members on the Chicago council, approximately 14 percent, or about 1,000, are Latinos. If those Latinos are included, the more accurate number of Hispanic office-holders currently surpasses 6,600. See *2009 National Directory of Latino Elected Officials*, NALEO Education Fund, vii.

5. In 1993, the Census Bureau predicted that 39 million Hispanics would be living in the United States by 2010, 13.2 percent of the total population. That number, the bureau said, would grow to 80 million by 2050, or 21 percent of the total projected population. Just before the 2000 Census, however, the bureau upped its prognostication to 98 million Hispanics by midcentury. Then, in 2008, it noted in a new report that the Latino population had surpassed 46 million that year, or 15 percent of all residents, causing it to revise its numbers again. See *Hispanic Americans Today*, Current Population Reports, P-23-183, U.S. Department of Commerce (Washington, D.C.: U.S. Government Printing Office, 1993), 2; Randolph E. Schmid, "Twice as Many Americans by 2100," Associated Press, January 13, 2000; "An Older and More Diverse Nation by Midcentury," U.S. Census Bureau News, August 14, 2008.

6. Damien Cave, "The Immigration Gap: Baby Boomers Are Backing Arizona's Tough New Law While Young People Are Rejecting It," *New York Times*, May 18, 2010.

7. Brentin Mock, "Immigration Backlash: Hate Crimes against Latinos Flourish," Southern Poverty Law Center, Intelligence Report, Winter 2007, no. 128, https://www.splcenter.org/fighting-hate/intelligence-report/2007/hate-crimes-against-latinos-rising-nationwide; Federal Bureau of Investigation, "FBI Releases 2008 Hate Crime Statistics," November 29, 2009, https://archives.fbi.gov/archives/news/pressrel/press-releases/fbi-releases-2008-hate-crime-statistics.

8. Caroline Wolf Harlow, "Hate Crime Reported by Victims and Police," U.S. Department of Justice, Bureau of Justice Statistics Special Report, November 2005, https://bjs.ojp.gov/library/publications/hate-crime-reported-victims-and-police.

9. Eduardo Zepeda, Timothy A. Wise, and Kevin P. Gallagher, "Rethinking Trade Policy for Development: Lessons from Mexico under NAFTA," Carnegie Endowment for International Peace, December 2009, 13, http://www.carnegieendowment.org/files/nafta_trade_development.pdf. Projections on the undocumented population of the U.S. have been debated for years. In 2018, the Department of Homeland Security estimated there were nearly 12 million as of January 1, 2015. The Pew Research Center, using U.S. and Mexican census figures, estimated a lower number of 10.5 million in 2017, while the nativist Federation for Immigration Reform claims a far larger 14.5 million as of 2019. See Elaine Kamarck and Christine Stenglein, "How Many Undocumented Immigrants Are in the United States and Who Are They?" Brookings Institution, November 12, 2019, https://www.brookings.edu/policy2020/votervital/how-many-undocumented-immigrants

-are-in-the-united-states-and-who-are-they/. I've chosen 11 million as an admittedly imperfect estimate. See also "Illegal Aliens: Despite Data Limitations, Current Methods Provide Better Population Estimates," U.S. Government Accountability Office, August 5, 1993, http://www.gao.gov /products/PEMD-93-25; Brad Knickerbocker, "Illegal Immigrants: How Many Are There?" *Christian Science Monitor*, May 16, 2006; Roberto Gonzalez Amadador and David Brooks, "México, el Mayor Expulsor de Migrantes del Planeta, Dice BM," *La Jornada*, April 16, 2007. For declining Mexican share of undocumented population, see Jeffrey S. Passel and D'Vera Cohn, "Mexicans Decline to Less Than Half of U.S. Unauthorized Immigrant Population for the First Time."

10. Heiner Schulz, "Foreign Banks in Mexico: New Conquistadors or Agents of Change?" Wharton Financial Institutions Center Working Paper no. 06-11, April 22, 2006, https://papers.ssrn.com/sol3/papers.cfm?abstract_id=917149.

11. Tracy Wilkinson, "Mexico Agricultural Subsidies Are Going Astray: A Fund to Help Poor Farmers Compete with U.S. Imports Is Instead Benefiting Drug Lords' Kin and Officials," *Los Angeles Times*, March 7, 2010.

CHAPTER 1: CONQUERORS AND VICTIMS

1. Tzvetan Todorov, *The Conquest of America* (New York: HarperCollins, 1984), 4–5; Adam Smith, *The Wealth of Nations* (1776), ed. Edwin Cannan, vol. 2 (London: University Paperbacks, 1961), 141. (The other for Smith was the discovery of a passage to India.)

2. William M. Denevan, *The Native Population of the Americas in 1492* (Madison: University of Wisconsin Press, 1992), xvii–xxix. Also Jack Weatherford, *Indian Givers: How the Indians of the Americas Transformed the World* (New York: Fawcett Columbine, 1988), 158; Alvin Josephy Jr., *The Indian Heritage of America* (Boston: Houghton Mifflin, 1991), 71; and Francis Jennings, *The Invasion of America: Indians, Colonialism and the Cant of Conquest* (New York: W. W. Norton, 1976), 30.

3. Estimates range from 7 to 18 million. See David J. Weber, *The Spanish Frontier in North America* (New Haven, CT: Yale University Press, 1992), 28. Also Jennings, *The Invasion*, 30.

4. Bernal Díaz del Castillo, *The Conquest of New Spain* (London: Penguin Books, 1963), 235.

5. Josephy, *The Indian Heritage*, 164.

6. Robert S. Gottfried, *The Black Death* (New York: The Free Press, 1993), 133–56, provides a provocative analysis of how the plague transformed medieval Europe.

7. Geoffrey Elton, *The English* (Cambridge: Blackwell Publishers, 1995), 111.

8. Ibid., 138–39; also Nicholas Canny, *The Ideology of English Colonization: From Ireland to America*, quoted in Jennings, *The Invasion*, 46.

9. Álvar Núñez Cabeza de Vaca, *Adventures in the Unknown Interior of America*, ed. and trans. Cyclone Covey (Albuquerque: University of New Mexico Press, 1990), 67.

10. Ibid., 123.

11. Todorov, *The Conquest*, 5.

12. Samuel M. Wilson, *Hispaniola: Caribbean Chiefdoms in the Age of Columbus* (Tuscaloosa: University of Alabama Press, 1990), 91–93, summarizes the dispute over Hispaniola's population, whose estimates run from 200,000 to 5 million; also Eric Williams, *From Columbus to Castro: The History of the Caribbean 1492–1969* (New York: Vintage Books, 1984), 33.

13. Jennings, *The Conquest*, 24–27.

14. Miguel León-Portilla, *The Broken Spears: The Aztec Account of the Conquest of Mexico* (Boston: Beacon Press, 1992), 124.

15. Ibid., 117–20.

16. Bartolomé de las Casas, *A Short Account of the Destruction of the Indies* (London: Penguin Classics, 1992), 19.

17. John A. Crow, *The Epic of Latin America* (Berkeley: University of California Press, 1992), 157–60. Modern scholars such as Benjamin Keen, however, have asserted that the claims of Spanish cruelty made by Las Casas and other Dutch, French, and Italian writers of his era were largely accurate and that the premise of a Black Legend itself that should be debunked. See Benjamin Keen, "The Black Legend Revisited," *Hispanic American Historical Review* (1969) 49 (4), 703-19, https://read.dukeupress.edu/hahr/article/49/4/703/157405/The-Black-Legend-Revisited-Assumptions-and.

18. Josephy, *The Indian Heritage*, 302–3; Alice B. Kehoe, *North American Indians: A Comprehensive Account* (Englewood Cliffs, NJ: Prentice Hall, 1992), 251–52.

19. Ibid., 252–53.

20. Bernard Bailyn, *The Peopling of British North America* (New York: Vintage Books, 1988), 116.

21. Weatherford, *Indian Givers*, 158; and Josephy, *The Indian Heritage*, 322.

22. Díaz, *The Conquest*, 82.

23. Kathleen Deagan, "St. Augustine and the Mission Frontier," *The Spanish Missions of Florida*, ed. Bonnie G. McEwan (Gainesville: University of Florida, 1993), 99.

24. Simon Collier, Thomas E. Skidmore, and Harold Blakemore, *The Cambridge Encyclopedia of Latin America* (New York: Cambridge University Press, 1992), 193.

25. Jennings, *The Invasion*, 111.

26. Ibid., 53–56.

27. Ibid., 247.

28. Ibid., 251.

29. William Bradford, *Of Plymouth Plantation, 1620–1647*, ed. Samuel E. Morrison (New York: Alfred A. Knopf, 1952), 24.

30. Crow, *The Epic*, 192–208, gives an excellent summary of the Spanish missionary experience.

31. Josephy, *The Indian Heritage*, 319–20.

32. Weber, *The Spanish Frontier*, 106, 307, 309.

33. Bailyn, *The Peopling of British North America*, 96.

34. Nancy Rubin, *Isabella of Castile: The First Renaissance Queen* (New York: St. Martin's Press, 1991), 11–12; also Crow, *The Epic*, 149.

35. Hugh Thomas, *Conquest: Montezuma, Cortés and the Fall of Old Mexico* (New York: Simon & Schuster, 1993), 652, n. 17.

36. Leslie Bethell, ed., *Colonial Spanish America* (New York: Cambridge University Press, 1987), 20; also Clara E. Rodríguez and Héctor Cordero-Guzmán, "Placing Race in Context," *Ethnic and Racial Studies* 15, no. 4 (London: Routledge, October 1992), 527.

37. Verena Martínez-Alier, *Marriage, Class and Colour in Nineteenth-Century Cuba: A Study of Racial Attitudes and Sexual Values in a Slave Society* (Ann Arbor: University of Michigan Press, 1989), 42–79.

38. Herbert S. Klein, "Anglicanism, Catholicism, and the Negro Slave," in *Slavery in the New World*, ed. Laura Foner and Eugene D. Genovese (Englewood Cliffs, NJ: Prentice-Hall, 1969), 146.

39. Herbert S. Klein, *African Slavery in Latin America and the Caribbean* (Oxford, UK: Oxford University Press, 1986), 169–70.

40. U.S. Census Bureau, "1790 Census: Return of Whole Number of Persons Within the Several Districts of the United States," https://www.census.gov/library/publications/1793/dec/number-of-persons.html.

41. Some 60 percent of freed slaves, and virtually all of those freed unconditionally by masters, were young women—suggesting that personal unions between white masters and female slaves played a critical role in forging the freed population of the Iberian colonies. See Klein, *African Slavery*, 227.

42. Santo Domingo counted 80,000 free colored and 15,000 slaves in 1788; Puerto Rico, 22,000 slaves and 104,000 free colored in 1820; and Mexico, 10,000 slaves and 60,000 free colored in 1810. Klein, ibid., 221.

43. Louis A. Pérez Jr., *Cuba: Between Reform and Revolution* (New York: Oxford University Press, 1995), 86.

44. Klein, *African Slavery*, 225–26.

45. Crow, *The Epic*, 216.

46. J. H. Elliot, *The Old World and the New, 1492–1650* (New York: Cambridge University Press, 1970), 75–77.

47. Larry Neal, *The Rise of Financial Capitalism: International Capital Markets in the Age of Reason* (Cambridge, UK: Cambridge University Press, 1990), 10.

48. Herbert Aptheker, *The Colonial Era* (New York: International Publishers, 1959), 10–12.

49. Philip Foner, *Labor and the American Revolution* (Westport, CT: Greenwood Press, 1976), 7; also Bailyn, *The Peopling*, 120–22.

50. Bailyn, *The Peopling*, 37–42.

51. Ibid., 147, n. 40.

52. Crow, *The Epic*, 217.

53. Margaret Ellen Newell, *Brethren by Nature: New England Indians, Colonists and the Origins of American Slavery* (Ithaca, NY: Cornell University Press, 2015); also Juliana Barr, "From Captives to Slaves: Commodifying Indian Women in the Borderlands," *Journal of American History* 92 (2005): 19–46.

54. Aptheker, *The Colonial Era*, 36, 40; also Bailyn, *The Peopling*, 60–61.

55. Patricia Nelson Limerick, *The Legacy of Conquest: The Unbroken Past of the American West* (New York: W. W. Norton, 1987), 68–69.

56. Bailyn, *The Peopling*, 66–67.

57. Aptheker, *The Colonial Era*, 56.

58. For discussion of *mayorazgos*, see Bethell, *Colonial Spanish America*, 283–85; Crow, *The Epic*, 162, 257.

59. Thomas, *Conquest*, 8.

60. Quoted in Bruce E. Johansen, *Forgotten Founders: How the American Indians Helped Shape Democracy* (Boston: Harvard Common Press, 1982), 9.

61. Clark Wissler, *Indians of the United States: Four Centuries of Their History and Culture* (New York: Doubleday, Doran, 1940); Henry Steele Commager, *The Empire of Reason: How Europe Imagined and America Realized the Enlightenment* (New York: Anchor Press/Doubleday, 1977); Felix Cohen, "Americanizing the White Man," *American Scholar* 21, no. 2 (1952); Weatherford, *Indian Givers*, 132–50.

62. Johansen, *Forgotten*, 13.

63. Weatherford, *Indian Givers*, 128.

64. Ibid., 54.

65. Thomas Jefferson, *Notes on the State of Virginia*, 9th American ed. (Boston: H. Sprague, 1802), 287.

CHAPTER 2: THE SPANISH BORDERLANDS AND THE MAKING OF AN EMPIRE

1. George W. Crichfield, *American Supremacy: The Rise and Progress of the Latin Republics and Their Relations to the United States under the Monroe Doctrine* (New York: Brentano's, 1908), vol. 1, 268–99.

2. Jack Ericson Eblen, *The First and Second United States Empires: Governors and Territorial Government, 1784–1912* (Pittsburgh: University of Pittsburgh Press, 1968), 17–51, summarizes the pressures on the Founders to expand the country's territory; Malcolm Rohrbough, *The Land Office Business: The Settlement and Administration of American Public Lands, 1789–1837* (New York: Oxford University Press, 1968), says, "Land was the most sought after commodity in the first half-century of the republic, and the effort of men to acquire it was one of the dominant forces of the period"; Charles Grant, *Democracy in the Connecticut Frontier Town of Kent* (New York: Columbia University Press, 1961), 13–27, documents how land speculation was rampant among settlers from earliest colonial times; and Arthur Preston Whitaker, *The Spanish-American Frontier: 1783–1795* (Lincoln: University of Nebraska, 1927), 47, says, "The importance of the land speculator in the history of westward expansion in the United States . . . can hardly be exaggerated."

3. Lester D. Langley, *The Americas in the Age of Revolution, 1750–1850* (New Haven, CT: Yale University Press, 1966), 107, 111, 163.

4. Jacques Barbier and Allan J. Kuethe, eds., *The North American Role in the Spanish Imperial Economy, 1760–1819* (Manchester: Manchester University Press, 1986), 16.

5. Peggy Liss, "Atlantic Network," in *Latin American Revolutions, 1808–1826*, ed. John Lynch (Norman: University of Oklahoma Press, 1994), 268–69. Also Crow, *The Epic*, 418–20.

6. Lynch, *Latin American Revolutions*, 6.

7. In the viceroyalty of Peru, where natives made up 90 percent of the population, Inca chief José Gabriel Condorcanqui killed the local governor in 1780 and proclaimed the reestablishment of the Inca Empire. He crowned himself Tupac Amaru II, after the last Inca emperor (who had been beheaded by the Spaniards), abolished slavery, and raised an army of thousands with which he attacked the colonial capital of Cuzco. Spanish troops finally captured and beheaded him in 1781, but it took three years of fighting and eighty thousand deaths to restore order. The same year Tupac Amaru was executed, twenty thousand Indians and mestizos from the area around Socorro in the viceroyalty of New Granada (Colombia) marched on the city of Bogotá to protest escalating sales taxes. For a fine summary of the Tupac Amaru rebellion, see Crow, *The Epic*, 404–8; and for an unsympathetic view, see Melchor de Paz, "What Is an Indian?" in Lynch, *Latin American Revolutions*, 191–205.

8. The only place that Spain seemed to welcome Creoles was its colonial army, where they made up 60 percent of its officers. See Lynch, *Latin American Revolutions*, 17; also Tulio Halperin-Donghi, *The Contemporary History of Latin America* (Durham, NC: Duke University Press, 1993), 6–7.

9. Successive wars between Spain and England in the 1790s and early 1800s repeatedly cut the colonies off from trade with the mother country. Those interruptions gradually forced the Crown to allow contraband merchants from England and North America to trade openly with the colonies. As early as 1776, the United States was already Cuba's main trading partner. See Barbier, *The North American Role, 1760–1819*, 15; also Lynch, *Latin American Revolutions*, 10–11; also John Fisher, *Commercial Relations Between Spain and Spanish America in the Era of Free Trade, 1778–1796* (Liverpool: Centre for Latin American Studies, University of Liverpool, 1985), 16; also Halperin-Donghi, *The Contemporary*, 80–83.

10. David J. Weber, *The Mexican Frontier, 1821–1846: The American Southwest Under Mexico* (Albuquerque: University of New Mexico Press, 1982), 159; Alexander von Humboldt, *Political Essay on the Kingdom of New Spain* (Norman: University of Oklahoma Press, 1988), 37; and Desmond Gregory, *Brute New World: The Rediscovery of Latin America in the Early Nineteenth Century* (London: British Academic Press, 1992), 133.

11. Crow, *The Epic*, 609.

12. Ibid., 675.

13. R. W. Van Alstyne, *The Rising American Empire* (Chicago: Quadrangle Books, 1965), 87.

14. Quoted in Langley, *The Americas*, 240.

15. Henry Marie Brackenridge, *South America: A Letter on the Present State of*

That Country to James Monroe (Washington, D.C.: Office of the National Register, October 15, 1817), 24.

16. Apolinar Díaz-Callejas, *Colombia–Estados Unidos: Entre la Autonomía y la Subordinación. De la Independencia a Panamá* (Bogotá: Planeta Colombiana Editorial S.A., 1997), 93–98.

17. For a summary of how Henry Clay and Brackenridge urged immediate recognition of the United Provinces of Río Plata, but President Monroe refused their entreaties, see William F. Keller, *The Nation's Advocate: Henry Marie Brackenridge and Young America* (Pittsburgh: University of Pittsburgh Press, 1956), 221–22.

18. Harold A. Bierck, Jr., *Selected Writings of Bolívar*, vol. 1, *1810–1822* (New York: Colonial Press, 1951), 213.

19. Langley, *The Americas*, 194–95, 244–45; Halperin-Donghi, *The Contemporary History*, 76; for Venezuela policy, see Barbier, *The North American Role*, 174–75.

20. Bierck, *Selected Writings of Bolívar*, vol. 2, *1823–1830*, 603.

21. Chile abolished slavery in 1823, Central America in 1824, and Mexico in 1829; Venezuela, Ecuador, Peru, and Colombia took until the 1840s and 1850s because of resistance from slaveholder groups. See Simon Collier, *The Cambridge Encyclopedia of Latin America*, 142.

22. Gregory, *Brute New World*, 90–93; also Brackenridge, *South America*, 42.

23. At their apogee in the mid-seventeenth century, the Spanish missions numbered forty and ministered to 26,000 Christianized Indians. See Bonnie G. McEwan's *The Spanish Missions of La Florida* (Gainesville: University of Florida Press, 1993), xv. For an account of the escaped-slave problem, see Theodore G. Corbett's "Migration to a Spanish Imperial Frontier in the Seventeenth and Eighteenth Centuries: St. Augustine," *Hispanic American Historical Review* 54, no. 3 (August 1974).

24. Weber, *The Spanish Frontier*, 289; also Whitaker, *The Spanish-American Frontier*, 33–46, for a discussion of the interplay between Indian, Spanish, and North American.

25. Weber, *The Spanish Frontier*, 280–81, notes that between 1782 and 1792 the population of Louisiana more than doubled, from 20,000 to 45,000, largely as a result of Anglo American immigration, and Spain appointed an English-educated officer, Manuel Gayoso de Lemos, as commander of the Natchez District specifically so he could communicate with its many foreign subjects there.

26. Ramiro Guerra y Sánchez, *La Expansión Territorial de los Estados Unidos a Expensas de España y de los Países Hispanoamericanos* (Habana: Editorial del Consejo Nacional de Universidades, 1964), 102; also Weber, *The Spanish Frontier*, 297.

27. For a summary of Jackson's early land speculation, see Michael Paul Rogin, *Fathers and Children: Andrew Jackson and the Subjugation of the American Indian* (New York: Alfred A. Knopf, 1975), 81–100.

28. Among the early Texas filibuster attempts were: Philip Nolan, who was captured and shot with his band of invaders by Spanish soldiers in 1801; Aaron

Burr, who tried without success to organize an invasion in 1806 and was ordered arrested by President Jefferson. For those, see Charles H. Brown, *Agents of Manifest Destiny: The Lives and Times of the Filibusters* (Chapel Hill: University of North Carolina Press, 1980), 6–7; Mexican Bernardo Gutiérrez and former U.S. Army lieutenant Augustus Magee, who with more than eight hundred North Americans, Frenchmen, and Mexican revolutionaries invaded the territory from Tennessee and seized San Antonio in 1812 before being routed, and Connecticut adventurer Henry Perry, who in 1817 invaded Texas and marched on La Bahia. See Odie B. Faulk, *The Last Years of Spanish Texas, 1778–1821* (London: Mouton & Co., 1964), 134–37; and Mississippi merchant James Long, who invaded with three hundred men in 1819 in a failed attempt to establish the Republic of Texas. See Rodolfo Acuña, *Occupied America: A History of Chicanos* (New York: HarperCollins, 1988), 6.

29. Jorge Roa, *Los Estados Unidos y Europa en Hispano América: Interpretación Política y Económica de la Doctrina Monroe, 1823–1933* (Havana: Carasa, 1933), 167–78.

30. Henry Steele Commager, *Documents of American History,* vol. 1, *To 1898* (Englewood Cliffs, NJ: Prentice-Hall, 1988), 236–37.

31. Examples of where the United States either failed to act or supported outside intervention: Britain's seizure of Argentina's Malvinas (or Falkland) Islands in 1833; its seizure of Central American territory to expand British Honduras in 1835 and 1838; the French blockade and occupation of Veracruz in 1838; and Spain's reannexation of the Dominican Republic in 1861. In one especially outrageous case, the Clayton-Bulwer Treaty of 1853, the United States and England agreed to jointly control any Central American canal construction without consulting a single Central American leader. Only after the French occupation of Mexico in 1862, and Louis-Napoleon's installation of Austria's archduke as emperor, did the United States openly condemn a major European aggression, but even then Washington did little more than register official objections, embroiled as the nation was in its own Civil War. It was left to Benito Juárez and the Mexican people to defeat the French invasion. For a detailed examination of the violations, see Gaston Nerval, *Autopsy of the Monroe Doctrine* (New York: Macmillan, 1934), 155–81; also Luis Quintanilla, *A Latin American Speaks* (New York: Macmillan, 1943) 117–22.

32. Bierck, *Selected Writings of Bolívar,* vol. 2, 732.

33. John Francis Bannon, *The Spanish Borderlands Frontier 1513–1821* (Albuquerque: University of New Mexico Press, 1974), 213–14.

34. The Stillman family partner, Daniel Smith, the U.S. consul in Matamoros, had already begun to oversee more than thirty New Orleans companies that were buying wool and hides from the Mexican ranchers and shipping lumber to the United States. See Chauncey Devereaux Stillman, *Charles Stillman, 1810–1875* (New York: C. D. Stillman, 1956), 4–20.

35. Milo Kearney, *More Studies in Brownsville History* (Brownsville: Pan American University, 1989), 47–48, mentions some of those early Anglo settlers: In 1829, Henry Austin, a cousin of Stephen Austin, began running a ship from New Orleans up the Rio Grande to Mier; John Southwell initiated a

newspaper in Matamoros in 1834; and Robert Love a hat factory shortly afterward. Englishman William Neale arrived in 1834 and set up a stagecoach line from Matamoros to Boca del Río.

36. Acuña, *Occupied America*, 89, notes that of 784 marriages in Sonora (Arizona) between 1872 and 1899, 148 were of Anglo men to Mexican women, and only 6 of Mexican men to Anglo women. By the twentieth century, however, most intermarriage had stopped.

37. Carlos Castañeda, *Our Catholic Heritage in Texas, 1519–1933*, vol. 6 (New York: Arno Press, 1976), 217–18.

38. Ciro R. de la Garza Treviño, *Historia de Tamaulipas: Anales y Efemérides* (Mexico City: Princeton University Press, 1956), 96.

39. Quoted in Weber, *The Mexican Frontier*, 170.

40. Ibid., 10.

41. John Hoyt Williams, *Sam Houston: A Biography of the Father of Texas* (New York: Simon & Schuster, 1993), 81–100; also Guerra y Sánchez, *La Expansión*, 199.

42. Frederick Merk, *Slavery and the Annexation of Texas* (New York: Alfred A. Knopf, 1972), 206. See also José María Tornel y Mendivil, "Relations Between Texas of the United States of America and the Mexican Republic," 1837, in Carlos Castañeda, *The Mexican Side of the Texas Revolution* (Washington, D.C.: Documentary Publications, 1971), 328.

43. Reginald Horsman, *Race and Manifest Destiny: The Origins of American Racial Anglo-Saxonism* (Cambridge, MA: Harvard University Press, 1981), 117–228, gives an excellent overview of the racial supremacist theories prevalent in the United States at midcentury and how they were used to rationalize territorial expansion.

44. Anson Jones, *Memoranda and Official Correspondence Relating to the Republic of Texas, Its History and Annexation* (New York: Arno Press, 1973), 97–98.

45. John S. D. Eisenhower, *So Far from God: The U.S. War with Mexico 1846–1848* (New York: Doubleday, 1989), xviii.

46. Ulysses S. Grant, *Personal Memoirs of U.S. Grant*, vol. I (New York: Charles A. Webster & Co., 1885), 53.

47. Railroad interests in the East who were trying to build a southern railroad line to gold-rich California began pressing President Franklin Pierce for more Mexican land not included in the original Treaty of Guadalupe Hidalgo. Pierce authorized his ambassador to Mexico, James Gadsden, to negotiate the purchase of flatlands south of the Gila River in Sonora and Coahuila provinces, which would provide the best transit route. Gadsden, himself a railroad executive, succeeded in getting a strip of thirty thousand square miles—a territory equal in size to Scotland—for $10 million, and it was through that area that the Southern Pacific Railroad built its line. Weber, *The Mexican Frontier*, 274–75.

48. Juan Gómez-Quiñones, "The Origins and Development of the Mexican Working Class in the United States: Laborers and Artisans North of the Río Bravo, 1600–1900," in Elsa Cecilia Frost et al., *Labor and Laborers Through Mexican History* (Tucson: University of Arizona Press, 1979), 482–83.

49. Carey McWilliams, *North from Mexico: The Spanish-Speaking People of the United States*, edition updated by Matt S. Meier (New York: Praeger, 1990), 144–45. Also David Montejano, *Anglos and Mexicans in the Making of Texas 1836–1986* (Austin: University of Texas Press, 1987), 80–84.

50. McWilliams, *North from Mexico*, 136–39; also Gómez-Quiñones, "The Origins," 486–87.

51. Acuña, *Occupied America*, 148.

52. Jeffrey Marcos Garcilazo, *Traqueros: Mexican Railroad Workers in the United States 1870–1930* (Denton, TX: University of North Texas Press, 2012), 34.

53. McWilliams, *North from Mexico*, 135–36; also Gómez-Quiñones, "The Origins," 492–93.

54. In 1826, New York businessman Aaron H. Palmer founded the Central American and United States Atlantic and Pacific Canal Company, with Governor DeWitt Clinton as a board member. The firm won a concession to build a canal across the isthmus, then failed to get financing. See Karl Bermann, *Under the Big Stick: Nicaragua and the United States since 1848* (Boston: South End Press, 1986), 15–16.

55. Lester D. Langley, *The United States and the Caribbean in the Twentieth Century* (Athens: University of Georgia Press, 1989), 32–33.

56. Gustavus Myers, *History of the Great American Fortunes*, vol. 2 (Chicago: C. H. Kerr, 1910), 117–23; and Wheaton J. Lane, *Commodore Vanderbilt: An Epic of the Steam Age* (New York: Alfred A. Knopf, 1942), 85–86, summarize the steamship company shenanigans in Central America by Law, Vanderbilt, and others; for the Panama Railroad, see "History of the Panama Railroad," by Fessenden N. Otis, in *The Panama Canal: Readings on Its History*, ed. Paul Scheips (Wilmington, Del.: Michael Glazier, Inc., 1979), 25–52.

57. Albert Z. Carr, *The World and William Walker* (New York: Harper & Row, 1963), 33, 70; David Folkman, Jr., *The Nicaragua Route* (Salt Lake City: University of Utah Press, 1972), 43.

58. Quoted in Bermann, *Under the Big Stick*, 43–46.

59. Ibid., 46–50.

60. *New York Times*, December 15, 1854, 3.

61. Bermann, *Under the Big Stick*, 63.

62. Brown, *Agents of Manifest Destiny*, 352–55.

63. Ibid., 348.

64. Bermann, *Under the Big Stick*, 71; Brown, *Agents of Manifest Destiny*, 346–58.

65. Jason M. Colby, *The Business of Empire: United Fruit, Race, and U.S. Expansion in Central America* (Ithaca, NY: Cornell University Press, 2013), 29.

66. Michael L. Conniff, *Black Labor on a White Canal: Panama, 1904–1981* (Pittsburgh: University of Pittsburgh Press, 1985), 17. Historian Jason Colby estimates as many as 300,000 West Indians traveled to Central America between 1850 and 1914, thus filling a major portion of the labor needs of U.S. and French railroad, canal, and agricultural firms. See Jason Colby, *The Business of Empire*, 7.

67. Díaz-Callejas, *Colombia–Estados Unidos*, 215–30.

68. Thomas Karns, *Tropical Enterprise: The Standard Fruit and Steamship Company in Latin America* (Baton Rouge: Louisiana State University Press, 1978), 3–4.

69. Aviva Chomsky, *West Indian Workers and the United Fruit Company in Costa Rica, 1870–1940* (Baton Rouge: Louisiana State University Press, 1996), 17–19.

70. For Stillman investments, see John Mason Hart, *Empire and Revolution: The Americans in Mexico Since the Civil War* (Berkeley: University of California Press, 2001), 24; for investor support of Juarez, see 10–19.

71. *New York Times,* June 5, 1868, cited in Hart, 30–31.

72. Ibid., 59–69, where author provides a detailed account of the role U.S. industrialists and Washington politicians played to install Díaz, and where he asserts that Lerdo's overthrow by Díaz "was the first engagement in which the American elite mustered itself against a duly constituted, elected, and internationally recognized government in what is now called the developing world."

73. Bryant Putney, "Protection of American Interests in Mexico," In *Editorial Research Reports 1938*, vol. I (Washington, D.C.: CQ Press, 1938), 197–212, https:// library.cqpress.com / cqresearcher/ document.php? id= cqresrre1938040700#H2_2. In the mining industry alone, the number of mine sites operated by American firms zoomed from 40 in 1884 to 13,696 twenty years later. See Hart, *Empire and Revolution*, 152.

74. Ibid., 511–25. See the complete list of the 160 Americans with the largest landholdings.

75. Acuña, *Occupied America*, 146–49; also John Kenneth Turner, *Barbarous Mexico* (Chicago: C. H. Kerr, 1910), 251–69. For wage gaps and debt peonage, see Hart, *Empire and Revolution*, 143, 280.

76. Arturo Morales Carrión, *Puerto Rico: A Political and Cultural History* (New York: W. W. Norton, 1983), 114.

77. John Quincy Adams, *The Writings of John Quincy Adams*, vol. 7, ed. Worthington C. Ford (New York: Macmillan, 1913–1917), 372–79.

78. Philip S. Foner, *The Spanish-Cuban-American War and the Birth of American Imperialism*, vol. 1: *1895–1898* (New York: Monthly Review Press, 1972), xvi.

79. Ibid., 42.

80. Louis A. Pérez Jr., *Cuba and the United States: Ties of Singular Intimacy* (Athens: University of Georgia Press, 1990), 18, 19, 24. Pérez reports that William Stewart of Philadelphia acquired La Carolina estate near Cienfuegos, a plantation of about 2,000 acres, worked by 500 slaves. Augustus Hemenway of Boston purchased San Jorge estate near Sagua la Grande in 1840, a property of more than 2,500 acres with 160 slaves. J. W. Baker from Philadelphia owned the 1,200-acre San Jose estate near Cienfuegos, which was worked by 700 slaves.

81. Ibid., 19–21. According to Pérez, the number of North American residents in Cárdenas increased from 1,256 in 1846 to almost 2,500 in 1862. So many

arrived that "in 1855, a new hospital was established in Havana exclusively to serve the needs of the North American community in Cuba."

82. Ibid., 47.

83. Ibid., 22. Eighteen hundred came in 1858 and 3,106 in 1859, according to Pérez.

84. Ibid., 57–63. Boston banker Edwin Atkins, for instance, began foreclosing on more than a dozen sugar estates in Cienfuegos in the 1880s. Eaton Stafford, a New York banking firm, gobbled up properties in the Cienfuegos-Trinidad area. The E&L Ponvert Brothers of Boston bought or foreclosed on several in Palmira, including the four-thousand-acre Homiguero plantation. And, in 1893, New Yorkers Benjamin Perkins and Osgood Walsh gained control of one of the largest sugar plantations in the world, the sixty-thousand-acre Constancia estate.

85. Stephen Schlesinger and Stephen Kinzer, *Bitter Fruit: The Untold Story of the American Coup in Guatemala* (New York: Doubleday, 1983), 66.

86. Lester D. Langley, *The United States and the Caribbean in the Twentieth Century*, 12.

87. Alfonso Lockward, *Documentos para la Historia de las Relaciones Dominico Americanas*, vol. 1, *1837–1860* (Santo Domingo: Editora Corripio, 1987), ix.

88. Bruce J. Calder, *The Impact of Intervention: The Dominican Republic During the U.S. Occupation of 1916–1924* (Austin: University of Texas Press, 1984), 2.

89. Emilio Rodríguez Demorizi, *Luperón y Hostos* (Santo Domingo: Editora Taller, 1975), 14, 31.

90. Carlos M. Rama, *La Idea de la Federación Antillana en los Independentistas Puertorriqueños del Siglo XIX* (Río Piedras, PR: Librería Internacional, 1971), 15–16; also Harold J. Lidin, *History of the Puerto Rican Independence Movement*, vol. 1, *19th Century* (Hato Rey, PR: Master Typesetting of Puerto Rico, 1981), 108–9.

91. Charles C. Tansil, *The United States and Santo Domingo, 1798–1873: A Chapter on Caribbean Diplomacy* (Baltimore: Johns Hopkins Press, 1938).

92. For a colorful account of the fight between Grant and Sumner, see William S. McFeely, *Grant: A Biography* (New York: W. W. Norton, 1981), 332–55.

93. Roberto Marte, *Cuba y la República Dominicana: Transición Económica en el Caribe del Siglo XIX* (Santo Domingo: Editorial CENAPEC, 1988), 350.

94. Roger Plant, *Sugar and Modern Slavery: A Tale of Two Countries* (London: Zed Books, 1987), 13–14; also Marte, *Cuba y la República Dominicana*, 436–37.

95. See Frank Moya Pons, *The Dominican Republic: A National History* (New York: Hispaniola Books, 1995), 265–78.

96. Foner, *The Spanish-Cuban-American War*, vol. 1, 261.

97. Ibid., 258–59.

98. Ibid., 270.

99. Pérez, *Cuba and the United States*, 100.

100. Foner, *The Spanish-Cuban-American War*, vol. 2, 368–70.

101. Foner, *The Spanish-Cuban-American War*, vol. 1, 281–310.

102. Schlesinger, *Bitter Fruit*, 67; also Colby, *The Business of Empire*, 69–70.

CHAPTER 3:
BANANA REPUBLICS AND BONDS

1. Scott Nearing and Joseph Freeman, *Dollar Diplomacy: A Study of U.S. Imperialism* (New York: B. W. Huebsch, 1925), 16.

2. Angel Rivero, *Crónica de la Guerra Hispano Americana en Puerto Rico* (New York: Plus Ultra Educacional Publishers, 1973), 502.

3. Mini Seijo Bruno, *La Insurrección Nacionalista en Puerto Rico, 1950* (Río Piedras, PR: Editorial Edil, 1989), 8–9.

4. James L. Dietz, *Economic History of Puerto Rico: Institutional Change and Capitalist Development* (Princeton, NJ: Princeton University Press, 1986), 87–88; also José Trías Monge, *Puerto Rico: The Trials of the Oldest Colony in the World* (New Haven, CT: Yale University Press, 1998), 12–13.

5. Some estimates are that coffee farms in Puerto Rico lost 40 percent of their real worth through that devaluation. Delma S. Arrigoitia, *José de Diego, El Legislador: Su Visión de Puerto Rico en la Historia, 1903–1918* (San Juan: Instituto de Cultura Puertorriqueña, 1991), 322–26.

6. Juan R. Torruella, *The Supreme Court and Puerto Rico: The Doctrine of Separate and Equal* (Río Piedras, PR: Editorial de la Universidad de Puerto Rico, 1988), 53.

7. Dietz, *Economic History*, 88.

8. Torruella, *The Supreme Court*, 59.

9. Dietz, *Economic History*, 94–95.

10. Norma Valle Ferrer, *Luisa Capetillo: Historia de una Mujer Proscrita* (San Juan: Editorial Cultural, 1990), 66.

11. Charles H. Allen, "First Annual Report, Charles H. Allen, Governor of Puerto Rico," in *Documents of the Puerto Rican Migration*, ed. Centros de Estudios Puertorriqueños (Research Foundation of the City of New York, 1977), 11.

12. The agents for the planters were New York labor brokers Williams, Dimond and Company, and Macfie and Noble, a plantation equipment importing company that had offices in several Puerto Rican port cities. See Norma Carr, *The Puerto Ricans in Hawaii: 1900–1958* (University of Michigan doctoral dissertation, 1989), 87; also *Documents of the Puerto Rican Migration*, 13–42; also Blase Camacho Souza, "Boricuas Hawaiianos," in *Extended Roots: From Hawaii to New York, Migraciones Puertorriqueñas*, ed. Centro de Estudios Puertorriqueños (New York: CUNY, 1988), 8–10.

13. The bulk of those contracted cane workers came from the coffee-growing sections of the island, which had been devastated by the worst hurricane in the island's history, San Ciriaco. The storm struck Puerto Rico on August 8, 1899, and killed three thousand. See Dietz, *Economic History*, 99.

14. *Congressional Record*, 64th Cong., 1st Sess. (May 5, 1916). Cited in Ronald Fernandez, *Cruising the Caribbean: U.S. Influence and Intervention in the Twentieth Century* (Monroe, ME: Common Courage Press, 1994), 113.

15. Pérez, *Cuba and the United States*, 118.

16. Langley, *The United States and the Caribbean*, 38.

17. Foner, *The Spanish-Cuban-American War*, vol. 2, 481; Langley, *The United States and the Caribbean*, 38. For a detailed catalogue of direct U.S. investments in Cuba in 1924, see Robert W. Dunn, *American Foreign Investments* (New York: The Viking Press, 1926), 119–33.

18. Nearing and Freeman, *Dollar Diplomacy*, 178–81.

19. Langley, *The United States and the Caribbean*, 64–65.

20. Louis A. Pérez Jr., *Cuba Under the Platt Amendment, 1902–1934* (Pittsburgh: University of Pittsburgh Press, 1986), 140.

21. Ibid., 229.

22. Gary R. Mormino and George E. Pozzetta, *The Immigrant World of Ybor City: Italians and Their Latin Neighbors in Tampa, 1885–1985* (Urbana: University of Illinois Press, 1987), 64–69.

23. "There were, of course, innumerable demands for American armed intervention, especially from certain people representing commercial interests," he recalled. "Every request was flatly rejected." What Welles never divulges in those memoirs were his repeated requests to Roosevelt—later revealed in his secret State Department correspondence—for an American invasion, all of which the president rebuffed. For Welles's account, see Sumner Welles, *The Time for Decision* (New York: Harper, 1944), 193–99. For a detailed version of Welles's insidious role, see Pérez, *Cuba and the United States*, 186–201.

24. Louis A. Pérez Jr., *Cuba Between Reform and Revolution* (New York: Oxford University Press, 1995), 276–312, provides an excellent summary of the Batista years.

25. Luis A. Diez Castillo, *El Canal de Panamá y Su Gente* (Panama: 1990), 26.

26. Langley, *The United States and the Caribbean*, 35–37. Also Walter LaFeber, *The Panama Canal: The Crisis in Historical Perspective* (New York: Oxford University Press, 1970), 29–46. David Healy, *Drive to Hegemony: The United States in the Caribbean, 1898–1917* (Madison: University of Wisconsin Press, 1988), 77–94, argues that Roosevelt did not possess prior knowledge of the revolt but instead jumped quickly to back the rebels. Bunau-Varilla, however, in his firsthand account of the conspiracy, described his meetings with Roosevelt and Hay, wherein he alerted them to the imminent rebellion, and he claimed that both he and U.S. officials attempted to avoid any appearance of coordination. See Phillipe Bunau-Varilla, *The Great Adventure of Panama* (New York: Doubleday, Page & Company, 1920), In any event, there seems little doubt that the arrival of a U.S. Navy ship in Colón on November 2, the day before the revolt, and U.S. recognition of the revolutionary government by November 6 assured a victory for the secession uprising.

27. Some twenty thousand came from Barbados, amounting to 40 percent of all the adult males on that island at the time! See Conniff, *Black Labor on a White Canal*, 29; also David McCullough, *The Path Between the Seas: The Creation of the Panama Canal, 1870–1914* (New York: Simon & Schuster, 1977), 476.

28. During those ten months, 656 West Indians died, compared with 34 Americans. While Black workers were three times the number of white workers, they had nearly twenty times the number of deaths. See McCullough, *The Path Between the Seas*, 501.

29. Ibid., 31–35.

30. Calder, *The Impact of Intervention*, 3; also Frank Moya Pons, *The Dominican Republic: A National History*, 279–82.

31. In 1921, when some marines shot a British citizen—a Black plantation worker from Saint Kitts—in cold blood, C. M. Ledger, the British chargé d'affaires in San Pedro, demanded an investigation of the "reign of terror" by the marines. See Calder, *The Impact of Intervention*, 133–83, for an in-depth view of the occupation and guerrilla war.

32. Already a subsidiary of the U.S.-owned South Porto Rico Sugar Company, Central Romana would nearly quadruple in size to more than half a million acres by the 1960s and would later become one of the Caribbean pearls in the worldwide empire of the giant Gulf and Western Corporation. See Plant, *Sugar and Modern Slavery*, 14.

33. Calder, *The Impact of Intervention*, 91–114, gives an excellent overview of land and sugar policy during the occupation; also Edward S. Herman and Frank Brodhead, *Demonstration Elections: U.S.-Staged Elections in the Dominican Republic, Vietnam, and El Salvador* (Boston: South End Press, 1984), 19.

34. Plant, *Sugar and Modern Slavery*, 14–15.

35. For the 1902–3 sugar harvest, for instance, the planters imported three thousand laborers from the English-speaking Caribbean to the Dominican Republic. See Plant, *Sugar and Modern Slavery*, 17.

36. Calder, *The Impact of Intervention*, 99.

37. Following his arrival in the country in 1922, Welles got the military government to secure $6.7 million in public works bonds through the U.S. firm of Lee, Higginson & Co.; in 1924, after the new civilian president Horacio Vázquez took office, Welles pressured him to borrow another $3.5 million through Lee, Higginson and use part of the money to pay an inflated price for the assets of the failed American-owned Water, Light and Power Company of Puerto Plata and Santiago; subsequently, Welles persuaded Vázquez, despite the president's dissatisfaction with Lee, Higginson, to arrange a new $10 million loan in 1926; he even got Vázquez to pay $150,000 to the firm of a lady friend to erect a luxurious Dominican embassy in Washington. See José Ortega Frier, *Memorandum Relativo a la Intervención de Sumner Welles en la República Dominicana* (Santo Domingo: Ediciones de Taller, 1975), 89–94. According to Dominican historian Frank Moya Pons, by the time the occupation ended, the country's $10 million foreign debt had climbed to $15 million. See Moya Pons, *The Dominican Republic*, 339.

38. Ramón Alberto Ferreras, *Trujillo y sus Mujeres* (Santo Domingo: Editorial del Nordeste, 1982), gives an account of Trujillo's many attacks on women.

39. By 1899, five U.S. companies had investments of nearly $3 million in Bluefields. See Langley, *The United States and the Caribbean*, 46–49; Bermann, *Under the Big Stick*, 123–50; Gregorio Selser, *Sandino: General of the Free* (New York: Monthly Review Press, 1981), 28–40.

40. Bermann, *Under the Big Stick*, 137–40.

41. Ibid., 142–45; Healy, *Drive to Hegemony*, 152–57.

42. Ibid., 143.

43. Ibid., 144; Langley, *The United States and the Caribbean*, 50–52; also Colby, *The Business of Empire*, 85. Bermann, Langley, and Colby all cite more active involvement by the U.S. government in the revolt, while noted historian Dana Munro in *Intervention and Dollar Diplomacy in the Caribbean* (1964), 167–86, ascribes less imperialist motives to U.S. actions and posits that the Taft administration remained neutral during the 1909 revolution. Munro, however, would later serve as a state department official in charge of Latin American affairs and also as president of the Foreign Bondholders Protective Council, which may have colored his view of events in the region.

44. Healy, 155–56. Also Rafael de Nogales, *The Looting of Nicaragua* (New York: Robert M. McBride & Company, 1928), 93–95; for Huntington-Wilson quote, see Benjamin Harrison, "The United States and the 1909 Nicaragua Revolution," *Caribbean Quarterly* 41, no. 3/4 (September–December 1995), 49, https://www.jstor.org/stable/40653942. The author notes that Washington's minister to Nicaragua and Costa Rica "estimated that 90 to 95 percent of all foreign investment in Nicaragua was American by 1894."

45. They awarded themselves and their cronies in Nicaragua exorbitant payments for damages incurred during the war against Zelaya. Chamorro alone got $500,000.

46. Bermann, *Under the Big Stick*, 157–61.

47. For Chamorro and Díaz, see Langley, *The United States and the Caribbean*, 102–3; for Sandino, see Colby, *The Business of Empire*, 152–53.

48. H. H. Knowles, a former ambassador to both Nicaragua and the Dominican Republic, condemned the U.S. presence during a speech at Williamstown, saying: "We have used the Monroe Doctrine to prevent European countries sympathetic to those republics from coming to their aid. Instead of sending them teachers, instructors, and elements of civilization, we send them hunters of usurious banking concessions, avaricious capitalists, corrupters, soldiers to shoot them down, and degenerates to infest them with every disease." See Selser, *Sandino: General of the Free*, 80–81.

49. Langley, *The United States and the Caribbean*, 109; Selser, 174–77; also Tom Barry and Deb Preusch, *The Central America Fact Book* (New York: Grove Press, 1986), 272.

50. By 1920, there were ninety-nine branches of American banks in the region. See Barbara Stallings, *Banker to the Third World: U.S. Portfolio Investment in Latin America, 1900–1986* (Berkeley: University of California Press, 1987), 65–67.

51. Ibid., 71.

52. See Jason M. Colby, *The Business of Empire*, 175–197; Eduardo Galeano, *Open Veins of Latin America: Five Centuries of the Pillage of a Continent*, trans. Cedric Belfrage (New York: Monthly Review Press, 1973), 124–29.

53. Stallings, *Banker to the Third World*, 84, 187. In the early 1950s, Latin America represented only 4 percent of annual "portfolio investments" of U.S. companies in the world; that figure skyrocketed to nearly 41 percent of world investments by 1979.

54. Galeano, *Open Veins*, 246–47.

55. Schlesinger and Kinzer, *Bitter Fruit*, xii.
56. McWilliams, *North from Mexico*, 152.
57. Ibid., 169; also Acuña, *Occupied America*, 177; Zaragosa Vargas, *Proletarians of the North: A History of Mexican Industrial Workers in Detroit and the Midwest, 1917–1933* (Berkeley: University of California Press, 1993), 6.
58. McWilliams, *North from Mexico*, 169.
59. Acuña, *Occupied America*, 153.

CHAPTER 4: PUERTO RICANS

1. The Census Bureau counted 7,364 in Manhattan's Spanish Harlem and around the Brooklyn Navy Yard. Joseph Fitzpatrick, *Puerto Rican Americans: The Meaning of the Migration to the Mainland* (Englewood Cliffs, NJ: Prentice Hall, 1987), 38.
2. U.S. Census Bureau, "Puerto Rico Population Declined 11.8% from 2010 to 2020," August 25, 2021 https://www.census.gov/library/stories/state-by-state/puerto-rico-population-change-between-census-decade.html. For Puerto Ricans in the United States, see "Hispanic or Latino Origin by Specific Origin, 2019 American Community Survey 1-Year Estimates," September 13, 2018, https://data.census.gov/cedsci/table?q=B03001%3A%20HISPANIC%20OR%20LATINO%20ORIGIN%20BY%20SPECIFIC%20ORIGIN&tid=ACSDT1Y2019.B03001&hidePreview=true.
3. This and much of the early González family history is pieced together from extensive interviews by the author during 1992–1993 with Graciela Ramos, Pura Morrone, Sergio González, and Ana Meléndez, the surviving children of Teófilo and María González; with my mother, Florinda Guillén; with her brother, Heraclio "Pancho" Rivera; with my uncle Charley Meléndez; and with several members of the González clan of the second generation, my many cousins.
4. Dietz, *Economic History of Puerto Rico*, 55.
5. For an account of the role of the Puerto Rican scouts in the U.S. invasion, see Rivero's *Crónica de la Guerra Hispano Americana en Puerto Rico*, 473–87.
6. Earl Parker Hanson, *Puerto Rico: Land of Wonders* (New York: Alfred A. Knopf, 1960), 77.
7. Ibid.
8. While Puerto Ricans earned 63 cents daily in 1917, Hawaiian cane cutters earned 97 cents and Cubans $1.26. Between 1923 and 1930, the return on capital of the four largest U.S. corporations averaged 22.5 percent; and from 1920 to 1925, three U.S. sugar growers (Central Aguirre, South Porto Rico, and Fajardo) distributed more than $60 million in dividends to shareholders while accumulating only $20 million for reinvestment. In other words, 75 percent of the companies' earnings were leaving the country to shareholders' pockets. See James Dietz, *Economic History of Puerto Rico*, 110–11, 139.
9. Ronald Fernández, *The Disenchanted Island: Puerto Rico and the United States in the Twentieth Century* (New York: Praeger, 1992), 116; also Dietz, *Economic History of Puerto Rico*, 175.

10. Kal Wagenheim and Olga Jiménez de Wagenheim, *The Puerto Ricans: A Documentary History* (Maplewood, NJ: Water Front Press, 1998), 179–82.

11. Seijo Bruno, *La Insurrección*, 35.

12. Gerald Meyer, *Vito Marcantonio: Radical Politician, 1902–1954* (Albany: State University of New York, 1989), 27–29, gives an in-depth look at Marcantonio.

13. Author's interview with Eugenio Morales.

14. See interview with Teodoro Moscoso, former head of industrial development for Puerto Rico in documentary *Manos a La Obra: The Story of Operation Bootstrap*, Center for Puerto Rican Studies of the City University of New York.

15. Juan González, "The Turbulent Progress of Puerto Ricans in Philadelphia," *Bulletin of the Center for Puerto Rican Studies (CPRS)* 2, no. 2 (Winter 1987–1988): 34–41; also Eugenio Rivera, "The Puerto Rican Colony of Lorain, Ohio," *Bulletin of CPRS* 2, no. 1 (Spring 1987): 12–14; for a fine chronicle of the Lorain workers and the evolution of that city's Puerto Rican community, including oral accounts from the migrants themselves, see Eugenio Rivera, "La Colonia de Lorain, Ohio," in *The Puerto Rican Diaspora: Historical Perspectives*, eds. Carmen Whalen and Victor Vasquez (Philadelphia: Temple University Press, 2005); for a summary of the substandard conditions the Indiana contract workers from Puerto Rico faced, see James B. Lane and Edward J. Escobar, *Forging a Community: The Latino Community in Northwest Indiana, 1919–1975* (Bloomington: Indiana University Press, 1987), 205–10. Note that earlier editions of my book misidentified the recruiting firm as H. G. Friedman Labor Agency.

16. Frank Santana was a teenage Puerto Rican gang member who made front-page headlines in 1955 when he murdered a white boy. Facing the electric chair if convicted, he pleaded guilty to second-degree murder and was sentenced to twenty-five years to life. See "Gangster, 17, Admits Slaying Model Boy, 15," *New York Daily News*, May 2, 1955. Likewise, Salvador "Capeman" Agron was captured after a sensational manhunt, and subsequently convicted for the fatal 1959 stabbing of two white boys in a gang fight in the Hells Kitchen area of New York. Agron, who was eventually pardoned by Governor Nelson Rockefeller after spending nearly two decades in jail, was the subject of a controversial and short-lived Broadway musical by Paul Simon. See "Slew Two 'Because I Felt Like It,' Says Capeman," *New York Daily News*, September 3, 1959.

17. Richie Pérez, "From Assimilation to Annihilation: Puerto Rican Images in U.S. Films," *Centro Bulletin* 2, no. 8 (Spring 1990): 8–27.

18. Fortunato Vizcarrondo, *Dinga y Mandinga* (San Juan: Baldrich, 1942); Toni Morrison, "On the Backs of Blacks," *Time*, December 2, 1993.

19. In his autobiography, published only a few years before his death in 2016 at the age of 98, Gerena Valentín denied ever being a member of the Communist Party, while acknowledging that he "worked closely with the men and women who belonged to the Party and I owe a great deal of my knowledge about organizational strategy and tactics to them. With many of those Communist Party members I forged a profound friendship." See Carlos Rodriguez-Fraticelli, ed., *Gilberto Gerena Valentín, My Life As a Community Activist, Labor*

Organizer, and Progressive Politician in New York City (New York: Center for Puerto Rican Studies, Hunter College, 2013), 87. For a description of the rise of the Congreso de Pueblos, the federation of the social clubs, see 108–17.

20. While the definitive account of Puerto Rican involvement in the 1960s upheaval and how it affected the overall society has yet to be written, those interested in that period, and especially the Young Lords, should see Alfredo López, *Puerto Rican Papers: Notes on the Re-emergence of a Nation* (New York: Bobbs-Merrill Company, 1973), 321–39; and Michael Abramson, *Palante: Young Lords Party* (New York: McGraw-Hill, 1971).

21. Author's interview with Eddie Palmieri.

22. The film *The Battle of Algiers* was regularly shown by the Young Lords in education classes within the organization and in street showings to the community.

CHAPTER 5: MEXICANS

1. The World Bank estimated Mexico's population at nearly 129 million in 2020 with 43.9 percent below the poverty line. World Bank, "Country Profile, Mexico," https://databank.worldbank.org/data/views/reports /reportwidget.aspx?Report_Name=CountryProfile&Id=b450fd57&tbar =y&dd=y&inf=n&zm=n&country=MEX.

2. U.S. Department of Homeland Security, *2019 Yearbook of the Immigration Statistics* (Washington, D.C., 2021).

3. Conan T. Wood, "Cerralvo as the Mother City of the Lower Rio Bravo Valley," in *Selections from the Collected Papers of the Lower Rio Bravo Historical Society: 1949–1979*, vol. 1 (Harlingen, TX: Lower Rio Bravo Valley Historical Society, 1982). Wood presented this talk to the society on October 28, 1964, 1–3.

4. J. B. Wilkinson, *Laredo and the Rio Bravo Frontier* (Austin, TX: Jenkins Publishing Company, 1975), 11–12.

5. Florence Johnson Scott, *Historical Heritage of the Lower Rio Grande* (San Antonio: Naylor, 1937), 8–21; *Royal Land Grants North of the Rio Grande, 1777–1821* (Rio Grande City, TX: La Retama Press, 1969), 1–17.

6. Ana Josefa de la Garza, a relative of the captain, married a son of Blas Canales Jr., José Antonio Canales, in 1755.

7. A Canales family member, José López, founded Lopeño, which still exists just outside Mier, according to family members and a Texas State Historical Society marker at Lopeño.

8. Wilkinson, *Laredo and the Rio Bravo Frontier*, 17–27; also Florence Johnson Scott, *Historical Heritage of the Lower Rio Bravo*, 8–21; also Robert J. Rosenbaum, *Mexicano Resistance in the Southwest* (Austin: University of Texas, 1981), 33–39.

9. Florence Johnson Scott, *Royal Land Grants North of the Rio Bravo*, 1777–1821, 7.

10. Jóse Joaquín Canales, great-grandson of the original pioneer, served as a town councilman in Monterrey for more than thirty years and as mayor

three times. His cousin, the Reverend Manuel María Canales, founded the area's first public school in 1812, led the citizens of Monterrey in publicly swearing allegiance to the new Mexican government after independence, and later represented the city in the national legislature. See Israel Cavazos Garza, *Diccionario Biográfico de Nuevo León*, vol. 1, *A–L* (Monterrey: Universidad Autónoma de Nuevo León, 1984), 70–71.

11. John S. D. Eisenhower, *So Far from God: The U.S. War with Mexico, 1846–1848* (New York: Doubleday, 1989), 103. Originally a Federalist who had twice rebelled against the tyranny of President Santa Anna and even welcomed Texas adventurers in his army, Canales made peace with the Mexican government by the mid-1840s and received a colonel's commission in the army. Soon after, along with the notorious General Ampudia, he turned back one invasion by a group of Texas filibusters at the Battle of El Rosillo in Mier. During that battle, Ampudia and Canales captured 250 Anglo prisoners and executed 17 of them on orders of President Santa Anna. The victory earned Canales a promotion to general.

12. John C. Rayburn and Virginia Kemp Rayburn, *Century of Conflict, 1821–1913: Incidents in the Lives of William Neale and William A. Neale, Early Settlers in South Texas* (Waco, TX: Texian Press, 1966), 57–61.

13. Pat Kelley, *River of Lost Dreams* (Lincoln: University of Nebraska Press, 1986), 46–71.

14. Montejano, *Anglos and Mexicans*, 43.

15. Author's interview with Canales family member Santos Molina.

16. *The Tejano Yearbook: 1519–1978: A Selective Chronicle of the Hispanic Presence in Texas*. Compiled and edited by Philip Ortego y Gasca and Arnoldo De León (San Antonio: Caravel Press, 1978), 41.

17. Imelda Garza, who was born in 1923 and is the great-granddaughter of Gervacio Canales Sr., recalls one lynching her older brothers, Flavio and Fernando, told her they witnessed in 1917. "They were walking in the fields between two ranches," Imelda said, "and they came across a Texas Ranger who they'd never seen before. They watched from hiding as the Ranger stopped a *mojaito* [wetback or illegal immigrant] and just hung him from a tree." Author's interview with Imelda Garza.

18. Montejano, *Anglos and Mexicans*, 28.

19. Florence Johnson Scott, *Royal Land Grants North of the Rio Bravo, 1777–1821*, 62–67.

20. Judge J. T. Canales, "Juan N. Cortina Presents His Motion for a New Trial," in *Selections from the Collected Papers of the Lower Rio Bravo Valley Historical Society, 1949–1979*, vol. 1, 78–79.

21. Montejano, *Anglos and Mexicans*, 41.

22. Ibid., 79.

23. George Durham, *Taming the Nueces Strip: The Story of McNelly's Rangers* (Austin: University of Texas Press, 1962), 29.

24. Charles W. Goldfinch, *Juan N. Cortina, 1824–1892: A Re-appraisal* (Chicago: University of Chicago, 1949), 33.

25. The U.S. government accused him of being a cattle thief and smuggler, but

a Mexican commission appointed by President Benito Juárez, which also investigated the conflict, concluded that while some men he recruited did engage in cattle rustling, Cortina had not promoted the stealing and was in fact the victim of a smear campaign by powerful Texans. The Mexican commission went on to accuse major Texas landowners King, Billy Mann, and Patrick Quinn of directing extensive theft of cattle on the Mexican side of the river. See Gabriel Saldivar, *Historia Compendiada de Tamaulipas* (Mexico City: Academia Nacional de Historia y Geografía, 1945), 197–98.

26. Arnoldo De León, *Tejanos and the Numbers Game: A Socio-Historical Interpretation from the Federal Censuses, 1850–1900* (Albuquerque: University of New Mexico Press, 1989), 42–43.

27. Author's interview with Fiacro Salazaar.

28. McWilliams, *North from Mexico*, 152.

29. Author's interview with Imelda Garza.

30. John Chávez, *The Lost Land: The Chicano Image of the Southwest* (Albuquerque: University of New Mexico Press, 1984), 113–15.

31. Author's interview with Santos Molina.

32. McWilliams, *North from Mexico*, 309–17.

33. Estimates on the number of Mexican Americans who served in the war vary substantially. For the higher end of half a million, see Zaragosa Vargas, *Crucible of Struggle: A History of Mexican Americans from Colonial Times to the Present Era* (New York: Oxford University Press, 2011), 255; for a lower end of 350,00, see "Los Veteranos—Latinos in WWII," National World War II Museum, https://www.nationalww2museum.org/sites/default/files/2017-07/los-veteranos-fact-sheet.pdf; see also McWilliams, *North from Mexico*, 232.

34. Chávez, *The Lost Land*, 121–24.

35. Author's interview with Sandra Garza.

36. Author's interview with Mary Velasquez.

37. Gutiérrez notes in his autobiography, "Willie actually believed that loyalty to the Democratic Party was a must for us, but I vehemently disagreed with him. This ideological and philosophical disagreement between us was never resolved." See José Angel Gutiérrez, *The Making of a Chicago Militant: Lessons from Cristal* (Madison: University of Wisconsin Press, 1998), 187; also Armando Navarro, *La Raza Unida Party: A Chicano Challenge to the U.S. Two-Party Dictatorship* (Philadelphia: Temple University Press, 2000), 41.

38. Ignacio García, *United We Win: The Rise and Fall of La Raza Unida Party* (Tucson: Masrc, 1989), 161–64.

39. Author's interview with Diane Garza.

40. Robert R. Alvarez Jr., *Familia: Migration and Adaptation in Baja and Alta California, 1800–1975* (Berkeley: University of California Press, 1991).

CHAPTER 6: CUBANS

1. Alejandro Portes and Alex Stepick, *City on the Edge: The Transformation of Miami* (Berkeley: University of California Press, 1993), 129.

2. Mormino, *The Immigrant World of Ybor City*, 63–77.

3. Richard R. Fagen, Richard A. Brody, and Thomas J. O'Leary, *Cubans in Exile: Disaffection and the Revolution* (Stanford, CA: Stanford University Press, 1968), 17.

4. The disparity in wealth between those who left and those who stayed was enormous. According to one study, at a time when 60 percent of Cuba's employed males earned less than $900 a year, only 7 percent of the heads of households among the refugees earned less than $1,000, while half earned more than $4,000. And this study probably understates the disparities, because the richest Cubans did not even pass through refugee centers on arrival and thus were never surveyed. See Fagen, *Cubans in Exile*, 21–22.

5. Thomas D. Boswell and James R. Curtis, *The Cuban-American Experience: Culture, Images and Perspectives* (Totowa, NJ: Roman & Allanheld, 1984), 81.

6. Pérez, *Cuba and the United States*, 254; also "The Cuban Immigration 1959–1966 and Its Impact on Miami–Dade County, Florida," The Research Institute for Cuba and the Caribbean Center for Advanced International Studies, University of Miami, July 10, 1967, xiv–xv.

7. Portes and Stepick, *City on the Edge*, 126.

8. And while more than half of Cubans on the island had less than a fourth-grade education, only 4 percent of the refugees had failed to reach the fourth grade. See Fagen, *Cubans in Exile*, 19.

9. Portes and Stepick, *City on the Edge*, 129–32.

10. Ibid., 145–46. In 1979, 63 percent of a group of Cuban immigrants in a survey bought everyday goods in Cuban stores, but in a similar group of Mexicans in the country just as long as the Cubans, only 32 percent bought at Mexican stores. Also, in 1979, 49 percent of a sample of Cubans in the same survey were employed in Cuban firms, whereas only 15 percent of the Mexicans worked for a Mexican firm.

11. Ibid., 127–28.

12. Ibid., 146.

13. As Sylvia Pedraza has noted, they "were primarily young, single, working-class men with little education." Approximately 20 percent were Black or *mulato*, compared with just 7 percent of the Cubans who arrived between 1960 and 1964. Some 25 percent had been imprisoned in Cuba for various reasons, including violating the Cuban law of *peligrosidad*, or "dangerous behavior," which included public displays of homosexuality, but contrary to media reports, less than 2 percent of the *Marielitos* were convicted felons. See Silvia Pedraza, "Los Marielitos of 1980: Race, Class, Gender and Sexuality," *Annual Proceedings of the Association for the Study of the Cuban Economy*, November 30, 2004, https://www.ascecuba.org/asce_proceedings/los-marielitos-of-1980-race-class-gender-and-sexuality; also see Alex Larzelere, *Castro's Ploy—America's Dilemma: The 1980 Cuban Boatlift* (Washington, D.C.: National Defense University Press, 1980), 221–24. Nonetheless, within five years of the boatlift, South Florida counties estimated as many as 15,000 of the refugees had committed crimes in the state, and by 1990 more than 5,000 Mariel refugees were imprisoned across the country in federal or state correctional facilities for criminal offenses they'd

committed since their arrival. See Katie Springer, "Five years later, overriding crime is Mariel legacy," *South Florida Sun-Sentinel*, September 26, 1985, https://www.sun-sentinel.com/news/fl-xpm-1985-09-26-85021 00720-story.html; also David D. Clark, "The Mariel Cuban Problem," New York Department of Correctional Services, Division of Program Planning, Research and Evaluation, April 1991, https://www.ojp.gov/pdffiles1/Digitiza tion/142919NCJRS.pdf.

14. Author's interviews with Luis Del Rosario, from August 1994 to May 1996.

15. A 1960 study of one thousand Cubans in urban and semiurban centers concluded that 86 percent supported the revolutionary government, while a 1962 study of Cuban workers showed that 70 percent backed the government. See Lloyd A. Free, "Attitudes of the Cuban People Toward the Castro Regime in the Late Spring of 1960," Institute for International Social Research, Princeton, NJ, 1960; and Maurice Zeitlin, "Economic Insecurity and the Political Attitudes of Cuban Workers," *American Sociological Review* 31 (February 1966).

16. Author's interview with Manuel de Dios Unanue, May 1990, and Albor Ruiz, January 1998, both members of the Committee of Seventy-five.

CHAPTER 7: DOMINICANS

1. Jorge Duany, *Los Dominicanos en Puerto Rico: Migración en la Semi-Periferia* (Río Piedras, PR: Ediciones Huracán, 1990), 30–31; Gustavo López, "Hispanics of Dominican Origin in the United States, 2013," Pew Research Center, September 15, 2015, https://www.pewresearch.org/hispanic /2015/09/15/hispanics-of-dominican-origin-in-the-united-states-2013; Luis Noe-Bustamante, "Key Facts about U.S. Hispanics and Their Diverse Heritage," Pew Research Center, September 16, 2019, https://www.pewre search.org/fact-tank/2019/09/16/key-facts-about-u-s-hispanics/.

2. Bobby Cuza, "Hispanics Closing In on Whites as New York City's Largest Racial Group," NY1.com, October 13, 2021, https://www.ny1.com/nyc/all -boroughs/local-politics/2021/10/13/hispanics-closing-in-on-whites-as -new-york-city-s-largest-racial-group.

3. Hamlet Hermann, *Francis Caamaño* (Santo Domingo: Editora Alfa y Omega, 1983), 253; Edward S. Herman, *Demonstration Elections*, 30; also John Stockwell, *In Search of Enemies: A CIA Story* (New York: W. W. Norton, 1978), 160, 236; and Víctor Grimaldi, *El Diario Secreto de la Intervención Norteamericana de 1965* (Santo Domingo: Amigo del Hogar, 1989), 39–40; also Ramón Grosfoguel, "Migration and Geopolitics in the Greater Antilles," paper presented at Conference on Transnational Realities and Nation-States: Trends in International Migration and Immigration Policy in the Americas, the North-South Center, University of Miami, May 18–20, 1995.

4. Frank Moya Pons, *The Dominican Republic: A National History* (New Rochelle, NY: Hispaniola Books, 1995), 392.

5. Stockwell, *In Search of Enemies*, 236; also Edward S. Herman, *Demonstration Elections*, 22, and Grimaldi, *El Diario Secreto*, 37–40.

6. Much of the following account of the Luciano family history is from a series of interviews by the author with Estela Vázquez, Ana María Luciano, Amparo Sención, and Tony Sención, members of the Luciano family in New York and Santo Domingo.

7. John Bartlow Martin, *Overtaken by Events: The Dominican Crisis from the Fall of Trujillo to the Civil War* (New York: Doubleday, 1966), 35. See also Bernardo Vega, *Control y Represión en la Dictadura Trujillista* (Santo Domingo: Fundación Cultural Dominicana, 1986).

8. Author's interview with Arnulfo Reyes.

9. Hermann, *Francis Caamaño*, 145–47.

10. Ibid., 155–204. Also interviews with Estela Vázquez and Heraclio Rivera, an uncle of the author and survivor of the April revolution.

11. Grimaldi, *El Diario Secreto*.

12. Sherri Grasmuck and Patricia R. Pessar, *Between Two Islands: Dominican International Migration* (Berkeley: University of California Press, 1991), 24.

13. Ibid., 77.

14. Palmira N. Rios, "Acercamiento al Conflicto Dominico-Boricua," *Center for Puerto Rican Studies Bulletin* 4, no. 2 (Spring 1992): 46.

15. Amelia Estades Santaliz, "Sólido red para el tráfico de ilegales," *El Nuevo Día*, February 19, 1999.

16. U.S. Census Bureau, "Hispanic or Latino by Type in Puerto Rico, 2010," https://www.ncsl.org/documents/redistricting/puerto_rico_census_data _2010.pdf; see also U.S. Census Bureau, "Selected Population Profile in Puerto Rico, 2017 American Community Survey 1-Year Estimates," https:// centropr.hunter.cuny.edu/sites/default/files/data_sheets/ACS_17_1YR _Population_Profile_for_Puerto_Rico.pdf.

17. For Hostos, see Hostos Community College, Hostos Community College Student Profile, 2016, http://www.hostos.cuny.edu/Hostos/media/Office -of-the-President/Institutional-Research-Assessment/Profile-thru-S16 .pdf. For CUNY, see State University of New York, "New York Public University Systems Embark on Multilateral Academic Collaborations with Dominican Republic Education Ministries," December 7, 2018, https://www .suny.edu/suny-news/press-releases/dec-2018/12-7-18/academic -collaborations-with-dominican-republic.html.

18. Juan Gonzalez, *New York Daily News*, "Caribbean Labor Pains," August 2, 1991.

19. "Overview," World Bank in Dominican Republic, June 10, 2021, https:// www.worldbank.org/en/country/dominicanrepublic/overview.

20. According to a study in one Dominican city, Santiago, 20 percent of the households in 1981 were receiving regular aid from family members abroad. See Grasmuck, *Between Two Islands*, 71.

CHAPTER 8: CENTRAL AMERICANS

1. That number is nearly 400,000 fewer than the total estimated above to have arrived, but we must take into account that thousands inevitably returned

home after a few years of working illegally in the United States. Others were discovered by the INS and deported, and some of the 1.1 million counted as entering most certainly crossed the border several times and may have been double- or triple-counted.

2. For most recent population numbers, see U.S. Census Bureau, "Hispanic or Latino Origin by Specific Origin Universe: Total Population, 2017 American Community Survey 1-Year Estimates." See also Luis Noe-Bustamante, "Key Facts about U.S. Hispanics and Their Diverse Heritage."

3. Ibid., 251.

4. World Bank Open Data, https://data.worldbank.org; Inter-American Development Bank, *1996 Annual Report* (Washington, D.C.), 130–31; also Barry and Preusch, *The Central America Fact Book*, 225; on current education situation in Guatemala, see Manuel Orozco and Marcela Valdivia, "Educational Challenges in Guatemala and Consequences for Human Capital and Development," *Inter-American Dialogue*, working paper, 2017, https://www.thedialogue.org/wp-content/uploads/2017/02/Educational-Challenges-in-Guatemala-and-Consequences-for-Human-Capital-and-Development-1.pdf.

5. Robert S. Kahn, *Other People's Blood: U.S. Immigration Prisons in the Reagan Decade* (Boulder, CO: Westview Press, 1996), 11.

6. Inter-American Development Bank, *1996 Annual*, 133.

7. Sarah J. Mahler, *American Dreaming: Immigrant Life on the Margins* (Princeton, NJ: Princeton University Press, 1995), 174, shows INS approval rates for asylum requests from socialist countries that were not even at war were far more disparate—68.2 percent from Romania, 76.7 percent from the USSR, and 64.9 percent from China.

8. Maurice Belanger, "A Chronology of the Treatment of Central American War Refugees in the U.S.," National Immigration Forum, 1997.

9. Adam Clymer, "Poll Finds Americans Don't Know Positions in Central America," *New York Times*, July 1, 1983.

10. Between 1949 and 1964, 2,969 Nicaraguan officers were trained at the school. Costa Rica, with 1,639, was second. See Willard F. Barber and C. Neale Ronning, *Internal Security and Military Power: Counterinsurgency and Civic Action in Latin America* (Columbus: Ohio State University Press, 1966), 145.

11. Christopher M. White, *The History of El Salvador.* (Westport, CT: Greenwood Publishing Group, 2009), 76–80; also Robert W. Taylor and Harry E. Vanden, "Defining Terrorism in El Salvador: 'La Matanza,'" *The Annals of the American Academy of Political and Social Science* 463 (1982): 106–18; also John A. Booth and Thomas W. Walker, *Understanding Central America* (Boulder, CO: Westview Press, 1993), 37–38; on Hernandez outlawing labor unions, see Americas Watch Report, *Labor Rights in El Salvador* (New York, 1988), 11–12.

12. Alberto Martín Álvarez, *From Revolutionary War to Democratic Revolution: the Farabundo Martí National Liberation Front (FMLN) in El Salvador*, eds. Véronique Dudouet and Hans J. Giessmann. (Berlin: Berghof Transitions Series. Resistance/Liberation Movements and Transition to Politics, 2010).

For events leading up to the Soccer War and its aftermath, see Tim L. Merrill, *Honduras: A Country Study*. 3rd ed. (Washington, D.C.: Library of Congress, 1995), 40–41, 264; for early Salvadoran migration to the United States, see Nadia Y. Flores-Yeffal, and Karen A. Pren, "Predicting Unauthorized Salvadoran Migrants' First Migration to the United States between 1965 and 2007," *Journal on Migration and Human Security* 1, no. 14 (2018), 1–14; for Medrano and ORDEN, see Christopher White, *The History of El Salvador*, 87, 92.

13. John A. Booth and Thomas Walker, *Understanding Central America* (Boulder, CO: Westview Press, 1993), 135–39, summarizes the pivotal role of grassroots church activism.

14. For a concise account of the elections and coups of 1972 and 1977, see White, *The History of El Salvador*, 83, 93–94.

15. Ibid., xxiii; also Mario Lungo Uclés, *El Salvador in the Eighties: Counterinsurgency and Revolution* (Philadelphia: Temple University Press, 1996), 137–48.

16. For assassination of Bishop Oscar Romero and killing of Catholic nuns, see White, *The History of El Salvador*, 99–101. For U.S. aid, see Mario Lungo Unclées, *El Salvador in the Eighties*, 97.

17. Piero Gleijeses, *Shattered Hope: The Guatemalan Revolution and the United States, 1944–1954* (Princeton, NJ: Princeton University Press, 1991), 88–90.

18. Carol Smith, ed., *Guatemalan Indians and the State: 1540 to 1988* (Austin: University of Texas Press, 1992), 141–42.

19. For more on the Arévalo period, see Walter LaFeber, *Inevitable Revolutions: The United States in Central America* (New York: W. W. Norton, 1993), 113–19; also Schlesinger and Kinzer, *Bitter Fruit*, 37–43; and Booth, *Understanding Central America*, 42–43.

20. Gleijeses, *Shattered Hope*, 32–38.

21. Barry and Preusch, *Central America Fact Book*, 225. For details of the 1954 CIA coup, see Schlesinger and Kinzer, *Bitter Fruit*; also Richard H. Immerman, *The CIA in Guatemala: The Foreign Policy of Intervention* (Austin: University of Texas Press, 1982), 161–86.

22. U.S. General Accounting Office, "Central American Refugees: Regional Conditions and Prospects and Potential Impact on the United States," July 29, 1984, 3.

23. Kahn, *Other People's Blood*, 11–24, provides a summary that is highly critical of U.S. refugee policy. Aristide R. Zolberg, "From Invitation to Interdiction: U.S. Foreign Policy and Immigration Since 1945," in *Threatened Peoples, Threatened Borders: World Migration and U.S. Policy*, eds. Michael S. Teitelbaum and Myron Weiner, 137–52, shows how refugee policy for Central America, much as in the rest of the world, has always been dictated by U.S. foreign policy interests.

24. Author's interview with Ana Sol Gutiérrez, August 18, 1998.

25. Jacqueline María Hagan, *Deciding to Be Legal: A Mayan Community in Houston* (Philadelphia: Temple University Press, 1994), 48–68; also Roberto Suro, *Strangers Among Us: How Latino Immigration Is Transforming America* (New York: Alfred A. Knopf, 1998), 38.

26. Suro, *Strangers Among Us*, 44–48.

27. Anne-Marie O'Connor, "Refugees in Florida Cheer Prize, Guatemalans Want Asylum," *Atlanta Constitution*, December 6, 1992.

28. Author's interview with Carlos Vaquerano, August 1998.

29. Author's interviews with Angela Sanbrano, CARECEN of Los Angeles, August 1998, and Benito Juárez, Guatemalan Support Network of Houston, May 1998.

30. Author's interview with Mario González, August, 1998.

31. Author's interview with Gerónimo Campo Seco, August 1998.

32. "Researcher Says Mayans Adapt Well," United Press International, November 24, 1987; "Mayan Refugees Seek New Lives in the United States," Associated Press, July 10, 1984.

33. Juan Williams, "Black Power's New Dilemma: The D.C. Establishment That Fought for Civil Rights Faces a Latino Demand for Justice," *Washington Post*, May 12, 1991.

34. Author's interview with Ana Sol Gutiérrez, August 18, 1998.

35. American Immigration Council, "Immigrants in Maryland," 2017, https://www.americanimmigrationcouncil.org/sites/default/files/research/immigrants_in_maryland.pdf.

36. For Guatemalans, it was 75.7 percent, and for Salvadorans, it was 76.3 percent in 1990, while the U.S. average was 65.3 percent. See Portes, *Immigrant America*, 68.

37. Farhan Haq, "U.S. Labor: Guatemalan, U.S. Workers Unite Against Case Farms," Inter Press Service, August 16, 1996; also Craig Whitlock, "Immigrant Poultry Workers' Struggle for Respect Draws National Attention," *News & Observer*, Raleigh, North Carolina, November 30, 1996.

38. U.S. Census Bureau, "2013–2017 American Community Survey 5-Year Estimates." For an account of how Dalton's carpet and chicken-processing industries became magnets for Mexican migrants and fueled the growth of the city's Hispanic population, see James D. Engstrom, "Industry and Immigration in Dalton, Georgia," in *Latino Workers in the Contemporary South*, eds. Arthur D. Murphy et al. (Athens: University of Georgia Press, 2001), 44–56.

39. Mireya Navarro, "Guatemalan Army Waged 'Genocide,' New Report Finds," *New York Times*, February 26, 1999; also John M. Broder, "Clinton Offers His Apologies to Guatemala," *New York Times*, March 11, 1996.

CHAPTER 9:
COLOMBIANS AND PANAMANIANS

1. Michael L. Conniff, *Black Labor on a White Canal*, 137.

2. U.S. Department of Justice, *1996 Statistical Yearbook of the Immigration and Naturalization Service* (Washington, D.C.: U.S. Government Printing Office, 1997), 27–28.

3. Luis Noe-Bustamante, "Key Facts about U.S. Hispanics and Their Diverse Heritage."

4. Author's interview with Monica Manderson, January 21, 1995.

5. David McCullough, *The Path Between the Seas: The Creation of the Panama Canal 1870–1914* (New York: Simon & Schuster, 1977), 575.

6. Ibid.

7. Conniff, *Black Labor*, 31–35; also McCullough, *The Path Between*, 576–81.

8. Conniff, *Black Labor*, 6.

9. Ibid., 49–61.

10. Ibid., 91.

11. Author's interview with Vicente White, February 10, 1993.

12. Conniff, *Black Labor*, 121–23.

13. Ibid., 136–37.

14. Ibid., 140–41.

15. Galeano, *Open Veins of Latin America*, 116.

16. Alonso Salazaar, *Born to Die in Medellín* (New York: Monthly Review Press, 1990), 6–8; also Galeano, *Open Veins*, 116–19; and Crow, *The Epic*, 800.

17. Salazaar, *Born to Die*, 7.

18. Alan Gilbert, *The Latin American City* (London: Latin American Bureau, 1994), 63.

19. Human Rights Watch, *War Without Quarter: Colombia and International Humanitarian Law* (New York: 1998).

20. Quoted in Crow, *The Epic*, 803.

21. "Bogotá Halts Unit Faulted Over Rights," *New York Times*, May 25, 1998; see also "Colombia—A Killing Every 20 Minutes," Reuters, January 14, 1997.

22. Author's interview with Carlos Malagón, January 27, 1995.

23. Author's interview with Beatrice Uribe, February 4 and 6, 1995.

24. Author's interview with Gloria Uribe, May 1992.

25. Germán Castro Caycedo, *El Hueco: La Entrada Ilegal de Colombianos a Estados Unidos por México, Bahamas y Haití* (Bogotá: Planeta Colombiana Editorial S.A., 1989), 13–34, gives a Colombian journalist's extraordinary eyewitness account of how the immigrant smuggling operation worked.

26. James Petras and Morris Morley, *Latin America in the Time of Cholera: Electoral Politics, Market Economics, and Permanent Crisis* (New York: Routledge, 1992), 21; also Crow, *The Epic*, 803–4.

27. Author's interviews with several New York City detectives and Colombian community leaders during 1991 and 1992.

28. Author's interview with William Acosta, March, May, December 1992, November 1995, February 1998.

CHAPTER 10:
THE RETURN OF JUAN SEGUÍN

1. *A Revolution Remembered: The Memoirs and Selected Correspondence of Juan N. Seguín*, ed. Jesús F. de la Teja (Austin, TX: State House Press, 1991), 90.

2. Ibid., 1–70. De la Teja provides an excellent summary of Seguín's life. For Cisneros's election, see Thomas Weyr, *Hispanic U.S.A.: Breaking the Melting Pot* (New York: Harper & Row, 1988), 116.

3. For 2016, see U.S. Census Bureau, "Voting and Registration in the Election of November 2016," May 10, 2017, Table 2, "All Races" and "Hispanic"; for 1976, see U.S. Census Bureau, "Voting and Registration in the Election of November 1976," March 1978, Table 2, https://www2.census.gov/programs -surveys/cps/tables/p20/322/tab02.pdf.

4. Among the raft of recent studies are: Rodolfo de la Garza and Alan S. Yang, *Americanizing Latino Politics, Latinoizing American Politics* (New York: Routledge, 2020); Marion Orr, Domingo Morel, and Luis R. Fraga, *Latino Mayors: Political Change in the Postindustrial City* (Philadelphia: Temple University Press, 2018); Heather S. Mohammed, *The New Americans?: Immigration, Protest, and the Politics of Latino Identity* (Lawrence: University Press of Kansas, 2017); Ricardo Ramírez, *Mobilizing Opportunities: The Evolving Latino Electorate and the Future of American Politics* (Charlottesville: University of Virginia Press, 2015); Matt A. Barreto and Gary M. Segura, *Latino America: How America's Most Dynamic Population Is Poised to Transform the Politics of the Nation* (New York: PublicAffairs, 2014); Lisa García Bedolla, *Latino Politics* (Malden, MA: Polity, 2014); Rodolfo Espino, David L. Leal, and Kenneth J. Meier, *Latino Politics: Identity, Mobilization, and Representation* (Charlottesville: University of Virginia Press, 2008).

5. Juan Gómez Quiñones, *Chicano Politics: Reality & Promise, 1940–1990* (Albuquerque: University of New Mexico Press, 1990), 60.

6. The average factory wage in the South in the early 1900s was $10 a week, while the city and state poll taxes sometimes totaled $2.75. See Chandler Davidson, *Race and Class in Texas Politics* (Princeton, NJ: Princeton University Press, 1990), 18–23.

7. As early as 1915, however, William E. Rodriguez, a socialist lawyer and son of a Spanish immigrant, had become the first Hispanic elected to the Chicago city council. See Jerry Crimmins, "John Marshall marks a century since its first Latino graduate," *Chicago Daily Law Bulletin*, November 27, 2012, https://news.jmls.uic.edu/wp-content/uploads/2012/11/Rodriguez-Nov27 .pdf.

8. Gómez Quiñones, *Chicano Politics*, 53–60, 73; and National Association of Latino Elected Officials, *1996 Election Handbook*, 20; for 2018 figures on Hispanic Elected officials, see NALEO Educational Fund, "National Directory of Latino Elected Officials, 2018," https://naleo.org/wp-content /uploads/2019/10/2018_National_Directory_of_Latino_Elected_Offi cials-1.pdf, but it should be noted that exact comparisons with figures for the 1990s are not possible because NALEO changed its methodology for counting Latino officeholders over the years.

9. James Jennings and Monte Rivera, *Puerto Rican Politics in Urban America* (Westport, CT: Greenwood Press, 1984), 31–32.

10. Sherrie Baver, "Puerto Rican Politics in New York City: The Post–World War II Period," in Jennings and Rivera, *Puerto Rican Politics in Urban America*, 44.

11. Linda Chavez, *Out of the Barrio: Toward a New Politics of Hispanic Assimilation* (New York: Basic Books, 1991), 40.

12. *Rodriguez v. Texas*, May 3, 1954, 347 U.S. 475.

13. Gómez Quiñones, 87. Also Manuel Del Valle, "Developing a Language-Based National Origin Discrimination Modality," *Journal of Hispanic Policy* 4, no. 22, 75. John F. Kennedy School of Government, Harvard University.

14. John F. Stack and Christopher L. Warren, "Ethnicity and the Politics of Symbolism in Miami's Cuban Community," *Cuban Studies* 20 (Pittsburgh: University of Pittsburgh Press, 1990), 13.

15. Examples were the Miami assassinations of Luciano Nieves and Rolando Masferrer in 1975 and of Ramon Donesteves in 1976; and the murders of Carlos Muñiz Varela and Eulalio Negrín in Union City, New Jersey, in 1979; for furthering dialogue with Cuba, see Max Azicri, "The Politics of Exile: Trends and Dynamics of Political Change Among Cuban-Americans," *Cuban Studies* 11 (Pittsburgh: University of Pittsburgh Press, 1981 and 1982), 62–66.

16. From 1961 to 1965, an average of 2,400 Cubans became citizens each year, but after the new law, those numbers grew steadily each year. In 1970 alone, 20,888 Cubans became citizens. See Silvia Pedraza Bailey, "Cubans and Mexicans in the United States: The Functions of Political and Economic Migration," *Cuban Studies* 11 (Pittsburgh: University of Pittsburgh Press, 1981), 89.

17. William Neuman, "Dominican Candidates in New York Tout Their Pioneer Status, but History Is Complicated," *New York Times*, June 27, 2016.

18. Among the most well-known of many actions taken by members of the Cuban underground in non-Cuban issues were the 1973 Watergate break-in, which included three former CIA Cubans in Howard Hunt's "plumbers" group, and the fatal bombing that same year of the Chilean ambassador to Washington, Orlando Letelier, where two members of the Cuban Nationalist Movement were initially convicted, then acquitted in a retrial. See Azicri, "The Politics of Exile," 62–66; also Peter Dale Scott and Jonathan Marshall, *Cocaine Politics: Drugs, Armies, and the CIA in Central America* (Berkeley: University of California Press, 1991), 23–50.

19. Dan Balz, "Hispanics Use New Voting Rights Act to Reshape Texas Politics," *Washington Post*, April 25, 1983.

20. Gary Rivlin, *Fire on the Prairie: Chicago's Harold Washington and the Politics of Race* (New York: Henry Holt, 1992), 348–57.

21. Jennings and Rivera, *Puerto Rican Politics*, 54.

22. Among the victories were those of Ralph Acosta and City Councilman Angel Ortíz in Philadelphia, state representative Americo Santiago in Bridgeport, city councilman Eugenio Caro in Hartford, state representative Nelson Merced in Boston, Board of Education member Nancy Padilla in Rochester, Gutiérrez and Santiago in Chicago.

23. But even among Hispanic voters, Puerto Ricans (79 percent) were the most pro-Washington, followed by Mexicans (68 percent) and Cubans (52 percent). Rod Bush, *The New Black Vote: Politics and Power in Four American Cities* (San Francisco: Synthesis, 1984), 150–51.

24. Alejandro Portes, Juan M. Clark, and Manuel M. López, "Six Years Later, the Process of Incorporation of Cuban Exiles in the United States: 1973–1979," in *Cuban Studies*, July 1981–January 1982, 11.

25. Dade County did not officially change its name to Miami-Dade County until 1997. See https://web.archive.org/web/20070403184943/http://www .miamidade.gov/info/government.asp.

26. María Cristina García, *Havana USA: Cuban Exiles and Cuban Americans in South Florida, 1959–1994* (Berkeley: University of California Press, 1996), 113–15.

27. Thomas D. Bowell and James R. Curtis, *The Cuban American Experience: Culture, Images and Perspectives* (Totowa, NJ: Rowman & Allanheld Publishers), 69.

28. Stack and Warren, "Ethnicity and the Politics," 16–17.

29. Ibid., 19.

30. Alejandro Portes, "The Rise of Ethnicity: Determinants of Ethnic Perceptions Among Cuban Exiles in Miami," *American Sociological Review* 49, no. 3 (June 1984): 395.

31. Ibid., 20–24.

32. Stack and Warren, "Ethnicity and the Politics."

33. Institute for Puerto Rican Policy, *The Puerto Rican and Latino Vote in the 1984 NYS Democratic Presidential Primary* (New York: April 5, 1984); also Institute for Puerto Rican Policy, "Puerto Ricans and the 1988 Presidential Elections" (New York: November 7, 1988); also Univision Network Poll, June 1, 1988.

34. Institute for Puerto Rican Policy, *The 1989 Mayoral Election and the Charter Revision Vote in New York City* (New York: November 1989).

35. Frances Fox Cloward and Richard A. Piven, *Why Americans Don't Vote* (New York: Pantheon, 1988), 115–16.

36. Institute for Puerto Rican Policy, *The Dinkins Administration and the Puerto Rican Community: Lessons from the Puerto Rican Experience with African-American Mayors in Chicago and Philadelphia* (New York: February 1990).

37. A widely quoted voter opinion analysis after the referendum by the nonpartisan Field Institute found a majority of Black Californians (52 percent–48 percent) voted in favor of Proposition 187, while a *Los Angeles Times* exit poll reached the opposite conclusion (53 percent of Blacks opposed, and 46 percent in favor). See "California Opinion Index, A Summary Analysis of Voting in the 1994 General Election," The Field Institute, 1995, https://web .archive.org/web/20101020160337/http://field.com/fieldpollonline /subscribers/COI-94-95-Jan-Election.pdf. Subsequent academic studies appear to support more the *Los Angeles Times* results. See Irwin L. Morris, "African American Voting on Proposition 187: Rethinking the Prevalence of Interminority Conflict," *Political Research Quarterly* 53, no. 1 (2000): 77–98.

38. In one exceptional year, 2007, an unusual surge in citizenship applications rose to 1.3 million, nearly double that of the previous years, largely as a result of efforts by the Obama campaign and the Democratic Party to increase voter eligibility among Hispanics for the 2008 election. See Jie Zong and Jeanne Batalova, "Naturalization Trends in the United States," Migration Policy Institute, August 10, 2016, https://www.migrationpolicy.org/article /naturalization-trends-united-states#historical.

39. U.S. Department of Homeland Security, *Yearbook of Immigration Statistics: 2008* (Washington, D.C.: Office of Immigration Statistics, 2009), 52–53.

40. Alejandro Portes and Rubén G. Rumbaut, *Immigrant America: A Portrait* (Berkeley: University of California Press, 1996), 117–18. For 2010 naturalization rates, see Portes and Rumbaut, *Immigrant America*, 4th ed., 187–91. The authors make a convincing argument that Mexicans and Central Americans, as mostly unskilled migrant laborers from countries that are geographically close to the United States, possess reduced ability and resources to naturalize, compared with more skilled migrant populations from Asia and even Africa, and also less incentive to do so given the "reversibility" of their migration, that is, their ability to return easily to their homeland.

41. U.S. Department of Commerce, *Hispanic Americans Today* (Washington, D.C.: U.S. Government Printing Office, 1993), 15.

42. Cristina Escobar, "Extraterritorial Political Rights and Dual Citizenship in Latin America," *Latin American Research Review* 42, no. 3 (2007), 51.

43. B. Drummond Ayres Jr., "The Expanding Hispanic Vote Shakes Republican Strongholds," *New York Times*, November 10, 1996.

44. National Association of Latino Elected Officials, *1996 Latino Election Handbook*, 4.

45. Angelo Falcón, "Beyond *La Macarena*: The New York City Latino Vote," *Hispanic Link Weekly Report*, November 25, 1996, 4.

46. Ayres Jr., "Expanding Hispanic Vote Shakes Republican Strongholds"; see also "Despite Rapid Growth, Hispanic Vote May Play Only a Limited Role in Fall Presidential Contest," *Wall Street Journal*, September 30, 1996.

47. Falcón, "Beyond *La Macarena*."

48. Los Angeles voter exit poll conducted by the Tomás Rivera Policy Institute, *La Opinión*, and KVEA-TV, April 8, 1997.

49. Dan Whitcomb, "Once Again, L.A. Pledges to End Police Brutality," Reuters, May 8, 2007. Also Patrick Range McDonald, "Who Fixed Los Angeles? Not Former Mayor Antonio Villaraigosa, Say His Fiercest Critics," *Politico*, March 5, 2014, https://www.politico.com/magazine/story/2014/03/who-fixed-los-angeles-villaraigosa-legacy-104305.

50. As far back as the 1980s, a U.S. politician of partial Salvadoran ancestry, John Henry Sununu, became a national fixture in the Republican Party and the scion of a New Hampshire political dynasty. Sununu served as that state's seventy-fifth governor (1983–1989) and later as White House chief of staff under President George H. W. Bush. Born in Havana, Cuba, in 1939, he was the son of Victoria Dada, a Salvadoran national, and John Saleh Sununu, an American film distributor whose family ancestry was Lebanese and Palestinian. Two of John H. Sununu's sons, John Edward and Christopher Sununu, went on to their own political careers—John Edward as a U.S. senator from New Hampshire and Christopher Sununu as that state's governor. But the Sununus always identified more with their Lebanese roots and generally were not regarded as Hispanic leaders.

51. Rakesh Kochhar, Richard Fry, and Paul Taylor, "Wealth Gaps Rise to Record Highs Between Whites, Blacks and Hispanics," Pew Hispanic Center,

Social and Demographic Trends, July 26, 2011, https://www.pewresearch
.org/wp-content/uploads/sites/3/2011/07/SDT-Wealth-Report_7-26-11
_FINAL.pdf.

52. Reid J. Epstein, "NCLR Head: Obama 'Deporter-in-Chief,'" *Politico*,
March 4, 2014, https://www.politico.com/story/2014/03/national-council
-of-la-raza-janet-murguia-barack-obama-deporter-in-chief-immigration
-104217. For a more nuanced examination of Obama's immigrant removal
record, see Muzaffa Chisti, Sara Pierce, and Jessica Bolter, "The Obama
Record on Deportations: Deporter in Chief or Not," Migration Policy Institute, January 26, 2017, https://www.migrationpolicy.org/article/obama
-record-deportations-deporter-chief-or-not; also "All Presidents Are Deporters in Chief," *New York Times* editorial, July 14, 2019.

53. See Zev Chafets, "The Post-Hispanic Hispanic Politician: Will Julián Castro, the 35-Year-Old Mayor of San Antonio, Be the Next Great Latino
Hope on the National Stage?" *New York Times Magazine*, May 9, 2010.

54. They included state senators Efraín Gonzalez and Israel Ruiz, and city
council members Angel Rodriguez of Brooklyn and Miguel Martinez of
Manhattan. In 2009, state senator Hiram Monserrate was expelled from
that body following a misdemeanor conviction for assaulting his girlfriend.

55. Brian J. Connolly, "Promise Unfulfilled? Zoning, Disparate Impact and Affirmatively Furthering Fair Housing," *Urban Lawyer*, Fall 2016, American
Bar Association, https://www.jstor.org/stable/26425568. Daniel Marans,
"The Federal Government Failed Homeowners: How Much Blame Does
Julián Castro Deserve?" *HuffPost*, April 22, 2019, https://www.huffpost
.com/entry/julian-castro-housing-policy-foreclosure_n_5cbde8c1e
4b032e7cebb3daf.

56. Some have claimed Supreme Court justice Benjamin Cardozo was, in fact,
the first Hispanic on the court. Appointed by President Hoover in 1932,
Cardozo was descended from Sephardic Jews who migrated to the United
States from Portugal during the eighteenth century. Modern Hispanic lead-
ers, however, generally view the terms "Hispanic" and "Latino" as referring
to the Spanish-speaking peoples of Latin America and thus do not regard
Cardozo as Hispanic. See Neil A. Lewis, "Was a Hispanic Judge on the
Court in the '30s?" *New York Times*, May 26, 2009.

57. Sheryl Gay Stolberg, "A Trailblazer and a Dreamer," *New York Times*, May
27, 2009; see also Juan Gonzalez, "Day of pride for Latinos as Obama nomi-
nates Sonia Sotomayor for Supreme Court," *New York Daily News*, May 27,
2009.

58. Richard Wolf, "'The People's Justice': After Decade on Supreme Court,
Sonia Sotomayor is Most Outspoken on Bench and Off," *USA Today*, August 12, 2019.

59. Marc Lacey and Julia Preston, "Some Setbacks Aside, Latinos Reached
Milestones in Midterm Races," *New York Times*, November 6, 2010.

60. For Senate filibuster battle, see Scott Wong and Shira Toeplitz, "DREAM
Act Dies in Senate," *Politico*, December 18, 2010, https://www.politico.com
/story/2010/12/dream-act-dies-in-senate-046573; for protests against

Obama, see Peter Wallsten, "President Obama Bristles When He Is the Target of Activist Tactics He Once Used," *Washington Post*, June 10, 2012.

61. For DACA announcement, see "Remarks by the President on Immigration," Office of the Press Secretary, the White House, June 15, 2012, https://obamawhitehouse.archives.gov/the-press-office/2012/06/15/remarks-president-immigration; for data on DACA recipients, see Brian Harper, "Get the Numbers: Immigration Enforcement in the Trump Era," *Americas Society/Council of the Americas*, August 14, 2018, https://www.as-coa.org/articles/get-numbers-immigration-enforcement-trump-era; for 2012 exit polls, see Mark Hugo Lopez and Paul Taylor, "Latino Voters in the 2012 Election," Pew Research Center, Hispanic Trends, November 7, 2012, https://www.pewresearch.org/hispanic/2012/11/07/latino-voters-in-the-2012-election/.

62. Michael D. Shear, "Obama, Daring Congress, Acts to Overhaul Immigration," *New York Times*, November 20, 2014. For Secure Communities, see Kate Linthicum, "Obama Ends Secure Communities Program as Part of Immigration Action," *Los Angeles Times*, November 21, 2014.

63. "Here's Donald Trump's Presidential Announcement Speech," *Time*, June 16, 2015.

64. U.S. Census Bureau, Current Population Survey, November 1976 and November 2008.

65. U.S. Census Bureau, "Voting and Registration in the Election of November 2018," April 2019, https://www.census.gov/data/tables/time-series/demo/voting-and-registration/p20-583.html.

66. Pew Research Center, "Dissecting the 2008 Electorate"; also U.S. Census Bureau, Current Population Survey, "Reported Voting and Registration by Race, Hispanic Origin, Sex, and Age, for the United States: November 2008."

67. U.S. Department of Health and Human Services Office of Minority Health, "Profile: Hispanic/Latino Americans," October 12, 2021, https://minority-health.hhs.gov/omh/browse.aspx?lvl=3&lvlid=64.

68. Southwest Voter Registration Project, "SVREP President's Report #1 (2008): The Latino Voter Registration Surge in 2008."

69. Center for Democracy and Election Management, Building Confidence in U.S. Elections: Report of the Commission on Federal Election Reform (Washington, D.C.: Center for Democracy and Election Management, American University, 2005).

70. Justin Levitt, "The Truth about Voter Fraud," Brennan Center for Justice, 2007, 4, 18.

71. For summary of the Shelby case and its impact, see "*Shelby County v. Holder*, a Case Summary," Constitutional Accountability Center, https://www.theusconstitution.org/litigation/shelby-county-v-holder-u-s-sup-ct; also Van Newkirk II, "How *Shelby County v. Holder* Broke America," *Atlantic*, July 10, 2018, https://www.theatlantic.com/politics/archive/2018/07/how-shelby-county-broke-america/564707; for Brennan Center report, see Zachary Ross and Wendy R. Reiser, "This Is the Worst Voter Suppression We've Seen in the Modern Era," Brennan Center for Justice, November 2,

2018, https://www.brennancenter.org/blog/worst-voter-suppression-weve
-seen-modern-era. For detailed examinations of the modern voter suppression movement see Carol Anderson and Dick Durbin, *One Person, No Vote,
How Voter Suppression Is Destroying Our Democracy* (New York: Bloomsbury,
2018); also Ari Berman, *Give Us the Ballot: The Modern Struggle for Voting
Rights in America* (New York: Picador, Farrar, Straus and Giroux, 2016).

72. "Trump's Voter-Fraud Commission Itself Is a Fraud," *Washington Post*, July
18, 2017; Robert Farley, "Trump's Bogus Voter Fraud Claims Revisited," Fact-
Check, January 25, 2017, https://www.factcheck.org/2017/01/trumps-bogus
-voter-fraud-claims-revisited; Michael Tackett and Michael Wines, "Trump
Disbands Commission on Voter Fraud," *New York Times*, January 3, 2018.

73. Brian Holmes, "Wilder's All-Latino Leadership a First for Idaho," 7KTVB
.com, February 10, 2016, https://www.ktvb.com/mobile/article/mb/enter
tainment/places/idaho-life/wilders-all-latino-leadership-a-first-for-idaho
/39583219; for Yakima, see "Third Latina elected to Yakima City Council,"
Seattle Times, November 6, 2015, https://www.seattletimes.com/seattle
-news/3rd-latina-elected-to-yakima-city-council/.

74. Abigail Hess, "29-year-old Alexandria Ocasio-Cortez Makes History as the
Youngest Woman Ever Elected to Congress," CNBC, November 7, 2018,
https://www.cnbc.com/2018/11/06/alexandria-ocasio-cortez-is-now-the
-youngest-woman-elected-to-congress.html. For the Squad, who included
Ilhan Omar (D-MN), Ayanna Pressley (D-MA), and Rashida Tlaib
(D-MI), see: Anna North, "How 4 Congresswomen Came to be Known as
'The Squad,'" *Vox*, July 17, 2019, https://www.vox.com/2019/7/17/20696474
/squad-congresswomen-trump-pressley-aoc-omar-tlaib.

75. Britanny Mejia, "Latino Voters Tired of Being Taken for Granted by Baf-
fled Democratic Campaigns," *Los Angeles Times*, November 5, 2020;
Murtaza Hussain, "Nonwhite Voters Are Not Immune to the Appeal of
Right-Wing Populism," *The Intercept*, November 6, 2020, https://theinter
cept.com/2020/11/06/election-results-trump-voters-of-color/; Jennifer
Medina, "How Democrats Missed Trumps Appeal to Latino Voters," *New
York Times*, November 9, 2020; Nicole Chavez, "'There's No Such Thing as
the Latino Vote.' 2020 Results Reveal a Complex Electorate," CNN, No-
vember 9, 2020; Marcela Valdes, "The Fight to Win Latino Voters for the
GOP," *New York Times Magazine*, November 23, 2020.

76. U.S. Census Bureau, "Voting and Registration in the Election of 2020,"
April 2021, https://www.census.gov/data/tables/time-series/demo/voting
-and-registration/p20-585.html. The most accurate early analysis of the
Latino vote from the UCLA Latino Policy and Politics Initiative, which is-
sued a full report in January 2021. See Rodrigo Domínguez-Villegas, Nick
Gonzalez et al., "Vote Choice of Latino Voters in the 2020 Presidential
Election," UCLA Latino Politics and Policy Initiative, January 19, 2021,
https://latino.ucla.edu/wp-content/uploads/2021/01/Election-2020
-Report-1.19.pdf.

77. The much-cited 65 percent–32 percent split among Latino voters for president, for example, came from the National Exit Poll that the Edison

Research firm has conducted for the major broadcast networks every election since 2004, a survey criticized in the past because it undersamples voters who are Spanish dominant, those with less education, and those who live in majority Latino voting precincts, and because it oversamples precincts in Cuban-American communities, which historically have tended to vote more Republican. "It is an example of the worst possible poll that has somehow become believed as 'official' or 'fact' by folks in the media," said UCLA political scientist Matt Barret, who consulted for the Biden campaign. Author's interview and email correspondence with Matt Barreto, November 30 to December 8, 2020. See also Matt A. Barreto, Tyler Reny, and Bryan Wilcox-Archuleta, "Survey Methodology and the Latina/o Vote: Why a Bilingual, Bicultural, Latino-Centered Approach Matters," *Aztlán* 42, no. 2 (Fall 2017): 211–27, http://mattbarreto.com/papers/barreto_reny_wilcox _aztlan.pdf.

78. 2020 American Election Eve Poll, https://electioneve2020.com/poll/#/en /demographics/latino; For historic trends of Hispanic vote for president, see "Portrait of the Electorate: Table of Detailed Results," *New York Times*, November 3, 2010, https://archive.nytimes.com/www.nytimes.com/inter active/2010/11/07/weekinreview/20101107-detailed-exitpolls.html.

79. Reliable figures on voter participation would not be available until mid-2021, when the Census Bureau released its periodic survey of U.S. voters. The Edison poll, the one used by all the major media firms, initially estimated that Latinos composed 13 percent and African Americans 13 percent of the 159 million Americans who voted in 2020. If true, that would have meant an even higher number of Latinos voted—20.6 million. But like everything else about the Edison poll, Barreto insisted its numbers were unreliable "random guesses." As for the Biden margin among Latinos in the battleground states, preliminary estimates by UCLA's Latino Initiative researchers found that in Arizona, where Biden prevailed by just 12,000 votes, Latino voters delivered a net margin to him (after subtracting pro-Trump Latino votes) of 312,000; in Pennsylvania, where Biden won by 82,000, the net Latino vote for him was 116,000; in Wisconsin, where he won by 20,500, the net Latino Biden vote was 44,300.

80. The National Association of Latino Elected Officials' (NALEO) annual tally of Hispanic officeholders placed the tally at 6,749 in a 2019 report, its most recent. The number has fluctuated wildly over the years, largely because changes in procedures for selecting school district board members in Chicago and New York in the early 2000s reduced a large number of elected Latinos in those cities. See *National Directory of Latino Elected Officials 2018*, NALEO Education Fund, 2019, https://naleo.org/wp-content /uploads/2019/10/2018_National_Directory_of_Latino_Elected_Offi cials-1.pdf; also *1994 National Roster of Hispanic Elected Officials* (NALEO Education Fund, 1995), viii.

81. U.S. Census Bureau, "State-by-State Visualizations of Key Demographic Trends From the 2020 Census," October 8, 2021, https://www.census.gov /library/stories/state-by-state.html.

CHAPTER 11:
IMMIGRANTS OLD AND NEW

1. As Julia Young notes, today's nativists "have an outlet that earlier generations did not: a president who not only seems to agree with many of their
   arguments, but who also stokes the flames of this nativism so explicitly and
   aggressively." See Julia G. Young, "Making America 1920s Again? Nativism
   and U.S. Immigration, Past and Present," *Journal on Migration and Human
   Security* 5, no. 1 (2017): 228.

2. The "zero tolerance policy," announced by Attorney General Jeff Sessions
   in April 2018, declared the existence of a "crisis" at the Southwest border,
   one that the federal government would meet with "an escalated effort to
   prosecute those who choose to illegally cross our border." It soon led to tens
   of thousands of detentions and criminal prosecutions of migrants apprehended at the border and, in the case of families, to the separation of thousands of children from their parents. See "Attorney General Announces
   Zero-Tolerance Policy for Criminal Illegal Entry," Department of Justice,
   Office of Public Affairs, April 6, 2018, https://www.justice.gov/opa/pr/attor
   ney-general-announces-zero-tolerance-policy-criminal-illegal-entry.
   Also "The Trump Administration's 'Zero Tolerance' Immigration Enforcement Policy," Congressional Research Service, February 26, 2019, https://
   fas.org/sgp/crs/homesec/R45266.pdf. Also Ted Hesson and Lorraine
   Woellert, "DHS and HHS Officials Blindsided by 'Zero Tolerance' Border
   Policy," *Politico*, October 24, 2018, https://www.politico.com/story/2018/10
   /24/dhs-hhs-zero-tolerance-family-separations-935340.

3. For detentions, see Christopher Sherman, Martha Mendoza and Garance
   Burke, "US Held Record Number of Migrant Children in Custody in
   2019," *Associated Press,* November 12, 2019, https://apnews.com/015702af
   db4d4fbf85cf5070cd2c6824. For child deaths, see Molly Hennessey-Fiske,
   "Six Migrant Children Have Died in U.S. Custody. Here's What We Know
   About Them," *Los Angeles Times*, May 24, 2019. The U.S. Border Patrol has
   confirmed 7,505 migrant deaths at the Southwest border between 1998 and
   2018—an average of nearly 5 per week for the past thirty years. See "Southwest Border Deaths by Fiscal Year," U.S. Border Patrol, https://www.cbp
   .gov/sites/default/files/assets/documents/2019-Mar/bp-southwest-border
   -sector-deaths-fy1998-fy2018.pdf. Several media accounts, as well as some
   scholars and immigration advocates, however, assert the agency's figures
   significantly understate the actual toll by not counting, for example, those
   who drown but whose bodies end up on the Mexican side of the border. See
   Bob Ortega, "Border Patrol Failed to Count Hundreds of Migrant Deaths
   on US Soil," *CNN*, May 15, 2018, https://www.cnn.com/2018/05/14/us
   /border-patrol-migrant-death-count-invs/index.html; also Karl Eschbach
   et al., "Death at the Border," *The International Migration Review* 33, no. 2
   (Summer 1999): 430–54; and Jeremy Slack and Daniel E. Martínez, "The
   Geography of Migrant Death: Violence on the U.S.-Mexico Border," in
   Handbook on Critical Geographies of Migration, eds. Katharyne Mitchell
   et al. (Cheltenham, UK: Edward Elgar Publishing, 2019), 142–52.

4. "Immigrants Stage Massive Protest in Chicago," Reuters, March 10, 2006.

5. Mark Johnson and Linda Spice, "Thousands March for Immigrants," *Milwaukee Journal*, March 23, 2006.

6. Alfonso Gonzales, "The 2006 *Mega Marchas* in Greater Los Angeles: Counter-Hegemonic Moment and the Future of *El Migrante* Struggle," *Latino Studies* 7, no. 1 (2009), 42. Gonzales later expanded his article into a more detailed, groundbreaking study of the immigrant rights movement. See Alfonso Gonzales, *Reform Without Justice: Latino Migrant Politics and the Homeland Security State* (New York: Oxford University Press, 2014).

7. Gonzales, "The 2006 *Mega Marchas*," 41.

8. "500,000 March in L.A. against Immigration Bill," *Washington Post*, March 25, 2006; Aileen Torres and Kate Howard, "Immigration March Draws Thousands," *Nashville Tennessean*, March 30, 2006.

9. Thomas Korosec and Cynthia Leonor Garza, "The Immigration Debate: Rally Floods Dallas Streets: Police Estimate between 350,000 and 500,000 in Peaceful Crowds," *Houston Chronicle*, April 10, 2006, http://www.chron.com/disp/story.mpl/front/3782888.html.

10. Gonzales, "The 2006 *Mega Marchas*," 47–49; Juan Gonzalez, "On the Streets of New York, Solidarity Reigns," *New York Daily News*, May 2, 2006.

11. In "The 2006 *Mega Marchas*," 36–38, Alfonso Gonzales does an excellent job tracing the personal histories of several key organizers of the 2006 protests and how they came together in Los Angeles to form what Gonzales dubs the Latino Historic Bloc. I summarize his main findings here.

12. "Modern Immigration Wave Brings 59 Million to U.S., Driving Population Growth and Change Through 2065," Pew Research Center, Hispanic Trends, September 28, 2015, https://www.pewresearch.org/hispanic/2015/09/28/modern-immigration-wave-brings-59-million-to-u-s-driving-population-growth-and-change-through-2065/.

13. Pastora San Juan Cafferty, "The Language Question: The Dilemma of Bilingual Education for Hispanics in America," in *Ethnic Relations in America: Immigration, the Cities, Lingualism, Ethnic Politics, Group Rights*, ed. Lance Liebman (Englewood Cliffs, NJ: Prentice Hall, 1982), 106.

14. Carl Wittke, *Refugees of Revolution: The German Forty-Eighters in America* (Philadelphia: University of Pennsylvania Press, 1952), 185.

15. Ibid., 182, citing *Westbote*, July 28, 1854; also *New Yorker Staatszeitung*, April 1, 1854.

16. Joseph Fitzpatrick, *The Stranger Is Our Own: Reflections on the Journey of Puerto Rican Migrants* (Kansas City: Sheed & Ward, 1996), 99–100.

17. Wittke, *Refugees of Revolution*, 178.

18. Portes and Rumbaut, *Immigrant America*, 159–64.

19. Michael Novak, *The Rise of the Unmeltable Ethnics: Politics and Culture in the Seventies* (New York: Macmillan, 1972), 86.

20. Ibid., 86; also Harold Cruse, *Plural but Equal: Blacks and Minorities in America's Plural Society* (New York: William Morrow, 1987), 104–5.

21. Michael Teitelbaum, "Right Versus Right: Immigration and Refugee Policy in the United States," *Foreign Affairs* 59, no. 1 (Fall 1980): 26–27.

22. Richard D. Lamm and Gary Imhoff, *The Immigration Time Bomb: The Fragmenting of America* (New York: Truman Talley Books, 1985), 85, 93.

23. "INS 'Enforcement Deficit' Tied to Law: Voluntary Compliance Provision Fails to Deter Hiring of Illegals," *Washington Post*, February 2, 1995.

24. "Sealing Our Borders, the Human Toll," American Friends Service Committee, 6–7.

25. "The Browning of America," *New York Times*, April 9, 1990; "A Land of Immigrants Gets Uneasy About Immigration," *New York Times*, October 14, 1990; "Calculating the Impact of California's Immigrants," *Los Angeles Times*, January 8, 1992; "A Flood of Illegal Aliens Enters U.S. Via Kennedy," *New York Times*, March 18, 1992; "Fixing Immigration," *New York Times*, June 8, 1993; "Politicians Discovering an Issue: Immigration," *New York Times*, March 8, 1994.

26. Peter Brimelow, *Alien Nation: Common Sense about America's Immigration Disaster* (New York: Random House, 1995), 57. Such comments ignored the reality that at least one Latin American country, Panama, saw its entire ethnic and racial character transformed in the early 1900s when the U.S.-backed Panama Canal Company imported massive numbers of West Indians to build the Panama Canal. Brimelow would later go on to found the white nationalist website VDare in 1999, and is reportedly close to other white supremacists, such as Richard Spencer, of the National Policy Institute and Jared Taylor, founder of the white nationalist American Renaissance website. As recently as 2017, during remarks at an American Renaissance conference, Brimelow stated: "Hispanics do specialize in rape, particularly of children. They're very prone to it, compared to other groups." See Jane Coaston, "Peter Brimelow and VDare, the White Nationalist Website with Close Ties to the Right, Explained," *Vox*, September 24, 2018, https://www.vox.com /2018/8/22/17768296/peter-brimelow-vdare-kudlow-white-house-racism.

27. U.S. Immigration and Customs Enforcement 2008 *Annual Report*, 17.

28. Julia Preston, "Immigrants' Families Figuring Out What to Do after Federal Raids," *New York Times*, December 16, 2006.

29. William Johnson, "Smithfield Workers Arrested in Immigrant Raid," Labor Notes, January 28, 2007, https://labornotes.org/2007/01/smithfield-workers -arrested-immigrant-raids.

30. "Immigration Sting Nets More than a Hundred Arrests," Missourinet, May 22, 2007, https://www.missourinet.com/2007/05/22/immigration-sting-nets -more-than-100-arrests/.

31. "More Than 165 Arrested in Immigration Raid," *Los Angeles Times*, June 13, 2007.

32. "Pilgrim's Pride Plucked in Immigration Raids," Forbes, April 16, 2008, https://www.forbes.com/2008/04/16/pilgrims-pride-immigrant-markets -equity-cx_mlm_0416market36.html?sh=22eac79a4fc2.

33. "Nearly 600 Detained in Mississippi Immigration Raid," *USA Today*, August 26, 2008.

34. Margot Mendelson, Shayna Strom, and Michael Wishnie, "Collateral Damage: An Examination of ICE's Fugitive Operations Program,"

Migration Policy Institute, February 2009, Executive Summary, 1–2, http://www.migrationpolicy.org/pubs/NFOP_Feb09.pdf.

35. Chiu, Egyes, Markowitz, and Vasandani, "Constitution on ICE," 10.

36. Ibid., 16–17.

37. Ibid., 9–10.

38. Ibid., 12.

39. Jesse McKinley, "San Francisco Bay Area Reacts Angrily to Series of Immigration Raids," New York Times, April 27, 2007.

40. Clint Bolick, "Mission Unaccomplished: The Misplaced Priorities of the Maricopa County Sheriff's Office," Goldwater Institute, Policy Report No. 229, December 2, 2008, 9, https://goldwaterinstitute.org/2008-12-02 -maricopa-sheriff.

41. "America's Worst Sheriff (Joe Arpaio)," New York Times, December 31, 2008, http://theboard.blogs.nytimes.com/2008/12/31/americas-worst-sheriff -joe-arpaio/.

42. Robert Barnes, "Supreme Court Rejects Much of Arizona Immigration Law," Washington Post, June 25, 2012.

43. Marcelo Ballvé, "Immigrant Advocates Say Immigration Enforcement Worse Under Obama," New America Media, March 9, 2010, https://www .facingsouth.org/2010/03/immigrant-advocates-say-immigration -enforcement-worse-under-obama.html.

44. The group included Republicans such as Arizona's John McCain and Jeff Flake, South Carolina's Lindsey Graham, and Florida's Marco Rubio, as well as Democrats Chuck Schumer of New York and Richard Durbin of Illinois.

45. "Why Immigration Reform Died in Congress," NBC News, June 30, 2014, https://www.nbcnews.com/politics/first-read/why-immigration-reform -died-congress-n145276.

46. Nicholas Kulish and Mike McIntire, "An Heiress Intent on Closing America's Doors: How a Nature Lover Helped Fuel the Trump Immigration Agenda," New York Times, August 15, 2019; also Jason DeParle, "Shift Against Immigration Lifted a Young Firebrand: How a Movement Allowed Miller to Lead a Crusade from the White House," New York Times, August 18, 2019. See also "Mainstreaming Hate: The Anti-Immigrant Movement in the U.S.," A report from the Center on Extremism of the Anti-Defamation League, November 29, 2018, https://www.adl.org/the-anti -immigrant-movement-in-the-us#the-politics-of-immigration.

47. Julie Hirschfeld Davis and Maggie Haberman, "Trump Pardons Joe Arpaio, Who Became Face of Crackdown on Illegal Immigration," New York Times, August 25, 2017.

48. Mexicans represented a far lower portion that year (52.3 percent) of the total number of unauthorized migrants in the country. See Angela Gonzalez-Barrera and Jens Manuel Krogstad, "What We Know About Illegal Migration from Mexico," Pew Research Center, June 28, 2019, https:// www.pewresearch.org/fact-tank/2019/06/28/what-we-know-about-illegal -immigration-from-mexico.

49. Apprehensions in 2007 were 80 percent lower than the record year of 2000. See John Gramlich and Luis Noe-Bustamante, "What's happening at the U.S.-Mexico border in five charts," Pew Research Center, November 1, 2019, https://www.pewresearch.org/fact-tank/2019/11/01/whats-happening -at-the-u-s-mexico-border-in-5-charts/.

50. Author's analysis of figures from "U.S. Border Patrol Apprehensions by Sector Fiscal Year 2019," U.S. Customs and Border Protection, October 29, 2019, https://www.cbp.gov/newsroom/stats/sw-border-migration/usbp-sw -border-apprehensions#). According to the Migration Policy Institute, "In 2008, Mexicans comprised more than 90 percent of apprehensions. By fiscal 2019, Guatemalans, Hondurans, and Salvadorans represented nearly three-quarters of apprehensions, with two-thirds composed of families or unaccompanied children." See Randy Capps, Doris Meissner et al., "From Control to Crisis: Changing Trends and Policies Reshaping U.S.-Mexico Border Enforcement," Migration Policy Institute, August 2019, https:// www.migrationpolicy.org/research/changing-trends-policies-reshaping -us-mexico-border-enforcement.

51. Anil K. Sinha and Shikah Srivastava, "Comparative Study on Recovery and Reconstruction: A Case for an International Platform," International Recovery Platform, 2003, https://www.recoveryplatform.org/assets/publication /ADRC_Comparative_Study.pdf; for drought, see Gena Stephens, "Changing Climate Forces Desperate Guatemalans to Flee," *National Geographic*, October 23, 2018, https://www.nationalgeographic.com/environment/2018 /10/drought-climate-change-force-guatemalans-migrate-to-us/; also Anna Catherine Brigada, "Nearly 60% of Migrants from Guatemala's Dry Corridor Cited Climate Change and Food Insecurity as Their Reason for Leaving," Univision, May 11, 2018, https://catholicclimatemovement .global/nearly-60-of-migrants-from-guatemalas-dry-corridor-cited -climate-change-and-food-security-as-their-reason-for-leaving; also "Central American Migration: Root Causes and U.S. Policy," Congressional Research Service Report IF11151, June 13, 2019.

52. For President Trump's inaugural speech, see https://www.politico.com /story/2017/01/full-text-donald-trump-inauguration-speech-transcript -233907; for crime rates, see Lauren Brooke-Eisen, "America's Faulty Perception of Crime Rates," Brennan Center for Justice, March 16, 2015, https://www.brennancenter.org/our-work/analysis-opinion/americas -faulty-perception-crime-rates.

53. Dara Lind, "'Immigrants are Coming Over the Border to Kill You' is the Only Speech Trump Knows How to Give," *Vox*, January 9, 2019.

54. For "American phenomenon," see Freddy Funes, "Removal of Central American Gang Members: How Immigration Laws Fail to Reflect Global Reality," *University of Miami Law Review*, October 1, 2008, 304–5. Also Clare M. Ribando "Gangs in Central America," Congressional Research Service Report for Congress, July 27, 2007, 3, https://www.justice.gov/sites /default/files/eoir/legacy/2013/11/08/crs%20gangs_07.pdf; See also "Transnational Organized Crime in Central America and the Caribbean: A Threat

Assessment," United Nations Office on Drugs and Crime, September 2012, 28.

55. U.S. Department of Homeland Security, *Annual Report, Immigration Enforcement Actions: 2017*, March 2019, https://www.dhs.gov/sites/default /files/publications/enforcement_actions_2017.pdf. Mexico, was by far the biggest receiving nation for "criminal alien removals," with 992,170, followed by Guatemala (96,086), Honduras (92,238), and El Salvador (64,547), according to my calculation the annual figures.

56. "El Salvador's Crisis of Perpetual Violence," International Crisis Group, Latin America Report, no. 64, December 19, 2017, 13; Ana Arana, "How the Street Gangs Took Central America," *Foreign Affairs* 84, no. 3 (May–June, 2005): 98–110, https://www.jstor.org/stable/20034353. See also United Nations Office on Drugs and Crime (UNODC), *Transnational Organized Crime in Central America and the Caribbean: A Threat Assessment*, September 2012, 27. For El Salvador prison population, see "World Prison Population List, Eleventh Edition," Institute for Criminal Policy Research, October 2015, https://prisonstudies.org/sites/default/files/resources/down loads/world_prison_population_list_11th_edition_0.pdf. Gonzales, *Reform Without Justice, Latino Migrant Politics and the Homeland Security State*, 99–120, details how U.S. aid spurred the Mano Dura policies and he provides first-hand accounts of the experiences of repatriated Salvadoran males at the hands of local police.

57. UNODC, *Transnational Organized Crime*, 5, 28. Sonia Nazario, "Pay or Die," *New York Times*, July 28, 2019. The author found some bus company owners were forced to pay 30 to 40 percent of all their revenue in extortion fees to multiple gangs, with police or government officials often complicit in extortion schemes.

58. UNDOC, *Transnational Organized Crime*, 16. Randy Capps, *From Control to Crisis*, 18, notes that in 2018, murder rates per 100,000 were down to 51 in El Salvador, 41 in Honduras, and 22 in Guatemala. For individual cities, see "The world's most dangerous cities," *The Economist*, March 31, 2017, https:// www.economist.com/graphic-detail/2017/03/31/the-worlds-most -dangerous-cities. For impact of deportations on murder rates, see Christian Ambrosius and David Leblang, "Exporting Murder: US Deportations & the Spread of Violence," Free University of Berlin, School of Economics and Business, discussion paper, August 21, 2018, https://refubium.fu-berlin.de /bitstream/handle/fub188/22750/discpaper2018_13b.pdf?sequence=3&is Allowed=y. For unaccompanied minors, see Michael A. Clemens, "Violence, Development, and Migration Waves: Evidence from Central American Child Migrant Apprehensions," Center for Global Development, Working Paper 459, July 2017, 1–2, https://www.cgdev.org/publication/violence -development-and-migration-waves-evidence-central-american-child -migrant.

59. UNDOC, *Transnational Organized Crime*, 59–62. For increasing arms sales from U.S., see Alex Yablon, "Trump Is Sending Guns South as Migrants Flee North," *Foreign Policy*, March 8, 2019, https://foreignpolicy

.com/2019/03/08/trump-guns-honduras-central-america/; for smuggling of guns south of the border, see Chelsea Parsons and Eugenio Weigand Vargas, "Beyond Our Borders: How Weak U.S. Guns Laws Contribute to Violent Crime Abroad," Center for American Progress, February 2, 2018, https://www.americanprogress.org/issues/guns-crime/reports/2018/02/02 /445659/beyond-our-borders/; also Topher McDougal et al., "The Way of the Gun: Estimating Firearms Trafficking Across the US–Mexico Border," *Journal of Economic Geography* 15, no. 2 (2015): 297–327, https://academic .oup.com/joeg/article/15/2/297/929819.

60. Doris Meissner et al., "Immigration Enforcement in the United States: The Rise of a Formidable Machinery," Migration Policy Institute, January 2013, 9. Ironically, Meissner, the report's lead author, served as Commissioner of the Immigration and Naturalization Service under Bill Clinton, when the modern era of mass deportations began.

61. Mark Motivans, "Immigration, Citizenship, and the Federal Justice System, 1998–2018," U.S. Department of Justice, Bureau of Justice Statistics, August 2019, https://www.bjs.gov/content/pub/pdf/icfjs9818.pdf.

62. Zolan Kanno-Youngs, "Pentagon Investigator to Examine $400 Million Border Wall Contract Awarded to G.O.P. Donor," *New York Times*, December 12, 2019. Also Jaden Urbi, "Here's Who's Making Money from Immigration Enforcement," CNBC, June 29, 2018, https://www.cnbc.com/2018 /06/28/companies-profiting-immigration-enforcement-private-sector -prison-tech.html; "Here Are the Companies Poised to Profit from the Trump Wall," *MarketWatch*, February 25, 2019, https://www.marketwatch.com /story/here-are-the-companies-poised-to-profit-from-the-trump-border -wall-2019-02-22; Ted Hesson, "15 Companies that Profit from Border Security," ABC News, April 15, 2013, https://abcnews.go.com/ABC_Univision /Politics/15-companies-profit-border-security/story?id=18957304.

63. Immigrant Legal Resource Center, "The Rise of Sanctuary: Getting Local Officers Out of the Business of Deportations in the Trump Era," January 2018, https://www.ilrc.org/sites/default/files/resources/rise_of_sanctuary -lg-20180201.pdf. For Trump executive order, see William Cummings, "Federal Appeals Court Rules Trump's Sanctuary City Order Unconstitutional," *USA Today*, August 1, 2018.

64. Peniel Ibe, "Trump's Attacks on Legal Immigration System Explained," American Friends Service Committee, October 3, 2019, https://www.afsc .org/blogs/news-and-commentary/trumps-attacks-legal-immigration -system-explained. Also Michael D. Shear and Zolan Kanno-Youngs, "Trump Slashes Refugee Cap to 18,000, Curtailing U.S. Role as a Haven," *New York Times*, September 26, 2019.

65. Nicole Narea, "The Trump Administration Just Inked Another Deal Making it Harder to Seek Asylum in the U.S.," *Vox*, September 25, 2019, https:// www.vox.com/policy-and-politics/2019/9/25/20883831/trump-asylum -honduras-agreement.

66. Alan Gomez, "The Six Countries 300,000 Must Return to With End of TPS Program," *USA Today*, October 15, 2018. Also Catherine E. Shoichet,

"Federal Judge Temporarily Blocks Trump Administration from Ending TPS," CNN, October 4, 2018, https://www.cnn.com/2018/10/03/politics/tps-preliminary-injunction/index.html.

67. "Federal Judges in 3 States Block Trump's 'Public Charge' Rule for Green Cards," National Public Radio, October 11, 2019, https://www.npr.org/2019/10/11/769376154/n-y-judge-blocks-trump-administrations-public-charge-rule. "The Trump Administration's Proposed 'Mixed-Status' Housing Rule is Another Form of Family Separation," American Civil Liberties Union, July 10, 2019, https://www.aclu.org/blog/immigrants-rights/trump-administrations-proposed-mixed-status-housing-rule-another-form-family; also Xavier Arriaga, "'Mixed Status' and 'Public Charge' Rules: Attacks on Immigrants' Access to Housing," National Low-Income Housing Coalition, June 12, 2021, https://nlihc.org/sites/default/files/AG-2021/06-12_Attacks-Immigrants-Access-Housing.pdf.

68. Portes and Rumbaut, *Immigrant America* (4th Edition, 2014), 123.

69. Belinda I. Reyes, "Dynamics of Immigration: Return Migration to Western Mexico," Public Policy Institute of California, January 28, 1997.

70. Michelangelo Landgrave and Alex Nowrasteh, "Criminal Immigrants: Their Numbers, Demographics and Countries of Origin," Immigration and Policy Brief no. 1, Cato Institute, March 15, 2017. Also Anna Flagg, "The Myth of the Criminal Immigrant," *New York Times*, March 30, 2018.

71. Jeffrey S. Passel and Rebecca L. Clark, *Immigrants in New York: Their Legal Status, Incomes and Taxes, Executive Summary* (Washington, D.C.: The Urban Institute, 1998), 4–8; also "Calculating the Impact of California's Immigrants," *Los Angeles Times*, January 8, 1992.

72. Portes and Rumbaut, *Immigrant America*, 285–90.

73. Europe's population jumped from 140 million to 260 million in the hundred years between 1750 and 1850. By 1900, it had increased to 400 million. (See *World Almanac and Book of Facts*, 1993 [New York: Pharos Books, 1992].) We can only imagine what social conditions would have been like in a twentieth-century Europe if emigration had not been available as a safety valve. In contrast, Latin America, which counted 100 million inhabitants in 1930, skyrocketed to nearly 450 million in 1990. (See Alan Gilbert, *The Latin American City*, 26–27.) Thus, the region took a mere 60 years to achieve a population increase that took Europe 150 years. That population explosion has been worsened by the economic stagnation of the past few decades.

74. United Nations, Department of Economic and Social Affairs, "World Population Prospects 2019: Highlights," https://population.un.org/wpp/Publications/Files/WPP2019_Highlights.pdf.

75. Petras and Morley, *Latin America in the Time of Cholera*, 14.

76. In 1980, per capita gross domestic product was $2,315, but fourteen years later, it had dropped to $2,218. See Inter-American Development Bank, *Annual Report, 1994*, 103.

77. Raymond J. Mataloni, "U.S. Multinational Companies: Operations in 1995," in *Survey of Current Business*, October 1997, 62–63. Inter-American

Development Bank, *Annual Report, 1996*, 126. Also Aaron O'Neill, "Latin America and the Caribbean: External debt from 2011-2021," Statista, June 9, 2021, https://www.statista.com/statistics/698958/external-debt-of-latin -america-and-the-caribbean/; also United Nations Economic Commission for Latin America and the Caribbean, "Financing for development in the era of COVID-19 and beyond: Priorities of Latin America and the Carib- bean in relation to the financing for development global policy agenda," March 11, 2021, 3, https://www.cepal.org/en/publications/46711-financing -development-era-covid-19-and-beyond, and "Foreign Direct Invest- ment in Latin America and the Caribbean," 12, https://www.cepal.org /en/publications/type/foreign-direct-investment-latin-america-and -caribbean.

78. Manuel Orozco, Laura Porras, and Julia Yansura, "Remittances to Latin America and the Caribbean in 2018," *The Dialogue*, April 2019, https://www .thedialogue.org/wp-content/uploads/2019/04/2018-NumbersRemittances .pdf. For total U.S. foreign aid in 2008 of $36 billion (including military as- sistance), see Connie Veillette and Susan B. Epstein, "State, Foreign Opera- tions and Related Programs: FY 2008 Appropriations," Congressional Research Service, December 14, 2007, https://sgp.fas.org/crs/row/RL34023 .pdf; For 2017 total remittances from the U.S., see Pew Research Center, "Re- mittance Flows Worldwide in 2017," Pew Research Center, April 3, 2019, https://www.pewglobal.org/interactives/remittance-flows-by-country/.

79. Handlin, *The Uprooted*, 7.

80. Portes and Rumbaut, Immigrant America, 11. Similar patterns were been found in studies of Dominican immigrants in the 1990s. For more recent figures, see Jens Manuel Krogstad and Jynah Radford, "Education levels of U.S. immigrants are on the rise," Pew Research Center, September 14, 2018, https:// www.pewresearch.org/fact-tank/2018/09/14/education -levels-of-u-s-immigrants-are-on-the-rise/.

81. James D. Cockcroft, *Outlaws in the Promised Land: Mexican Immigrant Workers and America's Future* (New York: Grove Press, 1986), 49.

82. Francisco E. Balderrama and Raymond Rodriguez, *Decade of Betrayal: Mexican Repatriation in the 1930s* (Albuquerque: University of New Mexico Press, 1995), 120–22.

83. Cockcroft, *Outlaws in the Promised Land*, 67–75; also McWilliams, *North from Mexico*, 238–40.

84. U.S. Census Bureau, "Census Bureau Estimates Nearly Half of Children Under 5 Are Minorities," press release, May 14, 2009; also U.S. Census Bu- reau, "Annual Estimates of the Resident Population by Sex, Single Year of Age, Race, and Hispanic Origin for the United States: April 1, 2010 to July 1, 2018," 2018 Population Estimate, https://www.census.gov/newsroom/press -kits/2019/detailed-estimates.html; also T. J. Matthews and Brady E. Ham- ilton, "Total Fertility Rates by State and Race and Hispanic Origin, United States, 2017," *National Vital Statistics Report* 68, no 1, Centers for Disease Control, January 10, 2019, https://www.cdc.gov/nchs/data/nvsr/nvsr68 /nvsr68_01-508.pdf.

85. Lawrence Auster, "The Forbidden Topic," *National Review*, April 27, 1992. "Immigration will have to become an increasing part of the solution, not just in the U.S. but throughout the industrial world," Auster warns.

CHAPTER 12:
SPEAK SPANISH, YOU'RE IN AMERICA!

1. Sam Howe Verhovek, "Mother Scolded by Judge for Speaking Spanish," *New York Times*, August 30, 1995.
2. India's population is larger, but the majority of its people speak neither English nor Hindi, the two official languages. See Karen Zeigler and Steve Camarota, "67.3 Million in the United States Spoke a Foreign Language at Home in 2018," Center for Immigration Studies, October 29, 2019, https://cis.org/Report/673-Million-United-States-Spoke-Foreign-Language-Home-2018; also Stephen Burgen, "US Now has More Spanish Speakers than Spain—only Mexico has more," *The Guardian*, June 29, 2015, https://www.theguardian.com/us-news/2015/jun/29/us-second-biggest-spanish-speaking-country.
3. Arthur M. Schlesinger, *The Disuniting of America* (New York: W. W. Norton, 1992), 27–28, 122.
4. James Crawford, *Hold Your Tongue: Bilingualism and the Politics of "English Only"* (Reading, MA: Addison-Wesley, 1992), 30–39; also Pastora San Juan Cafferty, "The Language Question," in Liebman, *Ethnic Relations in America*, 108.
5. Crawford, *Hold Your Tongue*, 46.
6. Ibid., 42–44.
7. Weber, *The Mexican Frontier*, 16.
8. Ibid., 51–52; also Rosina Lozano, *An American Language: The History of Spanish in the United States* (Oakland: University of California Press, 2018), 5, 81, 102; and Laura E. Gomez, "Race, Colonialism, and Criminal Law: Mexicans and the American Criminal Justice System in Territorial New Mexico," *Law & Society Review* 34, no. 4 (January 2000): 1132, 1139–40.
9. Juan F. Perea, "A Brief History of Race and the U.S.–Mexican Border: Tracing the Trajectories of Conquest," *UCLA Law Review* 51 (2003): 299–300.
10. Ibid., 44.
11. Elise DuBord, "La Mancha de Plátano: Language Policy and the Construction of Puerto Rican National Identity in the 1940s," *Spanish in Context* 4, no. 2 (2007): 241–62; also Roamé Torres González, *Idioma, Biligüismo, y Nacionalidad: La Presencia del Inglés en Puerto Rico* (San Juan: Editorial de la Universidad de Puerto Rico, 2002); and Jorge A. Vélez, "Understanding Spanish-Language Maintenance in Puerto Rico: Political Will Meets the Demographic Imperative," *International Journal of the Sociology of Language* 142 (2000): 5–24.
12. Loida Figueroa, *Tres Puntos Claves: Lares, Idioma y Soberanía* (San Juan: Editorial Edil, 1972), 37–51; Crawford, *Hold Your Tongue*, 241–45; also Rosina Lozano, *An American Language*, 243–52.

13. Schlesinger, *The Disuniting of America*, 107.

14. Manuel del Valle, "Developing a Language-Based National Origin Discrimination Modality," 54–56.

15. *García v. Gloor*, 618 F. 2nd 264.

16. Carlos A. Pedrioli, "Respecting Language as Part of Ethnicity: Title VII and Language Discrimination at Work," *Harvard Journal on Racial and Ethnic Justice* 27 (2011), 102, https://harvardblackletter.org/wp-content/uploads/sites/8/2012/11/HBK103.pdf.

17. *EEOC v. Premier Operator Services, Inc.*, 113 F. Supp. 2d 1066, 1073 (N.D. Tex. 2000).

18. *Garcia v. Spun Steak Co.*, 998 F.2d 1480, 1487-89 (9th Cir. 1993).

19. U.S. Equal Employment Opportunity Commission, "Skilled Healthcare Group, Inc. to Pay up to $450,000 for National Origin Discrimination," April 14, 2009, https://www.eeoc.gov/eeoc/newsroom/release/archive/4-14-09.html; also U.S. Equal Employment Opportunity Commission, "Wisconsin Plastics to Pay $475,000 to Settle EEOC National Origin Discrimination Lawsuit," May 26, 2017, https://www.eeoc.gov/eeoc/newsroom/release/5-26-17.cfm.

20. D. E. Gevertz and A. C. Dowell, "Are English-Only Policies in the Workplace Discriminatory of National Origin?" American Bar Association, March 13, 2014.

21. European Charter for Regional or Minority Languages, Council of Europe, May 11, 1992, http://conventions.coe.int/treaty/en/Treaties/Html/148.htm.

22. Tamar Lewin, "Citing Individualism, Arizona Tries to Rein In Ethnic Studies in School," *New York Times*, May 13, 2010.

23. Edward W. Said, *Culture and Imperialism* (New York: Alfred A. Knopf, 1993), xii–xiii.

24. Ibid., xxv.

25. Clara Rodríguez, *Latin Looks: Images of Latinas and Latinos in the U.S. Media* (Boulder, CO: Westview Press, 1997), 21–33, summarizes many of these studies.

26. Ibid., 73–179.

27. Stacy L. Smith, Marc Choueiti, and Katherine Pieper, *Inclusion or Invisibility? Comprehensive Annenberg Report on Diversity in Entertainment, Media, Diversity, & Social Change Initiative*, USC Annenberg, February 22, 2016, 18, https://annenberg.usc.edu/sites/default/files/2017/04/07/MDSCI_CARD_Report_FINAL_Full_Report.pdf.

28. For film roles, see Darnell Hunt et al., "Hollywood Diversity Report 2018: Five Years of Progress and Missed Opportunities," UCLA College of Social Sciences, February, 2018, 21, https://socialsciences.ucla.edu/wp-content/uploads/2018/02/UCLA-Hollywood-Diversity-Report-2018-2-27-18.pdf; for movie audiences, see Parker Morse, "The Importance of Hispanic Audiences to the Entertainment Biz," *The Marketing Insider*, August 30, 2018, https://www.mediapost.com/publications/article/324337/the-importance-of-hispanic-audiences-to-the-entert.html.

29. Carlos Aguilar, "The American Latino Experience: 20 Essential Films Since 2000," *New York Times*, October 1, 2020.

30. Ward Alan Minge, *Acoma: Pueblo in the Sky* (Albuquerque: University of New Mexico Press, 1991), 11–15.

31. Gaspar Pérez de Villagrá, *Historia de la Nueva México*, 1610, trans. and ed., Miguel Encinias, Alfred Rodríguez, and Joseph P. Sánchez (Albuquerque: University of New Mexico Press, 1992).

32. Roberto Esquenazi-Mayo, ed., *El Padre Varela: Pensador, Sacerdote, Patriota* (Washington, D.C.: Georgetown University Press, 1990).

33. Nicolas Kanellos, *A History of Hispanic Theater in the U.S.: Origins to 1940* (Austin: University of Texas, 1990), 2–4.

34. José Martí, *Our America: Writings on Latin America and the Struggle for Cuban Independence*, ed. Philip S. Foner (New York: Monthly Review Press, 1977), 88.

35. Kanellos, *A History of Hispanic Theater*, 44–70.

36. John Storm Roberts, *The Latin Tinge: The Impact of Latin American Music on the United States* (New York: Oxford University Press, 1999), 24–27.

37. Ibid., 27–30, 36–41.

38. Ibid., 44–45, 50–55.

39. Ruth Glasser, *My Music Is My Flag: Puerto Rican Musicians and Their New York Communities, 1917–1940* (Berkeley: University of California Press, 1995), 54–82.

40. Roberts, *The Latin Tinge*, 76–126.

41. Manuel Peña, *The Texas-Mexican Conjunto: History of a Working-Class Music* (Austin: University of Texas Press, 1985), 51–59.

42. Roberts, *The Latin Tinge*, 97.

43. Melissa Castillo-Garstow, "Latinos in Hip Hop to Reggaeton," *Latin Beat*, March 2005, http://www.brownpride.com/latinrap/latinrap.asp?a=hiphoptoreggaeton/index.

44. García, *Havana USA*, 117.

45. Rebecca Mead, "All About the Hamiltons," *New Yorker*, February 9, 2015, https://www.newyorker.com/magazine/2015/02/09/hamiltons.

46. Crawford, *Hold Your Tongue*, 21.

47. Rosina Lozano, *An American Language*, 73.

48. Richard Rodriguez, *Hunger of Memory: The Education of Richard Rodriguez* (Toronto: Bantam Books, 1982), 3.

49. "New York's Bilingual Bureaucracy Assailed as School Program Grows," *New York Times*, January 4, 1993.

50. Pérez de Villagrá, *Historia de la Nueva México*, 120.

CHAPTER 13: FREE TRADE

1. For a discussion of the key pillars of neoliberalism, see John Williamson, *Did the Washington Consensus Fail?* (Washington, D.C.: Peterson Institute for International Economics, 2002); also Ximena de la Barra and Richard A. Dello Buono, *Latin America After the Neoliberal Debacle* (Lanham, MD:

Rowman & Littlefield, 2009); also Juan Carlos Moreno-Brid, Esteban Pérez Caldentey, and Pablo Ruíz Nápoles, "The Washington Consensus: a Latin American Perspective Fifteen Years Later," *Journal of Post Keynesian Economics* 27, no. 2 (2004–2005): 345–65.

2. Dani Rodrik, "Goodbye Washington Consensus, Hello Washington Confusion? A Review of the World Bank's Economic Growth in the 1990s: Learning from a Decade of Reform," *Journal of Economic Literature* 44, no. 4 (2006): 973–87; also Charles Gore, "The Rise and Fall of the Washington Consensus as a Paradigm for Developing Countries," *World Development* 28, no. 5 (2000): 789–804.

3. Julian Berger and Alex Bellos, "U.S. 'Gave the Nod' to Venezuelan Coup," *The Guardian*, April 17, 2002, https://www.theguardian.com/world/2002/apr/17/usa.venezuela; also Juan Forrero, "Documents Show C.I.A. Knew of a Coup Plot in Venezuela," *New York Times*, December 4, 2002. The CIA was aware beforehand of precise details of the coup plot yet chose not to alert Chávez, while key figures in the Bush administration's Latin America policy, including Elliot Abrams, John Negroponte, and anti-Castro extremist Otto Reich—all veterans of the 1980s Iran-Contra fiasco in Central America—met with the Venezuelan coup plotters in the months before the failed attempt. See El Vulliamy, "Venezuela coup linked to Bush team," *The Observer*, April 21, 2002.

4. Juan Manuel Karg, "Nueva Guerra Jurídica en América Latina," *Página12*, February 4, 2018, https://www.pagina12.com.ar/92381-nueva-guerra-juridica-en-america-latina.

5. See Ernesto Londoño, Julie Turkewitz, and Flávia Milhorance, "Leftists Are Ascendant in Latin America as Key Elections Loom," *New York Times*, January 4, 2022.

6. Mira Wilkins, *The Emergence of Multinational Enterprise: American Business Abroad from the Colonial Era to 1914* (Cambridge, MA: Harvard University Press, 1970), 110.

7. National Labor Committee Education Fund, "Paying to Lose Our Jobs," September 1992, 7.

8. Price Waterhouse, *Update of Baseline Study of Honduran Export Processing Zones, Report to United States Agency for International Development* (Washington, D.C.: 1993), 63.

9. Galeano, *Open Veins of Latin America*, 198.

10. Ibid., 203–6.

11. Alfred E. Eckes Jr., *Opening America's Market: U.S. Foreign Trade Policy Since 1776* (Chapel Hill: University of North Carolina Press, 1995), 47, 52.

12. United Nations Conference on Trade and Development, *Investment-Related Trade Measures* (New York: 1999), 7; Precise figures on the share of world trade conducted by multinational enterprises among themselves are difficult to quantify, given that many nations do not track them regularly, thus estimates vary significantly. See Nick Shaxson, "Over a third of world trade happens inside multinational corporations," Tax Justice Network, April 9, 2019, https://www.taxjustice.net/2019/04/09/over-a-third-or-more-of

-world-trade-happens-insidemultinational-corporations/. Other recent reports reflect similar percentages on intra-firm international trade. See Csilla Lakatos, Fanziska Ohnsorge, "Arm's-Length Trade: A Source of Post-Crisis Trade Weakness," World Bank Policy Research Working Paper No. 8144 (Washington, D.C., 2017), https://openknowledge.worldbank.org /handle/10986/27647; also Kim Moody, *Workers in a Lean World: Unions in the International Economy* (New York: Verso, 1997), 48–49. Also Raymond J. Mataloni Jr., "U.S. Multinational Companies: Operations in 1995," in *Survey of Current Business*, October 1997, 50; also Doug Henwood, "Clinton's Trade Policy," in *Free Trade and Economic Restructuring in Latin America*, eds. Fred Rosen and Deidre McFadyen (New York: Monthly Review, 1995), 32.

13. United Nations Development Programme, *Human Development Report 1998* (New York: Oxford University Press, 1998), 30. Larry Elliot, "World's 26 Richest People Own as Much as Poorest 50%, says Oxfam," *The Guardian*, January 20, 2019, https://www.theguardian.com/business/2019/jan/21 /world-26-richest-people-own-as-much-as-poorest-50-per-cent-oxfam -report.

14. Moody, *Workers in a Lean World*, 130–32.

15. Barry and Preusch, *The Central America Fact Book*, 309.

16. Originally enacted as Section 262 of the U.S. Revenue Act of 1921, and later renamed Section 931, the exemption from federal taxes for U.S.-owned businesses operating in territorial possessions was aimed at assisting American firms in the Philippines. In 1948, Puerto Rico's government, led by Luis Muñoz Marin, passed its own Industrial Tax Exemption Act, which also offered complete exemption from Puerto Rico income, property, and municipal taxes to new firms—popularly known as triple-tax-exemption. Congress amended that exemption in 1974 and renamed it Section 936. See Ann. J. Davidson, "A Credit for All Reasons: The Ambivalent Role of Section 936," *The University of Miami Inter-American Law Review* 19, no. 1 (October 1, 1987), 97–136.

17. Dietz, *Economic History of Puerto Rico*, 210–12.

18. Ibid., 226–28.

19. Augusta Dwyer, *On the Line: Life on the U.S.-Mexican Border* (London: Latin American Bureau, 1994), 6.

20. Author's interview with Othal Brand, mayor of McAllen, Texas, and president of Griffin and Brand, June 1993.

21. Dwyer, *On the Line*, 8.

22. Ibid., 42.

23. *NAFTA's Broken Promises: The Border Betrayed* (Washington, D.C.: Public Citizen Publications, 1996), 5–6; also *La Industria Maquiladora en Reynosa y Matamoros*, Centro de Estudios Fronterizos y de Promoción de los Derechos Humanos (Tamaulipas, Mexico: 1992), 5. Also Robert E. Scott, "Manufacturing Job Loss: Trade, not Productivity, Is the Culprit," Economic Policy Institute, August 11, 2015, https://www.epi.org/publication /manufacturing-job-loss-trade-not-productivity-is-the-culprit/.

24. *La Industria Maquiladora*, 10; also *Mexico, No Guarantees: Sex Discrimination in Mexico's Maquiladora Sector* (New York: Human Rights Watch, August 1996).

25. Saskia Sassen, "Why Migration?" in *Free Trade and Economic Restructuring in Latin America*, 277–78.

26. U.S. Department of Homeland Security, *Yearbook of Immigration Statistics: 2019*, https://www.dhs.gov/immigration-statistics/yearbook/2019.

27. "NAFTA's Legacy for Mexico: Economic Displacement, Lower Wages for Most, Increased Migration," Public Citizen Global Trade Watch Factsheet, October 2019, https://www.citizen.org/wp-content/uploads/NAFTA-Factsheet_Mexico-Legacy_Oct-2019.pdf.

28. Inter-American Development Bank, *Annual Report* (Washington, D.C.: 1994), 103.

29. In 1981, the average hourly factory wage in Mexico and Hong Kong was the same, $1.80. But, by 1987, the Hong Kong wage had risen to $2.11, while Mexico's had dropped to $0.71. See *La Industria Maquiladora*, 3.

30. Dwyer, *On the Line*, 17.

31. *La Industria Maquiladora*, 34.

32. Ibid., 36.

33. J. Dougherty, "U.S.-Mexico Commission Fails to Stop Sewage Plaguing Border," *The Revelator*, March 29, 2018, https://therevelator.org/sewage-plaguing-border; also Tim Vanderpool, "The Festering Sanitation Crisis at Our Border," National Resources Defense Council, December 3, 2018, https://www.nrdc.org/onearth/festering-sanitation-crisis-our-border; also Chloe Jones, "A different kind of border crisis; it's not about security or immigration, it's about sewage," *Cronkite News*, May 7, 2019, https://cronkitenews.azpbs.org/2019/05/07/mexico-arizona-border-wastewater/.

34. Sanford J. Lewis, *Border Trouble: Rivers in Peril: A Report on Water Pollution Due to Industrial Development in Northern Mexico* (Boston: National Toxic Campaign Fund, 1991), 4–8. See also Mary E. Kelly, "Free Trade: The Politics of Toxic Waste," NACLA, September 25, 2007, https://nacla.org/article/free-trade-politics-toxic-waste.

35. Michael Beebe, "Mallory Plant Is Long Gone: Some Say It Left Grim Legacy," *Buffalo News*, March 11, 1987; also Juan Gonzalez, "The High Costs of 'Free' Trade," *New York Daily News*, January 22, 1992; also Dwyer, *On the Line*, 66–68.

36. *NAFTA's Broken Promises*, 25.

37. *Endangered Rivers of America: The Nation's Ten Most Endangered Rivers and Fifteen Most Threatened Rivers for 1993*, American Rivers (Washington, D.C.: April 20, 1993), 1.

38. Author's interview with Domingo Gonzáles, Coalition for Justice for the Maquiladora Workers, Brownsville, Texas, June 1993; also Sanford J. Lewis, *Border Trouble*, 8.

39. Ibid., 20–25; also Texas Department of Health, *An Investigation of a Cluster of Neural Tube Defects in Cameron County, Texas*, July 1, 1992; also Linda Diebel, "Mexico's Futuristic Nightmare," *Toronto Star*, March 13, 1993.

40. *NAFTA's Broken Promises*, 29–34; also Texas Department of Health Services "Liver and Intrahepatic Bile Duct Cancer in Texas," Texas Cancer Registry, November 2018, 11 and 24, https://www.dshs.texas.gov/tcr/data/cancersites/Liver-Cancer-in-Texas-Web-Report.pdf.
41. National Labor Committee, "Paying to Lose Our Jobs," 17–22.
42. Ibid., 23.
43. Ramona Hernández, Francisco Rivera-Batiz, and Roberto Agodini, "Dominican New Yorkers: A Socioeconomic Profile," Dominican Research Monographs (New York: CUNY Dominican Studies Institute, 1995), 14.
44. Apparel exports to the United States from the region increased 688 percent between 1980 and 1991. See National Labor Committee, "Paying to Lose Our Jobs," 23–24. For 2019 figures, see World Integrated Trade Solutions, "United States Clothing and Textile Imports by Country in U.S.$ Thousand in 2019," World Bank, 2019. https://wits.worldbank.org/CountryProfile/en/Country/USA/Year/LTST/TradeFlow/Import/Partner/by-country/Product/50-63_TextCloth.
45. National Labor Committee, "Paying to Lose Our Jobs," 39–41.
46. National Labor Committee Education Fund, "Free Trade's Hidden Secrets: Why We Are Losing Our Shirts" (November 1993), 9.
47. Price Waterhouse, *Update of Baseline Study*, 11–12.
48. Juan Gonzalez, "Exploitation's Always in Fashion," *New York Daily News*, July 25, 1995.
49. "Casos Especiales Durante el Período del 23/06/95 al 29/06/95," Oficina de Tutela Legal del Arzobispado, Comisión Arquidiocesana de Justicia y Paz, San Salvador, El Salvador, C.A.
50. Price Waterhouse, *Update of Baseline Study*, 50.
51. National Labor Committee, "Paying to Lose Our Jobs," 24–25.
52. Edmund L. Andrews, "How Cafta Passed House by 2 Votes," *New York Times*, July 29, 2005.
53. Estimates are that Mexico spent some $30 million lobbying for the passage of NAFTA, more than twice the previous record of foreign lobbying, which was Kuwait's spending of $10 to $12 million before and during the Persian Gulf War. See "Trading Game," by the Center for Public Integrity, May 27, 1993, and "Mexico Buys Free Trade," by Don Hazen, in *Facts and Fictions About "Free Trade"* (New York: Institute for Alternative Journalism, 1993), 89–92.
54. "NAFTA Trade-off: Some Jobs Lost, Others Gained," *New York Times*, October 9, 1995.
55. Author's interview with Othal Brand, mayor of McAllen, Texas.
56. Nancy J. Perry's "What's Powering Mexico's Success," *Fortune*, February 10, 1992, 109–15.
57. Jorge G. Castañeda, *The Mexican Shock: Its Meaning for the U.S.* (New York: The New Press, 1995), 36.
58. See Lee Hudson Teslik, "NAFTA's Economic Impact," Council on Foreign Relations Backgrounder, July 7, 2009; also "The Effects of NAFTA on U.S.-Mexico Trade and GDP," U.S. Congressional Budget Office report, May 2003.

59. Bruce Campbell, "False Promise: Canada in the Free Trade Era," Economic Policy Institute Briefing Paper, April 2001, http://www.epi.org /pages/briefingpapers_nafta01_ca/.

60. The deficit in goods was slightly offset by a growing U.S. surplus in services sold to Mexico ($8.7 billion in 2007), but it still remained at historically high levels. See Office of the United States Trade Secretary, "U.S.-Mexico Trade Facts," July 23, 2009, http://www.ustr.gov/countries-regions/americas /mexico; also U.S. Census Bureau, "Trade in Goods with Mexico," https:// www.census.gov/foreign-trade/balance/c2010.html.

61. Robert E. Scott, Carlos Salas, and Bruce Campbell, "Revisiting NAFTA: Still Not Working for North America's Workers," Economic Policy Institute Briefing Paper no. 173, September 28, 2006, 9, http://www.epi.org/publica tions/entry/bp173/.

62. Ibid., 3.

63. David Brauer, "Factors Underlying the Decline in Manufacturing Employment Since 2000," U.S. Congressional Budget Office report, December 23, 2008, 2, 4, https://www.cbo.gov/sites/default/files/110th-congress-2007 -2008/reports/12-23-manufacturing.pdf.

64. Zepeda, Wise, and Gallagher, "Rethinking Trade Policy." See also Kevin P. Gallagher and Lyuba Zarsky, "Sustainable Industrial Development? The Performance of Mexico's FDI-Led Integration Strategy," Global Development and Environment Institute, Fletcher School of Law and Diplomacy, Tufts University, February 2004, 44–45. For 2012 *maquiladora* employment, see INEGI, "Indicadores de Establecimientos Con Programa IMMEX, Cifras Durante Febrero de 2019," April 29, 2019, https://www .inegi.org.mx/contenidos/saladeprensa/notasinformativas/2019/est_immex /est_immex2019_04.pdf. For changes in government census, see INEGI, "Síntesis Metodológica de la Estadística del Programa de la Industria Manufacturera, Maquiladora y Servicios de Exportación," 2015, http://internet .contenidos.inegi.org.mx/contenidos/Productos/prod_serv/contenidos /espanol/bvinegi/productos/nueva_estruc/702825075521.pdf.

65. Zepeda, Wise, and Gallagher, "Rethinking Trade Policy," 10, 13.

66. Anne Vigna, "NAFTA Hurts Mexico, Too," Agence Global, June 1, 2008; also Zepeda, Wise, and Gallagher, "Rethinking Trade Policy," 12–13; also Mark Weisbrot, Lara Merling, Vitor Mello, Stephan Lefebvre, and Joseph Sammut, Did NAFTA Help Mexico? An Update After 23 Years (Washington, D.C.: Center for Economic and Policy Research, March 2017) 14, http:// cepr.net/images/stories/reports/nafta-mexico-update-2017-03.pdf?v=2).

67. Elisabeth Malkin, "NAFTA's Promise Unfulfilled," *New York Times*, April 13, 2009, B1.

68. Zepeda, Wise, and Gallagher, "Rethinking Trade Policy," 13.

69. For a splendid account of the food disaster NAFTA has produced, see Alyshia Gálvez, *Eating NAFTA: Trade, Food Policies, and the Destruction of Mexico* (Oakland: University of California Press, 2018). For diabetes, see Jason Beaubien, "How Diabetes Got To Be the No. 1 Killer in Mexico," National Public Radio, April 5, 2017, https://www.npr.org/sections/goatsandsoda

/2017/04/05/522038318/how-diabetes-got-to-be-the-no-1-killer-in
-mexico. For obesity rates, see Organization for Economic Co-operation and
Development, Obesity Update 2017, https://www.oecd.org/els/health
-systems/Obesity-Update-2017.pdf.

70. Ibid.; also Zepeda, Wise, and Gallagher, "Rethinking Trade Policy," 14. For
$16 per hour wage earners, see, "Only 269,000 Mexicans Earn More Than
US $16 per Hour, or 308 Pesos," *Mexico News Daily*, August 30, 2018,
https://mexiconewsdaily.com/news/only-269000-mexicans-earn-more
-than-16-per-hour/. For 2017 wage gap, see "Average wage in the manufacturing sector in Mexico compared to the United States from 2015 to 2017."
Statista, 2019, https://statista.com/statistics/882757/mexico-average-wage
-manufacturing-sector-compared-us/. Harley Shaiken, "Mexico's Labor
Reform: Opportunities and Challenges for an Improved NAFTA," testimony before the Subcommittee on Trade, Committee on Ways and Means,
U.S. House of Representatives, June 25, 2019, https://docs.house.gov/meet
ings/WM/WM04/20190625/109703/HHRG-116-WM04-Bio-ShaikenH
-20190625.pdf.

71. For wage increase, see Mark Weisbrod et al., "Did NAFTA help Mexico . . ."
For poverty rate, see International Monetary Fund, "Mexico's Economic
Outlook in Five Charts," November 8, 2018, https://www.imf.org/en/News
/Articles/2018/11/07/NA110818-Mexico-Economic-Outlook-in-5-Charts.
For social programs, see Gerardo Esquivel and Guillermo Cruces, "The
Dynamics of Income Inequality in Mexico since NAFTA," Economía 12,
no. 1 (2011), https://www.jstor.org/stable/41302974.

72. "Remittance Flows Worldwide in 2017," Pew Research Center.

73. United Nations Statistics Division, United Nations Commodity Trade Statistics Database, 2008. For 2017 data, see World Bank. (n.d.). Mexico trade
summary. World Integrated Trade Solution, https://wits.worldbank.org
/CountryProfile/en/Country/MEX/Year/LTST/Summary.

74. Heiner Schulz, "Foreign Banks in Mexico: New Conquistadors or Agents of
Change?" Wharton Financial Institutions Center Working Paper No. 06–
11, April 22, 2006, 3, 8–10; also Monica Campbell, "Chase Is On for the
Whole *Enchilada*," *The Banker*, June 2, 2004.

75. John Lyons, "Mexican Officials Prod Banks to Boost Lending," *Wall Street
Journal*, March 22, 2004, A17; also Campbell, "Chase Is On."

76. Estimates for Mexican cartel drug trafficking revenues from sales in the
United States vary wildly. See Salvador Rizzo, "Do Mexican cartels make
$500 billion a year?" *Washington Post*, June 24, 2019; also "2010 Interna-
tional Narcotics Control Strategy Report (INCSR), vol. 1," U.S. State Department, Bureau of International Narcotics and Law Enforcement Affairs,
March 1, 2010, 432, https://2009-2017.state.gov/documents/organization
/137411.pdf. See also Laura Y. Calderón, Kimberly Heinle, Octavio Rodríguez
Ferreira, and David A. Shirk, "Organized Crime and Violence in Mexico:
Analysis Through 2018," Justice in Mexico, Department of Political Science
and International Relations, University of San Diego, April 2019, https://jus
ticeinmexico.org/wp-content/uploads/2019/04/Organized-Crime-and

-Violence-in-Mexico-2019.pdf. For 2018 murder rate, see Jon Martín Cullell, "México Cerró 2018 con un Promedio de Casi 100 Homicidios al Día en Plena Ola de Violencia," *El País*, July 25, 2019, https://elpais.com/internacio nal/2019/07/25/mexico/1564063543_114010.html.

77. Roberta S. Jacobson, "U.S.-Mexico Security Agreement: Next Steps for the Merida Initiative," deputy assistant secretary of state testimony to U.S. House of Representatives Committee on Foreign Affairs, May 27, 2010, https://2009-2017.state.gov/p/wha/rls/rm/2010/142297.htm.

78. "2010 International Narcotics Control Strategy Report (INCSR)," 435–36; For 2017, see "Illegal Opium Poppy Cultivation Increases in Mexico," Reuters, January 12, 2018, https://www.eluniversal.com.mx/english/illegal -opium-poppy-cultivation-increases-in-mexico.

79. Tracy Wilkinson, "Mexico Agricultural Subsidies Are Going Astray: A Fund to Help Poor Farmers Compete with U.S. Imports Is Instead Benefiting Drug Lords' Kin and Officials," *Los Angeles Times*, March 7, 2010.

80. Mary Botari, "Trade Deficit in Food Safety: Proposed NAFTA Expansions Replicate Limits on U.S. Food Safety Policy That Are Contributing to Unsafe Food Imports," Public Citizen, July 2007, 4, http://www.citizen.org /documents/FoodSafetyReportFINAL.pdf; also Thomas Hargrove, "A Russian Roulette of Food Poisoning in the American States," Scripps Howard News Service, November 11, 2006. Also L. Hannah Gould et al., "Outbreaks of Disease Associated with Food Imported into the United States, 1996–2014," *Emerging Infectious Diseases Journal* 23, no. 7 (March 2017), https://wwwnc.cdc.gov/eid/article/23/3/16-1462_article#tnF1.

81. De la Barra and Dello Buono, *Latin America*, 28.

82. Isidro Morales-Moreno, "Mexico's Agricultural Trade Policies: International Commitments and Domestic Pressure," in Managing the Challenges of World Trade Organization Participation: 45 Case Studies, eds. Peter Gallagher, Patrick Low, and Andrew Stoller (World Trade Organization, 2005), www.wto.org/english/res_e/booksp_e/casestudies_e/case28_e.htm.

83. For an excellent summary of these new social movements, see De la Barra and Dello Buono, *Latin America*, 51–77.

84. De la Barra and Dello Buono, *Latin America*, 77, no. 8.

85. Raúl Zibechi, "Regional Integration after the Collapse of the FTAA," International Relations Center (Silver City, NM: November 21, 2005), 2–4.

86. Ibid., 1–2.

87. For Venezuela, Bolivia, Ecuador, and Brazil, the span of years was 2002 to 2007; for Argentina, it was 2002 to 2006. See "Social Panorama of Latin America, 2009," United Nations Commission for Latin America and the Caribbean, 9–11.

88. Jake Johnston and Stephan Lefebvre "Honduras Since the Coup: Economic and Social Outcomes," Center for Economic Policy and Research, November 2013, http://cepr.net/documents/publications/Honduras-2013-11-final .pdf; also Clayton M. Cunha Filho et al., "A Right-to-Left Policy Switch? An Analysis of the Honduran case under Manuel Zelaya," *International Political Science Review* 34, no. 5 (2013): 519–42.

89. The Honduran military claimed to be following an arrest order against Zelaya issued by that country's Supreme Court, after Zelaya refused to accept a court order that he not proceed with a non-binding referendum calling for a new constituent assembly. But the United Nations, the Organization of American States and the European Union all immediately condemned the military actions as an illegal coup, and in 2011, a Honduran Truth Commission reached the same conclusion. See "Honduran Truth Commission Rules Zelaya Removal Was a Coup," BBC, July 7, 2011, https://www.bbc.com/news/world-latin-america-14072148. For U.S. role in the coup, see Lee Fang, "During Honduras Crisis, Clinton Suggested Back Channel with Lobbyist Lany Davis," *The Intercept*, July 6, 2015, https://theintercept.com/2015/07/06/clinton-honduras-coup/; also Jake Johnston, "How Pentagon Officials May Have Encouraged a 2009 Coup in Honduras," *The Intercept*, August 29, 2017, https:// theintercept.com/2017/08/29/honduras-coup-us-defense-departmetnt-center-hemispheric-defense-studies-chds/.

90. For a riveting account of the repression during the post-coup years in Honduras, see Dana Frank, *The Long Honduran Night: Resistance, Terror, and the United States in the Aftermath of the Coup* (Chicago: Haymarket Books, 2018), 52–93. For the murders of journalists, see *Informe Anual Sobre El Estado General de Los Derechos Humanos en Honduras, Año 2013*, Comisionado Nacional de lo Derechos Humanos (CONADEH), 39, http://app.conadeh.hn/Anual2013/informes/CONADEH_2013.pdf. For the case of Berta Cáceres, see "Berta Cáceres: Seven Men Convicted of Murdering Honduran Environmentalist," *The Guardian*, November 29, 2018, https://www.theguardian.com/world/2018/nov/29/berta-caceres-seven-men-convicted-conspiracy-murder-honduras. For a broader report of repression after the coup, see "Preliminary Observations concerning the Human Rights Situation in Honduras," Inter-American Commission on Human Rights Report, Organization of American States, December 5, 2014, https://www.oas.org/en/iachr/media_center/PReleases/2014/146A.asp. For the federal indictment of Juan Antonio "Tony" Hernández, which listed his brother, President Juan Orlando Hernández, as an unindicted co-conspirator, see *U.S. v. Juan Antonio Hernandez*, S2-15-CR379, https://www.justice.gov/usao-sdny/press-release/file/1113821/download. At least fifteen other former senior officials of the Honduran government have been indicted or convicted in U.S. or Honduran courts for drug trafficking, moneylaundering or racketeering since 2015. They include former president Rafael Callejas Moreno, a former Supreme Court president, a former vice-president of the National Congress, the one-time mayor of the country's largest city, San Pedro Sula, a former head of the national telecom company, and a half-dozen members of the Honduran congress. See "Report to Congress on Corruption in El Salvador, Guatemala, and Honduras," U.S. State Department, May 18, 2019, https://torres.house.gov/sites/torres.house.gov/files/05-16-19.State_.Report-on-Corruption-El-Salvador-Guatemala-Honduras.pdf.

91. Mateo Crossa, "Maquiladora Industry Wages in Central America Are Not Living Wages," Center for Economic and Policy Research, May 20, 2015,

https://cepr.net/maquiladora-industry-wages-in-central-america-are
-not-living-wages.

92. Banyan Globalm, USAID/Guatemala Gender Analysis Final Report 2018, United States Agency for International Development, September 14, 2018, 74, https://banyanglobal.com/wp-content/uploads/2018/10/USAID -Guatemala-Gender-Analysis-Final-Report.pdf.

93. Equipo de Investigaciones Laborales (EIL)/Red de Solidaridad de la Maquila (RSM), "Salarios de Maquilas en Centro América 2018 e Inciativas Internacionales por un Salario Digno," October 2018, 20, https://www .maquilasolidarity.org/sites/default/files/attachment/Salarios_maquila _centroamérica_EIL_RSM-Oct2018.pdf.

94. From 120,000 *maquila* workers in 2011, Honduras grew to 167,009 by 2019. Nicaraguan employment went from 103,000 in 2011 to 123,000 in 2019. For Honduras figures, see Equipo de Investigaciones Laborales (EIL)/Red de Solidaridad de Maquilas (RSM), *Los Salarios Mínimos de Maquila y las Canastas Básicas de Alimento en Cuatro Países de Centroamérica 2019* (San Salvador, Octubre 2019), 8, https://www.business -humanrights.org/sites/default/files/documents/Salarios_minimos_ma quila_2019.pdf. For Nicaragua figures, see "Menos Empleos en Zonas Francas," CentralAmericaData.com, June 4, 2019, https://www.centralam ericadata.com/es/article/home/Menos_empleo_en_zonas_francas.

95. "'Neoliberal,' 'Corrupción' y 'Pueblo,' entre las Palabras Que Más Dijo AMLO en Primer Discurso," *El Financiero*, January 12, 2018, https://www .elfinanciero.com.mx/nacional/neoliberal-corrupcion-y-pueblo-entre-las -palabras-que-mas-dijo-amlo-en-su-primer-discurso.

96. As López Obrador describes them, the previous transformations of Mexico were the original revolution for independence against Spain in 1810, the War of Reform led by Benito Juárez (1857–1860) that culminated in the official separation of church and state, and the Mexican revolution of 1910 that overthrew Porfirio Díaz. He thus proclaimed his movement as aiming at social revolution.

97. "Mexico to Raise Base Wage, New Leader Pledges More Hikes to Come," Reuters, December 17, 2018, https://www.reuters.com/article/us-mexico -politics-wages/mexico-to-raise-base-wage-new-leader-pledges-more -hikes-to-come-idUSKBN1OH07H; Rodrigo Cruz, "Lo Que Sabemos de las Pensiones a Adultos Mayores Que Dará AMLO," January 1, 2019, https:// www.eluniversal.com.mx/nacion/politica/lo-que-sabemos-de-las -pensiones-adultos-mayores-que-dara-amlo. For critiques of AMLO, see Mary Beth Sheridan, "AMLO is Mexico's Strongest President in Decades. Some Say He's Too Strong," *Washington Post*, November 29, 2019; also Christopher Lenton, "AMLO's Tumultuous First Year in Office Creates New Energy Environment in Mexico," Natural Gas Intelligence, December 3, 2019, https://www.naturalgasintel.com/articles/120366-ngi-2020-amlos -tumultuous-first-year-in-office-creates-new-energy-environment -in-mexico. For the Maya Train, see Martha Pskowski, "Mexico's 'Maya Train' Is Bound for Controversy," CityLab, February 22, 2019, https://www

.citylab.com/environment/2019/02/mexico-travel-mayan-train-yucatan -tourism-economic-development/583405/.

98. Daniel Blue Tyx, "A Labor Spring for Mexico's Maquilas?" North American Congress on Latin America, March 1, 2019, https://nacla.org/news /2019/03/01/labor-spring-mexico's-maquilas. For the new labor reform, see M. Angeles Villareal, "USMCA and Mexico's New Labor Law," Congressional Research Service, May 22, 2019, https://fas.org/sgp/crs/row /IN11123.pdf; also "Catching Up on the Labour Reform #2: Mexico Budgets for the Transition," Maquila Solidarity Network, December 2019, https://www.maquilasolidarity.org/sites/default/files/resource/Mexico -Budgets-for-the-Transition_Dec_2019.pdf.

99. The final pact required that 75 percent of autos sold in North American be made from cars and auto parts that originated in the region (up from 62.5 percent under NAFTA), and that 40–45 percent of the value of those cars and trucks be made by workers paid an *average* $16 per hour—a figure that could only be met today by workers in the United States and Canada, but the provisions left a loophole in the future possible for outsourcing to Mexico a portion of the industry's research and skilled jobs, according to U.S. auto unions that opposed the deal. See Courtney Vinopal, "These four changes helped Trump and Democrats agree to the USMCA trade deal," *PBS Newshour*, December 11, 2019, https://www.pbs.org/newshour/economy/making-sense/these-4 -changes-helped-trump-and-democrats-agree-to-the-usmca-trade-deal. Also "Redo of USMCA Better Than Original NAFTA After Yearlong Effort to Improve Trump's 2018 deal," Public Citizen, December 10, 2019, https:// www.citizen.org/news/unions-consumer-groups-and-congressional -democrats-achieve-removal-of-big-pharma-giveaways-and -strengthening-of-labor-environmental-standards-and-enforcement/.

100. Annette Lin, "AMLO's Crumbling Promise to Migrants," North American Congress on Latin America, July 24, 2019, https://nacla.org/news/2019/09 /17/amlo's-crumbling-promise-migrants.

101. Ted Piccone, "The Geopolitics of China's Rise in Latin America," Brookings Institution, *Geoeconomics and Global Issues*, Paper 2, November 2016, https:// www.brookings.edu/wp-content/uploads/2016/11/the -geopolitics-of-chinas-rise-in-latin-america_ted-piccone.pdf. By 2017, more than a quarter of Latin America's mining and oil exports and 16 percent of its agricultural exports were going to China. See Rebecca Ray and Keehan Wang, "China-Latin America Economic Bulletin, 2019 Edition," University Global Development Policy Center, 2019, 4, https://www .bu.edu/gdp/files/2019/02/GCI-Bulletin-Final-2019-1-1.pdf. See also Vijay Prashad, "The US Is Doing Its Best to Lockout China from Latin America and the Caribbean," *Peoples Dispatch*, November 4, 2020, https://peoples dispatch.org/2020/11/04/the-us-is-doing-its-best-to-lock-out-china -from-latin-america-and-the-caribbean/. For data on 2018 Latin American debt to China, see Kevin P. Gallagher and Margaret Meyers, "China-Latin America Finance Database," InterAmerican Dialogue, 2019, https://www .thedialogue.org/map_list. See also Alfonso Serrano, "China Fills Trump's Empty Seat at Latin American Summit," *New York Times*, April 13, 2018.

102. Kenneth Rapoza, "Hugo Chavez Cancer Conspiracy Theories Resurface After Death," *Forbes*, March 6, 2013, https://www.forbes.com/sites/ken rapoza/2013/03/06/hugo-chavez-cancer-conspiracy-theories-resurface -after-death/#7c2c0c5d4f1a. Also Mike Whitney, "The Strange Death of Hugo Chávez: an Interview with Eva Golinger," Counterpunch, April 22, 2016, https://www.counterpunch.org/2016/04/22/the-strange-death-of -hugo-chavez-an-interview-with-eva-golinger/.

103. Alexander Main, "The Right Has Power in Latin America, but No Plan," Jacobin, August 3, 2019, https://jacobinmag.com/2019/08/latin-america -united-states-donald-trump-right-wing. For Haiti elections, see Mark Weisbrot, "Haiti's election: a travesty of democracy," *The Guardian*, January 10, 2011, https://www.theguardian.com/commentisfree/cifamerica /2011/jan/10/haiti-oas-election-runoff.

104. "Poverty in Latin America Remained Steady in 2017, but Extreme Poverty Increased to the Highest Level since 2008, while Inequality has Fallen Notably since 2000," press release on *Social Panorama of Latin America 2018*, report of United Nations Economic Commission for Latin America and the Caribbean, January 15, 2019, https://www.cepal.org/en/pressreleases /poverty-latin-america-remained-steady-2017-extreme-poverty -increased-highest-level.

CHAPTER 14: PUERTO RICO, U.S.A.: POSSESSED AND UNWANTED

1. For poverty levels, see Lara Merling, Kevin Cashman, Jake Johnston, and Mark Weisbrot, "Life After Debt in Puerto Rico: How Many More Lost Decades?" (Washington, D.C.: Center for Economic and Policy Research, 2017), http://cepr.net/images/stories/reports/puerto-rico-2017-07.pdf. For comparative median household incomes, see U.S. Census Bureau, "2013–2017 American Community Survey 5-Year Estimates, Selected Economic Characteristics." For federal net transfers to Puerto Rico, the Census Bureau discontinued in 2012 a Consolidated Federal Funds Report that specifically tracked such data, while the Puerto Rican government's own ability to report such information has become unreliable because of its continuing financial crisis, but a Bureau of Economic Analysis tracking of net federal transfers to all U.S. territories provides a comparable best estimate, since Puerto Rico represents most of those transfers, see "Unilateral Current Transfers, Net: Adjustment for U.S. Territories and Puerto Rico," St. Louis: Federal Reserve Economic Data, 2020, https://alfred.stlouisfed.org/series ?seid=B1655C1A027NBEA&utm_source=series_page&utm_medium =related_content&utm_term=related_resources&utm_campaign=alfred.

2. Joshua Barajas, "Hurricane Maria's Official Death Toll Is 46 Times Higher Than It Was almost a Year Ago. Here's Why," *PBS Newshour*, August 30, 2018, https://www.pbs.org/newshour/nation/hurricane-marias-official -death-toll-is-46-times-higher-than-it-was-almost-a-year-ago-heres-why.

3. Lewis portrayed the Rios family, an intergenerational dysfunctional group with a history of prostitution and other social problems. He popularized the

term "culture of poverty" to describe individuals who became accustomed to living at the margins of society. See Oscar Lewis, *La Vida: A Puerto Rican Family in the Culture of Poverty, San Juan and New York* (New York: Random House, 1966). Before Lewis, a controversial 1963 report on New York's welfare system by Julius Horwitz, a consultant to the New York State Senate, asserted that New York City's public assistance program had succeeded in "perpetuating Negro and Puerto Rican dependency and in creating a vast sick body of tortured, frightened, dependent children who have succeeded in overwhelming all of the moral and social institutions of New York City." See "Horwitz, Report on Relief Charges Southern Negroes, Puerto Ricans Do Come to New York and Demand Welfare," *New Pittsburgh Courier*, April 27, 1963. That same year, Daniel Moynihan and Nathan Glazer published *Beyond the Melting Pot*, in which they claimed one of the chief problems in race relations in the city was the "disproportionate presence of Negroes and Puerto Ricans on welfare." See Glazer and Moynihan, Beyond the Melting Pot (Cambridge, MA: MIT Press, 1963). Likewise, in 1990, sociologist Marta Tienda concluded Puerto Ricans were "part of the urban underclass," and were more prone than other ethnic or racial groups to a welfare lifestyle due to "family background effects." See Marta Tienda, "Welfare and Work in Chicago's Inner City," *The American Economic Review* 80, no. 2 (February 1990): 372–76; also Lydia Morris, "Women without Me: Domestic Organization and the Welfare State as Seen in a Coastal Community of Puerto Rico," *The British Journal of Sociology* 30, no. 3 (1979): 322–40, https://www.jstor.org/stable/589911.

4. Chavez, *Out of the Barrio*, 140.
5. Héctor Cordero Guzmán, "Lessons from Operation Bootstrap," in Rosen, *Free Trade and Economic Restructuring in Latin America*, 79; also James Dietz and Emilio Pantojas-García, "Puerto Rico's New Role in the Caribbean: The High-Finance/Maquiladora Strategy," in *Colonial Dilemma: Critical Perspectives on Contemporary Puerto Rico*, eds. Edwin Meléndez and Edgardo Meléndez (Boston: South End Press, 1993), 108.
6. According to a 1964 report to Congress by the Commonwealth of Puerto Rico, over 40 percent of companies that started with local tax exemptions closed their doors when those exemptions expired. See Fernández, *The Disenchanted Island: Puerto Rico and the United States in the Twentieth Century* (New York: Praeger, 1992), 208.
7. U.S. General Accounting Office, *Tax Policy: Puerto Rico and the Section 936 Tax Credit*, June 1993, 3.
8. Ibid., 9; also Congressional Budget Office, "Potential Economic Impacts of Changes in Puerto Rico's Status Under S. 712," April 1990, 7; also Emilio Pantojas-García, *Development Strategies as Ideology: Puerto Rico's Export-Led Industrialization Experience* (London: Lynne Rienner Publishers, 1990), 117–18.
9. Those 110 firms had three hundred factories operating then. See Pantojas-García, *Development Strategies*, 114.
10. Ibid., 115–16.
11. Ibid., 153. According to Pantojas-García, Abbott Laboratories listed 71

percent of worldwide profits from Puerto Rico; Digital Equipment, 57 percent; Union Carbide, 25 percent; Pepsi-Cola, 21 percent; and Motorola, 23 percent. For pharmaceutical industry tax benefits and worker compensation in 1975, see U.S. Department of the Treasury, "The Operation and Effect of the Possessions Corporation System of Taxation," First Annual Report, June 1978, 40–41.

12. The twenty-two drug company subsidiaries in Puerto Rico averaged 77.5 percent return on operating income in 1983, compared with the mainland average of 18.7 percent for pharmaceuticals. See GAO, *Tax Policy*, 52–53.

13. Kelly Richmond, "Drug Companies Fear Loss of Tax Exemption," *New Jersey Record*, November 8, 1993. For a detailed account of Congressional efforts to reduce the Section 936 tax benefits, see U.S. Senate, Joint Committee on Taxation, "An Overview of Special Tax Laws Related to Puerto Rico and an Analysis of the Tax and Economic Policy Implications of Recent Legislative Options," staff report, June 23, 2006, 50–55, https://esta disticas.pr/files/BibliotecaVirtual/estadisticas/biblioteca/USC_OSTR RPR.PDF.

14. This compared with $5.1 billion in Canada and $4.6 billion in Germany. While the size of U.S. investment in Canada was twice that of Puerto Rico's, the island's rate of return on investment is more than twice Canada's—a phenomenal 23.7 percent. See Pantojas-García, *Development Strategies*, 167; for lost federal revenues, see U.S. General Accounting Office, "Pharmaceutical Industry Tax Benefits of Operating in Puerto Rico," May 1992, 14.

15. Government of Puerto Rico Planning Board, "External Trade Statistics Puerto Rico 2016," February 2017.

16. Puerto Rico Planning Board, *Economic Report to the Governor 1995*, March 1996, chap. 5, 11.

17. "Democrats Attack Permanent Tax Exemption for Profitable Territorial Subsidiaries Bill," *Puerto Rico Herald*, October 18, 2002. See also U.S. General Accounting Office, *Puerto Rican Fiscal and Economic Trends*, 81 (Washington, D.C.: May 1997), https://www.gao.gov/assets/ggd-97-101.pdf. For recent job losses, see Commonwealth of Puerto Rico, Department of Labor and Human Resources, *Puerto Rico Economic Analysis Report 2015–2016* (San Juan: 2016), https://www.doleta.gov/performance/results/Annu alReports/docs/2017_State_Plans/Economic_Reports/Puerto %20Rico/PR%20Economic%20Analysis.pdf. Manufacturing jobs had dropped from 158,000 in 2000 to 112,000 in 2009—see Puerto Rico Planning Board, "Statistical Appendix of Economic Report to the Governor, May 17, 2010," Table 33.

18. U.S. GAO, *Puerto Rican Fiscal and Economic Trends*, 15, 6.

19. U.S. GAO, *Puerto Rican Fiscal and Economic Trends*, 61; Puerto Rico Planning Board, "Net Manufacturing Domestic Income," Statistical Appendix, Table 12.

20. U.S. GAO, *Puerto Rican Fiscal and Economic Trends*, 65.

21. Puerto Rico was surpassed by the Netherlands ($77.7 billion), Luxembourg ($62.4 billion), United Kingdom ($45.7 billion), Bermuda ($42.9 billion), Ireland ($42 billion), and Switzerland ($40 billion). It was, however, far

ahead of Japan ($12.1 billion), France ($9.5 billion), Mexico ($8.7 billion), and China ($7.8 billion). See Raymond J. Mataloni, "U.S. Multinational Companies, Operations in 2006," *Survey of Current Business*, November 2008. For Puerto Rico, see Puerto Rico Planning Board, "Statistical Appendix of Economic Report."

22. "Más del 20% del PIB Se Va en Gastos Tributarios," *Sin Comillas*, September 23, 2019, https://sincomillas.com/gobierno-publica-informe-de-gastos-tributarios-para-el-2017/; also Abner Dennis, "A Tax Haven Called Puerto Rico," *LittleSis*, February 19, 2020, https://news.littlesis.org/2020/02/19/a-tax-haven-called-puerto-rico/.

23. For comparative world labor participation rates, see World Bank, "Labor Force Participation Rate, Total (Percentage of Population Ages 15+), Modeled ILO Estimate," September 2019, https://data.worldbank.org/indicator/SL.TLF.CACT.ZS. For historical unemployment rate, see Federal Reserve Economic Data, "Unemployment Rate in Puerto Rico, 1976–2019," https://fred.stlouisfed.org/series/LAUST720000000000003A; also U.S. GAO, *Puerto Rican Fiscal and Economic Trends*, 11.

24. Salim Hurth, "Hired Labor's Share of Income is Lowest in Puerto Rico," The Heritage Foundation, Issue Brief No. 4502, December 29, 2015, http://thf-reports.s3.amazonaws.com/2015/IB4502.pdf.

25. Jaime Bofill Valdés, "Comportamiento de Diversas Variables Macro-Económicas de Puerto Rico y de la Trayectoria de Crecimiento entre Puerto Rico y Estados Unidos Durante 1950–94," *Boletín de Economía* 1, no. 1.

26. In 1989, for instance, pharmaceutical companies gave a mere $1 million in charitable contributions in Puerto Rico while earning more than $3 billion in profits from their operations there. See GAO, *Tax Policy*, 64.

27. The term "Jones Act" can refer to one of several U.S. laws. The 1916 Jones Act, also known as the Philippine Autonomy Act, provided for a transitional autonomous government for the Philippines. The 1917 Jones-Shafroth Act created a civilian government for Puerto Rico and granted U.S. citizenship to island residents. The Jones Act (Merchant Marine Act of 1920) established the nation's cabotage laws.

28. Colin Grabow, "New Reports Detail Jones Act's Cost to Puerto Rico," Cato Institute, February 25, 2019, https://www.cato.org/blog/new-reports-detail-jones-acts-cost-puerto-rico. For federal subsidies, see U.S. Government Accountability Office, "Maritime Security: DOT Needs to Expeditiously Finalize the Required National Maritime Strategy for Sustaining U.S.-Flag Fleet," August 2018, GAO18-478, 12, https://www.gao.gov/assets/700/693802.pdf.

29. U.S. Commission on Ocean Policy, *An Ocean Policy for the 21st Century, Final Report*, 2004, 192; also "U.S. Trade with Puerto Rico and U.S. Possessions, 2004," U.S. Census Bureau, http://www.census.gov/prod/2005pubs/annl04tx.pdf. For 2018 shipments, see "U.S. Trade with Puerto Rico and U.S. Possessions, 2018," https://www2.census.gov/library/publications/2019/economics/ft895-18.pdf. See also AFL-CIO Executive Council Statement, "Support of the Jones Act," October 21, 2017, https://aflcio.org/about/leadership/statements/support-jones-act.

30. "Report by the President's Task Force on Puerto Rico's Status," March 2011, 82–83, https://obamawhitehouse.archives.gov/sites/default/files/uploads /Puerto_Rico_Task_Force_Report.pdf.

31. Angel L. Ruiz and Fernando Zalacain, "The Economic Relation of the United States and the Puerto Rican Economies: An Interregional Input-Output Approach," *Boletín de Economía* 3, no. 1 (Unidad de Investigaciones Económicas, Universidad de Puerto Rico, September 1997).

32. Torruella, *The Supreme Court and Puerto Rico*, 257–59. For Medicaid, see Judith Solomon, "Puerto Rico's Medicaid Program Needs an Ongoing Commitment of Federal Funds," Center on Budget and Policy Priorities, April 22, 2019, https://www.cbpp.org/research/health/puerto-ricos -medicaid-program-needs-an-ongoing-commitment-of-federal-funds; for lost funds from SSI, see Kobre & Kim, "Independent Investigator's Final Investigative Report," The Financial Management & Oversight Board for Puerto Rico, August 20, 2018, 39.

33. Luis R. Dávila Colón, "The Blood Tax: The Puerto Rican Contribution to the United States War Effort," *Review of Colegio de Abogados de Puerto Rico*, November 1979. Also W. W. Harris, *Puerto Rico's Fighting 65th U.S. Infantry, from San Juan to Chorwan* (San Rafael, CA: Presidio Press, 1980); also Nicolás Santiago Ortíz, *Korea 1951, La Guerra Olvidada: El Orgullo de Haber Sobrevivido* (Río Piedras, PR: Esmaco Printers, 1991).

34. Shannon Collins, "Puerto Ricans Represented Throughout U.S. Military History," Department of Defense News, October 14, 2016, https://www .defense.gov/News/News-Stories/Article/Article/974518/puerto-ricans -represented-throughout-us-military-history. Exact counts for Puerto Ricans who served or were killed in U.S. wars are difficult to tally, since not all who enlisted from the fifty states necessarily identified as being of Puerto Rican heritage. Defense Department records as of June 2019, for instance, list 15 deaths of soldiers during Operation Enduring Freedom who originally resided in Puerto Rico, but 26 deaths of those whose "ethnicity" was Puerto Rican, suggesting that 11 were U.S.-resident Puerto Ricans. For the various campaigns of the Iraq and Afghanistan wars, the DOD found a total of 80 deaths of service members who self-identified as of Puerto Rican heritage, of whom 53 were from the island. See "American War and Military Operations Casualties: Lists and Statistics," Congressional Research Service, updated September 24, 2019, https://fas.org/sgp/crs/natsec/RL32492.pdf. A much bigger number, however, is claimed by the island-based anti-war group, Madres Contra La Guerra, which identified by name 123 soldiers of Puerto Rican heritage from either the island, the United States, St. Croix, or Panama who were killed between 2003 and 2014. It is thus likely that the actual number of Puerto Rican fatalities is greater than the official count. See Madres Contra La Guerra, http://madrescontralaguerra.blogspot.com.

35. Richard Goldstein, "The Big Mango," *New York*, August 7, 1972, 24, quoted in Manuel Maldonado-Denis, *The Emigration Dialectic: Puerto Rico and the USA* (New York: International Publishers, 1980), 76–77.

36. Raymond Carr, *Puerto Rico: A Colonial Experiment* (New York: Vintage Books, 1984), 294, 297.

37. Chavez, *Out of the Barrio*, 159.

38. Frantz Fanon, *The Wretched of the Earth* (New York: Grove Press, 1963), 210–11.

39. Quoted in Torruella, *The Supreme Court and Puerto Rico*, 223.

40. Arturo Morales Carrión, *Puerto Rico: A Political and Cultural History*, 326–30.

41. Chavez, *Out of the Barrio*, 159.

42. Daniel P. Moynihan, *The Negro Family: The Case for National Action* (Washington, D.C.: U.S. Department of Labor, March 1965).

43. Palmira Ríos, "Export-Oriented Industrialization and the Demand for Female Labor: Puerto Rican Women in the Manufacturing Sector, 1952–1980," in Meléndez, *Colonial Dilemma*, 89–92.

44. Clara E. Rodríguez, *Puerto Ricans: Born in the U.S.A.* (Boston: Unwin Hyman, 1989), 86.

45. "Hispanics of Puerto Rican Origin in the United States, 2007," Pew Research Center Fact Sheet, July 13, 2009, https://www.pewresearch.org/his panic/2009/07/13/hispanics-of-puerto-rican-origin-in-the-united -states-2007/.

46. Katherine T. McCaffrey, "Social Struggle against the U.S. Navy in Vieques, Puerto Rico: Two Movements in History," in Kal Wagenheim and Olga Jiménez de Wagenheim, *The Puerto Ricans: A Documentary History*, 4th edition (Princeton, NJ: Markus Weiner Publishers, 2008), 334–45; also Ronald O'Rourke, "Vieques, Puerto Rico Naval Training Range: Background and Issues for Congress," Congressional Research Service, December 17, 2001, https://www.everycrsreport.com/reports/RS20458.html.

47. Matthew Hay Brown, "Military Exercises Left Toxic Waste, Residents and Experts Claimed," *Orlando Sentinel*, January 18, 2003; also Elba Díaz and Arturo Massol-Deya, "Trace Element Composition in Forage Samples from a Military Target Range, Three Agricultural Areas, and One Natural Area in Puerto Rico," *Caribbean Journal of Science* 39, no. 2 (2003): 215–20; also Cruz Maria Nazario, John Lindsay-Poland, and Déborah Santana, "Health in Vieques: A Crisis and Its Causes," Fellowship of Reconciliation Task Force on Latin America and the Caribbean, June 2002, https://groups .google.com/g/soc.culture.puerto-rico/c/Woj1bZYUIYU?pli=1.

48. Mike Melia, "Former Marine Becomes Face of New Vieques Battle," *New York Times*, October 11, 2009.

49. Mike Allen and Roberto Suro, "Vieques Closing Angers Military, Hill GOP," *Washington Post*, June 15, 2001.

50. In May 2009, the author covered the Vieques protest during a visit to the range by the Reverend Jesse Jackson and Cardinal Roberto González, the archbishop of San Juan, both of whom openly backed the civil disobedience movement. Governor Rosselló personally welcomed the Jackson delegation to Puerto Rico. Later, during a private meeting with the commander of Roosevelt Roads Naval Base, the civil rights leader warned the commander, "These people don't want you here; it's time to leave." See also "Puerto Ricans Protest Plan to Resume Navy Training," *Los Angeles Times*, February 22, 2000.

51. In April 2001, the Reverend Al Sharpton, Robert F. Kennedy Jr., actor Edward James Olmos, famed Puerto Rican singer Danny Rivera, and Jackie Jackson, the wife of the Reverend Jesse Jackson, were all arrested in Vieques. So were two Puerto Rican members of Congress, New York's Nydia Velázquez and Chicago's Luis Gutiérrez, while the third, New York's José Serrano, was similarly arrested in an anti-navy protest in front of the White House. See O'Rourke, "Vieques, Puerto Rico Naval Training Range: Background and Issues for Congress."

52. Ibid.

53. Ivonne Acosta, *La Mordaza: Puerto Rico, 1948–1957* (Río Piedras, PR: Editorial Edil., 1989). Gives the best account of the gag law and persecution of *independentistas*.

54. For an account of the FBI subversion campaign against the independence movement during the 1967 referendum, see Ronald Fernández, *The Disenchanted Island: Puerto Rico and the United States in the Twentieth Century*, 214–19. Also Juan Manuel García-Passalacqua, "The 1993 Plebiscite in Puerto Rico: A First Step to Decolonization," *Current History* 93, no. 581 (March 1994): 78.

55. For a thorough discussion of the Carter administration debate, see Beatriz de la Torre, "El Plebiscito Nació en la Era de Carter," in *Puerto Rico y los Estados Unidos: El Proceso de Consulta y Negociación de 1989 y 1990*, vol. 2, 1990, eds. Juan Manuel García-Passalacqua and Carlos Rivera Lugo (Río Piedras, PR: Editorial de la Universidad de Puerto Rico, 1991), 10–21.

56. Edgardo Meléndez, "Colonialism, Citizenship and Contemporary Statehood," in Meléndez, *Colonial Dilemma*, 41–52.

57. Congressional Budget Office, "Potential Economic Impacts," 26–27.

58. García-Passalacqua, "The 1993 Plebiscite," 103–7.

59. Most directly threatened by default were a handful of obscure but extremely important firms known as monoline insurers, which provide insurance for investors on a huge portion U.S. municipal bonds, and who stood to lose up to $26 billion if there was major write-down of Puerto Rico's debt. If any of those monoline insurers were to collapse because their exposure, borrowing could potentially rise on all municipal bonds. See Lydia O'Neal "Puerto Rico Crisis: Bond Insurers Fight to Avoid Paying Claims," *International Business Times*, November 8, 2017, https://www.ibtimes.com/political -capital/puerto-rico-crisis-bond-insurers-fight-avoid-paying-claims -2611224. Also Jayden Sangha, "Current Status of Puerto Rico Debt Restructuring," Municipal Bonds Risk Management, March 20, 2019, https:// www.municipalbonds.com/risk-management/current-status-of-puerto -rico-debt-restructuring/.

60. White House, "Puerto Rico Hill Update: Muni Market Impacts," press release, March 18, 2016. But in 2019, the president of a bond issuer trade group warned: "The risk of contagion is real. Everyone will pay." See "Puerto Rico's Bankruptcy: 'The Risk of Contagion is Real,'" Association of Financial Industry Insurers, April 16, 2019.

61. For a detailed acount of how Republican Senators Strom Thurmond and Bob Dole executed their steal amendment in 1984 to deny Puerto Rico's

ability to seek protection from creditors under federal law, see the majority opinion of U.S. First Circuit Appellate Judge Juan Torruella in *Franklin California Tax-Free Trust v. Puerto Rico*, 805 F.3d 322 (1st Cir. 2015).

62. *Commonwealth of Puerto Rico v. Sanchez-Valle et al.*, No. 15-108, June 9, 2016, https://www.supremecourt.gov/opinions/15pdf/15-108_k4mp.pdf.

63. *Commonwealth of Puerto Rico et al v. Franklin California Tax-Free Trust et al.*, No. 15-233, June 13, 2016, https://www.supremecourt.gov/opinions /15pdf/15-233_i42j.pdf.

64. Back then, Clinton was able to appoint all the board members only in "consultation" with Congress, and each was required to be a resident of the district. See Michael Janofsky, "Congress Creates Board to Oversee Washington, D.C.," *New York Times*, April 8, 1995.

65. Van R. Newkirk II, "Puerto Rico Enters a New Age of Austerity," *Atlantic*, May 5, 2018, https://www.theatlantic.com/politics/archive/2018/05/puerto -rico-enters-a-new-age-of-austerity/559565/; also Lara Merling and Jake Johnston, "Puerto Rico's New Fiscal Plan: Certain Pain, Uncertain Gain," Center for Economic Policy and Research, June 2018, 4–12, https://cepr .net/images/stories/reports/puerto-rico-fiscal-plan-2018-06.pdf. For austerity measures in education see, Rima Brusi and Isar Godreau, "Dismantling Public Education in Puerto Rico," in *Aftershocks of Disaster: Puerto Rico Before and After the Storm*, eds. Yarimar Bonilla and Marisol Lebrón (Chicago: Haymarket Books, 2019), 234–49.

66. Puerto Rico Commission for the Comprehensive Audit of the Public Credit, "Pre-Audit Survey," July 1, 2016, 1–2, http://big.assets.huffingtonpost.com /Puerto_Rico_Commission_Interim_Report.pdf.

67. Financial Oversight and Management Board for Puerto Rico (FOMB), Special Investigation Committee: Independent Investigator's Final Investigative Report (San Juan: August 20, 2018), 27, 46–47, 87, https://bibliote caap.files.wordpress.com/2018/09/fomb-final-investigative-report-kobre -kim-20180820.pdf.

68. Ibid., 26–29; for Goldman Sachs banker's faulty memory, see 432. The control board later sought to declare invalid more than $6 billion in bonds issued in 2012 and 2014, see "Motion of the Financial Oversight and Management Board of Puerto Rico . . ." April 2, 2019, Case No. 17-BK-3283 (LTS), 9.

69. "Professional Fees in Puerto Rico Restructuring Pass $400 Million," *Bloomberg Law*, June 6, 2019, https://news.bloomberglaw.com/bankruptcy -law/professional-fees-in-puerto-rico-restructuring-pass-400-million; Luis J. Valentín Ortiz, "Puerto Rico's Fiscal Control Board, Parallel Government Full of Lawyers and Consultants," Puerto Rico Center for Investigative Journalism, August 1, 2018, http://periodismoinvestigativo.com/2018 /08/puerto-ricos-fiscal-control-board-parallel-government-full-of -lawyers-and-consultants/.

70. John Bacon, "Why Puerto Rico Faces a Monumental Recovery Effort," *USA Today*, September 26, 2017; also "Hurricane María Updates: In Puerto Rico, the Storm 'Destroyed Us,'" *New York Times*, September 21, 2017; also Erin K. Bessette-Kirton et al., "Landslides Triggered by Hurricane María:

Assessment of an Extreme Event in Puerto Rico," *GSA Today* 29, no. 6 (June 2019), https://www.geosociety.org/gsatoday/science/G383A/article .htm; Frances Robles and Luis Ferré Sadurni, "Puerto Rico's Agriculture and Farmers Decimated by María," *New York Times*, September 24, 2017.

71. Umair Irfan, "Puerto Rico's Blackout, the Largest in American History, Explained," *Vox*, May 8, 2018, https://www.vox.com/2018/2/8/16986408 /puerto-rico-blackout-power-hurricane; Charley E. Willison, Phillip M. Singer, Melissa S. Creary et al., "Quantifying Inequities in US Federal Response to Hurricane Disaster in Texas and Florida Compared with Puerto Rico," BMJ Global Health 2019, 4, http://dx.doi.org/10.1136/bmjgh-2018 -001191.

72. Omaya Sosa Pascual, "Nearly 1,000 More People Died in Puerto Rico after Hurricane María," Puerto Rico Center for Investigative Journalism, December 7, 2017, http://periodismoinvestigativo.com/2017/12/nearly-1000-more -people-died-in-puerto-rico-after-hurricane-maria/; Sarah Lynch Baldwin and David Begnaud, "Hurricane Maria Caused an Estimated 2,975 Deaths in Puerto Rico, New Study Finds," CBS News, August 28, 2018, https:// www.cbsnews.com/news/hurricane-maria-death-toll-puerto-rico-2975 -killed-by-storm-study-finds.

73. Alexia Fernández Campbell and Umair Irfan, "Puerto Rico's Deal with Whitefish Was Shady as Hell, New Records Show," *Vox*, November 15, 2017, https://www.vox.com/policy-and-politics/2017/11/15/16648924/puerto -rico-whitefish-contract-congress-investigation; also Michael Biesecker, "Whitefish Energy Get U.S. Contracts after Puerto Rico Ouster," AP News, October 9, 2018.

74. Kate Aronoff, "There's a Shady Puerto Rico Contract You Didn't Hear About," *The Intercept*, October 31, 2017, https://theintercept.com/2017/10/ 31/puerto-rico-electric-contract-cobra/; "FEMA Deputy Regional Administrator, Former President of Cobra Acquisitions, LLC, and Another Former FEMA Employee Indicted for Conspiracy to Commit Bribery, Honest Services Wire Fraud, Disaster Fraud, Among Other Charges," U.S. Justice Department, press release, September 10, 2019, https://www.justice.gov /usao-pr/pr/fema-deputy-regional-administrator-former-president-cobra -acquisitions-llc-and-another. Strangely, the firm well-connected to the former Obama official cornered this contract while Mastec, the company with decades of ties to conservative Republicans in Florida, was initially awarded a $500 million portion of the Puerto Rico rebuilding, but then shut out by Tribble. Mastec has long been operated by the sons of Jorge Mas Canosa, the deceased leader of the extreme anti-Castro Cuban community of Miami. See the civil racketeering complaint filed by Mastec in federal court in Miami, Mastec Renewables Puerto Rico, LLC v. Mammoth Energy Services, Inc. and Cobra Acquisitions, LLC. 1:20-cv-20263-RNS.

75. Patricia Mazzei and Agustín Amendariz, "FEMA Contract Called for 30 Million Meals for Puerto Ricans: 30,000 Were Delivered," *New York Times*, February 6, 2018.

76. Zeeshan Aleem, "Puerto Rico's Week of Massive Protests, Explained," *Vox*, July 22, 2019, https://www.vox.com/2019/7/20/20701898/puerto-rico -protests-ricardo-Rosselló-resign-ricky-renuncia-text-scandal; also Oliver Laughland, "Puerto Rico Governor Ricky Rosselló to Quit after Weeks of Protest," *The Guardian*, July 25, 2019, https://www.theguardian.com/world /2019/jul/25/puerto-rico-governor-ricardo-Rosselló-to-quit-after -weeks-of-protest; also Luis J. Valentín and Carla Minet, "The 889 Pages of the Telegram Chat Between Rosselló Nevares and His Closest Aides," *Centro de Periodismo Investigativo*, July 13, 2019, https://periodismoinvestigativo .com/2019/07/the-889-pages-of-the-telegram-chat-between-rossello -nevares-and-his-closest-aides/.

77. José Trías Monge, *Puerto Rico: The Trials of the Oldest Colony in the World* (New Haven, CT: Yale University Press, 1998), 64. For a full discussion of early colonial policy, see 36–76.

78. Roger Bell, *Last Among Equals: Hawaiian Statehood and American Politics* (Honolulu: University of Hawaii Press, 1984), 1–5; also Lawrence H. Fuchs, *Hawaii Pono: A Social History* (New York: Harcourt, Brace & World, 1961), 406–14.

79. From "Testimony Before the Co-Coordinators of the Interagency Working Group on Puerto Rico on the Future of Puerto Rico," June 22, 1995, at the White House, in *Cambio XXI*, Washington, D.C., 11–25.

EPILOGUE

1. U.S. Census Bureau, *Statistical Abstract of the United States: 1997* (Washington, D.C.: U.S. Government Printing Office, 1997), Table 12.

Index

Note: Italicized page numbers indicate material in photographs or illustrations.